Windows Into Literacy

Assessing Learners, K-8

Lynn K. Rhodes
Nancy L. Shanklin

HEINEMANN
Portsmouth, NH

HEINEMANN
A division of Reed Publishing (USA) Inc.
361 Hanover Street
Portsmouth, NH 03801–3912

Offices and agents throughout the world

Acknowledgments begin on page xx.

Every effort has been made to contact the copyright holders and students for permission to reprint borrowed material. We regret any oversights that may have occurred and would be happy to rectify them in future printings of this work.

Library of Congress Cataloging-in-Publication Data

Rhodes, Lynn Knebel.
    Windows into literacy: assessing learners, K-8/
Lynn K. Rhodes, Nancy L. Shanklin.
      p.   cm.
    Includes bibliographical references (p.).
    ISBN 0-435-08757-6
      1. Literacy—United States—Evaluation. 2. Language arts
(Elementary)—United States. 3. Language arts (Elementary)—
United States—Case Studies. I. Shanklin, Nancy Leavitt.
II. Title.
LC151.R46   1993
372.6—dc20   92-25297
                                     CIP

Designed by Jeffrey R. Pierce

Printed in the United States of America on acid free paper

93 94 95 96 97   7 6 5 4 3 2 1

Contents

Chapter Six: Writing Processes and Products

Chapter Seven: Emergent Reading and Writing

▨ Chapter Eight: Understanding and Challenging Traditional Forms of Evaluation

▨ Chapter Nine: Literacy Collections

Preface

This preface is intended to present our beliefs about effective literacy assessment, to suggest some significant barriers to making literacy assessment more effective, and to provide an overview of this book. We wrote the book with a wide audience in mind. Since individual readers will approach it with their own questions and concerns, the overview will help them make choices that best serve their purposes.

using assessment to inform literacy instruction

We believe that effective literacy assessment is an integral part of literacy instruction: effective assessment takes place most often in the midst of instruction and informs that instruction. In whole language classrooms, where the curriculum is child-centered, assessment data are the foundation of instructional planning for groups of students and for individual students. In "child-centered" classrooms, the teacher makes instructional decisions based on what she knows about each student's strengths, interests, and needs. The teacher rather than textbook publishers formulates the curriculum, using many kinds of materials, sometimes textbooks, to support learning. A teacher who plans the curriculum to take advantage of students' strengths and interests and to meet students' needs gathers the information needed for planning through the process of continual assessment.

As teachers, we know that each child has differences in personality, history, background knowledge and values, all of which affect literacy learning. Although this book focuses on various aspects of reading and writing, it is important to remember that we must go beyond the assessment of literacy if we are to take advantage of students' strengths and interests and meet their academic needs. Ultimately, students will need to use reading and writing as tools for learning in many facets of their lives.

The story of Evette, which follows, reminds us that each child is unique, and that it is important to gather information about the whole child, even when our focus is on the teaching of literacy. It also demonstrates how assessment can be used to plan instruction for the individual within a group of children.

Evette is an intermediate grade student who struggles with literacy. Her experience was recorded by her Chapter I teacher, Connie Timmons, in a Reflection Log for a university class. In order to highlight particular aspects of the story, especially with regard to assessment, we have recorded our thoughts to the right. Our notes will serve to highlight some of our values and provide a preview of some of the areas covered in this book.

Experience

I have worked with Evette for two years. She is a bright, articulate girl. She is also emotional and often feels outrage at school for the treatment and education she is receiving. She verbalizes her anger at being confronted with daily gang activity and peer pressure. One day, she screamed at the boys, "If you keep up all this gang colors stuff, the only way I'll feel safe coming to school will be naked!"

Evette sits with me after class, struggling to read notes meant for her mom because her mom is illiterate. She is frustrated because her mom's school experience was so miserable that she doesn't like to come to school. She says that her mom won't come to conferences anymore because the teachers always stick a bunch of papers (Evette's work) in her face to look over, and she can't read them.

Evette struggles to read and write. It is amazing to me that she has such a hard time. Her first independent goal this year was to quit getting stuck on little words when she reads. She describes the words that get in her way as "very simple, first grade, short little words."

Evette read for me, and I did a miscue analysis on her reading of *Freckle Juice* (Blume, 1971). All of her miscues were on longer, more unusual words, often on proper nouns. Frustrated sighs accompanied the self-corrections. This is a change from her reading in the past. She did predict some "little words" incorrectly but self-corrected them.

It was fun to show Evette what kinds of words she miscued and that her "stumblings" were actually self-

Notes

Although this book focuses on the assessment of literacy, knowing the whole child is important to understanding the child's struggles and progress with literacy. Here, Timmons provides a picture of Evette's personality, her views of schooling, and her values.

Timmons describes another important facet of Evette's literacy: her familial history, the impact it has on Evette, and Evette's feelings about it. In this book, we will suggest including parents in the process of assessment. This is a challenge when parents are illiterate and/or harbor negative feelings about schools.

Timmons engages Evette in setting her own goals in reading and writing. She also engages Evette in describing her own reading problems in the process of setting goals. In this book, we will talk about the importance of metacognition and how it enables students to think about themselves as readers and writers.

Timmons checked Evette's perceptions of her reading problems against her reading behavior (both miscues and sighing). To do this, she collected what is known as a performance sample of Evette's reading. What Timmons observed was different from Evette's description of her reading problem and her past behavior as a reader. Since Timmons had worked with Evette for two years, she knew that the reading problem Evette described had been true in the past.

Timmons draws Evette into reconsidering her reading ability and her problems by sharing the assessment data with her. She also tells Evette her

corrections. I told her that self-corrections may seem like problems when she reads aloud, but that I doubted that they were a big deal when she reads silently. Evette's perception of her reading was inaccurate, not because she didn't see what she did but because of the misplaced importance she placed on getting every word right all the time.

Often Evette grins a special grin when she truly believes what I say, and she finds it reassuring that maybe she isn't hopelessly meant to be a non-reader like her mom. She is not one to appreciate shallow praise and is very skeptical of the "good job" stuff handed out so easily by teachers. Well, I got one of her smiles. It has almost nothing to do with me—the smile is very private. But I always know that she has accepted the positive things I have said when she smiles like that. Her head drops and turns away a little. She blushes slightly and her lips, though firmly stuck together, curl up just a little on the sides. She seems to fight believing that she is doing something right, but gives into it just a little. These moments are very special for me. I want to look inside and see if I've broken down any major walls. I almost feel that Evette is made of strong concrete blocks and I am a pick—unfortunately, not a pick ax, but more a dentist's tool—patiently chipping away at the misconceptions, the poor instruction, the preconceived notions about her ability, and her fear of turning out just like her mom. Sometimes it makes me want to throw another tidbit of praise, but I've learned that it usually ruins the moment because it isn't as sincere and she isn't part of the discovery. Evette likes to be part of the assessment and judgment, rather than having it done to her.

Evette continued to read *Freckle Juice* independently. We decided that she might want to keep track of those words giving her trouble, and we could take a look at them later. This process reaffirmed that she wasn't having trouble with the little words. We also

own conclusions—why she sees the self-corrections as positive rather than negative. Timmons decides that working on Evette's perception of reading will be a priority.

We know of no checklist or other assessment instrument that captures what Timmons has captured here. What she knows about Evette is the result of carefully observing and recording assessment information about many interactions she and others have had with Evette. She uses this sort of information, as well as the information she has collected about Evette's literacy in performance samples, to make instructional decisions about how to approach Evette as a person and as a reader.

It is also clear that Timmons has used Evette's reactions to her teaching to gauge its effectiveness. She has learned, again from observing Evette, about the type and timing of praise that is most helpful to Evette's development. In fact, Timmons does not always offer praise. What she does offer is feedback that recognizes, in very specific ways, what Evette does as a reader. As we noted earlier, she pulls Evette into the process of looking at the assessment data. Like a good writer, Timmons shows more than tells. She shows Evette who she is as a reader rather than tells her who she is.

In suggesting to Evette that she keep track of the words that cause difficulty, Timmons not only provided Evette with more data to confirm the original conclusion, she also triangulated her data. That is, she collected data from silent reading and used it to check the original observations she had made of Evette's oral reading. Also, it was Evette

discovered something else—when she went over the words (in an isolated list) with me, she knew them. We went back to the context to see what happened. Sometimes she had miscues on the previous word, and the word she got stuck on was the one that followed. She didn't trust that the word was right because it's the one that didn't make sense. We talked about how it wasn't a matter of her knowing words but making sense of text. The little smile was quickly shaded by the thoughtful realization that she had major changes to make in the way she read.

Evette finished *Freckle Juice* independently and said it was the first chapter book she had ever read alone. Smile. When I talked with her about the book, she had little to offer in the way of a retelling. She did have a big question: "*Why* did he want freckles?" As she turned to me, I realized that there was a smattering of freckles across her nose. Evette wrote a story called *Anti-Freckles*.

Days and weeks passed as we continued to change the way Evette viewed reading. During a group reading of a very difficult book, *On My Honor* (Bauer, 1986), our group became very articulate about our strengths and weaknesses as readers along with the "heavy" issues raised by the story. The students fluctuated between not wanting to read because of the difficulty level and dark themes, and wanting to read ahead and peek at the ending to finish and understand. They often begged me to read the book aloud to them, and Evette's voice rang the loudest. Her claim, "But I'll understand it better. I miss too much when I read it myself," had often worked in the past as I weighed the importance of the content. But now I knew if I read the book to them, I wouldn't be rewarded with a smile. So I stuck to my guns, and we experimented with ways to read the book together so that they had more support for the process of making

who collected the data this time because the teacher gave her responsibility for doing so.

In the process of analyzing the new assessment data, Timmons and Evette discovered something new about Evette's reading that had not been clear before. As a result, Evette began grappling with an important but complex fact of reading—that she needed to focus on text meaning rather than on word recognition or meaning alone.

Again, Timmons gathers assessment information about Evette's literacy, this time from Evette's announcement about a "first" and her own observation of the telling smile. Though she was not satisfied with Evette's retelling, she did not assume from it that Evette did not understand the story. On the contrary, she realized that Evette understood the story well enough to make a connection between the book and herself. Timmons capitalized on this and encouraged rereading and greater comprehension by involving Evette in some writing on a topic of interest.

Wanting to challenge and extend the reading abilities of Evette and the other readers in the Chapter I group, Timmons chose an emotional "grabber" for the group to read. She hoped that such a book would keep them engrossed and reinforce the primacy of meaning construction as they read. When the students got frustrated with the difficulty of the book, she involved them in problem solving. Together, they figured out how to understand content even when they didn't know all the words. They also considered how much time and patience would be needed to read the book—issues often difficult for children like Evette.

Timmons also continued to encourage the students to consider reading metacognitively. That is, they talked about what they did well and needed to do better as readers, all the while maintaining their focus on the content of the book.

sense and understanding the content. We charted how many days it was going to take us to finish the book. Although we were sometimes fatigued and frustrated, we were nearing the finish.

Three days before the date we had set as the completion date, we couldn't stand it anymore and finished the book. We read through our lunch hour, getting to the cafeteria just before it closed. And we all cried, even Sam, at the end. When the story was finished, all we could do was look at each other. We didn't need to talk, we didn't want to talk. We sat in silence, with an occasional sigh, or shake of the head, or a verbalization like "geez." We walked down to lunch together. Evette looked down at her feet the whole way, smiling.

Later in the year, this group of students wrote commercials on school success, and we shared them via videotape with parents, classmates, and administrators. The principal viewed the video and asked Evette's group what it felt like to look at themselves on TV. In my head, I predicted a range of answers and recognized the surface level responses that could be made. Evette stared into nothingness and whispered, "Memories." The principal got more serious, as did we all. Someone asked Evette, "What do you mean?" Evette answered, "I mean I look at how I used to read and how I read now." I asked, "What's the difference? How has it changed?" Each child talked about his or her own reading and the reading of the other members of the group: "Tanya was so shy and wouldn't read aloud." "Yeah, I didn't have much confidence." "I stumbled over words a lot and I couldn't spell." "Yes, you could, Sam. You could always spell." "Well, I couldn't read so good, and now I can just go along the words." I added, "That's fluency, Sam. You are a fluent reader now." Then Sam turned to the principal and said, "And Evette, it's amazing. She doesn't know a lot of the words, but she seems to know the defi-

Ah, the satisfaction of finishing a wonderful book. No comprehension questions, no retellings. Instead: tears, sighs, and speechlessness. In this book, we'll explain how to assess comprehension by having children talk and write about books. Certainly, Timmons and the group used talk to sort out the meaning of the book as they read it. But Timmons didn't need to talk again at this point in order to assess either comprehension or satisfaction. Talking and writing are not always necessary in order to know that a child has comprehended a book.

In another section of her Reflection Log Timmons noted, "What went right in Evette's group was our constant assessment of our individual tryouts of reading strategies. We did a lot of group conferring about individual reading strengths, weaknesses, and needs together." When the principal unsuspectingly asked a question and Evette made her quiet observation in response, the students took the opening and revealed how they had learned to assess and affirm not only their own but also each other's growth as readers.

Timmons also noted that she had not realized how important it would be for her to institute peer conferences in reading and writing: "I saw that they could actually coach and confer with each other on learning issues. They had learned to make thoughtful, specific, and sincere comments. They had learned to respect each other's praise and help. Prior to this, I had always viewed peer conferences as a substitute for the better teacher conference, and at times, as a stalling technique for the overworked teacher." In light of Evette's response to Sam's assessment of her reading, Timmons realized that she needed to provide more vehicles, including peer conferences, so students could hear and learn from each other.

Timmons's careful integration of instruction and assessment had a powerful impact on a group of children who "would die before they would hang around together." Timmons carefully observed each of the children she describes as "entirely dif-

nitions. Like she would look at all the words around and know what it all meant. Like she always got it." The conversation between the students and principal continued, but I was looking at Evette. Her head was down, and I could barely see her face. She knew I was staring at her. She looked up and got very rigid. She had turned bright red. Her lips were pressed tightly together as if she was trying not to smile, but the smile curled up anyway. She was shaking. My eyes started to water. I heard the old Carole King song in my head: "I feel the earth move under my feet; I feel the sky come tumbling down, come tumbling down." I envisioned a recent video of the Berlin wall falling and the hoards of people tearing at it. It wasn't just me and my dentist's pick. It was our whole Chapter I group that did it. We pulled down a section of the wall. Evette and I stared into each other's eyes and shared the moment.

ferent readers and different personalities," using the information she gathered. To shape each child as an individual and to shape the group as a community that would support each child's literacy development, she engaged Evette and the others in becoming increasingly responsible for their own and one another's literacy assessment, learning, and development.

For Timmons, assessment is integral to literacy instruction. It is primarily a process of observing students during instructional interactions with printed materials and with people, and of reflecting on and analyzing the meaning of what she observes. She uses the information she gathers to make instructional decisions that help the class and the individual children in the class to advance their literacy.

To gather this information, Timmons observes students during instruction, collects occasional performance samples, interviews students as they work in order to find out about their attitudes, interests, and perceptions of reading and writing, and reviews the work students have gathered in their folders and portfolios. These methods of gathering assessment data, along with analysis of the data collected, are the foundation for Timmons's instructional planning.

Where do standardized, norm-referenced tests and criterion-referenced tests fit into Timmons's assessment of her students? Because she is a Chapter I teacher, she gives a standardized, norm-referenced test each spring, under a federal mandate, to Evette and the other students she serves. In addition, the students take district criterion-referenced tests three to five times a year in their regular classrooms. Knowing where Evette scores in relation to the other children on norm-referenced tests does not help Timmons decide what Evette needs to understand and learn in order to become a more effective reader. Norm-referenced tests are useful only for gauging how large groups of students are doing in relation to other large groups of students—and only on a particular test. Evette's test scores reconfirm that she belongs in the Chapter I program.

The results of the district criterion-referenced tests are not helpful to Timmons's instructional planning either. For one thing, the theory underlying the tests is different from the theory Timmons uses in her teaching. The tests are skills-based, while Timmons bases her instruction on whole language theory. For another, almost all of the skills are tested in isolation from reading whole text. Even the comprehension section of criterion-referenced tests are replete with difficulties—such as brief (sometimes only a sentence) texts that focus on words and literal meaning. Certainly, better scores on these sections might provide at least an indication that a student like Evette is becoming a more effective reader. Yet the student's attitude toward these frequently given tests is often so poor that teachers cannot trust the results to represent a student's reading ability even as defined by the tests.

barriers to effective literacy assessment

There are three barriers to the assessment recommendations we make in this book: the primacy of norm-referenced tests, too much testing and too little assessment, and a lack of teacher involvement in the assessment process. We list the primacy of norm-referenced tests first because it underlies the other two. If norm-referenced tests did not play the major role they do in schools, there would be less testing and teachers would likely be more involved in the assessment process than they are.

Norm-referenced tests are not likely to disappear from the American education scene anytime soon. (They do not play such a large role in other countries, including Canada.) The American public has a great deal of faith in the instruments and the scores; witness the media attention the results receive in most newspapers during the late spring and early summer. Basal reader tests and criterion-referenced tests are close cousins of norm-referenced tests. In fact, many teachers use these tests to "prepare" students for norm-referenced tests.

Many people assume that norm-referenced tests will improve instruction and learning because they hold educators accountable to other groups, such as parents and the general public. But in fact, norm-referenced tests cannot help teachers improve instruction and learning. Most norm-referenced tests are given in the spring, at the end of the school year. At this point, a teacher cannot use the results to improve instruction. But even if the tests were given in the fall, the results could not help teachers improve instruction because they are expressed in numbers, not a form of information a teacher can use for instructional planning. Instead, the primacy of norm-referenced tests often results in teaching to the test. Since the tests are ill-conceived (see Valencia & Pearson, 1987; and Weaver's chapter on standardized tests, 1990), they have the opposite effect—they discourage school reform and the improvement of teaching and learning.

A recent *U.S. News & World Report* article (Tosh & Levine, 1991) stated that typical students face ten to twenty norm-referenced, standardized tests before graduation and that "130 million standardized tests are administered in public schools annually, at an estimated cost of $500 million" (p. 64). In addition, teachers also give other tests, many of them mandated by districts or by programs such as Chapter I. In the face of so much testing, teachers collect too little assessment information that will inform their instruction. At the same time, many teachers equate testing and assessment. They see assessment as something they must do, not something that could be of value to their teaching and students' learning. Because of the primacy of norm-referenced tests, relatively few teachers have been trained in the area of assessment. They need information about literacy development and literacy assessment techniques in order to be able to gather assessment data for instructional planning.

Thus, a shift from testing to assessment requires a major commitment to staff development. Reallocating some of the $500 million per year now used in the purchase and scoring of tests would certainly give a boost to staff development funding. Teachers with a knowledge of literacy development and literacy assessment techniques have the cognitive base and the confidence to be involved in formulating assessment procedures and practices that improve learning, improve instruction, and monitor the outcomes of instruction. All teachers, including whole language teachers, are concerned about accountability, but they need to be even more concerned about gathering the information that allows them to improve instruction and learning for the wide variety of students, like Evette, who deserve such attention.

This book is devoted primarily to providing information about the aspects of reading and writing that can be assessed and how assessing them can aid in planning instruction. The first chapter defines assessment and addresses what we see as the purposes of literacy assessment. We also discuss a number of principles that we believe ought to guide assessment. Finally, we provide an overview of the assessment process: collecting, recording, and analyzing data, and using the analysis to plan instruction and generate new assessment questions. An important part of this discussion is practical because we know how important the management of assessment is to making it an integral part of instruction.

We have made assessing literacy environments and instruction the subject of the second chapter in order to emphasize the key point that as teachers, we are responsible for assessing the impacts of literacy environments and of our instruction on students' literacy development. The chapter looks at students' literacy attitudes and interests, the notions of authenticity and of gradually releasing responsibility to students, and patterns of communication between teacher and student and among students themselves. All of these are important to providing effective contexts for literacy learning.

Students' perceptions about literacy events, reading and writing strategies, and themselves as readers and writers, are of vital importance to literacy development. In Chapter 3 we address the assessment of the metacognitive aspects of literacy. We show how to use questionnaires, interviews, and group discussions, often within everyday literacy events in the classroom.

Chapters 4 and 5 are devoted to reading abilities. In Chapter 4 we provide information about how to assess students in the process of reading. Tools such as miscue analysis uncover students' use of language systems and strategies during reading. Chapter 5 focuses on the assessment of the "product" of reading—comprehension. Assessment techniques—such as interviews, think alouds, and retellings—can be used to collect performance samples or to construct literacy events that focus on comprehension.

Chapter 6 reviews various approaches to the assessment of writing with particular emphasis on students' writing processes, including spelling, and written products. We introduce the Authoring Cycle Profile as a systematic means of analysis and describe procedures for collecting writing samples and for holistic and analytic scoring of these written products. The final section includes suggestions for assessing students' writing during literacy events.

Because the same assessment techniques are not always applicable to students who cannot yet read independently, Chapter 7 is devoted to emergent reading and writing. We critique readiness tests and review various performance samples. The majority of the chapter portrays the assessment of reading and writing during literacy events that are common in whole language classrooms.

In Chapter 8, we discuss the use of standardized, norm-referenced tests in the assessment of literacy. In particular, we address the difficulties in defining literacy, how test results might be communicated to those who are interested, the statistical methods used to create norm-referenced tests, and the ability of norm-referenced tests to measure literacy. In addition, the chapter contains extended discussions of grading, progress reports (including report cards and conferences), and special education staffings.

Chapter 9, on the topic of literacy collections, includes information on reading and writing folders and on current-year and permanent portfolios. We see such literacy collections as the best place to save the products that students generate as they engage in reading and writing. They are also sources of information for teachers. We see literacy collections as an important part of the process of refining what we know about students' literacy, particularly their progress as literacy users over time.

Chapter 10 looks at the educational change process as it relates to assessment. If some or all of the information in this book is new and the ideas make sense to you, you will want to change the ways you approach literacy assessment. This chapter helps you consider the process of fostering personal change. The chapter also addresses the issue of being a change agent, which is helpful in generating a more widespread acceptance of your ideas about literacy assessment. If you find personal change challenging or if you are already committed to being a change agent, you may want to read this last chapter first.

special features of the book

Although this book is packed with information about literacy assessment, information alone is not enough. It must be combined with reflection. We have included two features to highlight the importance of reflection: "Reflections" and "Teacher Reflection."

The "Reflections" section is intended to encourage you to consider several views of the information we have provided. These sections appear at the beginning of each chapter because a number of the suggested activities are best done before further reading. Other activities ask you to react to information you encounter in the reading. Each "Reflections" section includes many more activities than you'll want to do, but we hope you'll choose those that best serve your purposes and interests as you explore the various facets of literacy assessment.

Most chapters end with a feature we have titled "Teacher Reflection." Each "Teacher Reflection", written by a teacher, is about a single topic that relates to the preceding chapter. The author reflects on some aspect of literacy assessment and instruction by telling a story about the change she experienced in her thinking and her practice. These reflections show how teachers invent and adapt assessment techniques to the unique contexts in which they work and their own particular purposes. You may enjoy turning to the "Teacher Reflection" pieces first.

A handbook of assessment instruments is available to accompany this book. The handbook contains many of the instruments we refer to throughout the text. Some are not available elsewhere, and others were too long to include here. The instruments are organized under the following categories: Reading, Writing, Emergent Reading and Writing, Literacy at Home, Program Placement, and Assessing the Teaching of Literacy. The authors have given permission for the instruments to be copied for teacher use in assessment. Our assumption is that teachers will adapt the instruments and procedures for particular contexts and particular students.

getting started: a gentle word of advice

A reviewer has referred to the "overwhelming" amount of information included in this book. "Thorough" is a word often applied to both of us, and it apparently applies to the way we have approached our topic. However, we don't want you to be overwhelmed. We know that when we are overwhelmed, we become discouraged and unable to act, and we wrote the book to encourage educators to take action in the area of literacy assessment.

If the size of the book seems daunting, we urge you to look through it and read what is of greatest interest to you. Each chapter is comprehensive and stands on its own. Once you have identified those aspects of literacy assessment that bother you the most and framed your questions about literacy assessment, you can choose those parts of the book that address those needs.

In the final chapter, we talk about how to keep change manageable. Here are some ideas from that chapter that may be worth thinking about preliminary to your reading:

- Identify one or more colleagues who also want to consider changes in assessment. Working with others will help you clarify your thinking, provide you with the support you need, and help you solve problems.

- Don't try to change too much at once. Define one change you'd like to make in literacy assessment and figure out a comfortable starting point for that change.

- Find your own pace. The pace of change is an individual matter and the result of a number of factors. You may need to be patient with yourself.

- When you think you are ready, challenge yourself to take some risks. You know that when students take risks, they learn. So will you.

references

Blume, J. (1971). *Freckle Juice*. New York: Dell Yearling.

Tosh, T. & A. Levine. (1991). Schooling's big test. *U.S. News & World Report*, 110 (17), 63-64.

Valencia, S. & P.D. Pearson. (1987). Reading Assessment: Time for a change. *The Reading Teacher*, 40 (8), 726-733.

Weaver, C. (1990). *Understanding Whole Language*. Portsmouth, NH: Heinemann.

Acknowledgments

We certainly didn't know it at the time, but this book started in 1984 when we began four years of work with the Denver Public Schools elementary Chapter I program. On a weekly basis, we worked with over seventy-five Chapter I teachers and their students, two administrators, and two teachers who served as resource specialists for the program. We were charged with helping the teachers change their instructional practices from a skills-based approach to one based in whole language.

From the beginning it was clear that assessment would play a major role in helping teachers reconsider their teaching of reading and writing. As we worked with the teachers on whole language instructional theory and practice, they began requesting information about assessment instruments and procedures that would match their instruction. When we introduced some of these assessment techniques, we found that the teachers' views of the reading and writing processes changed dramatically. As the teachers' views changed, so did their instructional and assessment practices.

We learned a great deal in the process of working with the Chapter I teachers as they reconsidered and realigned their literacy instruction and assessment. The reality of their instructional situations was brought home to us weekly. We thank the teachers themselves as well as Rosalie O'Donague and Mary Ann Bash, the DPS Chapter I administrators, for the gift of four years with their teachers. And we thank Mary Ann Bash again and the two Chapter I resource teachers, Debbie Milner and Wendy Downie, for countless hours of talk about literacy instruction and assessment.

Our university teaching during and after our years of working in the Denver Public Schools has served to refine and broaden our understanding not only of the relationship between assessment and instruction but also of many particular techniques for literacy assessment. Working with teachers from the wide variety of situations a university graduate program attracts has affected our thinking a great deal. In particular, we thank the teachers whose classroom practicums we supervised; without them, our thinking would not have been challenged to the extent it has been.

We have also learned a great deal more about literacy assessment as we wrote this book—from many of our fellow teacher-educators across the United States and Canada and beyond. It never ceases to amaze us how differently we read articles and hear presentations when we are writing about a topic ourselves.

As we wrote and revised, we also continued to learn about assessment from working with the teachers who wrote the "Teacher Reflection" pieces for this book: Jan Bennett, Lori Conrad, Bonnie DeFreece, Marty Frampton, Maureen Holland,

---

Gloria Kaufmann and Kathy Short, Kathy Mestnik, and Carol Wilcox. We thank each of them for their thoughtful contributions.

We also want to thank a number of others who contributed by allowing us to share their own work or their students' work and who thus shaped our thinking in significant ways: Sheryl Allen, Joann Briggs, Carolyn Burke, Arlene Chenoweth, Ann Christensen, Mark Clarke, Jean Anne Clyde, Karen Condit, Linda Darcy, Kathy DeZengremel, Pat Dykstra, Carrie Ekey, Marge Erickson, Jackie Eversley, Catherine M. Felknor, Tammy French, Linda Gherardini, Mary Giard, Karen Grossman, Jeanne Gustafson, Mary Hellen, Lynn Hayes, Mary Ellen Hitchins, Kathy Hoerlein, Karen Holesworth, Linda Hoyt, Joyce Jelinek, Judy Jindrich, Judy Lampert, Mary Ann Lillis, Lorraine Marzano, Linda McFadyen, Jeanne McLaughlin-Powers, Sue Monaco, Lori Murray, Rose O'Dorisio, Ellen Rawson, Pat Reser, Sharon Reiling, Ron Schuster, Roseanne Schwartz, Tammy Smiley, Connie Timmons, Roxanne Torke, Debra Vicksman, Kay Williams, Crystal Winter, Lori Wiese, and Sherry Wise. Many other teachers have also influenced our thinking in our graduate classes and in staff development work. We are indebted to them all.

We hope that you will begin or continue the study of literacy assessment in the spirit in which we wrote this book. There is still much to be learned, and we hope you will join with us in learning more.

Credits

The authors and publisher thank those who granted permission for the use of the following copyrighted material:

Appendix C   Reprinted by permission from Loughlin, Catherine E. & Martin, M.D., *Supporting Literacy: Developing Effective Learning Environments*. (New York: Teachers College Press, copyright © 1987 by Teachers College Columbia University. All rights reserved.)

Figure 2.3   From *Grand Conversations: Literature Groups in Action*, ed. by R. Peterson & M. Eeds. Copyright © 1990 by Karen Smith. Reprinted with permission of Scholastic, Inc.

Figure 2.6   Observational checklist from "A child-based observation checklist to assess attitudes toward reading" by Betty S. Heathington & J. Estill Alexander. *The Reading Teacher*, April 1978, pp. 769-771. Reprinted with permission of Betty S. Heathington and the International Reading Association.

Figure 3.1	Figure 3 from "Developing metacognitive awareness" by Suzanne E. Wade & Ralph Reynolds. *Journal of Reading*, October 1989. Reprinted with permission of Suzanne E. Wade and the International Reading Association.
Figure 4.1	From *Understanding Reading: A Psycholinguistic Analysis of Reading and learning to Read* by Frank Smith. Copyright © 1985 by Frank Smith. Reprinted by permission of the author.
Figure 4.3	From *Clifford at the Circus* by Norman Bridwell. Copyright © 1977 by Norman Bridwell. Reprinted by permission of Scholastic, Inc.
Figure 4.4	From *Frog and Toad All Year* by Arnold Lobel. Copyright © 1976 by Arnold Lobel. Reprinted by permission of HarperCollins Publishers.
Figure 4.5	From *The Great Gilly Hopkins* by Katherine Paterson. Copyright © 1978 by Katherine Paterson. Reprinted by permission of HarperCollins Publishers.
Figure 4.6	From *Julie of the Wolves* by Jean Craighead George. Text Copyright © 1972 by Jean Craighead George. Reprinted by permission of HarperCollins Publishers.
Figure 4.7 and 4.9	From *Lincoln: A Photobiography* by Russell Freedman. Copyright © 1987 by Russell Freedman. Reprinted by permission of Clarion Books/Houghton Mifflin Company. All rights reserved.
Page 210	"When I read a good book" by Jennifer Rose. *The Reading Teacher*, October 1989. Reprinted with permission of Jennifer Rose and the International Reading Association.
Figure 5.4	Adapted from "Retelling stories as a diagnostic tool" by Leslie M. Morrow. In *Reexamining Reading Diagnosis: New Trends and Procedures*, ed. by Susan M. Glazer, Lyndon Searfoss, & Lance Gentile. 1988. Reprinted with permission of the International Reading Association.
Figure 5.6	From "Assessing free recall" by Charles Clark. *The Reading Teacher*, January 1982. Reprinted with permission of Charles Clark and the International Reading Association.
Appendix D	From "You get lost when you gotta blimmin' watch the damn words: the low progress reader in the junior high school." *Topics in Learning and Learning Disabilities* 3(4), 16-30. Copyright © 1984 by Pro-Ed Inc. Reprinted by permission.
Figure 6.1	Reprinted and adapted with permission of Jerome C. Harste, Kathy G. Short, with Carolyn Burke: *Creating Classrooms for Authors* (Heinemann Educational Books, Portsmouth, NH, 1988).

Figure 6.11   From "Team for success: guided practice in study skills through cooperative research reports" by Beth Davey. *Journal of Reading*, May 1987. Reprinted with permission of Beth Davey and the International Reading Association.

Figure 7.1   From "Young children's responses to one-to-one story readings in school settings" by Leslie M. Morrow. *Reading Research Quarterly*, Winter 1988. Reprinted with permission of Leslie M. Morrow and the International Reading Association.

Page 327   Adapted from "Children's emergent reading of favorite storybooks: a developmental study" by Elizabeth Sulzby. *Reading Research Quarterly*, Summer 1985. Reprinted with permission of the International Reading Association.

Table 8.1   National Assessment of Educational Projects, *The Reading Report Card: 1971-1988*.

Page 414   From *Portfolio Assessment in the Reading-Writing Classroom* by Tierney, Carter, & Desai, 1991. Reprinted with permission of Christopher Gordon Publishers.

Table 9.1   From "Assessment and accountability in a Whole Literacy Curriculum" by Kathryn H. Au, Judith A. Scheu, Alice J. Kawakami, & Patricia A. Herman. *The Reading Teacher*, April 1990. Reprinted with permission of the International Reading Association.

Chapter One

Reflecting on Literacy Assessment

reflections

☐ What do you believe are the purposes of literacy assessment? Jot down your ideas before reading this chapter and compare them with ours after you have read it. What did you not consider that we think is important? What did we not consider that you think is important?

☐ Write a learning log entry in which you reflect on what you see as the potential value of assessment to you as a teacher. Share your entry with other teachers who have reflected on the same question.

☐ Look over what we have proposed as principles of literacy assessment. Which are principles you have thought about in the past? Which are new to you? Choose one new principle that is of interest and talk about it with someone else.

☐ On what do you base your decisions about what to teach? What sort of role does observation play in your instructional planning? What must you rethink to ensure that your instruction is more often based on your observation of students?

☐ Teachers may worry that assessment instruments largely determine what they teach. Others see this as a positive force. In what ways do the assessment instruments you use determine what you teach? Consider ways in which this might be positive or negative.

☐ How much assessment data do you record on a daily basis? If you record a great deal, talk with others about why you do so. If you record only a little, talk with others about why. After you have read this chapter, talk with the same people again about the issues you raised in the first conversation.

☐ Many teachers find that assessment is a difficult area for them. What parts of assessment come most easily or naturally to you? What parts are most difficult? Why?

☐ If you have attempted or implemented ways of assessment, such as checklists, anecdotal records, collecting work in reading/writing folders and so on, think about the difficulties you encountered in recording, analyzing, and using the information. Consider some possible solutions for these difficulties as you read this chapter.

> The nation's specialists in reading and writing recognize that our assessment instruments largely determine what we teach. As long as standardized survey tests, state and large-district assessment tests, and program-related criterion tests in commercial systems continue to stress single skills and discrete elements of reading and writing, we will find these skills and elements stressed in our classrooms (Squire, 1989, p.4).

Assessment can be an empowering force for documenting and guiding literacy development. Assessment is empowering when, after learning that a high-risk first grader is interested in bears, a teacher shows the child books about bears and the child says, "I want to learn to read this book." It is a positive force when a fourth grader sets himself the goal of learning to read chapter books, and his teacher designs activities to support his reading of a Cam Jensen mystery he has chosen. It is also a positive force when a teacher observes that a number of students are enthusiastic about dramatization and capitalizes on their interest by teaching them to write scripts from stories they enjoy, thus increasing their reading and writing opportunities.

Assessment can likewise be empowering for teachers because it can serve as a tool for reflecting on and improving teaching. Assessment provides information about whether students are making progress as readers and writers, but it also provides insights into teaching techniques that have made a difference in students' learning. Assessment helps us see why some students may be making little or no progress so that we can implement changes that would make more effective learning possible.

Knowledge about how to gather and analyze useful assessment data to make decisions about instruction is crucial to teachers in socio-psycholinguistic, child-centered classrooms. In such classrooms, cues about instruction come largely from learners themselves rather than from the next lesson in a textbook. Through assessment teachers can discover students' interests, strengths, and areas of developmental need to help them become more literate. There is a special responsibility that accompanies the operation of such classrooms: to assess well in order to guide development and document its occurrence.

Considerable attention is currently being paid to the assessment of literacy development. In the past two decades we have learned a great deal about the reading and writing processes, reading and writing development, and how context influences both. However, because many tests do not reflect this new knowledge, reading and writing educators are working on developing "instruments as good as our eyes" (Brickell, 1976) to document progress. Ultimately, the issue is not just the nature of the tests but how the tests determine the curriculum. Deep concern about these issues is reflected in the 1988 International Reading Association Resolution on Assessment:*

> Reading assessment must reflect advances in the understanding of the reading process. As teachers of literacy we are concerned that instructional decisions are too often made from assessments which define reading as a sequence of discrete skills that students must master to become readers. Such assessments foster inappropriate instruction . . . . Be it therefore

> *Resolved* that the International Reading Association affirms that reading assessments reflect recent advances in the understanding of the reading process; be it further

> *Resolved* that assessment measures defining reading as a sequence of discrete skills be discouraged . . . .

We want to help teachers and other educators revalue (Goodman, Smith, Meredith & Goodman, 1987) or reconceive assessment as an empowering force using the most recent research about reading and writing processes, development, and teaching. We believe that teachers should draw on assessment information to decide how best to support students' literacy development.

Let us explain what we mean by assessment and why we have chosen, in general, to use this term rather than evaluation.** For us, the word *evaluation* connotes making judgments about students' products that result in a mark, score, or grade, judgments that often have little connection with the teacher's instructional plans. In contrast, the term *assessment* implies the process of carefully collecting or recording and analyzing students' literacy products and processes in a way that establishes a strong connection between the assessment data and the teacher's instructional plans.

In practice, evaluation and assessment are not always neatly delineated. For example, an assessment can result in a grade (and therefore also function as an evalu-

---

* Complete texts for the 1988 and 1991 IRA Resolutions on Assessment are reprinted in Appendixes A and B.

** The terms *assessment* and *evaluation* are used interchangeably by some educators. Other educators, who differentiate between assessment and evaluation, define the terms in ways that are different from how we have defined them here. When talking about assessment and evaluation, it is important to find out what others mean to ensure a convergence of concepts, even if using different terminology.

ation) although it is used as the basis for ongoing instructional decision making. It is also possible to evaluate (and thus grade) students' reading and writing processes. In actual practice, however, we would argue that students are constantly evaluated but seldom assessed. Students' products are constantly marked, scored, or graded, but those evaluations have little impact on the teacher's ongoing instructional plans. (The only instructional decision that evaluations seem to have an impact on is group placement or the levels to which students are assigned in materials such as basals and spelling programs.) Yet little information is recorded and analyzed in most classrooms for the sake of ongoing instructional planning, and few teachers plan the next day's or week's instruction by reviewing this information. Instead, in many classrooms, curriculum guides determine the content and sequence of instruction.

We do not mean to imply that we object to the evaluation of students' reading and writing. What we do object to is the degree to which scored, marked, and graded products dominate the lives of teachers and students. (In a recent observation of a fourth-grade class, for example, we noticed that each student turned in five pieces of work from the morning's reading and language arts classes for grading.) It is far more educationally beneficial for assessment to take the upper hand, and for only a small amount of assessment information (including process information) to form the basis for evaluation. With that in mind, we give the word *assessment* the upper hand in this book along with the concepts it represents. When we use the word *evaluation,* it is because the information being discussed has little potential to affect a teacher's ongoing instructional plans or decision making in a way that is significant or positive. Assessment information can always be marked or graded, although we will argue in Chapter 8 for far less marking or grading.

purposes of literacy assessment

The most basic reason to conduct literacy assessment is to gather information in order to plan literacy instruction. This assumes a view of teaching as a process of making decisions about curriculum on the basis of observations about students' strengths, needs, and interests. The International Reading Association's resolutions on assessment issues (1991; see Appendix B) reflect this basic reason for conducting literacy assessment in its two aims for assessment: "monitoring the outcomes of instruction at the level of the school, the community, the state or province, or the nation," and "providing input information to the teacher and the pupil for the guidance and improvement of instruction and learning."

In this section, we will present seven purposes for assessment, all of which relate to the basic reason for conducting assessment—to plan literacy instruction that recognizes students' strengths and interests and addresses their needs. In Figure 1.1, we have categorized these seven purposes under IRA's aims for assessment. Although the first aim is an important one (and more aligned with our definition of evaluation

---

"For the guidance and improvement of learning. . ."

> To determine what development is occurring.

> To identify a student's strengths and weaknesses in reading and writing.

"(For) the guidance and improvement of instruction. . ."

> To discover the power of your teaching.

> To learn more about the development of reading and writing.

> To sharpen the quality of your observations and your confidence in them.

"Monitoring the outcomes of instruction. . ."

> To have information about a student as a reader and writer to share with others.

> To assess program strengths and weaknesses and guide staff development.

Figure 1.1   Purposes of literacy assessment

than assessment), it is also the one that has received the most support and attention in the recent history of schooling. For this reason it is listed last as "Monitoring the outcomes of instruction" and has two purposes associated with it.

The other five purposes are related to IRA's second aim, "providing input information to the teacher and the pupil for the guidance and improvement of instruction and learning." Because we view this aim as the more important and the more closely related to the overall purpose of using assessment to plan instruction, we have divided it into two separate aims, "for the guidance and improvement of learning" and "for the guidance and improvement of instruction," each associated with several purposes.

As we discuss each of these seven purposes, we will briefly introduce topics such as anecdotal records, miscue analysis, self-assessment, and metacognition. Although these topics are not explained here, each will be developed in considerable detail in later chapters.

◼ ◼

to determine what development is occurring

The first of the two purposes that directly focuses on student learning recognizes the importance of using a developmental approach in gathering and analyzing assessment information. It is important for teachers to relate assessment information to their knowledge of developmental criteria. It is not very helpful to know simply that in writing, a child spells most words wrong. That same statement may apply to a number of children, but a child who is using a letter name strategy to spell words will benefit from different instruction than a child who is using random letters to spell words, even though both are spelling most words unconventionally. A knowledge of spelling development and of appropriate instruction for various stages of development will ensure that the children get the specific teaching they need to continue to make developmental progress.

It is also important for teachers to relate past assessment data to current assessment information to determine how a child has developed. Roseanne Schwartz, a Denver Public Schools Chapter I teacher, saves her miscue analysis data from the spring so she can compare these results with the oral reading and retelling of returning students in the fall. She is particularly interested in seeing whether progress in particular aspects of reading has been maintained, has declined, or has increased over the summer and in getting some sense of why. She shares all of this information about their reading development with students and uses it to write individual educational plans at the beginning of the year, to make initial instructional decisions, and even to think ahead to the following spring about what she can do to encourage students' reading over the next summer.

Teachers can help students understand and appreciate their growth as readers and writers if they share information with students, as Schwartz does, and involve students in self-assessment, including setting goals in reading and writing. In so doing, teachers help students become aware of their own responsibility for their literacy development.

to identify a student's strengths and weaknesses in reading and writing

In the assessment of reading and writing, it is important to uncover weaknesses so that they may be addressed, but it is equally important to uncover strengths so that they may be recognized and used in making plans to bolster a student's confidence as a learner. Recognizing what a student does well helps the student understand that he is already a capable learner and that we consider it our job to extend the student's capabilities. Within such a positive affective and cognitive context, it is easier for both teacher and student to address the student's weaknesses.

Jamaal, a second grader and a new reader, is a good illustration of this point. When assessing Jamaal's writing abilities and his attitude, his teacher learned that he loved to write. She loaned him two markers for the evening and suggested that he might like to do some writing at home. As she hoped, he arrived the next day with a story he had written about his dog being sick and going to the veterinarian. On subsequent days, he told several other stories and wrote them down. But Jamaal's reading was another matter. When he attempted to read, he would skip many of the words he didn't know, sound others out but end up with nonsense words, make real word substitutions that made no sense, and fail to self-correct. His attitude toward reading was one of avoidance; he clearly didn't enjoy his encounters with books.

Jamaal's teacher decided to capitalize on his positive writing attitude and used his own writing, along with language experience stories that he dictated, to help him learn to revalue reading and to extend his skills as a reader. He began to read his written and dictated stories repeatedly, which slowly built his confidence and skill as a reader and changed his attitude toward reading. Gradually he came to understand that stories by other writers carry the writer's message, which was supposed to make sense to him as an audience and a reader.

Identifying a student's interests is another way of capitalizing on his strengths. For example, when Martin's teacher conducted an interest inventory with him, she found that he was interested in learning more about Indians. She suggested that he might like to read *Sign of the Beaver* (Speare, 1983), a book about the relationship between a white boy and an Indian boy in the late 1700s. This book would also allow her to work with Martin on his reading of more complex sentences and his use of context to determine the meaning of unknown words, two areas that were difficult for him. Later Martin revealed that he was part Cherokee and that his grandfather lived on a reservation in Oklahoma. When he told his teacher about how his grandfather had taught him to make arrows, she encouraged him to write this story for his book on Indians. Martin decided to call his grandfather to interview him about questions that came up in his reading.

Of course, it is also important to identify a student's strengths and weaknesses in using reading and writing strategies. Jake, a third grader, made a number of semantically unacceptable miscues while he was reading orally yet could give a full retelling of most of the stories he read. It appeared that he was mentally making sense, perhaps even mentally self-correcting his miscues, since his comprehension was good. Because he read weekly to a first grader, Jake's teacher decided to help him learn to use the meaning he was obviously constructing to self-correct his miscues.

A few sessions with a tape-recorded version of Jake reading helped him understand why his reading didn't make sense to others; he quickly learned how to read orally so that his first-grade reading buddy could get more from their sessions together. The teacher used her knowledge of Jake's reading strength, his ability to construct meaning, to help him with his weakness, his lack of attention to meaning construction in his oral reading. She also involved him in assessing his own strengths and weaknesses and encouraged him to become aware of what he was doing as a reader.

to discover the power of your teaching

The first two assessment purposes were aligned with IRA's aim to improve learning. However, the IRA assessment aim of "providing input information to the teacher and the pupil for the guidance and improvement instruction and learning" includes giving attention to improving of instruction. Although instruction and learning are integrally linked, teachers often assess student learning without reflecting on the teaching that is the basis of such learning.

Teachers who assess students have data that will allow them to discover the power of their teaching. Assessment data can reveal that students have truly learned the lessons they have been taught. One teacher we know found that writing samples and interviews helped her see that her students had learned to pay attention to the meaning they were constructing, a major lesson she had been teaching about writing. Most of the students' writing had become clearer and more interesting. When students talked about writing in their interviews, they mentioned creating meaning as the aspect of writing they attended to. At the same time, however, she also observed that students were not attending to editing for the sake of their readers. Students had learned to focus on meaning, but they had begun to ignore conventions. Since they had started the year quite concerned about the conventional use of spelling, punctuation, and capitalization, she realized that she needed to help them see that conventions were important for readers of their writing.

Assessment helps teachers uncover how teaching has affected learning in positive ways and how it has affected learning in unexpected or unwanted ways. In other words, it helps them discover the power of their own teaching. Once they understand the effects of their teaching on students' learning, they can adjust their teaching where necessary to change the direction of learning—or give themselves a much-deserved pat on the back!

to learn more about the development of reading and writing

The more teachers know about the development of reading and writing, the easier it is for them to achieve the first assessment purpose, to determine how students are developing. Careful reflection on assessment information often teaches us things we did not know about the development of reading and writing. Because learning more about these areas affects the knowledge base we bring to our literacy observations in classrooms, this indirectly benefits the students whose literacy we observe and analyze.

At University Hills Elementary School in Boulder, Colorado, teachers have begun to keep portfolios of children's reading and writing that will be passed on from year to year over a seven-year period. They are interested in learning what these folders will tell them about the spurts and plateaus in children's literacy development. We suspect that teachers will also find these portfolios useful in learning about the developmental range that is typical at any grade level, which should, in turn, spur dialogue about how best to meet these wide-ranging needs.

Even when teachers can only look at children's work over one school year (rather than over a whole school career, as schoolwide portfolios allow), much developmental information can still be gained. One team of teachers met on a monthly basis and brought along the work of students about whom they were currently concerned or curious. Spreading out each child's assessment data chronologically and encouraging one another to comment on what they observed helped them begin to see developmental patterns more clearly and to understand the similarities and differences in their students' development.

When Mary Ann Lillis and Crystal Winter, kindergarten and first-grade teachers in Douglas County, Colorado, analyzed children's work to learn more about development, they decided to use their clearer understanding of spelling development to do a presentation for parents. Using children's writing, the teachers gave the parents a concrete view of how children in their classrooms typically developed as spellers. This study led the teachers to discuss how they could better coordinate their efforts at supporting spelling development across kindergarten and first grade. Eventually, the second-grade teacher also became involved and began to consider the implications of spelling development for instruction.

■ ■

to sharpen the quality of your observations and your confidence in them

Many teachers find that the act of collecting and analyzing assessment information enables them to sharpen the quality of their observations and increases their confidence in those observations. Some teachers note, for example, that writing down what they observe students say and do encourages them to attend more consciously to what they are seeing and hearing, to focus their observations. Because teachers capture detail about students and their literacy in the assessment information they record, they begin to see and hear significant data even when they are not recording them.

Recording assessment information also encourages teachers to generate new assessment questions. One teacher commented, "As I review my notes on the kids, sometimes even as I write them, I realize what else I need to find out." The teacher who writes "Shawn is the leader in this situation" during buddy reading is apt to find herself wondering what it is about particular literacy situations that brings out or constrains Shawn's leadership. A teacher who jots a note about a student who supplies his partner with words at the least hesitation during buddy reading is likely to wonder if this "rescue behavior" is common among the other pairs of students reading together. As the teacher observes such behavior over the next few days, she gets better at spotting it and gains greater confidence in her ability to identify it during other situations in which students don't give each other time to work out problems.

The quality of teachers' observations and their confidence in themselves can also be positively influenced by working with other teachers. Teachers can achieve this purpose in two ways. They can simply read and talk about each others' assessment data—what it means to them, what it makes them wonder about, and so on. The teacher who took the notes will probably find that he has questions about them even a few days later; a colleague will very likely have even more. All these questions will lead to more detailed and focused data collection and recording.

Another possible approach is to have a second educator record assessment data about the same children. This can often be done by enlisting another teacher's help during planning time, by asking an administrator to set aside some time, or by having a teacher friend observe a tape-recorded lesson including the student. Comparing one set of data with another helps teachers assess the quality of their own and will perhaps lead to recognition of new aspects of a child's reading or writing behavior. Two pairs of eyes may focus on some of the same things, but they will also see different things. One educator might gather interesting and useful information that will encourage another teacher to grow in confidence and experience.

to have information about a student as a reader and writer to share with others

Along with the teacher who has responsibility for the students, there are others who are often interested in assessment data. This leads us to two final purposes for literacy assessment, both of which are related to the IRA aim of "monitoring the outcomes of instruction." Outcomes of instruction can be monitored for individual students, the focus of the purpose we will discuss here, and for levels beyond the individual student, the focus of the next and final assessment purpose.

Assessment information can be a powerful force in demonstrating to parents, other teachers, and even the students themselves what they can do and the progress they have made. Of course, this can help to spur a student's further development as a user of literacy. Often conferences with parents and other teachers in which assessment information is shared can help them understand more successful alternative ways to work with a child. Assessment data can also document particular concerns about a child and provide the foundation for a discussion with other concerned parties who might be able to help the student progress as a reader and writer. In addition, assessment information can be a vehicle for encouraging higher quality dialogue about learning and schooling among teachers and between parents and teachers.

Assessment information is also of vital importance to students themselves. All students need to hear about their successes, and some need to learn to value reading and writing as important in their lives. Adam is one such child. Though promoted to fifth grade, Adam had little confidence in himself as a reader and writer, nor could he articulate what strategies he used. He participated in a summer school program for children who were having difficulties with literacy. All summer, Adam's teacher talked with him about good strategies she observed him already using and worked with him to add new ones. By the end of the summer Adam was growing much more confident that he could read and write and would be able to keep up with next year's class.

Reporting to parents is more effective when supported by assessment information because teachers have a record to substantiate their view of a student's ability, attitude, and progress over time. Because the teacher can relate details of the student's literacy in the classroom, parents leave conferences with a sense of how well the teacher understands their child's literacy. Specific examples pulled from anecdotal records, for example, can help parents see their child as the teacher does. Without such records, specific memories and details about what students do as readers and writers can be lost.

Assessment data are also very helpful in situations where more than one teacher has responsibility for a student (such as conferences between a Chapter I and regular classroom teacher) or in staffings for special education. The data are likely to leaven the test information provided by others and supply important clues about which instructional contexts are supportive of the student's learning and which are not.

■ ■

to assess program strengths and weaknesses and guide staff development

Finally, assessment data can also serve as a way of monitoring instructional outcomes at levels beyond the individual student—"at the level of the school, the community, state or province, or the nation" (IRA, 1988). In our purpose statement above, "program" is a broad reference to large numbers of students who receive particular services (such as Chapter I), who have a similar curriculum (for example, writing process), or who are organized geographically (by school, state, or nation).

When assessment is done well, the information collected for monitoring purposes can be valuable to teachers. Its value depends on teachers' input into decisions about which instruments are used and how they will be used. This, in turn, depends on how close the "program" is to the level of the classroom. Teachers can have far more input about assessment when data are collected to make school-based decisions than they can if data are collected for use by district or national policy makers. We will discuss two examples, one in reading and one in writing, in which teachers' involvement in assessment in order to monitor instructional outcomes has improved the quality of teaching and of students' learning.

The first example has to do with reading at the level of Chapter I, a school district program. In our initial assessment work with the Denver Public Schools' elementary Chapter I program (see Shanklin & Rhodes, 1989), we suggested areas in which assessment was needed: screening of students to determine program eligibility; program monitoring as required by the U.S. Department of Education; pre-post assessment of reading and writing, including changes in attitudes and interests; and ongoing assessment of reading and writing to guide instruction. Program administrators and Chapter I teachers reviewed existing instruments in each area and determined which ones needed developing. After we had developed initial versions of these instruments, they were critiqued by program administrators and selected teachers prior to use, and revised in response to their input. After the instruments had been field tested, we gathered further teacher comments and made further revisions. If teachers were dissatisfied with the instruments for particular populations of students (such as emergent readers), they created others that were then adopted by the program.

In this example, assessment information was used in a number of ways: to help teachers plan instruction, to aid program administrators in determining issues and topics for staff development, and to provide the federal government with data it requires of all Chapter I programs. Of course, the teachers found the assessment instruments that were most like their instruction most useful in their instructional planning and the norm-referenced test data required by the federal government least useful in their instructional planning. At the same time, however, program administrators were able to utilize the wide variety of information that was collected in determining priorities in staff development.

A second example has to do with monitoring instructional outcomes in writing at a school level. For several years the English Department at Flood Middle School in Englewood, Colorado, has used analytic scoring of writing samples each spring to gauge students' progress. The results have helped them spot areas where teaching and learning have been successful as well as areas that could be improved. Teachers then address these areas with the same group of students in the next grade and are encouraged to make adjustments to ensure that the incoming group of students also focuses on these areas. In staff development sessions some teachers have dealt with the weaknesses uncovered by the data, some teachers have explored problems in university course work, and most recently they have instituted peer coaching.

In these examples, although data were collected to monitor instructional outcomes, they were also useful for other purposes. In one, they helped improve the learning of individual students. In both, they helped teachers and educators in charge of staff development to determine how best to improve instruction. It is not always possible to satisfy these varied assessment needs when gathering information for the community, the state or province, or the nation, but when teachers are involved in determining how instructional outcomes will be monitored, there is a greater possibility that teaching and student learning will be strengthened by the results.

principles of literacy assessment

New knowledge about the reading and writing processes and how they develop has resulted in new concepts about how literacy can be assessed (Farr & Carey, 1986; Pearson & Valencia, 1987; Johnston, 1987). Each chapter of this book will discuss these advances and their implications in more detail, but here we would like to introduce eleven principles we believe should guide the assessment of literacy (see Figure 1.2).

assess authentic reading and writing

In evaluation, there is always concern about validity: Does the test truly measure what it claims to measure? In reading and writing evaluation this translates to: Does this test truly measure reading and writing? This concern about validity relates to assessment as well. It is equally important that we concern ourselves with assessing what we have defined and value as real or authentic reading and writing.

Reading and writing experts generally agree that students are not reading and writing unless graphophonic, syntactic, and semantic cueing systems are available to them. Yet many standardized, norm-referenced tests fragment reading and writing into isolated skills or require the use of isolated cueing systems. For example, the vocabulary sub-test of a typical norm-referenced test consists of finding a synonym or meaning for an isolated word or a word highlighted in a phrase. Although this is usually counted as part of the "total reading" score, we do not define this as reading because it does not allow students to deal with vocabulary in the context of a whole text. In such tests, students cannot use syntax or semantics to determine the meaning of vocabulary as they do in normal reading situations.

The treatment of the skills that tests assume add up to writing on norm-referenced tests is no different. Students' ability to control elements of writing is tested outside of the act of writing; or their ability to punctuate text correctly, for example, is tested in situations in which they do not have to orchestrate all language cueing systems in responding to the punctuation problems posed by the test.

We need to assess reading and writing while students are reading and writing whole texts and thus able to draw on available cueing systems. Then it is possible to observe whether a student utilizes information from several sentences to infer the meaning of an unknown word or understands the meaning of vocabulary about which the author provides little or no information. In writing, it is possible to see if students punctuate the simple and complex sentences they use in their writing conventionally, and if they don't, whether it is because they don't know how to or because they haven't attended to that aspect of writing.

Principles of Literacy Assessment

Assess authentic reading and writing.

Assess reading and writing in a variety of contexts.

Assess the literacy environment, instruction, and students.

Assess processes as well as products.

Analyze error patterns in reading and writing.

Consider background knowledge in the assessment of reading and writing.

Base assessment on normal developmental patterns and behavior in reading and writing.

Clarify and use standards in the assessment of reading and writing.

Use triangulation to corroborate data and make decisions.

Involve students, parents, and other school personnel in the assessment process.

Make assessment an ongoing part of everyday reading and writing opportunities and instruction.

Figure 1.2   Principles of literacy assessment

In addition to these considerations, if we want to assess authentic reading and writing we also need to be concerned about the pragmatics of reading and writing—the social situations in which they take place. If we want to know how students can read and write for communicative purposes that they themselves control to a large degree, there is little value in assessing reading and writing in testing situations where others control the purposes, the timing, the response format, and so on. We may arrive at inaccurate judgments about students' abilities on the basis of such tests. For example, a student who performs poorly at pronouncing the isolated nonsense words on the Woodcock Johnson Psychoeducational Battery may be able to use graphophonic knowledge effectively in whole text that he reads for enjoyment.

For these reasons, we recommend that students' reading and writing be assessed while they read and write whole texts for real communicative purposes. The assessment may not always result in a neat score, but we can be more certain that it is valid and that we have assessed reading and writing according to our definitions of these processes.

■ ■

assess reading and writing in a variety of contexts

If it is desirable to assess students' literacy as they engage in authentic reading and writing, it is also desirable to assess students' reading and writing abilities in a variety of contexts. Reading and writing are context-specific. Every time we read something, the act of reading is different, even reading the same text again. The same is true of writing.

Assessing literacy in a variety of contexts provides insights into students' strengths and weaknesses as readers and writers. In the middle grades, for example, it is not uncommon to discover students whose comprehension of narrative materials is good but whose comprehension and strategy knowledge in content-area texts are poor. In addition, we often gain significant insights by listening to students read orally and retell *and* read silently and retell. For some students, silent reading is conducive to more effective comprehension, while for other students, oral reading seems to support comprehension.

In writing, students' abilities and the processes they use can vary greatly depending on a change in context, such as the writing topic. For example, when Meredith was asked to write a story, at first she wrote a tall tale, a form she had recently learned in school. Her major concern was for correct spelling, and she did little revision. When asked to write a true story about herself, however, she thought a minute and then began to write about the death of her dog. From the revisions she made as she wrote, it was evident that Meredith was monitoring her text for meaning and inventing spellings for words she didn't know but wanted to use ("tomers" for "tumors").

Students' test scores or the notes teachers record about them reflect only how they did on one particular day and at one particular time and with one particular reading or writing task. It is not possible to know whether such a performance is representative if the assessment is conducted on a one-time basis only. How credible is a single assessment if an allergic child's mental functioning has been impaired by overexposure to allergy-inducing substances on test day? Or if a child has had a fight on the way to school? In addition, students often do not try their best on tests because they do not realize that important decisions are made largely on the basis of test scores. When we asked a group of fifth-grade minority students what they thought their spring norm-referenced test scores would be used for, they had no idea that these scores would highly influence what classes they would take in middle school the following year.

We need to assess students' reading and writing in a wide variety of contexts. Only then can we ensure that we are able to describe their reading and writing well. As we will suggest, we can also use our knowledge of how students read and write in various contexts to determine what contexts will encourage them to read and write most effectively.

assess the literacy environment, instruction, and students

Since literacy always occurs within a context and its use is specific to that context, it is not sufficient to assess students' literacy and ignore context. This context includes the classroom learning environment as well as literacy instruction. In the next chapter, we suggest that an assessment of the classroom learning environment should include attention to several important areas: the literacy demonstrations a teacher provides, the amount of time students are engaged in reading and writing, how students' attitudes and interests affect the classroom environment, and the authenticity of the classroom's literacy events. An assessment of literacy instruction should include attention to several additional areas: how the teacher gradually releases responsibility for literacy to students and the communication patterns within the classroom. If these elements of the context are excluded from assessment, a teacher may be in danger of finding literacy problems only "in" a student rather than recognizing that it is the context—the literacy environment and instruction—that may be problematic and should be adjusted to enable the student to develop as a reader and writer.

Admittedly, it is often easier to assume or decide that the problem is in the student rather than to make changes in the literacy environment or in our methods of instruction. Too often, we try to fit the square-pegged student into the round hole that is the classroom rather than trying to "square" the classroom so the student who is struggling can not only fit but thrive. A poignant story of a young boy named Patrick in *Learning Denied* (Taylor, 1990) is a frightening example of this. On the basis of a single preschool screening assessment, Patrick was identified as having perceptual difficulties, and when he did not learn to read quickly in school, more and more testing "proved" to the school personnel's satisfaction that something was wrong with him. Although Patrick's parents and Taylor, a literacy expert, requested that the curriculum be adjusted in particular ways to take advantage of Patrick's learning strengths, it was not done. Meanwhile, Patrick was learning to read increasingly more complex texts through an adjusted curriculum during home tutoring sessions. But the school personnel insisted that the problem was all Patrick's and that it was neither necessary nor vital to assess the school's literacy environment and instruction. As a result, Patrick stopped trying to learn at school even as he was learning to read outside of school in a context where the instruction was designed to fit him.

For the sake of Patrick and all our students, we need to be willing to assess the literacy environment and instruction we are providing and to change it to help students learn more effectively. In the process, we, and those with whom we work, may also modify our beliefs about literacy teaching, learning, and assessment.

assess processes as well as products

Traditionally, we have assessed products in students' reading and writing. In reading, we have checked students' answers to comprehension questions yet rarely gained insight into the reading processes they used to arrive at their answers. (The usual assumption is that there is a single answer, which can be marked or scored. Questions that have more than one answer often are not asked because they can't be easily evaluated.) In writing, we have evaluated students' compositions yet rarely gained insight into the process students used to generate the writing. Though we believe it is useful to continue to assess and evaluate products in both reading and writing, we find that the products are far more meaningful if we also gather information about students' in-process thinking and their reading and writing strategies.

Observing students' oral reading miscues, for example, provides teachers with insights about how children interrelate graphophonics, syntax, and semantics to construct meaning as they read. Examining a student's miscues can often yield information that is helpful in assisting the student with more effective strategies for constructing meaning. We can also learn a great deal by observing a youngster struggle with vocabulary in an illustrated story without ever referring to the pictures for help.

In writing, we can learn about a student's thinking and writing strategies by observing the student at various points during the process. It may be obvious why a student doesn't write much when we observe the student stopping frequently in the process of writing a story to ask about the spellings of words. We can also learn a great deal when we give a student a chance to revise a text the day after it was written, and the student reads it back, aware that parts don't really make sense but unwilling to change how the paper "looks" by revising.

Observing not only the products of reading and writing but also the processes by which they are generated allows us to know when change begins to occur in students' language processes—in their thinking and in their strategies—before we actually see significant progress in their products. The hope such documentation provides can sustain both a teacher's and a student's efforts to improve.

■ ■

analyze error patterns in reading and writing

It has long been recognized that analyzing errors in children's oral language is a powerful way to observe their language learning. Error analysis provides us with insights about the language rules and strategies children are using, and it also shows us what they are attempting to learn about language and the difficulties they are encountering along the way.

Error analysis is also important in discovering what students know about literacy. By analyzing the differences between what a student reads or understands in a text and what the text actually says, we can gain insight into the student's current reading strategies and the difficulties the student is encountering as a reader. Likewise, by analyzing the differences between a student's writing and accepted writing conventions, we can gain insight into the student's writing strategies, what the student is currently attempting in writing, and the difficulties the student is encountering. We also learn a great deal by asking students about these differences: Do they realize that they made errors, do they have ideas about how to correct them, and what was their thinking in making them?

Error is an expected part of language use. We all make mistakes as readers and writers. These mistakes have a special name in the field of reading—miscues (Goodman, 1973). The term *miscue* is intended to signal that not all language errors are a problem and that errors help us understand the rules and strategies language users employ in reading the text. Although the occasional error can be interesting and useful, it is the errors that occur in patterns which are most helpful to a teacher's understanding of what students are trying to do as readers and writers. Weaver (1982) points out that "semantic and syntactic growth are normally accompanied by errors in language use" (p. 443). She shows that students who are experimenting with new words and syntactic structures can be expected to make errors in their writing and that these reveal patterns of growth and difficulty. As Weaver also points out, counting the errors is not helpful to student or teacher, but observing the patterns and analyzing the reasons behind them helps the teacher guide students in adjusting their reading or writing to accommodate their new understanding.

consider background knowledge in the assessment of reading and writing

Current theories about the processes of reading and writing contend that background knowledge plays an important role in the construction of meaning. When readers possess background knowledge about a subject, their ability to understand what they are reading about that subject is enhanced. When writers have background knowledge about topics and potential audiences, their content improves and their fluency often increases.

Students may not have a reading problem per se but may experience difficulty with a particular passage because it is unrelated to their background knowledge. In one form of the *Basic Reading Inventory* (Johns, 1988), for example, the fifth-grade passage is about camping and fishing while the sixth-grade passage is about Halloween. Inner-city children from the Denver area consistently read and comprehend the sixth-grade passage better than they do the fifth-grade passage. Although they live near the mountains, many inner-city children have never been camping or fishing, but going on Halloween outings and reading Halloween books are common experiences. Thus, the "harder" sixth-grade passage is actually easier for them to read and comprehend.

Lack of experience or background knowledge in other aspects of reading also affects students' comprehension. Knowing about how texts are structured can affect how well students understand a particular text. Students who sense the structure of a text they've read retell it more coherently and with greater detail than students who do not.

In writing, problems related to background knowledge are most prevalent when topics are assigned to students. If students have no input in choosing a topic, they may know little about it and write a short piece that does not necessarily reflect their writing capabilities. Students who have little experience in particular genres, such as reports, also encounter difficulty as writers even when they know their topic well.

■ ■

base assessment on normal developmental patterns and behavior in reading and writing

The simplest concepts in education are often the most perplexing. Having adopted a more process-oriented view of reading and writing over the last two decades, literacy researchers and educators have discovered more about the development of various aspects of reading and writing. Yet they are also aware that there is much more to learn, not only about predictable developmental patterns but also about how individuals follow developmental expectations and deviate from them.

Teachers can learn about developmental patterns in two ways: by studying what researchers have learned and by studying their own students. Though it is helpful to have a firm knowledge base and a familiarity with the terminology of literacy development from reading research, it is also important to have the intuitive "feel" about reading and writing development that comes from personal observation. If teachers are to collect the most relevant assessment data and use it as a basis for good instructional decisions, it is vital that they learn the parameters of children's normal development as readers and writers and continue to add to that learning over their teaching careers.

Teachers who have the best intuitive sense about students' reading and writing development are often those who have some knowledge of development beyond their current grade level, perhaps from moving between grades as teachers. Special education and Chapter I teachers frequently need to work with normally developing readers and writers at a wide variety of grade levels in order to retain an intuitive sense of normal development. If they fail to keep this knowledge up to date, teachers may make judgments about students' progress that are based on extremely limited (or even unknowingly fabricated) views of what readers and writers actually do as they become more literate.

This principle is also important in communicating students' progress to parents. Parents have not had the experience of working with a hundred fourth graders over four years when they arrive at their judgment of how their own fourth-grade child is progressing in reading and writing. Teachers can help them understand what is normal development at a particular grade level by revealing to them what they see in the child's work and how they have arrived at these judgments. Test scores and report card grades cannot provide this important developmental information.

clarify and use standards in the assessment of reading and writing

Without clearly defined and consistently applied standards for analyzing students' reading and writing, we cannot communicate what we have learned in ways that others will consider trustworthy. Though we may have confidence in our own assessment data, it is also important that others have confidence in our assessment data. Valencia (1990) puts the matter this way: "Trustworthy instruments will require clarity of standards. . . . Clarity will come from us, literacy educators, who are knowledgeable about research and instruction, have valuable practical experience with children, develop expertise at creating, implementing, and evaluating alternative assessments, and engage in ongoing dialogue with our colleagues to establish a shared vision" (p. 61).

Another word for trustworthiness is reliability. Just as assessment needs to be valid, it also needs to be reliable. Reliability means that we can assume that the assessment data, and the conclusions derived from it, will be the same from (trained) person to person and across time in the "same" contexts (although, of course, contexts are never exactly the same). At the heart of the issue, however, is that others can trust or have faith in assessment information and its interpretation.

How are we to clarify standards? Certainly, an important aspect of this question is knowing and using what is currently understood about the nature of the reading and writing processes and about developmental characteristics in reading and writing. This means that we need to stay abreast of what researchers discover about the reading and writing processes and to continue to study the development of reading and writing in the children we teach.

Another element contributing to the clarification of standards is, as Valencia puts it, the "ongoing dialogue with our colleagues to establish a shared vision." It is not enough to read what researchers tell us; we must talk with the other members of our educational community in order to develop a *shared* understanding of what we read and what we ourselves observe in our students.

In addition to clarifying standards, we must also apply consistent standards to students' processes and products. Again, this is often best done through dialogue. We have observed teachers participating in reliability training sessions prior to scoring students' writing samples, and we are always reminded of how powerful the talk that surrounds such training is. Teachers not only clarify what the standards for scoring mean, they also work hard to become consistent at applying those standards in their own scoring of students and in comparison with their colleagues. By talking, they clarify the standards and the process of applying them consistently in their own classrooms.

Formal reliability sessions like these contribute a great deal to teachers' confidence in approaching the assessment of reading and writing through observation in their classrooms. In addition, teachers become increasingly able to communicate standards to parents, to other school personnel, and, most important, to students.

Let us end this discussion with a caveat: As important as reliability is, it is not really possible to be consistent in our judgments. After all, the reading and writing behaviors we are trying to assess are some of the most cognitively complex activities in which human beings engage. We can only work to increase the degree of reliability or trustworthiness. As Farr & Carey (1986) state, "[An educator's] concern with reliability is whether the results from one test given at one time will be generally the same as the results of the same test given at a slightly different time. The answer is that they will not. This means the information provided by any test is only an estimate of the information one is attempting to gather" (p. 137).

This takes us back to the importance of assessing reading and writing in a variety of contexts. It also moves us forward to our next two principles, using triangulation in assessment and involving others in assessment. If data are consistent (or if we can figure out why they are inconsistent) across various contexts, across various assessments, and from assessor to assessor, we can more easily assume that they are as reliable as possible.

■ ■

use triangulation to corroborate data and make decisions

"Triangulation" means that one draws conclusions and acts only after similar information emerges from multiple—often three—data sources, hence the term. Too often, we come to conclusions and make decisions about individual students and programs without using multiple means of gathering information.

For example, in one local school district, plans were made to document the progress of children in both whole language and traditional classrooms using only the Iowa Test of Basic Skills. But to conduct an effective study we would argue that other data need to be collected. How many books do children read in each type of classroom? How many strategies can they talk about to deal with unknown words? In Adams 12, a school district in the Denver area, these types of data were gathered (Hagerty, Hiebert, & Owens, 1989). They showed that children in what the researchers labeled "whole language" classrooms did as well as children in "traditional" classrooms on a norm-referenced instrument, read more books, and were able to discuss more reading strategies. Of course, triangulation is facilitated by planning ahead and deciding what kind of data one is interested in examining rather than thinking about it at the end of the school year when often only norm-referenced test scores are available.

When instructional decisions are made about individual students, triangulation provides a fuller, richer, and more trustworthy picture. Sometimes the data appear to be contradictory. A student may perform inadequately on the norm-referenced test section on comprehension and write a detailed and well-organized retelling in the classroom, but give a poor summary of a novel in a book talk to his classmates. Does the student comprehend well or not? When a student reveals good comprehension in one setting but not in another, we need to think about what it was in those other settings that did not allow the student to do as well as he appears to be able to do. We'd want to ask: Does the student generally not perform well on norm-referenced tests? Why? Had the student read the book before he gave the book talk? Was he uninterested in it? Is the student generally shy or ineffective in oral presentations? It is also possible, of course, that the excellent retelling was an aberration. Perhaps the student had so much background information on the topic in the retelling, compared to the other two settings, that it made a major difference in his comprehension. Or did the student do the written retelling at home and get help? These questions are important ones, not to be dismissed lightly. They all lead to a greater understanding of the student's strengths and weaknesses and thus allow the teacher to support the student's growth in comprehension with appropriate instruction.

We can approach questions like these in different ways. First, we could interview the student as yet another important source of information. If we showed the student in our example all three pieces of comprehension data and asked him to explain the discrepancies that puzzled us, he might be able to clarify what happened. We could also continue to observe the student in other situations in which he demonstrates comprehension, keeping our questions in mind. In this way we'll gain a clearer sense of the student's abilities and be able to make solid instructional decisions to support the student's development.

involve students, parents, and other school personnel in the assessment process

The students themselves, their parents, and other teachers and school personnel who interact with students may all see aspects of a student's literacy that teachers don't see or see in a different light. Their perspectives on students' literacy development, the literacy environment, and instruction are also helpful in gaining a more complete and richer understanding of students as literacy users.

Involving students in self-assessments can have many benefits. When students are asked to assess their own progress, they are challenged to reflect on the strategies they use as well as the strategies good readers and writers use. As part of this "metacognitive" self-assessment, students often clarify the reasons behind their reading and writing behaviors, which can help teachers make better decisions about how to assist their literacy development. Self-assessment also encourages students to monitor their own efforts in implementing new or revised literacy behaviors and to set their own goals as readers and writers. When students can see their own progress, their self-esteem increases, along with their confidence that they are—or can be—proficient readers and writers.

Often we think that parents are involved in assessment only when teachers are sharing information with them about their child's progress in school. The assessment process may start in this unidirectional way, but parents can become more involved. They have important information about their children's reading and writing that teachers do not have access to—except through parents' comments or students' self-reports. After all, parents see children reading and writing in many literacy contexts in the world outside of school. Because parents usually know their children better than anyone else, they can also supply important clues to help teachers adjust the literacy environment and instruction so their children can better succeed in school.

Finally, it is important to involve other teachers and school personnel in the assessment process, especially when students are involved in special programs or when a particular student is a puzzle. When students are involved in special education or Chapter I programs, the special program teacher and the regular classroom teacher should be collaboratively involved in that student's assessment and instruction. They see the student in different contexts and instruct and interact differently with the student. Together the teachers can learn about what literacy environments and instruction are most supportive of the student's learning so that they can help the student more effectively. Teachers who work together like this often become more willing to try new teaching strategies that have been found to be successful elsewhere. And this kind of collaboration in assessment and instruction is more likely to result in the student's successful transition out of the program.

Even when a student is not receiving instruction from more than one teacher, the observations of other teachers or school personnel can often be helpful when the student's teacher cannot figure out how to best assist him. In such cases, asking another teacher to observe the student during planning time, or having the student spend some time in the other teacher's class, may open up new avenues of thinking about the student. Sometimes administrators like the principal or district reading coordinator, have schedules that are more flexible for this kind of observation.

make assessment an ongoing part of everyday reading and writing opportunities and instruction

Because assessment is intended to inform and guide instruction, it needs to be pursued in an ongoing manner, not only for evaluation at the beginning and end of the school year. The most informative kind of assessment occurs on a daily basis during everyday reading and writing in the classroom.

Our premise in this book is that most assessment should be an integral part of instruction. While students participate in literature circle discussions, for example, teachers can jot anecdotal notes to record their observations. In addition to or in place of teacher assessment, students can complete and discuss self-assessment forms that focus on how the discussion went during the literature circle.

To make assessment an ongoing part of reading and writing, the teacher and the students together must establish routines that allow students to become increasingly independent readers and writers. This is possible even in kindergarten classrooms. Teachers must understand and become increasingly effective in recording, analyzing, and using assessment information so that they can continue to meet the literacy needs of their students.

recording, analyzing, and using assessment information

In order to record and analyze assessment data, there are a number of points to consider. First, you need some tools for recording data. Second, it's important that you find the time to conduct assessment. Third, you need to decide ways to record and analyze assessment data that best suit your requirements and needs. Finally, it helps to consider specific techniques that will make assessment manageable. In this section we will deal with each of these topics.

assessment tools

We wish we could include a clipboard with this book; that's how important we think it is! A clipboard provides a good writing surface in all instructional situations so you can capture the fleeting moments of the school day. It also serves as a reminder to record data. So, if you don't own one, we'd suggest that you get one— it will become a valued companion.

Besides a clipboard, you'll need a pen or pencil, of course, preferably one on a string that can be attached to the hole in the clip, and paper to write on. A clipboard will hold any paper that is standard size (8½ by 11 inches) or smaller (note the "or smaller"—we'll talk later about the usefulness of small pieces of paper) and a variety of thicknesses. Thus, you can be quite flexible about what you decide to write on during instruction. We recommend that you use loose paper on a clipboard rather than a bound notebook, since it is easier to organize and reorganize and allows flexibility in dealing with information.

finding time

Recently, as we listened in on a discussion about assessment, we overheard a teacher say, "I just don't have time for assessment. I don't want to give up working with children to keep records." While we applaud the teacher's desire to work with children, we question her conclusion.

There are at least three periods in a teacher's day when assessment can be conducted: during planning, during instruction, and during review of student products. When it occurs during the school day, planning time allows teachers to work with an individual or a small group in order to collect more detailed data than they can when all students are present. It may seem odd or even prohibitive to use planning time in this way, but if teaching students (rather than teaching curriculum) is your focus, mental and written assessment data are vital in formulating instructional plans. If some students are a puzzle, figuring out some pieces of the puzzle in a more focused assessment setting may facilitate planning and instruction.

Reviewing student work may occur after planning but certainly feeds directly into it. As you respond to and evaluate student products, you can note what you observe about the reading and writing of individuals and groups of students. An individual student may be attempting something new in her writing that can be extended; that should go into your notes about the student. Or students' science logs may reveal that almost the entire class appears to have a misconception about what conclusions can be drawn from that day's science experiment. In that case, a note about the misconception and about the few students who seem to "get it" may be helpful. Perhaps those students could do the experiment again and explain their thinking, or the class could try another experiment that contradicts their current conclusions.

In other words, time spent in reviewing student products can also be time for collecting assessment data. In order to celebrate learning, try making notes about what students can do now that they couldn't do before. It is helpful to have notes about where students apparently need help or information to aid in planning future instruction. If recording ongoing assessment data is new to you, give yourself enough time to try it out. Gradually you will begin to see it as a valuable resource for your teaching.

Of course, you spend the major part of your day working with students, so it is also important to consider how to find time to conduct assessment during the school day. In general, it is easier (and more useful) to record assessment data when you are not directly "in charge" or at least when you are not having to manage students' behavior. If you are always talking to students, you cannot easily record information. If students are independently engaged in reading and writing, how-ever, you can afford to record assessment data. There are a number of times when students read or write independently:

- **SSR.** Sustained silent reading (or whatever it's called in your classroom) is an ideal time to assess students. Spend part of your time reading your own book and part recording assessment data. Conferences can provide even more data than observing students as they read silently.

- **SSW.** Sustained silent writing (or whatever it's called in your classroom) is a time when it's even easier to take notes because everyone else is writing, too. Sit with some students and observe what you can about their writing process. Of course, you'll want to spend some time doing personal writing as well.

- **Reading or writing workshop.** Students not only work independently during workshop periods, they also interact with each other and with you, giving you plenty of time to listen and record. In fact, writing down what you see and hear will help you look and listen better.

- **Reading or writing in any content area.** Students should have a variety of opportunities to read and write in all their content areas. As they work on various projects, you can record information about their successes and problems, much as you do during reading or writing workshop.

- **Conferences.** Conferences (which can occur during any of the four previous situations) typically offer a great deal of data, which can be recorded as you listen during the conference and immediately after it. Consider involving students in record-keeping of what they did and learned during the conference.

- **Authors' circles.** When students share their writing with each other, the teacher usually sits with the listening students as a participant. With a clipboard on your lap, it's easy to record your observations of the author and the students' responses.

- **Discussion circles.** When students discuss literature they've read, occasionally sit outside the circle and observe rather than always direct or enter into the conversation. You can learn a great deal not only about students' reading but also about their interactions with each other and the impact of those interactions on learning. When participating in the group, do so for part of the time and record assessment data for part of the time.

- **Talking about reading and writing.** Have regular discussions about what students perceive they are learning during reading and writing instruction. In the beginning, the talk is likely to be surface-level and repetitive, but as you continue to ask students to reflect on what they are learning and on the processes they use to read and write, they will become better at it and provide rich assessment data.

As you can see, recording assessment data requires that you establish an environment in which students can work without always depending on you to manage their time and responsibilities. When you spend less time being "in charge," you have more time to record the kind of information that will be helpful in expanding students' learning opportunities and horizons.

As we have mentioned, another way to find time to record assessment data is to give students the responsibility for self-assessment. Of course, students will need to be taught how to observe themselves, how to pinpoint difficulties, how to pat themselves on the back for specific positive behaviors, and how to set instructional goals. But as you teach students to do these things, you will also begin to solidify them for yourself, establish with the students a culture of responsibility, and gain important information in the process.

ways to collect and record assessment data

There are several ways to collect and record assessment data: by testing students, by conducting performance samples, by observing, by interviewing students, and by filing students' products in folders. In practice, teachers do not approach these as discrete actions; two or more are often used in tandem with each other. Here we want to consider the advantages and disadvantages of each.

testing

Tests, either commercial or teacher-made, are the most obtrusive of the various approaches to assessment. Students are aware that they are reading or writing so the teacher can evaluate—grade or score—their reading or writing. Testing typically is least like authentic reading and writing. The tasks are usually not the kind of reading and writing that go on in whole language classrooms, there are often time constraints, and no choices are provided to students. Answers are right or wrong and are not analyzed to uncover students' thinking processes. Testing can only reveal what the student does in a very limited setting, that of the test, administered once in a short time period, and containing only the sorts of tasks that were tested.

performance samples

Like tests, performance samples are primarily done to provide assessment data, although the reading and writing children are asked to do are like the reading and writing they do in the classroom. Since performance samples can also be obtrusive, we recommend that they be collected in settings that are more like instructional settings than testing settings. The *Emergent Reading and Writing Evaluation* (Rhodes, 1993) has been used with many children, who did not perceive it to be any different from what they usually do in the classroom except that they worked individually with the teacher, who took more notes than usual.

Unless performance samples are normed or standardized, or require the teacher to observe the students' processes closely, it is possible to collect samples as children do authentic reading and writing in ordinary instructional situations. A teacher could use the *Authoring Cycle Profile* scoring sheets (Rhodes, 1993) as he observed a number of students write an invitation to their parents to attend a school function. The invitations would become the writing products that are scored in the product portion of the scoring system.

Although performance samples, like tests, generate data from only a single setting, they do have one advantage, which can be expressed as the notion of "dynamic assessment" (Wood, 1988). Unless they are standardized, the reading or writing tasks can be adapted to reveal what the child knows. If the student appears "stuck," for example, the teacher can suggest another approach that will more fully engage the child in reading or writing and thus observe what the student is capable of in a more supportive situation. Of course, notes should be taken about the student's reading and writing in the usual as well as in the adapted situation.

The notion of a performance "sample," however, often connotes a product. It is not unusual for teachers to collect writing samples without taking notes about the process the students used and to evaluate only the samples themselves. Certainly, teachers could observe the process, as is the case in the *Authoring Cycle Profile* we mentioned earlier. And although the writing is usually done in a single setting, there is no reason why a writing sample cannot include all the drafts of a piece that has been published since they will provide evidence of the process students used to draft, revise, and edit as they moved toward publication. In reading, performance samples of in-process behavior can be collected by tape-recording students' oral reading or "think alouds."

◼ observation

As a method of collecting information for assessment, observation has numerous advantages. Probably the major one is that it permits information to be recorded in a multitude of literacy situations and settings, yielding rich data—both product and process—about what students can do. When observation takes place during everyday reading and writing events, it is not obtrusive; it is an integral part of the authentic reading and writing students do on a daily basis.

Observations can be recorded in two ways: anecdotal records and checklists, which include rating scales. Anecdotal records are the notes written by the teacher during or after an observation. The best are descriptive; they capture an event with enough detail so that the teacher can consider it again at a later time. Because the nature of anecdotal records is entirely up to the teacher, they can be used to record details about virtually anything that seems significant. However, the teacher must be expert in what to look for in reading and writing if anecdotal records are to be useful in later instructional planning. The teacher must understand the developmental nature of reading and writing, the processes of reading and writing, and how both might vary in different literacy contexts. (For more information on anecdotal records, see Rhodes & Nathenson-Mejia, 1992.)

Checklists are often used by teachers during or after instruction to record observations. Those constructed by reading and writing experts may be helpful in guiding teachers to look at readers and writers in ways that are different. For example, regular classroom teachers were asked to use a rating scale to judge whether children's miscues made sense in order to help identify appropriate students for Chapter I in the Denver Public Schools. (See the *Classroom Teacher Judgment Rating Scale*,

Rhodes, 1993.) As a result, many teachers found themselves listening to what students read in new ways.

Teachers who have a broad knowledge base about reading and writing often design their own checklists. But these same teachers often find that the open-ended nature of anecdotal records is more suitable for capturing the rich literacy behaviors and events in their classrooms.

Because assessment checklists are static and students are not, a single checklist, no matter how well designed, will not be suitable over an entire school year. Students develop as readers and writers and your goals for them change, so your checklists must also change. In addition, the same checklist is not always suitable for all the students in one class, particularly when the students vary widely in their abilities and interests. An urban first- and second-grade combination classroom we know includes some students who do not understand that print is meaningful and stable from one reading to the next and others that are capably reading chapter books. Different checklists will have to be developed to capture a variety of information about these youngsters if they are to be used for all youngsters.

If you are in a dilemma about whether you would prefer to collect observation data using anecdotal records or checklists, consider the issues we have raised here. Many teachers use both. They find checklists to be efficient in recording the same sort of information from one student to the next and anecdotal records more helpful in capturing what cannot be easily confined to a checklist—the essence of the child's reading and writing.

interviews

Interviews are designed to uncover children's thinking about reading and writing and to illuminate teachers' observations of them as readers and writers. Although students are often not entirely aware of what they do when they read and write, what they say may help teachers understand those processes better.

Interviews can be conducted as separate entities or as part of instruction. Some interviews, like Carolyn Burke's *Reading Interview* (Y. Goodman, Watson, & Burke, 1987; reprinted in Rhodes, 1993), include a series of preplanned questions. Some are designed to be given orally. Others, often called "surveys," are designed to be responded to in writing. Whether given orally or in writing, interviews with preplanned questions can be more informative if teachers follow up on interesting or confusing responses by asking further questions.

Interviews may also be conducted within instruction. Asking open-ended questions—for example, "Tell me what you are doing here" and "Why do you suppose your teacher asked you to do this?"—as a child is reading or writing is often informative. When a visitor asks such questions, the child understands that it is his job to explain what goes on in the classroom and why. If the child's teacher asks the same questions, the child is more likely to view them as a test of whether or not he listened to instructions. We've seen some teachers overcome this problem by letting students know that the questions are designed to find out whether or not students have understood their teaching.

Other interview questions asked as you stop next to students at work sound less like a "test," however, and more an expression of interest in what the students are doing. "How are you doing with . . . ?" or "How is it going?" are often good beginnings. In general, we then try to focus on the process the student is using to do the task. For example, if you are a resource teacher helping several students in a more traditional classroom, you might hear "I'm having trouble answering these questions" when you sit down next to a student who has been assigned to answer end-of-chapter questions in the textbook. "Tell me how you're going about trying to answer the questions" is likely to uncover the source of the student's problem and provide you with some insight into how best to help. (See Nicholson's interviewing tips in Appendix D in Chapter 5.)

folders and portfolios

Folders are another way to collect assessment data. Students usually have separate reading and writing folders in which they keep finished and ongoing work. Although all the students' work can be of interest to teachers, folders are easier to manage if the work filed in them is selected from all the work the student has done. Some teachers prefer two sets of folders (one for selected work and one for all the rest), while other teachers prefer to have students regularly clean out their folders and take the excess home.

Collecting assessment data in folders is relatively simple to manage if students are involved. Even very young students can learn to date their papers. (Try a rubber date stamp; you'll be surprised how few forget.) Each student can also be involved in selecting his best work to keep in the folders the teacher uses for assessment. Or the teacher may decide that particular projects are destined for the students' current-year portfolios. At the end of the year, a final selection of this already-selected work can be included in the students' permanent portfolios—folders that are especially designed to reveal their achievements and progress through the actual work they have done over their school years. (See Chapter 9 for more information about folders and portfolios.)

We know one teacher who provides time each month for her students to select what they consider to be their best piece or pieces of work in reading and writing. She also gives them time to look back over the pieces they have previously selected and see what they have learned to do over the year. If you ask students to write down their own observations about how they've progressed, your job will be easier, and the students' ideas about how they are growing as readers and writers can inform your instructional planning.

A group of teachers in Bloomington, Indiana, have discovered a way to "file" students' writing in a more public forum. They provide each student with a 9-by-12-inch space on one of the bulletin boards in the classroom. At the end of each month, each student selects his best piece of writing to display for others to read. The newest piece (dated) is tacked on top of the old pieces, creating an instant record of writing growth for anyone who wants to flip through the year's pieces (Harste, 1989).

The key to effective assessment is to use several of these ways of collecting data. Decide which are most helpful to your goals. If your goal is to provide better information for making daily plans, emphasize observational data. If your goal is to provide a developmental picture of a student's progress to others, supplement observational data with performance samples, folders, and portfolios. If your goal is to provide others with comparative data, norm-referenced tests can be helpful. You need to decide on your goals and then determine which ways of collecting data will help you reach those goals. If you have a variety of goals, you'll want to try a variety of ways of collecting data.

analyzing data

Recording assessment information may or may not include data analysis, which requires that you make some judgments or come to some conclusions about what the information you have gathered means. In the case of a checklist or rating scale, you have already mentally analyzed the data and what you have recorded is the result of that analysis—your judgments or conclusions. In contrast, writing folders or tapes of oral reading contain information that still requires analysis. Anecdotal records, too, must be analyzed, although you may find that you have already done much of the analysis as you took down the information and may even have recorded some of the analysis.

Your thinking about when you will analyze assessment data will have a major impact on your decisions about how you record information. We know teachers who spend a great deal of time recording information but then don't spend time analyzing it. Gathering samples of student writing in folders is not useful unless you take time to analyze the work in those folders on a consistent basis.

The analysis includes making inferences from data, looking for developmental trends and patterns within individuals and across students, and identifying both strengths and weaknesses in learning and teaching. It also includes conferences with students to check your perceptions against theirs and help them set goals.

Teachers make inferences about students' reading and writing on the basis of tests, performance assessment, observations, and other kinds of assessments. Sometimes those inferences are made explicit, as in some anecdotal notes. At other times, it is possible to develop a hypothesis from assessment information and to check it (using triangulation) against other assessment data or to collect more data.

Looking for developmental trends or patterns of behavior is also an important aspect of analysis. In fact, such trends or patterns are often what enable us to make inferences about students' reading and writing. Consistent patterns of behavior may mean that the students know whatever it is you are observing, or it may mean that they don't know it. You may see, for example, that the most effective readers consistently produce miscues that make sense, while the least effective readers consistently produce miscues that do not make sense. Comparing the patterns of your most and least effective readers and writers is often a helpful way to decide what the less effective readers and writers need to learn.

Inconsistent behavior usually means that a student is attempting to learn something or do something new. It's often a sign that the student needs more information. Students need help to see when and how they are using some aspect of written language effectively and encouragement to use what they've discovered in those situations where they have been less effective. If you help students see the inconsistent patterns you have spotted, they can do something about them.

Looking for patterns is far easier if you have a good working knowledge of how students develop as readers and writers. For example, if you know how spelling develops, your observation of patterns can be quite precise and thus more helpful in planning instruction. If young children use the letter "h" to represent the sound "sh," a mini-lesson on how the sound is spelled in books will often be all the children need to move their understanding forward.

If you know about students' reading and writing at your grade level and at the grade levels above and below, you can consider how the data about students look in comparison. You may notice that many of your fourth graders are showing a great deal of interest in mysteries. From past experience with intermediate grade students, you know that this is not only unusual but also developmentally advanced, since it is usually fifth and sixth graders at your school who are most interested in that genre.

Looking for patterns will also enrich your understanding of how children develop as readers and writers. In many ways, what you are doing is teaching yourself about literacy development just as researchers do when they collect and analyze data on developmental patterns, making your job of analysis even easier the next time.

It is also important to look for strengths and weaknesses in students' reading and writing. For example, when we see reluctant readers who like to write, we can use writing to help them reconceptualize reading as meaningful. After all, the texts they read are written by authors like themselves. Assessment can almost always uncover areas in which students have succeeded and areas in which they can grow.

Finally, it is important to find time for analysis. Because planning for instruction ought to be firmly grounded on assessment, one of the best times to analyze data is in advance of planning. Begin planning with the question, "What do the students need to learn or experience next on the basis of what I've recently observed?" In your daily planning sessions, review written assessment information either to confirm the instructional plans you have in mind from mental "notes" or to uncover new directions that you might not have considered. To manage this, some teachers review a certain number of folders each day and the anecdotal records they've made that day.

In addition, consider reviewing assessment information during some of the time you spend meeting with other teachers. If you have grade-level meetings, ask the group to look over the folders of some specific students, perhaps those who are your most and least effective writers or those that you don't feel that you know very well yet. What did each of you learn about the students whose folders you examined? What information can you share? What can you learn together? If you are a resource or Chapter I teacher, consider holding conferences with regular classroom teachers about the students' assessment data. Together you can examine the students' work in the regular classroom and in the special classroom and think about effective ways of supporting the students' development. One of the reasons assessment data is not analyzed more is that many teachers avoid activities that isolate them from other adults. If talking with other people about what your students are doing is helpful in getting that job done, establish routines that make assessment analysis a social activity.

You might also consider sharing the data with the students and their parents. Preparing for a parent-student-teacher conference includes reviewing the assessment information on a student to help you identify what you want to celebrate with the parents and to formulate instructional plans that will meet the child's needs. But don't overlook the conference itself as a setting in which analysis might take place. It is not at all uncommon to uncover patterns you haven't noticed before as you talk with the child and parents. In fact, they may share something that helps you see the student's work in a new way.

beyond analysis

Although it doesn't always happen in the linear fashion in which we are presenting it here, recording and analyzing assessment data are followed by instructional planning, reflection on teaching, and the generation of further assessment questions. Once patterns of success and difficulty are uncovered for both individuals and groups of students, teachers can use this information to plan instruction based on their knowledge of students' current literacy development. Students who have similar instructional needs can be grouped together. Individual needs can be addressed within the documented strengths of the student.

Instructional planning also involves creating support systems for student learning outside the classroom. Report cards, parent conferences, student conferences, and special education staffings are all opportunities for planning. Specific examples of a child's achievements and problems derived from assessment data help parents and other school personnel to see the child from the teacher's viewpoint and provide clues about what contexts are and are not supportive of the child's learning in various situations in school as well as out of school.

Using assessment data to plan instruction encourages teachers to generate further assessment questions, not only about students' learning but also about their own teaching. Teachers become more aware of how students interpret their instruction. In addition, analysis leads to a more focused assessment of individuals and literacy events. Recording assessment data for one student or about one event often leads the teacher to look for similar patterns in other students and other events.

For example, a teacher took the following anecdotal notes while students read together:

> Brooke & Larry reading a Nate the Great story together—switching off at each paragraph. Brooke jumps in to correct Larry or give him a word at the slightest hesitation.

> Aaron & Shawn reading—switching off after every 2 pgs. Shawn loves the story—keeps telling Aaron the next part will be funny & chuckling as he reads aloud. Shawn is the leader in this situation. He interrupts with immediate help when Aaron hesitates with a word.

The teacher used these notes to plan how these students could assist each other without shifting the responsibility for reading from the reader. She also used the notes to consider other issues:

- Are other students "rescuing" each other as these students are?

- What effect will the planned lesson have on students' interactions over words during paired reading?

- What other interactions do students have with each other over ideas in the story when they read in pairs? [Her notes about Shawn led her to wonder this.]

- Do different pairings make a difference in how readers interact with each other? What kinds of pairings are optimal?

- In what other situations is Shawn a leader? What can be done to further encourage that side of him?

The teacher has now gone beyond analysis to plan instruction and reflect on her teaching. In the process, she has generated a number of new assessment questions. Thus, a new cycle of recording and analyzing begins.

making assessment manageable

Even before considering what will make assessment manageable, it is vital that you make a commitment to the importance and efficacy of assessment as an integral part of instruction and instructional planning. If you believe, like the teacher quoted earlier, that assessment robs you of time for instruction, finding ways to institute assessment as a part of your everyday routine will not be a priority.

We have already considered various ways of finding time to record and analyze assessment data and some issues that may influence the time you devote to assessment. However, there are other techniques we have observed that will also help make assessment more manageable. A major one is giving students responsibility for assessment, a strategy that is also likely to support their learning. Recording data involves students in understanding the processes of reading and writing and viewing themselves critically. They will benefit from looking carefully at what they do and how they do it. If they can learn to observe themselves, they can learn how to change the ways they read and write in increasingly flexible and effective ways. Throughout this book, we'll offer examples that show how students can be involved in self-assessment.

We have mentioned that you may need to assess different students in qualitatively different ways. You should also consider quantitative differences. We have already alluded to the fact that it may be important to collect more assessment information on students who are not progressing as they ought to be in school. Consider collecting some data on everyone while you collect more detailed data on those students who are not engaged readers and writers. The additional information will help you focus on how best to assist those students in becoming more effective and willing readers and writers. When special circumstances present themselves, such as an upcoming special education staffing or the arrival of a new student, again consider differential assessment. Don't feel that you need to have the same set of assessment data for all students. It is hardly ever necessary for effective or efficient instructional planning.

If you are in charge of twenty-five or more students, you cannot possibly collect or analyze assessment information on each student on a daily basis. Consider an observational rotation that works for you, perhaps a weekly or biweekly schedule that encourages you to observe each student carefully. Again, however, consider observing those students who need greater support and attention on a more frequent basis.

One technique that has worked well for a number of teachers who record anecdotal notes is the use of yellow stick-on notes. One teacher, who has twenty-five students, plans to record information on five per day during reading and five per day during writing. At the beginning of the reading/writing periods, the five students are represented by five stick-on notes affixed to the teacher's clipboard, each labeled with a student's name and the date. In addition, blank notes are also affixed to the clipboard for recording important information about other students who are not scheduled for observation. When a student is experiencing problems, a note is affixed to the clipboard for that student more often. The teacher uses these stick-on notes to remind her about which children she needs to focus on. Later in the day, she transfers the notes to each child's page of chronologically organized anecdotal records in a notebook (a folder also works) and reviews them in relation to other dated notes she has previously made about each child. If the notes raise a new assessment question, as they sometimes do, she prepares a new note with the question(s) listed on it. If the question is particularly important, the teacher puts the new note with the next day's collection on the clipboard. If the question can wait until the next scheduled recording date, the note with the question stays in the notebook until the appropriate day.

Another way to making assessment manageable is to figure out, often through trial and error, the most efficient ways to record information from instructional settings. One teacher who was new to anecdotal records found herself repeatedly recording the same information about her first graders' spelling: "Is beginning to use vowels," "represents all the sounds that can be heard in the words," "sounds words out loud," and so on. She realized that she could record this information more efficiently if she developed a checklist for spelling. At the same time, she continued to make anecdotal notes on other aspects of the children's writing that were idiosyncratic or difficult to represent on a checklist. Repeated recording of the same information and the inability to capture important information are usually the two problems that alert teachers to the fact that they may need to adjust how they are recording data.

Finally, you will want to think about how you are going to record and analyze assessment data and stay sane doing it. You may be a person who needs to make changes in steps. If so, consider tackling only reading *or* writing first. Or consider tackling a particular aspect of one or the other—some question you find particularly important. Or you may be a person who cannot tolerate the theoretical imbalance or practical inconsistency that will result in making changes in steps. If so, make the sweeping changes that you long for, but be patient with yourself. Don't invest hours in creating beautiful folders or checklists in the beginning; it's too hard to throw them out or change them when you find that they don't work the way you hoped. And even if the checklists work, don't assume they'll work for long—they'll need to change as your students change. Just because something doesn't work at first, don't give up. If your students gave up because something didn't work, you wouldn't be pleased. Expect no less from yourself. Work out the problems you encounter with anyone who is willing to listen and help you reflect, including your students.

teacher reflection teacher reflection

Maureen Holland, the author of our first "Teacher Reflection," is a fourth-grade classroom teacher in a school located in a relatively affluent area of south metro Denver and a recent graduate of the Reading and Writing Program at the University of Colorado at Denver. Over the past six years, Maureen has moved from being a skills-based teacher who relied on basals, a language arts textbook, and spelling workbook to a process-oriented teacher who bases her instruction on her assessments of children's strengths and weaknesses and a curriculum that children see as authentic. Maureen feels that this change has resulted in greater learning and has improved children's attitudes toward literacy.

Maureen began making changes in her instruction by trying out individual reading and writing strategy lessons. Gradually making adjustments and achieving success with these lessons, she moved to creating her own version of Writing Workshop and then Reading Workshop. She found that something was still missing—an adequate assessment plan that would allow her to keep abreast of children's ongoing progress. Her focus on assessment over the past two years has been the final step she needed to communicate and feel confident about her decision-making abilities as a teacher. Maureen provides a powerful demonstration of a mature teacher who uses self-reflection to improve her anecdotal notetaking and encourage students' learning.

Documentations of a kidwatcher

Maureen Holland

"I like sports—soccer, baseball, and basketball. I like school, it's the work I hate," Zach wrote on his survey.

Jonathan proclaimed loudly, "I hate to write. You can't make me write!"

"I am a slow reader. I don't go fast. I am a terrible reader," Cody disclosed during our reading interview.

"I hope you're easy on me, I'm not very good in school," confided April, while giving me a hug.

These revealing statements were among the first recorded in my anecdotal notebook. Strongly feeling that traditional assessment of students' finished work, or products, was not enough, I attempted to uncover a more complete picture by becoming a "kidwatcher." I began by having students complete an interest inventory. I then interviewed students about their attitudes and perceptions about themselves as readers, writers, and learners. I wanted to add in-process observations and conferences with students in some organized and efficient way.

Collecting and organizing anecdotes

"Brittany is a socializer who finds fault easily; she needs to be shown the positive side of things."

"Cody works at a slower pace. Needs lots of patience."

"Anthony is a very bright student; has some problems with social interactions because of his intelligence."
—from end-of-year reports by previous teachers

To organize my observations and anecdotal notes I used a three-ring notebook, 2½ to 3 inches thick with colored dividers for each student, writing my students' first names in alphabetical order on the tabs. I inserted the information sheet passed on from the previous teachers, added interest surveys, student self-assessment sheets, and notes from individual reading and writing interviews I had conducted. Later I included a reading miscue analysis and writing sample for each student.

I found that using pregummed labels (approximately 2 by 3 inches) worked well for jotting down notes. I could keep sheets of these labels in my grade book, on a clipboard I used while circulating during reading and writing workshops, and in various places around the room, so that they were always available when I wanted to record some comment or observation.

I observed students during silent reading, reading circle discussions, Authors' Circle, peer conferences, and throughout the reading and writing process. I conferred with students during reading and writing workshops and recorded observations on comprehension, strategies employed, and comments students made about their own reading and writing. Students were comfortable with my notetaking because it became so routine.

Dating each entry and giving a brief reference to the setting (for example, Writing Workshop, peer conference, and so on) was helpful. I abbreviated common words and wrote fragmented sentences. Later, usually during my planning time, I would transfer the labels to the anecdotal notebook.

Learning from mistakes

> "When I make a mistake, I feel really embarrassed," admitted Jonathan.
>
> "I say I made a mistake, so what. I just shake it off, and go on," advised Ryan.
>
> Kate revealed, "After I make a mistake, I go back and try again."
> —from a self-assessment sheet, "I'm Proud to Be Me!"

Rather than try to take anecdotal notes for all subjects, I decided to concentrate this year on the areas of reading and writing. I began by writing down in-process observations and summaries of reading and writing conferences. Early on, I discovered that many of my comments were too vague. "Creative story," "descriptive vocabulary," and "good use of mechanics" did not give me enough information about the writer. I began to quote lines or phrases from the children's work with more specific comments.

> 12/8 (Authors' Circle)—"On a hot desert day, during a drought . . ." Opening sentence establishes setting. Mentions a pond in middle of story. Would there be a pond in a hot desert during a drought?
>
> 1/14 (Edit conference)—Expresses ideas in complete thoughts. Uses capital letters correctly at beginning of sen-

tences. Uses appropriate punctuation at ends of sentences. No attempt to paragraph.

Striving for more consistency

"I think I did better because my grade went up. But I still want to improve my mechanics. When I am a professional writer, I must have good mechanics."
—from a student self-assessment/goal-setting sheet

While sharing my anecdotal notebook with some colleagues, I discovered that for some students I had copious notes and comments, while for others I had only a few. I had unconsciously collected more notes for those students who were behavior problems and those who were struggling academically. My method of gathering notes had been too haphazard. I determined that a more systematic collection was needed.

The pregummed labels I used came six to a sheet. At the beginning of each week, I wrote the names of my students on these labels and kept them on my clipboard. Each day I would focus on gathering notes for the six students listed on one sheet. Blank labels were readily available for additional observations and notations on students who needed follow-up conferences or mini-lessons. This method seemed to work better. I did not neglect those quiet or average students that often get overlooked. I could easily record at least one note or comment for every student each week.

Emerging patterns

10/4 (Writing Workshop)—Good voice in piece. Expresses ideas in complete thoughts. No attempt to paragraph.

10/11 (Revision conference)—Attempting to elaborate on ideas by using dialogue. Needs mini-lesson on use of quotation marks.

10/18 (Reading log entry)—Very few misspellings. Written vocabulary not as expressive as verbal. Afraid to risk misspelling a word? Used quotation marks in dialogue. Need to indent for each new speaker.

10/25 (Writing Workshop)—Indented twice in new story. Use of quotation marks more consistent. Using descriptive language. Some invented spellings.

By documenting strengths as well as needs, I began to see certain patterns emerging. The above notes record one student's progress over a period of four weeks. Using error patterns I was able to assess students' progress, plan instruction, and evaluate my own teaching.

It became apparent from other entries that I overemphasized recording the language mechanics (punctuation, capitalization, spelling, and so on) of my students. I needed to focus more on language expression, comprehension, and strategic thinking processes. I began by asking more process-oriented questions of my students during conferences. When I worried that Matt was spending too much time illustrating rather than writing, he informed me, "I always draw a picture first. It lets me see my character and what he'll be doing." When I asked Jenny what she was thinking as she stared off into space for almost ten minutes, she enlightened me: "I do most of my prewriting and planning in my head. I just think about it for a long time, and then I know what to write." Brittany told me, "I have to talk about it (the story) with a friend. Then I know that it will be good."

Enhancing parent communications

"I was proud of Anne for sharing her poem with the class during Authors' Circle. This was the first time she had volunteered to share a piece. She told me afterwards that she had been very nervous, but she was glad she had shared. The kids responded very positively to her poem."
—Teacher comment from Thursday folder

"When Zach feels insecure about something, he begins to act like a clown to cover up his own feelings of inadequacy," revealed his mother.

"Sorry about the missing assignments," responded Darren's mom. "His dog died this week and he has been having a hard time coping."

Sharing insights, comments, and progress with parents became easier using my anecdotal notebook. Each Thursday I would send home the students' papers in a pocket folder along with a cumulative comment sheet. The parents were encouraged to respond to my comments, ask questions, relate concerns, and keep me informed of their observations, attitudes, or problems at home. This written dialogue was invaluable in communicating with parents about their child's progress, and also revealed to me parental support, concerns, and values. Often I gained important missing pieces to the puzzle, when parents responded to my concerns or questions. At the end of each quarter, I added the written dialogue to my anecdotal notebook.

Cody's story

Cody recognized that he read more quickly when he read silently. He did his oral reading in a monotone voice, but his retelling skills were good. I observed that Cody needed a lengthy wait time before answering a question.

> "I like to read to myself, but not out loud to anyone else.
> My mom reads to my younger sister, but not to me.
> Sometimes I listen in. When I try to read to my sister, she
> just gets bored. I guess I just read too slowly and without
> much expression."
> —Excerpt from Cody's reading interview

Sharing this information with Cody's mother proved to be an important step. She had been unaware of his interest in the bedtime stories, but intended to include him on a regular basis from then on. She informed me that in second grade, Cody had suffered embarrassment when children had teased him about his reading aloud during round robin reading groups.

Cody set goals for himself to improve his oral reading and to learn to read faster. He would practice reading picture books out loud throughout the week before sharing them with his first grade reading pal each Friday. Sometimes we would tape his oral reading of these stories. He slowly gained confidence in his oral reading ability.

When I helped Cody activate his own background knowledge before reading and to chunk words together during reading, Cody was able to increase his pace while reading silently. His comprehension continued to be good, and at the end of the year he was reading lengthy novels and many nonfiction books.

Cody wrote on his third-quarter self-assessment and goal setting sheet, "I think I am reading much better now. I am trying to put in more expression when I read out loud."

Admittedly, being a kidwatcher and documenting findings does take time. But it is time well spent! I used my anecdotal notes to plan lessons and to reflect on the effectiveness of my teaching. My rapport with students was strengthened; they felt I recognized their efforts and respected their ideas. Looking at students' in-process thinking, in addition to evaluating final products, gave me a more valid picture of what children were doing in reading and writing and more confidence in evaluating student progress on reports to parents and report cards.

Conclusion

As you finish this first chapter and continue you may share the feelings and experiences of Carol Wilcox:

> In the past ten years, my view of assessment has changed
> dramatically. In college, I had a course on methods of evaluation;
> in that class we learned how to find standard deviation, mean
> and mode, and that a true-false test had to have at least 25 items
> to be valid.

> In my first two years of teaching, I don't think I worried much about evaluation. Instead, I believed that if I taught something, my students naturally learned it.
>
> In the following three years, my school's test results came under district scrutiny. During that time, I viewed evaluation as something done TO me and my students. Preparing my low-income, minority students for standardized tests took time away from REAL teaching, and the results told me little I did not already know.
>
> It is only in the past two years that I have come to view evaluation as a tool for monitoring progress and making instructional decisions.

Even when Wilcox began to reconsider the purpose of assessment, it took her time, effort, and reflection to begin to apply practical routines and techniques that allowed her to use assessment as a tool for observing students' literacy progress and making more effective instructional decisions.

Involving yourself in collecting and analyzing assessment data will help you grow as an observer and recorder and, in turn, enlarge your understanding of the reading and writing processes and how children develop as readers and writers. We have found that more teachers are successful with literacy assessment if they start simply and don't overwhelm themselves or expect too much of themselves at first. Learning to conduct effective literacy assessment is a gradual, ongoing process of refining and changing instruments, routines, and techniques. It is important to maintain a risk-taking attitude and to find ways to continue reading, sharing, and learning with other professionals.

appendix A

Adopted by the 1988 Delegates Assembly

International Reading Association

Resolution on Assessment

Background

Reading assessment must reflect advances in the understanding of the reading process. As teachers of literacy we are concerned that instructional decisions are too often made from assessments which define reading as a sequence of discrete skills that students must master to become readers. Such assessments foster inappropriate instruction.

We are concerned that inappropriate assessment measures are proliferating for the purpose of school by school, district by district, state by state, and province by province comparisons. The expansion of such assessments aggravates the issue of educational decision making based upon an inaccurate definition of reading. Be it therefore

Resolution

Resolved that the International Reading Association affirms that reading assessments reflect recent advances in the understanding of the reading process; be it further

Resolved that assessment measures defining reading as a sequence of discrete skills be discouraged and that the International Reading Association opposes the proliferation of school by school, district by district, state by state, and province by province comparison assessments.

appendix B

Adopted by the 1991 Delegates Assembly

International Reading Association

Resolutions on Literacy Assessment

The International Reading Association supports literacy assessment that recognizes and addresses the complex nature of literacy, that is built on goals and standards having broad societal endorsement, and that takes into account background differences among students.

Literacy is a complex process that contributes to people's ability to function in society, to more fully realize their intellectual and psychological potential. Literacy assessment must address this complexity by using a variety of observations, performance measures, and extended response items; it must assess literacy by the use of quality texts of various genres and a range of literacy tasks in a variety of settings. Educational leaders and agencies must explore new forms of assessment, must treat such assessments as tentative and experimental, and must set long-range literacy assessment research agendas—thereby avoiding quick, but ineffective, "fixes."

Literacy assessment must build on broad educational goals that have wide societal support and must evaluate students' performance against agreed-upon standards. Educators have a professional responsibility to provide leadership in defining the goals and standards. Such formulations should be developed through the active participation of teachers and students and must be reviewed and endorsed by a broad range of citizens.

All assessment must be purposeful. Two major purposes for literacy assessment are: 1) to inform learning and instruction; and 2) to address accountability concerns, that is, evaluating program effectiveness. As educators we have a responsibility to show that our instructional efforts result in expanded literacy among the students and citizens of our nations. Ideally, the same assessment measures and procedures should address both major purposes of assessment. However, given our imperfect understanding of the processes and dynamics underlying literacy and the limitations inherent to assessment procedures, we are often forced to focus on one major purpose or the other. For example, large-scale test results have been seriously limited in their ability to guide learning and instruction, but limitations in funding and techniques for validly aggregating such data limit their use in addressing large-scale program evaluation issues, at least for the present. Because the **primary** purpose of assessment is to inform learning and instruction, assessment designed to address accountability needs should not be permitted to interfere with or detract from the essential purpose of guiding learning and teaching.

Literacy assessment must respect and acknowledge intellectual, cognitive, language, social, and cultural differences. Therefore, assessment procedures must be flexible and allow for a variety of legitimate responses, while taking into account the variable contexts of opportunities for learning that confront children in different settings and from differing backgrounds.

As an international organization, an important goal of the Association is to support resolutions that will promote literacy worldwide. However, assessment issues and traditions vary significantly from nation to nation and across cultures. Assessment resolutions with global implications require extensive study and consultation. Since many among the leadership and membership of the Association have the greatest amount of experience with assessment issues in the United States and Canada, these resolutions apply most specifically to these two countries. However, they may well apply to other countries. Units and affiliates of the Association are encouraged to study these resolutions from their own national, regional, and cultural perspectives and to endorse them, comment upon them, expand upon them, and develop positions and applications appropriate to their particular needs and situations. In this manner, guidelines, resolutions, and positions on assessment that are more globally appropriate can and will be forthcoming.

The resolutions that follow reflect the continued commitment of the International Reading Association to provide leadership in improving, revising, and redesigning traditional assessment procedures and measures. They are intended to encourage innovative assessments which incorporate current theory, research, and instructional practice. These resolutions build upon an earlier set of resolutions which were endorsed by the Delegates Assembly of the Association in 1988 and reaffirmed by that group in 1990. Since 1988, however, there has been much discussion, exploration of alternate forms of assessment, and expression of concern for limitations and abuses of testing. Therefore, it is timely to expand the Association's position on literacy assessment. These expanded resolutions focus on the effectiveness of assessments, the assessment development process, the content and form of assessments, and the need for appropriate interpretation of assessment findings.

I. Improving the effectiveness of assessment procedures and measures

Whereas . . . educators and researchers concerned with literacy assessment are effectively using sampling procedures to increase the usefulness of assessments and reduce the amount of time individual students and teachers must devote to assessments for large-scale monitoring purposes, and

Whereas . . . many current reading measures used in the early grades may lead to narrowly focused instruction which insufficiently addresses the language and cognitive skills that become increasingly essential to literacy beyond the early grades, and

Whereas . . . students and educators must strive to attain the highest standards of literacy, and whereas much testing effort has, instead, focused on comparing students, districts, provinces, and states, and

Whereas . . . young children are especially vulnerable to negative experiences with tests, and

Whereas . . . reducing the number of tests administered in school will result in more time for learning and instruction while conserving financial resources. Be it therefore

RESOLVED that large-scale assessments for the purpose of evaluating program effectiveness, as at the national or state and provincial levels, be implemented on a sampling basis. Sampling approaches are economical and allow the use of more sophisticated, authentic tasks which often require more time for administration and increased resources for scoring and analysis; be it further

RESOLVED that the International Reading Association supports efforts to develop standards for literacy attainment that are applied to authentic texts and call for authentic tasks; be it further

RESOLVED that the International Reading Association opposes the proliferation of school by school, district by district, province by province, and state by state comparison assessments; be it further

RESOLVED that where large-scale assessments of outcomes for program evaluation purposes are deemed necessary, such assessments not be imposed on learners before age 9 (grade 4); be it further

RESOLVED that the International Reading Association provide leadership at the national, state, provincial, and local educational levels to review current testing patterns and practices to reduce the volume and proliferation of inappropriate or unproductive assessments.

II. **The importance of how assessments are developed**

Whereas . . . literacy assessments are often used to make important decisions affecting students, teachers and schools. Be it therefore

RESOLVED that literacy assessments be based upon broad goals and standards developed through consensus of a wide range of involved citizens, teachers, teacher educators, researchers, and representatives of professional organizations such as the International Reading Association; be it further

RESOLVED that literacy assessments be developed on the basis of the best available theory, research, and practice. The International Reading Association, through the professional talents and knowledge of its members and working with related professional organizations, will provide information and assist in creating opportunities to focus discussion, support and encourage research, and promote sound decision making about literacy assessments.

III. The importance of assessment content and philosophy

Whereas . . . teaching and learning are influenced by the form and content of assessment instruments which often have powerful personal, political, and professional implications, and

Whereas . . . there have been significant advances in our understanding of reading, writing, and language as complex, constructive, and dynamic processes, and in our understanding that definitions of reading as a hierarchical sequence of discrete skills lead to inappropriate assessment and foster inappropriate instruction, and

Whereas . . . students in most educational settings come from varied cultural, social, and ethnic backgrounds and are faced with a diversity of learning opportunities. Be it therefore,

RESOLVED that literacy assessments must be based in current research and theory, not limited by traditional psychometric concepts, and must reflect the complex and dynamic interrelationship of reading, writing, and language abilities critical to human communications; and therefore, to better inform teaching and learning, be it further

RESOLVED that literacy assessments must incorporate a variety of observations, taking into account the complex nature of reading, writing, and language, and must also include high quality text, a variety of genres, and a range of authentic literacy tasks; be it further

RESOLVED that assessments must reflect a broad based consensus about age-appropriate literacy tasks for students taking into account the learning opportunities that have been provided for children in schools and communities; be it further

RESOLVED that to be of use in the improvement of instruction and learning literacy assessments need to reveal change over time at the level of the individual child; be it further

RESOLVED that literacy assessments must be designed to eliminate bias toward students whose language, cultural, social, and ethnic backgrounds may be different from those of the majority population.

IV. The importance of appropriate interpretation and use of assessment results

Whereas . . . the International Reading Association recognizes that one valid purpose for assessment is monitoring the outcomes of instruction at the level of the school, the community, the state or province, or the nation, and that a second valid, and distinct, purpose for assessment is to provide input information to the teacher and the pupil for the guidance and improvement of instruction and learning, and

Whereas . . . large-scale assessments for the purpose of monitoring outcomes and classroom assessments for the guidance and improvement of instruction and learning presently require different approaches and techniques appropriate to the needs of those who use assessment results, and

Whereas . . . large-scale assessments do not address the question of how to improve teaching and learning and because such data are subject to misinterpretation and error when applied to small groups or individuals. Be it therefore

RESOLVED that users of assessment results recognize the importance of considering a variety of observations, procedures, and instruments; be it further

RESOLVED that users of assessment results take into account the specific purposes for which assessments are made and the settings in which assessments are conducted; be it further

RESOLVED that where large-scale assessments are conducted for the purpose of monitoring outcomes, results should not be reported for individual pupils, classes, or schools.

references

Brickell, H. (1976). Needed: Instruments as good as our eyes. *Journal of Career Education, 2* (3), 56–66.

Farr, R., & R. Carey. (1986). *Reading: What can be measured?* Newark, DE: International Reading Association.

Goodman, K. (1973). Miscues: Windows on the reading process. In K. S. Goodman (Ed.), *Miscue analysis: Applications to reading instruction.* Urbana, IL: National Council of Teachers of English.

Goodman, K., E.B. Smith, R. Meredith, & Y. Goodman. (1987). *Language and thinking in school.* Katonah, NY: Richard C. Owen.

Goodman, Y., D. Watson, & C. Burke. (1987). *Reading miscue inventory.* Katonah, NY: Richard C. Owen.

Hagerty, P., E. Hiebert, & M. Owens. (1989). Students' comprehension, writing and perceptions in two approaches to literacy instruction. In S. McCormick & J. Zutell (Eds.), *Cognitive and social perspectives for literacy research and instruction* (pp. 453–460). The 38th Yearbook of the National Reading Association. Chicago: National Reading Association.

Harste, J. (1989). *New policy guidelines for reading.* Urbana, IL: National Council of Teachers of English.

International Reading Association. (1988). Resolution on assessment. Newark, DE: International Reading Association.

———. (1991). Resolutions on literacy assessment. Newark, DE: International Reading Association.

Johns, J. (1988). *Basic reading inventory* (4th ed.). Dubuque, IA: Kendall Hunt.

Johnston, P. (1987). Assessing the process, and the process of assessment, in the language arts. In J. Squire (Ed.), *The dynamics of language learning* (pp. 335–357). Urbana, IL: National Council of Teachers of English.

Nicholson, T. (1984). You get lost when you gotta blimmin' watch the damn words: The low progress reader in the junior high school. *Topics in Learning and Learning Disabilities, 3* (4), 16–30.

Pearson, P.D., & S. Valencia. (1987). Reading assessment: Time for a change. *The Reading Teacher, 40* (8), 726–732.

Rhodes, L.K. (1993). *Literacy assessment: A handbook of instruments.* Portsmouth, NH: Heinemann.

Rhodes, L.K., & S. Nathenson-Mejia. (1992). Anecdotal records: A powerful tool for ongoing literacy assessment. *The Reading Teacher, 45* (7), 502–509.

Shanklin, N., & L.K. Rhodes. (1989). Transforming literacy instruction. *Educational Leadership, 46* (6), 59–63.

Speare, E.G. (1983). *Sign of the beaver.* New York: Dell.

Squire, J.R. (1989). Tracing the development of reading and writing. In J. Mason (Ed.), *Reading and writing connections* (pg. 1–6). Boston: Allyn and Bacon.

Taylor, D. (1990). *Learning denied.* Portsmouth, NH: Heinemann.

Valencia, S. (1990). Alternative assessment: Separating the wheat from the chaff. *The Reading Teacher, 44* (1), 60–61.

Weaver, C. (1982). Welcoming errors as signs of growth. *Language Arts, 59* (5), 438–444.

Wood, K. (1988). Techniques for assessing students' potential for learning. *The Reading Teacher, 41* (4), 440–447.

Wixson, K. (1986). Reading (dis)ability: An interactionist perspective. In T. Raphael (Ed.), *Contexts of school-based literacy* (pp. 131–148). New York: Random House.

Chapter Two

2

Literacy Environments and Instruction

reflections

☐ Before reading this chapter, consider the physical literacy environment of your classroom, especially the use of space and materials and their probable impact on students' literacy growth. After reading the chapter, use Loughlin and Martin's *Survey of Displayed Literacy Stimuli* (see Appendix C) and consider the environment again. What are your conclusions about the probable impact of the classroom literacy environment on your students' literacy growth?

☐ Choose a couple of the more and less effective readers or writers in your class and observe them using either the *Inventory of Classroom Reading Use* or the *Inventory of Classroom Writing Use*, or both. What can you conclude about the literacy opportunities you are providing for more and less effective readers and writers? about the literacy opportunities more and less effective readers and writers are initiating for themselves?

☐ Before reading the chapter, jot down what you think "authentic reading" and "authentic writing" are. Then list everything students read and wrote on the last day you taught them and assess the authenticity of each reading or writing event according to your definitions. After reading the chapter, return to your assessment and adjust it where necessary.

☐ Read the chapter section entitled "Reading and Writing Interest." Try out one assessment that piques your interest.

☐ Videotape your students giving a tour of the classroom and explaining how various materials and spaces are used. Use the students' comments to assess the learning environment and the place of literacy in it. You might also consider using the tape at back-to-school night.

☐ Think of a strategy or a skill you have learned to use independently—it may or may not relate to your literacy. Make a list of all the things you remember doing that contributed to your learning. If you place them in their order of occurrence, how did you gradually take responsibility for your own learning and use of this strategy or skill? In a group, share your example with others.

☐ Consider a reading strategy such as predicting, dealing with unknown words, or self-monitoring your reading for understanding. What is a possible sequence of lessons for gradually releasing responsibility for use of this strategy to students? What factors went into your decision making about this sequence?

☐ Record one or more student-led, small-group discussions in your classroom. What did students learn from each other? What are the positive qualities of students' responses to one anothers' peer transactions? What areas need improvement? How could you help students improve in these areas?

☐ Record your teaching of a reading comprehension lesson, readers' workshop sharing session, writing mini-lesson, or Authors' Circle. Examine your lesson for the following qualities:

1. How did you encourage students' personal interpretations and responses?

2. What questions did you ask (list them) that encouraged a divergence of response and problem solving? If you altered your questions during the course of the lesson, what were the effects?

3. How did you encourage risk-taking in your lesson? What evidence do you have that students did or did not take risks?

4. How did the nature of your transactions (IREs, wait time, turn taking, receiving comments and reflecting, and scaffolding) help or hinder students' understanding?

Literacy assessment must look carefully at both the student's learning environment and the instruction she has experienced. Assessment that focuses only on the student assumes that reading or writing difficulties are "in" the student. Assessment that includes an examination of the literacy environment and instruction assumes that the successes and problems a student experiences are the result of a complex network of dynamics that involve not only the student, but also the learning environment and instruction. As teachers, we have considerable control over these two factors. We can adjust either or both to enhance students' literacy development.

One teacher who has considered how the classroom environment and instruction have influenced the learning and attitudes of her students is Gloria Kauffman, at the time a third-grade teacher in Millersburg, Indiana. (See Chapter 9 for a "Teacher Reflection" by Kauffman and Short.) The assessments her students have written are indicators of her success in creating an effective instructional environment. One third grader reflected on the differences between last year's classroom and this year's:

> I'm totally diffrent in my life because of what's changed durring the year. Last year the things I learned seemed to go in one ear and out the other one. But this year information wants to stay in my head. We arent assigned seats or grops. We choose what to read, write and think. We are aloud to talk about our wrok. Last year we weren't aloud to talk at all. I learned that we are all teachers and learners.

A boy in the same classroom reflected more specifically on various aspects of the curriculum:

> I am getting better in writing because in this room every subject connects to others. When I read I learn in writing.
> In this room we also work together and share what we know. That way everyone knows more in the end.
> When I try to revise my own stories I think they are good because I wrote it. When someone else looks at my story they can point out my mistakes.
> In some of the lit. circles I've been in we came up with some good ideas to discuss. When I was in *the big wave group* I felt that I was growing alot in being able to understand the deep down meaning of the book and how the author wrote the book.
> In math, we don't *just* want the answer because that can't help at all. We want how and what and why. The book is just warm up, the real thinking is in expirements and all the other hands-on learning.

Because the children in Kauffman's classroom have talked so much about their experiences, their writing is very revealing. Not all students are as metacognitively aware as Kauffman's, but the impact of the classroom environment on students is equally great in either positive or negative ways in other classrooms. With this in mind, we want to consider the assessment of learning environments for literacy and literacy instruction. We'll focus first on a particular instructional structure which encourages students to assume responsibility for reading, writing, and learning, then on communications between teacher and students and among students themselves about literacy. Our discussion will move beyond the classroom to literacy environments and communications outside of school settings, which also have a strong influence on students' literacy development. So that you can assess the instructional structure and communication both within and beyond your own classroom with a more critical eye, we'll provide information and examples about both aspects of literacy instruction. But first let's consider the learning environment which shapes the context of literacy instruction.

assessing the classroom learning environment

The environmental conditions necessary for literacy learning to take place include demonstration, engagement and sensitivity (Smith, 1988b). When people read and write or when reading and writing artifacts or products are available, they demonstrate to learners what reading and writing are and how they are done. When students engage in someone else's literacy demonstration or read or write on their own they enact the adage, "I do and I understand." Engagement does not occur, however, unless a student is open or "sensitive" to it. Frank Smith defines sensitivity as "the absence of any expectation that learning will not take place or that it will be difficult" (1988b, p. 193).

Demonstration, engagement, and sensitivity are sufficient for literacy learning to take place, but here we are concerned that students learn about authentic rather than inauthentic literacy. We want students to read and write in situations where they construct meaning for purposes beyond instruction or evaluation and where they are agents of control over print use and the conduct of the literacy event (Edelsky, 1991). In many classrooms, students see and engage in inauthentic literacy activities or exercises. As a result, teachers have to work hard to get students to "transfer" what they have learned in exercises to reading and writing for their own genuine communicative purposes. But when students see and engage in authentic, real-world reading and writing, they learn how to do authentic, real-world reading and writing.

Although we'll explore the notions of demonstration, engagement, sensitivity, and authenticity separately, the discussions of each will overlap because they do not operate as separate entities in learning environments. Then we'll expand our discussion and explore ways you can assess the literacy environment in your classroom. Assessing that environment is an important and fascinating undertaking; it will help you understand how to make adjustments to increase the likelihood that students will become more effective readers and writers. (See Graves, 1991, and Loughlin & Martin, 1987, for additional support in building a literate environment.)

literacy demonstrations

As the most effective and experienced reader and writer in the classroom, the teacher is a key figure in demonstrating literacy concepts to students: how the reading and writing processes work, what attitudes adults have toward reading and writing, what materials are available for reading and what kinds of writing are possible, why we read and write and so on.

Students who see their teacher's eyes fill while reading *Where the Red Fern Grows* (Rawls, 1961) come to understand that people can react to books emotionally. Students who give their teacher suggestions about her writing in the Authors' Circle and then hear the revised piece the next day come to understand that revision is an expected and valued part of the writing process. But students who see their teacher grade papers during sustained silent reading time learn that reading is for children, not for adults. They may also conclude that reading is done for practice, not for enjoyment; otherwise, why doesn't their teacher read? Students who are asked to copy a thank-you note to a guest speaker from the chalkboard rather than compose their own learn that adults value the use of perfect conventions in writing over personal meaning.

As children witness demonstrations of literacy over time, they derive a cumulative definition of reading and writing. Of course, home demonstrations of literacy can offset school demonstrations. As a result of seeing positive demonstrations of literacy at home, many students talk about the reading and writing they do in school quite differently from that which they do at home. Too often, they develop two categories—reading and writing done "for fun" and for communicative purposes at home, and reading and writing "work" (inauthentic with no communicative purpose) at school.

How can you assess the demonstrations you provide to students? Consider the reading and writing you've done in the last day or so while spending time with students. Divide a piece of paper into two columns and list each demonstration in the left-hand column (remember that anything the students have witnessed is a demonstration—whether you intended it as such or not). Then put yourself in the students' shoes and consider what they might have learned from observing you and write that in the right-hand column. As an illustration, we'll repeat and expand upon two examples we presented earlier.

Demonstrations I Provided	What Students Might Have Learned
1. I read my writing in Authors' Circle and asked for suggestions. I wrote down the suggestions.	1. The teacher values writing enough to do it herself. The teacher values students' ideas about her writing. The teacher thinks it's important to hear others' ideas about writing. Revision is an expected and valued part of writing. How to keep track of others' suggestions.
2. I graded papers during SSR.	2. Reading is for children, not for adults. Reading is not enjoyable to the teacher. Grading papers is more important than reading.

Now look over what your students have learned from your demonstrations of reading and writing. Especially if the literacy demonstrations the students are receiving elsewhere (at home) are limited, are you satisfied with what you are "teaching"? If not, work backwards by listing what you'd like your students to learn in the right-hand column. And then consider what you need to demonstrate so they can learn those things. We will say more about this later.

If you want to delve into literacy demonstrations even further, you can assess those the students in your classroom provide for each other in the same way you assessed your own. In classrooms where students interact with each other a great deal during literacy activities, the literacy demonstrations they provide for each other are also important.

Classroom artifacts also demonstrate a great deal about reading and writing and how they are done. "Artifacts" are usually defined as objects or materials of some kind, but we want to expand that to include not only literacy materials but also the arrangement of those materials in the classroom.

Literacy materials and how they are organized in space can demonstrate a great deal to students about reading and writing. A classroom in which books are displayed in a number of places (such as a reading corner; an area containing Japanese costumes, maps, informational books, and novels set in Japan; a shelf for books about guinea pigs next to the cage) demonstrates that books are important and may be used for enjoyment and for gaining information. A well-stocked publishing center demonstrates to children that writing for an audience is important, that the students have significant ideas to communicate to others, and that text can be prepared for publication in a number of ways.

Loughlin & Martin's (1987) classroom assessment focuses on whether materials and their organization will encourage and invite students to engage in literacy activities, but it is also helpful in considering what space and materials tell children about reading and writing. *The Survey of Displayed Literacy Stimuli* (see Appendix C) provides a vehicle for examining each area of the classroom for 1) the pattern of distribution of "literacy stimuli," or materials and spaces, and 2) the kinds of literacy stimuli, or materials and spaces.

Using a sketch of your classroom, make a list for each area. Then assess each area's materials and spaces as you *sit* in it; Loughlin and Martin argue that the only materials and spaces that demonstrate literacy to students are those that are at eye level when the students are sitting. Then survey child-generated text; directions for daily activities; different kinds of books, recording materials, and reference sources; books and other print related to nearby materials, objects, or pictures; and the presence of functional labels and display space for children's work.

Using Loughlin and Martin's survey summary sheet, you can assess the level of demonstrations provided by classroom materials and space overall and the level provided by each area. In addition, the survey sheet permits you to analyze the extent to which students generate literacy demonstrations for each other, how much and where students can locate and use functional print, the extent to which there are interesting materials to read and write about in the environment, the intensity of support for written communication, and the extent to which the use of books is fostered.

▪ ▪

literacy engagement

Of course, people and artifacts can demonstrate reading and writing and how they are done, but unless students engage in reading and writing in concert with others and on their own, they will not achieve literacy learning. Opportunities to engage in reading and writing are key to students' progress. Teachers encourage engagement not only by providing demonstrations but also by providing time and a variety of literacy experiences.

Time to read and write connected discourse (whole stories, poems, informational material, and so on) is an important ingredient in a student's literacy learning. Allington's (1980) finding that students spend an average of seven minutes per day reading in school reveals serious problems in the area of literacy engagement. As Frank Smith emphatically states, "Children learn to read [and write] by reading [and writing]" (1988b). It's simply not possible to become an effective literacy user without engaging in reading and writing for a great deal of time.

Students can assist teachers in assessing the amount of time they spend reading and writing, both at home and at school. For example, sustained silent reading is a school routine that encourages engagement in reading. It is easy enough for either a teacher or a student to keep track of how much time is scheduled and how much is actually used on a daily/weekly/monthly basis for reading. But it is also important that students recognize and assess their engagement in such opportunities. After all, teachers can provide opportunities that students don't take advantage of; a student who reads for only a few minutes during a lengthy reading period is not taking advantage of the reading opportunity the teacher has provided. The form in Figure 2.1 (also in Rhodes, 1993) allows a teacher to assess the degree of engagement in sustained silent reading, often called DEAR time.

Drop Everything and Read (DEAR)

Name _____ Date _____

1. How much time did you spend reading during DEAR time today?

   all the time   most of the time   some of the time   not at all

2. If you didn't spend all the time reading, why didn't you?

3. What will help you so that you'll spend all your time reading the next time we have DEAR time?

Figure 2.1   DEAR Self-assessment

This assessment is filled out by the students in order to establish in their minds that they are responsible for their participation in DEAR time and to structure class discussions of problems that arise. For example, pooling students' responses to the third question will help students generate solutions such as having reading material ready at the beginning of each reading period, developing possible ways to refocus their wandering attention, and so on.

Once the sustained silent reading period is established, occasional self-assessment will keep students mindful of their responsibility to remain engaged in reading during the period. The same self-assessment might be handed out randomly to students from time to time to keep tabs on the engagement level in the class and any new problems that may have arisen. In addition, you might want to observe or interview particular students about whom you are concerned by using the form in Figure 2.2 (also in Rhodes, 1993), which is analogous to the one for students. When your observations of a student are not in accord with the student's self-evaluation, it probably signals a need for a conference.

Drop Everything and Read (DEAR)

Name _____ Date _____

Reading material_____ # minutes_____

1. How much time did you spend reading during DEAR time today?

   all the time   most of the time   some of the time   not at all

2. If not all of the time, what appeared to be the source of difficulty?

3. Source of difficulty determined through: observation   interview

---

Figure 2.2   DEAR Assessment

Literature Study Contract

Name _____ Date _____

During the week of _____, I agree to read the book entitled _____

_____. This book has a total of _____ pages. I will pace myself

according to the schedule below.

M	T	W	TH	F	SA	SU
_____	_____	_____	_____	_____	_____	_____

I kept close to my planned schedule.   Yes _____ No _____

I finished the book on time.   Yes _____ No _____

I did not finish the book. I am on page _____.

Student's signature _____

Parent's signature _____

Teacher's signature _____

Figure 2.3   Literature Study Contract

Students' engagement in reading can also be assessed in the home environment. For example, Peterson & Eeds (1990) propose a contract developed by Karen Smith, a former sixth-grade teacher in Arizona, which also functions as a self-assessment. The contract (see Figure 2.3) is intended to encourage home engagement in reading a piece of literature that will be studied in school the following week. The contract asks students to plan and assess their reading time. If home reading is to be a recurring assignment, students who had difficulty fulfilling the contract might benefit from discussing what their problems were and what they might do in the future to meet the terms of the contract.

As we said in introducing this section, teachers encourage literacy engagement through the provision of the time and a variety of literacy experiences. It is possible that students will have plentiful amounts of time to read and write but a narrow range of reading and writing experiences. It is not surprising, for example, to find that students read mostly realistic fiction when their teacher also gravitates toward that genre. Nor is it surprising that students don't gather and use information to provide specific details in their writing if the teacher hasn't helped them analyze how authors go about doing so. Through their selection of tasks, activities, materials, and lesson, teachers can influence the varieties of reading and writing opportunities that students choose.

Students can help in the assessment of reading and writing they are engaged in by doing their own record-keeping. For example, students can list the titles and authors of the books they have read in their reading folders. Such a book-reading record can be used to analyze the variety of reading students have undertaken. Students can be asked if they ever reread books and why. They can also analyze their genre preferences by deciding which books can be classified as realistic fiction, historical fiction or biography, nonfiction, fantasy, poetry, and so on. This kind of analysis is often a useful way to help students refocus their reading or writing, to challenge them to try something new, or to broaden the reading and writing they engage in. Including students in the analysis usually results in far more understanding and involvement than if teachers analyze the records on their own and communicate their findings to students.

An observation instrument developed to assess both the amount and the variety of opportunities students have for reading is the *Inventory of Classroom Reading Use*. The instrument is useful for assessing the environment you provide for students because you observe not only the extent to which students engage in various kinds of reading but also whether the reading is student- or teacher-initiated. The "teacher-initiated" column allows you to assess whether you are providing the varied opportunities students need to engage in reading if they are not engaging in these activities on their own. The *Inventory of Classroom Reading Use* (CAWLs, 1993) and *Inventory of Classroom Writing Use* (Conrad, 1993), an analogous instrument, may be used to assess the variety of writing in which students engage. Both instruments may be found in *Literacy Assessment: A Handbook of Instruments* (Rhodes, 1993.)

One fourth-grade teacher who used the *Inventory of Classroom Reading Use* saw a recurring pattern in her observations of students' engagement in various kinds of reading and the level of support she was providing for them to grow in this area. The inventory for Ginelle shown in Figure 2.4 was filled out in October. It reveals that Ginelle was reading a very narrow range of fiction and did not use reading for informational purposes.

Many of the girls in the class had the same sort of profile. Many of the boys in the class also read a narrow range of material, though it tended to be almost exclusively nonfiction. As the teacher completed the inventories, she realized that she needed to help the students read more widely and in genres other than those they were currently choosing to read on their own. The fact that she could not mark the "teacher-initiated" column helped her understand that her curriculum and learning routines were permitting children to read narrowly. She also realized that other routines were having a positive impact on the amount of reading students were doing; almost all the students were marked in the high ranges for items 7 and 8.

On the basis of her findings, the teacher began to highlight high-quality literature from a variety of genres in her read-aloud time and to incorporate a variety of good fiction and nonfiction tradebooks into science and social studies classes. She also talked with students about various genres and asked them to record the genre of each book they read. By February, as Figure 2.5 shows, there was a considerable difference in the kind of reading Ginelle and others in the class did.

Name *Ginelle*   Grade **4th**

Teacher _____   Date   **10/90**

An Inventory of Classroom Reading Use

To what extent does the student:

	Not at all	A little	To some extent	To a large extent	To a great extent	Teacher-initiated	Student-initiated
1. Utilize available environmental print? (posters, cafeteria menu, notices to go home)	A	**B**	C	D	E	☐	☐
2. Seek specific information from printed material? (maps, yellow pages, directions)	A	**B**	C	D	E	☐	☑
3. Gather related information for a specific purpose from a variety of sources?	**A**	B	C	D	E	☐	☐
4. Engage in a wide variety of book reading? *Babysitters' Club almost exclusively.*	**A**	B	C	D	E	☐	☐
5. Engage in reading materials at various difficulty levels? (easy to hard for child)	A	**B**	C	D	E	☐	☐
6. Seek/follow up the reading of a piece of material with related reading? (another book by the same author, another book on the same topic) *All B.C. books -- some Judy Blume*	A	B	**C**	D	E	☑	☑
7. Choose to read during "choice" time?	A	B	C	D	**E**	☑	☑
8. Engage fully in reading during sustained silent reading periods?	A	B	C	D	**E**	☑	☑

Comments:

_____

Figure 2.4   Inventory of Classroom Reading Use

The teacher could clearly see that the actions she had taken (as recorded in the "teacher-initiated" column) had paid off in the range of materials the students were reading. She hoped that she would be able to put more checks in the "student-initiated" column by the end-of-year checkpoint, to indicate that the students were more independent in engaging in a wide variety of reading on their own.

| Name | Ginelle | Grade | 4th |
| Teacher | | Date | 2/91 |

An Inventory of Classroom Reading Use

To what extent does the student:

	Not at all	A little	To some extent	To a large extent	To a great extent	Teacher-initiated	Student-initiated
1. Utilize available environmental print? (posters, cafeteria menu, notices to go home)	A	B	*C*	D	E	☑	☐
2. Seek specific information from printed material? (maps, yellow pages, directions)	A	*B*	C	D	E	☐	☐
3. Gather related information for a specific purpose from a variety of sources?	A	B	*C*	D	E	☑	☐
4. Engage in a wide variety of book reading? *Has branched out to Betsy Byars, Katherine Patterson and others*	A	B	*C*	D	E	☑	☐
5. Engage in reading materials at various difficulty levels? (easy to hard for child)	A	B	*C*	D	E	☑	☐
6. Seek/follow up the reading of a piece of material with related reading? (another book by the same author, another book on the same topic) *Has chosen to read other non-fiction related to our science and social studies topics*	A	B	C	*D*	E	☑	☑
7. Choose to read during "choice" time?	A	B	C	D	*E*	☑	☑
8. Engage fully in reading during sustained silent reading periods?	A	B	C	D	*E*	☑	☑

Comments:

_____

Figure 2.5 Inventory of Classroom Reading Use

sensitivity

Smith (1988b) states that engagement in literacy will not occur unless the student is "sensitive" to engagement. The student must approach literacy activities confident that engagement and learning are possible. Although teachers don't often sit over a cup of coffee discussing sensitivity, they do talk about their students' attitudes and interests and how they affect the students' engagement in literacy. Smith's notion of sensitivity can be thought of as a container for a student's attitudes and interests. Together they determine how open a student is to a particular literacy activity. Students need to feel that tasks will not be too hard and that they can learn from them.

Students' attitudes and interests not only affect their own engagement in literacy, they often affect the literacy environment of the classroom: the literacy demonstrations that are available to other students and the engagement of other students in literacy events. For example, students who don't enjoy writing won't write much and therefore won't become good at writing. When students don't write, they can't provide demonstrations of writing for other students. When students who don't like to write engage in writing, they often demonstrate a dislike of writing as well as ineffective writing strategies. Attitudes and interests are contagious (Moawad, 1982).

These affective aspects of literacy are important because they have a major impact on students' literacy growth. As Sanders (1987) states, "the interplay between affect and cognition [is] clearly observable, and it is ultimately the workings of both together that contribute to [a child's] . . . growth as a literate person, and indeed as a human being" (p. 631).

▥ attitude toward reading and writing

Students' attitude toward reading and writing plays an important role in the literacy development of all students, no matter how proficient they are. Reed (1979) says of students who are becoming literate, "How a student feels about reading [or writing] can, to a large extent, determine the ultimate success that the student will have in learning to read" (p. 149). Estes (1971) says of the student who has developed the ability to read and write, "How students feel about reading [or writing] is as important as whether they are able to read [or write], for, as is true for most abilities, the value of reading [writing] ability lies in its use rather than its possession" (p. 135). You cannot assume that students who are effective readers and writers have a good attitude toward literacy; nor can you assume that students who are ineffective readers and writers have a poor attitude toward literacy. Both affective aspects of literacy and students' abilities need to be considered in instructional planning (Roettger, 1980).

Several different techniques may be used to assess students' attitude toward reading and writing. The most unobtrusive is to take anecdotal records about students' spontaneous remarks during such activities as story time or conferences, about their level of enjoyment when they go to the library, and so on. (Refer to the beginning of Maureen Holland's "Teacher Reflection" in Chapter 1 for anecdotal record examples on attitude.) If the use of instruments is warranted or helpful, the *Inventory of Classroom Reading (Writing) Use* can help you to infer attitude from use.

More focused observations may be made of attitude indicators: the number of library books students carry home with them, the number of books students have read during a grading period, or even the number of books that are worn from use

Observational Checklist

Name _____ Date _____

In the two-week period, has the child:	Yes	No
1. Seemed happy when engaged in reading activities?	_____	_____
2. Volunteered to read aloud in class?	_____	_____
3. Read a book during free time?	_____	_____
4. Mentioned reading a book at home?	_____	_____
5. Chosen reading over other activities (playing games, coloring, talking, etc.)?	_____	_____
6. Made requests to go to the library?	_____	_____
7. Checked out books at the library?	_____	_____
8. Talked about books s/he has read?	_____	_____
9. Finished most of the books s/he has started?	_____	_____
10. Mentioned books s/he has at home?	_____	_____

Figure 2.6   Observational Checklist

at the end of the school year. A ten-item observational checklist (see Figure 2.6) developed by Heathington & Alexander (1978, p. 770) may be helpful to use as is or to adapt. The checklist is intended to be filled out for individual students over a two-week period.

You may need to adapt this checklist to mirror what you value, how you spend your time in the classroom, and what the routines of the school are. For example, if students are allowed to go to the library only once a week, they are not likely to ask to go to the library—not because of a poor attitude toward reading but because they know they can only visit the library at the scheduled time. In such cases, item 6 in the checklist would not be a helpful indicator of attitude toward reading. You could also adapt this checklist to observe students' attitude toward writing.

Questionnaires or surveys are another favored way to assess attitude toward reading and writing. There are several published reading attitude surveys (Atwell, 1987; Estes, 1971; Heathington & Alexander, 1978; McKenna & Kear, 1990) and a few writing attitude surveys (Atwell, 1987; Daly & Miller, 1975; Emig & King, 1985). One reading attitude survey, the *Elementary Reading Attitude Survey*, or ERAS, was developed and norm-referenced for students in grades 1 to 6. It uses a Lickert scale of "Garfield" expressions (from a broadly smiling to a scowling Garfield) that younger students find easy to understand. The ERAS assesses students' attitudes about recreational reading as well as their attitudes about academic reading. It has the advantage of being suitable for group administration and may be copied for classroom use from McKenna & Kear (1990) or from Rhodes (1993).

Although the ERAS can be helpful in assessing reading attitude, several items that assess attitude toward academic reading may prove problematic for some teachers. The survey is intended for use beginning in first grade, but most teachers of young children will not find "How do you feel about using the dictionary?" age-appropriate. In fact, we wonder if there aren't better ways for teachers at any grade level to assess academic reading attitude than to ask about dictionary use. In addition, in view of two of the other items intended to assess academic reading attitude—"How do you feel about doing reading workbook pages and worksheets?" and "How do you feel about taking a reading test?"—the survey seems designed for traditional basal and test-bound classrooms. These items and others designed to assess academic reading need to be examined critically, but the way the test is printed makes it easy enough to substitute questions that better reflect the curriculum you offer to students.

The *Denver Reading Attitude Survey* and the *Denver Writing Attitude Survey* (Davis & Rhodes, 1993; in Rhodes, 1993) were developed for use in an intermediate-grade research project, in part because we believed the only published writing attitude survey we located for elementary students (Daly & Miller, 1975) was daunting. The reading survey was designed to parallel the writing survey in content and format. The two surveys gather information about what and how much students read and write (a measure of engagement), their confidence in their reading and writing, and their beliefs about the importance of reading and writing in their lives. They are based on the attitude measurement work done by the National Assessment of Educational Progress (see Applebee et al., 1990; Langer et al., 1990; Mullis & Jenkins, 1990).

In the Middle (Atwell, 1987) includes both a reading survey and a writing survey designed for middle-grade students. The surveys not only tap students' habits, interests, and attitudes but also elicit their perceptions about reading and writing. Because the surveys consist of a set of questions to which students give written responses, the teacher who administers them needs to do a qualitative analysis of the students' responses. But they can easily be adapted to elicit particular information important to the teacher who decides to use them.

Because the purposes behind attitude questionnaires are often transparent to students, they are best used in conjunction with interview or observational data about students' attitudes. Students' responses on such surveys are not always true indications of their attitudes; students sometimes modify their responses when they know what their teacher's preferred answers are. Observations permit you to check the questionnaire data against actual student behavior; in this case, use of reading and writing. Interviews permit you to extend or clarify questionnaire responses; they may also help you get at aspects of attitude that questionnaires cannot; such as the causes of a particular attitude. Uncovering causes may be of significant use in helping students construct more positive literacy attitudes.

One important aspect of attitude that does not appear to receive much attention in questionnaires, checklists, or interview questions is risk-taking. Students sometimes believe reading and writing need to be error-free. With selected students, sometimes referred to as "perfectionists," difficulty with risk-taking permeates most of what they do. It is a general attitude, not just an attitude toward reading and writing. In a mild form of perfectionism, students find risk-taking difficult in new or unfamiliar situations, while in familiar situations they will take more risks. Other students approach reading and writing—but not other areas of their lives— with the idea that they need to be error-free. Usually these students have learned this attitude from past instruction, from teachers or others who conveyed the belief that reading means reading the words on the page correctly and that writing means spelling correctly.

An example is Rita, a second grader who spent thirty-two minutes committing a "story" of six words to paper, each word spelled correctly. When Rita was asked why she thought the writing had taken such a long time, she responded, "I was thinking of a story I could spell" (Rhodes, 1981). A lack of fluency can often be traced to a student's fear of taking risks or store of knowledge about reading and writing. Rita's response clarified immediately that her lack of fluency was a risk-taking problem. Students' responses to a teacher's puzzled "Why?" often help the concerned teacher understand the nature of the difficulty. The question is worth asking; otherwise, we may conclude that students don't have the knowledge to write, rather than that they have an attitude toward risk-taking that is a barrier to using the knowledge they do have.

reading and writing interests

In addition to assessing students' attitudes toward reading and writing, it is also helpful to assess their interests—the topics, genres, purposes, authors, and even particular titles they prefer when they read and write. Students' interests are affected by their literacy environment, which includes the interests of teachers and other students. Many teachers assume that the reason to assess students' interests is to be able to make connections between their interests and the curriculum more easily. If a student is interested in dinosaurs, the teacher can help the student locate books about dinosaurs.

This is an important way to use this information, but it can also be used to determine possible ways to *expand* students' interests. Part of our responsibility as teachers is to broaden the world for children, to introduce new topics, genres, authors, titles, and purposes to them. Unless students have been exposed to something, they don't know whether they're interested in it.

Probably the most common way to assess student interests at the beginning of the school year is with an interest inventory that requires brief responses to questions. These questions sometimes tap interests that could be related to reading and writing indirectly: "What are your hobbies and collections?" but some are more direct: "What kinds of stories do you like best?" or "What kinds of writing have you tried?" and "What kinds of writing do you most like to do?" As you look over the following "interest" inventory (see Figure 2.7), note that like many surveys it assesses both attitude and interest. Interest inventories like this one are meant to be used (too many of them disappear into files) so that you and the students can learn about each other's

Reading Interest Inventory

Name _____ Date _____

1. Do you like to read?

2. What kinds of stories do you like best?

3. What is the name of your favorite book?

4. Name any book you have read more than once. Write how many times: _____

5. Write the name of any book you didn't like and tell why.

6. Do you ever read a book instead of watching TV?

7. Have you ever read a book because one of your friends said it was good?

8. Give the names of some books you have at home.

9. What are your hobbies and collections?

10. Do you read a book if you have seen the movie or TV program based on it?

11. Name some of the movies you've liked best.

12. What do you want to be?

Figure 2.7   Reading Interest Inventory

interests. Familiarity with each other's interests helps to create a community of learners.

Learning about each other's interests through interest inventories can be done in a variety of ways. Individual responses about pets, hobbies, and similar things can be shared in small groups or in focused "show-and-tell" sessions. Or information on the types of writing students have tried could be the basis for a number of writing mini-lessons designed to help students understand how many kinds of writing there are and to encourage them to challenge themselves when they write. In other words, consider students' written responses on an interest inventory as the *beginning* of a continuing conversation about their lives and the relationship of reading and writing to their lives. In this way, students' interests can become an integral part of the literacy environment in the classroom.

Another way to assess students' reading and writing interests is to analyze the students' records of books they've read and pieces they've written. (This only works if these are students' choices. If they reflect the teacher's assignments, the analysis reveals only the *teacher's* interests.) You will often see patterns: favorite topics, genres, or authors in both lists, and genres, topics, and even purposes for writing in those records. As we suggested in our discussion of students' attitudes, it is beneficial for students to be involved in their own record analysis. The analysis of reading and writing interests helps students to become aware of the decisions they make about what to read and write. And if it is shared with other students, it helps them broaden their ideas about available options.

One important aspect of student interest that is almost never assessed is students' understanding of the source of their interest and their ability to generate interest. Ortiz (1983, p. 113) argues very convincingly that, "a large number of students take statements like, 'That book is boring' as absolute statements, as if interest were a quality of the material rather than a state of mind in which to approach it or to be achieved by interaction with it. They are unaware of their responsibility to generate interest." According to Ortiz, students don't need to be taught how to generate interest because they do it all the time in a variety of situations. What they do need to learn is how to transfer those techniques to situations where they don't automatically find themselves interested. "Because they are unaware of their ability to generate interest, they do not think of using it deliberately when reading" (Ortiz, 1983, p. 115).

Though Ortiz does not address assessment directly, she includes several aids that are conducive to assessment. The first is a list of interview questions, such as:

- How do you decide what to read?

- Where does interest come from?

- Who controls interest?

- Is interest inherent in the books we read, objects, we see, things we do, or is it brought to texts, objects, and activities by people?

- Have you ever been bored by something at one time and interested in it at another? If so, how can you account for this?

In addition, she describes an activity that provides an excellent assessment opportunity. She passes out a different page of a telephone directory to each student in class and tells the students that it is their responsibility to make the page interesting to read. They are directed to write down what they intend to do and then proceed to do it. Ortiz's description of this lesson suggests several questions that might guide your observations:

- Who is initially resistant to the assignment and for how long?

- What do students who are resistant notice about others who are not? (Ortiz talks to these students at their desks and asks this question.) What does this tell them? Does it seem to motivate them to find ways to make the page interesting?

- Who is still resistant at the end of the exercise? What are their reactions to the ideas and discussion that follow?

- Could students analyze and name what they did in order to become interested? Are they able to discuss how they might use these same techniques to generate interest in other reading material they initially find uninteresting?

authenticity

Though an elusive concept, authenticity is an important aspect of the literacy environment in the classroom and in the school. As we said earlier, we are concerned not only that students engage in reading and writing but that they engage in authentic rather than inauthentic reading and writing. Thus, although demonstration, engagement, and sensitivity are sufficient conditions for learning, a fourth condition, authenticity, ensures that students are learning to read and write rather than learning to handle decontextualized reading and writing exercises.

◼ defining authenticity

Dictionaries define something as authentic if it is "genuine" or "real." In the classroom, students should engage in reading and writing opportunities that are genuine or real, where all the cues for meaning construction are available. Reading and writing should be done for real reasons—the same communicative purposes for which literacy is used outside of school. The students themselves should have a large degree of control over the literacy event—what materials they will use, what they will do with them, the amount of time they will devote to the event, what their purpose is, and so on.

Copying the letter "t" twenty times for a handwriting lesson is not authentic writing. There is no potential meaning in the print, no underlying communicative purpose, and it is the teacher, not the students, who is in control of the event. In contrast, the student's letter (Figure 2.8), written to complain about how the school librarian (whose name has been removed) treated the important matter of choosing books, is an example of authentic writing. The child conveyed her point of view on a matter that was very important to her and chose the form her complaint would take.

Once we get beyond such obvious activities, however, whether something is authentic or not becomes more difficult to judge. For example, is writing about "What I Did During the Summer" on the first day back at school authentic writing? Certainly, it has potential to be meaningful. If the students are asked to write "What I Did During the Summer" as a starting point for catching up on each other's activities, the writing might serve a genuine purpose, and the students are more likely to take control of important aspects of the writing event. On the other hand, if students write the piece and hand it in for the teacher to evaluate, the purpose is primarily evaluative rather than communicative, and the teacher has the greatest control over the event. Under such circumstances, the situation is less likely to be authentic. (We say "less likely" because it is always possible that some students will generate an authentic communicative intent and take control in such a situation.) If "the reader's [writer's] purpose is to comply with an assignment or to prove competence, those are sufficient grounds to experience that event as a [reading/writing] exercise" (Edelsky et al., 1983, p. 261).

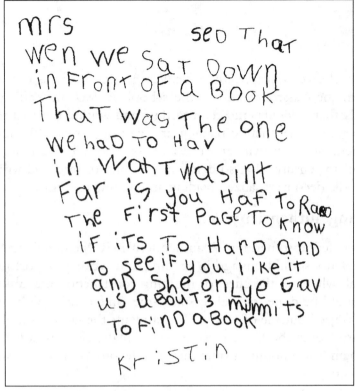

mrs
seo Thar
wen we sat Down
in Front oF a Book
That was The one
we haD To Hav
in Waht wasint
Far is you Haf to Raeo
The First PaGe To know
iF iTs To HarD anD
To see iF you like it
anD She onLye Gav
us aBouT 3 miimits
To FinD a Book

KrisTin

Figure 2.8   Student's letter

Teachers give many reading and writing assignments that seem "realistic" and thus make the judgment of authenticity difficult (Edelsky, 1991; Edelsky & Draper, 1989). For example, if a teacher asks students to write diary entries as if they were the entries written by the main character in a book, is that authentic writing? Or if the teacher has the students pretend that their bicycles are broken and they need to find a local repair shop in the yellow pages, is that authentic reading? The reading and writing in these two cases may be realistic, but they are not authentic as long as the students engage in them only as an assignment. The primary purpose of both assignments is to practice something, but it is the teacher who determines the what, why, and how of that practice. If, on the other hand, some students create genuine purposes for such assignments and take control of the events, the reading and writing can become authentic for those students. For example, a boy may actually have a broken bicycle and end up using the assignment for his own real-life purpose: to locate a bicycle repair shop close to his house in the yellow pages and call for information. That student's primary purpose is not practicing use of the yellow pages, but accomplishing his own real goal. (Note that practice occurs anyway.)

What is challenging, given the nature of schools and schooling, is engaging students in doing things such as using (and learning to use) the yellow pages when a real purpose for doing so arises and assessing a student's reading and writing within the literacy events that are authentic for that student.

increasing authenticity

We would suggest three ways to begin increasing the authenticity of reading and writing in your classroom. First, provide students with literacy materials and opportunities that let them use language cues in natural social contexts.

Second, provide students with choices. When students choose the materials they will use, the activities they will engage in, and the timing of those activities, the chances are greater that they will discover genuine purposes for reading or writing.

Third, follow students' leads. Sometimes these leads are very direct: "Can we make a chart about all these dinosaurs?" But often they're more subtle, expressed vaguely or simply through a child's enthusiasm. A student who says, "I wish Stephen Kellogg would come to Denver!" could be encouraged to write the author to see if he was planning to visit or at least to establish written contact with him. The kinds of things students ask to do or wonder about are usually lead-ins to authentic reading and writing. Children are naturally focused on communicating (unless they have learned not to be). In classrooms where choices are available and there is an emphasis on learning about aspects of the world, they will often suggest or hint at doing things that involve interacting with others about what they are learning.

You can assess how authentic the reading and writing in your classroom is in several ways. Begin by listing reading and writing events (including the materials that are used) over a certain period of time, such as the most recent day of school. Then create a column for each of the following questions and use them to analyze how authentic each event was for students:

- Are all language cues present? Are students reading or writing whole texts in a natural context?

- Is the primary purpose for reading or writing a communicative one? Were the students reading or writing primarily for the sake of enjoyment, to learn something about the world, or to explore or expand their thinking, or were they reading or writing primarily to practice something or because you wanted to evaluate something?

- What choices did the students have?

- Did the students provide leads? Did you follow them?

The information from this kind of assessment can help you set goals that will encourage engagement in more authentic reading and writing. If you provide "realistic" opportunities for reading and writing in your classroom, such assessment is also likely to encourage you to stretch yourself.

authenticity within assessment

If you agree with Edelsky & Draper (1989) that "there are two purposes which, if predominant, render reading (writing) a mere exercise: compliance and displaying proficiency" (p. 205), you must conclude that much of the assessment done in schools examines inauthentic reading and writing. In most assessments, the teacher is in control of the where, what, when, and how of the event. Students understand that the purpose is to prove proficiency rather than to communicate, and many assessments provide no way for students to read or write in meaningful ways because the assessment materials are made up of fragmented language exercises.

Even realistic performance samples, such as writing samples and retellings, are assessments of inauthentic reading and writing because they give students few (if any) choices. Such assessments are indeed realistic: the student has access to all language cues and may even be asked to pretend to be in a social situation where the reading or writing is intended to communicate. ("Pretend that your best friend just walked in and you want him to hear what this story was about. Tell him about the story.") But the fact is, you cannot be sure that you have observed what the same student would do in an authentic reading or writing situation (one in which the student decides to tell his friend about the story).

In authentic reading and writing students are constructing meaning to communicate and have substantial control of the event. In the assessment of authentic reading and writing, the students usually have no idea that the teacher is conducting an assessment; even when they do, they do not see it as the primary purpose. Because everyday literacy events are the most likely occasions for assessing authentic reading and writing, we have devoted a section of a number of chapters to "Assessing Within Literacy Events."

This doesn't mean that we won't on occasion recommend the use of realistic tests and performance samples. Information gathered from such assessments can be useful in some situations if you keep their limitations firmly in mind:

- Standardized test information is sometimes required, as in the case of Chapter I pre- and post-testing. If you must gather standardized test information, it is best to do so with a realistic reading or writing assessment.

- Realistic reading or writing assessments can help you to narrow your focus in authentic reading or writing events so that you have a better idea of what to look for and can do so more efficiently.

- Realistic assessments help teachers develop a more observant eye. For example, learning to record and analyze miscues using the standard (realistic) procedures will allow you to observe and analyze reading behaviors that occur in authentic oral reading situations.

There may be other situations in which this approach to assessment is the most feasible. But you should always remember that assessment data, no matter how realistic the situation, may not represent what students actually do during authentic reading and writing. We believe that you must always analyze data gathered through realistic reading and writing performance samples in light of what you observe students doing when they are engaged in authentic reading and writing. To do any less is to discount a fundamental principle.

assessing literacy instruction

Just because literacy instruction takes place, it does not necessarily follow that student learning also takes place. Assessment becomes the "bridge" that allows teachers to gauge the gap between their instruction and students' learning. Observing and assessing students' behaviors helps us understand what students have learned from our instruction. If change is necessary it may be in the instruction, not "in" the students.

gradual release of responsibility model of instruction

We will begin our discussion of literacy instruction by considering the Gradual Release of Responsibility Model of Instruction (GRR) (Pearson & Gallagher, 1983). This model (see Figure 2.9, adapted by Rhodes & Dudley-Marling, 1988) provides an important philosophical base for literacy communications. In the GRR model, students' learning begins with a teacher-led discovery lesson or a demonstration of a strategy, language convention, or task. Then, by using methods that gradually withdraw support over time, the teacher releases more and more responsibility for using the strategy, convention, or task to the students themselves until, finally, they are able to use it independently. We will discuss each of these areas in more depth.

demonstration and discovery

When students are ready to learn something new, one of a teacher's most powerful instructional techniques is demonstration. (We are defining "demonstration" here more narrowly than in our previous discussion in this chapter.) Demonstra-

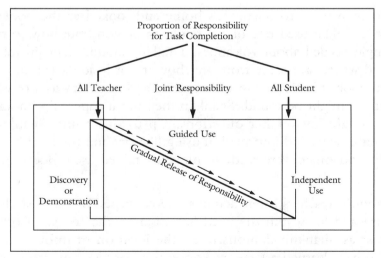

Figure 2.9 The Gradual Release of Responsibility Model of Instruction

tion refers to showing students how to do something and talking about it. Demonstration is different from explanation. As a teacher shows students how to use a strategy or convention or how to do a task, she "thinks aloud," articulating the thoughts that go through her mind as a proficient literacy learner. This offering of hints and tips, which involves talking about why adjustments are made, thus reinforcing the action with explanatory language, are what make demonstration a powerful teaching technique. In contrast, explanation is purely verbal. Students are left to make the connections with action on their own.

In deciding that students are ready for a particular demonstration lesson, the teacher needs to have thought through carefully exactly what it is she eventually wants students to be able to do independently. Holding this image in mind, the teacher can be more focused in thinking aloud.

Here is a story that will illustrate the process. Seventh-grade Angie, Shanklin's "little sister" in the Big Sister program, needed to write a science report on a land form. She chose volcanoes. At her middle school, students were allowed to check out only two books at a time from the media center. Thus, at school she had three potential sources available: two books and an encyclopedia. Angie told Shanklin that she was having trouble finding time to go to the media center and so far had only been able to find one book on her topic that was not already checked out. Shanklin decided to demonstrate to Angie how she might find other books on volcanoes at the public library that she could check out. They went to the library, and Shanklin showed Angie how to use the computer to look up volcanoes in the children's collection, look for useful book titles, talk with the librarian about where to find the books by using the call numbers, and then locate the books. As Shanklin did these tasks, she talked with Angie about what she was doing and why. When they found the books, Angie decided on several that looked interesting to her. Shanklin observed that Angie used only the book covers to make these choices, but she said nothing at this point about using the table of contents or checking copyright dates to see if the books really contained up-to-date information.

The two then went to Shanklin's home and looked at the books Angie had checked out. Shanklin used one of the books to demonstrate how to find information that Angie needed about volcanoes. Thinking aloud, Shanklin told Angie that she wondered where lava came from and how it got inside a volcano. She showed Angie how to look at both the table of contents and the index to spot where answers to her questions might be found. Shanklin then put a paper clip on any pages that she thought might answer her questions. Up to this point, Shanklin had been demonstrating how to find information using libraries and books at her disposal. By now Shanklin and Angie were ready to move to guided use of locating information in books.

In classrooms, teachers often demonstrate concepts for those students who are ready to learn and for whom the need has arisen in the course of other authentic activities, just as Shanklin demonstrated the location of information to Angie. Students who have learned a strategy, convention, or task can also give demonstrations to their peers.

Instead of demonstration, teachers may opt to construct a discovery lesson, to develop situations in which students are likely to make discoveries about a strategy, convention, or task for themselves. Often the technique of asking students to make comparisons is used to structure a discovery lesson. For example, one teacher noticed that her students' stories, though well-formed, would be far more interesting to readers if the students used dialogue. The teacher decided that setting up contrasts between scenes that had dialogue and those that did not would help students discover the differences and begin to infer rules for writing dialogue. She began by reading one version of a fairy tale that used very little dialogue. Then she read another version that contained a great deal of conversation among the characters. She asked students which version they liked better and why. Once they had discovered the value of dialogue, she directed them to the written dialogue in order to discover how dialogue is presented and punctuated.

▧ guided use

In the GRR model, a teacher moves from demonstration or discovery to guided use. The teacher plans for repeated use of the strategy, convention, or task, each time encouraging students to become more independent. Gradually, students fill in parts of the process themselves.

A number of principles can help you generate guided-use lessons that gradually release responsibility to students:

- The teacher assumes that she will need to provide multiple opportunities for the students to use the new learning in a guided manner before independent use is possible.

- The teacher continues to demonstrate but gradually encourages students to take over thinking aloud.

- As the students take over thinking aloud, the teacher moves to observing the student's use and giving feedback. She offers help when needed, sometimes in the form of a question that directs students to observe something or think about what might come next.

- The teacher structures use in such a way that students work together. After the teacher has worked with the class, she forms small groups that work together, perhaps moving to pairs. In these groups, students engage in exploratory talk. Gradually, this external talk among peers is internalized to become a kind of inner speech that students rely on when they work independently.

- The teacher uses self-assessment in thinking about how use of the strategy, convention or task has gone and why.

- The teacher uses a guide for students to follow that provides them with information or a structure for the learning. The guide may be prepared as part of the introduction to the learning and may be used by groups working together, but it is also used as a final support for the individual student just prior to independent work.

Let's return to the story of Angie to illustrate some of these principles. As we said, Shanklin felt she now needed to engage Angie in some guided use of the books to find information about volcanoes. They both looked through books to find an answer to a question that Angie posed. Engaging in a parallel activity kept Shanklin from offering too much help and making Angie nervous; it also continued to provide a demonstration that Angie could borrow from. As Shanklin worked on her own task, she observed Angie, giving feedback where needed. They then shared what they had found, in the process assessing how each had gone about locating the information. Shanklin wrote down the steps Angie used so that Angie could follow them as a guide. As Angie located information to answer her next question, Shanklin went to the kitchen to fix a snack, leaving only the guide to support her. When she returned with the snack, Shanklin asked Angie to talk about how she went about finding the information.

In this one-on-one setting Shanklin could not follow the principle that students depend on each other for assistance, but she did draw on other principles to release responsibility gradually. First, Shanklin assumed that multiple opportunities for guided use would be necessary. She provided a demonstration that Angie could borrow from, observed and provided feedback when needed, asked Angie to talk about the process she used for locating information, engaged Angie in self-assessment of her use of the process, and provided a guide sheet to serve as a resource in continuing the same process. In classroom settings, students may be encouraged to provide support to each other as an intermediate step. Peer revision, peer editing, paired reading, and paired study methods are some of the options. As a teacher you can learn about students' understanding of what you are teaching by observing them in such situations.

◼ independent use

The teacher does not always have to push learners toward independence. As use of a strategy causes reading to be more meaningful or writing to communicate more effectively, students move toward independence themselves because they want to have control and to make sense on their own. But sometimes students lack confidence and must be nudged along. This is particularly true of poor readers and writers, who may like the attention they receive from their teacher's support. We jokingly refer to this as the "Mother Hover" effect and encourage teachers to give children more responsibility gradually and consciously so they become more independent. This is easier to accomplish when you have a very clear sense of what you want students to do independently even before the initial demonstration or discovery lesson.

To illustrate independent use let's return to the story of Angie a final time. Angie was able to use the rest of the books she checked out to find answers to most of her questions herself. What happened the next time she had a report due, this time on bobcats, is of great importance. She went to the public library, only a short walk from school, by herself. With the librarian's help at the computer, she learned that the only books on bobcats were in the main library—not the children's library—on the second floor. She ventured out of the children's library to find the books, but she couldn't figure out where they were. All of these efforts she reported to Shanklin, before asking for her help the next weekend. The two went back to the library and Shanklin asked Angie where she thought the books might be. Shanklin observed that Angie was trying to use the Dewey decimal system (as her school did) to locate the books rather than the Library of Congress system the public library used. Shanklin thought aloud as she tried to find the right shelf and the books Angie wanted. The books were there and the bobcat report got written. The next time a report was due Angie found the books on her own and has done so ever since. In fact, Angie has told of going to the library after school with a group of friends and all of them helping each other locate books for reports.

Angie's story reveals several important concepts about independent use. First, Angie made the moves toward independence herself. With the second report, she didn't want Shanklin's help until she got stuck trying to find the books in a library that used a different shelving system than she was used to. Once she learned how, she became even more independent and the next time was even able to use her metacognitive knowledge to help friends when she went to the library with them. Helping her friends further cemented strategies for locating books in her mind and gave her more opportunities to ask questions of librarians. Like other students her age, she is very peer-oriented and has found her growing literacy a ticket to meeting a widening circle of friends who go to the library, talk about books, swap paperbacks, and give books to each other as presents.

Second, Angie's moves toward independence were not simply the result of copying a model. Angie didn't use the same material Shanklin used in her demonstration for her next report, so she had to generate the book and information location strategies and adapt them to new contexts, no matter how slight the difference. Through repeated and supported uses, Angie made the strategies her own, adapted them, and learned to use them in other situations.

Independent use of a strategy, convention, or task is not always straightforward, especially when the learning is complex. The totality of Angie's task, writing a report, has many facets, only a few of which we discussed here. It is made up of multiple tasks and multiple strategies, all of which may need to be demonstrated and gradually released to the student. Though the model of gradual release is straightforward for each task alone (or for more simple language concepts, such as learning the difference between it's and its), when the model is used to consider something as complex as writing a report, it is not simple. Students may require further demonstrations, especially if they are tackling a book that is harder to read or a topic that is more difficult to write about. This is what happened in Angie's case when she tried to locate books in a library with a Library of Congress classification system.

Finally, the GRR model must be carefully distinguished from mastery of subskills or subtasks. In the GRR model, the teacher helps students develop knowledge and strategies within an activity meaningful to them and about which they have made some choices. Most important is the fact that students see the whole process and its relation to meaning and communication from the very beginning. Then they learn to use new strategies, conventions, or tasks in the process of applying them rather than breaking them into subskills or subtasks, each of which must be mastered before moving on. Angie, for example, was not taught the Library of Congress system with worksheets; she learned to use it in the process of accomplishing something she wanted to do. In the GRR model, the activities are generally authentic, not done at the teacher's total direction, and encourage the development and use of higher order thinking and problem solving.

▪ assessing the gradual release of responsibility

In teaching a strategy, convention, or task to students, the most important question you can ask about students' use of the learning is: Am I gradually releasing responsibility to students? The teachers we work with usually report one of two discoveries when we introduce the concept of gradual release of responsibility. Some teachers realize that they seldom encourage students to become independent users of what is being taught. It was a group of these teachers who generated the "Mother Hover effect" quip that we referred to earlier. Concerned that students may not succeed at independent use, they don't allow them to take responsibility. It isn't that they don't release responsibility; many do. But they stop short of independent use. These teachers seem to benefit most by establishing a very clear picture in their minds of what independent use of a strategy, convention, or task they are teaching would involve and then working on continuing to release responsibility with that end in mind.

Other teachers after they teach something, often, immediately assume that students can independently use the learning. These teachers frequently feel frustrated, sometimes commenting that their students "just don't listen." As these teachers discover, they explain concepts to children rather than using demonstration or discovery techniques. They benefit from carefully planning, even rehearsing a demonstration, and then planning a series of lessons utilizing the principles discussed in the section on "Guided Use." Once they use the lessons they have planned and see the impact on students' learning, they replace "the students just don't listen" with "I know how to help the students learn."

Several other questions are also helpful in assessing specific aspects of your use of the GRR model:

- Do I have a clear idea about what I want students to be able to do independently?

- Am I demonstrating or helping students discover rather than explaining?

- Am I teaching in a way that will allow students to understand how they might apply the learning independently in other settings?

- What strategies am I using to gradually release responsibility to students? What other ideas could I try?

- How could I sequence the lessons to (more) gradually release more responsibility to the students?

- If the strategy, convention, or task is a complex one, have I considered all the aspects that students might need to learn?

Once you begin to move students toward independent use, you can ask yourself:

- How are the students responding?

- What do the students and I need to talk about?

- What further adjustments need to be made?

- Have I released too little responsibility or too much responsibility without sufficient support?

communication in literacy environments and instruction

Closely related to the gradual release of responsibility to students for their own learning is communication. In the remainder of the chapter, we will discuss communication between teacher and student and among students themselves. The communicative patterns that teachers and students use can help or hinder students' growing assumption of responsibility for their own learning. We will also discuss students' literacy-based communications outside of school with family members and friends.

Communication in the literacy environment includes transactions between teacher and student, among students themselves, and among students and others outside of the school environment. We have chosen to use the word "transaction" rather than "interaction" to suggest that in communicative events there is always the potential for fundamental transformation of ideas. By their nature, these exchanges can augment or hinder students' literacy development and their sense of responsibility for their own literacy as a tool for learning throughout life. But there are additional reasons to consider the nature of teacher-student (T-S) and student-student (S-S) communications. First, T-S and S-S transactions often reveal the extent to which instruction involves problem solving and higher order thinking or rote learning (Lucking, 1985). Second, these transactions often signal whether students feel that asking questions, thinking aloud, and taking risks are valued or that only correct answers receive positive recognition. Third, it is important to consider the nature of a teacher's transactions as she augments or hinders the gradual release of responsibility to students. What we say and how it contributes to students' development can have considerable impact on students' confidence in their own literacy abilities. In addition, work on literacy tasks with peers, which is often accompanied by talk, is a powerful way for students to move from guided use to independence.

As students use their communicative abilities to take more control of their own literacy and learning, they attain a sense of equal status with their peers and gain their appreciation. When students become more independent literacy participants, whether in the classroom, in afterschool activities, in social organizations, or at home, they become a part of each of these communities of learners. Their growing literacy is often a "ticket" to feeling that they have "joined" and can participate equally in such communities (Smith, 1988a). Competence as literacy learners in these settings in turn engenders further expectations of success, attention to demonstrations, increased engagement, and the independent pursuit of experiences in which literacy is a tool for action and learning.

We believe that sharing knowledge through verbal transactions to learn and to solve problems is, and will continue to be, a critical ability as we begin the next century. Most of the social and technological problems of today's world are very complex—indeed, only people who can work well together and look at problems from multiple perspectives will be able to ensure there is a world for future generations. Because of the challenges ahead we need to be effective in both oral and written communication (see Brown, 1991).

The implementation of literacy events such as a Reading or Writing Workshop, however, does not guarantee significant literacy transactions. A teacher can work with small groups of learners or hold individual conferences in workshops and still ask only literal questions or expose students to little of the variety of possible opinions about the meaning of a text. In this final section, therefore, we will examine how you can assess the effectiveness of T-S and S-S transactions within a classroom environment. We will also discuss the importance of learning about the nature of literacy transactions in other areas of students' everyday lives outside of school.

■ teacher-student communication

Central to most teachers' communications over literacy tasks are the questions they ask. Communication patterns can lead students to learn to ask and answer significant questions for themselves or hinder the growth of these abilities. We will explore two types of teacher communication patterns that involve questions: closed transactions and open transactions.

Characteristics of Closed Transactions. The most typical type of questioning pattern in classrooms is the IRE: I stands for a teacher-*I*nitiated question; R for the student's *R*esponse, and E for the teacher's *E*valuation of the student's response (Lehr, 1984; Watson & Young, 1986). Consider the following excerpt from a "comprehension check" conducted by a teacher after students had read "A Raccoon to Remember," a story in a basal reader. The teacher read each question from the teacher's guide to the basal reader.

Question 1   T: How did the campers at the campfire feel about Frosty?

S1: Happy.

T: Oh, come on. Natasha, what is your answer?

S2: He was friendly.

T: How did the campers feel about Frosty?

S3: They was glad—they broke out in a smile.

T: He was a kind, gentle animal.

Question 2   T: How did Frosty change the campers' minds about wild animals?

S4: [Reads from book] "At first he was very shy. And then he relaxed and peeked at the public again and again, always ducking back quickly afterwards, as if he couldn't bear to look." That's what it says in the book.

Question 3   T: What regular duties did Harriet have as ranger?

S2: To pick up litter.

T: No, that wasn't it.

S2: [Proceeds to read from her book.]

T: What were her duties, now?

S2: You want me to keep reading? [She continues where she left off in the book.]

T: Okay, stop right there—that's one thing.

S5: Clean the restrooms.

T: No, no, no. What does she do at evening time?

S4: Feeds Frosty.

T: Yes, feeds Frosty. And gives campfire talks.

This lesson contains clear examples of IRE binds. Although some of the questions could indeed be open to interpretation, the teacher is looking for her (the basal's) view of the correct answers, rather than calling for thoughtful responses and discussion. The teacher's guide suggests two more open questions that might have sparked discussion of important issues in the story: "What do you think Harriet meant by saying that Frosty 'began to have more public than he needed or was good for him?'" and "In many state parks, people are allowed to feed the animals, but in national parks, feeding the animals is forbidden. Which plan do you think is better? Why do you think that?" But time ran out before the students could get to these questions; in teacher guides questions like these are listed last.

When the teacher asks all the questions, there is no possibility of a gradual release of responsibility for comprehension to students. In such cases, students do not self-monitor their understanding. Rather, it is something "out there" that the teacher judges as right or wrong. Notice that one student says directly, "That is what the book says," and that in two cases students read from their books in order to respond to the teacher's questions. These students have learned that the teacher values using the text as an authority. The teacher's questions and her evaluations of students' responses do not encourage the students to consider the materials they read with thoughtfulness (Brown, 1991).

Closed transactions often occur because of problems related to the questions the teacher poses. If the questions can be answered with yes or no or just a few words, they elicit brief, correct answers but do not engender thinking about the text. You may think you are trying out a good question from a professional resource but in listening to a tape of the lesson realize that in subtle but important ways you have changed it. Or you learn that the question was fine but the students just don't know how to answer it. In the latter case, you may need to demonstrate how to respond or you may just need to continue to ask such questions over time (even though students can't answer them, it doesn't mean they aren't working on figuring out how to). You may also need to encourage more risk-taking and talk again about its value to learning.

Sometimes T-S transactions become closed because you have overestimated what students know or can do. Depending on the situation, you may need to build on students' background information, teach students the value of a reading strategy, or change texts because the current one is too difficult. In the "comprehension check," the difficulty that the students had in transacting with the text was partially due to the fact that none of them had ever visited a national or state park.

Teacher wait time is another important factor (Pearson, 1980; Rowe, 1986). When teachers don't wait long enough for students to formulate responses to thoughtful open questions, closed transactions often result. The student may answer "I don't know" or may fail to respond at all. Waiting is not always easy for teachers or students at first—it often makes them nervous. In addition, some students learn subconsciously not to try; if they don't answer immediately, the teacher will call on someone else. One way to increase wait time substantially is to ask students a thoughtful question and then let each one jot thoughts on scrap paper before beginning discussion. (You can also use this time to jot a response to the question so that you can participate in the ensuing discussion as a fellow literacy user.)

An exact parallel to IRE patterns in reading is hard to construct for communication about students' writing, since the reality is that unless the classroom emphasizes writing process techniques, few oral exchanges over writing occur. Instead, students write as if the teacher is the only real audience. The teacher then grades the paper, marking aspects of the writing as correct or incorrect. This routine can be thought of a series of "silent" IREs.

Characteristics of open transactions. Open transactions encourage students to give extended, plausible answers that demonstrate problem solving and thoughtfulness about the text and the issues raised through transaction with it. They have at least four important characteristics:

- Students construct meaning using the text as a blueprint. More than one interpretation is valued.

- Students take risks in developing their responses.

- Students share and extend each other's understanding of a passage. They receive and reflect back each other's ideas in ways that stimulate critical thinking.

- Students initiate some of the discussion, sometimes by posing questions of their own. Students respond to each other, not just to the teacher.

Consider, for example, a discussion among a first-grade teacher and a small group of her students after they read *Leo the Late Bloomer* (Kraus, 1971). To structure the discussion, the teacher asked the children to engage in the strategy "Save the Last Word for Me" (Harste, Short & Burke, 1988). In this strategy, students write a word, phrase, sentence, or longer section of text on the front side of a card and a personal response to that section of text on the back side of the card. Then each student reads his or her piece of text (the front side of the card) and asks others in the group to respond to it. After each of the students who wants to respond has done so, the initial reader of the text has "the last word" and reads the back side of her card. The following excerpt from a first-grade discussion of *Leo the Late Bloomer* in which this strategy was used exemplifies the four characteristics of open transactions listed above.

Teacher: Okay, Adam, you're next. Read to us what is on the front side of your card.

Adam: [reading what he wrote] He couldn't read.

Teacher: Who wants to comment on that?

Tara: Well, it makes me feel pretty sad because I think like, gee, it seems so magical that you can just say those words and know the exact ones to say and know how to fit it to the picture and I used to just pretend to read and I just looked at the pictures and said babaababaa.

Adam: Sara.

Sara: Well, it makes me feel like, well because, uh, I forgot what I was going to say. I wrote down the same part Adam did. [Reads] He couldn't read.

Teacher: Well, we'll let you read yours too then at the end. Jason?

Jason: Well, it makes me feel that I can't read, so that I have to practice every day.

Teacher: So it makes you think about how you have to practice learning to read. Okay, good. Adam, read us what you had to say about that ["He couldn't read."]

Adam: [turns over his card and reads] I felt sad for Leo because he couldn't read. I could read a little when I was little. I'm glad he could read at the end. I'm glad I can read now.

Teacher: Sara, since you wrote down the same one as Adam, read us what you wrote, too.

Sara: I wrote a little story. [She reads from her card] A long time ago, I couldn't read a single word. That was before first grade. And you learn to read in first grade. A few years later, I could read a book, a whole book!

Teacher:	Those were both good. Sara, it was interesting how you pretended like you were older in your story. Jason?
Jason:	[reading his card] I made it. Alice.
Alice:	It makes me feel happy because, like, he made it because he learned a lot of different things.
Sara:	Well, see it makes me feel like sorta when I was two years old and there was this tree about as high as the chalkboard, maybe a little higher, and my parents were real scared because I tried to climb it. I made it back to the bottom.
Teacher:	Did that feel good when you made it?
Sara:	Yeah.
Adam:	It makes me feel good because I made it lots of times.
Teacher:	Okay, Jason, why don't you read us what you wrote.
Jason:	[reading] At the end, he could do anything. I can do anything if I try.

Through the use of "Save the Last Word for Me," these young children are learning to construct personal meaning using the text as a blueprint. All of them had different responses to the text and each interpretation was valued in the discussion. The writing stage of the strategy gave the children plenty of time to consider what the text meant to them personally and made it easier for them to risk sharing their own thoughts.

This activity also encouraged students to respond to each other and not just to the teacher. For example, both Adam and Jason decided whom to call on. When the student "in charge" read her card, other students, in turn, addressed their comments to that student. At times, the teacher facilitated the children's turn taking and encouraged the students to listen intently by doing so herself. She received and reflected back students' ideas several times, including when she said to Jason, "So it makes you think about how you have to practice learning to read."

The characteristics of open transactions are also found in good discussions of writing, especially within Authors' Circles (Graves, 1983; Harste, Short, & Burke, 1988). Students receive and reflect when they tell what they believe they heard a writer read. Such exchanges allow the writer to know if her intended meaning has been communicated. The writer also controls the Authors' Circle so that the other children respond to that student in ways that help her consider revisions that might be helpful.

The kinds of open transactions over reading and writing that first occur as external dialogues with the teacher and the other students eventually become internal; students begin to use the external questions to guide their personal thinking. In this way, they gain greater control of the metacognitive strategies they can use to respond to text. (Metacognitive strategies will be discussed in depth in Chapter 3.)

Assessing teacher-student transactions. Since as a teacher you are normally a part of the transactions in a classroom, you will find it difficult to analyze the quality

Windows Into Literacy

of those transactions at the same time. We suggest that periodically you tape a reading or writing lesson so that you can examine your communications with children more closely and then replay it to analyze the discourse for features indicative of good discussions.

You may also take anecdotal notes about the nature of your discussions with students. Ellen Rawson, an eighth-grade English teacher, plans a book discussion with her students by constructing thought-provoking questions similar to those used in the Great Books program. Prior to the discussion she has the students form a circle with their desks so that everyone can see everyone else. As discussion proceeds, she uses a labeled seating chart to document who speaks (including herself) and the important contents of the discussion. While another teacher would have difficulty translating these anecdotal notes, she can use them during the discussion to see that all the students participate and after the discussion to ponder whether there are any other points she wants to discuss or clarify. In addition, she can also assess the impact of her questions (both quality and quantity) on the students' participation in the discussion. Other ideas and forms that can be used during a discussion to assess the transactions can be found in the "Discussions" section of Chapter 5 and in *Literacy Assessment: A Handbook of Instruments* (Rhodes, 1993).

You also can gain insight into your literacy transactions through peer coaching. When you coach another teacher, you often become more aware of the effects of that teacher's questions and comments on students' transactions with text in reading and writing. You may realize that you use similar or different language and begin to wonder about the impact of your language on students. Of course, asking another teacher to coach you in your classroom permits a direct assessment of your literacy transactions with students. At your direction, the coach can jot down actual dialogue for the two of you to discuss in the debriefing conference that follows the observation. (More can be found about coaching in Chapter 10.)

Other speech roles of teachers. Questions are not the only kind of verbal transaction between teacher and student that can be assessed. Teachers' use of praise and feedback to learning are other important types of communication. Feedback influences students' developing abilities and confidence as readers and writers. As their confidence as literacy learners and users increases, their self-esteem also grows.

In analyzing feedback, teachers may need to assess several features. One aspect of feedback has to do with whether the feedback focuses most on the meanings and language strategies involved in classroom activities or if instead it involves comments about behavior, following directions, and management. Teachers use feedback for all these purposes at one time or another, but it is the amount of each that must be examined. There are also equity issues: teachers need to provide feedback to all students, not just to those whose behavior demands it the most, and they need to examine whether their feedback is qualitatively different depending on students' gender, race, or abilities.

Through peer coaching or listening to a tape of your own teaching, you can consider whether the feedback you are providing has a healthy balance. Is it positive, praising something well done; is it constructive, involving students in problem solving; or does it consist of telling children that they have something wrong or need to change an answer? A related issue is whether the feedback is honest and delivered in a genuine manner.

Praise can be specific or general. Specific praise helps a student understand what she has done well. Lee & Rubin (1979) prefer to call it "recognition" because it *recognizes* or puts into words what the student has achieved: "I heard you read ahead in order to figure out two words—that strategy worked well for you." Recognition statements are more likely to provide information that allows students to make their own decisions and become responsible for them (Lee & Rubin, 1979). General praise ("Good job!" or a smiley-face stamp) may make a student feel good at the time, but the student is unlikely to understand what specifically is good or be able to verbalize how it might be accomplished again. As Lee and Rubin argue, praise is too often "given when children do what *we* want them to do" and that "it encourages children to depend on the teacher to tell them what they should or should not do" (1979, p. 13).

Edelsky, Draper & Smith (1983) have identified other types of teacher-student transactions. In examining Smith's instruction, they identified six other roles that teachers may play that result in different transactions between teacher and student. These roles are: lesson leader, information dispenser, scout leader, consultant/coach, neutral recorder, and preacher. Data from this study suggest that teachers' transactions in whole language classrooms go far beyond questioning and providing feedback. Much can be learned from studying verbal transactions that go beyond questioning and feedback. Other sources that may be useful for conducting more in-depth examination of T-S transactions include Cazden (1988), Lindfors (1987), and Short & Pierce (1990).

◼ peer communication in the classroom

As teachers we are also responsible for guiding how students in our classrooms engage in verbal exchanges with one another. When teachers are able to establish solid cooperative relations among students, many benefits to learning are possible. Encouraging communication among students can free teachers from the limitations of IRE response patterns and gradually release more responsibility for learning to students themselves.

When students work together in pairs or small groups, they have the opportunity to engage in exploratory or "first draft" speech (Barnes, 1992). Learners are much more likely to reveal questions, tentative hypotheses, inferences, connections to their past learning, and speculations in small groups than in large group discussions (Brause & Mayher, 1985), since the audience is small and more immediate, and students can interrupt to ask for further clarification. Within a classroom a teacher can construct groups that know each other and will work well together. As groups grow larger, learners feel that they must be more careful about their speech; interrupting easily to seek clarification becomes difficult. Talk tends to be less exploratory and more like "final draft speech." Thus, when teachers structure classrooms to allow personal transactions, they begin to increase the willingness of students to take risks.

Recently one of us observed two boys working side by side on reports about animals. One boy, who attended Chapter I, asked his neighbor several questions about how he should write down the information he was learning about a lynx. At one point the second boy showed the first what he needed to find and write about how many babies a lynx bore at one time. When the first boy couldn't find the information in his encyclopedia article, he asked the second boy for help, but the second boy couldn't find the information either. However, another boy sitting nearby was working on mountain lions. Concluding that mountain lions and lynxes were similar, the two approached the third boy to ask what he had found out about the number of babies and used that information. All of these information exchanges occurred without any teacher intervention.

Positive, productive peer transactions like these do not just happen on their own. In various ways, teachers structure events or activities in which peer communication can occur and then teach students how to communicate effectively within those activities. There are many literacy events in whole language classrooms that encourage peer communication: Authors' Circle, Readers' Theatre, literature circles, sketching, written conversation, community journals, dramatization, and so on (see Harste, Short, & Burke, 1988; also Whisler & Williams, 1990). Teachers often use cooperative learning tasks such as reciprocal teaching (Palincsar, 1987) that clarify the role of each student and help demonstrate appropriate forms of communication and higher order thinking. Within these literacy events, teachers help students learn how to communicate effectively with each other by teaching learners to offer each other recognition, appreciate different opinions and interpretations, use data to confirm particular answers, criticize in constructive ways, identify problems and generate potential solutions to problems, and so on.

When you are observing peer communication, it is helpful to keep in mind the principles that support learning. First, students need to listen actively to each other. They must speak loudly and clearly enough so that they can easily hear each other. Body language reveals clues about whether active listening is taking place; students who are leaning into each other and have their eyes on each other are likely to be listening. And certainly the students' comments and questions often indicate whether students are actively listening to one another. Students who build on or reflect back on each other's topics and respond to each other's concerns must hear each other. These characteristics are present in the following exchange between two third graders, who are working with others on a Readers' Theatre script and performance of *The Chocolate Touch* (Catling, 1952):

Jenny: I have a question for Mandy. When John went to the storekeeper, he said John would have the chocolate touch.

Mandy: Uh, uh! [No.] The storekeeper said he could pick any candy he wanted, but he didn't say anything about the touch.

Jenny: Well, I would have had more about the kind of candy he picked.

Mandy: It didn't make any difference—he'd get the chocolate touch from any candy.

In peer learning sessions, students ought to be attempting to help each other create meaning, either from what they are reading or in what they are writing. What is important in this process is that peers encourage each other to take risks. Peers can also encourage each other by offering recognition and constructive criticism. If teachers—or students themselves—articulate what they have done, there is a much better chance that they will be able to do it again or figure out how to do it better.

In peer learning there ought to be nearly equal amounts of talking and all should contribute as equally as possible to the task. With this in mind, groups need to be taught problem-solving techniques through which they generate alternatives, engage in critical evaluation of the ideas they have brainstormed, make decisions, and assign tasks. Too often, the student who is best at doing something is the one who becomes responsible in a group project. For example, the person who writes most easily is the one who does all the recording. Students need to understand that it is usually more important to give everyone an equal opportunity to learn rather than to get the task done more quickly or with a better result.

As students work together in Authors' Circles or in various literature discussion groups, teachers can observe their communications and log them by taking anecdotal notes or maintaining checklists. Instead of trying to catch all that is going on, we recommend focusing on one group or several individuals. A peer coach, aide, student teacher, or parent volunteer can help make observations. In writing conference groups or literature circles, it is possible to tape-record small groups on a rotating basis and then listen to these tapes soon after the group meeting and make notes. Consider also the benefits of having students listen to these tapes with you.

Listening to taped lessons discussing the quality of their responses right after the lesson encourages each student to be self-reflective about peer learning, to think as one who learns and one whose communications help others learn. Consider Lorraine Marzano's discussion after her fifth graders' participation in a lesson using "Save the Last Word for Me" (Harste, Short, & Burke, 1988):

Teacher: I want you to think about the activity that we just did, and I'd like to know what it was about the activity that you think was good. What did you learn from writing your responses to the literature along with sharing and listening to each other's responses. Who would like to start?

Neil: It makes you learn a lot because you may not have understood one of the parts, and they may have picked it and from that you learn more about other people—of how they feel.

Laura: I like it because I learn more about other people and how they feel about what they choose. Most people are honest, and it's hard not to be honest when you're in a group and you're talking.

Jim: I like it too. You learn more about it because you hear what other people think about the book. It's a good thing to know other people's feelings especially when they're your own age.

Devin: You learn a lot about other people's ideas and how other people's ideas are totally different from what you had in mind.

Kate: Before we started doing these activities on all the books, I didn't really get into the books, but when we got started on this activity I really got more interested in the book 'cause I knew I would understand it more if I tried harder.

Laura: Well, usually some of the things I write, I use because sometimes they're sayings [quotes], and I like to use those because it makes people more confident in what they can do.

communication in other literacy environments

Children have literacy-based conversations outside of school as well as in school. In fact, for young children especially, the nature of their literacy transactions with teachers in school is shaped by the literacy transactions that have occurred at home. In some cases, literacy has been valued at home, but little or no money is available to purchase books, pay library fines, buy paper, or supply crayons, pencils, and other writing implements. In other homes, money is available but since literacy itself is not valued, money is not spent on magazines, newspapers, books, extra paper, and so on. Neither of these is an environment conducive to literacy discoveries or communications that involve literacy learning.

The most extensive study of the literacy transactions between parents and children within their communities and the impact of these transactions on the children's success in school was completed by Heath (1983a, 1983b). (See also Leichter, 1984; Taylor, 1983; and Taylor & Dorsey-Gaines, 1988.) Heath studied children's literacy development in three cultural groups (middle-class white, working-class white, and working-class black) over a 10-year period. Among the groups she found interesting differences which influenced children's ability to adapt to the structures imposed at school. Heath believes that teachers can learn to communicate with children in more familiar ways that draw on their strengths. As students reach the intermediate grades, they can begin to study for themselves the different dialects, language functions, and so on used in their community and school. This helps them discover for themselves the principles of language variation and how to use language appropriate to various contexts.

A second area of research closely linked to the more general studies of family literacy is that of parent-child storybook reading (Altwerger, Diehl-Faxon, & Dockstader-Anderson, 1985; Baghban, 1984; Bissex, 1980; Butler, 1980; Doake, 1988; Hill, 1989; Taylor & Strickland, 1986). Parent-child storybook reading studies were initially of mothers reading to their preschoolers, but educators are becoming more and more aware of the important role fathers, other significant adults, and older siblings play as they read with young children.

Included in the *Literacy Assessment: A Handbook of Instruments* (Rhodes, 1993) are two sets of interviews to be adapted on children's uses of literacy and their attitudes toward literacy in their home environments. One interview is designed for the child and the second for the parents. The second (from the British Columbia Ministry of Education, 1990) also includes a questionnaire for the teacher so that multiple perspectives (child, parents, and teacher) on a child's literacy development may be brought together. Gathering and analyzing data from these interviews will help teachers better understand the strengths of children's home literacy and whether home and school literacy are at odds, necessitating parent education and/or the teacher's adjustment of instruction. Together the teacher and parents can review all three of the Canadian questionnaires to find out more about the child's literacy development and how it can be further supported at home and at school.

In some situations, it is not the parents who are literacy role models for children and assist in children's literacy development by answering questions, reading to the child, having the child read to them, seeing that books are borrowed from the library or purchased often as presents. Instead, literacy models may be guardians, grandparents, an aunt or an uncle, an older sibling, a boys' club leader, or a volunteer working with an immigrant family. In such cases, it is this person's transactions with the literacy learner that teachers want to support further. In the case of a Hispanic girl named Lisa in a special reading class at summer school, it was an aunt and uncle in their twenties, living with Lisa and the grandparents, who listened to her read every night and came to talk with the teacher about helping her improve her abilities.

In looking at literacy in home or social environments outside of the classroom, we must not shortchange the positive or negative influence of friends. Often literacy can be included in students' afterschool activities at school or at other social agencies. Gaining in importance are afterschool community programs in which students read and write for meaningful purposes (Moll, 1988). But peer influence can also be negative. For example, black students who begin to do well can be accused by other students of "acting white" (Fordham & Ogbu, 1986). Students can also be accused of being a "school boy" or "school girl" because their grades are very good, a situation that is especially hard for preadolescents and teenagers, since it sets them apart from the group.

We need to widen our assessments to look at all of these variables and how they might affect our ability to provide students with the best possible literacy instruction. Our students' literacy transactions with others outside of school may break down or need to be reconsidered. And there may be potential in other situations that we have not realized.

Conclusion

As teachers, we make many decisions about the nature of the literacy environments we create in our own classrooms. We can often make changes in the literacy environment and instruction that make literacy learning easier, more attractive, and more enjoyable for students. We can make sure that plenty of time is available for students to engage in reading and writing and help them learn to use their time wisely. We can offer students legitimate recognition for good work, and thus try to raise their sensitivity for the next literacy event. We can be on the lookout for situations that would necessitate doing authentic reading and writing. As teachers, we can also have some impact on children's home literacy environments, especially when parents want to collaborate with us. Finally, we need to consider the nature of our verbal communications with students and how we can gradually release responsibility for literacy strategies, conventions, and tasks to our students. By focusing on these elements we can truly begin to help our students join "the literacy club" (Smith, 1988a).

Lynn Hayes, a teacher we know, decided to take Smith literally. She got permission for interested students to eat in the classroom and developed a "Literacy Club" that met over lunch for eight consecutive weeks. Over lunch, they discussed what they had been reading that week. Some weeks they all agreed to read the same book; other weeks each reads her own book but all in the same genre. As part of the discussion, or after it, students engaged in book-related activities, such as sketching a favorite part of the story, developing character sociograms, or comparing one book with another.

As a culminating activity for the club and as a way to expose students to more content reading, Hayes proposed conducting studies of animals and going to the zoo. The students convinced her instead to go to the Botanic Gardens and to read about plants and flowers in advance of the trip. (Hayes thinks that these fourth and fifth graders were tired of the almost yearly field trips to the zoo and had never been to the Botanic Gardens.) After two weeks of reading about plants and flowers, they took their field trip. The teacher reported that the students were fascinated by what they saw, especially in the enclosed greenhouse/tropical area. They shared information they had learned in their reading as they came upon each plant.

These students had truly developed a "literacy club." In this final activity they had taken over and become independent literacy learners using their literacy to explore something new in their own lives.

appendix C

The Survey of Displayed Literacy Stimuli

EXHIBIT 1. SURVEY COVER PAGE/DIRECTIONS

The Survey of Displayed Literacy Stimuli can help determine the level of stimuli and support for spontaneous literacy behaviors in a learning environment. The Survey examines each area for information about the *pattern of distribution* of the literacy stimuli in the environment and compares one area to another. The Survey also shows the *kinds* of literacy stimuli offered within areas and within the whole environment.

How to Use the Survey

1. **Look at the classroom.** Make a sketch map of your classroom environment, showing its spatial organization. Divide the total into different areas, deciding boundaries, space, materials for each. Include *all* classroom space in these areas. List each area at the top of the survey record.

2. **Survey one area at a time.** Enter an area and sit so you can see all displayed materials from child's eye level. Begin the examination with the category definitions beside the survey record. *Count only those materials displayed at children's eye level or below.* Complete the recording for all literacy stimuli categories in one area before moving to the next area.

3. **Count one category of literacy stimuli at a time.** With the category definitions beside the survey record, count all visible literacy stimuli in a given category. *Recheck the definitions for each category when you are ready to count.*

    Look first at the category, then examine the area for items that belong in that category. Remember, you are searching for items that fit in a category; you do not try to find a category for each item you see. Record the number of instances in one category by tally or numeral before going on to the next category. Remember that *only* displayed items, at child's eye level or below, are counted.

4. **Yes or no categories.** The last five categories on the survey are not counted. Recheck the category definition. Then examine the area for presence of the stimulus described and record its presence or absence.

5. **Total.** To compare one area of the environment with another, total each column. This will show where the stimuli for literacy are in the entire environment.

To compare the relative emphasis on different categories of literacy stimuli, total the records across each row. This will show the variety of stimuli and support for literacy behaviors in the environment.

EXHIBIT 2. SURVEY RECORDING SHEET

Each item must be clearly visable and within child's eye level/range. Definitions attached.

Areas

Displayed Literacy Stimuli										Total by Category
1. Current child-generated messages, labels, stories.										
2. Messages about the current day.										
3. Displayed directions for activity.										
4. Sign-on charts or sheets.										
5. Different kinds of books.										
6. Different kinds of recording tools.										
7. Different kinds of recording materials.										
8. Different references.										
9. Print or writing segments related to nearby materials, objects, or pictures.										
10. Books related to nearby materials, objects, or pictures.										
11. Community culture/language books or print segments.										
12. Presence of empty display space.										
13. Presence of display tools.										
14. Presence of clearly legible handwritten or machine-printed segments.										
15. Presence of books with cover or page displayed.										
16. Presence of functional labels.										
Total per area										

Record Actual Count (items 1–11)
Record 1 or 0 (Yes or no) (items 12–16)

Date _____   Special Conditions _____

Number of areas surveyed _____

Classroom and Grade Level _____   Observer _____

EXHIBIT 3. SURVEY CATEGORY DEFINITIONS

Each item must be clearly visible, and at child's eye level or below.

1. **Current child-generated messages, labels, or stories (less than five days old):** These may be child-written or child-dictated. Determined by dated material or by asking. Groups of completed assignments displayed together are excluded. Items in this category may also be counted in other categories.

2. **Messages about the current day:** Schedules, assignments, notices, groupings, news, and announcements needed to work through the day. These are clearly related to events on the day of the survey.

3. **Displayed directions for activities:** Displayed tasks, cards, or charts that give directions for activities or procedures that children can carry out independently. Labels that explain how to operate equipment or care for material are excluded.

4. **Sign-on charts or sheets:** Teacher- or child-prepared charts or sheets, clearly displayed, that call for children to record information in print or symbol, or to sign names.

5. **Different kinds of books:** The number of different kinds of books available for children's access, displayed so they are clearly visible (i.e., trade, reference, child-made, magazines, etc.). The number of volumes is not counted.

6. **Different kinds of recording tools:** The number or different kinds of tools for children's use in recording events, ideas, information (i.e., pencils, crayons, chalk, tape recorders, etc.). Duplicates in an area are *not* counted.

7. **Different kinds of recording materials:** The number of different kinds of materials for children to record upon (i.e., audiotape, stationery, chart paper, chalkboard, drawing paper, etc.). Duplicates in an area are *not* counted.

8. **Different references:** Lists, pictures, charts, or other information sources children may use as references to help with ongoing activities. A set of references (i.e., encyclopedia) stored together is counted as one reference. Single volumes placed in different locations are counted. Duplicates in an area are *not* counted.

9. **Print or writing segments related to nearby materials, objects, or pictures:** Print placed close to pictures or other materials, with the contents of the print or writing clearly related to those materials in some way. Labels are excluded. Children's illustrated stories are excluded, unless they are related to other nearby materials.

10. **Books related to nearby materials, objects, or pictures:** Books located in combination with other materials, objects, or pictures, and whose contents are clearly related to those materials in some way.

11. **Community culture/language books or print segments:** Books and print segments written in children's home language, or reflecting home culture, in a fairly homogeneous linguistic/cultural community not ordinarily represented in educational materials.

12. **Presence of empty display space:** Empty space in the area that is clearly available for children to display their own work. This is not always labeled and can be determined by indications that materials have been displayed there, by something already displayed by not using all the space, or by asking.

13. **Presence of display tools:** Visibly displayed tacks, tape, label blanks, and/or other tools children can use to display materials.

14. **Presence of clearly legible handwritten or machine-printed segments:** Print and child or teacher writing, displayed on unpatterned background with empty space surrounding the print segment. Print or writing is large enough to be seen by children in the area.

15. **Presence of books with cover or page displayed:** Books in the area with the covers clearly visible, displayed, or with a particular page clearly visible.

16. **Presence of functional labels:** Working labels on holders, cabinets, or equipment that give information about contents, use, or procedure for use.

EXHIBIT 4. SURVEY SUMMARY SHEET

Observer _____   Date _____   Classroom _____   Grade/Age _____

AREAS: CATEGORIES:
No. areas surveyed _____   No. 1-11 categories in
                                                environment   _____

No. areas with all 1-10
categories   _____   No. 12-16 categories in
                                                environment   _____

No. areas with all 12-16
categories   _____

No. areas with category 11 _____

Functional Score   Child-generated Score   Communication Score
Categories: Category: Categories:
  2 _____   1 _____   1 _____
  3 _____   12_____
  4 _____   13_____
  8 _____   14_____
16_____
                                                             T _____
  T _____

Variety Score   Content Score   Book Use Score
Categories: Categories: Categories:
  5 _____   9 _____   5 _____
  6 _____   10_____   10_____
  7 _____   11_____   15_____
  8 _____
                                  T _____   T _____
  T _____

TOTALS

Categories 1-11 score   _____

Categories 12-16 score   _____

references

Allington, R. (1980). Poor readers don't get to read much in reading groups. *Language Arts, 57,* 872–876.

Altwerger, B., J. Diehl-Faxon, & K. Dockstader-Anderson. (1985). Read-aloud events as meaning construction. *Language Arts, 62* (5), 476–484.

Applebee, A.N., J.A. Langer, L.B. Jenkins, A.V.S. Mullis, & M.A. Foertsch. (1990). *Learning to write in our nation's schools: Instruction and achievement in 1988 at grades 4, 8, and 12.* Princeton, NJ: Educational Testing Service.

Atwell, N. (1987). *In the middle.* Portsmouth, NH: Boynton/Cook.

Baghban, M. (1984). *Our daughter learns to read and write.* Newark, DE: International Reading Association.

Barnes, D. (1992). *From communication to curriculum.* Portsmouth, NH: Boynton/Cook.

Bissex, G. (1980). *GNYS AT WRK: A child learns to write and read.* Cambridge, MA: Harvard University Press.

Brause, R. & J. Mayher. (1985). Learning through teaching: Language at home and in the school. *Language Arts, 62,* 870–875.

British Columbia Ministry of Education. (1990). *Primary program resource document. Primary program foundation document.* Province of British Columbia: Ministry of Education.

Brown, R.G. (1991). *Schools of thought.* San Francisco: Jossey-Bass.

Butler, D. (1980). *Cushla and her books.* Boston: Horn Book.

Catling, P. (1952). *The chocolate touch.* New York: Morrow Junior Books.

CAWLs (Coordinators/Consultants Applying Whole Language). (1993). Inventory of classroom reading use. In L.K. Rhodes (Ed.), *Literacy assessment: A handbook of instruments.* Portsmouth, NH: Heinemann.

Cazden, C. (1988). *Classroom discourse: The language of teaching and learning.* Portsmouth, NH: Heinemann.

Conrad, L. (1993). Inventory of classroom writing use. In L. K. Rhodes (Ed.) *Literacy assessment: A handbook of instruments.* Portsmouth, NH: Heinemann.

Daly, J.A., & M.D. Miller. (1975). The empirical development of an instrument to measure writing apprehension. *Research in the Teaching of English, 9,* 242–249.

Davis, W.A., & L.K. Rhodes. (1993). Denver reading and writing attitude survey. In L. K. Rhodes (Ed.), *Literacy assessment: A handbook of instruments.* Portsmouth, NH: Heinemann.

Doake, D.B. (1988). *Reading begins at birth*. New York: Scholastic.

Edelsky, C. (1991). *With literacy and justice for all: Rethinking the social in language and education*. London: Falmer Press.

Edelsky, C., & K. Draper. (1989). Reading/"reading"; writing/ "writing"; text/"text." *Reading-Canada-Lecture, 7* (3), 201–216.

Edelsky, C., K. Draper, & K. Smith. (1983). Hookin' 'em in at the start of school in a "whole language" classroom. *Anthropology and Education Quarterly, 14,* 257–281.

Emig, J., & B. King. (1985). Emig-King writing attitude scale for students. In W.T. Fagan, J.M. Jensen, & C.R. Cooper (Eds.), *Measures for research and evaluation in the English language arts*, Vol. 2, pp. 173–174. Urbana, IL: National Council of Teachers of English.

Estes, T.H. (1971). A scale to measure attitudes toward reading. *Journal of Reading, 15* (2), 135-138.

Fordham, S. & J. Ogbu. (1986). Black students' school success: Coping with the "burden of acting white." *The Urban Review, 18,* 176–206.

Graves, D.H. (1983). *Writing: Teachers and children at work*. Portsmouth, NH: Heinemann.

———. (1991). *Build a literate classroom*. Portsmouth, NH: Heinemann.

Harste, J.C., C.G. Short, & C. Burke. (1988). *Creating classrooms for authors*. Portsmouth, NH: Heinemann.

Heath, S. (1983a). *Ways with words: Language, life and work in communities and classrooms*. New York: Cambridge University Press.

———. (1983b). What no bedtime story means: Narrative skills at home and school. *Language and Society, 2,* 49–76.

Heathington, B.S., & J.E. Alexander. (1978). A child-based observation checklist to assess attitudes toward reading. *The Reading Teacher, 31* (7), 769–771.

Hill, M.W. (1989). *Home: Where reading and writing begin*. Portsmouth, NH: Heinemann.

Kraus, R. (1971). *Leo the late bloomer*. New York: Harper & Row Junior Books.

Langer, J.A., A.N. Applebee, A.V.S. Mullis, & M.A. Foertsch. (1990). *Learning to read in our nation's schools: Instruction and achievement in 1988 at grades 4, 8, and 12*. Princeton, NJ: Educational Testing Service.

Lee, D.M., & J.B. Rubin. (1979). *Children and language*. Belmont, CA: Wadsworth Publishing Co.

Lehr, F. (1984). Student-teacher communication. *Language Arts, 61,* 200–203.

Leichter, H.J. (1984). Families as environments for literacy. In H. Goelman, A. Oberg, & F. Smith (Eds.), *Awakening to literacy*, pp. 38–50. Portsmouth, NH: Heinemann.

Lindfors, J.W. (1987). *Children's language and learning*. Englewood Cliffs, NJ: Prentice-Hall.

Loughlin, C.E., & M.D. Martin. (1987). *Supporting literacy: Developing effective learning environments*. New York: Teachers College Press.

Lucking, R. (1985). Just two words. *Language Arts, 63*, 173–174.

McKenna, M.C., & D.J. Kear. (1990). Measuring attitude toward reading: A new tool for teachers. *The Reading Teacher, 43* (9), 626–639.

Moawad, B. (1982). *Increasing human effectiveness*. Tacoma, WA: Edge Learning Institute.

Moll, L. (1988). Some key issues in teaching Latino students. *Language Arts, 65*, 465–472.

Mullis, A.V.S., & L.B. Jenkins. (1990). *The reading report card, 1971–88: Trends from the nation's report card*. Princeton, NJ: Educational Testing Service.

National Assessment of Educational Progress. (1980). *Writing achievement: Results from the third national writing assessment (Vols. 1–3)*. Denver, CO: Education Commission of the States. (ERIC Document Reproduction Service No. ED 196 042, 043, 044).

Ortiz, R.K. (1983). Generating interest in reading. *Journal of Reading, 27* (2), 113–119.

Palincsar, A. (1987). Reciprocal teaching: Can student discussions boost comprehension? *Instructor*, January, 56–60.

Pearson, C. (1980). Can you keep quiet for three seconds? *Learning*, February, 40–43.

Pearson, P.D., & M.C. Gallagher. (1983). The instruction of reading comprehension. *Contemporary Educational Psychology, 8*, 317–344.

Peterson, R., & M. Eeds. (1990). *Grand conversations: Literature groups in action*. New York: Scholastic.

Rawls, W. (1961). *Where the red fern grows*. New York: Bantam Books.

Reed, K. (1979). Assessing affective responses to reading: A multi-measurement model. *Reading World, 19* (2), 149–156.

Rhodes, L.K. (1981). Making connections: "I had a cat." *Language Arts, 58* (7), 772–774.

———. (Ed.). (1993). *Literacy assessment: A handbook of instruments*. Portsmouth, NH: Heinemann.

Rhodes, L.K., & C. Dudley-Marling. (1988). *Readers and writers with a difference: A holistic approach to teaching learning disabled and remedial students.* Portsmouth, NH: Heinemann.

Roettger, D. (1980). Elementary students' attitudes toward reading. *The Reading Teacher, 33* (4), 451–453.

Rosenblatt, L. (1978). *The reader, the text, the poem: The transactional theory of the literary work.* Carbondale, IL: Southern Illinois University Press.

Rowe, M. (1986). Wait time: Slowing down may be a way of speeding up. *Journal of Teacher Education, 37*, 43–50.

Sanders, M. (1987). Literacy as "passionate attention." *Language Arts, 64* (6), 619–633.

Short, K., & K. Pierce. (1990). *Talking about books: Creating literate communities.* Portsmouth, NH: Heinemann.

Smith, F. (1988a). *Joining the literacy club: Further essays into education.* Portsmouth, NH: Heinemann.

Smith, F. (1988b). *Understanding reading.* New York: Holt, Rinehart & Winston.

Taylor, D. (1983). *Family literacy: Young children learning to read and write.* Portsmouth, NH: Heinemann.

Taylor, D., & C. Dorsey-Gaines. (1988). *Growing up literate: Learning from inner-city families.* Portsmouth, NH: Heinemann.

Taylor, D., & D. Strickland. (1986). *Family storybook reading.* Portsmouth, NH: Heinemann.

Watson, K., & B. Young. (1986). Discourse for learning in the classroom. *Language Arts, 63*, 126–133.

Whisler, N., & J. Williams. (1990). *Literature and cooperative learning.* Sacramento, CA: Literature Co-op.

Chapter Three

3

Metacognitive Aspects of Literacy

reflections

☐ Choose a few of the questions from the three categories of
"Questions to Ask About Students' Metacognition" (pp. 112–115)
and ask them of yourself—of your own reading and writing. What did
you discover about yourself that you had not previously thought about
or realized? What might you do with your discoveries?

☐ Conduct an interview with students of varying abilities with questions like those you asked yourself. Examine their responses in light of
the problems of self-reports outlined in this chapter. If there were any
responses that you found uninformative, think about what you might
do to obtain more informative ones. Try out your new strategy and
compare the resulting responses with the original ones.

☐ Interview students of varying abilities to gather their responses to a
question on the *Reading Interview* or *Writing Interview* about something they do during reading or writing (such as "Do you ever make
any changes in your writing? If so, what?"). Then compare their
responses to what the students actually do in reading or writing (that
is, the changes they actually make during the process). What did you
find out? What do your findings make you wonder about? What do
your findings mean for assessment and instruction?

□ Try out an assessment technique in this chapter that appeals to you—Wilcox's metacognitive conferring, self-evaluation, an interview, a questionnaire, or something else. Reflect on how it went. Revise the technique using what you learned and try it again.

□ Give your class a single question from this chapter to respond to in writing. Then conduct a group discussion centering on that question. How did the discussion go? Did the anecdotal records you took during the discussion add to the information you gained from each individual's written response? How will you use the assessment information you gained?

□ Consider the literacy activities your students are involved in. Using our description of "debriefing," debrief some aspect(s) of the activity with the students. Reread the section entitled "Metacognitive Debriefing of Literacy Activities" and critique the debriefing session with an eye toward future sessions.

Of all the aspects of literacy we discuss in this book, metacognition is the most recent one to receive attention. Because it is a rather new concept, we'll begin with a definition and discuss at some length why it is important to assess metacognition as an aspect of literacy. We decided to put this chapter before those dealing with the assessment of various reading and writing behaviors because, like attitude and interests, metacognition affects those behaviors. In addition, metacognition is the basis for self-assessment, which is a major tool in the assessment techniques we describe in subsequent chapters.

After we define metacognition and provide a rationale for assessing it as part of literacy assessment, we'll survey various ways to explore students' metacognition, including their metacognitive efforts during literacy instruction. There is still much to be learned about the assessment of metacognition and the instructional use of the information it supplies; however, we know enough to believe that it is likely to be of real use in planning literacy instruction for students.

what is metacognition?

Metacognition will make more sense if we consider an example. The example we'll provide is of Mike, a ninth-grade student, talking with one of us about the process he used to write an informational report for his English class on a topic of his choice. Mike has received the services of a learning-disabilities resource specialist since elementary school and was mainstreamed into a regular English class with the support of a specialist. Here is the final draft of Mike's report:

BURIAL CUSTOMS

After death a responsible person of the family gets in touch with a funeal director is licensed to embalm and prepare a body for burial the funeral director then then removes the body from the home or hospital once the body reaches the funeral home. It's arranged for burial. The procedure involves a lot of steps depending on cause of death and the funeral plans of the family. unless the body is going to be buried or cremated soon with in a day or so it is usally embalmed.

In Europe the body is washed wraped in cloth the cloth is called a shroud and placed in a coffin usually wooden it is traditional to have six sided coffin Now today the body is burid in cloths and placed in in casket and burid

The body is usally put on view in the funeral home during the funeral service then the family and friends gather to the service to morn and acknoledge the death of thier loved ones. When there is a large family the body is ussally taken to a church and viewed there at the church funeral services usally have prayers or a speech or eulgy in praise of the dead person and sometimes singing in praise of the dead. Reliliver and freinds maybe selected to carry the casket from the funeral home to the hurse or funeral car. These people are known as pallbears.

After the funeral services closes friends and Relitever ussually go to the cenatory following the hurse with the casket or coffin is sometimes put in a burial vault is a large cement or metal house. That is thightly sealed in the House the family is ussaly buried to gether they come and visit and bring flowers and pay respects.

After reading the piece and talking with us about problems he identified (lack of punctuation, missing words), Mike explained how he wrote it and referred to the various products he generated during the process—notes, a rough draft, and a final draft. In so doing, he metacognitively considered the process of writing he had enacted. As you read the transcript of this interview, consider how Mike's description of the writing process would inform instruction if you were his learning-disabilities or English teacher.

Interviewer: One of the things I'm interested in is how you went about doing this—how you went about the whole report-writing process. Can you line all these up in the order in which you did them?

[Mike arranges his rough draft, his notes, and his final draft.]

Interviewer: So, walk me through all this and tell me about it.

Mike: Well, first of all I didn't think that brainstorming was all that important 'cause I already had my idea. So I just got three or four books . . .

Interviewer: Oh, so brainstorming is to think of a topic, not to think about what you could write about with a topic?

Mike: Right. Because I usually just follow in order of the book. Like the first step would be the responsible person of the family goes to the funeral home, that happens first. So I just did that first. And went down the line.

Interviewer: Okay, so you decided that brainstorming wasn't going to be helpful.

Mike: Yeah, so I just got a couple of books and I read, and they all said about the same thing. So I just started on my rough draft, and then I got to class and I heard you needed notes so I did the notes. I didn't really have my notes at first, I just wrote some stuff down from my rough draft.

Interviewer: Okay, let's stop there—I need to understand some things. You read the books first. Did you write anything down or just read them?

Mike: I just read them. And then I picked the best one, the one that had the most information.

Interviewer: So you put all the other books aside and you just had the one book, the one you thought was best. How did you go from the book to this piece of writing [indicating the rough draft]?

Mike: I read the book over again, going from . . . Well, this book had like why we die. An explanation of why we die, and nature, and all this stuff. And I skipped over that and just went to customs. And I read down the line till the end, when they come and pay respects and when people usually come the day the person died or the day of the funeral to pay respects. Like, say somebody died in 1988, November 5, and then they would come back in the year 2000 on the same day. And then I read through the customs all over again, and then I started with . . . I just started writing it down.

Interviewer: When you started writing that down, what did you do with the book you had been reading?

Mike: I had it with me as a resource.

Interviewer: Did you leave it open?

Mike: Yes.

Interviewer: Next to you while you were writing?

Mike: Right.

Interviewer: And then how did you decide to write this first section [indicating the first paragraph of his rough draft]?

Mike: Well, at first I thought I'll just change a few words and copy down what the book says [laughter]. And then I think it was the day after we turned it [the rough draft] in, Mr. T. said that everything was written so beautifully and nobody used plagiarism, did they? And somebody said, "No, of course not." And so I just sort of went down the line just as the book, like there were some things I had to copy down. I had no choice.

Interviewer: Why?

Mike: Well, because that's the order they had to go into. I had to use some specific words and things like that.

Interviewer: Can you show me some examples of that?

Mike: Well, like the shroud. Right there [pointing to rough draft]— "body is washed," "cloth called shroud," things like that. I copied this: "The body is washed and wrapped in cloth and covered in a cloth called a shroud."

Interviewer: So you copied the whole sentence?

Mike: Yeah.

Interviewer: Now why did you decide to do that?

Mike: Because I needed this.

Interviewer: So you needed the information in that same way?

Mike: Right.

Interviewer: Can you show me a sentence somewhere that you didn't copy?

Mike: Well, the first one. I'm not sure what it said in the book right now but what I had written down was what the book mostly said was the leader of the family or the next person like the husband, if a child died, and I just wrote down "responsible person in the family."

Interviewer: So you made up this sentence that says, "After death the responsible person in the family gets in touch with the funeral director who's licensed to embalm and prepare a body for burial."

Mike: Uh huh. They did say, "Licensed to prepare and embalm the body."

Interviewer: But you took that part and put it in your own sentence.

Mike: Right.

Interviewer: And then what did you do after finishing the rough draft?

Mike:	I got to class, and I didn't know we absolutely had to have the notes, so I wrote down some notes real quick.
Interviewer:	These are the notes you were supposed to take [indicating the notes on the table]?
Mike:	Yeah. This was the brainstorming organization so I just wrote down the order that I went in, like the burial process, how the person goes, and the tools which would be the shroud and the casket, and the embalming, and the burial places, the funeral home, and headstones. I didn't do headstones though. And then I wrote down the family.
Interviewer:	Okay. And so this [indicating the notes] lists the major topics you're going to cover in here [indicating the rough draft] or that you did cover in here because these notes were written after the rough draft. And in the same order you covered it in. So this qualified for your notes for the teacher?
Mike:	Yes, supposedly [laughter].
Interviewer:	Okay, so after you got to class, you figured out you had to have notes, and you created the notes. Then what?
Mike:	I turned in the notes and the rough draft stapled together and then Mr. T. told us about plagiarism, and I started on this [indicating the final draft] and then we had three days to finish this [the final draft]. I started two of them and messed up real bad so . . .
Interviewer:	What do you mean you messed up?
Mike:	I made mistakes. You're supposed to have it real perfect and I didn't. Like a title I had to rewrite 'cause they didn't want that, and then I had written down the same title so I started over when I got finished with the whole thing. And I didn't notice till I was all the way done, that I had written "death" across the top.
Interviewer:	Oh, so you had to start over again?
Mike:	Yeah.
Interviewer:	So, essentially, you were just recopying the same thing so that it would be right?
Mike:	Right.
Interviewer:	So, when Mr. T gave you your rough drafts back, what did he say about them other than plagiarism? Did he write anything on your rough draft?
Mike:	No, he just wrote down that he knew that we had done it [the draft and notes]. Then he does the final copy—grades the final copy.
Interviewer:	I'm noticing on here [a list of the writing process steps that Mike also had] that you've got the words "revise" and "edit." Did you do either of these things?

Mike:	Yes, I did. My mother, she edited it.
Interviewer:	And did you do any revision? Do you know what revision is?
Mike:	Well, I sort of didn't. I just said, "Mom, would you edit?" and she did.
Interviewer:	What kinds of things did she do when she edited it?
Mike:	What she would say was "What's wrong with this sentence? What's wrong with this?"
Interviewer:	Oh, so she sat with you and went through it sentence by sentence and then you made the corrections?
Mike:	Yes.
Interviewer:	What did she have you work on?
Mike:	A lot of spelling. And I forget, as you can see, I forget to put in a lot of punctuation in my stories and things. Quite a bit. I just sort of go along and if I get started I forget to do stuff like that, and just keep on going and writing and writing.
Interviewer:	Before you sat down to work with your mother did you try to fix up a lot of those things yourself?
Mike:	No, because you had to have somebody else do it for you.
Interviewer:	Oh, that was the teacher's idea?
Mike:	Uh huh.
Interviewer:	Oh. One of the things I sometimes do with kids when they're working on a report like this is have them read their reports to each other and make suggestions and comments about things that they could do.
Mike:	Some did that. But I didn't have enough time to . . . Well, I did but I didn't have enough time to sit down with somebody during class 'cause I was doing other things.

As the interview with Mike shows, talk about the process of writing (or reading) can provide rich assessment data that will help a teacher plan instruction. It appears that Mike was interested in his topic and put a great deal of time into writing his report. In addition, he was aware of the teacher's requirements in writing the report and had fulfilled them—even with a sense of humor. It is also clear from the interview that Mike doesn't understand the function of brainstorming or notetaking in the process of writing a report. Nor does he understand the subprocesses of report writing, such as reading a number of books and integrating ideas from all of them or integrating his prior knowledge with what he learned from his reading. Much could be planned for Mike on the basis of this interview. Given his ability to articulate his experiences and a rationale for them and his openness to talking about the process, instruction is likely to pay handsome dividends.

Now that we've considered an example of metacognition, how is it defined in the research literature? Brown (1978) has probably defined it in the most simple terms: "knowing about knowing." *Metacognition* is a general and superordinate term that encompasses other "meta" terms sometimes found in the literature on literacy, such as "metacomprehension" and "metacomposition." *Metacomprehension* is knowing strategies for understanding text; it is usually accompanied by comprehension monitoring—an ongoing effort to self-assess and regulate comprehension. *Metacomposition* is knowing strategies for writing text; it is usually accompanied by composition monitoring—an ongoing effort to self-assess and regulate composition.

Metacognition is the term used most often because it is applicable to many aspects of reading and writing outside of comprehension and composition. In reading, for example, students can know strategies for figuring out unknown words and for choosing books. They can also know about text structures, about how to discuss a piece of literature, about the various genres of literature, and so on. In writing, students can know strategies for spelling words, for revising, and for editing. They can also know about how poets format poetry, how to help a fellow writer, and about various purposes for writing.

Note here that we are also applying metacognition to elements of teaching and learning in reading and writing. Because whole language classrooms are communities, it is important for the students in such communities to be aware of how to interact with each other during literacy instruction. Thus, it is advantageous for students to know how to discuss literature, how to provide suggestions to fellow authors, how to assist each other in reading or spelling unknown words, how to learn to read a book, and so on. When teachers establish classroom environments in which everyone is expected to teach and learn from everyone else, this awareness of how to learn and teach literacy contributes to the literacy learning in that environment.

Like all of us, students may be aware of some aspects of reading and writing but not others. In addition, students' metacognitive knowledge or strategies may not always be correct, effective, or appropriate. Clearly, merely knowing about comprehension, composition, or any other aspect of reading and writing or literacy instruction may not be effective knowing. During the interview about his piece on burial customs, Mike was metacognitive; he talked about composition and about how to compose with an awareness of the process he had used. What he knows about composition and how to compose, however, does not reflect what effective writers know. In fact, what Mike "knows" will be a barrier to improving his writing process and products; he needs to reconsider writing, to "know" different strategies and create a different knowledge base before his writing will improve. Yet Mike is able to be metacognitive about writing, just as an effective writer is. His metacognitive talk about the process of writing a report will assist his teachers in planning instruction—identifying what experiences and further metacognitive talk will help him learn more effective approaches to writing.

Misconceptions like Mike's are the result of instruction that does not reflect what effective writers do or of the student's own (mis)perceptions. Mike doesn't understand the functions of brainstorming and notetaking, how books can be used as resources in writing a report, and the role others should play in editing. All of these misconceptions have a negative impact on his ability to be an effective literacy user. Mike's current metacognitive knowledge and strategies are a barrier to his becoming a more effective writer of research reports. The same phenomenon is in operation when students know only that they should "sound out" words they don't know; a single-minded application of this strategy is a barrier to comprehending text.

Some educators speak of metacognition as an "executive control" that students use to manage their thinking and behavior in reading and writing. Students seem to understand the idea of metacognition better if you refer to it as an "invisible guide" watching over their reading and writing. It's as if they have guardians who observe and provide counsel about the reading or writing they are doing. The invisible guide makes them aware of such things as what the reading and writing task requires (task awareness), what strategies are useful in reading and writing (strategy awareness), and whether or to what extent the reading and writing was effective (performance awareness). By stepping outside themselves, students (or their invisible guides) may reflect on what is happening in reading or writing or literacy instruction at a particular moment. Or their reflection may be retrospective, thinking back on one experience or an accumulation of reading and writing experiences.

How does language affect metacognition? If students don't have the terminology ("rough draft," "revision," "word," "story map," "invented spelling," and so on) to express their awareness of aspects of reading and writing, we sometimes assume (correctly or incorrectly) that they are not aware of those aspects under discussion. Certainly, it is difficult to assess students' awareness if they don't have a way to communicate it. On the other hand, we have all taught students who use terminology they have picked up from us or from other teachers without understanding what it means. We proceed under the assumption that students' awareness and the language they use to express that awareness have a salutary effect on each other. Once students attach language to something, they can begin to sort out what the label means. And giving a label to something can make a student more aware of it. We want to develop both the awareness and the language for reading and writing strategies and knowledge so that one reinforces the other.

why assessment and instruction in metacognition?

Effective readers and writers are often aware of their reading and writing strategies, and they use this knowledge of strategies as well as other knowledge (such as about how texts are structured) to support and monitor their construction of meaning. When necessary, they use their knowledge and these strategies to "fix" the reading or writing problems they encounter. Young, ineffective, and less experienced literacy users are typically less aware of strategies in reading and writing and know less about various aspects of reading and writing. Even when less effective readers and writers are aware, they may experience difficulty talking about what they know. Sometimes they will talk only about those strategies that have been named during instruction, whether or not they use them. (To some degree this is true of all students.) Since effective readers and writers are typically more metacognitive, it is useful to discover which students are not, in order to help them to become more so and use this awareness in becoming more effective readers and writers.

Research supports educators' views about the importance of metacognitive instruction, especially for ineffective readers. According to a summary of the research by the Institute for Research on Teaching, "Students in low reading groups who receive such instruction [in metacognition] demonstrate better awareness and achievement than students of teachers who do not provide such instruction. . . . These students demonstrate higher achievement on a variety of traditional and non-traditional reading achievement measures than do other students" (1989, p. 1). Myers and Paris (1978) conclude that ineffective readers benefit from instruction about the strategies, goals, and parameters of proficient reading.

Most educators also consider attention to the instruction of metacognition beneficial to younger students. For example, Costa (1984) provides an example of a kindergarten teacher who enhances her students' metacognition and notes that the strategies are useful "independent of grade level and subject area" (p. 45). Later we will look at other examples of young children's metacognition and how it is supported and assessed.

Educators also believe that instruction in metacognition aids students in becoming more aware of the problems that arise in reading and writing and how to go about solving them. As Baker and Brown state, "an essential aim is to make the reader aware of the active nature of reading and the importance of employing problem-solving, trouble-shooting routines to enhance understanding. . . . Such self-awareness is a prerequisite for self-regulation, the ability to monitor and check one's own cognitive activities while reading" (1984, p. 376).

According to Casanave, "exactly what the invisible mental processes encompass—the 'triggers' that signal incomprehension, the corrective options that are considered, the strategies that are ultimately chosen—may always remain unknown. But by attempting to articulate these events, processes, and decisions, readers become more aware of their existence and consequently of the need to pay attention to them while reading" (1988, pp. 289–290).

Stewart and Tei make a similar point: "Knowledge of reading gives readers control. Though such knowledge usually stays out of conscious awareness, it enables readers to make better use of their resources" (1983, p. 37).

Of course, these same points may be made about writing and other skills. For example, in football practice, the coach and the players enhance metacognition to improve the players' performances. At the football game, the metacognitive strategies are not focused on; instead, the focus in on "playing." During the game, the player must improvise and respond to the situation and the moment, automatically invoking the knowledge and strategies that were metacognitively introduced, rehearsed, and discussed in practice sessions.

Another important reason to assess metacognition is that student-centered instructional planning needs to take the learner's point of view into account. Hansen (1989) claims, "We are not providing child-centered instruction unless we are paying attention to children's perceptions of what they want to learn and how" (p. 21). In the case of reading and writing, assessment can uncover the students' points of view—their perceptions of reading and writing and of themselves as literacy learners. Sometimes these perceptions are dysfunctional (reading is viewed as decoding rather than as meaning construction) or not valid (a student with good comprehension sees himself as a poor reader because he makes miscues) and will counter instructional support offered to the student. Uncovering these dysfunctional or invalid views provides teachers with the information they need to help the students reconsider reading and writing and gain more valid views of their capabilities. (See Rhodes & Dudley-Marling, 1988, for ideas about how to confront students' views of reading and writing and gain new insights about these processes.)

Finally, since we believe it is important for a student to engage in self-assessment, we need to discover what the student values (Hansen, 1989). What a student values about reading and writing, like what a teacher values, affects his assessment of reading and writing. If a student's dysfunctional perceptions get in the way of assessing progress or ability, the teacher's understanding of those perceptions will make it possible to help the student reconsider and expand his notions about what is important in literacy. Students who have developed appropriate awareness of the processes and strategies of reading and writing are in a position to be more effective in teaching themselves.

As you read about metacognition, you may wonder why we don't simply suggest observing students' use of reading and writing strategies and knowledge directly. After all, teachers can observe reading and writing behavior and infer a student's literacy strategies and knowledge from the observations. It is possible to infer the strategies students use to deal with unknown words by looking for repeated use or patterns in the miscues they produce during reading. It is also possible to infer the writing functions that students understand by analyzing the functions of the pieces they write over time.

Observation allows you to collect information on what you see a student do rather than on what the student says he does. This can often work well unless what you want to observe takes a long time. For example, it is likely to take months to observe all the writing functions a student knows. Likewise, we would have had to observe Mike over a number of class periods, in the library and at home, in order to understand his perception of the report-writing process; instead, we were able to gain a great deal of understanding in a relatively brief interview.

You will not find out from observation whether the student is aware of what he does as a reader and writer. As we have seen, students are not always metacognitively aware of what they do. But those who are aware of what they do as literacy users have greater control of the processes and are more likely to make use of their resources in solving the problems they encounter.

In this chapter's "Teacher Reflection," Carol Wilcox relates how she tells her students what she observes them doing in order to increase their awareness of the strategies they use. She infers their strategies from observing their reading and writing and describes the strategies so that they become metacognitively aware of them: "Today, when you came to a word you didn't know, I saw you skip the word and read to the end of the sentence, and then go back. Do you remember when you used to just stop and sit there, so you would forget what you were reading about?" Notice that, in using "remember when," Wilcox is also communicating values to students; she sees the "skip and go back" strategy as more effective than the strategy of stopping the reading process, at least in this situation. Thus, she not only describes the students' old and new behavior for them but also lets them know the value of the new behavior over the old. When you read her description of how her approach to metacognition changes over the school year, also note that she eventually turns the metacognitive thinking and assessment over to the students. By the end of the school year, students are metacognitively aware and able to use their knowledge for purposes of self-evaluation and goal setting.

questions to ask about students' metacognition

Assessing metacognition allows us to discover students' perceptions of themselves as readers and writers, the reading and writing they do, and the strategies they employ to solve the problems they encounter in reading and writing. But students sometimes use reading and writing strategies of which they are not consciously aware. And what students say they do, or what they know they should do, is not always enacted in their reading and writing. These problems need to be kept in mind as you review our questions about students' metacognition and frame your own. The response to any question is only a clue. It cannot be considered a definitive answer about what students know or think about the aspect of reading or writing under consideration. You will gain further insight when you compare students' responses to these questions to their actual reading and writing behavior.

Although we'll list examples of questions that focus on students' perceptions of themselves as readers and writers, on literacy activities, and on strategies separately, these areas overlap, and the students' replies will reflect that fact. Numerous questions are listed (some from Felknor, 1989; Y. Goodman, Watson, & Burke, 1987; Hansen, 1989; Miller & Yochum, 1988; Siu-Runyan, 1990; Sommers, 1989; and Wixson et al., 1984). Each one could provide the impetus for a lengthy conversation with students, particularly if you pose the question to a group of students who are accustomed to comparing, contrasting, and building on each other's ideas. To save time, you'll want to choose (or generate) questions that help you uncover students' thinking about those aspects of reading and writing you have determined to be important to their growth and development.

■ ■

students' perceptions of themselves as readers and writers

It is useful to ask students about their perceptions of themselves as readers and writers, since their perceptions can affect literacy learning (Tarone & Yule, 1989).

- Do you consider yourself to be a good reader? writer? Why or why not? How do you know?

- How did you learn to read? write? Who helped?

- What are the most recent things you have learned about yourself as a reader? as a writer?

- What would you like to learn next in order to become a better reader? writer? How might you go about learning that? Who might help?

- What things do you do well in reading? writing? What difficulties or problems do you have as a reader? as a writer? What do you do about them?

- What kinds of reading (writing) do you find easy to do? Do you find some things more difficult than others to read? write? What do you do about this?

- How has your reading (writing) changed in the last year (grading period, etc.)? Why?

- Did being in Chapter I (or some other special class) help you to improve your reading? writing? If so, how?

- What does your teacher do to help someone who is having trouble reading? writing? Is that what you would do if you were the teacher?

- Who do you think is a good reader? writer? What makes that person a good reader? writer?

- Why do you read? write?

- How do you decide which are your best pieces of writing? your favorite books?

Responses to questions like these will provide a profile of the students' perceptions about what they do well and not so well as readers and writers, memories about early instruction at home and in school, their own and others' control over their literacy learning, their literacy-learning goals and progress toward them, and so on. These questions focus on uncovering students' perceptions of themselves as readers and writers, but some also tap their perceptions of the reading and writing processes, literacy instruction, and the strategies they use.

literacy activities

Another useful kind of metacognitive question focuses on reading and writing activities, especially school literacy activities. The questions the interviewer asked Mike during the interview about writing a research paper on burial customs fit into this category. Such questions uncover the students' perceptions about the nature of reading and writing and its purposes, and how they perceive the literacy-related activities and instruction that they have experienced. Students' responses to these questions help you assess whether they understand and benefit from your instructional intent.

- How do you prepare for literature discussion groups? for Authors' Circle?

- What do you do with the ideas you get from others when you share your writing in Authors' Circle? when you talk about a book in literature discussion groups?

- How do you decide what to write about in your Reading Log? What sort of impact do you think the Reading Log has on your reading?

- How do you study for a test in ___(name of a class)___?

- How do you deal with difficult ideas in ___(textbook)___?

- How do you go about answering the questions at the end of the chapter in this book? on this test?

- How did you go about writing your science report? Did you find each of the steps (such as writing an outline, taking notes) your teacher required helpful? Why or why not?

- Why do you think your teacher wants you to read _____? to write _____?

- What kind of help did you get in reading _____? writing _____? Did you find it helpful? Why or why not? Will you need the same kind of help next time?

- How does your teacher decide which students are good readers? which pieces of writing are good ones?

Students' replies to questions about literacy activities not only provide you with information about the processes that students use in various reading and writing tasks, but they also provide a great deal of assessment information about the students' instruction and instructional routines. Do they have the same understanding you have of the reasons for instructional routines? If not, what is their understanding and how might that constrain their literacy progress or performance?

A third type of metacognitive question often asked of students uncovers the strategies they use in the process of reading or writing. If you are familiar with questions that tap metacognition, it is probably strategy questions that you are familiar with, since students' strategy awareness has been a major focus in research on metacognition. The following are examples of some of the questions that could be asked of students:

- How do you go about choosing topics to write about? books to read?

- How do you go about revising your writing? editing your writing?

- What sorts of problems do you encounter in reading? writing? What do you do about them?

- How do you know when you come across an idea in reading that you can't understand? What do you do about it?

- When you get stuck trying to express an idea in writing, what do you do?

- What do you do when you come to a word you don't know in reading? a word you don't know how to spell in writing?

- How do you decide what the most important ideas are to remember from reading? what ideas to include in writing?

- Where and when do you read (write) easily? Do you have a hard time concentrating? What do you do to help yourself concentrate?

- How do you know you have/have not understood something you've read? How do you know when you have/have not been successful in writing something? How do you know when you are ready for a test?

In addition to finding out what strategies students believe they use in various literacy situations, you can also find out what other strategies they are aware of by following up almost any of the above questions with several others:

- What else could you do? Do you ever try those things? Why or why not?

Students' perceptions about what they do often provide teachers with excellent ideas for broadening the strategies available to them. In addition, they allow teachers to help students reconsider those perceptions. For example, if students perceive writing as the correct use of conventions, they need instruction that will help them understand the meaning-based nature of the process.

assessing metacognition

There are three ways to assess students' metacognition: 1) with written questionnaires, 2) in oral interviews, and 3) in group discussions. All involve student self-reporting. Self-reports are another way teachers can observe a student's thinking about reading and writing. They yield powerful insights into students' reading and writing behaviors and performance. The interview with Mike is an excellent example. His report of the process he engaged in provides information that could not have been retrieved in any other timely way.

Self-reports have some inherent difficulties teachers need to consider so that they treat the information with caution and check its trustworthiness (Valencia, 1990) and reliability. The following are some of the potential problems teachers should keep in mind (Casanave, 1988; Garner, 1986; Meichenbaum et al., 1985; Wade & Reynolds, 1989; Wagoner, 1983):

- Students may not do what they say they do. Instead, they may provide responses that will please the teacher or answers they know the teacher wants to hear (from instruction and demonstration).

- Students may do more than they say they do. They may be unaware of some of the strategies they use as readers and writers or of the knowledge they have about reading and writing.

- Students may not accurately report past history (such as early reading experiences, instruction, and so on). This is probably because we have a tendency to make our memories fit our general view of the world, including our view of literacy. Students may create an idealized world rather than report what really happened.

- Students may misinterpret questions due to variations in adult-child language. When a student responds in a way that is outside the responses you expected, it is usually because the student did not interpret the meaning of the question as you intended it.

- Younger or less effective literacy users are less likely to articulate clearly what goes on inside their heads during reading and writing. The students may remember and think about what they do as readers and writers but do not have the language to explain it well.

- Younger students experience more difficulty in responding to questions about general processes, about hypothetical situations, and even about actual events when the interval between reading and writing and reporting is lengthy.

- Students find it easier to be metacognitive when they have reason to do so. Understanding and "buying" the purpose for talking about the processes of reading and writing, literacy tasks, and literacy instruction enhances the possibility of tapping students' metacognition.

- The more automatic the reading and writing behavior, the more unaware the students will be of it.

You can deal with some of these general difficulties by wording the questions you ask carefully. For example, you can secure more reliable or trustworthy responses to questions about actual events that have just occurred ("What things did you do well in the reading you just finished? What difficulties or problems did you have in the reading you just finished?") than to similar general questions ("What things do you do well in reading? What difficulties or problems do you have as a reader?"). If you ask the same questions over time and in a variety of situations that reflect the range of reading the student does, you can increase the trustworthiness of the information the student provides.

If self-reports are sometimes problematic, you will want to consider what questions to avoid. For example, since younger students find it difficult to respond to questions about general processes and hypothetical situations, it would be best to avoid such questions. At the same time, some questions can be reworded. You might obtain a more trustworthy response if you ask the students about concrete situations, such as what they did in a cross-age tutoring session. In fact, if students can watch a videotape of the tutoring session, they may be able to consider their actions with more metacognitive insight.

It is probably more productive to ask students questions about processes that are new to them or in which they have less experience. If students have no difficulty choosing books and have done it for a long time, it may be an automatic cognitive process they are not even aware of carrying out. But if students have been introduced to the notion of revision in writing recently and are encountering revision problems, revision is a likely topic for metacognitive exploration.

Certainly, students need to understand why they are being asked to consider various aspects of reading and writing metacognitively, just as they need to understand the reasons behind other instructional and assessment activities. If metacognitive talk or assessment is a natural and authentic part of the problem solving students do during literacy events, they will observe the positive effects of metacognitive talk. ("Assessing Metacognition Within Literacy Events," on pages 125–137, demonstrates how metacognitive talk and assessment can be a natural part of literacy events in the classroom.) When it is not evident to students why they are being asked to reflect on reading or writing in a metacognitive way, give them a brief and simple explanation. In most cases, the students' responses, even on individual questionnaires, ought to become grist for discussion in the classroom literacy community.

Each type of self-report—questionnaires, interviews, and group discussions—has its own specific advantages and disadvantages. As we explore each type, we'll also provide information on instruments that assess metacognition.

■ ■
questionnaires
***

Since questionnaires can be answered by an entire class at once, they are often chosen as a means of assessment in order to save administration time. Questionnaires usually call for short-answer responses (see the example in Carol Wilcox's "Teacher Reflection") or require the student to choose from among a list of multiple-choice responses. Sometimes, however, students are given lengthy oral interviews and asked to respond in writing; we consider these "interviews-turned-questionnaires." Especially for students who have difficulty with writing, responses to interviews-turned-questionnaires may not represent the thinking they might have verbalized in an oral interview.

Although multiple-choice questionnaires permit students to respond without writing, they have several disadvantages. A published questionnaire, the *Metacomprehension Strategy Index* (MSI) (Schmitt, 1990), will serve as an example. This twenty-five-item questionnaire is designed for middle and upper elementary students and explores the students' understanding of comprehension strategies before, during, and after reading. The directions call for students to choose one statement that "tells a good thing to do to help you understand a story better before (during, after) you read it" (Schmitt, 1990, p. 459). Here is one item from the MSI:

> After I've read a story it's a good idea to:
>
> A. Read the title and look over the story to see what it is about.
>
> B. Check to see if I skipped any of the vocabulary words.
>
> C. Think about what made me make good or bad predictions.
>
> D. Make a guess about what will happen next in the story. (Schmitt, 1990, p. 461)

We have three concerns about multiple-choice questionnaires like the MSI:

- Multiple-choice questionnaires put words into students' mouths. You cannot be sure that the answer the student marked is what he would have responded on his own.

- Metacognitive awareness at a recognition level (identifying the best response from among several) may not be sufficient in real reading situations where students must generate metacognitive strategies.

- The distractors (the A–D responses that are not the correct answer) are all metacognitive strategies; whatever a student chooses, he will have identified a metacognitive strategy whether or not he was aware of it. For that reason, it is important to determine what is really being tested. What seems to be tested in the item above is the student's understanding of "before," "during," and "after" as well as the student's view of reading; the "B" answer may indicate that the student views reading as decoding.

You need to examine the MSI and other instruments developed to assess metacognition with your own assessment purposes and your own theories and beliefs in mind. This heightens the authenticity (Valencia, 1990) of your assessment. Using the MSI, we'll demonstrate what we mean. One of our primary purposes in assessing metacomprehension would be to find out what strategies students use to understand text. The directions for the MSI call on students to identify "a good thing to do"—a teaching purpose, rather than what the student actually does to understand text—an assessment purpose. Thus, the purpose of the MSI is different from ours, but the directions could be changed to meet our purpose: "Choose the statements that tell what *you do* to understand a story better before (during, after) you read it."

We have another problem with using such instruments without carefully considering the theories we base our teaching on. The preferred response for the example item is: "Think about what made me make good or bad predictions." We don't like to talk about predictions in terms of "good, "bad," "correct," or "incorrect" because the terms lead students to assume that any prediction that does not come to fruition is a poor one. We try to help them see that most predictions are both logical and supportable, and that the author could have made a different choice that matched the student's alternate prediction. If we were to use this instrument, we would eliminate items like this because it is not congruent with how we want students to think about the processing of text. Because it does not match what we value in reading, it is not an authentic item for us to use in assessment.

Does all this mean that we would not use the MSI or other multiple-choice questionnaires? If we did, it would be with a clear sense of what the instrument could—and could not—tell us about students. We have found that instruments like these are most useful as discussion starters and as vehicles for teaching or reminding students of important strategies that may have gone unused or unnoticed. Students' responses could usefully be followed up with individual interviews or with group discussions that focused on metacomprehension strategies. Many of our difficulties with multiple-choice questionnaires diminish considerably if they are used in this way.

However, our preference in assessment is open-ended questionnaires that allow students to generate their own responses rather than identify someone else's response as the best available. Although the questionnaire responses that students generate are messier data, we find that they usually contain more useful information. We trust the validity of the responses students generate and thus would have more faith in instructional plans based on the information.

interviews

Interviews have the advantage of being oral. Because students typically say more than they write, oral responses contain richer information. In addition, the interviewer can easily follow up the original open-ended questions with others that clarify or further extend students' responses, resulting in even richer information. However, interviews are more time-consuming to give. Often a questionnaire can be given to a whole class in the time it takes to conduct an interview or two with individual students.

To remedy this, sometimes teachers decide to administer questionnaires to the whole class and then conduct follow-up interviews with selected students.

Interview questions designed to assess metacognition can have a variety of purposes, as a brief review of three interviews will reveal. *The Reading Comprehension Interview* (Wixson et al., 1984), designed for use with intermediate- and middle-school students, has fifteen open-ended questions. These questions tap the student's perception of the purposes of reading ("What is the most important reason for reading this kind of material?), criteria for evaluating comprehension ("How good are you at reading this kind of material? How do you know?"), and comprehension strategies ("If your teacher told you to remember the information in this story/chapter, what would be the best way to do this?"). The interview is conducted using the basal reader, content textbooks, and reading worksheets the student uses in the classroom so that the teacher can assess metacomprehension in several contexts and across a variety of materials. It is fairly obvious that this interview is designed for teachers who use textbooks in reading instruction, but the general idea and some of the questions could be adapted for assessments in classrooms using other materials such as trade books. It would also be interesting to use this general idea to generate an interview to assess students' perceptions of various kinds of composition.

A second type of interview can help you determine how students study for various content areas. We suggest that you develop interviews for each particular subject area you teach rather than giving students a generic study interview. Using interviews specific to a content area provides insights into the specific strategies students are using and whether they are effective for particular content areas and reading material. Following are the interview questions and the responses of two eighth-grade girls, one who earned good grades (GS) and one who earned poor grades (PS) in math the previous year. The interviews uncover marked differences in the girls' approaches to reading, writing, and studying math.

1. Did you need to read in your math class last semester?
   GS: Some. Didn't really have to, but it kinda helped.
   PS: No.

2. What did you read? Why?
   GS: Just the assignments, to be able to do the homework problems.
   PS: N/A

3. When you were reading your math textbook and you came to something that you didn't know, what did you do?
   GS: Usually looked in the back of the book to see if it was defined or just skipped over it.
   PS: N/A

4. Who is the best reader you know in math?
   GS: Student or adult? Out of students I know, I think probably I am.
   PS: The math teacher.

5. What makes that person a good reader?
   GS: I understand the words and know enough to ask questions when I don't understand.
   PS: Because she already knows what she's reading about so the book makes sense to her.

6. How much writing did you do in your math class last year?
   GS: A lot of numbers. None, if you mean words.
   PS: None, except maybe some notes to other students.

7. What kinds of things did you write in your math class last year?
   GS: Only numbers.
   PS: Only notes to other students.

8. What did you (or would you have to) do to get a good grade in your math class?
   GS: I kept up with my assignments and always had my notebook turned in on time.
   PS: Maybe I should have listened better when the teacher explained things and gave the assignments.

9. How did you prepare for your math exams?
   GS: Mostly from my notebook of assignments and some from my book.
   PS: I didn't.

10. Did you take your math book home with you the night before a test?
    GS: Yes.
    PS: No. Why? There isn't an assignment the night before a test.

11. How did you study for exams in your other classes?
    GS: Looked over my notes for those classes.
    PS: I didn't.

12. Did you keep a math notebook with your assignments in it?
    GS: Yes.
    PS: Yes.

13. If you had to memorize something for a math test, how did you memorize it?
    GS: Just wrote it down, over and over, until I could say it without looking.
    PS: Just looked at it before the test and used what I knew on the test.

14. How often did you take notes about what your teacher said in class?

    GS: Not very often. Only if he showed us how to do something a different way than it said in the book.

    PS: Never.

15. How often did you take notes from your textbook?

    GS: Never.

    PS: Never.

16. Looking back, do you think you could have done anything more to improve your grade in math last year?

    GS: Not really, since I got an A.

    PS: Yeah, I could have done my homework problems and studied for tests.

Nancy Collings, who is just entering teaching, conducted these interviews as part of her planning for an after-school math study program. Her interviews revealed much about these students' methods of studying math. The good student has reasonable strategies for reading her math textbook, although her math teacher did not require much reading. The poor student admits that she doesn't read her book, and her answer about why the teacher is a good reader gives clues to why not: this student finds that there are too many things in the math book she doesn't understand to sustain her reading. Neither student was exposed to math approaches that would include more emphasis on writing, particularly using learning logs or developing their own story problems. The good student has begun to develop a real method for studying for tests. She takes both her book and her notebook home the night before a test and looks them over to make sure she understands the material. She does any memorizing that may be needed by writing out formulas over and over until she can remember them. The poor student has no strategies for rereading her text or reviewing her notes before a test. The interview makes clear several ways in which Collings can proceed to make both reading and writing more useful tools in learning math for both students.

Another interview, one we use frequently, is the *Reading Interview* (in Y. Goodman, Watson, & Burke, 1987; Rhodes, 1993). Students' responses to the *Reading Interview* provide information about their view of reading and the strategies they use during reading. The word "something" in the first question ("When you are reading and you come to *something* you don't know, what do you do? Do you ever do anything else?") is used deliberately. The linguistic unit the student identifies (word, phrase, sentence, chunk of text, and so on) and the strategies the student generates allow the teacher to find out:

- How the student views reading.

- The problem-solving strategies the student is aware of and thinks he uses during reading.

- Whether the reader depends on outside help to solve problems in reading ("I ask my teacher").

Responses to the first question, "When you are reading and you come to something you don't know, what do you do?" from three different students will serve to illustrate the information available through such questions:

Shane: Try to sound it out. (Do you ever do anything else?) See if the vowels have an "e" marker on it—if there's a vowel marker. If the vowel is long, the "e" would be at the end of it. (Anything else?) Try to sound out all the other letters you can.

Seth: If it's an easy book, I skip it and then I'll probably catch what it is. If it's a hard book, I'll go ask someone. I really don't come to any words I don't understand because I have a pretty good vocabulary. Most of the things I've read, I've read before. (Do you ever do anything else?) Sometimes, if I find a couple words I don't know, I'll put the book away and go to another book—it'll probably be too hard for me.

Dave: Read back over it—the sentence I didn't understand. (Do you ever do anything else?) Then, if I don't really understand that, I usually go back farther.*

Shane defines "something" as word parts, Seth as words, and Dave as sentences or larger language units. Clearly, Shane views reading as a process of decoding while Dave views it as meaning-based. Although Seth focuses on words, he views them as having meaning he needs to decode, in contrast to Shane, who sees words as letters that need to be decoded to sounds. All three boys seem to rely on themselves to solve their own reading difficulties, unlike another youngster whose two strategies relied entirely on outside resources: "I ask someone. If someone's not around, I look up the word in the dictionary."

Seth appears to be aware of a greater number of strategies than the other two boys: skip the word and figure out its meaning from the context, ask someone the meaning of the word, locate a more suitable book. In contrast, even when Shane is asked to dig deeper for another strategy, all of them emanate from a "sound it out" strategy. Both of Dave's responses emanate from a "reread" strategy. It would be helpful to observe all three boys reading to see if they use strategies other than the ones they describe in the interview.

The first question these three boys answered is the most powerful one in the interview. The others serve to broaden and validate the information gained from it ("When a good reader the student has named comes to something s/he doesn't know, what do you think s/he does?"). In addition, some questions provide information about how the process of learning to read and school instruction might have influenced the student's thoughts and views about reading ("What would a/your teacher do to help someone having trouble reading?").

In addition to the *Reading Interview*, an analogous *Writing Interview* (Felknor, 1989; Rhodes, 1993) has also been developed. Both the *Reading Interview* and *Writing Interview* have analysis systems that permit teachers and program adminis-

---

* We are grateful to Carolyn Burke, who collected these interviews.

trators to use the instruments in pre- and post-test situations or in other situations where systematic analysis might be helpful. Chapter 7 and *Literacy Assessment: A Handbook of Instruments* (Rhodes, 1993), contain another interview (adapted from the *Reading Interview*) designed for emergent readers, the *Emergent Reader/Writer Interview*.

Lest our enthusiasm for the reading interview (and its spin-offs) muffle a message we feel strongly about, it bears repeating that these instruments, like all others, need to be reviewed carefully to determine whether they will meet your assessment purposes. If the instruments do not match your instruction or do not inform your instruction, they will not be worth the time it takes to administer them. Select and adapt these interviews and others with that in mind. Refer back to the section "Questions to Ask About Students' Metacognition" for other questions that may be useful.

Of course, the richest interviews are often those conducted in the midst of or upon completion of a reading or writing task about the task itself. (See the hints on classroom interviewing from Nicholson [1984] in Appendix D in Chapter 5.) Mike's interview is an example. By beginning with a broad question you'd like to explore and listening carefully to the student's responses in order to follow up with clarifying questions, you can gain a great deal of information.

■ ■

group discussions

Group discussions about metacognitive aspects of reading or writing can be considered a type of oral interview. You can encourage group discussions of metacognition by asking the same sorts of questions you might ask on a questionnaire or in an interview. Sometimes they occur as part of debriefing (talk about a literacy activity after it is over) or during problem solving shared by the group. Because group discussions are oral, they have the same advantages as the interview. Because they are conducted with a number of students at once, they have the "group" advantage of the questionnaire. If you intend to use these discussions as a source of assessment data, you'll need to tape the discussions or take extensive anecdotal notes as the students talk.

Depending on how the group discussion is structured, it may be more difficult for the teacher to discern how individuals in the group think metacognitively, since they often remind and teach each other about metacognitive aspects of reading and writing as the discussion proceeds. One way to structure a group discussion to ensure that you can follow individual thinking is to ask the students to respond individually (and in writing) to a questionnaire or an interview-turned-questionnaire prior to the group discussion. Thus, each student comes to the group discussion having already thought about and responded to questions on his own. As a result, what students contribute during the discussion is more likely to reflect their own thinking. In addition, you can also gather the students' written responses for further review after the discussion. We are not suggesting that the students share only what they put on paper; one value of this kind of group discussion is that it often generates more and deeper thinking than individuals do on their own.

An example that illustrates moving from an individual response to a group discussion comes from Jean Anne Clyde's classroom when she was teaching in Elizabeth, Colorado. In order to help her new fifth-grade class more quickly reconsider what was important in writing, she asked the students in the previous year's class and the students in her new class to complete a set of open-ended statements about writing. (The statements may be found in Rhodes & Dudley-Marling, 1988, p. 100.) The statements were analogous; that is, the sixth graders were given "When my teacher told us we were all authors last year, I . . ." and the fifth graders were given "When my teacher tells us that she knows we are all authors, I . . ." After each student had completed the statements, the two classes met to exchange their ideas about writing. Hearing their older peers discuss their previous year's writing experiences—how the experiences had affected their perceptions of themselves as authors and resulted in new insights about the writing process—helped the current fifth graders reconsider their writing and resulted in improved attitudes and fluency. Other examples of group discussions that focus on metacognition will be found in the following section.

assessing metacognition within literacy events

Many events in the classroom that involve literacy incorporate metacognition in one way or another and thus provide opportunities for assessment. Those we'll focus on include literacy activities that require metacognitive thinking, metacognitive debriefing, metacognitive conferences or group discussions, and self-assessment.

metacognitive literacy activities

Some literacy activities are specifically designed to foster metacognition. They require metacognitive thinking and are amenable to metacognitive assessment. Two examples are comprehension rating and reciprocal teaching.

Comprehension rating (Davey & Porter, 1982) makes students aware of comprehension monitoring. Students read a text that has been divided into parts (by the teacher or with subtitles). As they read, they rate their understanding of each part on a scale of 1 ("not sure at all") to 5 ("very sure"). In the discussion that follows, students compare their understanding of various parts, focusing on those that were difficult to understand. Students not only identify the difficult-to-understand parts but also explain why they might be difficult and what they did or could do to increase their comprehension.

In comprehension rating, there are several sources of assessment information. The ratings themselves can indicate which students are unaware of their difficulties in understanding text. These students will have marked a text portion with a 4 or 5 ("very sure" of their understanding) but not be any more able to render a coherent explanation of the text portion than other students who have marked the text with a 1 or 2.

The group discussion following the individual ratings also provides rich information—about students' ability to locate sources of comprehension difficulty and ways of dealing with them. For example, some students may identify factors in the text that have contributed to their comprehension problems, while others seem unaware that the problem could lie anywhere but in themselves as readers. Some will identify a lack of background knowledge about the topic as a contributing factor, while others will see the problem more narrowly as vocabulary knowledge. During the discussion, you can illuminate the number and nature of the strategies students can use to rectify the comprehension difficulties they've identified.

Reciprocal teaching (Berliner & Casanova, 1986; Herrmann, 1988; Palinscar & Brown, 1984, 1985) encourages students to become more metacognitively aware of how to comprehend text and, in the process, creates a multitude of opportunities to assess students' metacognitive skills and thinking. Once the teacher has taught and demonstrated four comprehension strategies—generating questions, summarizing, clarifying, and predicting—students take turns assuming the role of the teacher in using the strategies and in guiding other students to use them.

Here is an example of reciprocal teaching as it was engaged in by Karen Condit's fourth- and fifth-grade students:

Teacher:	Let's begin with the title. Tes, you begin as the teacher once we've read the title [The title is *S.O.S. from Earth*].
Tes:	[Reads the title herself and gives everyone else time to do so.] Okay, has everyone read the title?
Other students:	Yes.
Tes:	Okay, does anyone need anything clarified?
Dino:	I do. S.O.S. What is that?
Phil:	I know. It's like something that . . . like when you need help or something.
Tes:	I think it's soap. You know, those soap things.
Dino:	Oh, yeah! Those scrubbie things that you use on dishes and stuff.
Phil:	Oh, yeah! Like Brillo.

Sandra:	No, *S.O.S. from Earth* [reading title]. I think it's like a code or something. Like a call for help. Would the earth give soap?
Karl:	Yeah, we get soap from animals.
Teacher:	That's a good question, Sandra. I wonder what would make more sense in this title?
Dino:	Oh! That's what this little kid was saying when we were playing basketball. Someone was talking about this and he said "a warning." We were talking about the S.O.S., you know, and he said that—he said that it means "help." Oh, that little kid is smarter than me—he knew it.
Teacher:	Well, now you know it, Dino!
Sarah:	I don't get it. Why would the earth say "Help?"
Tes:	Any other questions?
Students:	[Silence.]
Teacher:	Let's read the first part to see if we get some of our questions answered.

As the students continue to use the process of reciprocal teaching with a text they are reading, the teacher has the opportunity to assess their questions about what has been read, their summaries of the parts of the text that have been read, what they want clarified, and how they go about clarification, and what predictions they make about upcoming parts of the text. In addition, the teacher also has the opportunity to observe other important aspects of comprehension as they arise. For example, as illustrated in the transcription of the lesson, the teacher could observe which students attend to the story as a whole (Sandra), which try to define words without attending to surrounding context (Tes), and which recall other times when they have heard the word used (Dino). Finally, it is important to assess the students' ability over time to remember and use the four comprehension strategies on their own, since this is an important precursor to their use of them during independent reading.

Teaching and assessment are very closely linked in comprehension rating, reciprocal teaching, and other metacognitive literacy activities. Assessment that is done prior to these activities shapes the teacher's initial decisions about what needs to be taught, the focus of the first metacognition lessons, and the amount of support and structure the teacher provides during each lesson. Assessment done in the midst of these activities may result in the teacher making on-the-spot decisions that refocus the lesson or that change the degree of support and structure offered to the students. In addition, assessment should uncover how students are progressing in their ability to monitor their comprehension and use particular comprehension strategies. Palinscar (1986) recommends tape-recording reciprocal teaching sessions and playing them back to identify progress over time. Students can also listen to these tapes for self-assessment purposes. Since the focus of these lessons is on the development of metacognitive skills and thinking as a means to more effective comprehension, the progress that teachers witness ought to be communicated to the students in specific ways. A teacher's description of the progress students make in metacognitive thinking serves to increase such thinking even further.

■ ■

metacognitive debriefing of literacy activities

Teachers whose students are most proficient at self-assessment are those who spend time demonstrating and coaching students through a *metacognitive debriefing* of literacy activities. Following a reading or writing activity, the teacher asks questions that encourage the students to reflect metacognitively on some aspect or aspects of the activity—the purpose of the activity, what went well, what didn't go well, and what might need to be done the next time. This is the kind of self-talk students need to be able to do in self-assessment.

The questions Mary Giard, a first-grade teacher in Bangor, Maine, asks her students are one example of various kinds of debriefing that might be done after reading or writing activities, including activities done for assessment purposes:

- How has keeping a list of all the books you have read helped you?

- How do you think that reading every day is helping you?

- When you are reading aloud with a buddy, how do you help that person? How does your buddy help you?

- Let's talk about how you've been responding to literature.

- How did we work today? Were you pleased with the way we worked? What might we want to change? What might we want to keep the same? (adapted from Siu-Runyan, 1990, pp. 34–35)

Excerpts from an actual debriefing conducted by Roxanne Torke, a first- and second-grade teacher in the Denver Public Schools, show how such a discussion might go. Some of Torke's second graders had spent two sessions in cross-age tutoring helping kindergarten students learn to read by buddy-reading with them. Torke began their first debriefing session by saying, "I haven't seen you read with the kindergartners and I haven't talked to you about it, so I don't know how it's going. What are you doing during buddy reading? What do you see your job as?" After the children talked for a while in response to this general inquiry, Torke encouraged them to be more specific by listing what they liked and didn't like about the tutoring. The children had a lot to say in response. For example, Maurice commented:

> I like how they . . . well, the one [kindergartner] I have, I like
> how he studies the book hard before he says a word because
> maybe he doesn't know anything and like he read I Know An Old
> Lady Who Swallowed a Fly and he didn't like that book so he still
> read it. That's what I like about him. I said, "I know an old lady
> who swallowed a fly" and he repeated me right after I finished
> with it. He couldn't read "I know an old lady who swallowed a
> fly" but he found out how I read it and then he read it.

Once the child-teachers had listed all they could think of about what they liked and didn't like about the tutoring, Torke helped them deal with what they didn't like. She said, "Let's talk about a couple of the things you don't like and let's see if we can solve some of these problems." One problem the child-teachers identified was that "they fool around." As the child-teachers talked, what they meant became clearer—that the kindergartners didn't always look at the words in the book when the child-teachers were reading or even when the kindergartners themselves were reading along with the child-teachers. Torke encouraged further conversation about this problem as follows:

Teacher: Now, what could you do about this? Have any of you found a way to solve that problem?

David: I have. I think you just ask them to look at the words.

Teacher: So you ask them to look. Like what do you mean? Let's say I'm your kid, okay? And you want me to read this page. And I'm saying, "Run, frog, run. Jump, frog, jump." Am I looking at the words? [Torke is looking at the ceiling as she says this.]

Students: No.

Teacher: How could you get me to look at those words?

David: "Please look at those words" [pointing to the words on the page as he talks].

Teacher: Good, you could point to the exact words you want me to look at, huh? Great, okay. So that's one thing. What else could you do when they fool around and look around the room when you want them to look at the book?

Jeremia: You could say "You're not going to get a job if you don't know how to read."

Maurice: It's really important you learn how to read quickly in kindergarten. Because if you get a job and you never read before, and then they send up a thing where you have to read what you're supposed to do, but then he goes, "What's it say, I don't know." And then they go, "I'm sorry, I can't help you." Mostly you can't get a job when you don't know how to read.

Jeremia: In kindergarten you need a running start because in second grade they teach you more how to read, and if you don't even know how to read that, and they give you different hard books and you don't even know how to read the other little books, you might feel sort of embarrassed.

Teacher: The trick is, though, how do you say that? Jeremia, let's say I'm the teacher and Lisa's my student. And she's kind of looking around, fooling around. And I say, "Boy, if you don't know how to learn how to read *now*, you're not going to ever get a job, and you're not going to know how to read in first grade and so you better pay attention!"

Maurice: No, that's not right. You say it in a nice way.

David: If you yell at her, she'll think you're playing with her and she'll just keep fooling around.

Jeremia: Or she might start crying or something.

Lisa: And she might be afraid of you.

Teacher: And then do you think she would be serious and work really hard?

Students: No.

Teacher: Then she might not try at all. Now, watch this. Is this better? [Turns to Lisa.] "Lisa, I really want to help you learn how to read this book. Is this a book you'd *like* to learn how to read? I notice that you're looking around the room. And it's really important that you point to the words while we read. Now, if you don't want to read *this* book, we could get a different one." Is that a better way to get her to pay attention?

Students: Yes.

Teacher: Why?

We are always impressed when we observe Torke working with students in this way. She listens to her students' responses and values them, then builds on them by connecting them in ways that produce new insights and occasionally by demonstrating another possible response. We are also impressed with her students' ability to think metacognitively. They are young, from low-income families, and most of them were inexperienced with print when they began school. In fact, this session is partly valuable because the second graders themselves are still struggling to become readers. Through talking about how to help younger children to become readers—by looking at the words and repeating text they've heard read—they are reminding themselves of what they need to do during reading instruction. Even though these children are what many would describe as "at risk," they are able to be metacognitive in this situation because Torke debriefs them frequently. They have learned how to reflect and how to use language to do so. To assist them, she provides debriefing opportunities and structures that encourage them to examine the reading or writing activities they are involved in critically, and she demonstrates with her own thinking and language how to be reflective and how to solve problems.

In the buddy-reading debriefing, Torke began with no assessment data of her own; she relied on her students to describe how buddy-reading was going. At other times Torke begins debriefing with her own assessment of an activity. Sometimes she tells the students what she sees as the problem: "Yesterday I noticed that . . . Let's talk and see what we can do about it."

However, she also uses the technique of letting students discover what the problem is for themselves. For example, during a discussion of *Annie and the Old One* (Miles, 1971), she noticed that the students too quickly agreed with the interpretation of the first student who spoke. The literature discussion didn't take off until she intervened to suggest that there were other possible interpretations. Torke wants literature discussions to extend each student's comprehension of the story beyond his personal interpretation. If students agree with each other rather than volunteer other interpretations, this goal can't be achieved.

In order to help the students see what she saw, Torke transcribed a tape she had made of the discussion and gave it to the students to read. After reading the discussion transcript with the group, she began the debriefing in this way:

Teacher: Now tell me what you think about how we talked about the story.

Jesse: It sounds really funny to us.

Erin: In some parts.

Jesse: Yeah, in some parts.

Teacher: What do you mean it sounds funny in some parts?

Jesse: Well, like you didn't know what you were saying or some . . . like Justin said, "Because, well, I just agree with Matt."

Teacher: Let's ask Justin. What was going on there, Justin, when you said, "Well, I just agree with Matt."

Jesse: [to Justin] Er . . . you just weren't sure what you were going to say?

Justin: Well, I was just, like, thinking real hard but then I sorta like forgot. I forgot what I was going to say.

Teacher: Oh, so you just said you agreed with Matt?

Justin: Yeah.

Teacher: Oh. What else do you think? Sarah?

Sarah: Some people, um, when they say this stuff . . . Sometimes when people say something, they say it just because they want to say something, maybe because they don't really understand it but they just keep on saying something.

Teacher: Oh, so you think people were saying things just to say things?

Sarah: Yeah.

Teacher: Like what?

Sarah: [referring to transcript] Like, um . . . when Joleen and Shelley said "I agree," it made me think they weren't really sure, but you asked them and they probably weren't sure about it.

Teacher: Hm. Did you do that, Joleen? Did you just say "I agree" because you didn't know what else to say when I asked you?

Joleen: Yeah.

Teacher: You did?

Jesse: Is that what you did, Shelley?

Shelley: [Nods head.]

The conversation about the transcript went on in a similar vein for a bit, with the students continuing to identify other places where they simply agreed with each other rather than trying, as one student put it, to "think better" about the story they had read. Then Torke turned the students' attention to what to do about the problem they had uncovered and why it was important to deal with it. Instead of scolding them or making them feel as if they couldn't discuss literature well, she let the students discover that agreeing with each other didn't lead to "thinking better" about literature. Then she involved them in taking steps to encourage each other to share different interpretations. Though this technique is time-consuming (another way to do it is to videotape the activity and replay the video during the debriefing), the fact that the students identified the problem themselves will help literature discussions extend children's comprehension, one of the teacher's goals.

conferences

Conferences are an excellent time to carry on metacognitive conversations and to use those conversations as a basis for assessment. In Carol Wilcox's "Teacher Reflection," it is clear that she uses both whole class and individual conferences to encourage metacognitive thinking. In the whole class conferences, metacognitive talk or conferring goes on with one individual while the group listens.

Wilcox makes the point that she does most of the metacognitive talking in the beginning of the year but by the end of the year she expects students to have taken over this responsibility. Since Wilcox does most of the talking, early conferences are less likely to result in assessment data. However, it is possible to gather assessment data by observing the students' verbal and performance responses to what she says. Toward the end of the year, when she asks, "Are you noticing any particular problems in your reading? How do you plan to solve those problems?" the situation reverses itself. Now there is plenty of opportunity for assessment. The information may be used on the spot or at a later point to plan instruction for students that will further their understanding.

A reading conference designed to focus on metacognitive assessment and instruction could revolve around a "wheel" of reading strategies like "The Mini Page Reading Wheel" (Debnam, 1989), that appeared in the children's section of Universal Press Syndicate newspapers. Such a wheel can be made by dividing a circle into as many sections as there are reading strategies you want to feature. The strategies can include those used before reading (i.e., "Think about what I already know"), during reading (i.e., "Reread what I don't understand"), and after reading (i.e., "Summarize what I've read"). The students can mount a copy of the circle on a piece of cardboard and fasten a needle or pointer to the center of the wheel with a brad.

As children read, they may be asked to choose a strategy from the wheel in advance, one they want to try out while they read. Or when they are finished reading they may be asked to identify a strategy they remember using. In either case, when the teacher confers with a student who has used the wheel, he or she will be able to ask the student for examples of how the strategy was used, allowing the student to reveal actual reading situations. This kind of conference has excellent potential for collecting assessment information.

■ ■

self-assessment and goal setting

As we have pointed out, at its heart self-assessment is metacognitive. It requires that students reflect, that they know about various aspects of reading and writing, and that they have the language to express that knowledge. The end result of self-assessment is goal setting, another classroom activity that also requires metacognition. Metacognitive activities such as reciprocal teaching, the metacognitive debriefings that follow literacy activities, and the conferences that focus on metacognition all contribute to the student's ability to assess his or her literacy effectively and set goals.

Self-assessment can range from being highly teacher-structured to being structured by the student. The examples of various self-assessments we provide in this section are teacher-structured to varying degrees, since students who are young and inexperienced require more structure if self-assessments are to encourage reflection on targeted aspects of reading or writing.

The *Strategy Record Chart* (Wade & Reynolds, 1989; see Figure 3.1) is an example of a highly structured self-assessment. Students have studied the strategies listed, so they are familiar with the language used to name them when they appear on the chart. In fact, this self-assessment chart is a reproduction of the teacher's strategy definition sheet, which the students have worked with over time. (As an alternative to a strategy list that is generated by the teacher and given to the students, the list could be generated by the students as a group.)

The format is also highly structured; students are to check off the strategies they use as they read and study a variety of passages over time. The yes/no response leaves little room for students to consider the reasons why they abandon particular strategies or use others with certain passages. In such highly structured self-assessments, it is important that students discuss what strategies they used and how, when, and why they used them (Wade & Reynolds, 1989, p. 10).

Another example of a highly structured self-assessment (see Figure 3.2) was developed by Marilyn Borger, a seventh-grade English teacher for the Cherry Creek Public Schools. It can be used with most textbooks to help students learn to monitor their textbook reading. You may want to customize the interview further to fit whatever content area textbook or other book you are using. As the format of Borger's checklist emphasizes, there are strategies to apply before reading, during reading, and after reading. Students can periodically fill out the checklist after they have read a section of the textbook. Teacher-student conferences may be held to compare the student's records with the teacher's sense of the student's abilities (from anecdotal notes or a similar checklist kept for each student).

Strategy Record Chart

	Passages							
	1st	2nd	3rd	4th	5th	6th	7th	8th
Observable strategies								
Highlight or underline text	—	—	—	—	—	—	—	—
Copy from the text	—	—	—	—	—	—	—	—
Write down in your own words	—	—	—	—	—	—	—	—
Outline	—	—	—	—	—	—	—	—
Draw a diagram	—	—	—	—	—	—	—	—
In-the-head strategies								
Look over before reading	—	—	—	—	—	—	—	—
Read at your usual rate	—	—	—	—	—	—	—	—
Read slowly	—	—	—	—	—	—	—	—
Go back and read again	—	—	—	—	—	—	—	—
Special attention; memorize	—	—	—	—	—	—	—	—
Put together ideas in your head	—	—	—	—	—	—	—	—
Relate to what you already know	—	—	—	—	—	—	—	—
Make a picture in your mind	—	—	—	—	—	—	—	—
Question or test yourself	—	—	—	—	—	—	—	—
Guess what will happen	—	—	—	—	—	—	—	—
Other	—	—	—	—	—	—	—	—

Figure 3.1   Strategy Record Chart

A midyear self-assessment of writing used by Ann Christensen in her first- and second-grade classroom in the Denver Public Schools is less teacher-structured (see Figure 7.11, p. 343). Students were asked to respond in three areas: "Things I can do well in writing," "Something new I've tried to do in writing this year," and "What I would like to learn so I can become a better writer." Christensen can rely on less structure in this questionnaire because she has talked with her students about similar issues all year; they are experienced in thinking metacognitively and can be expected to generate ideas of their own without the aid of a checklist.

Here are some of the responses Christensen's students gave:

Things I can do well in writing

- Write long stories.

- I put in commas and periods.

- I can put in sounds.

- I use good words.

- I can read my writing.

- Spell my words better.

- How to write faster.

- Think of good stories.

Something new I've tried to do in writing this year

- To take out lots of words in my writing.

- Spaces, capitals, handwriting, quotation marks.

- Spell better. Put more sounds in words.

- How to make better stories.

What I would like to learn so I can become a better writer

- I need to learn how to write little.

- Try to ignore (spelled "eggnor"!) other kids so I can write.

- Spell even better.

- Make better titles.

- How to get more ideas.

- Write longer books.

- Nonfiction.

- Editing.

Another self-assessment, the "Writer's Memo" (Sommers, 1989), has the same degree of structure as Christensen's but is used in self-assessing a specific piece of writing rather than writing progress in general. Although it was developed for college students, the idea of a writer's memo can be adapted to upper elementary and secondary classrooms. Students are provided with questions, which they answer in writing and then submit to the teacher along with the piece of writing. The questions have to do with one or more of the following:

- The process of writing the piece. (How did you select your topic? What problems did you have in writing this piece?)

- Student's feelings about the finished piece. (What is this piece's greatest strength? How does the final draft compare to the first one?)

- Information that will help the teacher respond effectively to the piece. (Why did you write this piece? Who is your audience for this piece?) (Sommers, 1989, pp. 175–176)

The final section of the writer's memo involves the student in structuring a part of the self-assessment by generating questions for the teacher to answer: "What questions would you like me to answer about your [writing]?" (Sommers, 1989, p. 176). This, as well as other questions about purpose and audience, allows the teacher to assess the piece of writing using more information about the student's intent as a writer and to direct some of the response to the student's individual needs or concerns as a writer.

Less structured assessment forms or questions can be used early in the school year, but the effort is likely to reveal that students have no clear sense of their potential goals or of what they do as readers and writers. Only when students begin to

Name _____

Place an X in the column to indicate the strategies you used for each reading assignment.

	Date	Date	Date	Date
Prereading				
1. I previewed by reading the boldface type announcing topics and subtopics of the reading assignment.				
2. I asked myself what I already knew about the topic.				
3. I used parts of the textbook as a resource during reading: glossary, table of contents, index, chapter headings and subheadings.				
4. I surveyed questions at the end of the assignment prior to reading.				
Reading				
1. I took time to look at pictures and read captions related to the text.				
2. I took time to look at and try to understand charts, graphs, and maps which related to the reading assignment.				
3. I slowed my reading rate down when reading technical passages.				
4. I skimmed when appropriate.				
5. I differentiated between main ideas and details in the text of the assignment.				
Postreading				
1. I summarized what I read, putting ideas in my own words.				
2. When I didn't understand or needed to clarify passages, I marked them lightly in pencil with a question mark.				
3. I can identify what I have learned from what I have read and I am able to add the information to my previous knowledge.				

Figure 3.2   Checklist used for reading

develop clear notions of goals and processes do open assessments really work well. Earlier in the school year, as you are building metacognitive knowledge about comprehension strategies, you might use the sort of self-assessment seen in Figure 3.3. It is structured so that students have to choose strategies from among those they have been talking about and using.

Later in the school year, when students have made the comprehension strategies a more automatic part of their reading, a less structured self-assessment can be used. At this point, it is helpful to find out what strategies students generate independently when they read. Figure 3.4 is an example of a less structured self-assessment that taps comprehension strategies just as the previous one did.

Name _____ Date _____

Title of reading material _____

Underline the strategies that you used to help yourself understand the book you are reading. Circle the strategy you used the most.

I thought about what I already knew.

I made predictions and read to see if they came out.

I reread what I didn't understand.

I made pictures in my head.

I asked someone to explain what I didn't understand.

Give an example of how you used one of the strategies.

Figure 3.3   A structured self-assessment form

Name _____ Date _____

Title of reading material _____

What strategies did you use today to help yourself understand the book you are reading?

Give an example of how one of the strategies you listed helped you understand something in the book.

Figure 3.4   A less structured self-assessment form

In *Literacy Assessment: A Handbook of Instruments* (Rhodes, 1993), you'll find a number of self-assessment forms which range from more to less structured.

In order to understand and then communicate her understanding of metacognition, Carol Wilcox compares learning to be a reader with learning to be a runner in this chapter's "Teacher Reflection." Until recently, Wilcox was a Literacy Resource Teacher at McElwain Elementary School in Adams County (Colorado) School District 12. McElwain is located in a working-class Hispanic neighborhood in the northern suburbs of Denver. As a Literacy Resource Teacher, Wilcox's primary responsibilities included working with teachers to help them plan and carry out quality literacy instruction. She often did demonstration teaching and assessment in classrooms at McElwain. Wilcox is especially interested in restructuring schools so that literacy instruction and assessment empower all learners, not just the learners in the mainstream culture. She is now pursuing this interest through her doctoral studies at the University of New Hampshire.

On running and reading

Carol Wilcox

Several years ago I purchased the most expensive pair of shoes I have ever owned and took up jogging, but I don't run if it's too hot or too cold, too wet or too windy, too light or too dark. In short, I am not an avid runner. I am, on the other hand, an avid reader. One would logically assume, then, that I would draw on my expertise as a reader in assessing children's literacy. Suprisingly enough, however, my growth as a runner has taught me far more about evaluating children's literacy than have any of my experiences as a reader.

Offering strategies

When I began running, my friends were more than willing to provide me with all kinds of advice: "Buy this kind of shoe," "Hold your arms the way I do," "Eat carbohydrates before you run." Their underlying message was "We know you want to get better at running. These are strategies good runners use. If you practice them, you will become a better runner, too." I began to accumulate a reservoir of good running strategies—tools that I could use to help myself improve.

Beginning early in September, I try to provide my young readers with the same kind of helpful advice. Each day, prior to reading groups or

Reading Workshop, I present one good reader strategy. Some of the strategy lessons I present to fourth, fifth, and sixth graders include:

- How to select an appropriate book.

- How to use title, cover, and chapter headings to make predictions.

- How to use background knowledge.

- How to use knowledge of text structure, author, and genre.

- How to use mental visualization to aid comprehension.

- How to deal with unknown words (such as reread, read to the end of the sentence and then go back, put in a substitute, and so on).

- How to know if reading is not making sense.

- What to do if reading is not making sense.

- How to use retelling to check understanding.

- How to use other readers as resources.

I decide which strategies to teach, and in which order, by watching students to determine which strategies they already employ and which strategies they need most for growth. After I have taught a strategy, I post it on a large chart on the wall. I refer to the "Good Reader" chart often and expect children to use it as needed. Having introduced good reader strategies, my next role is to help children begin consciously applying them to their own reading.

Supporting strategy use

Again, I find it helpful to remember my history as a runner. When I was starting to run, several friends ran with me almost every day. Recognizing that I was insecure about myself as a runner, they encouraged me constantly ("You're holding your arms exactly right." "Last week you could barely do two miles, and today we ran almost three." "I've noticed you're trying to eat healthier—that will help your running."). Their underlying message, "You're getting better at this," enabled me to begin thinking of myself as a runner.

In a similar way, I encourage my young readers' approximations. I engage in brief (often only two- or three-minute) conferences with individual students as the rest of the class is reading silently. Sometimes, I simply talk to children about their reading. At other times, I may ask a child to read a short passage from his or her book to me. My comments to children generally fall into three categories.

1. My favorite comment begins with the phrase "remember when . . ."

"Today, I saw you stop and really think about what you were reading when it didn't make sense. Do you remember when you used to just keep going, whether it made sense or not? You really are working at improving, aren't you?"

The message I wish to give children in a "remember when . . ." conference is, "You are growing, you are choosing to get better at reading."

2. I always acknowledge a child's attempt to use any strategy, no matter how faulty that attempt might have been.

"Today I saw you try to substitute when you came to a word you didn't know. Good readers use the substitution strategy frequently."

Often, I also seize this opportunity to demonstrate the strategy again by saying, "Would you like to see how I would have used substitution in that case?" The message I want children to hear is "It's great that you are choosing to use that strategy. I know that you want to use it correctly."

3. I frequently use conferences to help children apply a strategy I think they should be able to use.

"I noticed that when you got to the end of that chapter you were having a hard time remembering what it was about. I have a really simple strategy that I use to make sure I am remembering what I am reading. Can I demonstrate it for you?"

Because I am a firm believer in gradually releasing responsibility to students, I do most of the talking in our early conferences. Later in the year, however, I expect children to tell me what good reader strategies are working especially well for them. By midyear, my part in the conference might consist of simply saying something like, "Tell me a little about your book. Are there strategies that are working especially well for you? Are you noticing any particular problems in your reading? How do you plan to solve those problems?"

Taking anecdotal records

As I confer with children, I use computer labels to take notes on what strategies they are using effectively and what strategies they are attempting to use. I also record my goals for the children.

A typical label might read:

> 2/17 Chris ALDO ICE CREAM
> Chose because liked A. APPLESAUCE
> Goal: Use chapter titles for predictions

I place these labels on individual pages in a looseleaf notebook. Students know where the notebook is kept and are welcome to refer to their page or add to it at any time.

In addition to using conferences as a means of helping children become increasingly cognizant of good reading strategies, I frequently take time during mini-lessons or share sessions to interview children about their use of good reading strategies.

Learning to self-reflect

As children become more adept at verbalizing their good reading strategies, I ask them to begin writing about themselves as readers once a month. The following survey (Figure 3.5) provides them, and me, with a concrete written record of their changing views of themselves as readers. I introduce these questions one at a time over several weeks, placing special emphasis on *how* children know about themselves as readers. Each month, I confer with students about their surveys, discussing both their strengths and their goals. I place these surveys in individual student files, accessible to them or me at any time. The accumulated surveys act as a wonderful tool for "remember when . . ." conferences.

Thinking About Your Reading

Name _____ Date _____

Title _____

Author _____

Genre _____ Is this a new genre for you? _____

1. As far as difficulty, this book was   Easy   Just Right   Hard   (Circle one)
   I know this because _____

2. Something I did really well when I read this book was _____
   I know this because _____

3. Something I want to work on when I read my next book is _____
   I want to work on this because _____
   I plan to do this by _____

4. My best piece of written work for this book was _____
   I know this because _____

5. On a scale of 1–10 (1–YUCK, 10–GREAT) I would give this book a _____
   because _____

   Do you want to read something by the same author or in the same genre soon? _____
   Why or why not? _____

Figure 3.5   Survey form

If I have any doubt about my students' knowledge of good reading strategies or about their views of themselves as readers, comments from last year's fourth and fifth graders quickly dispel those doubts.

On analyzing the difficulty of a book:

"Just right—the words were fine, but the puzzle was hard, I didn't get all the clues."

"Hard—I was always having to look back in my memory to think of all the events that had already happened."

On what the reader is doing well:

"Using the back of the book to see if I think it will be exciting. I never used to pay attention to it, so then I would always abandon books because they were boring."

"My literature log, I don't tell the story anymore, I tell my feelings."

Most important, this self-assessment allows children to begin to think about how they need to *grow* and *change* as readers. In formulating their own plans for growth, they begin to assume the characteristics of mature readers, learners, and thinkers.

"I think the area I need to grow in is reading more books by authors I have never heard of before. I think this because I only read certain authors. I'm going to ask Nicole to help me choose something different, because she always reads great books."

"My goal is putting in a word for a word I don't know, because I take too much time figuring that word out, then I forget what the story is about. I might need some help in practicing substituting."

In her short story "Slower than the Rest," Cynthia Rylant tells the story of Leo, a child who has been placed in a class for slow learners: "Leo thought he would never get over that. He saw no way to be happy after that." One day, however, Leo wins a schoolwide award for a report on his pet turtle, Charley. "That night, holding the turtle on his shoulder, Leo felt proud. And for the first time in a long time, Leo felt fast."

This year, for the first time ever, I ran the Bolder Boulder in less than an hour. Rosa Mota, the winner of the women's elite class, ran the race in thirty-three minutes. I didn't care. I "felt fast." Most of the readers I know will never be the Rosa Motas of the reading world. By teaching children good reader strategies, helping children to verbalize their successes at using strategies, and setting goals for future growth, however, I hope that each child will leave my presence "feeling fast." For me, growth and empowerment are the major issues behind literacy assessment.

Conclusion

In reading and writing, metacognition refers to the student's conscious awareness of or knowledge about the reading and writing processes, reading and writing strategies, and himself as a reader and writer. Metacognition is typically accessed through self-reports on questionnaires, interviews, or group discussions. Although self-reports often reveal a student's knowledge about reading and writing and what the student does as a literacy user, they also reveal a student's values in relation to literacy. Knowing these things about a student enables a teacher to design instruction to develop the student's knowledge and, when necessary, to help the student consider aspects of reading and writing. Metacognition is an important key to literacy development. Not only does it permit teachers to find out how students think about reading and writing, it also permits students to have control over the processes. Confidence and control over these processes help to insure that students become lifelong learners who use their literacy to learn.

references

Baker, L., & A. Brown. (1984). Metacognitive skills and reading. In P. D. Pearson (Ed.), *Handbook of reading research* (pp. 353–394). New York: Longman.

Berliner, D., & U. Casanova. (1986). Should you try reciprocal teaching? Yes! *Instructor*, Jan. 1986, 12–13.

Brown, A. (1978). Knowing when, where and how to remember: A problem of metacognition. In R. Glaser (Ed.), *Advances in instructional psychology*. Hillsdale, NJ: Erlbaum.

Casanave, C.P. (1988). Comprehension monitoring in ESL reading: A neglected essential. *TESOL Quarterly, 22* (2), 283–302.

Costa, A.L. (1984). Mediating the metacognitive. *Educational Leadership, 41* (2), 43–48.

Davey, B., & S.M. Porter. (1982). Comprehension rating: A procedure to assist poor comprehenders. *Journal of Reading, 26*, 197–202.

Debnam, B. (1989). The mini page reading wheel. *The Mini Page*, March 1, *Rocky Mountain News*.

Felknor, C. (1989). Chapter I Writing Interview. Northglenn, CO: School District No. 12, Adams County.

Garner, R. (1986). *Metacognition and reading comprehension*. Norwood, NJ: Ablex.

Goodman, Y., D. Watson, & C. Burke. (1987). *Reading miscue inventory: Alternative procedures*. Katonah, NY: Richard C. Owen.

Hansen, J. (1989). *The Colorado Communicator* interviews Jane Hansen. *The Colorado Communicator, 12* (3), 1, 21–23.

Herrmann, B.A. (1988). Two approaches for helping poor readers become more strategic. *The Reading Teacher, 42* (1), 24–28.

Institute for Research on Teaching. (1989). Precis from G. Duffy & L. Roehler (in press). The tension between information-giving and instructional explanation and teacher change. In J. Brophy (Ed.), *Research on teaching: Vol. 1. Teaching for meaningful understanding and self-regulated learning*. Greenwich, CT: JAI Press.

Meichenbaum, D., S. Burland, L. Gruson, & R. Cameron. (1985). Metacognitive assessment. In S.R. Yussen (Ed.), *The growth of reflection in children* (pp. 3–30). New York: Academic Press.

Miles, M. (1971). *Annie and the old one*. Boston: Little, Brown.

Miller, S.D., & N. Yochum. (1988). Evaluating students' awareness of reading problems and the strategies they use to remediate them. Paper presented at the National Reading Conference, Tucson, Arizona.

Myers, M., & S. Paris. (1978). Children's metacognitive knowledge about reading. *Journal of Educational Psychology, 70*, 680–690.

Nicholson, T. (1984). You get lost when you gotta blimmin' watch the damn words: The low progress reader in the junior high school. *Topics in Learning and Learning Disabilities, 3* (4), 16–30.

Palinscar, A.S. (1986). Reciprocal teaching. In *Teaching reading as thinking* (pp. 5–10). Alexandria, VA: Association for Supervision and Curriculum Development.

Palinscar, A.S., & A. Brown. (1984). Reciprocal teaching of comprehension-fostering and comprehension-monitoring activities. *Cognition and Instruction, 1* (2), 117–175.

———. (1985). Reciprocal teaching: Activities to promote "read(ing) with your mind." In T.L. Harris & E.J. Cooper (Eds.), *Reading, thinking, and concept development: Strategies for the classroom.* New York: The College Board.

Rhodes, L.K. (Ed.). (1993). *Literacy Assessment: A Handbook of Instruments.* Portsmouth, NH: Heinemann.

Rhodes, L.K., & C. Dudley-Marling. (1988). *Readers and writers with a difference.* Portsmouth, NH: Heinemann.

Schmitt, M.C. (1990). A questionnaire to measure children's awareness of strategic reading processes. *The Reading Teacher, 43* (7), 454–461.

Siu-Runyan, Y. (1990). Make your students colleagues in learning. *The Colorado Communicator, 13* (3), 1, 31–37.

Smith, F. (1989). *Understanding reading.* New York: Holt, Rinehart & Winston.

Sommers, J. (1989). The writer's memo: Collaboration, response, and development. In C.M. Anson (Ed.), *Writing and response* (pp. 174–186). Urbana, IL: National Council of Teachers of English.

Stewart, O., & E. Tei. (1983). Some implications of metacognition for reading instruction. *Journal of Reading*, October, 36–43.

Tarone, E., & G. Yule. (1989). *Focus on the language learner.* New York: Oxford University Press.

Valencia, S. (1990). Alternative assessment: Separating the wheat from the chaff. *The Reading Teacher, 44* (1), 60–61.

Wade, S.E., & R.E. Reynolds. (1989). Developing metacognitive awareness. *Journal of Reading, 33* (1), 6–14.

Wagoner, S.A. (1983). Comprehension monitoring: What it is and what we know about it. *Reading Research Quarterly, 18* (3), 328–346.

Wixson, K.K., A.B. Bosky, M.N. Yochum, & D.E. Alvermann. (1984). An interview for assessing students' perceptions of classroom reading tasks. *The Reading Teacher, 37*(4), 346–352.

Yaden, D.B., & S. Templeton. (1986). *Metalinguistic awareness and beginning literacy.* Portsmouth, NH: Heinemann.

Chapter Four

4

Assessing Language Systems and Strategies in Reading

reflections

☐ When listening to a student read orally, what criteria would you use to decide if a book is too hard? too easy?

☐ Tape-record a student reading aloud both a predictable and a nonpredictable book or passage. What difference do you observe in the student's miscue patterns and reading strategies? Which text actually turned out to be more predictable for the reader? What effect did the predictability of the text have on the student's use of the language cueing systems and reading strategies?

☐ Tape-record a student's reading of one or more passages. What evidence do you find of:

predicting
substituting
inserting
repeating
self-correcting
using pictures
habitual associations
tunnel vision

☐ Use the *Classroom Reading Miscue Assessment (CRMA)* (see Rhodes, 1993 or Rhodes & Shanklin, 1990) to gather information on several good and poor readers. What do you learn about differences in the ways that good and poor readers process text?

☐ Make a video or audiotape of yourself listening to a student read and responding to the student. What kinds of miscue feedback do you find yourself providing for readers? What other feedback might you try?

☐ Choose a book you would like to read. At the end of each of your periods of reading, reflect upon your own reading processes in a learning log. The book you select ought to be one you want to read that has not been assigned for any academic class in which you are currently enrolled. Write a culminating reflection about what you learn from your learning log. What implications do these reflections upon your own reading processes have that might apply to your work with students? Use these questions as possible guides to your reflections:

- How did you go about choosing this book to read?
- In what environments do you find yourself reading this book? What effects do these environments have on your reading?
- Did you preview the book before you began to read?
- How? Did it help in any way?
- How is your background knowledge affecting your reading of this book?
- How do you know if you aren't comprehending?
- What do you do?
- How are you handling any vocabulary that you don't know?
- How do you find yourself adjusting your fluency to read this book?
- Have you found yourself doing any talking or writing about this book? How has that affected your comprehension?
- How have you gone about sharing or presenting your learning from this book?

In the last five years many teachers have begun to establish Reading Workshops or literature-based reading programs. These programs allow students to experience more personally meaningful reading and make it possible for teachers to demonstrate reading strategies to select individuals or small groups of students who need them. This kind of instruction is based on the assessment of students' developmental needs and contrasts sharply with many basal reading programs in which children are grouped, then read the same story and learn skills as prescribed by teachers' manuals and workbooks. Jackie Eversley, currently a middle-school teacher for the Aurora Public Schools in Colorado, describes her journey as a teacher from the basal reading program to Reading Workshop, and instruction based on her assessment of students' strengths and weaknesses:

> I thought that in moving from the elementary to the middle school level, I wouldn't have to worry about placing students in basal readers. My relief was short-lived, however. For while there are no reading groups, there are still students with a wide range of reading abilities. In middle school the problem of placement takes on more subtle overtones. Because there are not reading groups and less time is spent on oral reading, the undiscovered low reader can sit with a novel in front of her and be drowning for days or even for an entire reading unit, without the teacher being aware of the situation.
>
> While I certainly don't miss the reading groups, I now realize that the responsibility for correctly fitting novels and students rests with me. Learning more about reading assessment has better equipped me to deal with these ongoing problems in classroom reading situations.

In Reading Workshops or literature-based reading programs, teachers determine what reading strategies children are ready to learn. To match children's needs and instruction appropriately, teachers must learn to observe and assess children's reading processes as they read whole pieces of text. Sometimes a teacher observes that a student in Reading Workshop is continually changing books or is always off task. Reading difficulties rather than student motivation may be at the heart of the problem, and teachers need to learn to assess such instances.

In addition, within Reading Workshops it is unwise to assume that children can learn everything they need to know about the reading process simply by engaging in reading. Some students may be using reading strategies that are dysfunctional, and they need to reflect upon what good readers do. At other times new strategies need to be demonstrated because students are developmentally ready for them. Such careful matching of readers and strategy instruction helps students gradually become more independent and handle increasingly more difficult reading materials in reading workshops. Interest and strategy instruction help insure that students are able to read for understanding.

Assessing the reading process, however, is not an easy task. We cannot do it when children read silently. But we can look at the strategies they apply to oral reading of unfamiliar text. The miscues—a term coined by Kenneth Goodman to signify that deviations readers make from text are not necessarily negative—can become windows into students' mental processing. In this chapter we will examine students' miscues as they attempt to integrate the language cueing systems of graphophonics, syntax, semantics, and pragmatics to construct meaning. We will also discuss the reading strategies students apply to unknown words in text. We will examine the effects of other factors on comprehension both during and after reading in the next

---

chapter. Here we want to state directly something we hope you already assume by this point: we are not interested in calling behavior "reading" if it does not involve attempts to construct meaning.

Comprehension is not tied to correct oral reading in the ways that many people commonly assume: it is not always true that when you read something correctly orally you automatically comprehend it. Instead, all readers make some miscues, whether they read orally or silently. In fact, they must risk miscues in order to read fast enough to overcome the limitations of short-term memory. Readers catch their miscues when text stops making sense to them, and they self-correct. Thus, when engaged in the process, readers make integrated use of all four language cueing systems. By listening to students ready orally, teachers can make observations about their strategies for using these systems. When readers' patterns of miscues provide sentences that do not make sense, chances are comprehension is poor. Often the basic strategies that these readers use to approach text must be changed before they are truly capable of comprehending in ways that are more than vague or global. If students' comprehension is poor, it can be important to use miscue analysis to try to discover why: are the readers using the language cueing systems in an integrated way? Do they lack a repertoire of reading strategies for making predictions, dealing with unknown words in text, and so on?

theories of the reading process

To assess students' reading processes we need to know what is currently understood about reading and reading comprehension. It is hard to spot a reading problem or a potential area of development without a knowledge of how good readers process and comprehend text and a sense of the normal parameters of development. A solid knowledge of the reading process is also a prerequisite for deciding what to do instructionally once a reading problem or developmental need is assessed.

We will briefly review five theories that have greatly influenced current thinking about how the reading process operates and how it develops. They represent five of the most important influences, on the whole language movement especially, over the past twenty-five years. Many of these ideas about the reading process have been excellently reviewed by Weaver (1988, 1990).

Goodman's psycholinguistic theory of reading

Kenneth Goodman's theory of reading (Gollasch, 1982; K. Goodman, 1984, 1989; Y. Goodman, 1989; Watson, 1989) developed from his interest in examining readers' miscues for evidence of interrelated use of the four language cueing systems—semantics, syntax, graphophonics, and pragmatics. Goodman views the errors that are made while reading aloud as windows to the actual cognitive processing that occurs during reading. He calls these deviations from the text "miscues" rather than errors. He argues that such "errors" are natural to the process of reading, and that it is through monitoring for meaning that readers make corrections. His system was based on the sentence. Its most crucial aspect was whether a miscue resulted in meaning change, that is, misinterpretation of the deep structure of a sentence.

Goodman views reading as a process in which the reader deals with information and constructs meaning continuously. The process is the same regardless of age, and proficiency can exist at every level. The reading process involves readers in making predictions, confirming or disconfirming these predictions while reading, and integrating information from the text with their background knowledge to form solid, holistic interpretations of texts. Readers use their existing background information to help make predictions and remember in part by integrating their new learning with what they already know.

a schema theoretic view

A second view of the reading process has been developed by cognitive psychologists who postulate that persons use schemas to organize and remember information (Rumelhart, 1977). *Schemas* may be defined as interlocking knowledge networks in our minds. Comprehending text involves applying one's existing knowledge to make sense of and relate new information to old. More specifically in reading, cognitive theorists posit that readers make global semantic predictions that are gradually refined, while at the same time making focal predictions about, for example, what letter is likely to appear next in a word. We read by making and confirming or disconfirming these global and focal predictions simultaneously (Adams & Collins, 1979; Anderson & Pearson, 1984).

Breakdowns and lack of comprehension do occur (Mason, 1984). Sometimes readers lack schemas or fail to use knowledge they already have. The issue here is "schema availability." At other times readers have the schemas but fail to bring them into focus and are thus said to have problems with "schema selection." Finally, readers sometimes have schemas available and select to use them but are unable to maintain the schemas while reading. They have trouble with "schema maintenance."

Rosenblatt's transactional theory

The title of Louise Rosenblatt's book *The Reader, the Text, the Poem* (1978) captures the essence of her theory of the reading process. She believes that the reader brings to text all of her personal experiences along with the influence of her cultural milieu. The text is the black and white graphic display created by the author. The "poem," as she defines it, is not the text per se but the ongoing transaction between the reader and the text. The transaction is the meaning, but this meaning may not be the same for each reader. Her definition of transaction is key to her theory (Rosenblatt, 1985, 1988). The transaction between a reader and a text is not simply an interaction. When an interaction occurs, things meet or collide but neither necessarily goes away from the incident changed in some fundamental way. In contrast, during a transaction true change occurs for those involved.

The transaction or "poem" that each reader creates is individual. There is naturally a variety of responses to, meanings for, and interpretations of the same text depending on readers' background knowledge. These interpretations are each equally valid. What constitutes "knowledge" then is socially constructed among readers in a group.

Rosenblatt distinguishes between what she sees as two different kinds of reading—aesthetic and efferent. *Aesthetic* reading is reading that we do for pleasure. It includes all of the fiction and poetry that we read and is characterized by being open to a variety of reader interpretations. It is literature that often tells a story and entertains, yet at the same time may have a serious message. On the other hand, *efferent* reading is the reading readers do "to get things done." It often tends to be informational in nature and is often done in relationship to jobs. Rosenblatt's point is that we use different strategies to approach comprehension of what we read depending on our purpose for reading. Even what comprehension means and how it is shared varies between these two kinds of reading.

Eco's theory: the role of the reader

Umberto Eco has proposed one of the most current but complex theories of the reading process. According to his theory, reading can be placed within a larger theory of how individuals construct meaning from all sign systems, be they music, dance, drama, architecture, television, or whatever. The print on a page, like music or art, is simply another sign system that people use to interpret and communicate their understandings of the world. We will not discuss all of Eco's theory but only two ideas that seem particularly relevant to classroom teachers.

As readers we assign meaning to the graphics on the page in order to comprehend an author's message. Often these graphics have several potential meanings, but we agree to use common understandings and rules for constructing meaning that seem to fit with what the author is trying to say. Eco calls these rules *codes* and *subcodes*. Puns are funny and we delight in them because they allow us to demonstrate how codes and subcodes can be broken and lead to a variety of interpretations. Examining text for bias and recognizing propaganda mean, in fact, learning how to determine if authors have broken the codes we normally expect them to follow: to be truthful, to present all the facts, and so on. For the most part readers learn codes and subcodes through the use of language in everyday contexts with other people.

The notion of codes and subcodes leads to the concept of open and closed texts. *Open texts* are those for which there can be a variety of interpretations depending on readers' background knowledge and the number of potential meanings a text has. We appreciate most poetry and great literature as open texts because of the variety of possible interpretations. In contrast, the verbal descriptions that accompany blueprints to the control panels of a power plant need to be *closed texts*, with little or no variance in interpretation. Here we don't want a variety of interpretations, since critical mistakes could cost both money and lives.

Smith's socio-psycholinguistic theory

Frank Smith's book *Understanding Reading* is now in its fourth edition. The first edition dates back to 1971, making Smith's original work virtually concurrent with Goodman's. We are choosing to review Smith's socio-psycholinguistic theory last because the most recent edition of his theory acts as a good summary of developments in reading theory over the past twenty years.

One of the most significant features of Smith's theory is his discussion of the importance of nonvisual information to reading. He argues that the more nonvisual information we bring to print, the easier the reading will be and the more the likelihood that we will comprehend and retain information. For example, Shanklin has been attempting to read more about the national debt. It looks as if a lot of taxpayer money is going into this area that could be spent otherwise—say, on education. But Shanklin finds that reading in this area is slow going. Often she needs to read very carefully to understand individual parts of particular articles and then doesn't really remember everything without looking the whole article over again. The problem is that she doesn't possess much in-depth background information about finance, and thus has to pay close attention to all of the visual information on the page.

A second topic for which Smith is well known is his cogent argument against phonics as the key to learning to read. As Smith points out, we need 166 different phonics rules to explain English pronunciation. To memorize all of these rules and to understand where they do or do not apply would be a monumental task for any beginning reader. It is also interesting to contemplate that while many adults can articulate some phonics rules, we cannot articulate 166, yet we can *still* read. Something more must be going on. In addition, Smith argues that reading cannot be a simple matter of decoding from left to right. There are many words we do not know how to pronounce until we look to the right of the letter.

Smith also points out that even if we use phonics rules and pronounce words correctly, it doesn't necessarily mean that we understand what we are reading. Teachers sometimes assume that if a learner reads a passage aloud correctly, she understands. Yet Shanklin can read aloud articles in her news magazine about the national debt but not really be able to discuss the subject in depth when she is done.

One of Smith's most important contributions to theories of reading has been his rethinking of how the short- and long-term memory work and relate during reading. Smith demonstrates that the short-term memory takes in approximately three to seven bits of information each second. Although the number of bits does not vary a great deal, the actual amount of information processed depends on the makeup of each bit. Smith demonstrates that readers take in fewer than ten random letters in a second, but if ten or more letters are organized into words, readers take in considerably more "letters" because the brain has organized them into meaningful bits as words. Still more letters can be processed if the words are arranged in a meaningful syntactic order so that they form a phrase.

In *Understanding Reading* Smith presents a diagram of how he perceives the short-term and long-term memory working (see Figure 4.1). Note that the short-term memory resides within the long-term memory. The most salient feature here is that, while the short-term memory processes incoming information into meaningful units, it is the long-term memory that guides and suggests what types of meaningful units the short-term memory should look for. When the short-term memory gets overloaded and units are not meaningful, tunnel vision occurs. This happens most frequently when students don't have enough nonvisual background knowledge to bring to the text.

Twenty years ago Smith's theory, like Goodman's, was characterized as a psycholinguistic theory of reading. Most important to the theory was an understanding of linguistics and psychology as it relates to the minds of individual readers. More recently he has explored and added "socio" aspects of reading and learning to read to his linguistic and psychological tenets (we might add that Goodman has done the same).

Smith discusses the social nature of reading and learning to read through his concepts of demonstration, engagement, and sensitivity. As you will recall, these three concepts have already been discussed in some detail (see Chapter 2). Through the literacy *demonstrations* of others—parents, teachers, peers—we learn what read-

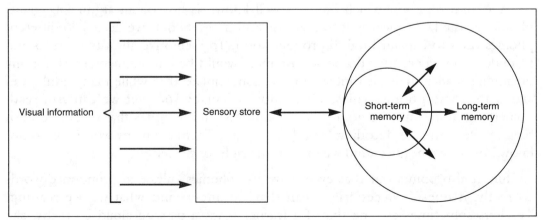

Figure 4.1   Smith's alternative diagram of memory

ing is and strategies for doing it. For many of us, parents or older siblings provided our earliest literacy demonstrations by reading to us. These demonstrations reflect important social aspects of reading and learning to read. *Engagement* is the amount of time actually spent in a literacy task. Engagement can occur alone or it can involve others. When it is social, some students will engage for longer periods of time and be more successful because they are assisting each other. *Sensitivity* relates to the degree that the learner expects learning to take place. Sensitivity is also social in that others can often encourage us or greatly discourage us as readers. The three terms can be defined separately, but they are best understood as acting together in real social contexts.

The final socio-psycholinguistic concept that Smith has coined is that of the "literacy club." Smith argues that learning to read is like joining a club. At first you are a novice among experts, but you get to see wonderful demonstrations from the experts, ask them questions, and engage in doing the activity and getting hints from them. Learning to read is just the same. Belonging to the club also means that you continue to engage in the activity in order to be considered part of the group. We join clubs because we have "sensitivity": we have an interest in the activity, think we'll enjoy it even more if we get better, and have every expectation that we will learn and contribute to the club. And that it will be fun!

Although there are some differences in these five theories, they tend to be more alike than different. All of them view reading as a constructive mental process, not just a passive reception of input from eyes scanning across a page. All recognize the important role of psychology in learning and in reading. Readers bring their background knowledge, organized into mental schemas, to each reading task. The nature of those schemas greatly affects learners' ability to read and comprehend passages of text. Some of readers' schemas relate to linguistics—especially how semantics, syntax, graphophonics, and pragmatics work together to create meaning. All five theories now recognize the important role of sociological variables in almost all reading contexts.

miscues: windows into the reading process

In their reading theories, Smith and Goodman have asserted that errors are natural to the reading process. Goodman calls such deviations from the print "miscues," a term not laden with the negative connotations of "error." Miscues occur naturally as readers try to keep up with the limitations of their short-term memory. For text to be comprehended, it must be processed through short-term memory to long-term memory in meaningful bits. Smith suggests that readers use schemas stored in long-term memory to make sense of and group incoming data into meaningful units. These schemas relate to readers' knowledge of the world, including the semantic, syntactic, graphophonic, and pragmatic cueing systems of language.

Miscues also occur because of the many "Englishes" that students speak (Lindfors, 1986). These "Englishes" may be a result of home dialects or the fact that English is a second language. This factor must be taken into account when considering students' miscues. Understanding students' home dialects or languages helps teachers to determine which miscues involve dialect or reveal features of children's native languages. In this way educators begin to understand that different "Englishes" do not imply intellectual inferiority.

the language cueing systems

The study of readers' miscues provides insights into how they integrate the language cueing systems during the reading process in order to construct meaning. This meaning construction during the process of reading is often called *ongoing comprehending*. The quality of readers' ongoing comprehending depends upon their ability to use the four language cueing systems in an integrated way. For readers to maintain ongoing comprehending, each sentence must sound like language and make sense at the same time. Problems with ongoing comprehending often provide clues to students' misinterpretations after reading. We would like to differentiate ongoing comprehending from readers' "comprehension" or final sense of the meaning of a text after reading. In this chapter we will focus on ongoing comprehending and in Chapter 5 on comprehension. We will begin by discussing each of the language cueing systems, defining each system and posing questions that can be asked in order to assess students' appropriate use of that system.

semantics

Semantics refers to the meaning system of language. Meaning is not lodged in individual words; words themselves have specific meaning only when they are embedded in the context of other language. The context in which a word appears gives clues to which meaning is intended. For example, the word "present" has two potential meanings and pronunciations depending on the sentence in which it is embedded. We can say, "I gave my friend a birthday present" or "I want to present our new chairperson." We have used the same word, but in each sentence a different meaning and pronunciation is intended. The correct one can only be determined when the rest of the context becomes known.

Semantics is an area in which specific content knowledge, separate from linguistic knowledge, also plays an important role in readers' ability to comprehend. Articles on the Commonwealth of Independent States are much easier to read if you have some understanding of the Russian Revolution and Russian history since 1900. It is also helpful to know the various states of the former Soviet Union, where they are located, and what important cities are in each. Such semantic knowledge provides readers with schemas they can use to unlock new information in text and mentally organize it to remember it. If readers' semantic knowledge in an area is weak, it can interfere with their ongoing comprehending.

Here are some questions to ask about a reader's use of semantics:

- Does the reader indicate through her miscues that she does not understand certain concepts or ideas presented by the author?

- Does the reader make omissions that disrupt the ongoing construction of meaning and comprehension?

- When the reader comes to an unknown word, does she put in a substitute to maintain meaning?

- Is the reader able to understand certain concepts and ideas even if she mispronounces words or phrases related to the concepts?

- Does the reader habitually associate the same words with each other? Are the associations disruptive to meaning? Examples would include was/saw, were/where, who/what, with/which, of/for/from. While each combination is graphically similar, if readers are also using semantic cues, they are unlikely to make these miscues.

- To what extent is the reader able to understand what the antecedents are for pronouns in the text?

syntax

Syntax refers to the grammar or ongoing flow of the language. That individual languages have this ongoing flow becomes most apparent in comparing the common sentence structures of different ones. In English, subject–verb–direct object is a common grammatical form. In many other languages the most common order is subject–direct object–verb. Children learn these rules naturally, often without being able to state them verbally, through hearing language spoken to and around them and through using language effectively to express themselves. Readers use their knowledge of grammar to predict what words are likely to appear next.

Syntax may also be thought of as occurring at higher levels of text organization than just the sentence. Different genres have different literary elements that typically occur in particular orders. For example, a story needs a problem before it can have a climax and a resolution to the problem. Or when a passage is a comparison, the text usually begins with how two concepts are alike and then explains how they are different. Readers anticipate these higher level syntactic organizational patterns and use them to help organize their efforts to construct meaning as they are reading and to remember information after reading.

Here are some questions to ask about a reader's use of syntax:

- Does the reader read certain words or phrases in her own dialect?

- Are the reader's insertions plausible given the syntax of her native language or dialect? Do they show that the reader is making predictions based upon her knowledge of syntax?

- Does the reader attend to punctuation as a clue to meaning?

- What sentence structures seem to give the reader difficulty?

- What types of corrections or adjustments does the reader make when her sense of the syntax begins to break down?

- Is the reader able to recognize and use common patterns of text structure to construct meaning as she is reading?

graphophonics

Graphophonics refers to the letter-sound system of language. Many people believe that this is the only system we use to read. If readers consistently rely only on graphophonics rather than use the cueing systems in combination, they simply cannot read fast enough to overcome the limitations of short-term memory. Thus, while readers use graphophonics in reading, they do so in conjunction with the semantic, syntactic, and pragmatic systems. People often assume that readers progress from left to right to decode graphophonic cues. Again, this is not true: frequently you cannot determine the sound of a vowel until you have processed what follows it.

Here are some questions to ask about a reader's use of graphophonics:

- Does the reader rely on the sound-letter similarity to the exclusion of thinking about constructing meaning?

- Does the reader focus only on the first letter and then say a word beginning with that letter without necessarily making sense in the story?

- To what extent does the reader overcorrect miscues that make no difference to the meaning?

- What consistent habitual associations does the reader make? Examples would include was/saw, were/where, who/what, with/which, of/for/from. While each combination is graphically similar, if readers are also using semantic cues, they are unlikely to make these miscues.

- Does the reader omit unknown words?

pragmatics

The pragmatic system of language refers to how individuals use language within a specific context. A child may not be able to read immediately the directions written by other children for feeding a new hamster. The child knows, however, how to read the directions for feeding the rabbit and predicts that this sheet clipped to the hamster cage is probably a set of directions for feeding it. Since the child wants to be the first to feed it, she looks at the sheet, expecting to find certain words and syntax phrases often found in other directions. When she comes to the new phrase "hamster food," graphophonics, syntax, semantics, and pragmatics help the child unlock the meaning of the phrase.

Here are some questions to ask about a reader's understanding of pragmatics:

- To what extent does the reader expect text to make sense?

- In what ways does the reader use cues from the environment to figure out what a text might say?

- To what extent is a reader able to understand what each character is saying in a written dialogue?

- In what ways does a reader converse with others about what a text might mean?

additional cueing systems within text

Pictures, captions, titles and subtitles, charts and graphs provide additional cues that proficient readers use to aid comprehension. If there is a good match between the text and other visuals, students will frequently use them in conjunction with semantics, syntax, graphophonics, and pragmatics to figure out unknown words. Moving away from using pictures as cues is one of the challenges children face in first learning to read the more extended text of chapter books.

Here are some questions to ask about a reader's use of additional cues in text:

- How does the reader use pictures in the text to figure out unknown words?

- How does the reader use pictures to confirm or disconfirm her understanding of the text's meaning?

- Is the reader confused by where and how pictures/figures are placed in relation to printed text?

- Is the reader able to read maps, bar graphs, and similar figures that are part of a text?

- In nonfiction materials, does the reader understand the function of main headings and subheadings and how those can be used to aid comprehension?

- In nonfiction materials, can the reader explain how bold or other special print is used, especially in relation to new vocabulary?

the relationship between miscues and comprehension

So far, our discussion of miscues may seem to suggest that there is a reasonably straightforward relationship between miscues and comprehension. Such, we must warn, is not always the case! Just because a student reads with few or no miscues, there is no guarantee that she understands what she has just read. For example, what happens when you read and then attempt to retell the following passage:

> Professor Thom's major research interest has been in topology and its applications—most recently to catastrophe theory. His earliest work dealt with manifolds and, in particular, cobordism of manifolds, a subject which asks when one manifold is the boundary of another. Not only did Thom answer the question, but he also developed some very beautiful and unexpected connec-

tions of cobordism theory with other areas of topology. The impact on the mathematical world was profound, and it was for this work that Thom was awarded the Fields Medal (the mathematicians' Nobel Prize) by the International Conference of Mathematicians in 1958.

Unique among pure mathematicians, Professor Thom became interested in applications of mathematics (particularly geometry) to other disciplines. He opened up an entirely new era in mathematics in his studies relating geometry to biology by a method he felicitously termed "catastrophe theory." Catastrophe theory is a device for explaining how discontinuities can arise as a result of continuously changing causes. Thom has proved that despite the almost endless number of discontinuous phenomena that can exist in all branches of science, there are only a certain number of different pictures or "elementary catastrophes" that actually occur.

When we ask teachers to read and retell this passage, they have many reactions. Most agree that they can read the words well; in fact, class members will volunteer to demonstrate their oral reading. Retelling the passage is another matter. Being able to say the words does not result in comprehension. Yet many teachers assume that students comprehend when they help them read a passage aloud correctly. They seem to be operating under the implicit assumption that if a student says all the words correctly she must understand the passage. Most of you probably found retelling this passage difficult because you lacked the background knowledge to really understand it. In addition, you may have found yourself looking at smaller and smaller syntactic and graphophonic units or concentrating so much on individual sentences or phrases that you forgot what you had just read. What is occurring is what Smith terms tunnel vision.

Sometimes when asked to read this passage, teachers just push it aside, thinking it another of those trick passages that professors use. But it's not. This was the biographical sketch on Professor Thom that appeared in the program for a speech he gave as a university guest lecturer. Some people do understand exactly what this passage says; in fact, most secondary math majors and several science teachers have understood the passage when it was used in a class on content reading.

Thus, word-perfect reading doesn't necessarily mean that comprehension has occurred. In fact, sometimes a reader may make many miscues yet demonstrate good comprehension of a passage. As we have pointed out, not all miscues are of the same quality. A teacher must consider how much a student's miscues affect the meaning of the passage to be able to gauge her comprehension of it. There are possible relationships between a reader's miscue patterns during ongoing comprehending and final comprehension:

High Quality Miscues — Good Comprehension
Low Quality Miscues — Poor Comprehension
High Quality Miscues — Poor Comprehension
Low Quality Miscues — Good Comprehension

High quality miscues are those that are semantically acceptable or represent miscues that are subsequently self-corrected because the text has stopped making sense. If miscue quality is high, then the number of semantically acceptable sentences a student reads in a selection will also be high. It stands to reason that if the quality of miscues is high, and thus semantic acceptability and ongoing comprehending are good, then the student is likely to demonstrate good comprehension of what she has read. It is this relationship between miscues and comprehension that we come to expect and strive for.

The second pattern, "low quality miscues — poor comprehension," seems equally plausible. If a student produces miscues that are semantically unacceptable and does not try to self-correct, then her miscues are of low quality. The result is that the student's ongoing comprehending is poor, and many sentences, as finally read, are semantically unacceptable. When a reader is unable to construct meaning as she is reading, it seems logical that her final comprehension of a passage will be poor.

The third and fourth relationships between miscues and comprehension are more difficult to understand. Sometimes a student will work hard at trying to read a text. Her ongoing comprehending will be adequate but final comprehension poor. It may be that, as in the Dr. Thom biographical sketch, the reader is able to pronounce the words quite well; the ongoing comprehending sounds good. However, the reader lacks sufficient background information to comprehend and discuss the author's intended meaning. This is what happened to most of us when we tried to read the Dr. Thom passage; only those in fields closely aligned to his really understood what the passage meant.

The fourth relationship, low quality miscues and good comprehension, seems the least plausible. Occasionally, however, it does happen. Two explanations seem most probable. Some readers make self-corrections in their heads but do not bother to self-correct errors out loud. As a result, their reading sounds poor to us although they are internally self-correcting and comprehending well. Another explanation is that some readers begin with low quality miscues, but the quality of their miscues improves as they become more engrossed in the book and understand better what is happening.

Rereading is another factor that can often affect the relationship between quality of miscues and comprehension. We are not suggesting, however, that students need to stare at a word for a long time. By rereading we mean rereading a book several times during several different sittings. The child's miscue patterns often change and with them the depth of personal understanding of the pictures and text.

The relationship between miscues and comprehension is often not an easy one to figure out, although it is an important one to examine. If a child's miscues frequently fail to maintain meaning and are not self-corrected, and the child's comprehension is also poor, then usually the child needs instruction in how to use the four language cueing systems better before she will be able to make significant gains in comprehension.

On the other hand, if the child's miscues are few but retelling poor, then usually the child needs to work on applying background knowledge and making predictions. During reading, a student in such a situation needs to focus more on confirming and disconfirming predictions than on getting the words right. Text structure can also be pointed out and used to aid retelling. Instructional strategies such as story maps, webbing, sociograms, drama, and comparisons that integrate comprehension can be taught. Much more will be said about comprehension in Chapter 5.

■ ■

examining readers' use of the cueing systems

In this section the miscue patterns of several readers—two primary children, two intermediate-grade students, and two middle schoolers—will be examined. These students represent a wide range of abilities, and their reading illustrates several of the issues we've raised above. We have chosen this method of presentation rather than illustrating each miscue type separately, because within the context of reading, one miscue usually does not occur apart from others. What we want to demonstrate is the complex thinking that teachers must do as they listen to children read passages aloud for assessment purposes.

So that teachers can reflect on miscue patterns and share this information, there are standardized procedures for marking miscues. Figure 4.2 illustrates a consistent way to mark miscues that can be easily learned and shared with others. If you are unfamiliar with this marking system and reading marked text, take a few minutes to read over the chart before you proceed. We aren't suggesting that you stop now to "memorize" the chart, but work to understand it and then use it to "hear" each of the six readers whose marked readings follow. As you work with these materials and try out some of the reflections at the beginning of the chapter, both marking and reading marked text will come easier. In fact, you will probably find that you know the chart without being conscious of having tried to learn it.

■ beginning readers

Let's start by looking at Tony, who is about to enter second grade. Tony was reading *Clifford at the Circus* for the first time. Figure 4.3 illustrates some selected miscues that he made in various parts of the story. Study his reading and think about how he made integrated use of the language cueing systems.

In his first miscue in line 3 Tony read "wanted" for "was." This miscue fit with both previous semantics and the syntax. The author of the story had already said that Elizabeth had a dog, so it makes sense that Tony would predict, especially from this information and the title of the story, that the circus "wanted" her dog. The syntax of "wanted"—that a verb will often follow a noun—also fit with the context "we saw a sign that said the circus." In addition, the "wa" was graphically similar to the first two letters in "was." It wasn't until Tony considered the phrase coming after the miscue that he realized "wanted in town" didn't make sense. He then went back and corrected to "was in town." Tony has demonstrated that he makes integrated use of the cueing systems and is self-monitoring his reading for meaning.

In the next section of text where Tony made miscues, he omitted the "s" on "lions and tigers." He must have predicted that there was only one lion and one

brothers bothers	Longhand superscriptions denote substitution miscues—oral observed responses that differ from expected responses to printed text.
∧	Insertion miscue (word not in printed text, added by oral reader). Example: Gwen∧ poured him a big glass. ***proudly***
(word)	Circled word or words; circled period or other punctuation indicates omission miscue—word in printed text, omitted in oral reading.
st-	In substitution miscues, partial word plus hyphen stands for partial word substituted in oral reading for text word.
Billy ⌐ cried	Reversal miscue of words in text by oral reader.
® ⌐Then he	In passages recording miscues, underlines denote repetitions—portions the reader repeats in oral reading.
© ⌐	Miscue corrected through regression. Example: © ***the*** ⌐Then he . . .
ⓤ© ⌐	Miscue with unsuccessful attempt at correction through regression. Example: ⓤ© ***All*** ⌐Tell me what you see . . .
Ⓐ© ⌐	Reader abandons correct form. Reader replaces an initially correct response with an incorrect one.
ⓓwith	Circled letter d preceding a miscue superscription denotes a variation in sound, vocabulary, or grammar resulting from a dialect difference between the author and the reader.
$	Nonword miscue. The reader either produces a nonword orally in place of text word or supplies a phonemic dialect variation. Examples: ***$ larther*** I sat in a large leather chair. ***$ cawed*** What his mother called him depended on what he did last.
+	Oral reader sounds out the word in segments. Example: ***$ sooth + thing*** I guess they do have a soothing sound.

Figure 4.2   Symbols, abbreviations, and other marks used in miscue analysis

---

tiger for Clifford to worry about. These miscues didn't seem to interrupt his basic comprehension of the story, and he chose to keep reading rather than go back to correct them. The next miscue of real interest was when Tony read "trainer" for "tamer" and again made no correction. "Trainer" and "tamer" have graphophonically similar beginnings and endings. Syntactically, they are also the same part of speech in that both are nouns. In addition, the author had previously referred to the "lion trainer" and this was the first time he has called him the "lion tamer." Tony did not correct this miscue, but little meaning was lost.

In the second part of the story, there is another good example showing Tony trying to use the language cueing systems in an integrated way to make meaning. He made several miscues here, which fit with the prior context, but because they did

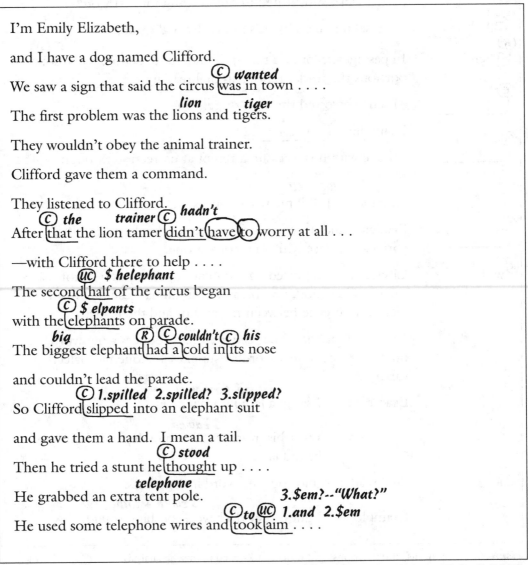

Figure 4.3 Tony, a second grader, reading *Clifford Goes to the Circus* by Norman Birdwell (1985). Collected by Linda Gherardini, Denver Public Schools.

Windows Into Literacy

not fit with the following context, Tony self-corrected. Particularly illustrative are his corrections on "slipped" and "thought."

We won't discuss all of Tony's miscues in the passage in order to leave some for you to analyze for yourself and give you a chance to think about how miscues provide insight into students' mental processing as they read.

In contrast to Tony, let's look at Chris, who was about to enter third grade. His marked reading of a story from one of the *Frog and Toad* books by Arnold Lobel, is shown in Figure 4.4.

As a reader, Chris is very different from Tony. From the very first line, we begin to suspect that his miscues may potentially affect his understanding of the story. His miscue of "coming" for "caught" made some sense. "Coming" also began with the same letter as "caught" and fit with the previous syntax. "Coming" was an easier word choice than "caught," a word that Chris may not have recognized in print. He also sounded out "r + an" for "rain" and was satisfied to leave it uncorrected, although it did not make sense. It is interesting that, after the mention of being wet in the next line, Chris had no trouble with "rain" in line 5.

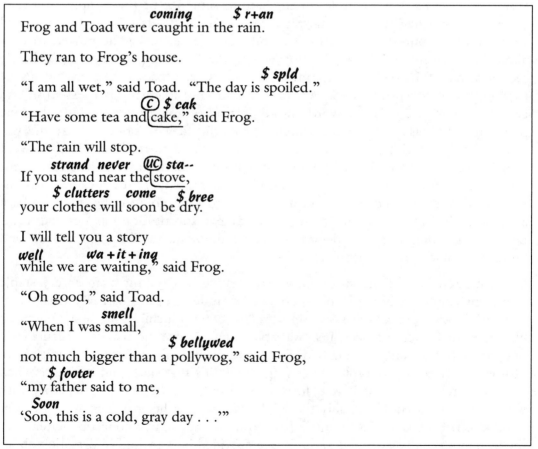

Figure 4.4   Chris, a third grader, reading *The Corner* by Arnold Lobel (1985). Collected by Tammy French, Denver Public Schools.

In line 3 Chris said "spld" for "spoiled." As with "r + an" for "rain," Chris sounded out the word but did not correct it or substitute another. He was willing to stick with graphophonically similar nonwords rather than attempt to make sense. Chris did self-correct his next miscue when he said "cak" for "cake." By now it seems clear that Chris is having trouble reading the story for meaning. His reading in lines 6 and 7 further confirms that he "reads" mostly by sounding out and has little ability to use semantics and syntax in conjunction with his knowledge of graphophonics.

◼ intermediate-grade readers

Although middle-grade readers can have miscue patterns similar to beginning readers, there are some types of miscue patterns that are more common to the middle grades (generally four to six). Notice the miscues Josh made as he began *The Great Gilly Hopkins* by Katherine Paterson, a chapter book that contains no pictures (see Figure 4.5). The sentences in this book, like those in most middle-grade materials, are longer and more complex than those in primary-grade books.

Josh's ongoing comprehension of this story seems to be quite good. Several of his miscues had little effect on the meaning and made the syntax more like his oral language patterns. For example, in the second sentence of the sample Josh read "She blew until her" rather than "She blew until she." His miscue "her" fit well with the prior context of the sentence and made sense, but as he started to look ahead he could see that "her" did not fit with the following context "could barely see the shape of the social worker's head." He ably went back to correct his miscue to read "she," which then fit with both the prior and following context. Josh also ended this sentence after the word "head" instead of going on to include the final prepositional phrase. Ending the sentence as he did fit with prior context and was more in keeping with the shorter sentences he is used to reading. He then went ahead to read the prepositional phrase but did not go back to reread the entire sentence to correct his placement of the period. We suspect that little meaning was lost through this miscue and that it did make sense to keep going rather than go back and correct it. In the next paragraph Josh made two substitution miscues that maintained the meaning to a large degree. He substituted "manner" for "maneuver" and "uncomfortable" for "unfortunate."

Josh's retelling of the story, however, was weak. Coming from a very stable home environment, he had no experience or understanding of the terms "caseworker," "foster home," or "social services," or of what a child's home life might be like under such circumstances. Josh was able to pronounce these words because each one, by itself, was not particularly difficult, and his use of graphophonics was good. However, it was the concepts underlying the words that he found difficult. When asked to retell what he had read, Josh focused only on the parts of the story with which he could identify—mainly that Gilly had gum in her hair and wasn't a very good kid. If his teacher had wanted Josh to understand these concepts better from the beginning of the story, she should have provided background information about foster homes, caseworkers, and so on. Another approach, however, would have been to let Josh continue reading, since one of the major things he might have learned by

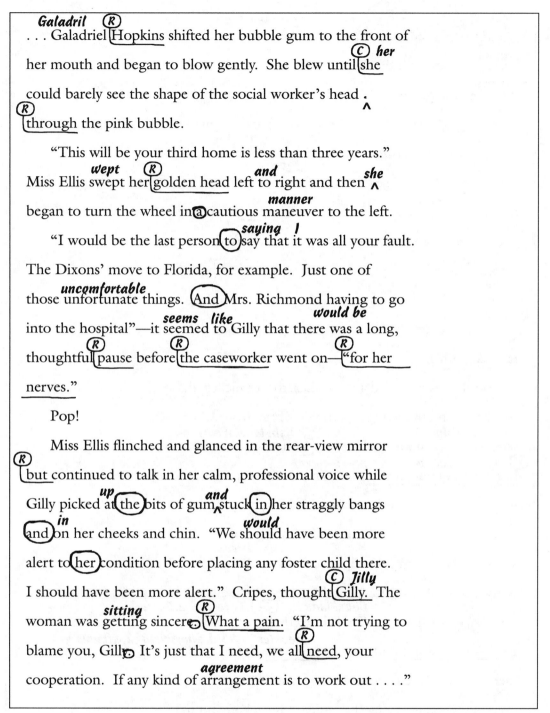

... Galadriel **Galadril** (R) Hopkins shifted her bubble gum to the front of her mouth and began to blow gently. She blew until (C) **her** she could barely see the shape of the social worker's head **.** ∧ (R) through the pink bubble.

"This will be your third home is less than three years."

wept (R) **and** **she**
Miss Ellis swept her golden head left to right and then ∧ **manner**
began to turn the wheel in (a) cautious maneuver to the left.

saying I
"I would be the last person (to) say that it was all your fault. The Dixons' move to Florida, for example. Just one of
uncomfortable
those unfortunate things. (And) Mrs. Richmond having to go
seems like **would be**
into the hospital"—it seemed to Gilly that there was a long, (R) (R) (R)
thoughtful pause before the caseworker went on—"for her nerves."

Pop!

Miss Ellis flinched and glanced in the rear-view mirror
(R)
but continued to talk in her calm, professional voice while
up **and**
Gilly picked at (the) bits of gum ∧ stuck (in) her straggly bangs
in **would**
(and) on her cheeks and chin. "We should have been more alert to (her) condition before placing any foster child there.
(C) **Jilly**
I should have been more alert." Cripes, thought Gilly. The
sitting (R)
woman was getting sincere. What a pain. "I'm not trying to
(R)
blame you, Gilly. It's just that I need, we all need, your
agreement
cooperation. If any kind of arrangement is to work out . . . ."

Figure 4.5 Josh, a fifth grader, reading *The Great Gilly Hopkins* by Katherine Paterson (1987). Collected by Sheryl Allen, All Souls Parochial School, Englewood, CO.

the time he finished the book was what these concepts mean. Then he could go back to reread to further enhance his understanding of the points he might have missed the first time.

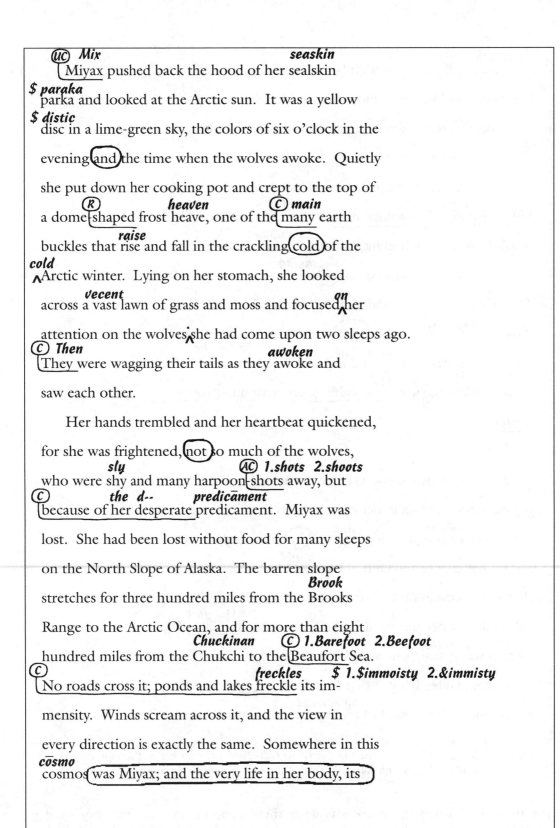

Figure 4.6   Maria, a fifth grader, reading *Julie of the Wolves* by Jean Craighead George.

Figure 4.6 Maria's reading
(continued)

The reading of Maria, a fifth grader, illustrates several other problems that are common to middle-grade students (see Figure 4.6). She is just starting to read *Julie of the Wolves*. How would you characterize the reading she is doing?

What is most interesting to note about Maria's reading is how her miscue patterns change when she goes from reading the highly descriptive first two paragraphs to the more narrative third paragraph. Maria made more meaning-changing miscues in the descriptive paragraphs: "heaven" for "heave," "vecent" for "vast," "predicá-ment" for "predicament," "immoisty" for "immensity." She was not familiar with the syntactic patterns of such language: note how she added a period after wolves in the first paragraph and then started a new sentence rather than process the upcom-ing adjective clause; she also said phrases several times as if she needed to repeat them to get the meaning now that she had rehearsed the confusing syntax. Some of the terms used to describe places in Alaska were unfamiliar to her. In the end, Maria self-corrected many of her miscues, but she made so many that one might wonder if she is going to understand any of this or if she will experience tunnel vision.

When she got to the third paragraph Maria began to read more fluently. She had fewer miscues and caught them quickly. When asked to retell what she had read, Maria omitted all detail from the descriptive passages but retold the basic narrative well. Maria reported that she did not really like to read. That seems understandable. Only by developing strategies for getting through more difficult descriptive passages will she be able to really enjoy reading. At first one might suggest that she read through the descriptive passages rather quickly (or, if they are really tough, even skip them!). If the descriptions subsequently seem particularly important to the story, she could reread them. A teacher could also encourage such second reading by designing activities such as making scenery and putting on a play, making a diorama, sketching a favorite scene, that encourage students to reread. At such times the teacher could also emphasize the beauty of the descriptive language by reading the passage to children and asking which particular images stand out for them. This would give students the opportunity to hear the syntax of more descriptive text.

■ middle-school readers

At the middle-school level many students find themselves exposed to a wider variety of types of reading, especially in relation to a new genres and content materials. Let's examine the reading of two students who are dealing with such problems. We'll begin with Janice's reading of a biographical passage about Lincoln (see Figure 4.7).

Although she is dealing with even more complex materials, Janice, like the middle-grade readers, is somewhat unfamiliar with the syntactic patterns in this passage. She omitted the period at the end of the first sentence, thinking that the sentence continued. She also read through the period at the end of the second sentence and connected the phrase "as a young man" to it. She then created a new next sentence that made sense: "He was sensitive about his lean-looking looks, but in time, he learned to laugh at himself." Thus, we see that Janice is beginning to find ways to deal with more complex sentence structure and to decide whether she needs to self-correct or not.

. . . At first glance, most people thought he was homely. Lincoln
thought so too, referring once to his "poor, lean, lank face." As a
young man, he was sensitive about his gawky looks, but in time,
he learned to laugh at himself. When a rival called him "two-faced" during a political debate, Lincoln replied: "I leave it to my audience. If I had another face, do you think I'd wear this one?"

Figure 4.7   Janice, a sixth grader, reading *Lincoln: A Photobiography* by Russell Freedman (1987). Collected in Jefferson County Public Schools, Golden, CO.

Janice made several meaning-changing miscues in the paragraph. She said "reflings" for "referrings," "several" for "sensitive," "revel" for "rival," "plital" for "political," and "detat" for "debate." In each case, it seems that she was relying on graphophonic and syntactic information and making no attempt to think about whether these miscues made sense. Although this excerpt is only part of one paragraph, Janice's miscues maintained similar patterns throughout the passage. She might do better if her teacher had previously read a book about Lincoln to the students, they had seen a film about Lincoln, or they had perhaps visited a Lincoln exhibit. They could also look at photographs of the times in the book and discuss how people looked and how pictures were taken. Then words such as "debate" and "political" and so on, which are associated with Lincoln, would not seem so foreign.

Finally, let's look at James, who is trying to read his seventh-grade science book (see Figure 4.8).

(Omits reading the heading for this section and the "you will find out" points.)

(R) Why would you want to put a telescope into space? One

(UC) $ amósphere

of the best reasons is to take it out of the atmosphere.

Think about the atmosphere outside your classroom

Hazel

right this minute. Is it clear? Foggy? Smoggy? Hazy?

The atmosphere prevents a clear view of space. It ab-

sorbs some energy from space. It blocks out some energy

. it takes   imagines

and at times makes the images from space look strange.

at (UC) $ ā-

It is like looking through a dirty window. The at-

mos´phere

mosphere is something astronomers would like to do

ob-

(UC) observ-   (UC) $ elīmat

without. Space observatories eliminate these problems. In a

space observatory the telescopes are outside the earth's

get   (R)

atmosphere. Will viewing be better? If the 5-m telescope

Palmar

on Palomar Mountain in Southern California were

(UC) $ amos´phere

above the atmosphere, it could see 50 times better.

Figure 4.8   James, a seventh grader, reading from his textbook, *Heath Earth Science* (1984).

James's problems with his science text are not unlike those of the other students we have discussed, but here we see how they are manifested in content reading. James read this passage in a very slow word-by-word manner, trying to pronounce each word. It is hard to figure out if he understood the concept of "atmosphere" or not. In some contexts he seemed to know the word, and in others he did not. This is not unusual, but a phenomenon normal to readers who are beginning to learn a word. He also miscued on "hazel" for "hazy," which indicates that his understanding of the concept of the atmosphere and different types of air is fuzzy at best. One wonders how much better James would do in reading this text if his teacher had first built up his background knowledge of topics like the atmosphere in space and telescopes.

In the next few sentences, James also miscues, reading "imagines" for "images" and "elimat" for "eliminate," and making no attempt to self-correct these miscues. It would seem that he is having a difficult time maintaining any ongoing comprehending. Indeed, James's retelling of the passage was very poor:

James: Stars. About, what was that word? A-atom-osphere?

Teacher: What else did it talk about?

James: About the stars and um, it talked about they don't know how many stars there could be. Or if there is even any.

Teacher: Did it say anything else?

James: It said there could be life on a . . . some planet. They don't know. It was just about outer space and stuff like that.

Teacher: Anything else?

James: Uh, no.

There are times when miscue analysis does not reveal information that helps to explain the nature of a student's reading problems. Sometimes the text that has been chosen for the student to read is too easy, and the student makes few, if any, meaning-changing miscues. If you can see that the student makes very few meaning-changing miscues in the opening fifty to one hundred words the student reads, then we would suggest that you stop the reader, explain that she is doing very well, but that you would like to give her something to read that is a bit more challenging. At other times, a student may read with few, if any miscues, but the reading is slow. The reader needs to develop fluency rather than new reading strategies themselves and would benefit from having many opportunities to read in order to learn to use strategies more rapidly and efficiently. A student may read perfectly aloud but have comprehended little. The problem may not lie in the student's use of the cueing systems in an integrated way but in other comprehension problems, such as the ability to activate background knowledge or to organize one's thoughts for retelling. These kinds of reading difficulties will be addressed in Chapter 5.

other factors interrupting readers' integrated use of cueing systems

There are other factors that can interrupt the reader's ability to integrate use of the cueing systems effectively. Teachers can make adjustments to these factors. We must always consider these additional areas in examining students' reading problems. These problems are not "in" the student but are ones for which we ourselves are responsible. We must make an effort to change our instruction if students are to have a chance to become better readers.

■ difficulty and predictability of the reading material

Several other factors can interrupt readers' integrated use of language cueing systems. Sometimes the material is simply too hard. Students' background knowledge is insufficient, and they cannot begin to make enough sense of the text to use syntax and semantics in an integrated way to assist in unlocking the graphophonics. You may have wondered if this was the case when Janice was reading the biographical passage about Lincoln. If we look at her reading of the next paragraph, we begin to suspect that it was (see Figure 4.9).

Janice made nine meaning-changing miscues in sixty-eight words. She needed to stop reading this text, which was simply too hard for her and didn't allow her to make interrelated use of the cueing systems in any way. Instead, it encouraged her to continue her overreliance on graphophonics, which probably contributes to her dislike of reading and perhaps school in general. Janice's needs would be better served if she was allowed to read a more simply written biographical passage that was more

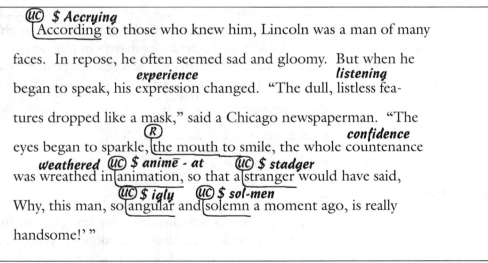

Figure 4.9   Janice, a sixth grader, reading *Lincoln: A Photobiography* by Russell Freedman (1987). Collected in Jefferson County Public Schools, Golden, CO.

directly related to her own background knowledge or if she was provided with background information.

influence of reading instruction

Sometimes the nature of the instruction that a student has received affects the ways in which she interrelates the cueing systems. The stories in some phonetically based texts are not very meaningful, nor does the language have a natural flow. As a result, students cannot effectively apply what they know to the content and sound of the language in a story. Often, even when those in trouble are given a more predictable text, they continue to make poor use of cueing systems. They need to be taught. In predictable materials, integrated cueing systems exist in the text. In phonetically based materials, other cueing systems are sacrificed in order to make only the graphophonic cues salient.

For example, let's think again about Chris, who read the *Frog and Toad* story. His teacher also asked him to read a more predictable book, *The Doorbell Rang*. At the beginning of the book, Chris used only phonetic strategies, just as he had in *Frog and Toad*.

> *A-*   *$tĕ*   *May*
> "I've made some cookies for tea," said Ma.
>   *$Vactorte*   *$trting*
> "Good," said Victoria and Sam. "We're starving."
> *$chrtery*   *$ben+where*   *May*
> "Share them between yourselves," said Ma.
>   *$bletted*
> "I made plenty."
>   *same am*
> "That's six each," said Sam and (Victoria)
>   *at*   *Gr+and+tume*   *$Vrt+e*
> "They look as good as Grandma's," said Victoria.
>   *sm+ell*   *Grand+ds*   *Same*
> "They smell as good as Grandma's," said Sam. . . .

Chris's miscue patterns gradually began to improve. As this predictable text supported his efforts to use other cueing systems besides graphophonics, what he needed most were the pictures, which he could look at while he thought about the ongoing meaning of the story. Several additional rereadings may help him gain fluency and discover new ideas in the text. Later in the story, Chris read three lines that were very similar to lines 5 through 7 with far fewer miscues:

>   *$Vaker*
> "That's three each," said Sam and Victoria.
>   *Gr+and*
> "They smell as good as your Grandma's," said Tom.
>   *$Han+ā+ăh*
> "And look as good," said Hannah.

feedback to miscues

Teachers' feedback to miscues also influences whether students learn to use the cueing systems independently. Parental feedback as children read aloud at home can also have a strong impact. The basic question is: What should a teacher or parent do when a child makes an oral reading error?

When Hoffman & Clements (1984) studied the reading groups in several different elementary classrooms, they learned that the feedback provided to students depended on the reading group in which they were placed. Only 27 percent of the miscues made by students in the high reading groups highly affected meaning; while 67 percent of the miscues made by students in the low group highly affected meaning. These results show that low readers do make more significant meaning-changing miscues. When students made miscues, those in the high group continued their reading 47 percent of the time (the miscues generally made sense) and self-corrected 24 percent of the time. In contrast, students in the low groups had no opportunity to respond to their miscues 52 percent of the time, because the teacher jumped in to offer feedback. Under such conditions these students rarely got to practice using strategies for correcting high meaning-changing miscues independently.

Teachers gave no feedback to the high groups 71 percent (47 percent plus 24 percent self-correction) of the time, told the student the word 16 percent of the time, and gave a cue that was typically semantic ("Now what are those things called?") 11 percent of the time. To the low groups teachers gave no feedback only 20 percent of the time, told the student the word 64 percent of the time, and gave a cue 16 percent of the time. The cue was typically a graphophonic cue ("Now how do you say c plus h?"). By calling attention only to graphophonics, the teachers did not encourage low-group readers to begin understanding and using information from semantics and syntax along with graphophonics in an integrated way.

Hoffman and Clements make several recommendations based on their study: Teachers should be tolerant of miscues that do not affect meaning and avoid stopping students to correct them. After a miscue, teachers should allow students to read to at least the end of the sentence, preferably to the end of a paragraph, or to begin the sentence again before providing further feedback. When providing feedback, teachers should focus their initial response on meaning rather than graphophonics. The teacher can ask the student to reread the sentence with the miscue or ask if what the student has read makes sense. Students can also be taught to make meaningful substitutions for unknown words as "place holders" that they can return to later if necessary.

After a miscue we may be able to wait longer before interrupting a student than you feel comfortable doing. This is because we want to see whether the reader will figure out a word through the context of the text by herself. Probably only at the end would we go back to discuss miscues that involved important concepts. Rather than correct the reader frequently while she is reading, after discussing the book we would be interested in what self-corrections the student made when rereading the book the next day.

These same suggestions for dealing with miscues also apply to parents (Mudre & McCormick, 1989). When parents continually interrupt their child's reading to correct miscues, much ongoing comprehending can be lost. Instead, parents need to let their child continue reading, especially if the miscues have little effect on meaning. With miscues that do change meaning, parents can stop their child at the end of the sentence, paragraph, or page and draw attention to the miscue. They can then provide her with clues: Now does (*miscue*) make sense here? What have they been talking about in the story? Does anything in the pictures give us a clue?

We know of several teachers who, when talking with parents, are beginning to discuss strategies for reading with children. Some, like Marty Frampton, whose "Teacher Reflection" appears at the end of this chapter, have parents listen to their child's reading. In discussing the reading, Frampton tries to suggest ways in which the parents might best read with their child. Another Chapter I teacher made a videotape illustrating how to select books and read with beginning readers, which parents can check out to view at home.

standardized techniques for miscue analysis

In this next section we will review five types of miscue assessment. All five are standardized in that they have written procedures for administering the instrument and coding and interpreting the data. Three of the most important considerations in deciding which form of miscue analysis to use are depth of knowledge about a student's reading, time available per student, and access to a text copy for marking as the student is reading. Although there are other forms of miscue analysis (Weaver, 1988; Kemp, 1987), we have elected to review those that we find most useful and that demonstrate the variety available.

classroom reading miscue assessment (CRMA)

The Classroom Reading Miscue Assessment (Rhodes, 1993) was developed by Consultants/Coordinators Applying Whole Language (CAWLs). The group had three goals: 1) to develop an alternative assessment that would provide information other than that from standardized tests about students as readers; 2) to develop an instrument that was not extremely time-consuming so that it could be integrated into classroom instruction on an ongoing basis; and 3) to develop an instrument that would encourage teachers to learn more about new views of the reading process and instructional strategies.

The CRMA measures a student's ability to read a complete text passage in relation to four questions:

- What percent of the sentences read by the child make sense?

- In what ways is the child striving for meaning?

Reader's name __RICHARD__   Date _____

Grade level __GR 4 - Chapter 1__ Teacher _____

Selection read __WOLF__ _____

Classroom Reading Miscue Assessment

I. What percent of the sentences read make sense?

	Sentence by sentence tally	Total
Number of semantically acceptable sentences	𝆏𝆏 𝆏𝆏 𝆏𝆏 𝆏𝆏 𝆏𝆏 𝆏𝆏 𝆏𝆏 𝆏𝆏 𝆏𝆏 𝆏𝆏 I	51
Number of semantically unacceptable sentences	𝆏𝆏 III	8

% Comprehending score:

$$\frac{\text{Number of semantically acceptable sentences}}{\text{Total number of sentences read}} \times 100 = \underline{86}\ \%$$

	Seldom	Sometimes	Often	Usually	Always
II. In what ways is the reader constructing meaning?					
A. Recognizes when miscues have disrupted meaning	**①**	2	3	4	5
B. Logically substitutes	**①**	2	3	4	5
C. Self-corrects errors that disrupt meaning	**①**	2	3	4	5
D. Uses picture and/or other visual clues	1	2	3	**④**	5
In what ways is the reader disrupting meaning?					
A. Substitutes words that don't make sense	1	**②**	3	4	5
B. Makes omissions that disrupt meaning	**①**	2	3	4	5
C. Relies too heavily on graphophonic cues	1	**②**	3	4	5

	No		Partial		Yes
III. If narrative text is used:					
A. Character recall	1	2	3	4	**⑤**
B. Character development	1	2	3	4	**⑤**
C. Setting	1	2	3	4	**⑤**
D. Relationship of events	1	2	3	4	**⑤**
E. Plot	1	2	3	4	**⑤**
F. Theme	1	2	3	**④**	5
G. Overall retelling	1	2	3	4	**⑤**
If expository text is used:	No		Partial		Yes
A. Major concepts	1	2	3	4	5
B. Generalizations	1	2	3	4	5
C. Specific information	1	2	3	4	5
D. Logical structuring	1	2	3	4	5
E. Overall retelling	1	2	3	4	5

Figure 4.10   Classroom Reading Miscue Assessment (CRMA) scoring sheet

- In what ways is the child arriving at nonsense?

- How well is the child able to retell what has been read?

As a student reads each sentence of a text, the teacher marks whether the sentence makes sense as the student finally left it. The teacher makes judgments, based on performance, about the student's strategies for constructing meaning on eight Lickert scale items. After the child retells what she has read, the teacher again marks Lickert scale items that judge the organization and completeness of the retelling. The instrument can be used with either narrative or expository text (see Figure 4.10). We will discuss specific sections of the CRMA in greater detail in the following sections.

selecting the text and preparing a retelling guide

In selecting a passage for a student to read during the CRMA, a teacher needs to choose a whole story or a selection that has a sense of completeness, such as a chapter or a section of a content book. The text should be one that the student has not previously read, and it should not be extremely brief or extremely long; probably three- to five-hundred words is reasonable. We would also recommend trying to select passages that relate to students' background, use natural language patterns, have well-formed narrative or expository structure, and contain pictures or other figures, if that is representative of what the student usually reads.

The text should be difficult enough that the student will make some miscues to allow you to observe the strategies the student uses to figure out unknown words. A reasonable guide is between one and nine semantically unacceptable miscues in the first one hundred words read. If the student makes no meaning-changing miscues in the first fifty to one hundred words, we would recommend telling the reader that she is doing a great job and that you would like to see how she does reading something a bit more difficult. If the student makes nine or more semantically unacceptable miscues in the first one hundred words, we would recommend stopping the student and telling her that you would like to switch to a different passage. Judgments need to be made quickly so that little administration time is lost finding a text at an appropriate level. If a teacher is familiar with the approximate level of text the student is reading from classroom instruction, selecting appropriate material should not prove difficult.

listening to a student read

In beginning a CRMA, you need to explain to the student that you would like her to read the passage aloud and after she finishes you are then going to ask her to retell all that she remembers about the passage. Tell the student that if she comes to a word she does not know, do what she would normally do if reading alone. Then if the student asks for assistance during the reading, gently remind the student, "Remember, do what you would do if you were by yourself." Or, "Remember, we are pretending that I'm not here."

Do not help the student with the reading in any way unless absolutely necessary to keep the reader involved in the task. If a reader is about to give up and you have already tried the phrases above, suggest that she skip the word or phrase and go on.

You need to discover the full repertoire of strategies the reader knows and uses when alone—and you won't if you offer help too readily.

▨ tallying ongoing comprehending

As a student is reading, the teacher needs to mark whether each sentence is semantically acceptable or unacceptable as the student finally read it. Marks can be made for each sentence in the boxes provided on the form (see Figure 4.10). Let's consider Richard, a fourth grader in a Chapter I program, who made the following miscues as he began to read the story *Wolf* by Alfred Payson Terhune.

> Wolf was not a friendly dog. He loved his master and
> *miss trees*
> mistress very much.

Richard had read the first sentence correctly, and a mark was placed in the semantically acceptable column. Richard miscued "miss trees" for "mistress" in the second sentence and did not go back to make any corrections even though it didn't make sense. As he finally left the sentence, it was semantically unacceptable, and a mark was placed in that column. Richard continued:

> But he didn't like other people.
> *doesn't*
> Wolf didn't seem to like other
> *How $ēver*
> dogs either. He hardly ever played with the other
> *Sunbank*
> collies that lived with him at Sunnybank Farm.

Richard reads sentence 3 correctly, so a mark is again placed in the semantically acceptable column. In the fourth sentence, Richard says "doesn't" for "didn't." Since this miscue does not change the meaning of the sentence and it is still semantically acceptable, a mark is again placed in that column. In the fifth sentence Richard makes three miscues: "how" for "he," "ēver" for "ever," and "Sunbank" for "Sunnybank." The first two miscues here change the meaning of the sentence and Richard did not correct them. While "Sunbank" is not exactly the same as "Sunnybank," since it is a proper name it would not be held against the reader. Thus, as Richard finally left the sentence, two of his miscues were not semantically acceptable, which made the whole sentence semantically unacceptable, and that column was marked. Richard's teacher continued to mark each sentence of his reading in this manner.

When Richard got to the end of the story, fifty-one of the sentences he had read were in the semantically acceptable box and eight were semantically unacceptable. This resulted in a comprehending score of 86 percent (meaning 86 percent of the sentences Richard read made sense). As Richard read further in the story, he began to make fewer miscues than he had in the opening paragraphs. He understood what was happening in the story better and his interest was high.

Marking sentences for semantic acceptability becomes more complex when students alter the sentence structures in the text by adding periods or reading through punctuation. In these instances, we have found it best to determine the semantic acceptability of each sentence the student breaks the reading into rather than worry too much about exact matches with the number of sentences in the passage. This decision is based on the fact that, in choosing to use the CRMA, you are *not* audio-taping and need to make quick judgments. This is a case of sacrificing perfect accuracy to save time.

■ making judgments about sense-making strategies

The next part of the CRMA form asks the teacher to make judgments about the sense-making strategies the student employed while reading the text. Thus, as the student is reading, in addition to making marks for semantic acceptability, you need to listen carefully for strategies the reader is or is not using to make integrated use of the cueing systems. You will want to observe whether a student recognizes when she has made a meaning-changing miscue. Often you can tell by the student's voice inflection, body language, or quizzical look. The student can recognize that she has made a miscue and that the text does not make sense but not have a repertoire of strategies for fixing it. Thus, you will need to observe whether the student can self-correct errors that disrupt meaning. Also, you need to observe whether she makes logical substitutions for unknown words or phrases and uses pictures or other visual clues to help construct meaning.

The next three questions act as a countercheck to the above questions. In observing strategies that disrupt meaning, a teacher needs to notice whether a student substitutes words that don't make sense or makes omissions that disrupt meaning. Finally, a teacher needs to judge whether the reader seems to rely too heavily on graphophonic cues.

After the student has finished reading but before proceeding to the retelling, mark the seven questions about strategies the reader is using. For each question, mark the Lickert scale. These are your first tentative judgments; you may want to think more about your markings after the session.

In Figure 4.10 you will notice that under "In what ways is the reader constructing meaning?" Richard's teacher has noted his ability to recognize when miscues have disrupted meaning, to make logical substitutions, and to self-correct miscues all as 1. These are qualities that are seldom found in Richard's reading. In contrast, she gave him a 4 rating for his use of picture and other visual clues. She was particularly impressed by the fact that Richard read the blurb about the author that appeared at the end of the story without being prompted.

For the three questions under "In what ways is the reader disrupting meaning?" this teacher gave Richard a 2 for substituting words that don't make sense and for relying too heavily on graphic cues. She gave him a 1 for making omissions that disrupt meaning because there was no evidence that he ever omitted; instead, he seemed to rely on graphophonics.

■ gathering and marking the retelling

After the student has finished reading and you have make judgments about her reading strategies, you need to ask the student to retell the passage. We recommend beginning by asking the student to tell you everything she remembers from the text. When the student finishes, ask her to think for a minute about whether there is anything more to add. You might say, "This was such a long story that I'm going to give you a minute to think of any other things you remember." Once you have completed this unaided retelling, you can ask more specific questions to get at items the student has left out.

You need to formulate the questions you ask carefully. They should be open-ended to elicit more than yes-no responses and to avoid introducing the student to information she has not previously mentioned. You must try to be sure to garner information in all the areas you will be asked to rate. Some good probes to use with narrative text are:

Character Recall:	Who else was in the story?
Character Development:	What else can you tell me about _____?
Setting:	Where did _____ happen? When did _____ happen? Tell me more about _____ place.
Events:	What else happened in the story? How did _____ happen?
Event Sequence:	What happened before _____? What happened after _____?
Plot:	What was _____'s main problem?
Theme:	What did you think (*the major character*) learned in the story? What do you think the author might have been trying to tell us in this story?

Good probes to use with expository text are:

Major Concept(s):	What was the main thing the author wanted you to learn?
Generalizations:	What other important information about _____ did the author tell you?
Specific Information:	Is there any other information you remember the author told about? What specific facts do you remember?
Logical Structuring:	How did the author go about presenting the information? (comparison, examples, steps in a process, etc.)

Once the student has completed her retelling, the teacher again makes judgments about areas of text comprehension using a Lickert scale. For narrative text the following areas are considered: character recall, character development, setting, events, plot, theme, and overall retelling. For expository text other criteria are rated: major concepts, generalizations, specific information, logical structuring, and overall

---

retelling. In the case of Richard, his actual retelling of *Wolf* was excellent. As Figure 4.10 shows, his teacher gave him 55 except for a slightly lower rating in his understanding of the theme of the story.

◼ what teachers learn

The CRMA provides teachers with much useful information for planning instruction. By listening to students read, teachers can learn the approximate level of difficulty of the material each student handles. The semantically acceptable score tells them how frequently the sentences sound like meaningful language. Teachers can observe what strategies students are using to construct meaning and how successful they are. They can also determine when meaning breaks down and what strategies students use ineffectively or not at all. Information on these areas is essential if Reading Workshop is to benefit all students. It helps teachers nudge children into books of appropriate difficulty and helps students learn new strategies so they can be more effective and independent readers.

In Richard's case, his comprehending score of 86 percent was quite good, although he read very slowly and did not always use effective reading strategies. Our instructional plans for Richard would include a great deal of emphasis on reading relatively easy material to gain fluency. We would work carefully with him to select books and suggest to his parents that time be set aside for Richard to read each evening. Participating in Readers' Theatre, doing buddy-reading, and reading to younger children would also increase his fluency. We would also work with Richard on learning to self-correct miscues that change meaning and on making meaningful substitutions. Learning to use these strategies would help to ensure that Richard's ongoing comprehending is good.

The retelling section of the instrument allows teachers to analyze students' comprehension strengths and weaknesses. For example, a student may have good recall of characters, their development, and the setting but not be able to retell the events in a logical sequence or identify the theme of the story. Information gained from either part of the instrument helps a teacher plan mini-lessons as part of Reading Workshop and points out areas to emphasize in literature circles. Since Richard's retelling was so complete, there is little to work on in his retelling of narrative texts except perhaps being more able and confident in talking about the themes of stories he is reading. Gaining more experience with theme fits in well with an emphasis on doing more reading in order to improve fluency. Since Richard, who has demonstrated his ability to comprehend narrative text, is in fourth grade, where content reading begins in greater earnest, we would also recommend that his teacher see how well he is able to read and comprehend his content textbooks.

Used periodically throughout the year, the CRMA can document students' development. In addition, what teachers learn from the CRMA about listening to students read can be very useful even without the form. They may simply listen and take anecdotal notes for these areas as students read to them during reading conferences.

▊ managing data collection

We believe it is worth finding the time necessary to complete a CRMA on each student. The information teachers gain about readers will help immensely in planning further instruction that meets individual student needs. One way to accomplish this goal is to assess two children per day for the first two to three weeks of school. You can listen to these two pupils read at various points in the day when others are doing individual seatwork. If you have an aide or parent volunteers, you can collect data while they supervise the rest of the class in another activity. If you have a student teacher or other special teachers who work with children from your room, you can organize so that both of you trade off listening to children read. If you are using Reading Workshop, you could listen to two children read during workshop time each day during the first few weeks.

If finding time during instruction is difficult for you, try scheduling one child before and one after school for the first few weeks. You might also be able to assess one child at lunch break and another at recess. Perhaps you could also make arrangements with the music, PE, or other teachers to assess several children during these periods over the first few weeks.

Collecting CRMA data again in January can document student growth and help you plan for the second semester. A final collection in May would allow teachers, children, and parents to look at growth across the whole school year. Or perhaps you would choose to give the full instrument only at the beginning of the year and use anecdotal notes and students' self-assessments to document development during the rest of the year. Or you could use the instrument to assess only those students whose progress is a subject of concern.

The CRMA may not provide many insights into the reading of very good readers starting at approximately fifth grade. When asked to read orally, these children tend to read any materials well. Of more value and perhaps also a more efficient use of time is to have them read materials silently and do written or oral retellings of what they have read or answer a few good comprehension questions in writing. (We'll say more about this in Chapter 5.) Students who do poorly on the silent reading comprehension checks could be assessed further using the CRMA.

▊ ▊

reading miscue inventory (RMI)

The *Reading Miscue Inventory* (RMI) (also see Rhodes, 1993) is a more in-depth method for examining a student's oral reading, ongoing comprehending, and subsequent comprehension. The *Reading Miscue Inventory* was originally published by Yetta Goodman and Carolyn Burke in 1972. The RMI is based on Kenneth Goodman's model of reading and the taxonomy he developed to classify types of miscues. It was revised in 1987 by Y. Goodman, Watson, and Burke, and it is this version that we will discuss here.

It is important to clarify from the outset why a teacher might choose to do an RMI instead of, or in addition to, the CRMA. The CRMA is designed to be used in a short period of time with all the children in a class or program. In order to keep the administration and scoring time short, it relies heavily on instant teacher judgment. In contrast, procedures in the RMI allow for more reflective teacher judgment, ensure more detailed accounting, and allow for a more in-depth analysis of a student's oral reading. When doing this more formal type of miscue assessment, the teacher marks the student's miscues on a copy of the text. The teacher also makes coding decisions about the nature of each miscue on separate forms that accompany the instrument. The current RMI has several alternative procedures for coding. Which procedure to use depends on the depth of information a teacher wants to know and the time available for coding.

In a regular classroom, the RMI is probably best used when in-depth analysis is needed on a small subset of readers who are experiencing reading difficulties. Using the RMI gives a much deeper picture of a child's reading strengths and weaknesses than the CRMA. It is also very useful to see if the results corroborate the CRMA or if the child does much better or worse. Often it is insightful to compare a child's reading of a narrative and a content text passage since children with reading problems will frequently do better with one type of text than the other. Most commonly, some children will be able to read and retell narrative text well but will not have developed strategies for reading content materials. The RMI is also useful for Chapter I or other special teachers who need to gather more in-depth information about a student's reading problems if they are to be alleviated. Used on a pre/post basis in such programs, the RMI can yield detailed information on improvements in students' reading strategies.

Y. Goodman, Watson, and Burke recommend that children read text one grade above their current reading level so that they generate some miscues. Texts chosen for the RMI can be narrative or expository and may be longer than those chosen for the CRMA. It is important that children read texts that have a sense of completeness, preferably all of a real children's book, a nonfiction article, or a chapter from a novel. In general, since the RMI is given to select numbers of students, the amount of time the reading takes is not quite the problem it is with the CRMA.

Data collection procedures for the RMI are quite similar to those for the CRMA. In terms of conducting the actual reading session, the only difference is that the student's reading is audiotaped. In the RMI all deviations from the print are marked, not just whether each sentence is semantically acceptable as the reader finally left it. Taping allows the teacher to double-check the markings and to mark any further miscues she was not able to catch while the student was reading.

In our experience, Procedure II of the RMI is most useful to classroom teachers. After listening to the child read and marking the text, the teacher is ready to begin coding miscues. It is important to determine what counts as a miscue to be coded. Figure 4.11 reviews the rules used in the RMI, Miscue Analysis Profile, and most informal reading inventories for counting miscues.

1. Insertions, omissions, substitutions, and reversals are coded as miscues regardless of whether they are subsequently corrected.

2. When a reader makes repeated attempts on a word, the first complete word or nonword substitution is coded as the miscue.

3. Partial substitutions which are *not* corrected are treated as omissions.

4. The following are *not* coded as miscues:

   a. Identical word repetitions and partial word repetitions.
   b. Partial repetitions that are corrected.
   c. Additional miscues that are made during a repetition.
   d. Proper nouns.
   e. Omission of whole lines of text.
   f. Misarticulations.
   g. Sound variations that involve dialect.
   h. Syllabication divisions within words.
   i. Pauses.

5. If a dialect miscue results in a change that is not grammatically acceptable (i.e., changes a plural noun to a singular noun or the tense of a verb), then it is counted as a miscue.

6. Repeated attempts made on an item across text occurrences are handled in one of the following ways:

   a. Each repeated omission and each repeated insertion is coded.
   b. Each repeated substitution of a function word (articles, prepositions, phrase and clause markers) is coded.
   c. Repeated identical substitutions of nouns, verbs, adjectives, or adverbs are coded separately each time the grammatical function of the word in the text changes.

7. When an initial miscue causes or is integrally related to another miscue, all is coded as a complex miscue on one line.

Figure 4.11   What counts as a miscue?

Now ready to use Procedure II of the RMI, the teacher is able to analyze miscue patterns in three significant areas: language sense, graphic and sound similarity of the word substitutions (miscues) in context, and retelling. In language sense, the teacher looks at each sentence the student reads and decides whether the sentence as finally read (with all self-corrections) is syntactically acceptable, and then semantically acceptable, and how much meaning change has occurred. Once these decisions have been made, patterns of strength, partial strength, and weakness can be determined. For example, a sentence that is both syntactically and semantically acceptable and results in no meaning change is labeled a strength. Each sentence in the entire selection is marked in this way.

Next, word substitutions are marked as highly, somewhat, or not graphically similar and similar in sound. Total miscues and total number of words read can be counted, and the number of miscues per one hundred words calculated. Repeated miscues across the text can be noted and observations made about their quality.

The retelling can be scored in several alternative ways. A teacher can simply decide to take anecdotal notes or to give the student's retelling a holistic score. A retelling guide can also be prepared and points assigned. In this way, a quantitative retelling score can be derived.

Although it is useful, Procedure II of the RMI does have some problems. Substitution miscues are monitored closely, but detailed notes about other types of miscues—especially omissions and insertions—are not noted separately. In addition, there is no procedure for counting how many miscues the reader self-corrected without setting up another column of the teacher's own making.

Procedure I of the RMI is more detailed than Procedure II and provides some solutions to the problems we have raised. Procedure I uses the most detailed format for examining reader miscues and this is the format recommended for research purposes. Each miscue throughout the entire reading is recorded and then analyzed on the basis of six questions. These questions ask about the syntactic acceptability of each miscue, the semantic acceptability of each miscue, the degree of meaning change, whether the miscue was self-corrected, the graphic similarity of the miscue, and sound similarity. From the answers to the six questions, a teacher can calculate a student's attempts at meaning construction and creating grammatical relationships for each miscue. From this information the teacher can calculate the percentages across the entire reading.

Although this format allows a teacher to keep track of self-corrections, it sacrifices the notion of noting the overall semantic acceptability of each sentence in favor of marking each miscue. It is obvious that this procedure can take much longer than marking each sentence and recording only substitution miscues, as in Procedure II. A computerized version of Procedure I is now available (Woodley, 1990). While all data must be entered, the program is efficient and saves some teacher time by performing all math calculations automatically and printing reader profiles.

miscue analysis profile (MAPro)

The *Miscue Analysis Profile* (MAPro) was developed by Altwerger and Resta (in press) as a somewhat simpler version of miscue analysis than Procedure I of the RMI that provides more information than Procedure II. Like the RMI, it is available in computer form. In addition to determining a reader's strengths and weaknesses, this version of miscue analysis suggests strategy lessons that can be used to address a reader's specific problems. Some experts have objected to this feature, arguing that it is too prescriptive and takes away teachers' decision-making power. We do not believe this was Altwerger and Resta's intent. Instead, the program is meant to generate strategy suggestions. The teacher decides which specific suggestions to implement (if any) and how to utilize the strategy lessons in authentic literacy activities. The addition of the strategies also facilitates staff development for teachers learning whole language methods.

Some insight into the history behind development of the MAPro may be helpful. At the time MAPro was developed, Resta was the North Area Chapter I Coordinator for the Albuquerque Public Schools and Altwerger was a faculty member at the University of New Mexico, whom Resta had recruited to facilitate staff development. As teachers began to learn whole language views of the reading process and reading instruction, it became apparent to Altwerger and Resta that new ways of measuring student growth beyond standardized tests would be valuable. At that time, the new edition of the RMI was just being written, and only the old manual using Procedure I was available. Altwerger and Resta wanted to use a format simpler than Procedure I of the RMI that would be more practical for teacher use, that could be computerized, and that could guide staff development efforts. They decided to develop their own form and involve teachers in the effort.

Because teachers were involved, the development of MAPro became a vehicle for helping teachers learn more information about whole language. Teachers also felt a stronger investment in using the instrument because it was meeting their own needs to assess students' strengths and weaknesses, document growth, and suggest potential strategy lessons. The original notebook of strategy lessons that accompanied MAPro was developed by the teachers in the program. Using MAPro, teachers in the North Area Chapter I program have subsequently been able to document students' reading growth. (We used MAPro with the Denver Public Schools Chapter I Program and were also able to demonstrate reading growth.)

Data collection procedures for MAPro are similar to those for the RMI. Altwerger and Resta suggest, however, that if MAPros are to be given to large numbers of students, it may be helpful for teachers to identify stories at different levels and to develop typed versions of the stories on which miscues can be marked and retellings guided. Doing such work individually is a time-consuming task; inter-rater reliability is better achieved when teachers work with commonly chosen texts.

Once the data are collected and the miscues have been marked, MAPro codes miscues in five different areas: miscue type, graphophonic similarity, syntactic acceptability, semantic acceptability, and self-correction. The analysis also reveals whether each sentence as finally left makes sense and then divides the retelling into seven areas that are scored using a Lickert scale.

We believe the MAPro has some potential advantages over both Procedure I and Procedure II of the RMI. There are important differences in the number of miscues that need to be coded in MAPro as compared to Procedures I and II of the RMI. With MAPro you need to code a representative sample from consistently running text of twenty-five miscues. With Procedure I of the RMI, you code all miscues across the entire reading passage, and with Procedure II only all substitution miscues across the entire reading passage. Using MAPro, a teacher can also document the specific types of miscues a student makes: complex miscues, reversals, omissions, and insertions. This information can be gained from Procedure I of the RMI, but it does not emphasize coding for this information. In Procedure II, only substitution miscues are noted, not other types a reader might make.

In the MAPro—somewhat like Procedure I of the RMI but different from Procedure II—the teacher is asked to mark whether each miscue is syntactically or semantically acceptable with the whole sentence in which it appears, with the prior context only, with the following context only, or with no part of the context. Engaging in this procedure encourages teachers to think in more depth about the prediction strategies students are or are not using.

Both MAPro and Procedure I of the RMI provide a self-correction column so that a teacher can monitor a student's reading for self-corrections. This feature is not available in Procedure II of the RMI. Both Procedure II of the RMI and MAPro allow tabulation of the number of semantically acceptable sentences that a student read. This is not a feature of Procedure I of the RMI. MAPro scores retellings differently from either Procedure I or Procedure II of the RMI, using the same measurement techniques as used in analytic scoring of students' writing. The retelling is broken down into several areas, depending on whether the material read was fiction or nonfiction, and a five-point Lickert scale is marked.

miscue analysis and informal reading inventories (IRIs)

Over the past ten years, many informal reading inventories (IRIs) have been revised to incorporate the concept of miscue analysis. One must review each inventory carefully, however, to determine whether concepts related to miscue analysis are being used accurately. Sometimes, even though the word "miscue" is used instead of "error," a teacher scores each deviation from text as wrong. In contrast, the theory underlying miscue analysis emphasizes that not all deviations from the text are of equal value, and they must be treated with a more sophisticated analysis system. In the most current informal reading inventories, this problem seems to be diminishing.

IRIs that include optional use of miscue analysis provide teachers with brief, graded, and ready-made passages. Thus, administration is less time-consuming. However, using these informal inventories has its limitations. First, the passages lack pictures. As a result, a teacher gets no sense of how a reader uses pictures to enhance comprehension. Second, while the texts are shorter, they are not necessarily better. One has to be careful to consider whether the short pieces are complete. When the passages are quite short, a teacher doesn't have the opportunity to see if the student's reading improves as she reads further. Third, when teachers choose reading passages, they will relate more closely to the curriculum and to the background experience of the students than the passages of commercialized tests. Finally, because the passages are graded, the inventories suggest that teachers can estimate the "level" of a reader more easily than is truly possible.

Thus, in our view, informal reading inventories involve trade-offs. If time for administration and staff development are quite limited, IRIs may be the only choice. In such cases, we recommend *The Basic Reading Inventory* (Johns, 1989) and *The Qualitative Reading Inventory* (Leslie & Caldwell, 1990) because of the way they treat miscue assessment.

running records

Last, we consider running records and standardized assessment procedures developed by Marie Clay. Their advantage lies in how they can be used to record systematic notes about students' reading during normal classroom activities. Thus, running records create a good bridge between this section and the next, which concerns ways to make observations about students' miscues as part of classroom instruction.

Clay developed running records to help teachers evaluate the difficulty of text, group children, and monitor the place and progress of children. Running records are similar to miscue analysis, but as Clay (1985) states: "[Running records are] more adapted to the teacher's needs in day to day activities of the classroom, particularly for those who teach young children" (p.17).

Running records do not require that the teacher have a separate copy of the text to mark, as do most miscue analysis procedures. Instead, the teacher keeps all of her marks on a separate piece of paper; any blank paper will do. To take the running record, the teacher makes a check on her sheet for each word a child says correctly; her checks match the number of words from the line of print in the book the child is reading. Markings quite similar to miscue analysis are used when children make deviations from the print. For example:

> When a child makes a miscue, write down the word in the text first, with the incorrect word the child said above. List each further attempt to the right of the original miscue with a slash in between.
>
> When a child makes a self-correction, the miscue is indicated as above, and then "SC" is written to indicate that a self-correction has been made.
>
> If a child leaves out a word, the word is written, and a dash written above. If a word is inserted, a dash is indicated for the text, and the word inserted written above.

There are other similar markings, including codes for teachers' offerings of limited help. Considering that running records were developed for beginning readers who may need limited teacher input to continue, this seems reasonable. Full explanations of running record procedures can be found in Clay (1985) and Kemp (1987).

We have found that many teachers of beginning readers prefer running records as a way to assess students' miscue patterns. One advantage of running records is that teachers do not need to have a copy of the text available, yet they have a system for recording miscues they can reflect on later. The texts read by beginning readers tend to be neither long nor complex. Clay (1985) reports achieving reliability coefficients for running records of first graders from teachers who have received training of .98 for correctly marking and scoring reading errors and .68 for scoring self-corrections.

Running records are more difficult to implement with older students who can read longer, more complex text quicker. When there are ten to fifteen words in a line of print, it becomes difficult (and tiresome) to accurately make a check for each word read correctly. Without a copy of the material to mark, it also requires great speed to make a check and then stop to record both text words and miscues when they occur. It is especially difficult if one thinks of intermediate-grade children reading five hundred to eight hundred-word texts. Thus, for teachers working with older students, running records may be less valuable. In such cases, teachers need to move to other procedures during instruction, such as taking anecdotal notes, making a mark for each semantically acceptable sentence, developing checklists that capture judgments about miscue quality, or using the CRMA. Using these procedures, the teacher can listen carefully and, instead of recording exact data, make judgments on the spot.

assessing the reading process within literacy events

All of these standardized methods of miscue analysis are excellent ways to assess a reader's use of the language cueing systems and ongoing comprehending, but they often tend to require interruptions in normal classroom instruction. In contrast, the everyday literacy events discussed in the following sections provide opportunities for teachers to make observations of children's use of language cueing systems and strategies and to record them. When conducting assessment during these activities, teachers may choose to assess the performance of one child or aspects of reading behavior across a whole group. We also discuss ways in which students can begin to self-assess their own integrated use of the cueing systems and ongoing comprehending.

cloze procedures

Cloze is an instructional technique often used to assess reading. Traditionally, cloze has been used as a standardized assessment procedure to determine whether selected material is within a student's reading ability (Pikulski & Tobin, 1982).

When it is used for this purpose, there are strict guidelines for leaving out every fifth word, which a student fills in with her best guess of the word the author actually used. In scoring, only exact replacements are accepted as correct; even synonyms that maintain the meaning are incorrect. The inference is that if a reader can fill in 40 to 60 percent of the blanks with the same word as the author, the text is within the reader's instructional reading level. Leaving out every fifth word, however, makes cloze very frustrating for many students. And teachers do not gain particularly good insights into children's actual strategies for using the cueing systems when words are left out so frequently and synonyms are not accepted.

In our view, the best use of cloze is as a classroom assessment/instructional procedure in which the teacher decides what words to leave out on her own. The teacher chooses to omit words that students can fill in if they are following semantic and syntactic cues within the text. Children can begin to work with cloze in this way even before they can competently read text. The teacher can read along in a book, stop, and ask the children to fill in the word that might follow next. This is called oral cloze and helps children learn to predict what may come next based on the semantics and the syntax of the on-going passage. Once children begin reading, graphophonic cues can be given as well by providing the first letter of the next word.

When filling in cloze activities, some children at first choose words that fit only the preceding context; they must be taught to consider the context following the word as well. Sometimes children at first fill in words that don't make sense. Then it is useful for a teacher to read back the text to see if the student can hear the parts that don't make sense and indicate them to the teacher. Sometimes a teacher may suspect that a student is having problems with a particular part of speech, such as prepositions or pronouns. This hypothesis can be checked out by selecting cloze blanks that relate to this part of speech. Finally, a teacher can create cloze blanks that relate to habitual associations a student makes. For example, this could involve "for" and "from." From listening to a child read a teacher might suspect that the child is having trouble with these words: one word is habitually associated with the other in an incorrect way. Use of cloze lets a teacher help a child differentiate between the associated words by thinking first about meaning within context.

Kemp (1987) presents some interesting new ways to use cloze as an assessment procedure. In preparing cloze passages, he suggests simply that blanks be balanced (not necessarily every X word) and that most parts of speech be sampled. He also suggests that cloze blanks can be rated using either exact replacements or what he calls "not exact replacements." He proposes that if "not exact replacements" are used, then a criterion of 70 percent may indicate a marginal level of comprehending; a 70–80 percent score, an instructional level; and more than 85 percent, an independent level.

Kemp gives several examples of good ways to format assessments that use cloze. He makes clear, however, that, like us, he is more in favor of cloze procedures than of cloze testing. He states:

The strongest argument in favor of cloze procedures (as distinct from testing) of under-achieving readers is that they may provide an excellent vehicle for discussions about language and words, and bring teacher and child together for a time when meanings, word chunks, phrases, alternative word choices, spelling, scanning, self-monitoring, prediction, self-correction and syntactic patterning can all be discussed, tested and enjoyed as the issues arise and without threat. (p. 163)

■ ■

reading conferences

In Writing Workshop a teacher can learn a great deal about students' composing processes by simply watching as they write. With reading this is not so easy. Clues to the process are not so overt. While you can tell some things about readers by watching them, to analyze progress and guide instruction a teacher often needs to ask a student to read aloud and discuss what she is reading. Both activities take place during reading conferences. Here we will concentrate on reading conferences that focus on assessment and the use of the cueing systems, reading strategies, and ongoing comprehending, and in Chapter 5 on conferences that focus on comprehension. Frequently, however, in actual classroom contexts emphasis on both may occur in a single conference.

Engaging in reading conferences with students means that you will have less time to read in class yourself and fewer opportunities to model your own love of reading. However, we would recommend doing some conferences with children while reading—especially with poor readers. Often it is only by listening to them read that you can get near the roots of their reading problems, suggest new methods to try out, and provide opportunities for practice with expert feedback.

Usually, a conference with a child over her reading will last ten minutes or less. As in a writing conference, a teacher needs to think of the reading conference as beginning even before she speaks to the student. Even before you approach the student, it is wise to stop just to observe her reading for a minute to two. How actively engaged does the student seem to be with the book? Is she deep in concentration? Does she seem amused by something she is reading? Is she looking carefully at the pictures?

You may also observe behaviors that may signal other problems. Do some students move their lips as they are reading? Under normal circumstances, proficient readers do not; otherwise, they would never learn to read more quickly than they can say words aloud. Some children use their fingers to point to individual words. Again, this encourages word-by-word rather than fluent reading and needs to be discouraged. Other children cover the pictures with their hands and never seem to look at them as clues to meaning.

After you pause to observe a student, approach her and ask open-ended questions that encourage the student to reflect:

- How's it going?

- How may I help you?

- Have you read any things you really found interesting, exciting, etc. today?

- What parts are you having trouble understanding?

- Show me a part that didn't make sense to you.

- What strategies have you tried?

As you begin to talk with the student, note the date of the conference, the name of the book, and the page number the student is on. By noting page numbers, especially when students are reading chapter books, you can see who is going slowly and needs to be encouraged to spend more time reading, increase her fluency, and so on.

If you decide to listen to the student read aloud, we'd recommend just asking her to continue from where she is. We'd say, "I just want to listen in." Try not to interrupt or correct the reader. If the student asks for assistance, use the situation as an opportunity to teach or reinforce a strategy rather than tell the student the word. Try to listen to a child read for three to five minutes.

While the child is reading, you may want to take anecdotal notes about the child's miscue patterns. You could also make marks to keep track of the number of semantically acceptable and semantically unacceptable sentences the child reads. When the child finishes or you stop her, you can ask the student to go back to selected sentences that did not make sense as she read them and discuss them further. Some questions you might use:

- Why did you leave out this word?

- You said (reader's word, nonword, or phrase) here.

- What do you think that means?

- Have you ever heard this (word, phrase, saying) before? What do you think it means?

- I noticed that you first said this word as _____ and then changed it to _____ later as you read. How did you figure out what the word was?

After the child finishes reading aloud, you may want to ask questions to gauge whether the student has comprehended what she has just read.

At the end of a conference, we recommend making anecdotal records of any reading strategies you talked about with the student. You may also want to write notes about what further instruction to provide. Records from conferences about the language cueing systems and reading strategies can be kept in several ways. You can keep anecdotal notes on a clipboard and place these in each child's folder or section of your assessment notebook. You could also use a checklist. Another alternative would be to make notes on a chart that is kept in a student's folder. A useful form that is a cross between a checklist and anecdotal records was developed by Kay Williams, a teacher for the Sheridan Public Schools in Colorado (see Figure 4.12).

```
┌────────────────────────────────────────────────────────────────────────────┐
│  Reading Profile for: _____        │
│                                                                              │
│  Date: _____    Text: _____        │
│                                                                              │
│                                                                              │
│  Comments: (retelling, comprehension, etc.)    Oral Reading:                 │
│                                                                              │
│                                                 ____ Confident               │
│                                                                              │
│                                                 ____ Slow                    │
│                                                                              │
│                                                 Reading Level:               │
│                                                                              │
│                                                 ____ Appropriate             │
│                                                                              │
│                                                 ____ Too easy                │
│                                                                              │
│                                                 ____ Too difficult           │
│                                                                              │
│                                                 New Vocabulary:              │
│                                                                              │
│  - - - - - - - - - - - - - - - - - - - - - - - - - - - - - - - - - - - - - - │
│                                                                              │
│  Instruction: (needs/topics/strategies)        Substitutions:               │
│                                                 Omissions:                   │
│                                                 Other:                       │
│                                                                              │
└────────────────────────────────────────────────────────────────────────────┘
```

Figure 4.12   Williams's cross between a checklist and anecdotal records

Three copies of the form fit on a single 8-by-11-inch sheet and are used for three observations of the same child. Anecdotal notes are kept on the left and information about the use of oral reading cues and strategies on the right.

You can also ask students to monitor their own miscues when they read silently. Jeanne Gustafson, a special reading teacher for the Littleton Public Schools in Colorado, has developed a self-assessment tool that asks students periodically to monitor their own use of the language cueing systems and reading strategies (see Figure 4.13).

Although a teacher cannot be sure that students' self-reports are accurate, self-assessments of this kind serve to remind students about the strategies they should be using to self-monitor their own reading. If a self-assessment seems askew, you can ask the student to read a part aloud to you to give you some indication of its accuracy.

■ ■

paired reading

Allowing two students to read together is a useful strategy that helps to bridge the gap between relying on the teacher too much and reading more independently. A teacher can learn about students' literacy development by observing their reading

My Reading Checklist

Student's name: _____

Date: _____ Text: _____

Oral _____ Silent _____

	Never	A little bit	Most of the time	Always
When I read I:				
predicted what might happen				
understood what I read				
wrote unknown words on bookmark				
If I came to a word I didn't know I:				
used picture clues				
read on and then went back				
put in a word that made sense				

My summary:

Questions I have:

Figure 4.13   The Gustafson self-assessment tool for students' use

and their interactions during paired reading and taking anecdotal notes, probably the most efficient way to collect such data. The following are some of the observations that could be made:

- What help does one reader give to the other? What do you learn from these exchanges regarding what each reader knows about reading?

- Do the readers give each other words or remind the one currently reading of strategies for figuring out unknown words?

- What strategies do the readers seem to know?

- Do the readers recognize when meaning-changing miscues have been made and try to do something about them?

- Do the readers use pictures to help them figure out unknown words?

- What is the nature of the spontaneous dialogue between the two students over the book?

Periodically, students can be asked to reflect upon their paired reading sessions. Discussions of such reflections can help to keep paired reading sessions productive. You might ask students some of the following questions about their paired reading:

- What book/chapter did you read?

- How well did you stay on task?

- How did you help your partner with her reading today?

- What else did you talk about in relation to the book?

- How would you rate your paired reading today?

For example, during a paired reading session, a second-grade teacher took two anecdotal notes as she observed the efforts of two pairs. In both pairs, this teacher observed the same problem—one reader taking over the responsibility for working out words from the other reader. Since she had notes on only two pairs of students, the teacher interviewed the class the next day about what they did to help classmates who encountered difficult words. In other words, she wanted to ascertain whether the pattern she had uncovered in these two situations was a more general problem. She learned that it was and then began to devote more time through mini-lessons, reading conferences, and self-assessments to strategies for dealing with unknown words.

reading to others

There are many literacy events that involve reading to others: reading to parents, reading to younger children, reading to elderly adults, creating a Readers' Theatre script and performing it, and recording a tape for the classroom listening center. Often reading to others involves rereading a piece several times in order to perform it fluently. With such rereadings, miscues often decrease and the cueing systems and reading strategies are used more efficiently. More discussion of the meaning of text seems to follow naturally as students discuss how to say a line, what a character might wear, and so on.

Again, anecdotal notes may be the best way to record observations as children rehearse and then read to others. For example, as they read a text the first time, you might notice that several first-grade readers miscue on the word "lives"; they keep reading "loves," which is graphically similar, and may be thinking that the bird in the story loves to be in the tree. A few children also miscue by reading "nut" for "nest." You decide that when students do a repeated reading of the book the following day, you will begin by having children retell and discuss the story from the pictures. Children may talk about where the bird "lives" and that he built a "nest" in the tree, both of which are very clear in the pictures. As children engage in rereading the story, you can notice whether the discussion helped them better use background knowledge they had built to read the new words.

In listening to children read aloud, you can make many observations about students' miscues. Virtually everything that can be noted in formal miscue analysis can be noted in a more informal manner here. One area we especially listen for is whether students go back to self-correct miscues that affect meaning. You may also notice children who do just the opposite. They correct all deviations from the print—even ones that do not affect meaning. That is, they overcorrect and often do not comprehend. Both extremes represent problems.

When young children read to their parents, parents also can make observations about their reading. These observations are frequently best shared during parent conferences, when further questions and discussion are possible with the teacher. In her "Teacher Reflection," Marty Frampton describes how she asks parents to listen to a tape of their child reading before each round of parent conferences throughout the year. Frampton uses these tapes to begin a dialogue with parents about their observations of their child's reading at home, how they go about helping, and what questions they have. She also uses this time as an opportunity to suggest strategies that parents might try when they listen to their child read.

One way that children can assess improvements in their oral reading for themselves is from the positive feedback they may receive. Many schools are organizing programs in which older students read to younger ones. Both groups of children benefit. The older students must find and practice reading the books they will read to younger children. As a result, they often read a large number of additional books in order to fulfill this authentic purpose. Rashida was a fourth grader who read very slowly and carefully, overcorrected miscues, and had poor comprehension. Her teacher felt that she would benefit from reading to younger children and convinced Rashida to visit a group of kindergartners to see what kind of books they liked and if they would like to hear her read to them. That got her hooked. Rashida worked hard to decide on two books to read and then practiced reading them aloud smoothly and quickly enough for the younger children to enjoy. Her teacher emphasized over and over that it was going to be important to read fluently and to go back only if a miscue didn't make sense. If she read too slowly or did lots of overcorrecting, the young children would lose interest and get wiggly. The day she was to read, Rashida came to school all dressed up, excited, and scared! With her teacher's last-minute encouragement, she went down to the kindergarten room, read the books, and did an excellent job. Rashida did this for several weeks, and gradually the quality of both her oral reading and her comprehension increased. By focusing on reading more fluently and correcting only if the text stopped making sense, Rashida was able to concentrate more on her comprehension.

retrospective miscue analysis

Sometimes Rashida read her text into a tape as part of her rehearsal for reading to the kindergarten children. Reading into a tape and playing it back to listen can be another good vehicle for a student's self-reflections and self-assessments. This is commonly called retrospective miscue analysis. We would caution, however, that such self-assessments of one's own miscues probably ought to wait until the reading problems a student might hear are few enough to be overcome (to ensure this, be sure the reading material is not too difficult). When students are very ineffective, listening to themselves on tape may be a defeating experience. We usually wait until we have a good sense of the reading materials the student can handle, the student's reading has begun to improve (and we believe the student can hear this on the tape), and we can talk about some very specific strategies that are still needed.

Marek (1989) talks about use of retrospective miscues with ineffective adult readers. An individual student listens to the tape with a teacher. The teacher and student stop the tape periodically to discuss why reading problems occurred and what other strategies might have been applied. We have found that listening to a recording of their own reading is especially helpful for students like Rashida, who overcorrect. At first we would sit with such a student and listen to the tape. We'd ask questions like "Did that make sense? Was this important and did you really need to go back and correct it? What would have happened if you had just kept reading? Was it necessary to correct this miscue?"

reader-selected miscues

Reader-selected miscues is a literacy event that asks students to monitor words that are giving them difficulty. On bookmarks students jot down each word, the sentence containing the word, and the page number. The teacher collects these bookmarks and looks over the words/sentences to determine common patterns, then addresses them in small group discussions. Students' gathering of words can provide the teacher with useful information. Students can also be encouraged to look for patterns in words that give them difficulty and to figure out strategies for dealing with them. When these words are logged and reviewed over time, students can see their real progress in terms of the new strategies they can use when they encounter other unknown words that could interfere with their comprehension. Students' knowledge of particular vocabulary grows as well.

The teacher's role is to assess reader-selected miscues for patterns that can be addressed. With a chapter book students might be asked to keep a separate bookmark for each chapter they read and record reader-selected miscues on it. When students have finished a chapter, the bookmarks could be collected and reviewed by the teacher, and common strategies to solve word problems discussed with the group.

Not long ago we developed a unit over the chapter book *Sign of the Beaver* (Rhodes, Shanklin, & Nathenson-Mejia, 1989). One of our goals was to get students to deal more independently with unknown words. This was a good book for working on this strategy because it contained several unusual words in contexts that provided support for figuring them out. We devised a self-assessment for students to use over the first three chapters. We located words that we felt were likely to give students difficulty and typed them out in their full context. We then asked students to check the strategy they had used to figure out the word. Here is an example:

> He had stood at one end of every log and raised it, one on top of the other, fitting the *notched* ends together as snugly as though they had grown that way. (p. 1)

_____ I already knew the word! It means _____.

_____ I put in a meaningful substitute: _____.

_____ I skipped it and kept going; little or no meaning was lost.

_____ I thought about what the author was talking about, thought about the flow of the author's language, looked at the sounds in the word, and figured it out and its meaning. The word means _____.

These choices focus students' attention on learning strategies for figuring out new words rather than on simply learning meanings for individual words. A Chapter I teacher who used this example in a bilingual classroom found that the students had no concept of a notch other than that you might "notch" a stick as a means of counting. She used Lincoln Logs and pictures to illustrate how logs for cabins are notched. The students were then able to return to the passage and talk about reading strategies they could apply to comprehend the meaning successfully.

teacher reflection teacher reflection

In her "Teacher Reflection," Marty Frampton provides a description of how she uses audiotaped recordings of oral reading to plan instruction, to keep parents informed, and to help students assess their own progress. Frampton is an experienced first-grade teacher at Cottonwood Creek Elementary in the public school system of Cherry Creek, a Denver suburb. Frampton has been a key figure in helping other district teachers revitalize their literacy instruction and develop ways to assess students that better fit their instruction and goals. The assessment technique she describes has also been used by teachers of older students in her building, who find it equally valuable.

Kids tapes inc.

Marty Frampton

One valuable assessment tool I use in the classroom is an audiotape. Once a month throughout the school year, I record each student reading a book or a piece of her writing. The audiotape of each child's reading is used for a variety of purposes. It provides parents with a clear picture of their child's reading and writing development. It gives the teacher information that helps her make instructional decisions for each child. The students enjoy reading to a parent volunteer, and they like to replay the tape to hear the progress they have made throughout the school year.

Taping procedures

For the first taping in September, I select four books that progress from an easy text to a very difficult text for children at the grade level I teach. I wait until we have had two to three weeks together in the classroom before I do the first taping so that each child feels comfortable with me. I have found that it helps to talk about the taping process with my students ahead of time. Since they bring their own blank audiotape as a part of their supply list, they are curious about how it will be used. They listen to a previous student's tape to understand the purpose and the process. They hear how each student starts the tape:

My name is _____ Today is _____.

I am going to read _____.

They hear the child start reading easy material and read hesitantly. As the year progresses, the reader becomes more fluent and the material more difficult.

For the first reading, I tape each child for approximately ten minutes in a quiet place. As they read through the series of materials I have chosen, I make sure the child is feeling comfortable and give nonverbal signals of encouragement (a pat on the back, a hand signal to indicate success). If the child is having difficulty reading even the easiest piece, I will read the selection, letting the child take the lead as much as possible. I will not proceed to the next reading sample with this child.

After I have repeated this process with every child, I listen to each tape at home and take a running record as I listen. I look closely at the substitutions, words skipped, words sounded out, and self-corrections that a child tries when she comes to an unknown word. As I record this information on the Reading Profile Sheet (see Figure 4.14), I replay in my mind exactly what the child said and did. This helps me evaluate the child's reading behavior. I can use the information on the tape to determine the reading material a child can handle. I always encourage my students to choose their own reading books, but occasionally I need to help with this decision. I use the running record to help me decide the reading strategies a child or a group of children need to be taught in order to become more independent readers.

In subsequent months parent volunteers oversee the taping. A child begins by self-selecting the book she wants to read into the tape. It may be the book the child is currently reading or one she read earlier. I encourage each child to read their selection to a friend before the taping so they feel comfortable with the words in the text. Sometimes a child may choose to read a piece of her own writing into the tape. After this reading, while she is still being recorded, each "author" is asked by a parent volunteer, "Why did you choose to read this book?" "What problem did you have writing this story?" "How did you solve it?"

As I look at selected parts of Megan's Reading Profile Sheet, it is clear to me that she is an emerging reader. She is willing to take risks with new words. She looks at beginning sounds and occasionally at ending sounds. She is reading for meaning because she self-corrects most words that don't make sense. Megan reads with beautiful expression and feels good about herself as a reader.

In the example recorded in February, Megan read *Do You Love Me*, a book she had written because she likes to make friends. She had a problem remembering what to write next. She solved this by asking her friend Krista to help. After listening to this part of Megan's tape, I decided to help her keep track of her ideas by using yellow stick-on notes to jot down a few key words that would help Megan remember what she wants to write about the next day.

After each month's taping, I listen to the tapes and record the information on the Reading Profile Sheet, just as I have done with Megan. I review the cumulative records as I go. It shows me how each student is growing and reveals or confirms areas in which the child could use assistance.

How tapes are used

These tapes help me make critical decisions about each child's reading. I can begin to assess whether a child is going to need special assistance or rapid promotion in reading during the school year. I am able to assess a child's strengths, difficulties, and areas of confusion.

I listen to hear if a child is self-monitoring while reading. If the child is self-correcting on a word, then I know the child is reading for meaning. If

Reading Profile

Name **Megan**

Date	Text	Reading Strategies				Other Comments
		Substitutions	Skips	Sounds out	Self-corrects	
9/19	Sing a Rainbow					Sang the words, read fluently.
	The Highway	House/highway			four/five	Took much longer to read, choppy.
9/19	Going to School	around/across	front buildings stairs doors	ba ... basement		Much too hard, didn't read beyond the third page.
11/13	Lazy Mary	want/won't			splat/splash	Very fluent, sang parts of it.
2/9	Do You Love Me by Megan				family/friend	1. Because I like to make friends 2. Remembering what to write next 3. By asking her friend, Krista, for help.

Figure 4.14   The Reading Profile Sheet

not, I might use cloze activities to help the child determine what word will make sense or help a child see that there are graphophonic cues that can be used to determine what an unknown word is. Sometimes, I will read back a page to the child the way she read it and ask if the child sees (hears) anything wrong. This helps the child begin to monitor her own reading. I will emphasize the importance of skipping a word, going on to the end of a sentence, and thinking of a word that would make sense in the blank.

My primary reason for taping is to see if children are becoming independent readers whose reading is improving. I have found that independent readers monitor their own reading, search for cues in words, reread, confirm their reading, self-correct, and figure out meaningful substitutions for unknown words. The running records I keep substantiate whether this is happening for each child. Finally, I can evaluate whether the text difficulty and the child's reading ability match. If they do not, I can assist the child with the next book selection and teach the reading strategies that will help each child grow.

Our first parent conference is in November. By then each child has been taped three times. I ask the parents to come to their conference twenty minutes early to listen to their child's tape. Outside the classroom I have set out their child's tape, a tape recorder with headphones, and a list of the books their child has read into the tape with the pages marked.

This is by far the most successful thing I have done to set a positive tone for conferences. After parents have listened to the tape, they bring the books into the classroom so we can talk about how their child read on the tape. Most often the progress is very easy to hear! I talk about all the good things their child is doing in reading by referring to the Reading Profile Sheet, point out the things that need to be worked on by looking at the page the child had difficulty reading, and model how I would help their child learn a particular strategy. This often gives parents a tool they can use to help their child read at home.

One nice result of having parents listen to their child read on tape is that they no longer ask which reading group their child is in. Instead, they ask questions like, "What books can I get for my child to read?" "How can I help my child read more fluently?" "Maybe I would have been a better reader if I had had this kind of a program!" The parents also develop a greater appreciation for their child's learning process. The emphasis is no longer on how children measure up but on how parents can continue to help their children become independent readers.

The children periodically listen to their own tape at a tape center in the classroom. They love to listen to their own voices and they are always amazed at the improvement they are making. Sometimes the child and I will listen to the tape together to assess how she read a particular story. Often the child will say, "Oops, I said that word wrong, the correct word is ___." Or they may say, "Boy, I can read that book much faster now." It is so much more effective for a child to discover her own errors and figure out a way to correct them. Listening to their own tapes proves to be a great self-evaluation tool for the children.

Audiotapes as part of portfolios

In the past, I have sent the audiotapes home with each child at the end of the school year. I enclose a note to the parents asking them to keep this treasure in a protected place because there is nothing more precious than listening to their child read favorite books and pieces of writing in the years ahead. Our school is now planning to use a portfolio next year that will follow each child from teacher to teacher. The audiotape will henceforth become a part of each child's portfolio. Parents will be able to take home the tape when their child finishes elementary school or moves to another school.

As children revisit their portfolios, we hope they will listen to the tapes and realize the progress they have made in reading and writing. There is usually room on the tape to continue taping the children as they move through the grades. After the following year's teacher has listened to a child's tape, she can develop strategies to help each child move forward in reading and writing. Parents can continue to listen to their child's tape before conferences as the child progresses from one year to the next.

Conclusion

We have outlined several theories about the reading process that have influenced reading assessment and instruction. Understanding these theories helps teachers to develop or select assessment procedures that are consistent with their approach to text. We discussed how the language cueing systems operate in relationship to one another and examined several forms of miscue analysis, a standardized assessment procedure that allows us to understand how students relate the language cueing systems as they read. We also discussed many classroom activities through which teachers can gather further information about students' miscues and reading strategies. These analyses help to pinpoint needed instruction that may either take place on the spot or be saved for future lessons. But our discussion of how students interrelate the cueing systems and their ongoing comprehension does not tell the whole story. We will take up additional questions about comprehension in the next chapter.

references

Adams, M., & A. Collins. (1979). A schema-theoretic view of reading. In R. Freedle (Ed.), *New directions in discourse processing*. Norwood, NJ: Ablex.

Altwerger, B., & V. Resta. (In press). *Miscue analysis profile software*. Katonah, NY: Richard C. Owen.

Anderson, R., & P. Pearson. (1984). A schema-theoretic view of basic process in reading comprehension. In P.D. Pearson (Ed.), *Handbook of reading research*. Newark, DE: International Reading Association.

Clay, M. (1985). *The early detection of reading difficulties* (3rd ed.). Portsmouth, NH: Heinemann.

Eco, U. (1970). *The role of the reader*. Bloomington, IN: Indiana University Press.

Gollasch, F. (Ed.). (1982) . *Language and literacy: The selected writings of Kenneth S. Goodman* (Vol. 1: Process, theory, research). London: Routledge & Kegan Paul.

Goodman, D. (1989). So why don't I feel good about myself? In K. Goodman, Y. Goodman, & W. Hood (Eds.), *The whole language evaluation book* (pp. 189–212). Portsmouth, NH: Heinemann.

Goodman, K. (1984). Unity in reading. In A. Purves & O. Niles (Eds.), *Becoming readers in a complex society*. The 83rd Yearbook of the National Society of the Study of Education: Part I (pp. 79–114). Chicago, IL: University of Chicago Press.

Goodman, K. (1989). Whole-language research: Foundations and development. *Elementary School Journal, 90*, 207–222.

Goodman, Y. (1989). Roots of the whole-language movement. *Elementary School Journal, 90*, 113–128.

Goodman, Y., D. Watson, & C. Burke. (1987). *Reading miscue inventory*. Katonah, NY: Richard C. Owen.

Hoffman, J., & R. Clements. (1984). Reading miscues and teacher verbal feedback. *Elementary School Journal, 84*, 423–439.

Johns, J. (1989). *The Basic Reading Inventory: Pre-primer through grade eight* (4th ed.). Dubuque, IA: Kendall Hunt.

Kemp, M. (1987). *Watching children read and write: Observational records for children with special needs*. Portsmouth, NH: Heinemann.

Leslie, L., & J. Caldwell. (1990). *Qualitative reading inventory*. Glenview, IL: Scott, Foresman.

Lindfors, J. (1986). Research currents: English for everyone. *Language Arts, 63,* 76–84.

Marek, A. (1989). Using evaluation as an instructional strategy. In K. Goodman, Y. Goodman, & W. Hood (Eds.), *The whole language evaluation book* (pp. 189–212). Portsmouth, NH: Heinemann

Mason, J. (1984). A schema-theoretic view of the reading process as a basis for comprehension instruction. In G. Duffy, L. Roehler, & J. Manson (Eds.), *Comprehension instruction: Perspectives and suggestions* (pp. 26–38). New York: Longman.

Mudre, L., & S. McCormick. (1989). Effects of meaning-focused cues on under-achieving readers' context use, self-corrections, and literal comprehension. *Reading Research Quarterly, 24,* 89–113.

Pikulski, J., & A. Tobin (1982). The cloze procedure as an informal assessment technique. In J. Pikulski & T. Shanahan (Eds.), *Approaches to the informal evaluation of reading* (pp. 42–62). Newark, DE: International Reading Association.

Rhodes, L.K., (Ed.) (1993). *Literacy assessment: A handbook of instruments.* Portsmouth, NH: Heinemann.

Rhodes, L.K., & N. Shanklin. (1990). Classroom miscue assessment. *The Reading Teacher, 44,* 252–254.

Rhodes, L.K., N. Shanklin, & S. Nathenson-Mejia. (1989). *Sign of the Beaver Link Pak.* Lakewood, CO: Link, the Language Company.

Rosenblatt, L. (1978). *The reader, the text, the poem.* Carbondale, IL: Southern Illinois University Press.

———. (1985). Viewpoints: Transaction versus interaction—a terminological rescue operation. *Research in the Teaching of English, 19,* 96–107.

———. (1988). *Writing and reading: The transactional theory.* Champaign, IL: Center for the Study of Reading, Technical Report No. 416.

Rumelhart, D. (1977). Toward an interactive model of reading. In S. Dornic (Ed.), *Attention and performance VI.* London: Academic Press.

Smith, F. (1988). *Understanding reading* (4th ed.). New York: Holt, Rinehart & Winston.

Watson, D. (1987). Reader-selected miscues. In D. Watson (Ed.), *Ideas and insights: Language arts in the elementary school* (p. 218). Urbana, IL: National Council of Teachers of English.

———. (1989). Defining and describing whole language. *Elementary School Journal, 90,* 129–142.

Weaver, C. (1988). *Reading process and practice: From socio-psycholinguistics to whole language.* Portsmouth, NH: Heinemann.

———. (1990). *Understanding whole languages: From principles to practice.* Portsmouth, NH: Heinemann.

Woodley, J. (1990). *Reading miscue inventory disk.* Katonah, NY: Richard C. Owen.

Books read by students for miscue analysis:

Bartholomew, R., & B. Tillery. (1984). *Heath Earth Science.* Lexington, MA: D. C. Heath.

Birdwell, N. (1985). *Clifford at the Circus.* New York: Scholastic.

Freedman, R. (1987). *Lincoln: A Photobiography.* New York: Clarion Books.

George, J. (1974). *Julie of the Wolves.* New York: HarperCollins Children's Books.

Hutchings, P. (1986). *The Doorbell Rang.* New York: Greenwillow Books.

Lobel, A. (1985). *Frog and Toad Together.* New York: HarperCollins Children's Books.

Paterson, K. (1987). *The Great Gilly Hopkins.* New York: HarperCollins Children's Books.

Chapter Five

5

Reading Comprehension

reflections

☐ Consider comprehension as a process that begins before reading, continues during reading, and goes on long after reading. List the questions you want to answer about your students' comprehension in one column. In an adjacent column, list various ways you can think of to answer these questions. Taking into account your instructional situation, generate specific plans for collecting the information you need to answer your questions and to use the answers in making instructional decisions. After you read the chapter, return to your ideas and think about them further.

☐ In which activities in your classroom do students demonstrate comprehension? Look back at the questions you listed for the first reflection activity. Can you answer the questions by observing the students in these activities? If not, can the activities be revised so that you can answer more questions?

☐ Tape-record one of your most proficient readers retelling a story. Tape-record one of your least proficient readers retelling a story. Analyze the differences before you read this chapter. Analyze the differences after reading this chapter.

☐ Choose a comprehension assessment technique other than retelling that is discussed in this chapter. Use the technique to assess the comprehension of a student who interests you for a particular reason. What did you find out about the student's comprehension and about the technique itself?

☐ Identify an upcoming literacy event (such as a book discussion) in which comprehension is the focus. Decide how you will gather assessment data during the event. What problems did you have and how will you solve them in the future? What did you discover about students' comprehension that you might not have discovered if you hadn't collected assessment data during the literacy event?

When I Read a Good Book
JENNIFER ROSE

When I read a good book,
I see the many lines of words
Running across the page like little ants scurrying across a log.
Pictures form in my mind
Like someone drawing on my eyelids.
And my brain deciphers words
As if I were reading the markings on an Egyptian tomb.

When I read a good book,
I hear myself reading in my mind like I'm reading aloud.
I hear the sounds in the book
Like the story is alive and next to me.
I hear the characters' voices
Like church bells ringing.

When I read a good book,
I feel like I am the character and always have been.
I feel the bad things in the book happen to me
Like someone has put a curse on me.
And I feel my imagination soaring like a bird in the sky,
When I read a good book.

(The Reading Teacher, October 1989)

The fifth grader who wrote this poem understands the nature of reading comprehension well enough to generalize about her reading experiences and make transparent some of the mental strategies she uses to comprehend stories. Jennifer

---

reflects on such things as seeing pictures in her mind, identifying with a character in the story, putting herself into the story, and using her imagination.

Jennifer provides us with some hints about the complexity of reading comprehension and about what's really important in reading a story, but her poem is not about what many tests consider important in comprehension: knowing literal information, being able to infer, and generating a main idea. Jennifer helps us understand that comprehension is complex, a deep response not only to text but to life itself.

In recent years, educators have come to understand that comprehension is a mental process of constructing rather than extracting meaning from text; that comprehension is a personal understanding of text; and that comprehension, even when it takes place privately, is a social process. We have also come to understand that each comprehension event is unique, since it is affected by a multitude of reader, text, and situational factors. As a result, comprehension assessment must be an ongoing process rather than an isolated event. Only by continually observing readers' interactions with a variety of texts in a variety of situations can we begin to understand the complex mental and social process of comprehension as Jennifer portrays it.

In this chapter, we'll discuss the dilemmas faced by anyone who assesses comprehension. After providing some questions typical of those we use to guide our assessment of comprehension, we'll detail major techniques that can be used to explore students' comprehension of text. In addition, we'll also discuss how to tap comprehension during literacy events and consider how comprehension assessment conducted during these events can be used to inform instruction.

the dilemmas and possibilities in assessing comprehension

Numerous dilemmas face anyone attempting to assess reading comprehension. However, once we understand them, they become possibilities.

process and product

Comprehension has traditionally been assessed almost exclusively as a product. Yet what we need to assess is a student's process if we are to teach the student to process text more effectively and thus improve the product. For this reason, in contrast to the focus on product in the instruments and techniques most commonly used to assess comprehension, the focus of our discussion about comprehension is on process. Valencia & Pearson (1987) point out the differences between the process view ("new view") that underlies the comprehension assessment ideas discussed here and the view underlying the product-oriented standardized and norm-referenced tests most commonly used in schools. Although some product measures are useful data banks from which to infer students' comprehension strategies, it is helpful to instructional planning if you can also gather information directly about the strategies students use to construct meaning. You can collect this kind of information even as students are tested on traditional measures of comprehension, such as multiple choice questions.

Judy Lampert, a Denver Chapter I teacher who was frustrated by her students' poor scores on standardized tests, obtained information on students' standardized test-taking processes by asking them to read aloud and think aloud while taking an alternate form of the district-mandated standardized test. She discovered that the students' ability to read and understand the passages (as determined by miscue analysis and think-aloud analysis) was quite good. On the other hand, she found that the students:

- Were unaware of distractors and often chose the first answer that could be right instead of reading all the answers in order to choose the best one.

- Did not ask themselves why they chose the answer they did.

- Did not always understand the questions. They seemed to be unfamiliar with some types of question stems. When the questions were rephrased, they could answer them.

- Tended to answer a question about what a character felt or thought by explaining what the student felt or thought instead.

- Tended to answer a question with what they knew instead of with what they read.

- Did not read the questions before reading the passage.

- Did not skim or look back in the text in order to answer questions. Instead, they answered from memory.

- Were thrown by the use of a synonym, instead of the word originally used in the text, in the answer choice.

In another study, Lampert compared students who scored well on standardized tests with her Chapter I students. She discovered that the good scorers approached the test as a challenging puzzle and maintained an attitude that they would do well on it. She also discovered that the good scorers typically loved to read—even tests. The Chapter I students, on the other hand, approached the test as a tedious task they simply needed to complete; they believed they would not do well on the test. She also found that the Chapter I students preferred test-taking strategies that did not require repeated reading (for example, to confirm an answer); they didn't like reading and used strategies that allowed them to read as little as possible on the test.

Armed with this information about her students' views and test-taking processes, Lampert was far better able to plan instruction that would enable her students to complete these tests as well as similar school tasks with more sophisticated strategies. The same is true of any situation in which comprehension is being assessed; process assessments often assist the teacher in uncovering the information that will be most helpful in planning instruction.

comprehension: a mental process

Because comprehension is a mental process, it can only be observed indirectly. This dilemma is compounded by the fact that the mental process is an evolving one, which often begins before the book is opened, changes as the book is read, and continues to evolve even after the book is closed.

Readers use a multitude of comprehension strategies in the process of constructing meaning from text: predicting, confirming and disconfirming predictions, using prior knowledge, making comparisons, rereading or reading ahead to deal with difficult ideas, visualizing, and so on. Although we cannot get inside readers' heads to observe comprehension, it is possible to infer comprehension strategies or make them more visible. In particular, comparing a student's comprehension of text with your own may assist you in inferring the thinking processes the student used in arriving at an interpretation. However, consider the differences between your and the student's comprehension as a way to gain insight into the student's thinking, not as a way to judge the "correctness" of his comprehension.

In addition, various techniques can make students' comprehension strategies more visible: interviews of students and in-process "think-alouds" are both helpful. Interviews can help students verbalize what they were thinking before, during, or after reading a text. For example, questions that uncover a student's thinking process can be asked when a student's retelling contains unexpected information. The teacher might say, "You said that. . . . What led you to that conclusion?"

"Think-alouds" are designed to uncover how the student thinks in the act of reading. After the student reads certain portions of the text, either orally or silently, the student "thinks aloud" about what he has read so far. Of course, much thinking aloud can also be observed during instructional activities. Students can be observed thinking aloud about the meaning of a story as they write a Readers' Theatre script.

Miscues can also be helpful indicators of the comprehension process, as we discussed in the previous chapter. If students' miscues indicate that they do not consider reading to be the construction of meaning, it's highly likely that this belief could be the root of their comprehension difficulties. Miscues can lead to insights about why and how a reader had difficulty understanding a concept presented in the text or why he misinterpreted the author's intentions.

comprehension: a social process

Reading is a transactional process (Rosenblatt, 1978) in which a reader constructs unique personal meaning using the text as a guide or blueprint. Comprehension is unique and personal because each reader brings his own personal background to the text and reads for his own purposes.

If comprehension is personally constructed, it is also socially constructed. The more similarity there is between one reader's background and the backgrounds of other readers, the more likely it is that the meanings they construct for a text will be similar. The readers' shared backgrounds are the foundation upon which they arrive at shared meaning. The meaning of text can also be extended when readers engage in social activities, such as sharing their personal meanings with each other. It is not at all unusual to find that our own understanding of a text is extended when we talk with others.

Because comprehension is socially constructed, we ought to take this into account in assessment. The dilemma is that traditional comprehension tests assume that all readers will arrive at the same meaning as those who constructed the test (and thus determined the meanings of the text). A related dilemma is that traditional comprehension assessments do not involve assessment of how students' comprehension is affected by social interchanges over text.

In discussions of text, students with different backgrounds are likely to reveal different personal meanings; encouraging students to talk about how they constructed their meanings may well uncover the reasons for such differences in comprehension. At the same time, discussion about text is likely to extend students' comprehension. Such discussion provides not only assessment data about students' personal comprehension but also the opportunity to assess students' evolving comprehension in response to social interaction. What we would hope to observe is that students' comprehension of text is broadened and deepened as the result of activities in which students share their personal interpretations.

factors that affect comprehension

Saying that a student has "poor comprehension" is like saying that family members have a "poor relationship." Until the source or sources of the "poor relationship" are understood, a therapist can't help the family members change their relationships. In the same way, it is imperative to understand the source or sources of comprehension difficulties before teachers can help students improve their comprehension. In addition, it is also helpful in instructional planning to understand which factors affect comprehension positively. Schell comments, "We can't automatically assume . . . instruction in understanding text is primarily what is needed" (1988, p. 14).

Three major categories of factors affect comprehension—the reader, the text, and the situation—and factors within and across each category interact in many ways. The following list charts major factors that affect comprehension.

The Reader
background knowledge
linguistic competence
reasoning ability
problem-solving ability
knowledge of reading strategies
knowledge of graphophonics
flexibility of reading strategies
purpose for reading
purpose for sharing what was read
interest
prior reading experiences
personal reading theory

The Text
text structure
density of concepts
topic
clarity of writing
print size/density
attractiveness
genre
vocabulary
language structures
text format
match between pictures and text
purpose of text (why written)

The Situation
degree of distraction/interruption
time provided
number of people involved
roles of people involved
purpose provided for reading
reading theory of teacher
reading strategies suggested
background information provided
who chose text
degree of text lookback permitted
silent or oral reading
support provided by teacher
activities assigned by teacher

The reader is often considered the source of difficulty when comprehension falters. Yet the list above suggests many other possible sources of difficulty within texts or within situations in which comprehension is taking place. A student's comprehension will vary with factors in the text, such as the length and structure of the text, the density of its concepts, the structure of sentences in the text, the vocabulary and conventions used, and so on. Comprehension will also vary with situational factors; such as whether the student reads orally or silently, what purpose is given for reading, what the teacher considers important in the text, what experiences the teacher has provided to increase background information, and so on. Once teachers understand that these factors affect comprehension, they find it necessary to assess the reading situation constantly to see what in the situation, the reader, or the text might have affected a student's comprehension either positively or negatively. They understand that a single measure of comprehension only hints at what *may* be a student's strengths and weaknesses. Though very little can be concluded about a student's comprehension on the basis of a single assessment, teachers can come to some useful conclusions on the basis of ongoing multiple assessments.

Once teachers have some understanding of the situations, text characteristics, and reader characteristics that influence comprehension in negative and positive ways, they have the power to know how to make adjustments that are likely to improve students' comprehension. So, although the variability of comprehension makes the teacher's job difficult, understanding that variability helps the teacher use it in powerful ways for the benefit of students. By noting the variations in readers, texts, and situations, teachers can begin to figure out optimal conditions for encouraging comprehension. If they understand, for example, that students are unlikely to have the background to read a science book, they can provide that background before they assign the reading.

Noting these variations can also help teachers uncover the sources of difficulty within the reader so that these can be addressed in instruction. For example, if it becomes clear that some students have difficulty comprehending texts that contain unusual vocabulary, the teacher may decide to help students learn how to figure out approximate meanings for vocabulary from surrounding text.

questions to ask about students' comprehension

It should not be surprising that our questions are shaped by the notion that comprehension varies each time it occurs and that we need to keep in mind the many factors in the reader, the text, and the situation that affect comprehension. Some questions we might have about the reader include:

- What prior knowledge or experience does the student have about the text topic? How does the student utilize that prior knowledge or experience?

- How well organized is the meaning that the reader constructs while reading the text?

- What is the relationship between the student's miscues and his comprehension of the text?

- How does the student relate the content of the text to other life experiences? to other reading experiences?

- What does the reader think his strengths and weaknesses are in terms of comprehending this text?

- What strengths and weaknesses in comprehension are evident in retelling, think-alouds, or other forms of comprehension assessment?

- Does the reader's interest in the topic affect comprehension? How?

- How is the student's response to text maturing over time?

- What strategies does the reader use to construct meaning?

- What information does the reader use to generate and confirm or disconfirm predictions?

- Does the reader use the same reasoning and problem-solving strategies displayed in other parts of his life in the process of comprehending text?

- How does the reader view the process of comprehension?

We are also concerned about how various texts affect students' comprehension. If we ask the above questions across a variety of texts, we should be able to understand what text features make comprehension more or less difficult for students. Some of the following questions are restatements of the previous questions, this time focusing on the texts themselves. Others are questions we consider it important to ask about the impact of text features on comprehension.

- How does ability to construct meaning vary from one text genre to another? How do strategies vary?

- How is the organization of the text reflected in the reader's retelling?

- How is the reader's comprehension affected by the complexity of the language structures used by the author?

- In what way is the reader's comprehension affected by the illustrations (or graphs or tables) in the text?

- How does comprehension vary when texts are written with highly controlled vocabulary and sentence length and when they feature more natural language?

- How is the reader's comprehension affected by stories that lack important story grammar elements?

It is also important to ask questions about the context or situation in which the readers are reading and reflecting on the text. Again, some of the following questions restate previous questions but with the focus on the situations in which texts are read. Others are questions we consider important to ask about the impact of the situation on comprehension.

- Who sets the purpose for reading and how does that affect the student's comprehension of text?

- How does the degree of authenticity of the context for reading affect the student's comprehension of text?

- Does the reader comprehend text differently in oral and in silent reading? How?

- How does rereading the text affect the reader's comprehension of it?

- How does talking with others about the text in the process of reading affect the reader's comprehension of text?

- How is the student's comprehension affected when the student reads alone as compared to paired reading?

- How and why does the students' comprehension vary from one situation to another?

The factors that affect comprehension (the reader, the text, the context for reading) are part of what shapes the questions we can ask about students' comprehension. Another important element to consider is what proficient readers do in order to comprehend text; these are the criteria against which we observe all students and make instructional decisions about what students need to learn to do. Observing your own comprehension and that of the proficient readers in your classes can help you understand what can be expected of students both in the comprehension process and in the comprehension product.

We'll list a few examples of the kinds of questions that might be asked. It is particularly important to explore these questions if you have been working only with ineffective readers for some time (for example, if you are a Chapter I teacher). An occasional assessment of an average or highly proficient reader will help you better define goals for the ineffective readers.

- What prior knowledge or experience does the proficient reader have about the text topic? How does the proficient reader utilize that prior knowledge or experience?

- What is the relationship between the proficient reader's miscues and his comprehension of text?

- What strategies does the proficient reader use to construct meaning?

- What does the proficient reader think his strengths and weaknesses are in terms of the comprehension of this text?

Finally, your instructional goals also ought to be a guide in deciding what kinds of information you want to collect about students' comprehension and thus, what questions you want to ask. Questions will be different in a situation in which students read fiction they have selected because of its relevance to their lives and in a situation in which you have assigned a nonfiction text about a science topic. You are more likely to be concerned with how students identify with characters in one situation and whether students can identify key facts in the other.

All the previous questions about students' comprehension assume certain instructional goals. "How does the reader utilize prior knowledge or experience in comprehending text?" for example, assumes that one of the teacher's goals in reading instruction is "the use of prior knowledge and experience." We recommend that you review the questions you decide to ask about students' comprehension with an eye toward whether the questions reveal the breadth of your instructional goals for the class and for individual students.

The questions we've listed are only some of those you may ask about your students' comprehension of text. It should be clear that assessing comprehension is no small task. Finding answers to even a few of these questions requires that you continually assess what students are doing and why they are doing it as the class experiences daily lessons that involve text comprehension. It should also be clear that assessing comprehension relies on a variety of ways of tapping students' understanding and will require that you know your students well. If you know what your students are interested in, what they have chosen to read in the past, and what their background experiences are, each assessment of comprehension is likely to be better informed by the accumulation of your knowledge and assessment data.

techniques for comprehension assessment

In this section, we will explore three major techniques that are useful in assessing comprehension—interviewing, thinking aloud, and retelling. We'll begin with interviewing and thinking aloud because they are most conducive to examining students' comprehension processes. Though they are really product measures, retellings will also be considered here because we find them the richest source of product data and because it is possible to infer useful information about a student's comprehension process from retelling. In this section and the one that follows, we'll show how the three techniques can be a part of everyday classroom activities.

interviewing

Interviewing can provide a variety of information: what students think about, what students do, sources of comprehension difficulty, the nature of students' confusion, ambiguity that exists in text material, how students use their prior knowledge to comprehend and do reading tasks, mismatches between students' everyday meanings and special meanings of content areas, how students may be completing tasks successfully without really understanding the text, and so on.

Interviewing can be conducted at any point in the reading process. It can also be done outside of the process, where you are likely to get a broader view of the student's comprehension process and less information about particular texts or situations that affect comprehension. Of course, the information you get has a great deal to do with the questions you ask during the interview and how you ask them. Interviewing two or three students during a work period often gives teachers plentiful information about what they need to clarify or teach that would be appropriate for many members of the class.

Asking interview questions that yield rich information is not easy to do. You need to be careful to avoid asking questions that alert students to the fact that they have responded incorrectly, that are double questions ("What do you think you have to do? What did the text tell you to do?"), or that guide students toward a correct answer or solution. Good interview questions are nondirective and reflective (probably the single most important one is "Why?"). They probe students' thinking and allow the teacher to follow the students' thought processes. These probes allow you to find out what students understand or misunderstand. "This [means] saying as little as possible, certainly less than the student. It also [means] encouraging the student to say a bit more, by asking 'What do you mean?' or 'mm' or 'yeah'" (Nicholson, 1989, p.1). Even when teachers ask good interview questions, students who are used to traditional questions often respond at first as if traditional questions are being asked.

Nicholson and his colleagues found that interviewing ineffective readers can be especially challenging; as Nicholson put it, they are "tough and wily" and make uncovering their thinking quite difficult. On the other hand, information can be gained that can strongly affect instruction. "The surface structure of the classroom can suggest to the teacher that content is being learned, while in the minds of pupils, there is only a maze of confusion. . . . As 'experts' in their own content areas, many teachers may simply have forgotten the little things that pupils are likely to find confusing" (Nicholson, 1984a, pp. 449–450). Interviewing can uncover these areas of confusion.

Nicholson (1984b) has compiled hints on classroom interviewing. They are reproduced in full in Appendix D and merit careful study. (They are applicable to questions that follow retellings and think-alouds as well.) The hints are helpful in learning how to gather the richest data in the most efficient ways—not only in reading but also in writing and related study skill areas such as research.

Interviewing can be done in the midst of a comprehension task such as listing important points to be remembered after reading a textbook chapter or finding details in the text in order to complete a drawing of a scene. In a study in secondary content area classrooms, Nicholson and his colleagues (1984a; 1984b) conducted "desk interviews" in order to find out how students coped with the reading demands in content area classes such as English, social studies, and science. As students worked on assignments at their desks, they were asked questions about the task, the knowledge needed to engage in the task, and the strategies they used to do the task. Although the questions are categorized to encourage the interviewer to consider each of these three areas, the areas are in fact interactive and students will not talk about them as if they are isolated. The "trigger questions" that follow are examples of those used to get the student talking initially; the follow-up questions are examples of those designed to keep the student talking—to amplify, justify, and clarify responses to the original question. (The questions are taken from Edwards, 1981a & 1981b.)

- **Task questions** are designed to discover how the student interpreted the comprehension task he was engaged in.

  Trigger question: What are you doing? (going to do?)
  Follow-up questions: Why do you have to do this? Can you give an example? What does the teacher want here?

- **Knowledge questions** are designed to find out what students need to know in order to engage in a comprehension task.

  Trigger question: How did you know that?
  Follow-up questions: Where did you get the information? What did you need to know? Are you having trouble? Why?

- **Strategy questions** are designed to uncover the strategies used by the student to comprehend text.

  Trigger question: How did you get to the answer? (are you going to get to the answer?)
  Follow-up questions: What was difficult? (easy?) What are you going to do next? Then what?

Interviewing can also be done in the course of a reading conference. As part of the conference, a few (keep it to a few) questions can help you understand the student's success or difficulty with a particular piece of material. If you confer with students frequently, you will have frequent opportunities to ask questions that help you illuminate their comprehension strategies over time. Some helpful questions are listed below (adapted from Y. Goodman, Watson, & Burke, 1987). Some may be used to begin the conference while others are best to asked in order to illuminate something the student has volunteered in the conference. Certainly, other questions will occur to you as appropriate follow-ups to comments students make in response to one of the listed questions. In any case, these are suggestions only.

- Is something in the text giving you trouble?

- Did you know concept (idea) before you began reading, or did you learn about it as you read?

- What have been the easiest (hardest) parts of the text to understand? Explain.

- Where did the text begin to make sense to you? (Become confusing for you?) Why?

- Have there been times when you didn't understand the text? Tell about those. (Find where they are in the text.)

- Have the pictures (diagrams, graphs) helped you? How? (or, Why not?)

- You said that you had difficulty understanding _____. Why do you think you had difficulty with that?

- I noticed you are frowning (asking for help, puzzled). What are you thinking about?

- Yesterday, you had a lot of difficulty understanding _____. Today, you seem to have had far less difficulty. Why do you think that's so?

All of these questions encourage metacognition in students. As we suggested in Chapter 3, such questions encourage them to be more aware of comprehension and how they go about the process of comprehension. Over time, the attention you give to students' comprehension processes through such interview questions may help them become better able to be reflective and self-assess their own comprehension.

thinking aloud

Think-alouds are "verbalizations of a reader's thoughts before, during, and after reading" (Brown & Lytle, 1988). The verbalizations may be spontaneous responses to reading text, a natural part of a comprehension activity, or procedurally encouraged in a think-aloud performance sample.

Think-alouds must be interpreted, usually by looking for patterns in what students say. In isolation, the reactions students verbalize have no significance; in context you will begin to see significance in them. An example: Rhodes (1979) did a study of ten first graders as they read two more and two less predictable texts. Almost all of the first graders commented spontaneously while reading the texts aloud. Although there were no apparent patterns in what individual children commented on, there were distinct patterns in what the children said as they read the more predictable books when compared with what they said as they read the less predictable books. Here are representative samples; see if you can discern the patterns.

Think-Alouds: More Predictable Texts

"Look what he's trying to do—pull out the leaf."
"He's going to trick him!"
"That's a new word I learned."
"Oh, I've never seen a wolf do that!"
"This is a funny story."
"If I were him, I wouldn't do that."
"I can't read all these words."
"The brick one [house] is safer."
"I hate this [the word 'granddaughter']."
"That's the end."

Think-Alouds: Less Predictable Texts

"I had that word. I forgot it."
"There's a lot of words I'm skipping because I have to."
"I don't know that word."
"I don't know where to go up to [how far to read]."
"Skip. I'll skip that over. I can't read it."
"He's taking it all."
"Now, I'm ready for the very last page."
"That's the end" [said after first two pages as a joke].
"I never had that word before."
"If this didn't stand for Mr., it'd be m+r+r+r."

You have probably figured out that the majority of the comments made in response to the more predictable texts (64 percent in the study) had to do with the meaning of the texts, while the majority of the comments made in response to the less predictable texts (67 percent in the study) had to do with word recognition. On the other hand, only 27 percent of the comments from the more predictable texts were about word recognition and only 7 percent of the comments from the less predictable texts were about meaning. The remainder of the comments (9 percent in more predictable and 26 percent in less predictable) were "situational," almost always having to do with keeping place in the story or determining the end of the story.

Think-alouds also occur naturally during many comprehension activities and can be most easily observed when students work cooperatively on these activities. Asking students to make prereading predictions about a text on the basis of its title and illustrations provides a great deal of think-aloud data. So does an activity such as preparing a Readers' Theatre script or reading and rereading the directions for an experiment in order to follow them. As the students talk together over the text, they refer back to its ideas and to the text itself, often thinking aloud about what it means. When students don't spontaneously talk about the reasons behind their meanings or the strategies they are using to comprehend the text, a few well-placed "Whys?" will usually encourage more strategy-oriented think-alouds.

■ procedures for eliciting think-alouds

If more detailed or formal data are required, teachers might use think-aloud procedures like those that follow. These procedures may also be used during instruction to help students monitor their own comprehension. Strategies such as "Say Something" (Harste, Short, & Burke, 1988, pp. 336–339) are instructional adaptations of these procedures.

1. Tell students that you want them to think aloud while reading and why you want them to do so.

   When you explain to students why you want them to think aloud, focus on how thinking aloud will benefit them. Thinking aloud increases their interaction with the text, thereby assisting them in comprehending more effectively. Of course, you can also use information gathered during the think-aloud for assessment. The students are more likely to provide less self-conscious and more natural information if you help them understand how thinking aloud benefits comprehension. Students also become more skilled at verbalizing their thoughts as they gain experience in doing so.

2. Show students where you want them to stop as they read the text in order to think aloud.

   Students can stop and think aloud almost anywhere, even before they begin reading. The stopping places and the amount of text between them will likely affect the kind and the amount of thinking aloud students do. In general, the more information you want, the more frequently the students should be asked to think aloud. On the other hand, you need to balance that concern with interrupting students' reading so much that it interferes with their comprehension.

   Teachers can try having students stop at places of their own choice or at the end of each page, paragraph, incident, sentence, subtitled section of text, and so on. Some students may require a mark at the places where they are to stop in order to remember to do so. In such cases, decide which points in the text are natural places for *you* as a reader to stop and think, and place the marks there. The stopping places you decide on or suggest will depend on the nature of the text (Is it sectioned in some way?) and on your knowledge of the students (Do they know what a paragraph is?).

   We have found it helpful to put a red star or dot in the text at natural thinking points to remind students to talk about what they are reading and thinking. In addition, some students benefit from a written reminder like this to refer to:

   When you see a red star, talk about:
       a. What you have read.
       b. What you were thinking about as you were reading.

3. Demonstrate and explain how to think aloud.

   You need to show and explain to students how thinking aloud works. The student reads silently and at each stopping point, he talks about the content of the text and what he was doing and thinking while reading it. In one study, the researcher directed the students to "talk about what happened in the story and about what you were doing and thinking as you read it" (Olshavsky, 1977).

In another study (Lytle, 1982, as discussed in Bean, 1988; Brown & Lytle, 1988), which looked at students' use of text structure, the researcher asked the students to "voice thoughts as news bulletins or play-by-play accounts of where you are intellectually as you figure out what the reading is about." These directions were designed for high school students. The younger your students are, the more you will want to demonstrate these strategies, and explain them in terms that are comprehensible to your students.

You can demonstrate thinking aloud as you read stories to children. If you think aloud during story time on a regular basis, the students will become familiar with how "thinking aloud" sounds and perhaps learn some new ways of thinking about text. You can also encourage them to think aloud during story time by inquiring what they were thinking as you read.

4. Have the student read the text.

In the case of think-alouds, the text is generally read silently. However, it could be read orally if you want to observe the interaction between the student's miscues and the think-aloud protocols he produces.

The think-alouds that follow were produced by Billy Jo and Allen, two sixth-grade boys identified as learning disabled, as they silently read "The Bicycle and How It Works" (Urguhart, 1981). So that you can follow what they were thinking as they read, the section of text the students commented about immediately precedes the think-aloud transcriptions.

> The year was 1816. There were no airplanes, no trains, and no cars. How did people get around? They walked, they rode on the backs of animals, or they used wagons or carriages. Then one day Baron Karl Drais Von Sauerbronn of Germany got tired of touring his land on foot or by carriage. He wanted a new and easier way to get around. So what did he do? He invented the bicycle.

Billy Jo: This is when they didn't have no cars, no planes, no trains, no nothin'. They just rode on horses pulling wagons and they rode on the back of horses and stuff; and then one day, Da, Dave V—, Van—. [Looks back at name in story.] Well, Dave, he got tired of walking so he invented the bicycle.

Allen: He was talkin' about, a long time ago, they didn't have any cars or anything. They had to ride on animals. And they finally invented a bicycle. I's thinking . . . I'd like to ride on a horse.

Teacher: What were you thinking about as you read it?

Billy Jo: Mmmm . . . If he wouldn't have got tired on his feet, there wouldn't be no such things as bikes! And if he wouldn't have invented the bike, there wouldn't be no bikes if he wouldn't have got tired like he did. So it's just about all tiredness, from walking.

The baron's bicycle was an immediate success. Within a few years, it began to be used in many different countries. But back then, a bicycle wasn't cheap. Believe it or not, in the 1800s, a bicycle cost the same as what $2,400 is in today's money. It took many years to develop a bicycle that was inexpensive enough for most people to buy.

Billy Jo: [pointing to text section] This one right here, in the 1800s a bicycle cost $2,400 and I think that if it cost that much, I wouldn't buy one! I wouldn't have enough m—, ooh, that's a big paragraph next! And I think if I had to buy a bike for that much, I think I'd be getting ripped off! [Laughter]

Allen: Back then, there wasn't a bicycle that was cheap. And I's thinking I wished there'd be [a] cheap [one].

Have you ever thought about how a bicycle is put together? Have you ever wondered how it works? A bicycle looks as though it is just a simple metal frame joining two wheels, with handlebars at the front and pedals. Each part may seem simple, but making it all work together took a lot of effort and a lot of thought. A frame without wheels would be useless because it wouldn't move. Wheels without brakes would be dangerous and difficult to stop. Brakes, wheels, and a frame without handlebars would be impossible to steer. Each part of the bicycle is important for the role it plays in the way the whole machine works.

Billy Jo: This one right here, it tells you about when they had the bicycle and there was no brakes. So Dave, he came up and invented brakes and it was a lot of work to invent them, to invent brakes. And I think if I didn't have brakes, like my bike does now, I'd still ride it, but in just a little bit they invented brakes, so nobody had to worry about stopping.

Allen: It's talkin' about each part that you put on the bicycle. They look simple but it ain't. And I's thinking . . . I'd want to put a bike together, too.

The frame of a bicycle holds all its parts together, much as your skeleton holds the parts of your body together. The frame should be both as strong and as light as possible. The first bicycle frame was made of wood. It held together two wheels, which were also made of wood. Later, steel and aluminum frames replaced the wood frames but steel was too heavy and aluminum was not strong enough. Finally, hollow steel was used as a frame. It was strong, it would not bend, and it weighed very little. So far, hollow steel has proved to be the best material with which to make bicycle frames.

Did you know that today most bicycles weigh about thirty pounds? Racing bicycles weigh even less. But years ago, bicycles weighed sixty pounds or more.

Billy Jo: The bike that they invented, it kept on falling apart because it was out of wood, and then all of sudden they invented the, they got steel, and then they started making bicycles out of steel. And I think that whoev—, it didn't say who got the steel, who got the idea to make the bike steel but I think it's pretty smart to do that.

Allen: In the olden days, it was, the bicycles was made out of wood. And I was thinking I'd rather have a metal bike than a wood bike.

We've seen what a bicycle frame is made of. But a bicycle can't go very far with just a frame. It needs wheels.

Take a look at the picture below. Do you see the hub? The hub is the center of the wheel. Do you see the axle? The axle is a metal bar inside the hub. The wheel turns on the axle. Do you see the rim of the wheel? The rim is the outside part of the wheel. It holds the rubber tire in place.

Now look at the spokes. The spokes are thick metal rods that connect the rim to the hub of the wheel. Spokes make the wheel stronger.

Billy Jo: When they invented the frame, they had to have something to make it, they can't just go on frames, so they invented the wheel with steel spokes and a wheel like a hub, like a hubcap, and then when they invented it, the whole thing was a lot better like that. And I think when they made the wheels steel, it made the whole thing a lot better to work with.

Allen: Oh, they's talkin' about the spo-, the spokes make the wheels stronger. And I's thinking . . . I wouldn't know how to, um, put a wheel on a bike.

Teacher: Is that what you were thinking as you were reading?

Billy Jo: It's so they can get like better when, like now, our rims are alunimin [sic] or whatever and steel, and back then they only had steel wheels. And then I think in the time being, whoever invented the aluminin [sic] wheel wanted to make the bike lighter. That's what I think.

In early days, wheels were made of wood and rimmed with iron. Imagine how uncomfortable that would be to ride on! These kinds of wheels could not absorb the bumps on road surfaces. In fact, bicycles that had these wooden wheels were called "boneshakers." That's because when you rode one of these bikes, you felt as though your bones were shaking.

Billy Jo: Back then all they had for wheels were wood, and then they invented steel but they had wood. And when they had wood, the wood always fell apart and it would break on them, so they invented the steel wheel. Let me see what I think . . . I was thinking since they had wooden wheels and then they came to the steel wheel and then they came to the alumunin [sic] wheel, probably the same person probably made all of the same wheels. If he lived long enough. That's what I was thinking.

Allen: They's talkin' about if you rode a wooden bike, your bones'd feel weird. And I was thinking . . . I wouldn't like my bones feeling weird. [Laughter]

Old-time tires weren't comfortable to ride on either. They were very hard. They were made of solid rubber. Then in 1888 rubber tires filled with air were invented. This type of tire is still used today. Air-filled tires are a great deal more comfortable to ride on. They are able to "give" with the road surface. This means they form an air cushion. The air cushion makes the ride smoother.

Billy Jo: This guy named Robert, he finally invented solid rubber to put air in, so you could put air in tires. And I think if it wasn't for Robert, all we would have is solid wheels, that's all we would have. [Long-drawn-out whisper] Wow!

Allen: 1888, rubber tires was filled with air and I's thinking. . . .

Teacher: You were thinking what?

Allen: I wasn't thinkin' of nothin'.

Tape-recording the think-alouds (as we have done) allows you to look for patterns in what each student has said. It may take you a while to develop an ear for patterns. As an alternative, jot down as much of what the student says as you can so that you have at least a partial written record. Of course, the more you analyze the think-alouds produced by students, the more easily you will be able to spot the patterns that are helpful to you in making instructional decisions. Take a few minutes and analyze Billy Jo's and Allen's think-alouds; make some notes about what you observe so that you can compare your analysis with ours in the next section.

If you feel that a student's think-alouds are inadequate, consider intervening to supply the support you believe will help the student produce more informative protocols. (A reminder like the one on page 224 will tell him what to do at each think-aloud point; such a chart was available to Billy Jo and Allen while they were reading.) You may find that the student produces a great deal of information about content but little about what he was doing to comprehend the text. If that's the case, you may want to ask direct questions to elicit more about the student's text processing.

You may also hear things that puzzle you as the student thinks aloud. We have found it is best to take notes and ask the student about those items after the reading. If you ask during the reading, you are likely to miss the opportunity to observe the student figure out the puzzling information on his own at a later point in the text. It is also difficult to avoid giving away information if you question the student about content during the reading. The student may rely on that information or assume it is so important that it becomes the focus of the remainder of the reading.

analysis of think-alouds

To begin, we'll analyze Billy Jo's and Allen's think-alouds as a way of elucidating how an analysis of think-aloud data might be conducted and what information might result. Like other data analysis, think-aloud analysis is dependent on your questions and interests as they relate to comprehension. As you will see, we were interested in finding out not only how well the boys' think-alouds reflected the author's intent and message but also what strategies the boys used in constructing meaning from the text. As you read, compare your own analysis with ours.

What struck us first was that both boys reveal a basic understanding of the author's intent and message. Allen's brief think-alouds reveal that he had the ability to summarize the main point of the section ("It's talkin' about each part that you put on the bicycle. They look simple but it ain't."). Allen's brevity was not always the result of summarizing, however. Sometimes, his think-aloud consisted only of one detail from the section, sometimes the last one. Thus, although Allen has the ability to summarize, he doesn't consistently use summarization in thinking about text.

Billy Jo's think-alouds include more of the author's detail than Allen's. We were also struck by Billy Jo's involvement in the text. There was wonder in his voice as he thought aloud about someone inventing something, why they did so, and how that invention had affected his life. Some of this wonder and interest is only apparent on the tape, although there is evidence even in the written transcript ("I think it's pretty smart to do that."). Even when the author did not provide reasons or only alluded to reasons for some of the refinements to bicycle design, Billy Jo did so overtly ("It made the whole thing a lot better to work with."). In contrast, Allen did not generate his own reasons and seldom repeated the author's reasons for why the bicycle is put together the way it is or how it was refined.

Both boys made connections between the text and their own lives. Billy Jo's think-alouds were usually connected closely to the author's intent. Allen's think-alouds contained highly personal connections ("I wouldn't like my bones feeling weird" and "I'd like to ride on a horse").

It is interesting that Billy Jo structures his think-alouds around the people who invented and refined the bicycle. In the first paragraph of the text, the author names the German inventor of the bicycle, and, although the author does not identify particular people as responsible for the refinement of the bicycle over time, Billy Jo does. He identifies "Dave" (his name for the German inventor) as responsible for inventing brakes, refers to "who got the idea to make the bike steel," "whoever invented the aluminum wheel," "probably the same person made all of the same wheels," and then fabricates "a guy named Robert" as responsible for the invention of air-filled tires. If Billy Jo had written the text, he probably would have structured it differently than the author did in order to highlight his own obvious interest in the people who invent things.

If you found your analysis of Billy Jo's and Allen's think-alouds difficult, you may find it helpful to study how some researchers have analyzed students' think-alouds. The frameworks created by Cakmak, Chase, & Kelleher (1989), Lytle (1982), Olshavsky (1977), and White (1980) are helpful in thinking about what to look for in think-aloud protocols. We'll use Olshavsky's framework to extend our analysis of Billy Jo's and Allen's think-alouds.

Olshavsky defines a strategy as "a purposeful means of comprehending the author's message" (Olshavsky, 1977, p. 656). By examining the think-alouds produced by the tenth graders in her study, she identified the following commonly used strategies. Examples of each strategy may be found in Olshavsky (1977).

1. Use of context to define a word: Reader uses information in the text to figure out the meaning of an unknown word.

2. Synonym substitution: When describing the content of the story, the reader uses a synonym in place of a word in the text.

3. Stated failure to understand a word: Reader identifies a word for which he cannot figure out a meaning.

4. Rereading: Reader states that he reads a portion of the text more than once.

5. Inference: Reader generates an interpretation on the basis of information in the story.

6. Addition of information: Reader adds information that was not in the text.

7. Personal identification: Reader makes a personal association with information in the text.

8. Hypothesis: Reader predicts meaning of the text, usually what will occur next.

9. Stated failure to understand clause: Reader identifies a clause for which he cannot figure out a meaning.

10. Use of information about the story: Reader relates information from part of the story to the theme of the story as a whole.

Using this framework, we can tentatively say the following about Billy Jo's and Allen's use of each strategy:

1. Use of context to define a word: Except for the inventor's name, which Billy Jo struggles with briefly, neither boy comments about using information in the text to figure out the meanings of unknown words.

2. Synonym substitution: Both boys make such substitutions. In the first section of the text, the author refers to people "riding on the backs of animals";

Allen comments about wanting to ride "on a horse" and Billy Jo comments about riding "on the back of horses."

3. Stated failure to understand a word: Neither boy identifies any word he didn't understand.

4. Rereading: Neither boy states that he reread a portion of the text nor do observations of their silent reading reveal such a strategy.

5. Inference: Billy Jo's think-alouds reveal a number of inferences that are not observable in Allen's. For example, Billy Jo comments that it must have been a lot of work to invent brakes, and he decides that one person could have invented wood, steel, and then aluminum wheels if the person had lived long enough.

6. Addition of information: Allen's think-alouds add no information. Instead he retells or summarizes what he has read. In contrast, Billy Jo adds information several times: he comments, for example, that "Dave" should be really important for inventing the bicycle but that he's pretty sure no one has ever heard of him.

7. Personal identification: Although both boys made comments that could be classified as "personal identification," Allen makes them more frequently ("I's thinking . . . I'd want to put a bike together, too."). Billy Jo's comments are more directly related to the author's point (how he'd feel ripped off having to pay $2,400 for a bike).

8. Hypothesis: Neither boy makes any predictions about upcoming text.

9. Stated failure to understand clause: As with words, neither boy identifies clauses for which they cannot figure out meaning.

10. Use of information about the story: Billy Jo's insistence on structuring the story around inventors' names and natures is an interesting example of relating information from part of the story (in this case, the first paragraph) to the story as a whole. Allen reveals no evidence of doing this.

We find Olshavsky's framework helpful in considering what else we could observe about a student's think-aloud, especially in the area of the strategies the student used during reading. When there is no evidence of certain strategies, you may overlook their importance. As an example, the framework helped bring to our attention the fact that neither boy reveals any evidence of monitoring his own comprehension, of bumping into or dealing with comprehension difficulties at a word or clause level. We cannot conclude that this means that the boys do not have comprehension difficulties or, if they do have them, that they deal with them ineffectively. But it does raise a question in our minds about the issue and helps us to realize that it's something we could explore in other assessments of the boys' reading.

On the other hand, we encourage you to go beyond frameworks like Olshavsky's in analyzing think-alouds. The information provided in think-alouds is not always easily categorized and should not be overlooked because a particular framework is used to examine students' reading. We made a number of observations about the boys' think-alouds (we're sure you made them too) that we would not have captured had we used only Olshavsky's framework.

Think-alouds have rich potential for assessing comprehension and for observing strategies students use in comprehending text. Analysis can focus on students, but think-alouds can also be helpful in understanding the effects of the text or the situation on students' comprehension in order to adjust them in ways that will improve comprehension.

■ ■

retelling

Unlike interviews and think-alouds, which provide in-process information about comprehension, retellings provide information about comprehension as a product. In our view, retellings provide far more information about a student's comprehension than do answers to the more common comprehension questions. You gain insight into if and how a student constructs his own meanings using the text as a blueprint. The student must decide what aspects of the text are important and how to organize the retelling. Retellings allow you to find out what a student knows without the support and the clues provided by your questions. As Johnston (1983) puts it, retellings are "the most straightforward assessment of the result of the text-reader interaction" (p. 54).

At the same time, retellings, like interviews and think-alouds, are messy data. Retellings can be considerably different, even for the same reader and text, depending on the situation in which the retelling is done. No two retellings are alike. In addition, as revealing as retelling a story can be, it can *never* represent a reader's total understanding of a text" (Y. Goodman, Watson, & Burke, 1987, p. 45). Thus, although analyzing a retelling can help us understand some aspects of a student's comprehension of a text, the conclusions we draw must always be conditional, and we must constantly reexamine them in light of other situations in which we observe the student's comprehension.

This section will detail the procedures for eliciting a free retelling and for asking questions afterwards, suggest ways to apply the ideas of dynamic assessment, and present various procedures for analyzing retellings that focus on those most useful to teachers (as opposed to researchers) who have limited time for conducting such analysis.

■ procedures for eliciting a retelling

It is helpful to decide beforehand what it is you want to find out about a student's comprehension; what you want to find out is likely to affect how you elicit the retelling. For example, you can find out:

- What the student thinks it is important to remember.

- What the student thinks it is important to retell.

- If the student's retelling fits the purposes set for reading.

- How the student structured and sequenced the retelling and if the structure and sequence matched that of the text.

- To what degree the student's responses are text-based or reader-based.

- How important the information that was retold was.

- How close the match between the text and the retelling was.

Retellings can be performance samples; the procedures we discuss are designed for that purpose. However, retelling is often a natural part of everyday classroom activities and certainly can be assessed in such circumstances by the observant teacher. In fact, Brown & Cambourne (1987) have devised an instructional procedure for groups of children that can easily be used for assessment, including student self-assessment. As we outline performance sample procedures, we'll attempt to elucidate how they might be varied or used in more naturalistic situations.

1. Select a text to read.

   Keep in mind such factors as the student's background and what you want to learn about the student's comprehension as you select reading material for a retelling. The student can also select a text on his own, which allows you to assess the student's comprehension of self-selected material.

2. Before the student reads the text, let him know that you will request a retelling after the reading.

   This step may be unnecessary if the student does a retelling as part of a classroom activity rather than in a more formal situation. In a Reading Workshop where the teacher holds individual conferences with students who are reading a variety of books, the students may be accustomed to summarizing what they are reading at the beginning of each conference.

   Students can be encouraged to retell a text for many authentic reasons. Whether the student views the retelling as an authentic activity or as a comprehension test (Harste & Burke, 1979) ought to be taken into account. Retelling a story for a friend who is looking for a good book to read is likely to produce different results than retelling a text for a teacher who is checking the student's comprehension.

3. The student reads the text.

   Unless you are also doing a miscue analysis, ask the student to read the text silently, allowing as much time as the student needs. (It may be useful to make a note about the length of time it takes the student to read the text.) Of course, when the student is required to read both orally and silently as part of everyday activities, comprehension ought to be assessed under both circumstances. If a retelling following silent reading is poor, have the student read another text or the same text again orally to see if comprehension is better. If a retelling following oral reading is poor, have the student read another text or the same text again silently. It is also possible to read the text to the student in order to assess listening comprehension. Then the student's listening and reading comprehension can be compared.

4. After the student has finished reading the text, ask him to put it aside and retell everything he can remember.

Although the procedure of setting aside the text is most often recommended, it sometimes leaves the impression of a "test." There are a number of other ways you might proceed that are less testlike and that may make it unnecessary to say anything about putting the book aside. For example, a student who decides to give his friend a story summary so he'll read a favorite book is unlikely to look back at the book in telling his friend about it. Nor is a student likely to look back at the book while reenacting a story with felt story characters on a flannel board.

When a student is provided with the opportunity to look back, it is interesting to observe how (or if) the student goes about the process of recovering information; poor readers often do not profit from look-backs (Davey, 1989). Even if you begin with a closed book retelling, you may want to allow look-backs if the student clearly needs some support for the retelling; that way you'll find out what a student is able to do in instructional situations in which readers can look back to remember and organize information.

Though it is best simply to listen after requesting a retelling, sometimes a student needs greater support. When necessary, give the student a prompt that encourages him to begin ("How about starting with 'Once upon a time?'") or to continue ("Then what happened?").

When a student has serious difficulty retelling a story, you will get information that will be helpful in instructional planning if you use the principle of dynamic assessment. Provide instruction you think will increase the student's comprehension and then observe its impact in a subsequent retelling. For example, you might ask the student to preview text features such as title and pictures to make predictions or formulate questions that will most likely be answered by the author. Or you may provide an overview of the structure of the story: "In this story, the main character has a problem. Figure out what it is. Then see how the character tries to solve and finally does solve the problem." After providing instructional support, ask the student to reread the story and retell it again.

5. Tape-record the retelling.

Tape-recording oral retellings allows you to recover information about the student's retelling you will not be able to acquire in any other way, but it is not always possible. If you observe a book discussion in which one student spontaneously does a retelling of a chapter for another student who didn't read it, it's impossible to insert a microphone into the middle of the retelling without changing it. In such cases, taking notes on the content of the retelling must suffice. If you have analyzed retellings more formally in the past, those analyses will guide you in determining what is most useful to listen for and record in such circumstances.

It is also possible to request written retellings from students. Written retellings offer two advantages: many students can produce a written retelling at the same time; and writing produces a product that can be examined in detail. Because writing a retelling slows down the thought processes and because writing can be revised, written retellings are sometimes more coherent than oral retellings. In Brown and Cambourne's (1987) retelling procedures, students compare and contrast each other's written retellings of the same text; in the process, they learn how to produce more effective retellings. However, especially when a student does not write fluently, the written retelling is apt to be a truncated version of what the student could have produced orally.

Written summaries are a type of written retelling; if produced effectively, a summary is shorter than a retelling and contains only the most important ideas instead of all that the student can remember. If a student has difficulty writing a summary, first check to see if he understands what a summary is, including the difference between a summary and a retelling of the whole text. You may also need to support the student by helping him identify important ideas in the text and underline them. Then assess the student's ability to compose a summary using the underlined ideas. This dynamic assessment allows you to discover the level and kind of support the student needs in order to be successful at such tasks.

6. When the student appears to have completed his retelling or indicates that he is finished, ask the student if there is anything more he would like to add.

Again, this is only possible in some circumstances. If it is possible, suggest that the student take a moment to think about what he read and consider whether any more can be said about the story. Give the student some thinking time; it is likely that more retelling will be forthcoming if you simply wait for it.

7. If desired, follow the free retelling with a guided retelling or questions.

Consider whether you want to elicit any further information and whether the circumstances permit it. In order to elicit more information, ask questions and allow the student to look back at the text to see if pictures or skimming the text provides support. Y. Goodman, Watson, & Burke (1987) suggest asking questions that directly follow up on what the student has already said and utilize only information already provided by the student. If the student retold the first and third of three episodes, you might say, "You told us about (first episode) and (third episode). What happened in between those two things?" Some helpful questions (from Y. Goodman, Watson, & Burke, 1987, p. 47) include:

Tell more about _____.

Why do you think _____ happened?

What problem was the story concerned with?

Describe _____ at the beginning of the story and describe _____ at the end of the story.

What happened after _____?

What do you think the author was trying to teach you?

Why do you think _____ did that?

It is also possible to use the analysis scheme you have chosen to help you determine the best questions to ask. If you are analyzing students' recall of story structure elements and a student has neglected to mention one, such as the setting, you could ask where and when the story took place. Or if you have divided the text into "pausal units" (see Clark (1982) later in our discussion), you can use the importance level of the units to determine what you want to ask the student about in your questions.

8. Analyze the retelling.

Such a short sentence for such a complex task! Analyzing a retelling requires thoughtful and specific decisions about what you want to assess. Thus, you have to reflect again on what it is you wanted to find out about the student's comprehension. Analysis can also be time-consuming. In general, the more detailed information you want from students' retellings, the more analysis time is required. There are many assumptions underlying the decision to analyze a retelling and how it is to be analyzed that are worrisome, given our knowledge about comprehension and about how students display comprehension. We will say more about this later.

When retellings are a spontaneous (rather than elicited) part of a literacy activity, the analysis of the retelling will probably be impressionistic, but it can also be guided by specific criteria. What is recorded is the result of the analysis. Here are anecdotal records from two different spontaneous retellings:

> Retelling of two chapters of *Indian in the Cupboard:* Andrew to David (sick & missed chapters yesterday). Great detail, even using some of the language of the story. Best retelling I've ever heard from A.—could be interest in story or that he had a real reason to retell well since D. really wanted to know what he had missed.

> Paired kids to retell what we had read yesterday before we went on. Heard Armisha spontaneously using "problem" & "solution" as if they were old familiar terms!

The specific criteria the teacher applied in listening to the *Indian in the Cupboard* retelling included the amount of detail, and the fact that the student recalled actual language from the story. On the other hand, she also recorded her impression that it was Andrew's best retelling. Recording her explanations will help her to consider good retelling situations in the future. In the second retelling note, it is clear that the teacher has taught the students about story elements and that what she has taught is guiding what she observes and records.

If the teacher has tape-recorded retellings, the analysis can be far more specific and detailed. In fact, a number of aspects of the retelling can be analyzed, since the retelling can be listened to as many times as is necessary for various purposes. If there is a reason to do so, all or part of the retelling can even be transcribed from the tape-recording for a closer look or for examples of what the student does.

There are a variety of qualitative and quantitative schemes for analyzing the comprehension displayed in retellings (and in other responses to text). We will present several here, not as schemes for you to adopt (unless they fit your purposes closely) but as alternatives for you to examine on your way to figuring out how you might devise your own schemes to fit your assessment purposes. It is also helpful to study the schemes so that you can fix in your mind what you can listen for when you hear a student retell or otherwise respond to a text.

using a checklist

Many teachers favor a checklist approach in their analysis of retellings, often supplemented with brief anecdotal records. Developing and copying the checklist are the only preparation necessary. However, adding anecdotal notes about the text that is retold, the context in which it is retold, whether the reading was oral or silent, and specific details of the retelling increase the effectiveness of the checklist in planning instruction. The same checklist can frequently be used to record comprehension in other settings: think-alouds, question answering, book discussions and so on. Instead of providing examples of comprehension checklists (these can be found in Hornsby & Sukarna, 1986; Irwin & Baker, 1989; Wood, 1988), we'll provide a list of possible items and formats for such a checklist. Using the items and formats, you can develop your own checklists to fit your instructional goals and circumstances.

The list of checklist items that follows is largely garnered from checklists that teachers have developed in our classes over the years. Note that we've categorized the items under "before," "during," and "after" reading to highlight the fact that comprehension can be assessed throughout the reading process. Some items (such as "uses background knowledge to predict") could appear in more than one category (under "during" in addition to "before" reading).

The list is infinitely malleable; you can add to it, take away from it, and reword any item on it. What you must do is decide which items best reflect your instructional goals and circumstances. We recommend that you avoid overwhelming yourself with items; select those that you consider most important at this time. Rethink the items on your checklist several times during the year. Consider constructing different checklists for different students, for different types of texts, and for different groups of students. (This is easy on a word processor.) Assessment should always fit your instructional purposes, and certainly those purposes will change over time, with texts, and from student to student.

Before Reading

Uses titles, pictures, captions, graphs, blurbs to predict.

Uses background knowledge to predict.

Intrinsically motivated to engage in reading.

During Reading

Is aware when text doesn't make sense.

Uses preceding text to predict.

Reads to answer own questions about text.

Reads "between the lines."

Understands and uses structure of text.

Rereads when comprehension difficult.

Changes reading mode (silent and oral) when comprehension difficult.

Gets help when comprehension difficult.

Reads at an appropriate rate for the text.

Able to identify concepts, language, or vocabulary that interfere with comprehension.

Searches efficiently for specific information.

After Reading

Extends comprehension through writing.

Extends comprehension through discussion.

Recalls important information.

Recalls sufficient information.

Summarizes main points.

Adjusts what is shared about the text for the audience.

Identifies story elements in text (characters, setting, problem, episodes, resolution).

States appropriate theme for story.

Uses text to support statements and conclusions.

Compares characters in text.

Retells fluently (length and coherence).

Links story episodes in narrative text; facts in expository text.

Uses author's language in retelling.

Uses own "voice" in retelling.

Before, During, or After Reading

Compares characters or incidents to self or experiences.

Compares this text to other texts.

Compares this text to media other than text.

Uses text to support statements and conclusions.

Identifies point-of-view.

Distinguishes between fact and opinion.

There are several checklist formats that teachers find useful. We'll present three formats along with some comments about the kind of situation in which each is likely to be most useful. Checklist items such as those above may be inserted in each of the formats where the phrase "checklist items" appears. The three formats are available for copying in *Literacy Assessment: A Handbook of Instruments* (Rhodes, 1993).

The first format (see Figure 5.1), a multiple-setting checklist for a single student, requires a copy for each student you want to assess. The advantage of using one checklist per student is that it is easy to spot progress or differences in the student's performance across time and in different contexts. Each vertical slot is labeled with the text and the date. You will need to develop descriptors and corresponding

Name _____

Checklist Items	Text read and date						

Notes

Date:

Date:

Date:

Date:

Figure 5.1   Multiple-setting checklist for a single student

| Name _____ | | Date _____ |

Title of text _____

Context _____

Checklist Items	+ ✓ − 0	Comments

Figure 5.2   Single-setting checklist for one student

marks to fill in the blanks (such as **+** : to a great extent; **✓**: to some extent; **−**: not at all; blank space or **0:** not observed in this setting). You may not observe a behavior in a particular setting because it was not appropriate in the setting, because the text was not conducive to the behavior, or because you were not present at the time the behavior was likely to have been observed. The notes at the end may include details not incorporated in the checklist but important for instructional planning, such as the context in which comprehension was assessed.

Title of text ______________________________

Date ____________ Context ______________________

Checklist Items	Students' Names							

Notes

Figure 5.3 Single-setting checklist for a group of students

The next format (see Figure 5.2), a single-setting checklist for one student, is useful in situations in which the teacher does more formal retelling analyses, probably on a regularly scheduled basis. (Denver Chapter I teachers collected retelling data in September, January, and May.) This format may also be useful with the students you are most concerned about in a regular classroom; you may find you need more detailed information in order to provide information to others or to plan instruction more effectively. Comparing the data on one checklist to data on another over time allows you to see progress or lack of progress in a student's retelling.

Student's name _____ Date _____

_____

Title of text _____

Context for retelling _____

Setting
   a. Begins story with introduction   <u>*1*</u>
   b. Names main character   <u>*1*</u>
   c. Number of other characters recalled   <u>*2*</u>
   d. Actual number of other characters   <u>*4*</u>
   e. Score for other characters (c/d)   <u>.5</u>
   f. Includes statement about time or place   <u>*1*</u>

Plot
   Refers to main character's goal or problem   <u>*1*</u>

Episodes
   a. Number of episodes recalled   <u>*4*</u>
   b. Actual number of episodes   <u>*5*</u>
   c. Score for episodes (a/b)   <u>.8</u>

Resolution
   a. Identifies solution to problem or goal attainment   <u>*1*</u>
   b. Ends story   <u>*1*</u>

Sequence
   Retells story in structural order: setting,
   plot, episodes, and resolution   <u>*1*</u>

   Highest score possible <u>10</u>   **Student's score**   *8.3*

Figure 5.4   Figuring a student's score

Again, you will need to develop descriptors and corresponding marks to use in the blanks. However, unlike the previous format, there is space for a comment about each checklist item. The comments should be recorded with the idea that they can provide clues about how to support the student's comprehension development.

The last checklist format (see Figure 5.3), a single-setting checklist for a group of students, is useful for teachers who want to collect information about students' comprehension during group literacy events such as book discussions. The checklist is designed to be used during one such setting and helps the teacher record data about the comprehension of each individual in the group. Of course, the problem with such a checklist and such a setting is that there is little time to record the detailed information that might be helpful in planning instruction for specific youngsters. At the same time, it does give the teacher a picture of how each student functions in a group setting. Again, you will need to develop descriptors and corresponding marks.

▓ assessing sense of story structure

As we suggested earlier, one aspect of a student's comprehension that can be assessed through retellings is the student's organization of recalled information (that is, use of story structure and sequences). The assessment may be done impressionistically or by generating an actual score.

Morrow's analysis (Morrow, 1988) of story structure produces a score. In order to conduct the analysis, the teacher summarizes each of the units that makes up the structure of a story or narrative: setting, plot or problem, episodes, and resolution. If the story is short enough, the teacher breaks the text itself into these units instead of summarizing.

After the student retells the story, the retelling is compared to the identified units in order to determine whether the student included each of the structural elements of the story. In addition, the student's sequencing of the story elements is compared with the sequence found in the text. The scheme in Figure 5.4 (adapted from Morrow, 1988) is used to figure the student's score.

Morrow's method for analyzing retellings is useful if the text being analyzed is a narrative and if story structure is the important feature the teacher wants to analyze. (No one has proposed such a retelling analysis for the various structures of expository material; we challenge you to try it.)

The units of Morrow's analysis are broad enough that a teacher experienced with the scheme could score the student's retelling without resorting to a tape-recording or written summary of story units. With a few notes about the characters and episodes the student mentions, the teacher can figure the derived scores at a later point. The advantage of this analysis scheme is that the same method can be applied to any narrative (unless it is poorly written and lacking some of the story elements). Thus, the teacher need only locate a sheet prepared with the above scheme in order to score even a spontaneous narrative retelling.

Story structure can also be scored more globally by giving each story structure unit a 1 (low) to 5 (high) score. The retelling scheme from the Classroom Reading Miscue Inventory is an example:

Setting	_____
Characters	_____
Problem	_____
Episodes	_____
Resolution	_____
Sequence	_____

A similar analytic scoring method using story structure descriptors may be found in Marshall (1983). It is set up in such a way that numerous students' retellings could be scored four times during the year.

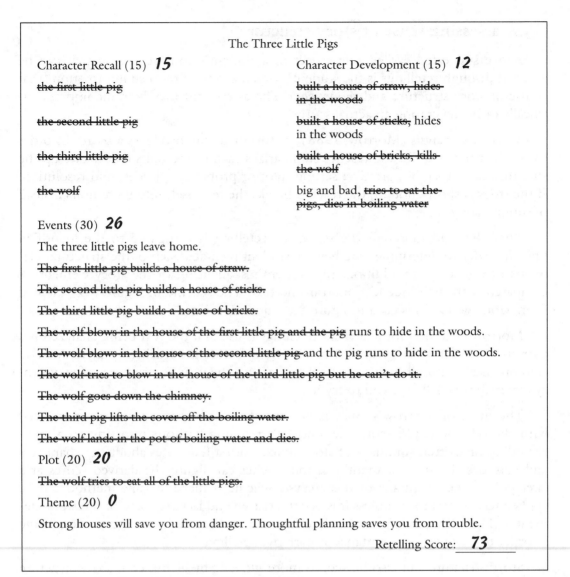

The Three Little Pigs

Character Recall (15) **15**

~~the first little pig~~

~~the second little pig~~

~~the third little pig~~

~~the wolf~~

Character Development (15) **12**

~~built a house of straw, hides in the woods~~

~~built a house of sticks,~~ hides in the woods

~~built a house of bricks, kills the wolf~~

big and bad, ~~tries to eat the pigs, dies in boiling water~~

Events (30) **26**

The three little pigs leave home.

~~The first little pig builds a house of straw.~~

~~The second little pig builds a house of sticks.~~

~~The third little pig builds a house of bricks.~~

~~The wolf blows in the house of the first little pig and the pig~~ runs to hide in the woods.

~~The wolf blows in the house of the second little pig~~ and the pig runs to hide in the woods.

~~The wolf tries to blow in the house of the third little pig but he can't do it.~~

~~The wolf goes down the chimney.~~

~~The third pig lifts the cover off the boiling water.~~

~~The wolf lands in the pot of boiling water and dies.~~

Plot (20) **20**

~~The wolf tries to eat all of the little pigs.~~

Theme (20) **0**

Strong houses will save you from danger. Thoughtful planning saves you from trouble.

Retelling Score: **73**

Figure 5.5   Retelling outline for *The Three Little Pigs*

content assessment

Probably the most common way to assess a student's retelling is to analyze its content, particularly in relationship to the content of the text itself. Unless the content of the retelling is scored holistically, scoring is usually done by comparing the student's retelling with a retelling outline of the text. When using such outlines, whether prepared by you or someone else, you should remember that the outline itself is also a retelling. It is a representation of the text that should be viewed as such when you "match" the student's retelling to it. Since we know that any retelling is only one representation of a text, comparing a student's retelling to a retelling outline is simply comparing one representation of the text to another. "If students produce alternate language, plots, themes, generalizations, or events that are appropriate, they should be considered acceptable options and scored accordingly" (Y. Goodman, Watson, & Burke, 1987, p. 101).

The original miscue analysis manual (Y. Goodman & Burke, 1972) and the revised manual (Y. Goodman, Watson, & Burke, 1987) contain information about developing and using retelling guides which permit you to assess the content match between the outline and the reader's retelling of the text. Typically, narrative outlines are divided into 40 points for character analysis and 60 points for events, while expository outlines are divided into 40 points for specific information, 30 points for generalizations, and 30 points for major concepts. Within each area, such as "events," points may be assigned to each listed item (that is, an event) on the basis of its importance in the text. A marked and scored retelling outline for the story of *The Three Little Pigs* might look like Figure 5.5.

Note that plot and theme receive a score as well as character analysis and events. Lee and Sadoski (1986) suggest that there are advantages to scoring plot and theme. Even if you elect not to score them, anecdotal information on a student's ability to state a plot and theme as part of the retelling should be recorded.

In using retelling outlines such as these, a tape-recording of the retelling to be scored is helpful but not necessary. If you know the story and outline well enough, it is possible to cross out the outline's content as the story is retold (as in *The Three Little Pigs* outline) and to figure the score afterwards. Jotting notes about what the student says may also be helpful. You may want to differentiate information recalled freely from information recalled in response to a question (you can use a straight line to cross out one kind of information and a wavy line to cross out another). A tape-recording should be considered if you plan to share the information with other teachers and with parents. It is much easier for them to understand how you arrived at your conclusions about the student's retellings if you have a tape for them to listen to in whole or in part. Tapes may also become a valuable part of a student's reading folder or portfolio.

Clark (1982) has developed an even more specific scoring system, which requires a written or tape-recorded retelling (see Figure 5.6). First, the text to be read is broken into "pausal units" (those places a good reader would normally pause during oral reading, including at punctuation and connectives), which are listed down the center of a page. To the left, the level of importance of each unit is indicated by a 1, a 2, or a 3. (Clark recommends that what you consider the most important units be assigned a 1, what you consider the least important units be a 3, and each of the remaining units a 2.)

To the right of each pausal unit is a blank. As the student retells what has been read, numbers are recorded in the blank for each pausal unit recalled. The first pausal unit recalled is assigned a 1, the second a 2, and so on (note that the first pausal unit recalled may be the fourth pausal unit listed). The blanks next to pausal units that are not recalled are left unmarked. In using Clark's system, we have sometimes simply placed a check in these blanks without keeping track of the sequence in which the students retold each unit.

On the basis of these data, the percentage of pausal units recalled may be calculated as well as the mean importance level of the recalled units. In addition, if you decided to record the sequence in which the students retold the text, it can be evaluated holistically.

If the teacher asks questions after the free retelling, Clark recommends that the importance level of the pausal unit be used to determine what might be asked. That is, the questions should be related to the most important ideas in the text. Answers to such questions can be recorded by placing an X or some other mark on the blank to the right of the pausal unit as shown in Figure 5.6. In this way, you can determine to what extent the student knew information not recalled in the free retelling situation.

Clark's retelling analysis is more detailed and time-consuming than most teachers will find useful, but it has several advantages. First, it is straightforward and can be done with either narrative or expository text. Second, the quantitative results can be helpful in some situations. It measures a student's recall of ideas at various levels of importance and can reveal differences between information freely recalled and information recalled in response to questioning. The analysis can be done over time, yielding information about how a student's comprehension varies with types of text and how the student is progressing.

Sample of recall (Billy, Grade 4)

Importance number		Pausal unit	Recall sequence
2	1.	The three were growing tired	1
3	2.	from their long journey	2
1	3.	and now they had to cross a river.	3
3	4.	It was wide and deep,	—
1	5.	so they would have to swim across.	4
1	6.	The younger dog plunged into the icy water	—
2	7.	barking for the others to follow him.	—
2	8.	The older dog jumped into the water.	—
3	9.	He was weak	—
3	10.	and suffering from pain,	—
3	11.	but somehow	—
1	12.	he managed to struggle to the opposite bank.	—
2	13.	The poor cat was left alone.	5
1	14.	He was so afraid	6
3	15.	that he ran up and down the bank	—
3	16.	wailing with fear.	—
2	17.	The younger dog swam back and forth	7
2	18.	trying to help.	—
1	19.	Finally,	—
1	20.	the cat jumped	—
2	21.	and began to swim near his friend.	—
3	22.	At that moment,	—
3	23.	something bad happened.	—
3	24.	An old beaver dam from upstream broke.	8
1	25.	The water cam rushing downstream,	—
2	26.	hurling a large log toward the animals.	—
2	27.	It struck the cat	9
1	28.	and swept him helplessly away.	—

Total number of units = 28
Number of units recalled = 9
Percentage recalled = 32%
Sequence evaluation = excellent
Mean importance level recalled = 1.9 (weak)

Figure 5.6   Sample of Clark's system of scoring and retelling

Windows Into Literacy

Different people may define "pausal units" in particular ways, but using specific linguistic analysis is unrealistic and unnecessary for teachers. What is important is that the person who defines the pausal units does so consistently. A publication that may be of help is the *Qualitative Reading Inventory* (Leslie & Caldwell, 1990), which parses graded narrative and expository texts into paraphrased units. You will still need to assign the level of importance of each unit in the various texts.

assessing comprehension within literacy events

A literacy event, in which students share their comprehension of text, can include retelling, thinking aloud, and interviewing. Teachers can assess comprehension during literacy events by using the assessment schemes we've discussed in this chapter or by keeping anecdotal records on what they observe. We'll talk about several kinds of literacy events that teachers commonly use to foster comprehension: prediction activities, discussions of reading material, literature and learning logs, book shares, various literature extension activities such as drama and art, and common comprehension tasks in content area classes. For each kind we'll suggest foci for teachers' assessment as well as ways that students might be involved in assessment.

prediction activities

Prior to reading a text, teachers frequently use techniques that can generally be described as prediction activities. Teachers may ask students who are about to read a novel to look over various features of the text, such as the title, cover illustration, author information, book blurb, and chapter titles. As the students think aloud about their findings, the teacher can record their predictions and questions about the text. Students frequently share information other students do not know and extend each other's ideas on what the book is likely to be about. The generated list of predictions and questions often provides teachers with assessment data about what the students are likely to comprehend and what they are likely to have difficulty with as they read the book.

Teachers can also assess the process by which students preview and use text features to activate their background knowledge and establish their purposes for reading the book. For example, do the students recognize that the author is one whose work they have read earlier and do they use what they know about the author's other writing to generate predictions and questions about the current book? Do the students understand the nature of book blurbs and use them to generate good predictions and questions? Can the students tie various chapter titles together to make well-founded predictions about the events in the book?

Students can also be involved in self-evaluation of their use of these strategies. Before beginning to read a novel but after a lesson in which they preview text features, students could fill out the following self-evaluation:

Name _____ Date _____

Circle the following things you used in coming up with predictions and questions today. Underline one that you think might be helpful to preview when you select a new book to read in the library tomorrow.

book title   book illustrations

chapter titles   author's name

information about author   "blurb" on outside of book

other: _____

Teachers often begin a study of a new topic or a novel with an activity designed to activate related background knowledge. Sometimes teachers decide that it is important to activate knowledge that will allow readers to identify with a character's situation in the book. This was the case with a language arts teacher in an urban middle school who decided to have her classes read *The Sign of the Beaver* (Speare, 1983) in order to support their study of the pioneer days of our country in social studies. The novel features a thirteen-year-old boy who is left to survive on his own in the wilderness for a number of months while his father fetches the remainder of the family.

Before they read the book, the teacher engaged the students in a prereading activity from a curriculum unit (Rhodes et al., 1989) on the book. The students were asked to draw a backpack and fill it with the items they thought would be necessary for surviving six months in the wilderness. By considering what was necessary for survival, they could better identify with the difficulties faced by the boy in the book. Each student drew and labeled items in their backpack.

As she observed the students, the teacher realized that they didn't have realistic notions about wilderness survival. Even after she stopped them to explain that there would be no electrical outlets, they "packed" battery-operated VCRs, TVs, and curling irons. Few students had enough outdoor experience to pack dried food, to consider a water bottle, or to think of such items as a knife or a blanket. Instead, they drew cases of Coke and packages of frozen pizza.

From the assessment data the teacher collected during this activity, she concluded that the students would have a very difficult time understanding the life of a boy on his own in the wilderness. In order to help the students develop more background and awareness, she made an instructional decision to invite a man who had recently returned from an Outward Bound wilderness experience to speak to her classes.

The man brought the backpack he had taken with him and explained the reason for including each item in it. He talked about how he felt about leaving behind television and other modern conveniences and what it was like to gather and trap food. He related how he spent his time and compared it to how he ordinarily spent his time. The students asked many questions that further clarified what a wilderness experience might be like. As they read about the dilemmas faced by the boy in the book, they referred back to the information the guest speaker had provided.

discussions

A common technique teachers use to encourage sharing of ideas and extension of comprehension is discussion. By discussion, however, we do not mean responses to teacher questions. Instead, we mean authentic and thoughtful talk among students (and possibly the teacher) about a text in which students share their understanding with each other and enlarge each other's sense of the text in the process. Eeds and Wells (1989) call such a discussion a "grand conversation."

Students need to know how to engage in discussions, especially if these are to be useful literacy events for assessment. If the teacher must constantly lead the group, he will find it difficult to take notes. If the group can hold a "grand conversation" without the teacher's constant supervision, the teacher has the time to observe and record some of what goes on. Observations can focus on comprehension of the reading material, on the discussion process itself, or on both.

Certainly much can be learned about the meaning students derive from a text as the result of listening to a discussion. During discussions, students frequently retell portions of the text, go back to the text to construct new meaning or to settle disagreements over meaning, think aloud about the meaning of the text and the meaning others have generated, and interview each other in order to clarify or extend thoughts about the text. The conversation is messy data—a variety of people talk, they repeat and build on what other members of the group say, they contradict each other. But, if there is good discussion, the teacher can come away from it with a better understanding of what he needs to address instructionally, and that is what matters.

In addition to assessing comprehension during discussion, teachers can also assess the discussion process itself. This information allows them to decide what the students need to learn in order to carry on more effective discussions. (And once the discussions become more effective, it becomes easier to assess comprehension.)

In order to evaluate discussion, it is necessary to consider the features of an effective conversation. One of the authors asked half of the teachers enrolled in her Children's Literature class to observe as the other half of the students had a discussion about a short story. On the basis of their observations of the discussion process, the teachers generated the list of "Discussion Process Questions" that follow to guide their observation of their own students in classroom discussions.

We recommend that you decide which of the questions are most important for you, given your impression of the current level of discussion skills among your students. The questions are not in any particular order, and some are more sophisticated than others. For example, summarizing what has been said during the discussion is not likely to be of concern if the students haven't yet learned how to stay on topic. The questions you decide to answer as you observe students should change as their discussions become more effective.

1. Are group members participating equally?

2. Is the group talking about the book? If the group gets off task, what strategies do they use to get back on task?

3. Did the group start talking about the book quickly?

4. Are group members clarifying comments when it is appropriate to do so? What strategies are they using (rephrasing, giving examples, asking someone else to say it in another way, etc.)

5. Is discussion staying focused on a topic long enough to develop the topic well?

6. Did anyone in the group provide an unusual insight that expanded the group's thinking about the book? How was that insight treated?

7. What evidence is there that people are listening or not listening to each other?

8. Is the group generalizing from the specifics of the book?

9. Are group members acknowledging each other through techniques such as using each other's names, eye contact, and so on?

10. Are group members inviting comment from each other through techniques such as asking each other questions, asking for another's point of view, and so on?

11. Are group members occasionally summarizing what has been discussed?

12. Are group members referring to the book in supporting their statements?

13. Are group members making connections between the book and their own experiences? Are they doing this in a way that does not move the focus from the book?

14. Are group members making connections between the book and other books, movies, or information?

15. Are group members accepting disagreement and using other members' opinions to expand what they are willing to think about in relation to the book?

16. Do group members acknowledge that there may be more than one point of view or interpretation of text?

17. Do group members give themselves time to think? That is, are they comfortable with silence?

18. Are group members speaking in loud enough voices?

The following form might be used by a teacher who wants to gather some initial assessment data on the discussion process. Following "amount of participation," the teacher simply lists students' names under the spot on the continuum that best represents the amount of each student's engagement in discussion. The question is very open-ended; it may be helpful to consult the previous list of questions to remember important discussion strategies. Since this question will determine what to teach students to do first in order to improve discussions, we would probably jot down no more than the two or three strategies we thought were most important at this point in their development.

Group and/or Book title _____

Date _____   Number of minutes of discussion _____

Amount of participation in discussion:

A great deal   Medium amount   None

What discussion skills do the students most need to learn?

Peterson and Eeds (1990, p. 71) have developed an assessment tool that helps teachers observe and assess students' preparation for and participation in literature groups. The assessment is divided into two parts: 1) preparation for literature study (whether a student brought a book to the group, contributed to developing a group reading plan, and took notes of places to share); and 2) participation in literature study (quality of responses, references to book to support ideas, modifications of responses where there was a reason to do so). Students could also use this as a self-assessment during a literature study and then compare their assessments to yours. The form could also be altered slightly to use as a guide in examining occasional video- and audiotapes of literature discussion groups.

Another assessment tool also included in Peterson and Eeds (1990, pp. 68–69) is an extensive response to literature checklist, which includes assessment of enjoyment/involvement, making personal connections, interpretations/making meaning, and insight into elements that authors control in creating a story. The assessment items under interpretations/making meaning are notable because they focus on processes that help to develop critical thinking about literature. They emphasize listening well and suspending beliefs in order to examine other perspectives. For example, two of the checklist items from this section (p. 69) are:

Is willing to think and search out alternative points of view.

Can modify interpretations in light of "new evidence."

Involving students in self-evaluation of the discussion process encourages them to see that the process is important and that it is their responsibility. A teacher used the following self-evaluation form (also in Rhodes, 1993) to help students assess their own participation and to encourage close listening. (Other ideas useful for self-evaluation of discussion may be found in Watson, 1987, pp. 209–211.)

Name _____ Date _____

Book title_____

How much did you participate in the discussion today?

about the right amount   too much

not at all   too little

What was an important contribution you made to the discussion?

What was an important idea expressed by someone else in the group during the discussion? (Identify the person and tell what he said.)

literature and learning logs

Literature and learning logs will be discussed in more detail in Chapter 6, but here we want to highlight how they can be used for comprehension assessment. Logs (or journals) may contain think-alouds written in the process of reading a text, retellings or summaries of sections of text, and interviews or dialogues between teacher and student (or student and student). There are plenty of data in logs to help the teacher assess students' understanding, misconceptions, biases, and questions about the text. In addition, when students have comprehension difficulties, what the student has written often offers clues to the sources of those difficulties.

As teachers regularly collect, read, and respond in writing to log entries, they can record assessment data. One fourth-grade teacher (Wollman-Bonilla, 1989, p. 118) found that many of her students' responses to literature fell into five categories:

- Opinions about plot episodes and characters.

- Direct expressions of personal engagement ranging from enthusiastic appreciation to placing the book within the framework of the child's life and concerns.

- Discussion of the author's style, language, and techniques.

- Reflections on the reading process and on expectations for narrative texts.

- Questions about vocabulary, language, or plot.

A categorization scheme such as this can help in assessing individual student and class responses to literature. As Wollman-Bonilla points out, "each child's work [is] very personal and unique in focus and insight." The response categories can help you identify each child's unique approach to responding to literature and identify how you might want to expand that approach.

Responses can also form the foundation for additional or dynamic assessment; the teacher can ask a question or pose a problem that encourages the student to think differently or within a different structure. A teacher can often spot common patterns that will lead to instruction if he pays attention to the types of responses students make, especially when they are reading the same book or reading about the same topic.

Teachers may ask students to share entries from their logs in class as a way to begin a discussion about some issue in the text. The teacher can then assess the shared log entries in much the same way he assesses discussions. In a situation like this, it is not uncommon to observe that students express conflicting interpretations about some issue in the text. How students use their own background information and the text itself to support their interpretations can provide a great deal of information about what to address next in instruction.

Teachers who demonstrate writing log entries may want to encourage students to try out the particular types of entries they have demonstrated. This can be done through self-evaluation. If the teacher has been demonstrating and encouraging students to make connections between issues in the book and their own lives, he might use a self-evaluation like this one:

Name _____ Date _____

Book title _____

1. In the last two weeks, how many log entries have you made? _____

2. In these entries, how many connections did you make between the book and your life? _____

Do *one* of the following. Circle the one you did.

A. If you answered "2" or more for question two above, turn in the entry with the best connection you think you made underlined in a color that shows up. In the space below, tell why you think this is the best connection you made between your own life and the book.

B. If you answered "0" or "1" for question two above, choose one of your entries from the last two weeks and revise it to make a connection between what you wrote about the book and your own life. Turn in the entry with the revision underlined in a color that shows up. In the space below, tell what you thought about in order to revise your entry.

Students can also assess their own ability to read narrative texts by reflecting on their log entries. In one column of a double-entry journal, a student lists the word, phrase, sentence, or paragraph that has made him want to respond along with its page number. In the other column, the student responds to the chosen part of the text. Once a week or so, students can be asked to read through their previous entries to discover ways in which their understanding of the book is growing and changing. This activity can also encourage rereading of particular passages to discover further nuances.

■ ■

book shares

———

Book shares can take many forms: oral, artistic, and dramatic. In a "book share," as defined here, students inform each other about books they have read and recommend particular titles to their classmates. A book share is a product of comprehension and as such, it almost always includes a brief retelling or summary of the text. As students do book shares, you can write anecdotal records, use a checklist, or even use one of the quantitative retelling procedures if students do a retelling as part of the book share. In addition to assessing the student's retelling of the text, you can also assess such things as the student's reading interests and purposes and what the student considers important in the text.

Students can be involved in self-assessment of book shares in a number of different ways. For example, if students have been asked to create a diorama to represent a scene from the book, they might also answer the following questions:

Name _____ Date _____

Book title/author_____

What scene from the story did you put in the diorama you shared with your classmates?

Why did you choose this scene?

Do you think your presentation of the diorama was effective in encouraging other students to read the book? Why?

art, drama, and other extension activities

When used effectively, extension activities take students back into a text in order to think about the text as a whole or some part of it. Unlike book shares, the primary purpose of a text extension is not to recommend the book for someone else's reading (though this can be a secondary purpose) but to revisit the book in a deeper way and with a particular focus. For example, the extension may encourage students to consider how a text is structured, how the author writes, or the nature of one or more story characters.

Text extensions may include dramatizing an entire story, doing a Reader's Theatre performance of one part of a novel, sketching a "bird's-eye view" of the setting of the story, trying out an experiment included in the text, comparing the facts in a piece of historical fiction set during the Revolutionary War to those in a history textbook, looking at how the characters' relationships with each other change in the course of the story, and so on.

As students become involved in text extensions, the teacher has an opportunity to observe not only their comprehension of the story as the activity begins, but also how and why it changes during the activity. The teacher can also observe how the students use the text and their background knowledge in generating and rethinking meaning. As students work, especially on collaborative projects, they think aloud about the meaning of the text, retell and argue over the significance of events, and ask each other questions or request information from each other. All of this provides data.

Of course, the students themselves can evaluate how the text extension has influenced their thinking about a text. If a group of students work together on a literary sociogram (Johnson & Louis, 1987), rearranging the circles representing the characters and discussing how the arrows representing the relationships between the characters are to be labeled, you might ask the following question when they finish their work:

Group members:_____

_____

The activity you just finished was designed to encourage you to think carefully about the relationships between the characters in the story. What do you understand now that you didn't understand before you began the activity?

This self-evaluation is open-ended and invites rather abstract thinking. As a result, students may not provide the information that you are seeking without some adjustments in how the self-evaluation is handled. Several kinds are possible. One is to have the students complete the self-evaluation as a group so that they can help each other think about the question. Second, you might provide the self-evaluation in advance of the activity so that the students can keep the question in mind as they work. Third, you might point out some of what you saw students learning in the process of doing the sociogram; this can be easily done as you move from group to group.

comprehension tasks in content areas

If students will be expected to engage in particular comprehension tasks in some content areas other than thinking aloud and retelling, it is important to gather information on how students perform on these comprehension tasks. It is common for students to have to answer various types of comprehension questions following the reading of a textbook. If so, it would be helpful to gather information on students' performance on such a task. Each student can read a textbook passage and then answer a variety of questions or they could respond to a three-level study guide or a QAR (Question-Answer-Response) guide (Vacca & Vacca, 1989). Another area to seek information about is students' ability to use all of the parts of their textbook and to read its charts and diagrams. You might try developing a locational guide in which you ask students to find, use, or interpret using tables of contents, glossaries, appendixes, maps, and so on. These comprehension tasks will begin to help you identify those students who have significant reading problems and which comprehension tasks students need more help with. If you organize in advance, all of the assessment passages and questions can link up with a unit topic that students are going to study.

Using comprehension tasks students will do in their classes, teachers will discover which students need more fine-tuned small group and individual analyses of comprehension difficulties. You might begin by doing a directed reading-thinking activity (Gillet & Temple, 1990) with students in small groups. Do students have adequate background knowledge? Do they make good predictions? Do they spontaneously begin to confirm and disconfirm their predictions? Can they find the answers they are seeking in text? You might also ask each student to do some reading aloud for you so that you can begin to make observations about the student's miscue patterns as they relate to comprehension of content texts.

Another way you can assess students' strategies and self-monitoring is through a Self-Monitoring Approach to Reading and Thinking (SMART) (Vaughan & Estes, 1986). In SMART, students are first asked to place a ✓ in the margin if they understand what they are reading and place a ? in the margin if they don't understand what they are reading. We would recommend asking students to do this at the end of each paragraph. Having given this direction to students, you can ask them to read silently or aloud depending on the nature of the information you are seeking. After students have finished reading, ask them to go back over the places in the text where they put question marks and see if they now understand them. If the idea remains unclear, ask students to specify what is causing the problem. Is it a word? A phrase? A relationship? If students come to understand this part of the passage by talking about it, have them change the ? to a ✓. Also ask them to think of things they might do (in a problem-solving manner) to further help with trouble spots. Note whether they mention using pictures, the glossary, going back to class notes, and so on.

Conclusion

In this chapter, we have portrayed comprehension as a complex process of meaning construction, which is affected by the social milieu in which it occurs. We have also argued that the traditional manner of testing comprehension does not take this current understanding of comprehension into account or help us uncover the processes or strategies students use in comprehending text—vital information if we are to help students comprehend text more effectively.

Because we are concerned about assessing the processes students use to comprehend text, we focused on comprehension assessment techniques that allow us to examine the processes as well as the products of comprehension. Because we want to know how students comprehend text in various social situations and how and why students' comprehension varies from one situation to another, we discussed various literacy events in which assessment techniques could be used to find out how to help students become more effective readers.

appendix D

Some Helpful Hints on Classroom Interviewing

DO

1. *Be friendly*. Sometimes it is better to start with a friendly, wide-open question before focusing on specifics. For example, "You look deep in thought—what are you thinking?"

2. *Focus*. Ask specific questions, but in an "open" way, so that the pupil thinks you are interested. For example, you might focus on strategies: "That's interesting—how did you work that out?" Or, you might focus on meanings: "Tell me more about _____. What does that mean to you?" Or, you might focus on the task: "How is the research going?"

3. *Probe*. Try to extend the interview, so that the pupil does most of the talking, and you are able to clarify what has been said. Try the following back-up questions:

   - Reflect. Turn the pupil's comment into a question. The pupil says, "I don't know that word. It was too hard." You say, "It was too hard?" Or, you could say, "What made it hard for you?"

   - Wait. Indicate that you would like to hear more by simply saying "mm" or "yeah," and then wait for the pupil to go on. Sometimes you have to wait a while.

   - Expand. Try to probe a bit more. The pupil says, "Yeah, when I first looked at it, I thought they meant coffee." You say, "Tell me how you thought it was coffee." Or, you could say, "I'm not with you. Could you tell me a bit more about why you thought it was coffee?" Try to be positive. Show that you are really interested. Play dumb if you have to.

4. *Keep on track*. Sometimes the pupil introduces other ideas into the conversation. Try to select the one that is most relevant. You can come back to the other ideas later. The pupil says, "This is hard. I've always had trouble reading. And I didn't understand it when you explained it." You say, "What parts are hard?" Or, you say, "I'd like to know more about the hard parts." The point is that the pupil has introduced some side-tracks. The personal problem ("I have trouble reading") can be followed up later. And the external excuse ("You didn't explain it properly") only begs the real question—why is it hard for that pupil?

5. *Tidy up*. Go over any points you may have missed. This is where you take the lead, simply to clarify points that you think might be important. You say, "Are there any other kinds of 'light' that are hard to understand?" Or, if you think the pupil has avoided some issues in the text, you point to those parts of the text and say, "What did this mean to you?"

DON'T

1. *Lead*. This is where the teacher guides the student toward an answer, using leading questions. The teacher is teaching—and it is very easy to do. The pupil is following your line of thinking, rather than the other way around. For example:

Yeah, well condensation turns into rain.
That's right. And where does the rain go to?
Onto the land.
And so what have you done there? You've completed a what?
Cycle.
That's right. Is that a bit clearer?
Mmm.

   This is the kind of question which we find hardest to avoid. It's too easy to help out, especially when the pupil seems lost. But often the pupil does have a meaning—so be on the lookout for warning signs. If the pupil says less than you do, then you are probably leading. Or if the pupil thanks you for helping out, then you know you were leading. The easiest clue to spot is the word "so." If you hear yourself saying it, then stop—you are asking leading questions. Now—how could you have improved on this interview? (See "answer" #1 at end of this section.)

2. *Rephrase*. Sometimes it is worth repeating what the pupil said. But it can go wrong, especially if you rephrase the pupil's words. This problem is easy to spot because pupils are quick to grasp onto your re-interpretation. For example:

Why did you think you got such a good mark for your report?
Cause I, um . . . describing.
You think you got your good mark because you used nice descriptive language? Do you agree?
Mmmm. (pupil grins)

Now—how could you have improved on this interview? (See "answer" #2 at end of this section.)

3. *Cue*. This is where you interpret slightly what the pupil said then, later in the interview, your own words come back to you through the mouth of the pupil. When this happens, you know you have changed the pupil's cognitive process toward your own way of thinking. For example:

What makes that diagram harder?
Cause it doesn't look like anything to me.
It doesn't look like anything? Can you not imagine it as the heart?
No.
Is that the main reason why it would be harder to understand?
Yeah. I just can't imagine it to be the heart . . . (Pupil repeats observer's comments). I just don't understand that one.

Now—how could you have improved on this interview? (See "answer" #3 at end of this section.)

---

4. *Pressure*. When time is short, it is tempting to hurry. But what happens is that the pupil clams up. For example:

> *What do you think the question is asking you to do?*
> Oh, sort of write a little . . .
> *Tell me in your own words.*
> To write a summary of what it means.
> *What's "it?" What "it" are you talking about?*
> Oh, just sort of parts of it, like . . .
> *What part?*
> That part there.
> *Why that part?*
> I forgot. (end of interview)

Now—how could you improve on this interview? (See "answer" #4 at end of this section.)

5. *Over-praise*. This is difficult. On the one hand, excessive praise can reinforce the teacher role—that is, the pupil goes along with your response. On the other hand, by being too neutral, you may lose an opportunity to get the pupil's confidence. Here is an example where praise influenced the pupil's thinking:

> *You're not quite sure where to go from here?*
> No. I could put that Mum and Dad found them ...
> *That's a good start.*
> Yeah. That's what I'll do.

Now—how could you improve on this interview? (See "answer" #5 at end of this section.)

A few more hints—When you first start interviewing pupils, keep a little card with you, made up of "focus" and "probe" types of questions. When you don't know what to ask say "mm"—this technique often works best of all. Be self-critical. Tape record some of your interviews, and analyze the transcripts, looking for "do's" and "don't's."

Some interviewing "answers." There are no answers, of course, in this kind of interviewing, where you have to think quickly. Yet there are guidelines that you usually try to follow, even if they sometimes do not work out:

#1. A better technique would have been to pursue the pupil's reasoning by using a "reflect" question—for example, "condensation turns into rain?" Then wait. The pupil will probably say more about what happens after the "rain." When you use this technique, sound interested, or else the pupil may panic, and think something is wrong.

#2. A better technique would be to fix on exactly what the pupil said, and simply repeat it, as if you are waiting for more information for example, just say "describing . . . " and wait.

#3. Here, the interviewer was leading, putting ideas into the pupil's mind, instead of letting the pupil explain. A better technique would be to get the pupil to expand—for example, say "I don't understand what you mean. Can you explain that to me?"

#4. Here, the interviewer was too pushy, and too fast. A better technique would be to slow down, wait for the pupil to finish, and make use of reflect questions—for example, you say "write a summary?" The pupil will sense that you do not understand, and will probably explain a bit more. Or you could try making encouraging noises, such as "mm" or "yes . . ." If the pupil seems to be talking at a tangent, try to get back to the point, by saying, "I'm a bit lost. When you say 'summary,' what does that mean to you?"

#5. Some pupils unconsciously look for praise and help—so they are really interviewing you in these situations, looking for someone else to help them. A better technique is to stay neutral—that is, look interested, say "mm," and wait, or else ask for clarification, such as "Tell me a bit more about that." After a while, the need for praise seems to go away. Pupils realize you are not going to make decisions for them.

Nicholson, T. (1984). You get lost when you gotta blimmin' watch the damn words: The low progress reader in the junior high school. *Topics in Learning and Learning Disabilities*, 3 (4), 16-30.

references

Bean, T. (1988). Organizing and retaining information by thinking like an author. In S.M. Glazer, L.W. Searfoss & L.M. Gentile (Eds.), *Reexamining reading diagnosis: New trends and procedures*, pp. 103–127. Newark, DE: International Reading Association.

Brown, C.S. & S.L. Lytle. (1988). Merging assessment and instruction: Protocols in the classroom. In S.M. Glazer, L.W. Searfoss & L.M. Gentile (Eds.), *Reexamining reading diagnosis: New trends and procedures*, pp. 94–102. Newark, DE: International Reading Association.

Brown, H. & B. Cambourne. (1987). *Read and retell*. Portsmouth, NH: Heinemann.

Cakmak, S., M. Chase, & C. Kelleher. (1989). *Think-aloud protocols as powerful tools for understanding the interactive reading process*. Research Symposium: Assessing Reading Holistically, National Reading Conference.

Clark, C. (1982). Assessing free recall. *The Reading Teacher, 35*(4), 434–439.

Davey, B. (1989). Assessing comprehension: Selected interactions of task and reader. *The Reading Teacher, 42*(9), 694–697.

Edwards, F. (1981a). Reading and learning in the junior secondary school: Progress and problems (Working paper one). Hamilton, New Zealand: University of Waikato.

Edwards, F. (1981b). Reading and learning in the junior secondary school: More progress and fewer problems (Working paper two). Hamilton, New Zealand: University of Waikato.

Eeds, M. & D. Wells. (1989). Grand conversations: An exploration of meaning construction in literature study groups. *Research in the Teaching of English, 23* (1), 4–29.

Gillet, J.W. & C. Temple. (1990). *Understanding reading problems: Assessment and instruction* (3rd ed.). Glenview, IL: Scott Foresman/Little, Brown Higher Education.

Goodman, Y.M. & C.L. Burke. (1972). *RMI manual: Procedures for diagnosis and evaluation*. New York: Macmillan.

Goodman, Y.M., D.J. Watson, & C.L. Burke. (1987). *Reading miscue inventory: Alternative procedures*. Katonah, NY: Richard C. Owen.

Harste, J.C. & C.L. Burke. (1979). Reexamining retellings as comprehension devices. Paper presented at the National Reading Conference, San Antonio.

Harste, J.C., K.G. Short, & C.L. Burke. (1988). *Creating classrooms for authors*. Portsmouth, NH: Heinemann.

Hornsby, D. & D. Sukarna. (1986). *Read on: A conference approach to reading*. Portsmouth, NH: Heinemann.

Irwin, J. & I. Baker. (1989). *Promoting active reading comprehension strategies*. Englewood Cliffs, NJ: Prentice Hall.

Johnson, T.D. & D.R. Louis. (1987). *Literacy through literature*. Portsmouth, NH: Heinemann.

Johnston, P. (1983). *Reading comprehension assessment: A cognitive basis*. Newark, DE: International Reading Association.

Lee, S. & M. Sadoski. (1986). Holistic evaluation of plot and theme. College Station, TX: Unpublished manuscript.

Leslie, L. & J. Caldwell. (1990). *Qualitative reading inventory*. Glenview, IL: Scott, Foresman/Little, Brown Higher Education.

Lytle, S.L. (1982). Exploring comprehension style: A study of twelfth grade readers' transactions with text. Ph.D. diss., University of Pennsylvania. *Dissertation Abstracts International, 43* (7), 2295-A.

Marshall, N. (1983). Using story grammar to assess reading comprehension. *The Reading Teacher, 36* (7), 616–620.

Morrow, L.M. (1988). Retelling stories as a diagnostic tool. In S. M. Glazer, L. W. Searfoss, & L. M. Gentile (Eds.), *Reexamining reading diagnosis: New trends and procedures*, pp. 128–149. Newark, DE: International Reading Association.

Nicholson, T. (1984a). Experts and novices: A study of reading in the high school classroom. *Reading Research Quarterly, 19* (4), 436–451.

———. (1984b). You get lost when you gotta blimmin' watch the damn words: The low progress reader in the junior high school. *Topics in Learning and Learning Disabilities, 3* (4), 16–30.

———. (1989). Research revisited: A study of reading in the secondary school classroom. *Language and Education, 3* (2), 1–11.

Olshavsky, J. (1977). Reading as problem solving: An investigation of strategies. *Reading Research Quarterly, 12* (4), 654–674.

Peterson, R. & M. Eeds. (1990). *Grand conversations: Literature groups in action*. New York: Scholastic.

Rhodes, L.K. (1979). Comprehension and predictability: An analysis of beginning reading materials. In R. F. Carey & J. C. Harste (Eds.), *New perspectives on comprehension*, pp. 100–131. Bloomington, IN: Indiana University School of Education Monographs in Language and Reading Studies.

———. (1993). *Literacy assessment: A handbook of instruments*. Portsmouth, NH: Heinemann.

Rhodes, L. et al. (1989). LINK Pak: *Sign of the beaver*. Lakewood, CO: LINK.

Rose, J. (1989). When I read a good book. *The Reading Teacher, 43* (1), 88.

Rosenblatt, L.M. (1978). *The reader, the text, the poem: The transactional theory of the literary work.* Carbondale, IL: Southern Illinois University Press.

Schell, L. (1988). Dilemmas in assessing reading comprehension. *The Reading Teacher, 42* (1), 12–16.

Shanklin, N. & L. Rhodes. (1989). Comprehension instruction as sharing and extending. *The Reading Teacher, 42* (7), 496–500.

Speare, E.G. (1983). *The sign of the beaver.* New York: Dell Publishing.

Urguhart, D. (1981). The bicycle and how it works. In *Hidden Windows.* Glenview, IL: Scott Foresman.

Vacca, R. & J. Vacca (1989). *Content area reading.* Glenview, IL: Scott Foresman.

Valencia, S. & P.D. Pearson. (1987). Reading assessment: Time for a change. *The Reading Teacher, 40* (8), 726–733.

Vaughan, J.L. & T.H. Estes. (1986). *Reading and reasoning beyond the primary grades.* Boston, MA: Allyn & Bacon.

Watson, D. (Ed.) (1987). *Ideas and insights.* Urbana, IL: National Council of Teachers of English.

White, J. (1980). A taxonomy of reading behaviors. Ph.D. doctoral diss., Southern Illinois University, Carbondale, IL.

Wood, K. (1988). Techniques for assessing students' potential for learning. *The Reading Teacher, 41* (4), 440–447.

Wollman-Bonilla, J. (1989). Reading journals: Invitations to participate in literature. *The Reading Teacher, 43* (2), 112–120.

Chapter Six

6

Writing Processes and Products

reflections

☐ What kinds of information would you like to gather in order to understand a student's ability to develop a piece from rehearsal to publication?

☐ Collect writing interviews and writing samples from several students using the *Authoring Cycle Profile* (in Rhodes, 1993). How does the writing interview inform and triangulate with the interpretation of each student's *Authoring Cycle Profile*?

☐ Look over your collection of writing interviews and writing samples. What writing problems do you find students having? Generate three strategies for addressing each problem.

☐ Collect writing interviews and writing samples from students at several different grade and ability levels. What do you learn about writing development from this experience? What seem to be the ways in which good writers are developing at these three levels: primary, intermediate, and middle school? What are the common characteristics of poor writers at each level?

☐ What are some ways in which you might help students assess the quality of their participation in peer conferences and Authors' Circle?

☐ Observe a student's writing process both with a computer and without it. What effect does the computer seem to have on the writer's process and the types of interaction she has with others over writing?

"How's my child's writing?" is a question parents often ask of educators. As a teacher, you may begin to wonder, "Are these parents really asking about the quality of their child's handwriting? Or her spelling? Or do they mean her ideas? Or are they talking about her ability to engage in the entire writing process?" It's hard to know, and we often find ourselves miscommunicating with parents about writing. Developing fair, complete assessments of writing abilities is not an easy undertaking.

Many standardized tests use very limited definitions of "writing." They assess spelling, grammar, punctuation, and capitalization. Being able to spell or use grammar, however, does not tell teachers whether students can organize ideas, select important details, write exciting leads, ask good questions of others' writing, or revise and edit their own pieces. Holistic and analytic assessments, which require students to write complete texts, have been developed as responses to these problems with standardized tests. Yet neither holistic nor analytic scoring of written products provides teachers with information about the actual processes students use to write.

Before we can consider students' written products and how to assess them, we feel it is important to look at and understand their writing processes. In this chapter, we will begin by outlining questions that can guide your observations of students' writing processes and subsequently their written products. We will then discuss methods of holistic and analytic scoring of writing samples. We will also introduce the *Authoring Cycle Profile*, an instrument we have developed to guide teachers' observations of students' writing processes and written products. The chapter will conclude with a discussion of literacy events and classroom assessments involving writing. Particular emphasis will be placed on spelling, ways to assess students' ability to do research and report writing, and several self-assessments of writing that encourage students to assume more responsibility for their understanding of the authoring cycle.

In this chapter, the view of the writing process we have adopted and adapted slightly is the Authoring Cycle presented by Harste & Short, with Burke (1988). We have altered the Authoring Cycle model to fit the concepts and terminology we have used throughout this book (see Figure 6.1). For "life experiences" we have substituted "rehearsing as part of authentic writing events." For the term "uninterrupted reading and writing" we have decided to use the more common term "drafting." We have broadened "Authors' Circle" to "conferring," which may include Authors' Circle but also adds conferring with the teacher, a parent, a peer, or a student-led group. We have decided to make revising more prominent, and in the editing phase to emphasize students' gradual assumption of responsibility for their own editing. Like the original Authoring Cycle, we have adopted the term "publishing," but to

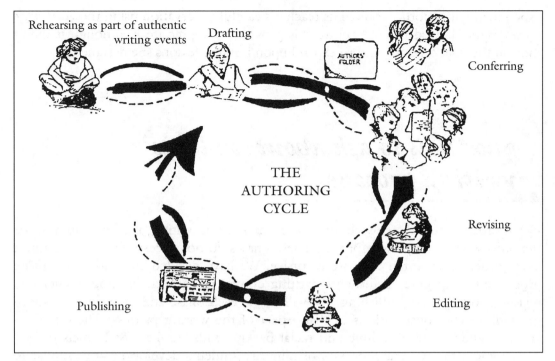

Figure 6.1   The Authoring Cycle

publishing we have added a section about observations that can be made of students' written products, which will be examined in terms of the message of the final product, its genre, and its adherence to conventions. At the end of the Authoring Cycle we have dropped the notion of strategy lessons and literacy invitations. Although these areas are very important, they link to the instruction that becomes an outgrowth of good assessment. These terms are defined in more detail in the section that follows. Please take a few minutes to study Figure 6.1 and refer back to it as you read the chapter.

By attempting to understand students' writing processes, teachers develop insights into their attitudes toward writing and to the features in their writing samples. Changes in students' writing processes can be the first clues to new development. They will often emerge here before they are evident in students' written products (Samway, 1987). To develop as writers, students must begin to take risks and experiment with new elements. Even if these experiments are abandoned by the final product, they can be further encouraged by a sensitive teacher.

One fifth-grade teacher used the *Authoring Cycle Profile* to observe Jeff. His favorite topic for writing was skateboarding. In fact, since the opening of school (it was now mid-October) this had been his only topic. In his story for the *Authoring Cycle Profile,* Jeff decided to try another topic. He experimented with writing about football until he decided that Eric, his main character, should be a skateboarder as well as a football player! As a result, the sense of topic focus in his "Eric" story was often fragmented, jumping between Eric the football player and Eric the skateboarder. But this piece represents potential growth for Jeff, since he did begin to experiment with another topic. His teacher's careful observation using the *Authoring Cycle Profile* allowed her to capture this growth, to appreciate it although it didn't show in the final product, and to expand upon it in the lessons she designed.

questions to ask about students' writing processes

In order to think deeply about what is involved in writing, teachers often divide the process into component phases. These phases do not necessarily occur in a neat linear order; more often they are recursive. We have decided to divide the writing process into engaging in authentic writing events, rehearsing, drafting, conferring, revising, editing, and publishing. We will define each phase and then pose questions to guide teacher observations of that aspect of the writing process. The questions apply to children of all ethnic and racial backgrounds. As Farr & Daniels (1986) have argued, the writing processes of minority students develop in ways similar to those of other children.

authentic writing events

When students write, it is important that they engage in authentic writing events (see Chapter 2) and see that their writing serves some meaningful purpose. As teachers, we don't always have the opportunity to observe how children's writing develops in response to their lives (Bissex, 1980). But we can be cognizant of clues to this development in our classrooms.

Adam, for example, began the year writing fiction. He never felt he had anything to say about his own personal life. But after his teacher had gained his trust and encouraged him to take risks, Adam ventured to write and publish a true story about his mother's attempts to drive a standard shift car in which she ended up running the car through the garage wall! When students enthusiastically received Adam's story in Authors' Circle, it gave him the courage to undertake writing a pamphlet with another student. The pamphlet was an outgrowth of another personal experience Adam had enjoyed—going to a transportation museum. With each subsequent piece, Adam became more concerned about getting his ideas about real events in his life on paper so that he could share them with others. Writing started to become a more authentic, personally meaningful experience. His confidence and self-esteem as a writer were bolstered, and he began to enjoy writing for the first time.

An environment that encourages risk-taking helps make writing activities more authentic. Taking risks requires that a writer put her critical self aside and simply try various ways of doing the writing at hand. Risk-taking involves faith that one's efforts will lead somewhere and the courage to begin. It is often helpful to have the support of others—praise for good ideas, listening ears, probing questions, and good suggestions. It also helps if a writer has succeeded before! As kindergartners and first graders, most children feel good about their writing. They haven't yet encountered external critics who tell them that they cannot write or developed harsh internal critics that do not believe in their own voices. In assessing children's writing, teachers must be careful not to be too harsh or reinforce children's self-criticism.

Some questions to consider about the authenticity of the writing a student undertakes include:

- Does the writer have authentic, personally meaningful reasons to write, a real message that she wants to convey—either to herself, as in a learning log, or also to others?

- Where did the idea for the writing come from—personal experience, an idea gleaned from another student's paper during Authors' Circle, a book?

- If a piece is to be shared with others, does the writer have a sense of the audience and the information she will need in order to communicate clearly?

- What sorts of risks is the writer willing to take in order to express her ideas?

- How would you characterize this writer's internal critic?

Information about these questions can be gathered informally from conferences with a student and from examinations of her writing samples over a period of time. Parents can also be encouraged to share their observations of the writing their child is doing outside of school.

rehearsing

Closely linked to the authenticity of writing tasks is the rehearsal that children engage in before writing. Sometimes, in fact, rehearsal starts even before students consciously decide to write. Rehearsal allows students to clarify the task and decide what method of communication would work best.

Children rehearse for their writing in many ways. They may draw pictures and use them as springboards for writing. As young writers mature, these initial pictures tend to be replaced by jot lists, story maps, or semantic webs of important ideas. Students sometimes get ideas from something they have read. Writers of all ages can share their ideas with other writers and in the exchanges generate, elaborate, and clarify their thinking before they begin to draft.

Some questions to consider about a student's rehearsal for writing are:

- In what ways does the writer think before drafting? Through drawing? Dramatization? A jot list, story map, or semantic web?

- What kinds of things does the writer say to herself, to the teacher, or to peers while rehearsing?

- To what extent does the writer confer with others about her ideas for writing? In what ways is this beneficial?

- In what ways does the writer use her reading as a springboard for writing?

- In what ways does the writer listen to others and help them generate ideas for texts?

drafting

Drafting refers to a writer's ability to put initial ideas on paper. More specifically, it involves fluency, strategies for spelling, and the ability to read and reread her own text proficiently.

fluency

When students begin to work on a piece, their fluency is often immediately apparent. Fluency refers to children's ability to assign language to thoughts and to write quickly so that they do not forget their ideas. Sometimes children are so concerned about writing neatly that they forget their thoughts. Or, when they are first learning to print or write in cursive, they cannot remember how certain letters are formed and lose what they want to say. At other times, children's fluency is hampered by an overconcern with correct spelling or even with how to spell words inventively.

Potential questions that can be posed about a writer's fluency include:

- How easily is the writer physically able to transcribe her ideas onto paper? How does the writer hold a pen or pencil? At what angle does the writer put her paper?

- Does the writer choose to erase or cross out in order to transcribe ideas quickly?

- Is fluency impeded by difficulties with spelling or by the writer's attitude?

spelling as a part of drafting

Spelling is most frequently considered a feature of final products. Actually, however, spelling is not just a product, it is a complex process that enters into the Authoring Cycle at several points. The questions and answers relevant to the issue of spelling depend on where a student is in the Authoring Cycle (drafting, revising, or editing her final product) and her level of spelling development.

Potential questions that can be asked about a writer's spelling during drafting are:

- Does the writer risk trying to spell words for which she does not know the correct spelling?

- What strategies does the writer use to spell unknown words?

- How does the spelling change between the draft or drafts and the final product? What does this reveal about how the writer handles spelling during drafting?

- What common spelling rules are second nature to the writer? That is, how does the writer spell when she is focusing on meaning?

- What seems to be the level of the writer's spelling development?

reading and rereading your own writing

By reading their own writing, writers can confirm that they have indeed said what they wanted to say. At the same time, rereading helps writers think of other ideas they may wish to include and allows them to correct errors. Reading one's own text during drafting helps overcome the limits of short-term memory (Smith, 1988).

Questions to ask about a student's reading and rereading of her own writing include:

- At what point in the writing and how frequently does the writer reread the text she is constructing?

- What does the writer do next—continue writing, make changes, talk to someone?

- What kinds of changes does the writer make in response to rereading?

- Does the writer read over the text only when she is finished drafting?

- To what extent must the writer be prompted by a teacher or a peer to reread?

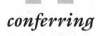

conferring

Before a writer begins to draft, as well as during and after writing, conferring offers the chance to rehearse ideas with classmates and often generates further ideas. It also allows a writer to obtain feedback about how well the message of the piece has been communicated. The feedback ought to be honest but handled so that the writer understands the strengths of the piece and how it could be made better. Students can confer with themselves, with the teacher, with other students, or as a part of Authors' Circle that includes teacher and peers.

Questions that can be asked about a student's conferring include:

- How willing is the writer to share the piece?

- In what ways does the writer's willingness to share vary from one situation to another (in the Authors' Circle, with the teacher, with a peer)?

- Does the writer competently read her piece in a strong, clear voice?

- How does the writer react to compliments from classmates?

- In what ways does the writer listen to questions and attempt to answer them during conferring or when making subsequent revisions?

- How does the writer keep track of suggestions?

revising

Revision refers to the changes writers make in the content of their pieces: adding information, deleting information to give a piece more focus, organizing ideas, trying out a different lead, selecting details to better illustrate a point, thinking of ways to show rather than tell what a character is like, and so on. "Re-vision" involves "re-seeing" the ideas in a piece of writing. As students become more proficient writers, they ought to be able to engage in self-revision, having internalized the kinds of questions most often asked by their audiences.

Questions that can be asked about a student's revision include:

- Does the writer make notes on the feedback from classmates in Authors' Circle and use them to make revisions?

- At what levels does the writer make revisions (for example, word, sentence, paragraph)?

- How does the writer add information?

- If the writer needs to reorganize information, does she use arrows, cut and paste, or have some other way to indicate these changes?

- Does the writer compose more than one lead or ending and determine which is better?

- In what ways does the final product effectively use transitions between sections?

editing

Editing is the process of making surface changes in a piece so that it conforms to the conventions of standard English (or of another language). Editing and revision are not the same. Normally, but not always, writers work first on revision to make sure that their ideas are clear and well organized and then address editing concerns.

If writers are to develop self-sufficiency, teachers must help them take more personal responsibility for editing. Children often need to be encouraged to attempt self-editing before going to the teacher or a peer. After trying self-editing, they still often benefit from working further with the teacher or with another student.

Questions that can be asked about a writer's ability to edit include:

- To what extent is the writer willing to edit her draft?

- Does the writer edit for several types of conventions at once or for each kind separately?

- What kinds of editing changes (spelling, periods, capitals, paragraphing, quotation marks, and so on) does the writer make?

- How does a writer's ability to edit a peer's piece compare with her ability to edit her own?

- To what extent is the writer able to locate and then correct spelling errors?

- What strategies does the writer use to find correct spellings?

publishing

Publishing refers to the final production and sharing of finished texts. These final products can take many forms—such as books, pamphlets, letters to relatives, bulletin board displays, letters to the editor, newspaper articles, reports, scripts, and poems. Publishing means "going public" with one's voice. It can turn out to be a positive or negative experience. Much depends on the audience, the quality of feedback the student has received during writing, and how the student has used the feedback.

Questions that can be asked about a student's publishing include:

- How does the writer describe the process of publishing? What seems to be her attitude toward such publishing?

- To what extent is the writer proud of her finished products? How and with whom have they been shared?

- What additional publishing would the writer like to do?

questions to ask about written products

Now that we have posed questions to guide teachers' observations of students' writing processes we will look at students' final products. Traditionally, these are what teachers have always assessed. Our point is that both processes and products are important. Improvement in the processes that students use to write will eventually lead to better products. We observe products to see when processes have become truly effective. We also observe them for clues to new development or to problems that need to be revisited. Our discussion of written products covers three areas: the quality of the writer's message, the writer's use of an appropriate form or genre, and the writer's control of conventions.

message

Writing leaves a trail of words that, unless the writing is for the writer alone, involves an audience. Writers want to know whether they have effectively communicated the messages they wanted to express.

Questions to ask about the message and function of the written product include:

- How clearly is the message communicated?

- Is the message elaborated with enough, but not too much, detail?

- To what extent does the piece use vocabulary appropriate to the topic?

- Does the piece have a sense of voice that is sincere and clearly the writer's own?

- Is the message well organized?

- Do the illustrations complement the message?

genre

Besides assessing the quality of the message, teachers will also want to look at the genre in which the message is expressed. Genre refers to the type of writing: letter, short story, poem, interview, report, and so on. Each genre is characterized by specific elements.

Questions about genre include:

- Has the writer selected an appropriate genre for her message?

- Having chosen a genre, does the writer demonstrate familiarity with the elements of the selected form?

conventions

Conventions are the surface features of the finished product: correct spelling, grammar, and punctuation. Conventions also include the quality of such details as the pictures, the book assembly, and the handwriting, typing, or quality of computer printout.

Questions to ask about conventions include:

- What is the final ratio between correctly and incorrectly spelled words?

- What seems to be the student's level of spelling development?

- Has the writer used a variety of sentence structures?

- Which grammar rules is the student able to apply? Which cause difficulty?

- Which punctuation and capitalization rules does the student seem to understand? Which remain unclear?

- To what extent is the student's handwriting clear and legible? Which letters does the student have difficulty forming correctly?

- Is the typing accurate?

- Is the final print clear and dark enough if from a computer?

- Do the illustrations enhance the text?

performance samples

Questions like those above about each part of the writing process tie closely to instruction. Answers to them are best gathered over time as part of classroom literacy events. At times, however, teachers may need to make one-time observations of students' writing. These single assessments are used to assess students' strengths and weaknesses in order to determine whether to admit particular students to a program, how to begin instruction, or in monitoring pre- and post-program gains. We will discuss three types of performance samples and their scoring: holistic, analytic, and the *Authoring Cycle Profile*. Holistic and analytic scoring measure only the final written product. The *Authoring Cycle Profile* also allows a teacher to analyze a student's work over the course of the writing process.

holistic scoring

In the past ten to fifteen years, holistic assessment of students' written products has been implemented in some school districts and special programs as a more valid measure of writing abilities and development than the spelling and grammar sections of standardized tests (Applebee, Langer, & Mullis, 1989). *A Procedure for Writing Assessment and Holistic Scoring* (Myers, 1980) is a short, highly readable book that explains in detail how holistic and analytic assessments are managed. In general, students are given a topic to write about, often in the form of a verbal prompt, and approximately thirty to sixty minutes to complete the task.

Extreme care must be given to the design of the topic (O'Donnell, 1984). Topics should be relevant to students' backgrounds so that they will have something to say. Authentic audiences and purposes for the writing should also be considered. In addition, if the prompt is to be read by students themselves, it needs to be written carefully so that any reading problems students have will not become a complication in determining how well they understood and developed their writing. In many situations it is a good practice to read the prompt to students.

As part of our research study, the Colorado Literacy Project, we have been developing alternative writing assessments to try out in a local school district. One topic the district currently uses at the intermediate grade levels is "my life as a headband." Students are asked to complete a piece about this topic in a one-hour sitting, including both a draft and final copy if they so choose. Some students find this topic "fun," but many do not. It is clear to them that there is no audience for the piece, and that they are writing it only for evaluation. In contrast, we designed a more authentic task that directed the teacher to read a letter from the school principal asking students to write letters with suggestions about how learning in their school could be improved. In advance, we persuaded each principal to read and reply in some manner to students' letters.

On the first day, students engaged in some discussion of the topic and wrote a draft. All the children had ideas and opinions, and could offer suggestions. They wrote believing that their letters would be read and, if they were convincing, that their suggestions would be acted on. On the second day, students were asked to revise their letters. On the third day, they were given time to complete any final editing and recopying they wanted to do. The principals followed up by reading all of the letters and writing a reply to each class or holding a discussion with them. In several schools student councils are now considering some of the students' suggestions for improving learning.

Children's writing samples are collected and then scored. If they are rated holistically, each receives a single score. Usually, this is a ranking of 1 to 4, 1 to 5, or 1 to 6, depending on how many categories have been deemed present or useful. To develop rubrics that describe a common "1" paper, a "2" paper, and so on, a subsample of all the writing samples is separated into piles reflecting the number of

Student ID# _____ Rater _____ Score _____

	1	2	3	4
Idea/Elaboration	Lacks understanding of task; no idea; no elaboration	Vague idea; understands task	Clear idea; moderate elaboration	Clear, perhaps original idea; well elaborated
Organization	No organized plan; reader unclear &/or confused; no paragraphing	Weak organized plan; reader unclear &/or confused; Inappropriate paragraphing	Some organized plan; reader has some sense of author train of thought; generally good paragraphing	Idea developed in logical sequence; reader has clear sense of author's train of thoughts; correct paragraphing
Complexity of Sentence Structure/ Usage	Many fragments &/or run-ons; many grammar & usage problems	Correct but very simple sentence structure; some grammar & usage problems	Some complex sentence structures; mostly conventional grammar & usage	Control of longer, complex sentences; correct grammar & usage
Spelling	Virtually all letter name or transitional; very few words spelled correctly	Basic sight words spelled correctly; problems with content words; ways to spell endings	Good overall spelling, occasional problem with: correct endings, homonyms, difficult content words	Almost all correct, an unusual content word may be misspelled
Caps/Punctuation	Virtually no caps or punctuation	Limited correct use of caps & punctuation	Caps good; punctuation okay, except for unusual constructions	Virtually all caps & punctuation correct

Yes	No	
_____	_____	Are there drafts?
_____	_____	Content focus on revisions? Substantial?
_____	_____	Mechanics focus on revisions? Substantial?
_____	_____	Adult intervention on revisions?

Figure 6.2 Analytic Scoring Guide from the Colorado Literacy Study

levels that have been predetermined or that seem to be present naturally. Raters agree on and record descriptors of papers at each level. These exemplar papers and descriptors serve to guide the raters, since they give a single score to each of the other papers. Normally, each paper is scored twice, each time by a different judge. If there is disagreement of more than two levels, the paper is also rated by a third person. Periodically, interrater reliability is checked, and if it seems to be falling, raters are asked to go back and look at the sample papers and the descriptors once again.

Holistic sampling allows a district to examine children's actual ability to compose text rather than just their performance on the spelling or grammar sections of a standardized test. In holistic assessments, however, the standard error of measurement for any single child is so great that using individual scores is invalid. Instead, the most valid use of the tests is to examine district trends. Additionally, while scores—say a 2 in the fall and a 4 in the spring—show significant progress, teachers have no idea in which specific areas children have improved or in which they need further work.

analytic scoring

Analytic scoring (also called primary-trait scoring) was devised to assess more specific areas of writing than holistic scoring does. When a district wants to do analytic scoring, normally a committee of interested teachers and administrators decides which characteristics of written products they think are important. Usually broad areas are selected, such as ideas, organization, grammar and usage, and conventions. Children's writing samples are then rated in these areas according to a scale—often 1 to 5 or 1 to 6. Descriptors are written for each of the areas. Figure 6.2 shows an example that was used to rate samples from the Colorado Literacy Study (Davis et al., 1992).

Analytic scoring can be useful to teachers at the beginning of the year if results are returned in a timely manner. Teachers can then adjust their instruction to concentrate on areas in which students demonstrate greatest need. End-of-the-year scores help teachers judge the effectiveness of their teaching and target curricular areas they need to revise for the following year (Olson & Swadener, 1984). Analytic scoring has also been adapted as a way to grade papers. If students are encouraged to help develop the rubric and assess their own work and that of their classmates, it can become a means for student self-assessment.

The differences between holistic and analytic scoring can be summarized as follows: Holistic scoring requires each judge to give a paper a single rating. It is relatively quick to do and can be used in gross ways to gauge program effectiveness. Analytic scoring results in several scores for each piece of writing. Numbers reflect raters' judgments across several areas of concern about students' written products. It takes longer, but it provides teachers with more useful information about specific areas of positive growth and areas that need further work.

authoring cycle profile

Neither holistic nor analytic scoring assesses students' actual writing processes. They can only assess students' written products. The *Authoring Cycle Profile*, developed by Shanklin and found in the handbook (Rhodes, 1993) that accompanies this book, is an instrument developed to assess children's writing processes as well as their written products. This instrument can be used with individual children in one-to-one settings or with small groups to collect information on a whole class over time.

The *Authoring Cycle Profile* is divided into four major areas: processes for drafting, conferring and Authors' Circle, revision and editing, and final product. These four areas, plus their subcategories, are similar to those found in the Authoring Cycle diagram in Figure 6.1. Areas to consider, corresponding to the questions about children's writing processes and products listed in this chapter, appear at the top. Each page has room for the names and anecdotal notes for up to six students at a time.

A teacher can make observations and take notes for a class of up to thirty students, covering their writing processes and final products, in one-hour sessions over eight school days. This schedule may seem rigorous and lengthy, but the information collected would be valuable in several ways, such as planning mini-lessons, organizing groups for lessons on particular writing strategies or conventions, and holding individual student conferences.

During this time the teacher might require the assistance of another adult, who would be responsible for the other children while she worked with specific groups. This could be a special teacher such as a Chapter I teacher who could also use the data to plan instruction, another member of a teacher's team, a parent volunteer, an administrator, a librarian, a music teacher, and so on. The helper could be asked to conduct tasks such as read-alouds, sustained silent readings, writing in literature or learning logs and entry sharing, and showing filmstrips on authors whose books children are reading.

On Day 1 of *Authoring Cycle Profile* data collection, the teacher would divide the class into five groups of approximately five students each. She would then begin to work with Group 1 by explaining the task and taking anecdotal notes as the children rehearsed and drafted their pieces. Groups 2 to 5 would be supervised by another adult. The *Authoring Cycle Profile* form suggests areas a teacher may want to observe during this forty-minute block.

On Day 2 the teacher would do the same initial assessment of rehearsal and drafting for Group 2. All the other groups would again be doing independent activities facilitated by another adult. Following the drafting, the teacher would call the whole class together for Authors' Circle. Students from Group 1 would share their pieces. On Day 3 the teacher would spent part of her time getting Group 3 started, taking notes on the Authors' Circle with students from Group 2 as featured authors, and observing the revising and editing of students from Group 1. By Day 4 students from Group 1 should have their final products ready for analysis. The cycle would continue in this manner until all the groups had finished their pieces.

There are many additional ways to use the *Authoring Cycle Profile*. A teacher could collect writing samples from all students at once and, using holistic or analytic scoring, decide which students need to be observed more closely during their whole writing process according to the *Authoring Cycle Profile*.

To be useful to teachers, information from instruments like the *Authoring Cycle Profile* needs to be collected during the opening weeks of school, preferably by the end of September, so that the results can truly influence instruction for the remainder of the school year. If teachers are to gain the responsibility as professionals for designing their own curricula, they need to plan the collection of assessment information carefully, even before school begins. All too often teachers and districts get off to a slow start and are still collecting and analyzing data in late October. End-of-the-year

Authoring Cycle Profiles are probably best collected in late April or May. In using the profile in a pre- or post-test manner, it is important for teachers to reread their initial profiles so that observations of growth in the same areas can be noted on the post-test.

assessing writing within literacy events

Performance samples are most often used to provide pre-and post-test information to determine program effectiveness and further guide program development. They may also be used to begin the year or to learn more about students who represent particular challenges. Of more help to teachers are new ways to collect on-going assessments of students' writing that document growth and help them make decisions about what kind of instruction to provide next (Lucas, 1988). Such ongoing assessment data can be collected during Writing Workshop or other literacy events that involve writing.

Ongoing assessment of writing in classrooms should involve teachers, students, and parents. As a practical matter, teachers do not have the time to collect all assessment data themselves and thus need to involve students. Participation often encourages students to learn more, to develop responsibility, and to increase their independence as writers. We will suggest teacher assessment and student self-assessment in the literacy events that follow. Bonnie DeFreece's "Teacher Reflection" at the end of the chapter outlines a powerful method for getting parents more involved in the assessment and development of their child's writing.

writing workshop

authoring cycle status

Teachers can learn a great deal about children's writing processes at the beginning of Writing Workshop if they quickly poll students about what they are going to work on or move around the room speaking to individual students. Children's answers reveal whether they understand various parts of the Authoring Cycle and can identify where they are in the cycle. Teachers can also discover where children are having trouble. When a student knows a final product is due soon but has been drawing, drafting, and abandoning new pieces for a week, the teacher can intervene. A chart that indicates students' Authoring Cycle status is a management tool that helps a teacher decide who needs help right away during workshop time (Atwell, 1987).

As another alternative, students can keep a chart indicating "the status of my writing" in their writing folders. Having children keep these charts encourages them to internalize parts of the writing process, decide where they are in the process, and set their own goals for moving through the Authoring Cycle. In conferring with a student or reviewing writing folders, a teacher can quickly consult the chart to spot where the child is in the cycle and if she needs to be nudged to move to the next area.

conferring

In Writing Workshop a teacher can arrange to confer with an individual student at any point during the Authoring Cycle. Likewise, a student can request a conference at any point. Teachers we know have devised four methods for keeping track of conferences. You may want to experiment with these methods, or others you devise, until you find one that works well for you.

The first method many teachers find successful is to keep anecdotal notes about conferring on a form in each child's writing folder. The advantage of this system is that no additional filing is needed, nor do teachers have to shuffle through the pages of a separate notebook to find anecdotal notes on a particular child.

The second method uses a form that lists all the students' names. The teacher records dates and anecdotal notes for all the children on this sheet. When grading or perusing students' folders, the teacher can also add additional notes to this form. It becomes a quick way for the teacher to check whether she has conferred with every student at least once in each two-week period.

In the third method, teachers take anecdotal notes on, or attach stick-on notes to, a writing assessment sheet. These are usually kept in a large notebook with dividers and pages for each child. These notes include observations and information about conferences with each student. When a student teacher or special teacher from an in-class program is present, this becomes an efficient way for both teachers to collect notes on children, file them, read them, and discuss their observations and subsequent teaching goals, which can be listed in a special right-hand column on each child's sheets.

Marty Frampton, a first-grade teacher in the Cherry Creek School District in Aurora, Colorado, has devised yet a fourth system for taking anecdotal notes. She makes observations about two students at a time on a sheet divided into two long columns, which she clips to her clipboard. The top of each child's column is devoted to writing and the bottom to reading. The writing section has five observational areas: topic selection, content, revision, participation in Authors' Circle, and ties between reading and writing. Because children's pieces are often short in the primary grades, she can usually gather all of this information in a day or two. She finds that she has time to make observations of six children (three sheets on her clipboard) per day.

Students can also assess their own peer conferences. In Lori Murray's fourth-grade classroom in the Adams 12 School District in Westminster, Colorado, a student wanting to confer with another fills out a conference form (see Figure 6.3). The student states what she wants to work on during the conference: spelling, capi-

```
Name _____ Date _____
I conferred with_____

                Requesting a Peer Revising and Editing Conference
Before you confer, be sure to have thought about and checked off each of these points:
_____ 1. Does all my information belong in this story or should some be crossed
            out?
_____ 2. I have answered three or more of the questions asked of me in the
            Authors' Circle.
_____ 3. I have checked my conventions sheet for all the writing conventions that I
            am responsible for.

_____

During this peer revising and editing conference, I want to work on:

        _____Title                    _____Spelling
        _____Organization             _____Capitals
        _____Ending                   _____Sentence Endings
```

Figure 6.3   Request for a peer revising and editing conference

tals, punctuation, title, organization, ending. Before beginning the conference, the student is asked to think about whether she has 1) checked to see that all of the information belongs in the story or decided what needs to be crossed out; 2) revised in response to three or more of the questions that were asked during Authors' Circle; and 3) checked the "my skills" sheet for all the skills she is responsible for and edited the piece for these things. Students sign up on the board in pairs when they are ready to confer. Only four pairs can sign up at a time, since this is the number of conference stations in the room. Students focus on one paper at a conference. Since Murray instituted this self-assessment form, the students' conferences have been much more focused, and they have been taking much more responsibility for revision and editing.

revising and the authors' circle

The Authors' Circle is an excellent place for observing children's development as writers and determining what they are ready to learn next. Notes help teachers track how children use feedback to make revisions, edit, and publish. Rather than attempt to keep this information in their heads, teachers benefit from developing methods for taking consistent notes. Kathy Mestnik, a second-grade bilingual teacher, has devised a form to keep notes about children's work from Authors' Circle through to publication. The form is divided into five columns, labeled *title of the piece*, *Authors' Circle comments*, *revision*, *editing*, and *publishing*. Under each, as reminders to herself, she has listed prompts about items she is looking for. For example, under *revision* for each student's piece she wants to observe and note elements of the genre, organization, and use of Authors' Circle comments. There is also room on the sheet

```
+--------------------------------------------------------------------------+
|                        Peer Conferring Guide                             |
|        You have decided to be the point monitor for Round 1 of your      |
|   group today. Please record on the sheet the names of each person in    |
|   your group, including yourself. For each person, circle the role they  |
|   are playing in this round of the group conference. You will change     |
|   roles after each writer has shared his/her piece. By the end of the    |
|   conference session, there should be a circle for each person around    |
|   each of the three roles: 1) shares writing, 2) secretary, and 3)       |
|   discusses the writing of others.                                       |
|        Your job as point monitor is to make a mark in the appropriate    |
|   blank under each person's name for "discusses writing of others" each  |
|   time that person speaks. When a group is working well, you will end    |
|   up with approximately an equal number of marks under each person's     |
|   name.                                                                  |
|        The job of the secretary is to use a separate piece of paper to   |
|   write down questions and suggestions from the group for the author and |
|   give them to him/her.                                                  |
|        To figure the total score for each group member, count each mark  |
|   for discussing the writing as one point.                               |
|                                                                          |
|   Name _____      Name _____        |
|                                                                          |
|   Shares writing          10 pts    Shares writing          10 pts       |
|   Secretary                5 pts    Secretary                5 pts       |
|   Discusses writing of others ___ pts  Discusses writing of others ___ pts |
|   Point monitor            2 pts    Point monitor            2 pts       |
|   Total                  ___ pts    Total                  ___ pts       |
|                                                                          |
|   Note: Continue development of the form for as many students as are in  |
|   a group. You may be able to create blocks for up to six students on    |
|   one standard-size page.                                                |
+--------------------------------------------------------------------------+
```

Figure 6.4   Peer Conferring Guide

to take notes about five of a child's pieces of writing. This allows Mestnik to assess improvements in revision and editing over time.

Other teachers take anecdotal notes about the Authors' Circle each day and use these notes to plan lessons. In one classroom where children were first beginning to work on how to confer as part of a group share, the teacher noticed that students did not give each other specific compliments or ask specific questions. The following day the teacher took anecdotal notes and this time she wrote down the specific questions the students asked. Listed on chart paper and read to the whole group, they became illustrations of the kinds of specific questions students could use. Not only did the feedback in Authors' Circle improve in quality, but students also began to successfully implement peer conferences.

At first, teachers may have to write down questions and suggestions for each student as they share in the Authors' Circle. Gradually, however, students can assume responsibility for keeping track of this feedback themselves. By the time they are in the intermediate grades especially, students can write down the questions asked or the suggestions offered right on their drafts or use stick-on notes provided for this purpose. Students can also tell classmates what they would like them to listen for or what they would like help with. In these ways, students become more involved in improving the quality of their own writing.

By the intermediate grades and middle school, students can operate more and more in their own Authors' Circles of four to six students. With some groups, no further monitoring is needed if the students are clear about their roles and the procedures. Simpson-Esper (1988) has developed a comprehensive checklist she uses to monitor individual student performance as part of student response groups. She looks for about ten elements under each of three areas: 1) identity within the response group, 2) use of suggestions, and 3) development of group interaction skills.

For students who need more structure, a form for running and evaluating small group conferences is helpful. Tammy Smiley, formerly of Sheridan Middle School in Sheridan, Colorado, has developed such a form using principles from cooperative learning (see Figure 6.4). The children are divided into groups of three. Student roles are: 1) writer who shares, 2) secretary who writes down comments, 3) and point monitor who keeps track of the person offering each comment. The two students who are not the writer are responsible for commenting on the piece. The roles rotate through the group and students get points for each one. By using the form, students learn appropriate procedures for working in small conference groups. Once students learn these roles well, it may be possible to dispense with the form.

Another kind of self-assessment suggested by Karen Spear in *Sharing Writing* (1988) helps students assess conference groups. Students are asked to respond to four questions in writing—two before and two after the conference. Prior to the group session, students are asked to list the strengths of their drafts and then to note any sticking points where they are still unsure. After the session, students must note the most essential contributions from members of the group for revising their pieces and list the modifications they plan to make in their drafts.

All of these ideas for student self-assessments emphasize learning to work together in Authors' Circles and various peer response groups. Atwell (1987), however, brings up another crucial point. One of the ultimate goals of Authors' Circles ought to be that students learn to do initial rounds of conferring on their own rather than immediately going to ask friends for their opinions. (This is part of the gradual release of responsibility discussed in Chapter 2.) To encourage a gradual assumption of personal responsibility for improving their own writing, Atwell suggests several questions that students can ask as they have writing conferences with themselves. We have found it best not to ask students to focus on too many questions a a time. We would not use all of Atwell's questions on a single piece of writing. Rather, we might focus on four or five items and change these as students demonstrate that they know they should check for these problems independently. Then new questions can be developed, or students can be asked to develop their own personal self-conference forms, which they will consult before going to confer with others. Some potential questions for self-conferring might be:

- Did I include everything I wanted to say?

- What is the best part of this piece; could I develop that part even more?

- Is my wording concise?

- Are my tenses consistent?

- Would it work better to organize this piece in another way?

```
┌─────────────────────────────────────────────────────────────────────┐
│                                                                       │
│   Name _____  Date_____             │
│                                                                       │
│   Title of my piece _____          │
│                                                                       │
│                        Editing Checklist                              │
│   _____  1.  I've shared my piece and made changes.               │
│   _____  2.  I've checked for periods.                            │
│   _____  3.  I've checked for capital letters.                    │
│   _____  4.  I've corrected my spelling.                          │
│                                                                       │
│   Author's comments:                                                  │
│                                                                       │
│                                                                       │
│                                                                       │
│   Tasks to learn:                                                     │
│                                                                       │
│                                                                       │
│                                                                       │
└─────────────────────────────────────────────────────────────────────┘
```

Figure 6.5   Editing Checklist

other literacy events involving writing

editing

Being the sole editors of students' papers is not a good role for teachers to play. Too often, however, students write rough drafts, give them to their teachers (or parents) for editing, and then recopy, making the changes teachers or parents have marked. Under such circumstances, students learn little about taking responsibility for polishing their own writing. Instead, writing becomes an assignment to complete, give to a more proficient writer to correct, and uncritically recopy in order to get a grade. When this is the process students use, they have little opportunity to internalize how to improve the quality of their writing or to feel a real sense of accomplishment from working through a set of ideas and communicating them well to others.

For editing to be of value to students, they must do it themselves. At first a teacher may need to work on editing directly with a student. The teacher negotiates what the piece is going to be edited for with the student and gets the student as involved as possible in finding errors. This process is different from the teacher taking the writer's paper, marking it elsewhere, and returning it for recopying. With time, a teacher can ask the student to edit her own paper before the two of them arrange a final editing conference. Often it helps if the teacher has made up an editing form listing items the student should look for. Students can also use such lists to guide peer editing.

For her middle-school Chapter I program, Tammy Smiley has also devised a peer-editing form. This form, which is quite long, is to be used after students have shared their pieces in Authors' Circle and made content revisions. The form lists all the writing conventions that have been taught and for which students are responsible. Depending on their developing abilities as writers, some students may not be responsible for all the items on the checklist. On the left-hand side are two columns, one for the student to use when self-checking each convention and the other for when two students do peer editing.

An editing checklist (see Figure 6.5) used by primary reading/writing specialist Mary Hellen of Adams County District 12 in Westminster, Colorado, is much simpler. Before having a final editing conference with the teacher, a student must make sure she is ready. The author is then asked for her comments. Janna wrote, "I like my 2 draft beder becuse it is loger." If a child has trouble completing these corrections, the teacher can then go over the concepts involved as part of her final editing conference with the student. The teacher can also note a child's progress and list new conventions for which she would like her to be responsible.

spelling

Learning to spell is a developmental process of gradual approximation that takes place over several years (Jongsma, 1990; Gentry, 1981, 1987; Nathenson-Mejia, 1989; Read, 1975). In fact, as literate adults, we are still learning to spell new words. Research over the past fifteen years has shown that spelling development occurs in the same ways as oral language development, especially when viewed within the larger perspective of learning to write. Parents and teachers celebrate the attempts young children make to communicate through oral language. They try very hard to understand the child's meaning even when the talk is not particularly clear or grammatically correct. Rather than directly correcting the child's language, they offer a model of how something might be said. They do not demand that children learn several words before attempting to communicate. They understand that the desire to communicate is what fuels the need to learn words. They do not expect immediate perfection from young children and trust that with time and experience their oral language will become more standard. Spelling needs to be considered from a similar perspective.

Spelling ought to be seen within the context of the whole writing process (Bean & Bouffler, 1988; Sowers, 1988). When children are required to learn to spell words correctly before they learn to compose, it stifles the writing process. Instead, teachers need to learn to analyze students' spelling development *within their writing* in order to understand what it is developmentally possible to teach students next—without squelching the development of the entire writing process. Teachers need to gather information about each student as a speller in three areas: level of spelling development, knowledge of common spelling rules, and spelling strategies used during drafting and editing. Additional information about students' attitudes toward

Stage	Definition	Example
Prephonemic	String letters and other "letterlike" symbols together without representing speech sounds in any systematic way.	DLD for "once" RZF for "witch"
Phonemic	Use one or two letters to represent the most salient sounds they hear in the words they write. May add a string of random letters after representing the sounds they hear so the words look the right size.	JD for "jumped" HD for "shed"
Letter-name	Use letters to represent all the sound features of words they write. The letters are often chosen on the basis of how closely the sound of the letter name matches the sounds heard.	LRND for "learned" PECT for "picked" MI for "my"
Transitional	Produce spellings that look correct because they employ many of the features of standard spelling—silent letters, endings, vowels in each syllable, digraphs, blends, etc. These features are sometimes used inconsistently or incorrectly. Standard spelling of frequently used words is often interspersed throughout their writing.	LURND for "learned" BUTUN for "button"
Derivational and Correct	Spell phonetically regular and irregular words correctly most of the time. They are able to think of other possible spellings to use when confronted with words that don't look right. They know/use alternative word forms (derivations) as well as prefixes, suffixes, contractions, word families, spelling patterns, and basic spelling rules to generate standard spellings.	SIGN for "sign"

Figure 6.6   Stages of spelling development

spelling and spelling strategies can also be gained from the writing interview (see Chapter 3).

Level of spelling development. When teachers begin to assess students' spelling, most start by attempting to determine the students' levels of spelling development. Many researchers have identified the same basic patterns in students' development but divide them in slightly different ways and give them slightly different names. We have adopted the scheme developed by Temple et al. (1988) (see Figure 6.6).

Information for analyzing students' levels of spelling development can be gathered in two ways: 1) by examining spellings in pieces they have written as part of Writing Workshop or other literacy events in the classroom, or 2) by looking at their spellings on carefully constructed word lists that use common spelling patterns. Although word lists have disadvantages (you cannot examine the spelling strategies students use as part of the writing process), when given at the opening of the school year they provide teachers with some quick information about the spelling levels of their new students. Asking students to spell words from a list is also helpful if stu-

| Name | Mindy | | Dates | 10/90 | 11/90 |

Group 1	Group 2	Group 3	Group 4
(and)	all	by	after
are	any	come	an
at	been	(get)	boy
be	day	go	cat
but	do	has	(did)
(can)	from	him	down
for	girl	his	give
have	good *gode*	how	here
in	had	know	just
(is)	he	like	long
it	her	little	new
(not)	(I)	make	old
of	if	(no)	put
on	me	or	said *sed*
that	(my) *mi*	our	she
(the)	one	(see)	take
this	out	them	their
to	so	then	three
we	some	two	were
will	there	(us)	who
with	they	was	
(you)	(up)	what	
your	very	which	
	when		

Figure 6.7   Monaco's list of frequently used words, marked for Mindy

dents are reluctant to take risks in spelling new words in their own writing. When lists are used with these students, the words the teacher pronounces challenge them to reveal what strategies they do know, even if they are uncertain about whether their spellings are accurate. We recommend the lists developed by Gillet & Temple (1990) as most useful.

To score a student's list and determine her level of spelling development, the teacher analyzes each spelling for the level of development it demonstrates; the level that characterizes most of the student's spellings is her level of spelling development. For example, if a writer has five letter-name spellings, two transitional spellings, and three correct spellings, her developmental level is letter-name.

Sue Monaco, a first-grade teacher for the Jefferson County Public Schools in Colorado, has developed an assessment procedure that documents students' growth in learning to spell frequently used words. This assessment is very reassuring to parents who are anxious to see their young children progress as spellers. Any list of frequently used words, preferably in alphabetical order, may be used. Once a month, Monaco reviews each student's lengthiest piece (or pieces) to see which words from the list each child has attempted and whether the words are spelled correctly. Each month she uses a different color marker to record the student's progress. As Figure

6.7 shows, by October Mindy had inventively spelled "good" and "my" from the list and had correctly spelled "I." By November she was able to spell the other circled words correctly and had attempted "said." In December Monaco reviewed another of Mindy's writing samples and marked more words, doing these in yet a different color. At parent conferences, she used the form to show Mindy's parents their daughter's progress in attempting new invented spellings and gradually learning correct spellings of frequently used words.

As we mentioned, the analysis of children's level of spelling development helps teachers decide what instruction is most appropriate to spur further development. The "levels" (actually categories would be a better word) are only meant to be descriptors that fit a majority of a child's spelling attempts. In addition, in doing an analysis of spelling from actual writing samples, it is important for teachers to consider whether they are looking at spelling in drafts or in what the writer considers a final product. Spellings in drafts are normally more rough and represent less reflective efforts than those found in final products, where students have had time to focus on demonstrating their best spelling.

Knowledge of common spelling rules. Teachers also need to determine the common spelling rules with which children are familiar. Here are seven of the most common (Gentry, 1987):

1. The rules for adding suffixes (changing y to i, dropping the final silent e, and doubling the final consonant).

2. The rule that English words don't end in v.

3. The rule that q is always followed by u in English spelling.

4. The rules for creating plurals (adding es to words ending in ch, sh, s, ss, and x, and changing f to v then adding es).

5. The rules for using periods in abbreviations.

6. The rules for using apostrophes with contractions and possessive words.

7. The rules for capitalizing proper nouns and adjectives formed from proper nouns.

Writing samples are the best source of information about students' knowledge and use of these rules. In writing samples, children are more likely to demonstrate both the rules they know and the ones they are confused about. Silva and Yarborough (1990) suggest that spelling errors break down into three types: those that are language/dialect-related, those that involve orthographic rules/conventions, and those that involve learned lexicon/visual memory. Each student's writing ought to be examined for these and other error patterns. Once an error pattern is identified, the teacher and student can work together to learn a new pattern.

Knowledge and use of spelling strategies. Writing samples can also provide information about the strategies students use for spelling during drafting and editing (Gable, Hendrickson, & Meeks, 1988; Wilde, 1989a, 1989b, 1990). Teachers can

Review of Categories for Misspelling Analysis

Each misspelling is examined to see if it fits into *one or more* of the following categories:

PURPOSE OF CATEGORIES	CATEGORIES
To observe the student's use of PHONETIC CUES.	1. The misspelling is Phonetic.
To observe the student's use of PHONIC CUES.	2. The misspelling is related to using Phonic cues.
To detect instances where the student could have used meaning and syntactic cues but did not, or did not have the knowledge to apply meaning and syntactic cues to create standard spellings.	3. The writer used the wrong form of a homophone. 4. A suffix is misspelled, misused, or omitted. 5. The misspelling has to do with the root within a word. 6. The misspelling has to do with punctuation.
To balance out misspellings with examples of standard spelling showing successful use of PHONIC and SYNTACTIC-SEMANTIC CUES.	7. Standard spellings revealing the successful use of Phonics or Syntactic-Semantic cues.
To note where penmanship interferes with spelling.	8. The apparent misspelling is due to penmanship.

Figure 6.8   Categories for misspelling analysis

best determine these strategies by observing children during the whole of the writing process (as in the *Authoring Cycle Profile*). They can observe whether the writer:

- Asks the teacher or a friend for a spelling.

- Primarily uses words she already knows how to spell correctly.

- Looks around the room or in books for spellings.

- Invents a spelling by thinking about the sounds.

- Thinks about how a word might look.

- Thinks about the base and prefixes and suffixes that go into a word.

- Crosses out rather than erases.

- Marks a word to come back to later for editing.

Writers may also employ some of these same strategies during editing along with several others. During editing a teacher can observe whether students:

- Can find their spelling errors on their own.

- Can fix spelling errors on their own.

- Try writing out a spelling several ways before picking the one that looks right.

- Think about spelling rules, for which they are accountable, and try to correct spelling errors.

MISSPELLING ANALYSIS
DATA COLLECTION FORM

Name of student _____ Date _____

School Group _____ Selection _____

Coding:	Meaning-related Categories		
1. Phonetic	3. Homophone	5. Root	7. Standard Spelling
2. Phonic	4. Suffix	6. Punctuation	8. Penmanship

STAN. SPELL.	MISSPELLING	ASSESSMENT	COMMENTS

7. STANDARD SPELLINGS	8. PENMANSHIP

Figure 6.9   Misspelling analysis data collection form

Buchanan (1989) has developed the most comprehensive method for collecting and analyzing data on children's spelling. The system she has developed encourages teachers to examine children's spelling for level of development, knowledge of spelling rules, and strategies. She suggests several activities through which teachers can collect samples of children's spellings for analysis: free writing, directed writing, cloze, retellings, dictated retellings, wordless books, students' own research on topics of interest, point-of-view stories, dictated lists, diagnostic dictation, and informal observation. Misspellings gathered through these means are then analyzed by category of error. Buchanan identifies eight categories (see Figure 6.8). A misspelling may fit into more than one category at a time.

Buchanan has also developed a convenient form the teacher can use to complete her analysis (see Figure 6.9). In the first column the teacher writes the standard spelling of each word; in the second, the student's misspelling; in the third, the category of the error; and in the last, additional comments. The teacher then notes any demonstrations that the student has learned a new spelling rule and finally records any penmanship problems that interfered with correct spellings.

Another form allows the teacher to analyze this information further by determining the percentage of words spelled correctly in the piece and commenting on the attitudes and strategies the student has. The areas covered are feelings about spelling, willingness to risk, interest in spelling, use of resources, willingness to do quick checks and edit, and ability to identify misspellings. The form also contains room for the teacher to plan further instruction for the child and compare this assessment to earlier samples.

Students can also be involved in their own spelling assessment, which encourages them to take more responsibility for their own spelling and develop a spelling consciousness. This consciousness will help them to suspect when a spelling is wrong and to take particular care over correct spelling when they edit. However, an emphasis on correct spelling, especially as part of editing, should not begin until students have developed some fluency in using invented spelling and in transcribing. For young writers, simply getting their messages down is hard enough. It deserves praise without putting undue emphasis on going back to edit for correct spelling. By late first grade or in second grade, many students begin to show interest in how words are spelled; as readers they have begun to notice correct spellings. If students are still using only invented spellings by third grade, the teacher needs to consider more direct ways to draw their attention to the conventions of correct spelling.

As students begin to show interest in correct spelling, they can be asked to self-edit their papers for spelling errors by circling them. They may need to do this when they have first completed a rough draft—especially if a child is an emerging reader and writer who has trouble remembering the word she has attempted to write. A child should receive help with these words so that she can read the draft smoothly in Authors' Circle. At other times, self-editing does not occur until after the child has made content revisions.

Teachers can learn from the spelling errors children make but also from the errors children do and do not catch as part of their self-editing. During drafting we often produce misspellings; the spellings may not totally reflect our level of spelling development or our knowledge of common spelling rules. What students choose to circle and their attempts at correction during editing often provide further insights into their current usage and areas of potential development.

After they have engaged in self-editing for spelling, students can be asked to work with their peers on further editing. Sometimes students are more willing and can spot errors in others' papers more easily than in their own. When students work together, teachers can also observe how they take in and subsequently use the spelling tips they give each other.

Writers can keep a spelling log of words they want to know how to spell and words that are problems for them. The log becomes a quick, easy-to-use reference for students to consult for correct spellings as part of drafting or editing. They can then be held accountable for spelling words from their logs correctly, especially as a part of editing.

Using a form similar to Figure 6.9, students might be asked to analyze the nature of their own spelling errors (using Buchanan's categories or ones they devise with their teacher) and make suggestions about how they might overcome these error patterns. Students can also be asked to keep track of whether they have consulted the editing checklists in their writing folders for the spelling rules they have learned. See Rhodes, 1993 for other assessment forms students may use to assess their own spelling.

journals, literature logs, learning logs

Writing as a way to think about our lives, the books we read, and what we learn is receiving more and more emphasis in classrooms. Students keep journals about the events, feelings, and people in their lives. Especially in Reading Workshop, students keep literature logs or write letters to their teacher or their peers about the books they are reading. As part of thematic units or middle school content area classes, students keep learning logs that hold class notes, brief in-class writings, summaries of materials read, observations from experiments, questions, predictions, and so on.

Many teachers believe that the writing in journals, literature logs, and learning logs should not be assessed. We would suggest that such writing can be assessed but not necessarily graded. As Fulwiler (1989) argues, "If journal writing is ever to achieve some measure of academic respectability, it too must be, to some extent, describable and understandable. In other words, how teachers respond to journal writing will depend on how well they can identify exactly what it is and does" (pp. 160–161).

First and foremost, journals, literature logs, and learning logs are collections of first draft writings. These writings fit into the category of expressive writing (Britton et al., 1975) which uses language close to the writer's self. Britton and his colleagues describe these as 1) thinking aloud on paper; 2) explorations of the writer's feelings, mood, opinions, and preoccupations of the moment; and 3) cases in which a writer may actively invoke a close relationship with his reader.

Graves (1989b) has studied the letters children have written to their teacher and peers about books they are reading in Reading Workshop. He noticed that three important features emerge over time: 1) engagement with the teacher over books, 2) engagement with characters in the books, and 3) engagement with the author.

After studying reading logs for a one-year period, Wilson (1989) found that they have specific characteristics. Her study focused on the logs of high school students, but her findings seem applicable to students at many levels. Wilson discovered that in logs where students are actively engaged, they admit confusion, ask questions, make connections, read with attention, identify with characters and authors, revise readings, question, and change.

Given this research base, we would suggest that teachers read students' work for these qualities and develop their own list to reflect their instructional goals. For example, if a teacher has been asking students to make connections between the books they are reading, they can look for evidence whether students are doing so in their journal entries. When teachers see that certain qualities are missing, they could decide to introduce them through mini-lessons.

researching and reporting

Many of the ways to assess how students use reading and writing to learn content link to their writing of reports. One technique is to ask students to develop questions that will guide their research and report writing. The quality of the questions provides information about a student's true interest in the topic and what she already knows. The questions also help a teacher understand the stance a student wants to take toward a particular subject.

Another approach is to have students develop and give surveys on the topics of their reports. These surveys are most valuable early in the research process. The talk accompanying the development of the surveys reveals a great deal of information about what students themselves do and do not know about their topics. Students need to reflect on the particular questions they want to ask fellow students, parents, teachers, administrators, and the public at large. Survey results lead to further reflection about the characteristics of the writer's audience and how to write the report if it is to be of interest to readers (Graves, 1989a).

Still other sources of useful information about students' comprehension are data charts (Koeller, 1982) or note cards (question/heading at the top, followed by the answer/information found and the citation of the source). The quality of the information can be an indicator of what students understand from their reading. In talking with students about data charts or note cards, you may need to probe more deeply. You may find that students have a wealth of information when they talk about a passage orally but find it hard to put the information in their own words and write it down.

In her book, *Information Alive! Information Skills for Research and Reading*, Gwen Gawith (1987) has developed teacher and student assessments to help students reflect during the researching process. Gawith suggests an excellent set of questions for teachers to use in conferring with a student or small group during a research project:

- How did this assignment make you feel about yourself as a researcher?

- At what stage did you feel most/least confident in your research?

- Did you discover any skills that you are going to need to learn or to practice before you feel confident as a researcher?

- Would it be worthwhile for you to "walk" me right through all six stages of your research to see whether we can spot where things could have been better for you?

Name/s

Title of project/topic

After this research, how do you feel about yourself as a researcher? (Mark your position along this scale)

```
Bleh!    1    2    3    4    5    6    7    8    9    10    Whoopee!
I don't feel so good about research                        I feel confident as a researcher, I did all the stages well!
```

EVALUATING THE RESEARCH PROCESS

Stage 1: Identifying information need and purpose
What did you find easy/difficult about (1). Deciding what you needed to know? (2). What you were going to produce? (3) What you already knew? (4) How to map it?

[1]

[2]

[3]

[4]

Stage 2: Identifying a variety of information sources and resources
What did you find difficult? Deciding on sources? Locating the resources? Locating the information in the resources using catalogues, indexes, etc? Were there enough resources? Right level?

Stage 3: Identifying, locating and analysing information in the resources
What did you find difficult:
- Reading, looking, listening, interviewing with purpose?
- Questioning, using 'W' questions?
- Analysing, comparing, collating information under main headings?
- Distinguishing bias, propaganda, prejudice, fact, opinion

Stage 4: Recording and organizing relevant information
What did you find difficult:
- Using notemaking techniques (layout, punctuation, notation)?
- Working out what was important enough to record?
- Using an inefficient method of recording eg, notes instead of photos?

Stage 5: Presenting the information
What did you find difficult:
- Trying to do too much, getting carried away?
- Not understanding enough about the form (eg. debate) of the presentation, and not asking 'What am I doing, for whom?'

Figure 6.10   Gawith's guide to evaluating the research process

- What would you do differently if you did the same assignment again?

- What do you think teachers could have taught or shown you earlier to make this sort of thing easier for you?

- If you were teaching a younger class, what would be the most important things you think they should know about doing this sort of work?

- What did this assignment say to you about information—what it is, where you find it, how it is organized?

Sample research report checklist			
Task	Target date (for completion)	Self rating of quality (1–6)	Teacher check
Planning			
1. Brainstorm questions			
2. Categorize the questions; write them as statements			
3. Identify sources			
4. Set timelines			
Researching			
1. Read widely			
2. Take notes			
3. Make card file of references used			
Organizing			
1. List the main topics			
2. Identify subtopics			
3. Insert the details			
4. Check for completeness			
Writing			
1. Do first draft			
2. Revise			
3. Check spelling			
4. Proofread			
5. Do final copy			

Figure 6.11   Davey's sample research report checklist

Gawith has also developed an excellent guide (see Figure 6.10) to encourage students to assess their research experience and their ability to use the research process to learn about a topic. The guide asks students to assess how they feel about themselves as researchers on a 1 to 10 point scale, whether they have been able to begin focusing their research and decide what form they want their final product to take, if they have attempted to think about what they already know and developed a map to organize information and clarify the research they need to do. It goes on to ask them to assess their ability to find a variety of information sources, to reflect on their ability to read or conduct an interview, and to consider whether they have asked good questions. The major focus at this point is on whether the student can gather information well. The final series of questions ask students to assess how well they were able to take notes, decide what to include, and analyze their information, and last, to assess how well they were able to communicate the information they learned.

Beth Davey (1987) has developed a method for having students write cooperative research reports. Students are divided into groups of two to five members. Although the teacher might suggest a broad theme, individual groups would brainstorm to determine the particular focus of their report. After deciding on the specific topic, each group would plan how they would go about their research. Using a research plan sheet to guide their thinking, the group would decide on the subcategories to investigate, the resources to use, and target due dates for notetaking, outlining, first draft, second draft, and final due date. Finally, they would decide exactly what each group member would be responsible for doing. The other steps in the process involve researching the topic, organizing the information, and writing.

To help students reflect upon their own progress, Davey has also developed a research report checklist (see Figure 6.11), which includes the important features of the research process. On the form the student writes the date she completes each step and gives a self-rating (1–6) on how well she did in each area. There is also room for the teacher to check off and rate (plus or minus) how well the student did with each step. This form allows the teacher to spot particular problems students are having as they complete their research and to teach mini-lessons to the whole group or small subgroups as appropriate.

Maureen Holland, a fourth-grade teacher from the Douglas County Public Schools in Colorado, whose teacher reflection appeared in Chapter 1, has developed student self-assessments to help her encourage students to be more independent as they complete projects. She uses a self-assessment for each thematic unit and varies her form depending upon her reading and writing goals for this particular unit:

Self-Assessment of _____ Report

1. How did using an outline* help me in my reading about [topic]?

2. How did using an outline help me organize my report?

3. What did I do well in writing this report?

4. What would I like to do better in my next report?

5. The easiest part of doing this report was . . .

6. The hardest part of doing this report was . . .

7. What I like best about doing this report . . .

8. Other things you would like to tell me about doing this report are . . .

   *Questions or a web or map could be substituted for an outline.

I-search papers (Macrorie, 1988; Jenson et al., 1989) also allow students to reflect upon their own research processes. Macrorie suggests that the I-search paper is a good way to introduce report writing to students. He encourages students to pick topics of real interest to them and suggests ways of going about collecting information that are similar to many of those listed above. Macrorie emphasizes activities like talking to experts, doing surveys, and watching films before going to printed materials. Unique to his approach is how he asks students to write up what they have learned, which encourages students to think about the entire process in a metacognitive way. He suggests that students divide their reports into four parts:

1. What I knew (and didn't know about my topic when I started out).

2. Why I'm writing this paper. (Here's where a real need should show up: the writer demonstrates that the search may make a difference in her life.)

3. The search (story of the hunt).

4. What I learned (or didn't learn. A search that failed can be as exciting and valuable as one that succeeded.)

Besides helping students self-reflect on their research methods, the I-search paper format allows the teacher to gain fascinating insights into the strategies students used to do their research. Teachers can see students' strengths and weaknesses and develop lessons to support further development when students undertake other projects.

teacher reflection *teacher reflection*

An area we have not covered in detail is that of communicating with parents about students' progress as writers. We have waited in order to let Bonnie DeFreece do so through her reflection as a Chapter I reading teacher in the Cherry Creek Schools, a suburban district of Denver. DeFreece is one of those teachers who understands the value of inventing curriculum and assessment techniques to fit a particular situation. She wanted to document students' progress and to communicate with parents about that progress. Although she sees fifty students on a daily basis, she decided to try out the writing assessment procedure she invented with a single group of Chapter I students and their parents. It helped her feel freer to revise the procedure as she discovered a need to do so.

As you read this piece, you may be pleased, as we were, by the responses that the parents of DeFreece's Chapter I students made about their children's writing. The comments were very positive and quite specific. Although she was too modest to say so, we were convinced that her comments provided an excellent model for the parents and gave them information about writing they could use in formulating their own comments. In this way, DeFreece not only included parents in the assessment process but also gave them the language and attitudes to talk with their children in beneficial ways about their writing.

"With our combined efforts, we may help her grow"

Bonnie DeFreece

During the last school year, Chapter I second graders carried home important documentation of their growth as writers. This documentation, a "Writing Progress" notebook, contained a piece of writing from each month, their own comments about each piece, and notes from me celebrating their growth as writers. The children's parents read the writings and the comments, and then added their thoughts, questions, and ideas to the books. The students proudly returned their books, eager to share what Mom or Dad wrote in their pages.

The students

The six second-grade students and their families represent a typical Chapter I class. Two of the students are on the wait list for learning disabilities testing. Two other students are adversely affected by family problems. Another student shares narratives verbally but struggles to express these ideas in written form. The sixth student is making progress as her developmental abilities allow her longer periods of sustained concentration.

I was amazed that the writing notebooks transcended the students' and families' problems. Every student and her parents participated in the writing activity. This experiment in shared writing assessment was so successful that I will extend it to include all grade levels in my Chapter I program next year. I may make minor changes, but the shared assessment process, which promoted new awareness for students, parents, and teacher, will become an important part of my writing curriculum.

Notebook procedures

The notebooks became the vehicle for recording and sharing the writing process. They were simply designed: I stapled white construction paper between two colored sheets of paper. Next year I'll make the notebooks more durable by laminating the covers and taping the stapled edges with book binding tape. The notebooks were titled,

" (Student's name) Writing Progress."

Once the notebooks were assembled, I planned five steps to include written participation from the student, the parents, and myself. A notebook entry from Stephanie's dinosaur report, "How Did They Become Extinct?" will serve to demonstrate these steps (see Figure 6.12).

The notebooks: a learning tool for students

I encouraged the students to select their favorite writings from a particular genre each month. On the month that I requested a piece of nonfiction writing, Stephanie chose her dinosaur report. Other months she selected from poetry, personal narratives, and journal writing. The variety of writing experiences assisted her in understanding these kinds of literature.

Asking the students to select a favorite piece required them to examine their writings. They used the knowledge about writing they had acquired through mini-lessons, conferences, and literature to make a decision. Stephanie's writing demonstrated her ability to write like the content book she read on dinosaurs, and she acknowledged this influence in her statement: "it [the book] hlpe my Reporet."

1. The student selects a piece of writing to be included in the note book. Stephanie selected a page from her dinosaur report and glued it into the notebook.

2. The student comments on the selected piece of writing. Stephanie decided to describe the prewriting process of

> I Raed a BOOK a buot
> What did Dinosawrlook
> like? it hlpe my Reporet.

3. The teacher comments on the selected piece of writing. I wanted Stephanie's parents to appreciate the work and the quality of the dinosaur report. I described the process she used in writing her report and supported her growth as a writer.

> Celebrate a Young Auther!
>
> <u>Writing Process</u> - During April the second graders studied about dinosaurs. They read books and compared and categorized information. They organized this information into a written report using student conferences to check for meaningful writing.
>
> <u>Organization and Language</u> - Stephanie chose to write a dinosaur report, "How Did They Become Extinct?" She wrote a lengthy report of twelve sentences and 61 words! She divided this topic into four divisions and wrote supporting information on each division. Her organization of this report will assist her understanding of paragraphs.
>
> <u>Mechanics</u> - Note that January's writing sample had no punctuation. Compare this to April's writing where every sentence ends appropriately with a question mark or a period. Stephanie is taking responsibility for her growth as a writer. Congratulations to her!

4. The parents comment on the selected piece of writing. Stephanie's parent, Jim B., confirmed that the notebook provided awareness of school and home cooperation in Stephanie's academic growth: "With our combined effort . . . "

> Parent Comment: I feel that Stephanie, has come a long way also. Not only in her writing skills, but also in her spelling. She is a very creative girl. Very imaginative. With our combined efforts, we may help her grow
>
> Jim B

Figure 6.12   Notebook entries from Stephanie's dinosaur report

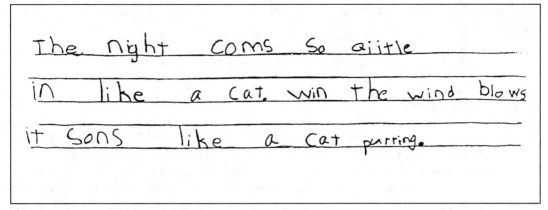

Figure 6.13 Justin's description of the night

During the month I asked the children to select a piece of poetry, Justin chose a piece he wrote describing the night creeping as softly as a cat into a room (see Figure 6.13).

As he struggled to explain his understanding of personification, I grabbed a pencil and wrote as he spoke, "I think this is my best poem because it's about the night and I think it sounds like a cat walking like the night." Justin distanced himself from his poetry to describe his thinking and writing. This reflection assisted his entry into the lifelong process of self-assessment.

In the beginning I wrote as the students dictated their comments. But the students soon understood the procedure and willingly wrote brief sentences about their writings.

In addition to monthly comments on their writings, I asked the students to write an overall evaluation at the end of the year (see Figure 6.14). Angie's comment acknowledged three benefits of the writing process:

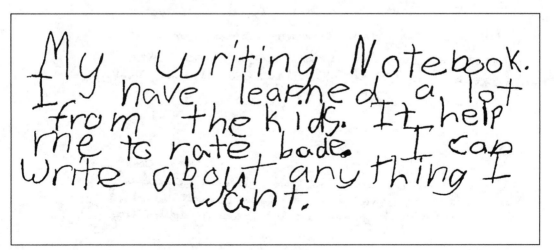

Figure 6.14 Angie's evaluation of her writing notebook

1. The social nature of the writing process as experienced in the class.

2. That writing assisted in her reading development.

3. That she experienced a new confidence in writing.

The notebooks: a learning tool for teachers

As I read the students' pieces I made notes on the concepts learned and the concepts needing reinforcement. This information assisted my planning for future mini-lessons and individual conferences. For example, as I read Stephanie's report, I noted that she understood the meaning of "extinct." She consistently used end punctuation, periods, and question marks. I also noted that she organized the dinosaur information into a book-like format: first she wrote a piece of information, next she posed a question about this information, and then she provided an answer for the question. By including questions for the reader in her report, Stephanie acknowledged the importance of thinking about and questioning the text during the reading process.

When making instructional notes from Justin's night poem, I observed many writing strengths: his poetic language, his use of word spacing, the

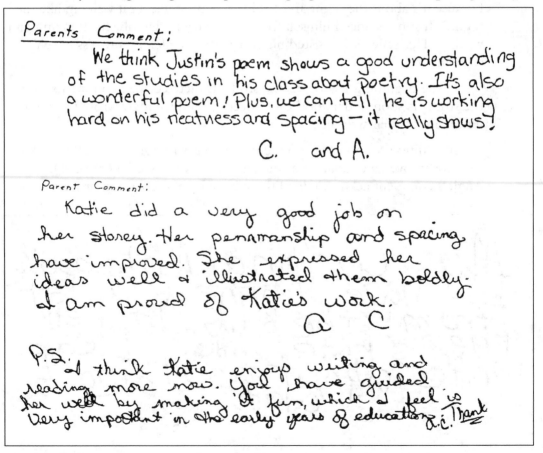

Figure 6.15 Parents' comments on the notebooks

legibility of his writing, his inventive spelling (qiitle/quietly), his knowledge of sight words (like, the, so), his inclusion of end punctuation, and his use of "ing" (purring). I noted that I would need to assist him in using capital letters and to discuss the differences between when/win.

In analyzing the students' writings I had a record of their writing strengths and needs. I used this information to inform parents, to plan mini-lessons and conferences, to celebrate the students' successes, and to encourage their continued growth as writers.

The notebooks: a learning tool for parents

Reading the parents' comments in the returning notebooks renewed my awareness that I was a partner in the education of six second graders (see Figure 6.15). All the parents acknowledged their children's progress in writing for meaning and in improving writing conventions. Justin's parents shared their pride in his night poem. Another parent's comments provided a thoughtful summation of her daughter's writing progress, including the change in her attitude.

The writing notebooks achieved far more than I had anticipated. The children, the parents, and I felt a sense of partnership, a sense of community in the learning process. The children's writings and comments helped me understand what they were learning, my own comments required me to study the children's writings carefully and be observant of their writing processes and products, and the parents' comments informed the children of parental pride in academic growth while providing me with additional information. Yes, Jim B., with our combined efforts, Stephanie and the other students *are* growing!

Conclusion

Over the past twenty years educators have worked to develop valid and reliable methods to assess whole pieces of student writing rather than just students' knowledge of spelling, grammar, and usage. In these new methods of assessment, students are given a topic to write about in a prescribed amount of time. Additional time is sometimes allowed for revision and editing of the draft. These pieces are then scored holistically or analytically by a group of raters who have been specially trained to achieve high interrater reliability. Bugs in these methods have gradually been worked out, and now some of the major testing corporations are even beginning to offer writing sample test options.

The problem with these measures is that they still do not assess the gradual development in writers' understanding and implementation of the writing process. As new process-oriented writing curricula enter the schools, teachers need ways to assess students' processes as well as their written products. We need to be able to

It was a cold November day and we were in orientation. Ms. _____ had a guest from a big busness company. Our school had a contest for the most improved writer in 4th grade. The winner would receive $25.00 dollas She would say the winner now.

I sat in my chair barely lustenig My mind was thinking of other things. Suddenly I heard my name announced. I just sat there. I couldn't beleve that I won. I was scard and they kept calling me up. Everyone was congratulating me I was so shocked that I couldn't move. I finally found enough courage to get up and get the money I felt so proud that I had written such a good piece.

I spent $15.00 dollars on baseball casds, and I still have the other ten dollars.

I think that I will always remember that day.

Figure 6.16 Student sample from the Coloroado Literacy Study (Davis et al., 1992)

document growth in students' rehearsal strategies, drafting, and fluency, their ability to respond to other writers' pieces in Authors' Circles, their revision strategies, their ability to self-edit, and finally their decisions about publishing. The *Authoring Cycle Profile* is an assessment that can help teachers to examine students' performance in these areas. This chapter has also outlined several other ways teachers can assess students' writing processes as part of their ongoing instruction. Students themselves can become involved in the reflection and assessment of their own abilities, leading to greater metacognitive knowledge about their own writing processes and responsibility for them. Our goal would be for all children to have an experience like Kent (see Figure 6.16), who won $25 for being the most improved writer at his school!

references

Applebee, A., J. Langer, & I. Mullis. (1989). *Understanding direct writing assessments.* Princeton, NJ: Educational Testing Service.

Atwell, N. (1987). *In the middle: Writing, reading, and learning with adolescents.* Portsmouth, NH: Boynton/Cook.

———. (1988). Making the grade: Evaluating writing in conference. In T. Newkirk & N. Atwell (Eds.), *Understanding Writing: Ways of observing, learning, and teaching, K–8* (2nd ed.), pp. 236–244. Portsmouth, NH: Heinemann.

Bean, W. & C. Bouffler. (1987). *Spell by writing.* Portsmouth, NH: Heinemann.

Bissex, G. (1980). *GNYS at WRK: A child learns to read and write.* Cambridge, MA: Harvard University Press.

Britton, J., T. Burgess, N. Martin, A. McLeod, & H. Rosen. (1975). *The development of writing abilities.* Urbana, IL: National Council of Teachers of English.

Buchanan, E. (1989). *Spelling in whole language classrooms.* Katonah, NY: Richard C. Owen.

Davey, B. (1987). Team for success: Guided practice in study skills through cooperative research reports. *Journal of Reading, 30,* 701–705.

Davis, A., M. Clarke, & L. Rhodes. (1992). *Colorado literacy study: Using multiple indicators to identify effective classroom practices for at-risk children in the language arts* (Contract No. R117-E00188-90). Washington, DC: Office of Educational Research and Improvement.

Farr, M. & H. Daniels. (1986). *Language diversity and writing instruction.* Urbana, IL: ERIC Institute for Urban and Minority Education, National Council of Teachers of English.

Fulwiler, T. (1989). Responding to student journals. In C. Anson (Ed.), *Writing and response: Theory, practice, and research*, pp. 149–173. Urbana, IL: National Council of Teachers of English.

Gable, R., J. Hendrickson, & J. Meeks. (1988). Assessing spelling errors of special needs students. *The Reading Teacher, 42,* 112–117.

Gawith, G. (1987). *Information alive! Information skills for research and reading.* Auckland, New Zealand: Longman Paul.

Gentry, J. (1981). Learning to spell developmentally. *The Reading Teacher, 34,* 378–381.

———. (1987). *Spell . . . Is a four-letter word.* Portsmouth, NH: Heinemann.

Gillet, J. & C. Temple. (1990). *Understanding reading problems: Assessment and instruction* (3rd ed.). Glenview, IL: Scott, Foresman.

Graves, D. (1989a). *Investigate nonfiction*. Portsmouth, NH: Heinemann.

———. (1989b). Research currents: When children respond to fiction. *Language Arts, 66,* 776–783.

Harste, J. & K. Short with C. Burke. (1988). *Creating classrooms for authors: The reading-writing connection*. Portsmouth, NH: Heinemann.

Jensen, J., J. Northrup, A. Alejandro, L. Arnold, & K. Coffey. (1989). Adapting the I-Search: A potpourri of topics and practices. *English Journal, 78,* 5:39–45.

Jongsma, K. (1990). Reading-spelling links. *The Reading Teacher, 43,* 608–610.

Koeller, S. (1982). Expository writing: A vital skill in science. *Science and Children, 20,* 1:12–15.

Lucas, C. (1988). Toward ecological evaluation. *The Quarterly of the National Writing Project and the Center for the Study of Writing, 10,* 1: 1+.

Macrorie, K. (1988). *The I-search paper*. Portsmouth, NH: Boynton/Cook.

Myers, M. (1980). *A procedure for writing assessment and holistic scoring*. Urbana, IL: ERIC Clearing House on Reading and Communication Skills and National Council of Teachers of English.

Nathenson-Mejia, S. (1989). Writing in a second language: Negotiating meaning through invented spelling. *Language Arts, 66,* 516–526.

O'Donnell, H. (1984). ERIC/RCS Report: The effect of topic on writing performance. *English Education, 16,* 243–249.

Olson, M. & M. Swadener. (1984). Establishing and implementing Colorado's writing assessment program. *English Education, 16,* 4: 208–219.

Read, C. (1975). *Children's categorization of speech sounds in English*. Urbana, IL: National Council of Teachers of English.

Samway, K. (1987). Formal evaluation of children's writing: An incomplete story. *Language Arts, 63,* 289–301.

Silva, C. & B. Yarborough. (1990). Help for young writers with spelling difficulties. *Journal of Reading, 34,* 34–53.

Simpson-Esper, M. (1988). Monitoring individual progress in revision groups. In Committee on Classroom Practices (Eds.), *Focus on collaborative learning*, pp. 93–97. Urbana, IL: National Council of Teachers of English.

Smith, F. (1988). *Understanding reading* (4th ed.). New York: Holt, Rinehart & Winston.

Sowers, S. (1988). Six questions teachers ask about invented spelling. In T. Newkirk & N. Atwell (Eds.), *Understanding writing: Ways of observing, learning, and teaching, K–8* (2nd ed.), pp. 562–70. Portsmouth, NH: Heinemann.

Spear, K. (1988). *Sharing writing: Peer response groups in English classes*. Portsmouth, NH: Boynton/Cook.

Temple, C. et al. (1988). *The beginnings of writing* (2nd ed.) Boston, MA: Allyn & Bacon.

Wilde, S. (1989a). Looking at invented spelling: A kidwatcher's guide to spelling, part 1. In K. Goodman, Y. Goodman, & W. Hood (Eds.), *The whole language evaluation book*, pp. 213–226. Portsmouth, NH: Heinemann.

———. (1989b). Understanding spelling strategies: A kidwatcher's guide to spelling, part 2. In K. Goodman, Y. Goodman, & W. Hood (Eds.), *The whole language evaluation book*, pp. 227–236. Portsmouth, NH: Heinemann.

———. (1990). A proposal for a new spelling curriculum. *Elementary School Journal, 90*, 275–289.

Wilson, N. (1989). Learning from confusion: Questions and change in reading logs. *English Journal, 78*, 7:62–68.

Chapter Seven

7

Emergent Reading and Writing

reflections

☐ Divide a sheet of paper into two columns. List the questions you want to answer about students who are emergent readers and writers in the first column. In the second column, list how you might get your questions answered.

☐ Compare your questions with the ones we've listed in this chapter. If you have listed some that are considerably different from ours, you may need to invent the means by which you will get your questions answered.

☐ In this chapter, we refer to an assessment instrument, the *Emergent Reading and Writing Evaluation*, a number of times. Prior to reading the chapter, review the instrument in some detail. It can be found in *Literacy Assessment: A Handbook of Instruments* (Rhodes, 1993).

☐ Use the *Emergent Reading and Writing Evaluation* with several students whom you perceive to be developmentally different, even though they are all emergent readers. What specific developmental differences did you uncover? What instructional decisions make sense, given the data you've collected? Having used the instrument, what new assessment questions do you have about the students?

☐ If your students have taken a standardized readiness test within the year, compare what you learned from that test to what you learned from giving the *Emergent Reading and Writing Evaluation.*

Children begin to read and write long before they "really read on the words" (as the young daughter of one of the authors so succinctly put it). Yet, because they do not read text conventionally, some of the observation and performance assessments for conventional readers are not as useful in uncovering the capabilities of these emergent readers and writers. This chapter undertakes an exploration of possibilities in emergent reading and writing assessment. The procedures in this chapter are for use with anyone who does not yet—or who is just starting to—"really read on the words," no matter what age. Like the goal of literacy assessment in general, the goal of emergent literacy assessment is systematically to create descriptive records of students' reading and writing over time and across literacy settings. This description and documentation can be used not only to plan instruction for individuals and groups but also to inform those who are interested in students' literacy development—parents, administrators, and other teachers.

Literacy assessment for emergent readers and writers has traditionally been based on a model of subskill development and instruction. That is, it is based on the idea that students need to perform well on shape, letter, sound, and word perception and discrimination, and on letter name and sound knowledge before they are "ready" to learn to read. In the next section we critique this subskill notion and the tests that embody it.

Then, after discussing what questions might best be asked about emergent reading and writing in order to focus assessment, we'll devote the bulk of the chapter to observational assessment within the literacy events that support students' development as readers and writers. The literacy events and assessments are based on current research about how children go about learning to read and write and what they learn in the process.

readiness tests

Traditionally, children who are not reading text independently are placed in "readiness" programs, and this placement is often determined through "readiness" tests. (For information on the use of readiness tests see Durkin, 1987.) Readiness programs and tests are based on the assumption that children must get "ready" to learn to read by learning a sequence of subskills, such as auditory and visual discrimination, letter names and sounds, and so on. In response to such programs and tests, a number of major professional organizations have developed position statements: "Literacy Development and Pre-First Grade" (see Appendix E, from Strickland & Morrow, 1989, pp. 160–161) and "Standardized Testing of Young Children 3 Through 8 Years of Age" (see Appendix F, from NAEYC, 1988, pp. 42–47).

Current developmental research (for reviews see Teale & Sulzby, 1986; McGee, Richgels, & Charlesworth, 1986) concludes that children engage in reading and writing events long before school and learn a great deal as they observe and participate in these events, with or without what readiness programs and tests consider prerequisite knowledge. Through their engagement in finding a particular kind of cereal at the supermarket, being read bedtime stories, sending a birthday card to Grandma, and observing family members write down phone messages, children develop as readers and writers before they enter school. Those experiences allow children to begin to understand the functions of print, story structure, book language, and the conventions of print, including sound-symbol or graphophonic knowledge. Because they are curious about all aspects of their world, children observe how others engage in literacy and ask questions about print. Certainly, this same learning can continue in school. And if children observe and participate in whole and meaningful literacy experiences in school instead of isolated and decontextualized subskill instruction, readiness is not an issue. Many older emergent readers understand this. When one fourteen-year-old emergent reader was about to begin individual instruction he said, "I really want to learn to read. But I don't want to learn the alphabet again first!"

We can highlight the shortcomings of readiness tests by comparing the principles of literacy assessment we outlined in the first chapter with how and what readiness tests measure. Clearly, the tests do not reflect what we know about effective literacy assessment practices, nor do they measure important aspects of learning to read and write.

Principles of literacy assessment tell us that . . .	Yet readiness tests . . .
Authentic reading and writing should be assessed in a variety of contexts.	Assess bits of knowledge believed to be prerequisite to reading and writing in a single test.
Assessment should be an integral part of instruction.	Are separate from instruction.
Processes should be assessed in addition to products.	Assess products only.
All language systems should be assessed in operation together.	Assess language systems separate from each other and focus on graphophonics in isolation.

(continued)

Principles of literacy assessment tell us that . . .	Yet readiness tests . . .
Analysis of error patterns yields important information about reading and writing.	Count errors against the child.
Background knowledge should be be considered in the assessment of reading and writing.	Disregard the fact that students whose background knowledge best matches the tested knowledge perform better on the test.
Normal developmental patterns and literacy behavior in reading and writing are the foundation of literacy assessment.	Do not reflect what is known about literacy development; test results are normed.
The literacy environment and instruction should also be assessed.	Only assess students.
Triangulation should be used to corroborate data.	Are often the sole basis for major decisions.

In a recent review of approximately twenty readiness tests, Stallman & Pearson (1990, p. 36) arrive at similar conclusions and note other difficulties as well. In their view, readiness tests:

- Are typically administered to a group of children rather than to an individual child.

- Take a long time to give (a little more than two hours spread over a few days).

- Rely a lot on asking students to fill in bubbles based on what the teacher says or what they see in a picture.

- Clearly emphasize (in almost half the subtests) sound-symbol knowledge.

- Involve recognition, not identification and production (the staples of reading), as the dominant level of cognitive processing. The group testing situation seems to be responsible for the dominance of recognition activities.

Stallman and Pearson's first three characteristics raise the important question of the appropriateness of formal testing for young children. It is highly unlikely that young children reveal what they know about reading in a formal testing situation where they must sit quietly in a large group and attend to a task that has no meaning for them, in a format with which they have no experience. Stallman & Pearson (1990, p. 38) note, "What dominates the whole enterprise when children actually take the [readiness] test is test-taking behavior—filling in bubbles, moving the marker, making sure everything is in the right place. These activities may be related to test taking, but they have nothing to do with reading." Teale (1990, p. 50) also addresses the issue of the appropriateness of readiness tests, but from a different vantage point: "When a child . . . takes one of these tests, the child is no longer engaging in the activity we want to measure. What is being measured is the child's ability to perform isolated skills rather than his or her skill at reading or writing."

Of course, multiple-choice tests for emergent readers have an inherent limitation: only one answer is correct. Kasten & Clarke (1989) used a recently developed readiness test based on more current developmental research, the individually administered *Metropolitan Early School Inventory—Preliteracy* (1986), and cited interesting examples of the limitations of this format.

> On subtest A ("What we read") . . . one strip contained pictures of a mixing bowl and spoon, a measuring cup with graduated lines, and a recipe. The child was asked to identify the one item someone would read. The manual lists the recipe as the sole correct response. However, in real life, measuring cups with graduated lines also contain print labeling. (p. 22)
>
> Another strip contains three pictures of open books. One book has blank pages, one has pictures showing and the other shows only print. (Again, the child was asked to identify the one item someone would read.) Children . . . would, according to the manual, be penalized for identifying other items [than the book with print] which could be justified as correct. As one kindergartner said, pointing to the book with pictures, "You can read this one, but the writing is on a different page." Another kindergartner said, pointing to the blank book which resembles a classroom journal, "You can read it if you write in it first." (p. 22).

In a review of the individually administered *Test of Early Written Language* (TEWL), Shanklin (1989) provides a similar example of writing assessment: "One question asks children to show where a story would begin on the back of a picture card. The correct answer is the upper lefthand corner. A child who wants to draw a picture first may not begin writing there, but this is not considered."

These examples reveal how easily teachers might arrive at conclusions that underestimate what students know about literacy even when relying on the results of tests that better reflect current developmental research on emergent literacy. We need more open-ended means of assessment to allow teachers to gather information about students that better reflect their thinking and capabilities in authentic literacy situations. This approach would be more helpful to teachers in instructional planning.

questions to ask about emergent readers and writers

Before we turn to various means for assessing the literacy knowledge of young children or older emergent readers, we must begin at the beginning, and ask what we want to find out about their literacy. You may be used to having the content of a test dictate what you find out about students' literacy, but that sort of thinking is actually backwards. It makes far more sense to decide what you want to find out first and then determine how you can best go about it. Otherwise, the tests, many of which have little or no foundation in developmental research about emergent reading and writing, dictate what we find out.

Certainly some of the questions about the assessment of reading and writing we've posed in earlier chapters are also appropriate for emergent readers and writers:

How familiar is the student with literature? with what types of literature?

How does the student define or view reading? writing?

What does the student read/write outside of school? How frequently and for what purposes?

Can the student retell stories in an organized, coherent fashion that reveals his knowledge about story grammar?

You might review earlier chapters for further questions. As in all literacy assessment, questions about emergent literacy should involve the process of coming to know, not just the product.

There are other questions we should ask when we think about the development of emergent readers and writers (no matter what their age). Some of these questions include:

Can the student fluently dictate an organized composition about a topic with which he is familiar?

Does the student attend to the print you write down as he dictates? Is he able to adjust the pacing of his oral composition to your speed in getting the composition onto paper?

To what degree does the student rely on print and on memory in order to read his own dictation immediately following the dictation? the next day?

Has the student established a consistent sense of the directionality of print?

Has the student established a consistent sense of "wordness" (what a word is as opposed to a syllable, a letter, or a phrase)?

Can the student match oral and printed language (voice-print match) in a familiar text?

How does the student read along with someone else once the pattern of a predictable text is established?

How can the student's "pretend reading" of a familiar book be characterized?

How can the student's written forms be characterized in comparison to conventional letter forms?

Is the student's spelling prephonemic, phonemic, or letter name?

How does the student attend to print in his environment? What does he know about such print?

Can the student recognize and write his name? Does he understand that his written name functions to identify things that are his?

Can the student identify the letters in his name? In other print that is meaningful to him?

Does the student ask questions that reveal an interest in how print works? What is the focus of those questions?

Of course, many other questions could also be asked; but our point here is that these kinds of questions are no longer of concern to teachers of students who are able to read and write text conventionally. These students can voice-print match, proceed from left to right in their reading and writing, recognize and write their name and the letters it contains, and are usually transitional or correct spellers.

assessing within literacy events

As we have pointed out, it is important to assess emergent readers and writers during actual literacy events. The more authentic the literacy event, the more useful the information it provides will be in planning instruction. Assessment procedures should be open-ended enough to allow students to choose how and when to respond. As Teale and colleagues (1987) emphasize, "Highly constrained procedures [such as traditional readiness tests] may seriously underestimate the [literacy] capacities of children whose styles of handling a complex task may not fit the way the task is posed. Especially important [are] informal assessments that resemble regular classroom activities" (p. 774).

The students themselves, their teachers, and their parents can all be a part of the assessment process. Literacy events that lend themselves particularly well to uncovering information about the literacy development of emergent readers and writers include:

- Reading and writing environmental print.
- Responding to books in read-aloud time.
- Responding to books in other ways.
- Shared reading.
- Independent reading.
- Shared writing.
- Independent writing.
- Drawing.
- Talking about reading and writing.

Although these literacy events are potentially authentic, they are not inherently authentic. A retelling (one way to respond to a book), for example, is more authentic if a student retells a story to a friend who didn't get to hear it than if the student retells the story to classmates who have just heard it.

In this section we'll explore the literacy events emergent readers and writers in whole language classrooms are typically involved in. We will present these events as distinct from each other, but of course, in the classroom they are often intertwined. The major focus of our discussion will be on possible observational assessment; however, some literacy events also result in products that can be assessed, and almost all observations within literacy events can be illuminated by informal interviews.

We'll also refer to performance sample assessments when they contain tasks that are similar to the literacy events under discussion. Emergent reading and writing performance samples can complement observations or provide greater documentation of students' literacy where it may be necessary for program requirements, reporting to others, staffings, and so on. The performance sample assessment we'll refer to most often is the *Emergent Reading and Writing Evaluation* (ERWE), which we developed in conjunction with staff and teachers of the Denver Public Schools Chapter I program (in Rhodes, 1993.) We find it more helpful than other performance sample assessments because it allows exploration of a wider range of literacy events in a single instrument. The ERWE builds on previous performance sample work, including that of Clay (1972, 1979), Goodman & Altwerger (1981), and McCormick (1981).

Because there are many more young than older emergent readers, we will refer primarily to this group; but most of what we say can be adapted for adult emergent readers, as a number of educators have shown (Davidson & Wheat, 1989; Fargo & Collins, 1989; Malicky & Norman, 1989; Padak, Davidson, & Padak, 1990; Padak & Padak, 1987; Rigg, 1981; Rigg & Taylor, 1979).

■ ■

reading and writing environmental print

Early childhood whole language teachers are fond of bringing environmental print into the classroom as reading material and encouraging children to create environmental print in their play. Teachers may ask students to bring in labels they can read to make an "I Can Read" bulletin board or an "I Can Read" book. They use these bulletin boards and books as reading material to talk with children about print.

Teachers can observe a great deal as children read environmental print. If a child brings in a Fruit Roll-Ups box, the teacher can watch for some of these things:

- Does the child point to the words "Fruit Roll-Ups" when he reads the label? If not, does he point at other words or at the picture?

- If he does point to the words "Fruit Roll-Ups," does he voice-print match (does the child say "fruit" when pointing to "fruit" and so on)?

- If the teacher needs to show the child where it says "Fruit Roll-Ups," can the child find the same words elsewhere on the box?

- If the teacher asks the child, "How do you know this says 'Fruit Roll-Ups,'" what does the child's response reveal about his knowledge of the function of print and of graphophonics?

- If the teacher asks the child to talk about other parts of the box, what does it reveal about the child's knowledge of pictures, the function of print, and so on?

Teachers who have set up grocery stores, restaurants, block corners and the like in their classrooms find it easy to encourage children to create environmental print for a variety of purposes. One group of boys created a "Do not touch" sign to watch over the creatures from *Where the Wild Things Are* (Sendak, 1963) that they were fashioning from clay. A girl made a sign for the classroom grocery store that said "Open" on one side and "Closed" on another. Another group of students made stop signs, railroad crossing signs, and street signs for a block city they created.

Again, teachers can observe children's writing of environmental print in these situations and learn about the importance of print to the children, the functions for which they use print, and their ability to handle the conventions of print, including their knowledge of graphophonics.

A performance sample assessment that includes the assessment of children's ability to read environmental print (among other aspects of emergent literacy) is the *Test of Early Reading Ability* (TERA) (Reid, Hresko, & Hammill, 1981, 1989). The TERA builds on research done by Harste, Woodward, & Burke (1984) in which children read environmental print in a variety of contexts—the actual label (or sign), a photocopy of the label (or sign), and a handwritten copy of the label (or sign). The first edition of the test was reviewed by Wixson (1985).

■ ■

responding to books during read-alouds

Read-aloud time is a regularly scheduled literacy event in early childhood classrooms. Often, early childhood teachers adopt the routine of reading an "old favorite" along with a "new book" each day so that children can benefit by hearing a variety of literature and repeated readings of particular stories. In addition, in many early childhood classrooms, teacher aides, visiting adults, or older children also read stories to individual children or small groups.

When an adult reads a book to children and encourages them to respond to it, the experience usually results in a rich literacy event, full of revealing instances of children's literacy knowledge and development (see Morrow & Smith, 1990). Many important questions about children's literacy development can be answered during story reading:

What is the locus and logic of children's predictions?

What is their understanding of genres, authors, dedications, and the like?

What connections do they make between their own experiences and the content of the story?

What connections do they make between the story being read and other stories or media?

What do they comprehend?

How do they interact with each other about books?

During group read-aloud time, the teacher can focus his attention on a couple of children and later record what he notices about their verbal and nonverbal responses, or he may want to take notes while someone else reads a story to the children. A special education teacher read a story to one first-grade class so that the regular teacher could observe the three special education students who were mainstreamed in her classroom. The first-grade teacher found that because she could focus on observing the three children, she could see what features of the text the students paid attention to and how the children interacted with the text and with the other students and decide how she might adjust her own instruction to help them become more engaged in reading. Of course, having someone else read to the children may mean that you won't be able to observe quite the same kinds of behavior that you would if you were reading to them, since differences in pacing, the kinds of questions asked, the other adult's ability to engage the children in the story, and so on can affect the children's responses. Nevertheless, such sessions are often helpful and provide a data base for comparing children's behavior.

Teachers who have arranged cross-grade matches of children can take notes as one child reads a story to another. One Chapter I teacher matched fifth- and first-grade Chapter I students and recorded this anecdotal note during the first week the children were together:

> Shawn (5th grade) is reading *Little Red Riding Hood* to Chris
> (1st grade). Reads very fluently and with occasional fine expression. Has the potential to really entertain young kids when he
> reads. Chris just listens attentively—no interaction between them.

The teacher realized that these students needed help in understanding how to interact with each other during story reading. Her instructional goal was to enable them to interact as parents and children do during storybook reading at home.

It is also beneficial to videotape a read-aloud session you conduct with students. If you use a tripod and aim the camera over your shoulder at the group, you can capture the children's interaction with the book without any assistance. This allows you to examine children's responses in some detail, and provides an opportunity to invite the students to view themselves and talk about the read-aloud.

When we think about what to observe during read-aloud time, we need to consider what we might look for before, during, and after reading the text. When we first read a book to children, we often hold it up without comment (other than perhaps reading the title) and ask which children are familiar with it and how they became so. Holding up a *Mother Goose* collection may spur the children who know some of these rhymes to recite a few. This will not only be a marvelous introduction to *Mother Goose* for the other children, but it will also tell you which children have encountered rhymes already. If several children know the story of *The Three Bears* when you hold the book up, you could request retellings of the versions they know, then read the story and ask the class to compare their classmates' versions to the one you have read.

This kind of prereading response helps you discover what children know about "the classics" of early childhood and gives you a general sense of their literary background. Another kind of prereading response can be encouraged when you hold up the book, read the title, and ask the students to guess what the book will be about. You will find out a great deal about the sources children use for prediction, the logic of their predictions, and about what they already know about the world and about literature.

If you permit children to continue to respond once you begin reading the story, you can find out more. If the students need encouragement, you can ask them to confirm or disconfirm the predictions they made before the reading or to compare the book with a version of the story they heard from a classmate. You can pause occasionally and ask the students for more predictions, and help them expand on the spontaneous comments they make during the story. As *The Three Little Pigs* was read to a group of first-grade children, they made these comments:

"He's going to trick him!"

"If I were him, I wouldn't do that."

"He's [the third pig] smart."

"I wish I could build a house."

In order to help the children elaborate on these spontaneous responses, the teacher might ask:

Student:	Teacher:
"He's going to trick him!"	"Do you think so? Why?"
"If I were him, I wouldn't do that."	"What would you do? Why?"
"He's [the third pig] smart."	"What makes you think that?"
"I wish I could build a house."	"If you had been a pig in this story, what kind of a house would you have built? Why?"

Comments like these, especially when students elaborate on them, reveal their understanding of a story, and its theme. Children's laughter or puzzled faces also reveal their comprehension or confusion. A well-placed question ("You look puzzled. What are you puzzled about?") may help children elaborate on responses they might otherwise keep to themselves. If you are reading a predictable book, you may find it interesting to observe who picks up and uses the pattern of the book to read along with you or makes predictions based on the pattern.

Instead of interrupting the story too frequently, you may want to save some of your questions and observations until you finish reading. Then you could say, "I noticed when [mention a particular event in the story] a number of you looked puzzled. Tell us what you were thinking." Or this might be the perfect time to have the children compare the versions they told earlier with the version they heard, or to review the predictions students made and consider whether the author might have written the story differently.

In her research, Morrow (1988) used a number of categories for recording children's story reading responses (see Figure 7.1). She found that they fell primarily in the category "Focus on Meaning." In the initial stages of the one-on-one read-aloud sessions each child had with an adult, the children also talked a great deal about illustrations ("Focus on Illustration"); toward the end of the study, a few children began to ask questions or make comments about print ("Focus on Print");

Categories for Recording Children's Responses

1. Focus on Story Structure
   a. Setting
   b. Characters
   c. Theme
   d. Plot episodes
   e. Resolution

2. Focus on Meaning
   a. Labeling
   b. Detail
   c. Interpreting (associations, elaborations)
   d. Predicting
   e. Drawing from one's experience
   f. Word definitions
   g. Narrational behavior

3. Focus on Print
   a. Questions or comments about letters
   b. Questions or comments about sounds
   c. Questions or comments about words
   d. Reading words
   e. Reading sentences
   f. Book management

4. Focus on illustration
   a. Questions or comments while eyes are focused on illustrations or fingers pointing to illustrations

5. Total number of questions

6. Total number of comments

Figure 7.1   Categories for Recording Children's Responses

---

although few of their responses indicated a concern for the structural elements of the story ("Focus on Structure"). Because these children came from "disadvantaged environments" and because they responded to text in an individualized story reading situation, their response patterns may be different from those of your students. Nevertheless, Morrow's categories are useful in assessing students' responses during read-aloud time and in using the resulting data to determine what you might demonstrate or encourage in future story reading sessions. Morrow (1990) provides an example of each type of response as well as teacher reactions during story reading that encouraged more and richer responses. In a more recent study, Morrow and Smith (1990) looked at children's verbal behaviors in whole class, small group, and individual story reading sessions using similar categories. They found that children interacted with the text as much in small groups as they did in individual reading sessions (and more than in whole class sessions) and that the small group sessions led to better story comprehension.

A performance sample of story reading is particularly important in cases where a child does not appear to be responding during group story readings or where the child's responses depend on those of other children rather than on personal interaction with the story. In such cases, it is helpful to conduct a one-to-one story reading to observe how the child interacts with the story when no one else is around to distract or support him. (Try this in a corner during sustained silent reading.) Use the routines and kinds of questions and encouragement you currently use during group story reading. Consider audiotaping the session for later analysis or for your records. It may also be useful to ask the child's parents about their observations of the child during story reading at home.

responding to books in other ways

Children's responses during read-aloud sessions are not the only way they reveal what they know about books and reading. One little girl who chose to paint during choice time decided to paint a picture of the caterpillar in *The Very Hungry Caterpillar* (Carle, 1969). In initiating this on her own, the little girl demonstrated her interest in the book, and her painting revealed her sensitivity to Carle's illustrations. When the girl's teacher asked her to talk about her painting with the class, she found out more about the child's obvious fondness for the book and her understanding of it.

The three-year-old son of one of the authors was playing outside one wintery day, moving his feet and dragging a stick through the snow to make three parallel tracks. When asked what he was doing, he replied, "I'm Peter." He was reenacting a scene from *The Snowy Day* (Keats, 1962) in which Peter makes three continuous tracks in the snow. Such responses to books are not uncommon in young children. Characteristically, "preschoolers and early primary children are inclined to use their bodies as they respond [to books] . . . They wiggle and bounce and clap and echo story actions as they listen" (Huck, Hickman, & Hepler, 1987, p. 122). Capturing these spontaneous responses with anecdotal records provides important details that can be shared with others.

Teachers can also encourage different kinds of response to literature. One first-grade teacher read a chapter of *Charlotte's Web* to her students every day. After each day's reading, the teacher asked one child to take the lead in summarizing the chapter which she recorded on chart paper. Another child drew a picture to accompany the chapter summary, once the class had talked about what might belong in the picture. The daily picture and chapter summary were displayed in the hall outside the classroom until the children had summarized and illustrated the entire story for others to read. Observing the lead student's summarization and the suggestions made by other students gave the teacher a great deal of information about how well children could listen, understand, and summarize or illustrate the major points in the story.

Karen Grossman, a first-grade teacher in the Denver Public Schools, provides time each day for small groups of children to chose an "old favorite" book to reread. They can choose a way to respond to the book from a list that hangs in the room:

Literary Projects

diorama
mobile
puppets
write different ending
book jacket
clay
cartoon strips
wordless picture book
transparency
write three things you learned

(Before adding each project choice to the chart, Grossman demonstrated it using the book she had read to the class that day.) When work time is over, each group presents its project, and the other students and the teacher assess its quality with a focus on what the student did well in responding to the book. The teacher makes sure to comment on inventive art techniques, interesting responses, and other original ideas (such as writing on the back of the paper bag puppets); these comments inevitably lead other students to try out the ideas, which enriches the general quality and inventiveness of their responses.

Of course, the teacher takes notes during work time and sharing time, not only about what books students are choosing and what projects they are doing, but also about their responses to the books and the ways in which they are working together on book projects that help each other to expand their comprehension. Particularly good or representative projects can be filed (a cartoon strip) or photographed (clay figures) for safekeeping in children's portfolios.

shared reading

Shared reading, including assisted reading, yields much the same kind of information as reading stories to children. But because students are able to observe the print while reading with a capable adult reader or with each other, shared reading also yields information on how they interact with print: directionality, graphophonic elements, frequently encountered words, strategies for dealing with new words, elements of punctuation, and so on. Whatever print conventions or strategies you decide to attend to in the process of shared reading are those about which you will discover the current level of students' understanding and use. (For information on shared reading with adult emergent readers, see Davidson & Wheat, 1989; Rigg & Taylor, 1979.)

Although anecdotal records are often the most effective way to record many aspects of shared reading, some teachers prefer a checklist. The one that follows may be used to record children's progress in learning about particular print conventions. (A lengthier example may be found in Heald-Taylor, 1987.)

	Beginning	Secure
Knows the function of print on a page.		
Reads left to right and top to bottom.		
Can voice-print match.		
Can locate a word by voice-print matching from the beginning of a sentence.		
Can locate frequently used words.		
Can locate repeating words and phrases.		
Uses graphophonic elements to aid in figuring out words.		
Uses picture cues to aid in figuring out words.		
Uses rhyming pattern to figure out words.		
Uses the meaning of the rest of the story to figure out words.		
Knows the function of periods.		

If the child has not demonstrated any knowledge of a particular convention, no mark is made. When the teacher recognizes that the child has begun to deal with the convention, he enters the date of the observation in the column labeled "beginning." When the child has become secure in his knowledge of the convention, the teacher enters the date of the observation under "secure." This kind of checklist enables the teacher to peruse information about individuals and groups quickly in order to plan which particular print conventions to attend to during instruction.

This checklist is also helpful for recording your observations after shared reading. Again, we recommend that you focus your attention on a couple of children during each shared reading session. You may want to keep a copy of the checklist on your clipboard as you conduct assisted reading with individual children during independent reading time. Consider using the checklist in both settings, observing what you can during shared readings and using individual assisted readings for recording other information.

If a detailed performance sample is needed or useful, the "Bookhandling" section of the *Emergent Reading and Writing Evaluation* (in Rhodes, 1993) suggests using a predictable book to examine what children understand about the features and conventions of text. Other bookhandling performance samples are Marie Clay's *Sand: Concepts About Print Test* (1972) and *Stones: Concepts About Print Test* (1979; reviewed by Goodman, 1981 and reprinted in Clay, 1982) and the "Bookhandling Knowledge Task" by Goodman & Altwerger (1985).

independent rereading

Independent reading is a rich source of assessment data about all readers. With emergent readers, independent reading usually means rereading a text that they have previously heard read to them. Whether or not the student "reads on the words," a student's rereading of a text can yield valuable information.

If you want to keep records of reading-like behavior, audio- or videotape the student's reading and compare the transcription with the text. (See Jan Bennett's "Teacher Reflection" at the end of this chapter for an example.) In the case of more conventional reading, tape recordings, miscue analysis, or running records can serve as evidence of the student's reading behavior.

Observing students' independent reading not only illuminates the process of reading, it also provides data about the kinds of books the student chooses to read, how the student chooses them, the quantity of rereading the student engages in, the level of engagement in independent reading, and so on. It is also interesting to observe whether students choose to spend their independent reading time engaged in reading by themselves or with someone else.

In the following sample (Figure 7.2), Kara, four-and-a-half-year-old daughter of one of the authors, read *Pete's Dragon*, a Walt Disney book that retells the film of the same name. Kara had seen the film two months earlier and had heard the story read by her mother twice, most recently five days before this reading was recorded. Before Kara began rereading, she arranged some stuffed animals on the couch and told them to get ready to listen to the story. Compare Kara's reading-like behavior with the actual text. What can you learn about her literacy? (As you read the transcript, jot down your observations about her language and literacy.)

Text

One day, a boy named Pete walked into a little town by the sea. Pete had no family but he did have a pet dragon named Elliott.

Elliott was a wonderful, friendly dragon. He had green scales and purple wings and a big, long tail—and he could fly! He could breathe fire out through his mouth. When he didn't want anyone to see him, he could make himself invisible!

Pete and Elliott soon found a cave to spend the night in. They had just settled in when they saw a young woman peering through the cave entrance.

"Hi," she said to Pete. "My name's Nora. What's yours?"

"I'm Pete, and this is my dragon, Elliott," Pete answered.

"It's kind of a cold place to spend the night, isn't it?" Nora asked Pete. "Why don't you stay at the lighthouse with my dad and me? I'd ask Elliott to stay, too but I'm afraid he won't fit."

Pete was sorry to leave Elliott alone in the cave, but the kindly dragon didn't mind. He was happy that Pete would have a nice, warm place to stay, anyway. So Pete moved into the big lighthouse with Nora and her father, Lampie.

The next day, Nora took Pete into town and bought him some new clothes. Then they went to the schoolhouse. Elliott went with them. He wanted to go to school, too.

When the teacher saw Elliott, she would not let him into the school. "I'm sorry," she told Pete, "but dragons are not allowed in school. Besides, Elliott won't fit!"

Elliott was sad, but he waited patiently outside on the playground. After a while, the children came outside for recess.

Elliott played with the children then, and they had lots of fun. They played ring-around-the-dragon and then dragon-in-the-middle. But soon the bell rang, and it was time for the children to go back in. Elliott was left alone again.

After school, Pete rode home on Elliott's back. They both noticed that the sky was

Kara

One day Pete and Elliott walked down the street near the lake.

They just found a cave to spend the night in. When they just settled in, a young lady peeked through the cave entrance. Nora said, "What's your name?" And Pete said, "My name's Pete. And this is my pet dragon." Pete said, "What's your name?" And Nora said, "My name is Nora."

"Isn't this a cold night to spend the night in?" "Yea." "I would ask Elliott to stay too but he might can't fit."

Pete was sorry Elliott . . . Pete would leave Elliott alone. But Elliott . . . Pete . . . I mean Elliott said . . . I mean Elliott was happy Pete would have a nice warm place to stay, to spend the night in.

One morning Nora and Pete went to buy Pete some new clothes.

When the teacher saw Elliott, he would not let him in. Pete went with him too because he wanted to go to school too but the minute the teacher saw Elliott, he wouldn't let him in.

He was sad but he waited patiently out on the playground. But pretty soon the children came out for russy, um russic . . . (she means "recess" and she knows she doesn't have the right word for it).

But in a little they played "Ring Around the Rosie" with Elliott and "Dragon in the Middle" with Elliott. But soon the bell rang and it was time for everybody to go in.

But when Elliott went in, Pete go back home on Elliott's back. But Pete said, "It's

Figure 7.2   Kara reading *Pete's Dragon*

Text *(continued)*	**Kara** *(continued)*
growing dark and cloudy. "Let's hurry, Elliott," Pete said. "It looks as though there's a storm coming."	getting dark. There's going to be a storm!" So they hurried home.
Later, Pete was eating dinner at the lighthouse with Nora and Lampie. Suddenly, there was a bright flash of lightning and a loud crash of thunder.	But when they got home, there was a big clap of thunder. Nora said, "My gracious. It might be a big storm. We got to check the lamp in case it runs out of fire."
"My goodness!" exclaimed Nora. "It must be a terrible storm. We'd better check the lamp." Nora and Lampie had to be sure the lamp in the lighthouse was lit all the time so ships could find their way to shore.	
As they tried to get the lamp lit, they heard a sound out at sea. "It's a ship's foghorn!" Lampie shouted. "If we can't get this lamp started, the ship will be lost! It'll run onto the rocks!"	Then he saw . . . then he heared a fog horn and it was a ship and he said "If we can't get this lamp started, then the ship would be lost and it would run onto the rocks." Elliott said, "This is a job for Pete." Elliott raced down the stairs to get Pete.
"This is a job for Elliott," said Pete. He turned and raced down the stairs.	
Pete ran along the beach to the cave. Big waves were crashing against the shore, and rain was pouring down. Pete found Elliott asleep in the cave.	But when he got downstairs, Pete was asleep. He kicked the big dragon's leg and he patted the big dragon's face.
"Wake up, Elliott! You've got to help us!" he cried. He shook the big dragon's leg and patted his face.	
Elliott woke up and rubbed his eyes sleepily. When Pete told him about the problem he jumped up. He left the cave and rushed to the lighthouse.	Elliott woke . . . waked . . . waked up but . . . and he told him about the problem. Elliott jumped up and ran
Elliott squeezed into the lighthouse and up the winding stairs. It was a tight fit because Elliott was a big dragon. When he reached the tiny room at the top, he took a deep breath. He blew a great blast of firy breath upon the wick of the lamp.	and he blowed . . . blowed a big, big blast of fire on the glass.
The lamp was lit again! Now the light shone brightly over the stormy sea. The ship was able to find its way safely to land.	
Elliott was a hero! Everyone was grateful to Pete and his dragon. Only one thing still made Elliott unhappy: He couldn't go to school with Pete and the other children.	He . . . Elliott was a hero but something still made Elliott unhappy. He still couldn't go to school.
The townspeople got together, and they made a decision. Whenever the weather was warm and sunny, classes would be held outside so that Elliott could watch and listen to everything that happened.	The kids talked about on sunny days they could go outside so what everybody happened . . . what everything happened, Elliott could hear it.
And the teacher agreed that maybe dragons should be allowed at school—well, Pete's dragon, anyway!	But . . . dragons could be allowed at school—but Pete's dragon anyway.

Figure 7.2   Kara reading *Pete's Dragon* *(continued)*

Certainly, a four-year-old child must have countless other experiences with literature before she is capable of recreating the content and language of a lengthy story in such detail after only three exposures. Although rereading is sometimes dismissed as "just memorized," "current research indicates that the child is not delivering a rote memorization; rather, the child is using strategic, effortful, conceptually-driven behaviors" (Sulzby, 1985, p. 470). For example, Kara's knowledge of story structure helps to support her efforts at remembering the particular content of this story, which she "slots" into story structure. Her knowledge of book language supports her in recreating the complex language structures that are found in books but not in the conversations of four-year-olds. Also of note is her excellent understanding of the use of dialogue in stories. And it is clear that she is quite proficient at using pictures to cue her reading, yet the text she creates stands alone and can be understood without reference to the pictures. Her "play" with language, particularly with new concepts and expressions, is informative, as are her occasional self-corrections of both content and grammar. Her intonations sound like reading rather than conversing.

And then, of course, there are the other important kinds of information to be gained from this setting. Kara's understanding that reading can function as a form of entertainment for herself and others is revealed in her selection of reading books to fill her time and in her use of stuffed animals as an audience for her reading. Also interesting is the extended attention of a small (and not always attentive) child to such a complex task. She read this book and several others to her animals before she moved on to another activity. Though Kara did not "read on the words" for almost two more years after this taping, is there any doubt that, at the age of four-and-a-half, she had already developed a sophisticated knowledge about books and what you do with them? Or that she had a well-developed love of books?

Sulzby's (1985) research on children's emergent reading of favorite stories has resulted in a classification scheme we find helpful in considering how a child's current independent reading behavior might be characterized and what behavior might be expected to occur next developmentally. Some of Sulzby's terms (1985) have been changed to be consistent with the terminology used in this book. The categories are listed from least to most mature:

Picture-governed reading

Story not formed: The child labels or comments upon discrete illustrations or the child reenacts the action of discrete pictures in a general way ("Look at that go."). In both cases, the wording does not reveal a story that the listener can understand.

Oral language-like story: The wording reveals a story that the listener can understand is a story, although it may be disjointed. The intonation used is that of storytelling as opposed to reading. Understanding the story requires that the listener see the pictures the reader is using as cues.

Written language-like story: The child sounds as if he is reading but is being cued mostly or entirely by the pictures rather than by the print. The story may be understood by the listener without reference to the illustrations. (Kara's reading of *Pete's Dragon* is a mature example of this category.)

Print-governed reading

"Reading on the words" with no meaning creation: The child refuses to read because he doesn't know the words or reads only the words he knows.

Reading with imbalanced strategies: The child reads the text using print cues but often produces nonsense by excessive sounding out, substituting words that make no sense, or omitting words. Or the reader may rely only on what he predicts or remembers when he encounters portions of text that are difficult.

Reading to create meaning: The child may read with few or many miscues but makes self-corrections using a variety of strategies in order to make sense of text.

Once children use more print to govern their reading (Sulzby's print-governed reading categories), information can be gained about the child's knowledge of print conventions by analyzing their oral reading miscues. This is true even if the child attends to print only when reading highly familiar or predictable text. (Information can be gained about children's knowledge of print long before this by analyzing their spellings.)

Checklists like the one in the "Shared Reading" discussion are helpful in situations when children's reading is print-governed. Miscue analysis and running records are also helpful. Although Chapter 4 provides detailed information on miscue analysis, some additional special markings are useful for emergent readers. You may need to invent others in order to describe the oral reading behavior of some readers.

Extra Miscue Markings for Emergent Readers

invented text	*the little dangerous wolf* . . . the big bad wolf
requests for help	*"What's that word?"* The great big ‸enormous turnip
teacher assistance (after a long pause)	The great big enormous turnip . . . (In margin, note assistance given: strategy suggested, word provided, assisted reading for the next 3 sentences, or whatever.)
observations on non-verbal responses	Put * in text at spot where non-verbal responses noted. Then describe response in nearby margin (looked at picture; frowned).

spontaneous comments	Put **✗** in text at spot where comment made. Then write comment within quotation marks in nearby margin ("He better watch out!").

Performance samples of reading-like behavior or emergent reading may be gathered most easily from individual children if you read a book to the whole class a couple of times before asking individual children to read it to you. In addition to rereading books for performance samples, you can also ask students to read their own dictation immediately after the recording of the dictation and again a day later. See the procedures for "Reading a Predictable Book" and the "First Reading" and "Second Reading" of a dictation in the *Emergent Reading and Writing Evaluation* (in Rhodes, 1993). Padak et al. (1990) explore the reading and rereading of dictations as an assessment procedure for adult emergent readers. Malicky & Norman (1989) use procedures similar to "Reading a Predictable Book" with adults, utilizing familiar songs as predictable text.

shared writing

Like shared reading, shared writing includes events in which a more proficient literacy user assists a writer by sharing the writing responsibility in some way. A great degree of assistance is provided when a teacher takes a language experience dictation, writing down a student's oral composition; the teacher takes responsibility for recording the student's message but the student has responsibility for generating the message. (For examples of how language experience is used with adult emergent readers, see Rigg, 1981; Rigg & Taylor, 1979.) A lesser degree of assistance is provided when a teacher helps a student discover and use strategies for labeling a picture he has drawn. Here the student is responsible not only for generating the message but also for recording what he and the teacher together decide needs to be encoded.

Shared writing, like shared reading, allows a teacher to work with a student in the "zone of proximal development" (Vygotsky, 1962), the distance between what a child can do independently and what he can do with guidance. This helps the teacher identify what the student is capable of working on next in the process of writing. The anecdotal note that follows was written after one of the authors conducted a shared writing with Eleanor, a first grader who had previously been writing only random letters (prephonemic spelling) during independent writing time in her classroom. Note how the teacher demonstrated to Eleanor what she needed to do for herself as a writer—how she moved Eleanor into the zone of proximal development by supporting the use of her knowledge—and how the teacher invited Eleanor to assess her own learning during the conference.

STRDAIPADENBSNO (Yesterday I played in the snow.)

STRDA = yesterday

I = I

PAD = played

EN = in

B = the (pronounced "the" as "du" and thought she was writing "D")

SNO = snow

Showed her how to stretch her words out like a rubber band—doing it almost on own by SNO. E does have a fairly good grasp of sound/letter relationships. However, she has a hard time isolating words and tracking words in sentences in her mind. That may hold up progress for a while. Asked her—at end—what she did in writing today that she hadn't done in previous writing. She said, "I listened to sounds." Told her to do it in her writing again tomorrow.

Although Eleanor's snow story is still unreadable (largely due to the lack of space between words), it is clear that she is capable of recording more than random letters when she writes. In this conference, Eleanor learned a major concept about writing, and her teacher gathered valuable assessment information. Her teacher now knows that Eleanor has graphophonic knowledge that she can be expected to use, but she also knows that Eleanor is going to need help in tracking and isolating words in sentences as she writes.

Shared writing also can be used in helping some students take more risks in their writing. When one of the authors recently worked with seven-year-old Lesley, she encountered great reluctance on the part of the child to write at all. The teacher offered to write down the first sentence the child dictated if the child would write the second. They shared the pencil, passing it back and forth until Lesley, who was focusing completely on what she wanted to say, forgot her reluctance and wrote several sentences in a row, surprising even herself.

Shared writing samples are often most useful in comparison with independently produced writing. It may be that a student composes well-structured stories when the teacher writes them down but that independently written stories are brief and disjointed in comparison. If performance samples are useful in some situations, the student's performance on the "Dictation" (shared writing) portion of the *Emergent Reader and Writer Evaluation* (in Rhodes, 1993) may be compared with the student's performance on the "Writing" (independent writing) portion of the same instrument.

independent writing

Long before many students are able to read conventionally, they write text independently. In so doing, they reveal what they know about the writing process and its conventions, but they also continue to refine their understanding of the process and its conventions, particularly if shared writing is part of the curriculum. (See Newman & Beverstock, 1990, for examples of the use of independent writing with emergent adult readers/writers.)

A number of books have traced the early development of writing through children's independent writing samples (see, for example, Clay, 1975; Harste, Woodward, & Burke, 1984; Newkirk, 1989; Newman, 1985; Schickendanz, 1990; Temple et al., 1988). A basic knowledge of writing development provides a way of assessing what a particular student does in writing in light of what students normally do as writers. This knowledge can be expanded by reading the experts' descriptions of writing development and also by observing and comparing students' writing, looking for patterns and developmental characteristics.

Spelling development has received a great deal of attention in recent years. Our favorite summary appears in *The Beginnings of Writing* (Temple et al., 1988). Research reveals that children move along a continuum of spelling development, passing through the following points:

Prephonemic spelling: Strings of letters, numbers and other letterlike forms that have no conventional relationship to expected spellings.

Phonemic spelling: One or a few letter sounds are captured in print (though not necessarily conventionally). Spellings cannot be read by others.

Letter name spelling: All (or almost all) of the letter sounds are captured in print with letter names. For example, the "y" in "baby" is likely to be represented as an "e." Spellings can usually be read by those who are familiar with rules used by letter name spellers.

Transitional: Visual features of words begin to be incorporated into spellings but are often used in situations where they are not appropriate. For example, "rain" may be spelled as "rane," a spelling that employs silent *e* in a word where silent *e* is not used.

Correct: Spellings regularly and correctly employ visual features of English. Of course, no one is ever a completely "correct" speller.

In the following section, we'll look at three writing samples to demonstrate those aspects of children's writing that you might observe: the function and intent of writing, the content and organization of the writing, and the use of conventions such as spacing, directionality, spelling, and punctuation. The samples are notes that first graders wrote on memo pads in Linda McFadyen's and Karen Holesworth's classrooms in Colorado's Jefferson County School District. They are sequenced developmentally from least to most conventional in spelling. The second and third notes were written by children who were "reading on the words" at the time of writing, while the child who wrote the first was not. This informal writing reveals some interesting aspects of the writing of individual children and the writing that goes on in the two classrooms.

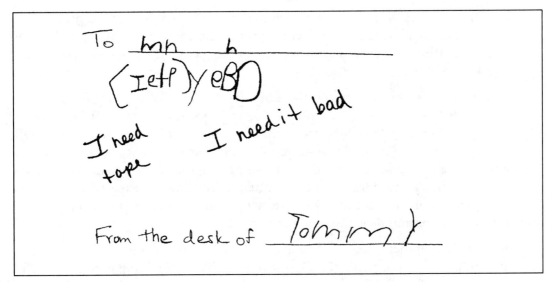

Figure 7.3   Tommy's note

In the first note (Figure 7.3), Tommy wrote to his teacher to request Scotch tape. It's clear that Tommy knows that writing can be used to make direct and emphatic requests. The note reads: (Ietop)yeBD ("I need tape. I need it bad."). In order to analyze Tommy's spelling, you have to know what Tommy said (he read his note to his teacher) and then look for sound/letter relationships. In previous notes, he wrote strings of letters that had no apparent relationship to his intended meaning. This note was one of the first attempts Tommy made to write letters that

Figure 7.4   Travis' note

graphophonically represented what he wanted to say. The "I," "top" for *tape,* and "BD" for *bad* provide information that he is now using early phonemic spelling strategies; that is, he realizes that there is a system for spelling and he is attempting to use it. Note that he has not used space to denote word boundaries, although he has used parentheses as markers to denote where the first thought ("I need tape") begins and ends and observes conventional directionality in writing left to right.

Travis's note (Figure 7.4) reveals that, like Tommy, he understands that writing can be used to make requests. In this note, Travis asks the age-old question in every classroom: kanIchaj Desg ("Can I change desks?"). Travis's spelling development is clearly more advanced than Tommy's; his note could be read by his teacher without his help. However, if you do not know the rules that letter name spellers typically invent, it may be difficult for you to read Travis' note on your own. Letter name spellers select letters whose names most closely represent the sounds they hear in the words they want to write. Thus, Travis uses a "j" to represent the final sound he hears in the word "change." It is also typical for letter name spellers to omit "n" in medial positions as Travis did in "change." One sign that Travis is beginning to represent sound/letter relationships more conventionally is his use of "ch" in the word "change." "Ch" and "sh" are typically represented by letter name spellers as "h"; if you listen to the sound produced when you say the letter "h," you will see why they select that letter.

In the last note (Figure 7.5), Steven writes to his friend David: I weLL DeDuKaT MY book to you AND Renee ("I will dedicate my book to you and Renee."). Here Steven uses writing to perform another function: to inform. Note the correct spelling of all but two words in his message. From his reading, Steven

Figure 7.5   Steven's note

has learned what words look like. He has begun to resemble a transitional speller, one who is learning the visual rules for spelling but who has not yet learned to apply them in all situations. His friend David has difficulty reading Steven's message and replied: Man I dont NO wat u sad ("Man, I don't know what you said!"). David's spelling is more like that of a letter name speller; note the difference between his and Steven's representation of the word "you," for example.

Although it is informative to look at single samples, judgments made about single samples may not stand up when we look at several samples by one student. The student's intent, the function of the writing, the audience the student is writing for, and other aspects of the writing situation can often affect the student's use of conventions in writing dramatically. That should not be surprising—you need only think about the differences you might observe if you examined two different pieces of writing you might do: a letter to the editor of your newspaper and a grocery list. At the same time, students may not use what they know as they write, which can be discovered if an adult does shared writing with a student. (Eleanor, in the previous section, is a good example.)

It is also necessary to observe the process of writing and to interview students if you are to learn as much as possible about their writing and make plans that will further their development. In an earlier chapter, we told about Rita, a second-grade girl who was asked to write a story—anything she wanted to write. Rita wrote her name quickly and then sat for quite some time, obviously deep in thought. Finally, she wrote the piece in Figure 7.6.

If we analyzed only this sample, we might conclude that Rita doesn't have many difficulties with writing. After all, her spelling is all correct, and she has used capitalization and punctuation correctly. We might only wonder why the story is so short and doesn't tell more about Rita's cat.

Because we were there during the writing process, we observed that Rita spent thirty-two minutes thinking and writing the sample and that she was not distracted by other things. That provided us with a great deal to wonder about. The puzzle

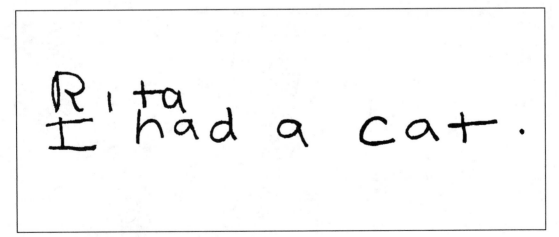

Figure 7.6   Rita's story

was solved when we asked Rita why it took her so long to write. She informed us, "I was thinking of a story I could spell." It turned out that Rita did not have a cat; she wrote about a cat because she could spell the word!

Performance samples of independent writing, such as the "Writing" portion of the *Emergent Reading and Writing Evaluation* (in Rhodes, 1993), may be helpful or necessary in some assessment situations. However, a performance sample that a student does not perceive as authentic is less likely to be as informative as the variety of writing samples the student produces as part of everyday classroom life. In addition, performance samples are likely to underestimate a student's writing capabilities. They also provide no information about important aspects of writing, such as the functions for which the student uses writing, because the writing situation is constrained; the writing is done as an assignment and a topic is provided.

drawing

Why include drawing in a chapter on the assessment of emergent reading and writing? There are several good reasons why such a discussion belongs here. First, drawing is a communication system, just as writing is. By observing the processes and products of drawing you can often gain insight about a child's approach to the writing process and its products. Second, when children write, the product typically includes the written text, a picture, and the oral commentary. "Children are 'symbol-weaving' (Dyson, 1986), constantly shifting among mutually supporting systems of representation—talking, drawing, and producing minimal text. Their 'writing' is a fabric formed of all these strands" (Newkirk, 1989, p. 37). Third, for many young children, drawing is more important than writing. Newkirk (1989, p. 65) also argues that "we dismiss too easily the value and complexity of children's drawing" and thus reduce children's capability for integrating graphics and text and for continuing to develop the perceptual abilities so key to observing the world.

Developmentally, children assign the majority of their time and energy to drawing when they first begin to communicate on paper. As they become better able to express themselves fluently in print and as the value placed on word-centeredness in schools takes over, drawing often becomes secondary and eventually non-existent. However, if we sit down to write with small children, our writing is likely to consist entirely of print, while theirs will often contain drawings.

It is interesting to observe the relationship between drawing, talking, and writing in children's products and in the process used to create the products. In the product, you can observe how much space is devoted to each and how one affects the meaning and display of the other. In the process, you can observe how the child uses talk to support drawing and writing, how each plays a role in communicating the child's intended meaning, and how the child moves between drawing and writing, writing, and talking.

In the picture in Figure 7.7, a kindergarten boy communicates through drawing. The drawing tells the story of a crocodile that is about to bite a boy. The child uses writing to clarify and to label: The "me" labels clarify that the two figures are actually the same boy at different points in time and space. The "sun" and "htoo"

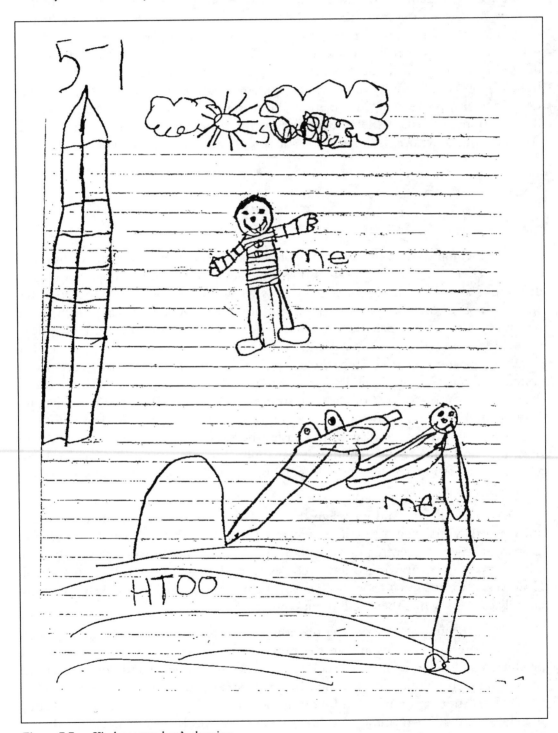

Figure 7.7   Kindergarten boy's drawing

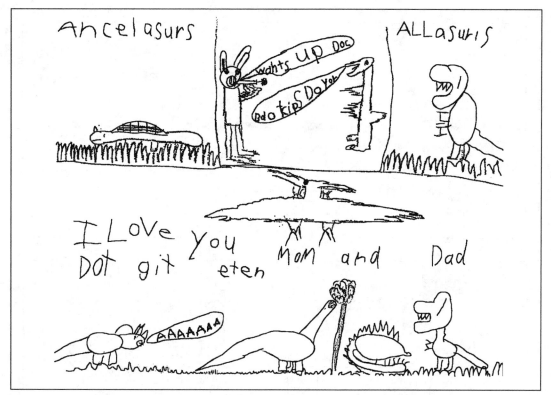

Figure 7.8 Eric's drawing

labels function to name the sun in the sky and the water (htoo is an invented spelling for H_2O!) in the river.

In contrast, Eric's writing (see Figure 7.8), adds information not available in the drawings. Two of the dinosaurs are labeled in the same way as in the drawing in Figure 7.7. However, in the middle picture at the top of the page, the characters are engaged in dialogue: "What's up, Doc?" and "You're despicable!" (The second sentence is written mostly right to left, adapting to the direction of the dialogue balloon coming out of the character's mouth.) The groan emanating from the mouth of the dinosaur in the bottom drawing is also dialogue. Finally, the caption "I love you, Mom and Dad. Don't get eaten" provides a message that the picture does not.

The writing/drawing combination, (see Figure 7.9), is quite sophisticated in several ways. First, it was done by a boy in the first few weeks of first grade over a period of days; the boy sustained the flow of the story over a period of time. Second, the action of the story is clearly revealed through a multiple frame strategy—like a series of movie frames (be sure to note the dog's receding tail in the last two pictures!). Third, the drawings and the writing are complementary; both could tell the story alone but together, they tell it more effectively. In fact, the writing reveals an action (the dog *made the cat* drop the piece of meat) that is not clear from the picture unless you note the cat's raised hair and understand its significance. In addition, it is not possible to illustrate something the text reveals: "The dog *thought* he had the piece of meat."

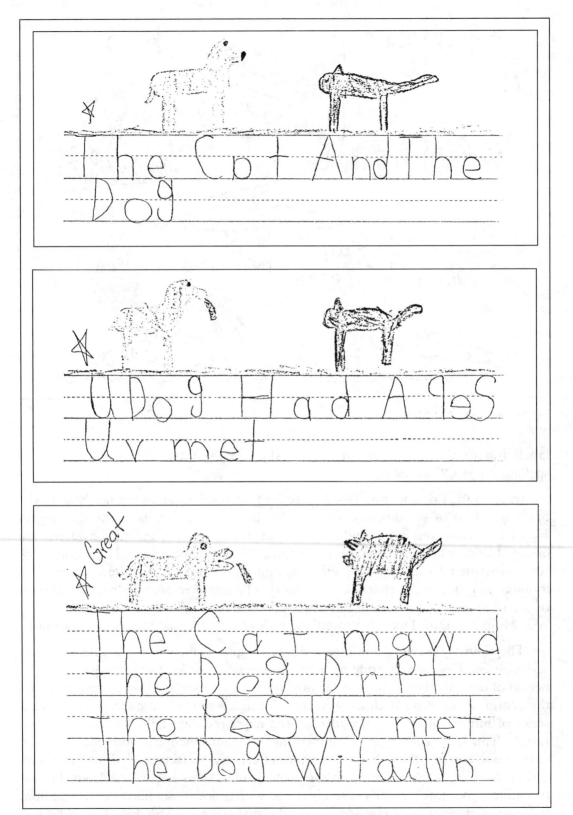

Figure 7.9 First grade boy's writing/drawing

Figure 7.9 First grade boy's writing/drawing
(continued)

In an excellent chapter about drawing and writing, Newkirk (1989, p. 59) lists seven ways (and notes that there may be others) in which drawing and text relate to each other in children's work. Because they may help you examine how children compose meaning, we list them here:

Text only. The text carries the only message, with no accompanying picture.

Picture only. The picture, unaided by text, represents the event, person, or object.

Picture and text—redundant. The text duplicates what is in the picture.

Imbalance—pictorial. The picture is far more specific and informative than the written text.

Complementary. Both text and drawing supply specific information, but the child decides which medium provides which information.

Imbalance—textual. The text provides most of the information.

General-specific relationship. The text identifies a general category, and the picture shows specific items in that category. For example, a child could draw a candy bar and label it "candy bar" (a redundant relationship) or he could call it "junk food" (a general-specific relationship.)

talking about reading and writing

As we said in Chapter 3, young children are capable of metacognitive behavior, of talking about reading and writing. This is particularly true when teachers support the development of metacognition by involving students in continually thinking and talking about the real reading and writing problems they encounter.

Learning to read a book is a reading problem peculiar to emergent readers. In Ann Christensen and Roxanne Torke's first and second-grade classroom, each child is encouraged to take responsibility for learning to read a new book by talking through the problem of going about the task. Problem solving begins with choosing a book that presents a challenge but that a child can learn to read over time. The class discusses at length how to choose books with these criteria in mind. Once they have chosen a book, the children also talk about ways to go about getting help in reading the book, ways to reread the book so they get better at it, and ways to know when they have learned to read their book.

All this talk about reading and learning to read tells teachers about students' current understanding of going about such a task. It also reveals what else students need to consider in order to succeed. At the same time, of course, the students are learning how to read and how to take responsibility for their own learning in this situation and in future situations.

Assuming that young children can think metacognitively and asking them questions about their reading and writing often yields interesting assessment data. Rita's reply to "Why did it take you so long to write this?" (Figure 7.6) is only one example. As we said in Chapter 3, "Why?" is probably our favorite question to ask when we are faced with an incident that puzzles us. Sometimes young children—and even adults—have difficulty answering such a question, but the question is often worth asking.

Particular interview questions may be useful in situations where teachers want to collect information about students' notions of reading and writing in a more organized fashion. Interviewing adult emergent readers/writers about their concepts of reading and writing is a fairly common procedure (see Fargo & Collins, 1989; Malicky & Norman, 1989; Padak, Davidson, & Padale, 1990; Rigg & Taylor, 1979). Teachers in the Denver Public Schools Chapter I program devised an interview for their young emergent readers and writers based on Burke's *Reading Interview* (Goodman, Watson, & Burke, 1987). The *Emergent Reader and Writer Interview* (in Rhodes, 1993) provides information about young children's views of themselves as readers and writers, their views of learning to read and write, and the support they have as readers and writers. When you read the interview in Figure 7.10, think about the instructional ideas and the other assessment questions that occur to you. (Remember that this is only one piece of information about the child.)

When students are asked to evaluate their own reading and writing, they talk about their reading and writing. In so doing, they develop greater metalinguistic awareness of the processes and of their role as responsible learners. Davidson & Wheat (1989) provide ideas about involving adults who are emerging readers/writers in plotting their progress in reading and writing. Ann Christensen and Roxanne Torke involve their first-and-second-grade students in self-evaluations. The examples in Figure 7.11 reveal a great deal about the first-grade writers who answered the questions and about the classroom in which they have been reading and writing all year.

teacher reflection   *teacher reflection*

As we were writing this book, we did some thinking about the use of videotapes in assessment, including their inclusion in portfolios; and we bemoaned the fact that we had not encouraged teachers in our classes to use them, nor did we know any teachers who did use them for assessment.

Then we attended the 1990 NCTE Spring Conference in Colorado Springs and met Jan Bennett, a first-grade teacher in Aspen, Colorado. It was her first conference presentation, and Jan had the misfortune of being scheduled to share an hour with a person who was unable to attend. In spite of the fact that she did not know this until she arrived at the conference, Jan easily kept her large audience's attention for a full hour with her description of how she conducted literacy assessment,

Name **Tamarah** Date **1**
Teacher _____ Grade **6**

Emergent Reader and Writer Interview

1. Tell me what kinds of things you read. **The Bad Wolf, Mother Goose, The 3 Little Bears, _Rhymes & Tales_**

   If positive response:
   Do you read (whatever child has mentioned) by yourself? (If no: Who helps?)
   yes

   If negative response:
   Are you learning to read?

   If yes: How are you learning to read and who is helping?

   Do you like to read? Why?
   yes -- Because I can learn a little bit about it (Q) Books, because it got good words in it.

   (learn a little bit about what?)

   Do you like to read? Why?

   If no: How do you think you'll learn to read and who do you think will help?

   Do you think you're a good reader? Why?
   Yes, cuz I know what the words says

   Do you want to learn to read? Why?

2. Who reads to you? or Who reads to you besides (whomever the child has named previously)?
   Nobody. I read by myself--my dad's in New Orleans.
   (Q: Does anybody else read to you?) My mom.

Emergent Reader and Writer Interview   **Rhymes & tales & all that stuff.**   111

3. Tell me what kinds of things you write. **I write ABC's. I write pictures of little girls & monsters.**

   If positive response:
   Do you write (whatever child has mentioned) by yourself? (If no: Who helps?)
   yes

   If negative response:
   Are you learning to write?

   If yes: How are you learning to write and who is helping?

   Do you like to write? Why?
   yes -- because it's fun. Because I can learn a lot about it (Q) Pictures and all that stuff.

   Do you like to write? Why?

   If no: How do you think you'll learn to write and who do you think will help?

   Do you think you're a good writer? Why?
   yes -- because I space & I don't write big.

   Do you want learn to write? Why?

4. Other information of interest:

Emergent Reader and Writer Interview by Instructional Assistance Project teachers Denver, Colorado. Reprinted by permission of Patricia Fernquist, Instructional Assistance Project Teacher Representative.

Emergent Reading and Writing   112

Figure 7.10 Tamarah's interview

NAME _Rachael M_   Writing Evaluation (Self)

Things I can do well in writing:

1. I Kan Sawnd owt wrS goD.

2. win I reD my stares I DaT haw a haB (bad) Time.

3. I LnD haw To mak sPasis.

4. win im riDen DaN wiR SaMn is TakeN I Til hos TakeN
   when someone's talking I tell who's talking
   rDaT BaTr

Something new I've learned to do in writing this year:

maK my riTen LuKe (look) prITe (pretty)
haw To DaT DereS in my STarE.

What I would like to learn so I can become a better writer: STarE.

1. I waT To lah _sentences_ haw To maK my SanTS (_sound_) SawnD BaTi

2. I waT To Irh haw To Tall oBaT DaT (_about_) aBowt owN SanTS.
   one _sentence_

3. I moIe info in senTeasa.

Figure 7.11 First-graders' self-evaluations

including her use of videotapes. When Jan played the videotaped readings of Neil, the child she refers to in her "Teacher Reflection," she clearly communicated the value of tapes for assessment, communicating with parents, and instructional planning.

Seeing is believing: videotaping reading development

Jan Bennett

To put the parents of my first-grade students in tune with their child's reading progress, I tape-record my students' reading. Then, at parent conferences, the parents can read the book while they listen to their child's oral reading of it. For years I had been satisfied with this method: I could explain to the parents how their child was approaching reading and the strategies that he or she was using. Tape-recording was a successful method at conferences and well worth the time I spent observing and taking notes on each child during a recording session.

Three years ago while doing some other work with videotaping in my classroom, it occurred to me that I could videotape each child reading for parent-teacher conferences. I promptly borrowed a videocamera from a parent of a student and videotaped each child. It was a tremendous hit with the parents. If I thought that they were happy with the audio recordings, they were delighted with the videos! Although the parents would have been happy just watching their child read, during conferences I was able to point out the strategies their child was using in order to read. If Johnny was "reading" along beautifully yet on an entirely different page, I could point that out. If Sarah was matching voice to print, I could point that out. If a child was using picture clues, it was easy to see. If a child struggled with a word, looked at the beginning sound, took in the meaning of the story, and then figured out the word, the parents could watch the process.

How to videotape

There was one problem with my videotaping: I had taped all the children on a single tape and spent a lot of time rewinding and fast forwarding to get to a particular child. When a parent who owned a popular local video store saw me struggling with one tape, he donated twenty-two tapes—one for each child in our class. Now I have someone videotape each child once every other month and I have set up a system for videotaping that works well. Here are five things to consider when beginning:

(1) **Locate tapes and a camera.** At the end of the first year, when the tapes had been donated, I had the parents bring in a blank tape and "trade" it

for the tape of their child reading over the course of the year. You could buy the tapes once and then begin the "trade" system, or you might have the children bring in a tape at the beginning of the year as part of their school supplies. Your librarian might be able to set you up with tapes.

Although many larger schools have video equipment, I have to depend on outside resources. The first year a parent allowed us to use a camera. Another year a local video store loaned us a camera for free. This year I paid a very small fee for the use of a camera from a local shop. Most athletic programs have cameras to tape games; the athletic director may let you borrow one from time to time.

(2) **Decide who will record.** A parent did the recording for our class the fist year, while for the past two I've had an aide. It helps to locate a person who can make a time commitment of one day (to tape twenty children) every other month. Since the person must be trained, it also helps to find someone who can do the job for the whole school year.

(3) **Find a place to record.** This should be a quiet room with as little interference as possible. Some places we have used have been the computer lab, the gym stage, the gym dressing room, the curriculum office, the principal's office, and the woodworking room. The room needs to be free of traffic and quiet so that noise doesn't interfere with the recording.

(4) **Train the recorder.** This is probably the most important of all. To get both the child and the book on camera a side view works best. The words can't be seen, but I can see how the child is using the words and pictures. I like the recorder to encourage the child to skip an unknown word and finish the sentence. If the child still does not know the word, then the recorder tells the child. Before reading begins, the recorder also picks a stopping place in a book that is too long. Usually five minutes of reading is adequate.

Since each videocamera varies in its operation, it is best to let the recorder become familiar with it before the first taping session. A tripod is not essential, but I find it extremely helpful for the quality of the tape and ease of operation. The person doing the recording can place the child and the camera in the correct position, announce the date of the taping session, and then be free to facilitate the child's reading.

(5) **Choose the books.** For the first recording, the child may choose any book to read. This helps the child with those feelings of being "camera shy" and also gives me a good idea of what the child is comfortable with. After the first recording I have the child choose from a number of books I consider to be at that child's level. The child always has the chance to choose the book before the taping session and read it, whether or not it is a new book to the child.

Using videotapes to assess literacy

At first, I wasn't sure how I'd use the tapes. I knew that there wouldn't be time to show each parent a child's whole tape at spring conferences—especially Whitney's because she took a novel in each time she read for the camera! Guilt was getting the best of me, so one afternoon after school I took down all the tapes and began viewing them.

I was amazed! I sat stunned as I saw the reading growth of each child unfold. I think it's similar to being around your toddler so much that you just don't see how much they have grown. I knew that my students were improving in reading but to be able to look at their reading in November and then in January and again in March—or to be able to look at a particular section over and over—was extremely powerful. Even Whitney (who I knew could probably read anything that I could) showed visible growth in her reading.

At that point I knew the tapes could be used for more than "showing off" the children to their parents, and I began using them to assess and study the children in my classroom.

Now I also use the tapes to help make decisions about whole group and individualized instruction and to create flexible groups. From this year's tapes, I have discovered that Brandon sounds out so many words he loses meaning. Ah! An individual mini-lesson needed on skipping the unknown word and reading for meaning. I can tell that Jeremy, Jessica, and Neil lose their place frequently and that all need reminders to "touch and read." I can see that Ashley carefully looks over the pictures before beginning to read a set of pages. I then notice that her own illustrations play a major part in her writings. I can tell that Tracey (Whitney's sister) finds joy in her reading; she pauses for a good laugh now and then or looks up and comments on some aspect of *her* novel. I can look again and see that Jessica doesn't have a firm grasp of periods. The benefits of "kid watching" are almost endless and I see something more almost every time I rewind and look again.

Neil's reading

Besides using the tapes to plan instruction, I also use them to document the reading progress of students over time. An example is Neil, who came to me from a kindergarten teacher unsure if he would benefit more from another year in kindergarten or from moving on to first grade.

November: In November Neil "retold" the story *The Red Rose* by looking at the pictures. He used book language and had a general sense of the story line because he was familiar with the book. He did not use print to help him make sense of the story or to follow the story line. At the end of the story—as told by Neil—the man gives the rose to Mrs. McGuire, who is a character from another book, *Fire! Fire! Said Mrs. McGuire.*

January: Neil had "memorized" *Go, Go, Go,* the next developmental step in the reading process. Although he was not pointing to the print (making me wonder if he did look at the print), when he misread the last page ("hop" for "ride") he looked at the beginning sound to jog his memory.

March: Neil had picked a simple, predictable book (*One, One is the Sun*) to read. As he began reading, he was not touching the words and seemed to be saying what appeared to be "memorized" text. On the second page, however, Neil made a miscue. From the miscue on, Neil began to point to each word and occasionally used pictures as clues.

April: Once again, Neil picked a simple, predictable book (*Fizz and Splutter*) to read but one that I considered at the next higher level of difficulty. The format was such that the same sentences appeared on each page. As part of the illustrations, a variety of words appeared to be coming from a magician's hat. Neil began by reading the repetitive sentences only, until the recorder had him reread the book in its entirety. Neil did as asked, using picture cues and beginning sounds to read the whole book. While Neil had little difficulty with any of the words, he became confused as to the order in which he thought the recorder wanted him to read. He lost some confidence and had difficulty with the last page.

I know from Neil's tapes that he is truly moving along the continuum towards becoming a reader. He can match voice to print, he employs meaning to predict a word, he always uses beginning sounds and occasionally ending sounds when reading, he understands that periods mean a full stop, he uses pictures for understanding print, and he is willing to take risks and try new books. Most of all, Neil shows a desire to read by choosing to read independently and frequently!

In videotaping first graders' reading, I have moved from using assessment to inform parents to assessment that also provides a basis for my instruction. I am able, as in no other manner of assessment, to study my students in depth, to look at a particular aspect of reading over and over again without interruptions, and to professionally interpret not only reading ability and progress but body language and confidence. As I analyze tapes and as I share them with parents, we focus on helping the child through assessment.

Conclusion

Many of the aspects of reading and writing assessment we have already discussed apply to emergent readers and writers, although some are not as useful in uncovering their capabilities and knowledge. In this chapter we briefly critiqued "readiness tests," posed assessment questions that are unique to emergent readers and writers, and highlighted classroom literacy events that lend themselves to the assessment of emergent readers and writers. The literacy events themselves are the kind that are most frequently found in whole language classrooms designed for young children, although a number of them are also used in the literacy instruction of older or adult emergent readers and writers. In addition, we discussed performance samples, which are open-ended and come closest to the literacy events we outline.

appendix E

Literacy Development and Prefirst Grade

A Joint Statement of Concerns about Present Practices in Prefirst Grade Reading Instruction and Recommendations for Improvement

- Association for Childhood Education International
- Association for Supervision and Curriculum Development
- International Reading Association
- National Association for the Education of Young Children
- National Association of Elementary School Principals
- National Council of Teachers of English

Prepared by the Early Childhood and Literacy Development Committee of the International Reading Association.

Literacy learning begins in infancy. Children have many experiences with oral and written language before they come to school.

- Children have had many experiences from which they build ideas about the functions and uses of oral and written language.
- Children have a command of language and of processes for learning and using language.
- Many children can differentiate between drawing and writing.
- Many children are reading environmental print, such as road signs, grocery labels, and fast food signs.
- Many children associate books with reading.
- Children's knowledge about language and communication is influenced by their social and cultural backgrounds.
- Many children expect that reading and writing will be sense-making activities.

Basic premises of a sound prefirst grade reading program

- Reading and writing at school should permit children to build upon their already existing knowledge of oral and written language.
- Learning should take place in a supportive environment where children can build a positive attitude toward themselves and toward language and literacy.
- For optimal learning, teachers should involve children actively in many meaningful, functional language experiences, including *speaking, listening, writing,* and *reading.*
- Teachers of young children should be prepared in ways that acknowledge differences in language and cultural backgrounds, and should emphasize reading as an integral part of the language arts as well as of the total curriculum.

Concerns

- Many prefirst grade children are subjected to rigid, formal prereading programs with inappropriate expectations and experiences for their levels of development.
- Little attention is given to individual development or individual learning styles.
- The pressures of accelerated programs do not allow children to be risk takers as they experiment with written language.
- Too much attention is focused upon isolated skill development and abstract parts of the reading process, rather than on the integration of talking, writing and listening with reading.
- Too little attention is placed on reading for pleasure; therefore, children do not associate reading with enjoyment.
- Decisions related to reading programs are often based on political and economic considerations rather than on knowledge of how young children learn.
- The pressure to achieve high scores on tests inappropriate for the kindergarten child has led to undesirable changes in the content of programs. Activities that deny curiosity, critical thinking and creative expression are all too frequent, and can foster negative attitudes toward language communication.
- As a result of declining enrollment and reduction in staff, individuals with little or no knowledge of early childhood education are sometimes assigned to teach young children. Such teachers often select inappropriate methods.
- Teachers who are conducting prefirst grade programs without depending on commercial readers and workbooks sometimes fail to articulate for parents and other members of the public what they are doing and why.

Recommendations

1. Build instruction on what the child already knows about oral language, reading and writing. Focus on meaningful experiences and meaningful language rather than on isolated skill development.
2. Respect the language the child brings to school, and use it as a base for language and literacy activities.
3. Ensure feelings of success for all children, helping them to see themselves as people who enjoy exploring both oral and written language.
4. Provide reading experiences as an integrated part of the communication process, which includes speaking, listening and writing, as well as art, math and music.
5. Encourage children's first attempts at writing, without concern for the proper formation of letters or correct conventional spelling.
6. Encourage risk taking in first attempts at reading and writing, and accept what appear to be errors as part of children's natural growth and development.

7. Use reading materials that are familiar or predictable, such as well known stories, as they provide children with sense of control and confidence in their ability to learn.

8. Present a model for children to emulate. In the classroom, teachers should use language appropriately, listen and respond to children's talk, and engage in their own reading and writing.

9. Take time regularly to read to children from a wide variety of poetry, fiction and nonfiction.

10. Provide time regularly for children's independent reading and writing.

11. Foster children's affective and cognitive development by providing them with opportunities to communicate what they know, think and feel.

12. Use developmentally and culturally appropriate procedures for evaluation, ones that are based on the objectives of the program and that consider each child's total development.

13. Make parents aware of the reasons for a broader language program at school and provide them with ideas for activities to carry out at home.

14. Alert parents to the limitations of formal assessments and standardized tests of prefirst graders' reading and writing skills.

15. Encourage children to be active participants in the learning process rather than passive recipients, by using activities that allow for experimentation with talking, listening, writing and reading.

appendix F

NAEYC Position Statement on Standardized Testing of Young Children 3 Through 8 Years of Age

Adopted November 1987

Statement of the problem

The practice of administering standardized tests to young children has increased dramatically in recent years. Many school systems now routinely administer some form of standardized developmental screening or readiness test for admittance to kindergarten or standardized achievement test for promotion to first grade. As a result, more and more 5- and 6-year-olds are denied admission to school or are assigned to some form of extra-year tracking such as "developmental kindergarten," retention in kindergarten, or "transitional" first grade (Miesels, 1987; Shepard & Smith, in press). Such practices (often based on inappropriate uses of readiness or screening tests) disregard the potential, documented long-term negative effects of retention on children's self-esteem and the fact that such practices disproportionately affect low-income and minority children; further, these practices have been implemented in the absence of research documenting that they positively affect children's later academic achievement (Gredler, 1984; Shephard & Smith, 1986, 1987; Smith & Shepard, 1987).

A simultaneous trend that has influenced and been influenced by the use of standardized testing is the increasingly academic emphasis on the curriculum imposed on kindergartners. Many kindergartens are now highly structured, "watered-down" first grades, emphasizing workbooks and other paper-and-pencil activities that are developmentally inappropriate for 5-year-olds (Bredekamp, 1987; Durkin, 1987; Katz, Raths, & Torres, undated). The trend further trickles down to preschool and child care programs that feel their mission is to get children "ready" for kindergarten. Too many school systems, expecting children to conform to an inappropriate curriculum and finding large numbers of "unready" children, react to the problem by raising the entrance age for kindergarten and/or labeling the children as failures (Shephard & Smith, 1986, in press).

The negative influences of standardized testing on the curriculum is not limited to kindergarten. Throughout the primary grades, schools assess achievement using tests that frequently do not reflect current theory and research out how children learn. For example, current research on reading instruction stresses a whole language/literacy approach that integrates oral language, writing, reading, and spelling in meaningful context, emphasizing comprehension. However, standardized tests of reading achievement still define reading exclusively as phonics and word recognition and measure isolated skill acquisition (Farr &Carey, 1986; Teale, Hiebert, & Chittenden, 1987; Valencia & Pearson, 1987). Similarly, current theory of mathematics instruction stresses the child's construction of number concepts through firsthand experiences, while achievement tests continued to define mathematics as knowledge of numerals (Kamii, 1985a, 1985b). As a result, too many school systems teach to the test or continue to use outdated instructional methods so that children will perform adequately on standardized tests.

The widespread use of standardized tests also drains resources of time and funds without clear demonstration that the investment is beneficial for children. Days may be devoted to testing (or preparing for it) that could be better spent in valuable instructional time (National Center for Fair and Open Testing, 1987).

Ironically, the calls for excellence in education that have produced widespread reliance on standardized testing may have had the opposite effect—mediocrity. Children are being taught to provide the one "right" answer on the answer sheet, but are not being challenged to think. Rather than producing excellence, the overuse (and misuse) of standardized testing has led to the adoption of inappropriate teaching practices as well as admission and retention policies that are not in the best interests of individual children or the nation as a whole.

Purpose

The purpose of this position statement is to guide the decisions of educators regarding the use of standardized tests. These administrative decisions include whether to use standardized testing, how to critically evaluate existing tests, how to carefully select appropriate and accurate tests to be used with a population and purpose for which the test was designed, and how to use and interpret the results yielded from standardized tests to parents, school personnel, and the media. Such decisions are usually made by school principals, superintendents, or state school officials. Teachers are responsible for administering tests and, therefore, have a professional responsibility to be knowledgeable about appropriate testing and to influence, or attempt to influence, the selection and use of tests. It is assumed that responsible and educated decisions by administrators and teachers will influence commercial test developers to produce valid, reliable, and useful tests.

Standardized tests are instruments that are composed of empirically selected items; have definite instructions for use, data on reliability, and validity; and are norm- or criterion-referenced (see definitions on page 359). This position statement addresses *tests*—the instruments themselves, and *testing*—the administration of tests, scoring, and interpretation of scores. This statement concentrates on standardized tests because such tests are most likely to influence policy. Nonstandardized assessments such as systematic observation, anecdotal records, locally or nationally developed checklists, or mastery tests developed by individual teachers (that do not meet the above criteria for standardization) play a vital role in planning and implementing instruction and in making decisions about placement or children. Decisions made on the basis of nonstandardized assessments should take into consideration the guidelines presented in this position statement.

The field of standardized testing is complex. Various types of standardized tests exist for various purposes. These include: achievement/readiness tests; developmental screening tests; diagnostic assessment tests; and intelligence tests (see definitions, page 359). The guidelines in this position statement apply to all forms of standardized testing, but primarily address the uses and abuses of achievement, readiness, and developmental screening tests.

Developmental screening tests are designed to indicate which children should proceed further to a multidisciplinary assessment, only after which a decision regarding special education placement can be made. School readiness tests are designed to assess a child's level of preparedness for a specific academic program (Meisels, 1987). As such, readiness tests should *not* be used to identify children potentially in need of special education services or for placement deisions (Meisels, 1986). Diagnostic assessments are designed to identify children with specific special needs, determine the nature of the problem, suggest the cause of the problem, and propose possible remediation strategies (Meisels, 1985). Intelligence tests are norm- or criterion-referenced measures of cognitive functioning (as defined by a specific criterion or construct) and are often used in diagnostic assessment. No single test can be used for all of these purposes, and rarely will a test be applicable to more than one or two of them. The uses and abuses of diagnostic assessments and intelligence tests have been well documented elsewhere and are beyond the scope of this position statement (Chase, 1977; Goodwin & Driscoll, 1980; Gould, 1981; Hilliard, 1975; Kamin, 1974; Oakland, 1977; Reynolds, 1984).

NAEYC acknowledges and endorses the *Standards for Educational and Psychological Testing* (1985) developed by a joint committee of the American Educational Research Association, American Psychological Association, and National Council on Measurement in Education. Standardized tests used in early childhood programs should comply with the joint committee's technical standards for test construction and evaluation, professional standards for use, and standards for administrative procedures. This means that no standardized test should be used for screening, diagnosis, or assessment unless the test has published statistically acceptable reliability and validity data. Moreover, test producers are strongly encouraged to present data concerning the proportion of at-risk children correctly identified (test sensitivity) and the proportion of those not at-risk who are correctly found to be without major problems (test specificity) (Meisels, 1984). NAEYC's position on standardized testing is intended not to duplicate, but to be used in conjunction with, the *Standards for Educational and Psychological Testing* (1985).

Statement of the position

NAEYC believes that the most important consideration in evaluating and using standardized tests is the *utility criterion:* The purpose of testing must be to improve services for children and ensure that children benefit from their educational experiences. Decisions about testing and assessment instruments must be based on the usefulness of the assessment procedure for improving services to children and improving outcomes for children. The ritual use even of "good tests" (those that are judged to be valid and reliable measures) is to be discouraged in the absence of documented research showing that children benefit from their use.

Determining the utility of a given testing program is not easy. It requires thorough study of the potential effects, both positive and negative. For example, using a readiness or developmental test to admit children to kindergarten or first grade is often defended by teachers and administrators who point to the fact that the children who are kept back perform better the next year. Such intuitive reports overlook the fact that no comparative information is available about how the individual child would have fared had he or she been permitted to proceed with schooling. In addition, such pronouncements rarely address the possible effects of failure of the admission test on the child's self-esteem, the parents' perceptions, or the educational impact of labeling or mislabeling the child as being behind the peer group (Gredler, 1978; Shepard & Smith, 1986, in press; Smith & Shepard, 1987).

The following guidelines are intended to enhance the utility of standardized tests and guide early childhood professionals in making decisions about the appropriate use of testing.

1. **All standardized tests used in early childhood programs must be reliable and valid according to the technical standards of test development (AERA, APA, & NCME, 1985).**

   Administrators making decisions about standardized testing must recognize that the younger the child, the more difficult it is to obtain reliable and valid results from standardized tests. For example, no available school readiness test (as contrasted to a developmental screening test) is accurate enough to screen children for placement into special programs without a 50% error rate (Shepard & Smith, 1986). Development in young children occurs rapidly; early childhood educators recognize the existence of general stages and sequence of development but also recognize that enormous individual variation occurs in patterns and timing of growth and development that is quite normal and not indicative of pathology. Therefore, the result obtained on a single administration of a test must be confirmed through periodic screening and assessment and corroborated by other sources of information to be considered reliable (Meisels, 1984).

2. **Decisions that have a major impact on children such as enrollment, retention, or assignment to remedial or special classes should be based on multiple scores of information and should never be based on a single test score.**

   Appropriate sources of information *may* include combinations of the following:

   - systematic observations, by teachers and other professionals, that are objective, carefully recorded, reliable (produce similar results over time and among different observers), and valid (produce accurate measures of carefully defined, mutually exclusive categories of observable behavior);

   - samples of children's work such as drawings, paintings, dictated stories, writing samples, projects, and other activities (not limited to worksheets);

   - observations and anecdotes related by parents and other family members; and

   - test scores, if and only if appropriate, reliable, and valid tests have been used.

     In practice, multiple measures are sometimes used in an attempt to find some supporting evidence for a decision that teachers or administrators are predisposed to make regarding a child's placement. Such practice is an inappropriate application of this guideline. To meet this guideline, the collected set of evidence obtained through multiple sources of information should meet validity standards.

3. **It is the professional responsibility of administrators and teachers to critically evaluate, carefully select, and use standardized tests only for the purposes for which they are intended and for which data exists demonstrating the test's validity (the degree to which the test accurately measures what it purports to measure).**

Unfortunately, readiness tests (based on age-related normative data) that are designed to measure the skills children have acquired compared to other children in their age range are sometimes used inappropriately. The intended purpose of such instruments is typically to provide teachers with information that will help them improve instruction, by informing them of what children already know and the skills they have acquired. In practice, however, teachers have been found to systematically administer such tests and then proceed to teach all children the same content using the same methods; for example, testing all kindergartners and then instructing the whole group using phonics workbooks (Durkin, 1987). The practice of making placement decisions about children on the basis of the results of readiness tests is becoming more common despite the absence of data that such tests are valid predictors of later achievement (Meisels, 1985, 1987).

4. **It is the professional responsibility of administrators and teachers to be knowledgeable about testing and to interpret test results accurately and cautiously to parents, school personnel, and the media.**

Accurate interpretation of test results is essential. It is the professional obligation of administrators and teachers to become informed about measurement issues, to use tests responsibly, to exert leadership within early childhood programs and school systems regarding the use of testing, to influence test developers to produce adequate tests and to substantiate claims made in support of tests, and to accurately report and interpret test results without making undue claims about their meaning or implications.

5. **Selection of standardized tests to assess achievement and/or evaluate how well a program is meeting its goals should be based on how well a given test matches the locally determined theory, philosophy, and objectives of the specific program.**

Standardized tests used in early childhood programs must have content validity; that is, they must accurately measure the content of the curriculum presented to children. If no existing test matches the curriculum, it is better not to use a standardized test or to develop an instrument to measure the program's objectives rather than to change an appropriate program to fit a pre-existing test. Too often the content of a standardized test unduly influences the content of the curriculum. If a test is used, the curriculum should determine its selection; the test should not dictate the content of the curriculum.

Another difficulty related to content validity in measures for young children is that many critically important content areas in early childhood programs such as developing self-esteem, social competence, creativity, or dispositions toward learning (Katz, 1985), are considered "unmeasurable" and are therefore omitted from tests. As a result, tests for young children often address the more easily measured, but no more important, aspects of development and learning.

6. **Testing of young children must be conducted by individuals who are knowledgeable about and sensitive to the developmental needs of young children and who are qualified to administer tests.**

Young children are not good test takers. The younger the child the more inappropriate paper-and-pencil, large group test administrations become. Standards for the administration of tests require that reasonable comfort be provided to the test taker (AERA, APA, & NCME, 1985). Such a standard must be broadly interpreted when applied to young children. Too often, standardized tests are administered to children in large groups, in unfamiliar environments, by strange people, perhaps during the first few days at a new school or under other stressful conditions. During such test administrations, children are asked to perform unfamiliar tasks, for no reason that they can understand. For test results to be valid, tests are best administered to children individually in familiar, comfortable circumstances by adults whom the child has come to know and trust and who are also qualified to administer the tests.

7. **Testing of young children must recognize and be sensitive to individual diversity.**

Test developers frequently ignore two important sources of variety in human experiences—cultural variations and variations in the quality of educational experiences provided for different children. It is easier to mass produce tests if one assumes that cultural differences are minimal or meaningless or if one assumes that test subjects are exposed to personal and educational opportunities of equally high quality. These assumptions permit attributing all variances or differences in test scores to differences in individual children's capacities. However, these assumptions are false.

Early childhood educators recognize that children's skills, abilities, and aptitudes are most apparent when they can be demonstrated in familiar cultural contexts. Because standardized tests must use particular cultural material, they may be inappropriate for assessing the skills, abilities, or aptitudes of children whose primary cultures differ from the mainstream. Language is the special feature of a culture that creates the greatest problem for test developers. There are many language varieties in the United States, some of which are not apparent to the casual observer or test developer. Although having a common language is definitely desirable, useful, and a major goal of education, testing must be based on reality. For non-native English speakers or speakers of some dialects of English, any test administered in English is primarily a language or literacy test (AERA, APA, & NCME, 1985). Standardized tests should not be used in multicultural/multilingual communities if they are not sensitive to the effects of cultural diversity or bilingualism (Meisels, 1985). If testing is to be done, children should be tested in their native language.

Conclusion

NAEYC's position on standardized testing in early childhood programs restricts the use of tests to situations in which testing provides information that will clearly contribute to improved outcomes for children. Standardized tests have an important role to play in ensuring that children's achievement or special needs are objectively and accurately assessed and that appropriate instructional services are planned and implemented for individual children. However, standardized tests are only one of multiple sources of assessment information that should be used when decisions are made about what is best for young children. Tests may become a burden on the educational system, requiring considerable effort and expense to administer and yielding meager benefits. Given the scarcity of resources, the intrusiveness of testing, and the real potential for measurement error and/or bias, tests should be used only when it is clear that their use represents a meaningful contribution to the improvement of instruction for children and only as one of many sources of information. Rather than to use tests of doubtful validity, it is better not to test, because false labels that come from tests may cause educators or parents to alter inappropriately their treatment of children. The potential for misdiagnosing or mislabeling is particularly great with young children where there is wide variation in what may be considered normal behavior.

Administrators of early childhood programs who consider the use of standardized tests must ask themselves: How will children benefit from testing? Why is testing to be done? Does an appropriate test exist? What other sources of information can be used to make decisions about how best to provide services for an individual child? In answering such questions, administrators should apply the foregoing guidelines.

The burden of proof for the validity and reliability of tests is on the test developers and the advocates for their use. The burden of proof for the utility of tests is on administrators or teachers of early childhood programs who make decisions about the use of tests in individual classrooms. Similarly, the burden of responsibility for choosing, administering, scoring, and interpreting a score from a standardized test rests with the early childhood professional and thus demands that professionals be both skilled and responsible. Ensuring that tests meet scientific standards, reflect the most current scientific knowledge, and are used appropriately requires constant vigilance on the part of educators.

Definitions

Achievement test—a test that measures the extent to which a person has mastery over a certain body of information or possesses a certain skill after instruction has taken place.

Criterion—an indicator of the accepted value of outcome performance or a standard against which a measure is evaluated.

Criterion-referenced—a test for which interpretation of scores is made in relation to a specified performance level, as distinguished from interpretations that compare the test taker's score to the performance of other people (i.e. norm-referenced).

Developmental test—an age-related norm-referenced assessment of skills and behaviors that children have acquired (compared to children of the same chronological age). Sometimes such tests are inaccurately called developmental screening tests.

Diagnostic assessment—identification of a child who has special needs, usually conducted by a multidisciplinary team of professionals; used to identify a child's specific areas of strength and weakness, determine the nature of the problems, and suggest the cause of the problems and possible remediation strategies.

Early children—birth through age 8.

Intelligence test—a series of tasks yielding a score indicative of cognitive functioning. Tasks typically require problem-solving and/or various intellectual operations such as conceiving, thinking, and reasoning, or they reflect an earlier use of such intellectual functions (e.g., in information questions). Standardized by finding the average performance of individuals who by independent criteria (i.e., other intelligence tests) are of known degrees or levels of intelligence.

Norms—statistics or data that summarize the test performance of specified groups such as test takers of various ages or grades.

Norm-referenced—a test for which interpretation of scores is based on comparing the test taker's performance to the performance of other people in a specified group.

Readiness test—assessment of child's level of preparedness for a specific academic or preacademic program. (See also achievement test and developmental test.)

Reliability—the degree to which test scores are consistent, dependable, or repeatable; that is, the degree to which test scores can be attributed to actual differences in test takers' performance rather than to errors of measurement.

Score—any specific number resulting from the assessment of an individual.

Screening test (also called *developmental screening test*)—a test used to identify children who *may* be in need of special services, as a first step in identifying children in need of further diagnosis; focuses on the child's ability to acquire skills.

Standardized test—an instrument composed of empirically selected items that has definite instructions for use, adequately determined norms, and data on reliability and validity.

Testing—the administration, scoring, and interpretation of scores of a standardized test.

Utility—the relative value or usefulness of an outcome as compared to other possible outcomes.

Validity—the degree to which a test measures what it purports to measure; the degree to which a certain inference from a test is appropriate or meaningful.

    Content validity—evidence that shows the extent to which the content of a test is appropriately related to its intended purpose. For achievement tests, *content* refers to the content of the curriculum, the actual instruction, or the objectives of the instruction.

Criterion-related validity—evidence that demonstrates that test scores are systematically related to one or more outcome criteria.

Predictive validity—evidence of criterion-related validity in which scores on the criterion are observed at a later date; for example, the score on a test with predictive validity will predict future school performance.

Selected resources

Cohen, R. (1969). Conceptual styles, culture conflict, and non-verbal tests of intelligence. *American Anthropologist, 71*(5), 828–857.

Cole, M., & S. Scribner (1974). *Culture and thought: A psychological introduction.* New York: Wiley.

Heath, S. (1983) *Ways with words: Language, life and work in communities and classrooms.* Cambridge, England: Cambridge University Press.

Heller, K. A., W.H. Holtzman, & S. Messick (Eds.). (1982). *Placing children in special education: A strategy for equity.* Washington, DC: National Academy Press.

References

American Educational Research Association, American Psychological Association, and National Council on Measurement in Education. (1985). *Standards for educational and psychological testing.* Washington, DC: Author.

Bredekamp, S. (Ed.). (1987). *Developmentally appropriate practice in early childhood programs serving children from birth through age 8* (exp. ed.). Washington, DC: NAEYC.

Chase, A. (1977). *The legacy of Malthus: The social cost of scientific racism.* New York: Knopf.

Durkin, D. (1987). Testing in the kindergarten. *The Reading Teacher, 40*(8), 766–770.

Farr, R. & R. Carey (1986). *Reading: What can be measured?* Newark, DE: International Reading Association.

Goodwin, W. & L. Driscoll (1980). *Handbook for measurement and evaluation in early childhood education.* San Francisco: Jossey-Bass.

Gould, S. (1981). *The mismeasure of man.* New York: Norton.

Gredler, G. (1978). A look at some important factors for assessing readiness for school. *Journal of Learning Disabilities, 11*, 284–290.

Gredler, G. (1984). Transition classes: A viable alternative for the at-risk child? *Psychology in the Schools, 21*. 463–470.

Hilliard, A. (1975) The strengths and weaknesses of cognitive tests of young children. In J.D. Andrews (Ed.), *One child indivisible*. Washington, DC: NAEYC.

Kamii, C. (1985a). Leading primary education toward excellence: Beyond worksheets and drill. *Young Children, 40*(6), 3–9.

Kamii, C. (1985b). *Young children reinvent arithmetic.* New York: Teachers College Press, Columbia University.

Kamin, L. (1974). *The science and politics of IQ.* New York: Wiley.

Katz, L. (1985). Dispositions in early childhood education. *ERIC/EECE Bulletin, 18*(2), 1, 3.

Katz, L., J. Raths, & R. Torres (undated). *A place called kindergarten.* Urbana, IL: ERIC Clearinghouse on Elementary and Early Childhood Education.

Meisels, S.J. (1984). Prediction, prevention, and developmental screening in the EPSDT program. In H.W. Stevenson & A.G. Siegel (Eds.), *Child development research and social policy.* Chicago: University of Chicago Press.

Meisels, S.J. (1985). *Developmental screening in early childhood: A guide.* Washington, DC: NAEYC.

Meisels, S.J. (1986). Testing four- and five-year olds. *Educational Leadership, 44,* 90–92.

Meisels, S.J. (1987). Uses and abuses of developmental screening and school readiness testing. *Young Children, 42*(2), 4–6, 68–73.

National Center for Fair and Open Testing. (1987, Fall). North Carolina legislature drops exams for 1st, 2nd graders. *Fair Test Examiner,* p. 3.

Oakland, T. (Ed.). (1977). *Psychological and educational assessment of minority children.* New York: Brunner/Mazel.

Reynolds, C. (Ed.). (1984). *Perspectives on bias in mental testing.* New York: Plenum.

Shepard, L. & M. Smith (1986). Synthesis of research on school readiness and kindergarten retention. *Educational Leadership, 44*(3), 78–86.

Shepard, L. & M. Smith (1987). Effects of kindergarten retention at the end of first grade. *Psychology in the Schools, 24,* 346–357.

Shepard, L. & M. Smith (in press). Escalating academic demand in kindergarten: Some nonsolutions. *Elementary School Journal.*

Smith, M. & L. Shepard (1987). What doesn't work: Explaining policies of retention in the early grades. *Educational Leadership, 45*(2), 129–134.

Teale, W.E. Hiebert, & E. Chittenden (1987). Assessing young children's literacy development. *The Reading Teacher, 40,* 772–776.

Valencia, S. & P. Pearson (1987). Reading assessment: Time for a change. *The Reading Teacher, 40,* 726–732.

references

Carle, E. (1969). *The very hungry caterpillar.* New York: Philomel Books.

Chittenden, E. & R. Courtney. (1989). Assessment of young children's reading: Documentation as an alternative to testing. In D. Strickland & L. Morrow (Eds.), *Emerging literacy: Young children learn to read and write* , pp. 107–120. Newark, DE: International Reading Association.

Clay, M. (1982). *Observing young readers.* Portsmouth, NH: Heinemann.

———. (1979). *Stones: Concepts about print test.* Portsmouth, NH: Heinemann.

———. (1975). *What did I write?* Portsmouth, NH: Heinemann.

———. (1972). *Sand: Concepts about print test.* Portsmouth, NH: Heinemann.

Davidson, J.L. & T.E. Wheat. (1989). Successful literacy experiences for adult illiterates. *Journal of Reading, 32* (4), 342–346.

Durkin, D. (1987). Testing in kindergarten. *The Reading Teacher, 40*(8), 766–771.

Dyson, A. (1986). Transitions and tensions: Interrelationships between the drawing, talking and dictating of young children. *Research in the Teaching of Writing, 20,* 279–409.

Fargo, J.E. & M. Collins. (1989). Learning from researching: Literacy practitioners and assessment of adults' reading progress. *Journal of Reading, 33* (2), 120–125.

Genishi, C. & A.H. Dyson. (1984). *Language assessment in the early years.* Norwood, NJ: Ablex.

Goodman, Y. (1982). Concepts About Print. In M. Clay, *Observing young readers,* pp. 83–88. Portsmouth, NH: Heinemann.

Goodman, Y. (1981). Review of Concepts About Print. *The Reading Teacher, 34* (4), 445–447.

Goodman, Y. & B. Altwerger. (1985). Bookhandling knowledge task. In *Bookshelf Teacher's Resource Book,* pp. 131–133. Jefferson City, MO: Scholastic.

Goodman, Y. & B. Altwerger. (1981). Print awareness in pre-school children: A working paper. Occasional Papers: Research Paper #4. Tucson, AZ: Program in Language and Literacy, College of Education, University of Arizona.

Goodman, Y., D.J. Watson, & C.L. Burke. (1987). *Reading miscue inventory.* Katonah, NY: Richard C. Owen.

Harste, J., V. Woodward, & C. Burke. (1984). *Language stories and literacy lessons.* Portsmouth, NH: Heinemann.

Heald-Taylor, G. (1987). Predictable literature selections and activities for language arts instruction. *The Reading Teacher, 41* (1), 6–13.

Hresko, W.P. (1988). *Test of early written language.* Austin, TX: Pro-Ed.

Huck, C., J. Hickman, & S. Hepler. (1987). *Children's literature in the elementary classroom.* New York: Holt, Rinehart & Winston.

Kasten, W.C. & B.K. Clarke. (1989). Reading/writing readiness for preschool and kindergarten children: A whole language approach. A Florida Educational Research Council Research Project Report. Sarasota, FL: University of South Florida.

Keats, E.J. (1962). *The snowy day.* New York: Viking Penguin.

Malicky, G. & C.A. Norman. (1989). The reading concepts and strategies of adult nonreaders. *Journal of Reading, 33* (3), 198–202.

McCormick, S. (1981). Assessment and the beginning reader: Using student dictated-stories. *Reading World, 21,* 29–39.

McGee, L., D. Richgels, & R. Charlesworth. (1986). Emerging knowledge of written language: Learning to read and write. In S. Kilmer (Ed.), *Advances in early education and day care,* vol 4. Greenwich, CT: JAI Press.

Metropolitan Early School Inventory-Preliteracy. (1986). Orlando, FL: The Psychological Corporation of Harcourt Brace Jovanovich.

Morrow, L.M. (1990). Assessing children's understanding of story through their construction and reconstruction of narrative. In L.M. Morrow & J.K. Smith (Eds.), *Assessment for instruction in early literacy,* pp. 110–134. Englewood, NJ: Prentice-Hall.

Morrow, L.M. (1988). Young children's responses to one-to-one story reading in school settings. *Reading Research Quarterly, 23,* 89–107.

Morrow, L.M. & J.K. Smith. (1990). The effects of group size on interactive storybook reading. *Reading Research Quarterly, 25* (3), 213–231.

NAEYC (National Association for the Education of Young Children). (1988). NAEYC position statement on the standardized testing of young children, three through eight years of age. *Young Children, 43,* 42–47.

Newkirk, T. (1989). *More than stories.* Portsmouth, NH: Heinemann.

Newman, A.P. & C. Beverstock. (1990). *Adult literacy: Contexts and challenges.* Newark, DE: International Reading Association.

Newman, J. (1985). *The craft of children's writing.* Portsmouth, NH: Heinemann.

Padak, N.D., J.L. Davidson, & G.M. Padak. (1990). Exploring reading with adult beginning readers. *Journal of Reading, 34* (1), 26–29.

Padak, N. & G. Padak. (1987). Guidelines and a holistic method for adult basic reading programs. *Journal of Reading, 30,* 490–496.

Reid, D.K., W.P. Hresko, & D.D. Hammill. (1981, 1989). *Test of early reading ability.* Austin, TX: Pro-Ed.

Rhodes, L. (1993). *Literacy assessment: A handbook of instruments.* Portsmouth, NH: Heinemann.

Rigg, P. (1981). Beginning to read in English the LEA way. *Reading English as a second language, moving from theory.* (Monograph 4 in Language and Reading), pp. 81–90. Bloomington, IN: Indiana University School of Education.

Rigg, P. & L. Taylor. (1979). A twenty-one year old begins to read. *English Journal, 68,* 52–56.

Schickedanz, J.A. (1990). *Adam's righting revolutions.* Portsmouth, NH: Heinemann.

Sendak, M. (1963). *Where the wild things are.* New York: Harper & Row.

Stallman, A.C. & P.D. Pearson. (1990). Formal measures of literacy assessment. In L.M. Morrow & J.K. Smith (Eds.), *Assessment for instruction in early literacy,* pp. 7–44. Englewood, NJ: Prentice-Hall.

Shanklin, N.L. (1989). Test review: Test of Early Written Language. *The Reading Teacher, 42* (8), 630–631.

Strickland, D.S. & L.M. Morrow. (Eds.) (1989). *Emerging literacy: Young children learn to read and write.* Newark, DE: International Reading Association.

Sulzby, E. (1985). Children's emergent reading of favorite storybooks: A developmental study. *Reading Research Quarterly, 20* (4), 458–480.

Teale, W.H. (1988). Developmentally appropriate assessment of reading and writing in the early childhood classroom. *Elementary School Journal, 89* (2), 173–183.

Teale, W.H. (1990). The promise and challenge of informal assessment in early literacy. In L.M. Morrow & J.K. Smith (Eds.), *Assessment for instruction in early literacy,* pp. 45–61. Englewood, NJ: Prentice-Hall.

Teale, W.H., E.H. Hiebert, & E.A. Chittenden. (1987). Assessing young children's literacy development. *The Reading Teacher, 40,* 772–777.

Teale, W.H. & E. Sulzby. (1986). *Emergent literacy: Writing and reading.* Norwood, NJ: Ablex.

Temple, C., R. Nathan, N. Burris, & F. Temple. (1988). *The beginnings of writing.* Boston: Allyn & Bacon.

Vygotsky, L.S. (1962). *Thought and language.* Cambridge, MA: MIT Press.

Wixson, S.E. (1985). Test review: Test of Early Reading Ability. *The Reading Teacher, 38* (6), 544–547.

Chapter Eight

8

Understanding and Challenging
Traditional Forms of Evaluation

reflections

☐ Explain to parents and students that you are interested in learning about their perceptions of norm-referenced test data. How do ways of reporting norm-referenced test data help them understand their child's strengths, needs, and progress. Ask some students why they think they take standardized tests every year. What happens to the information? Is it important to do well? Why or why not? Ask why they think they did well in one area of a standardized test and less well in another.

☐ Keep track of the amount of time you spend on testing and getting students directly ready for tests. Reflect carefully so that you don't forget any, including spelling tests! Discuss whether you think students are being over-tested. Use the same process to examine whether you over-grade students.

☐ What are some ways you could take the offensive or be a change agent (see Chapter 11) in relation to testing in your community? Brainstorm several ideas and then consider how to implement one or two of the best ones.

☐ Collect several articles from newspapers or popular magazines that discuss testing. Decide which articles are most accurate and informative, given what you have learned from this chapter. Also discuss what the articles reveal about involvement in and communication among groups involved in testing.

☐ In the section on norm-referenced tests, we have only discussed reading. Think what could be said about norm-referenced tests and the evaluation of students' progress in writing.

☐ Given the information in this chapter, critique your report card (and other forms of progress reports) and decide what changes you might want to consider. Interview both parents and students about their perceptions of report cards. For example, ask parents to tell you what they see as the value of report cards and what report cards tell them about their child's progress. Ask students why they think their grades went up or down and how you arrive at grades.

☐ Observe a staffing and critique it in light of what is presented in this chapter. Decide what assessment data you might like to collect and how you will do so for future staffings of students in your classroom. Also consider how you can profitably enter into the staffing process to ensure that the student's strengths are reported and utilized in planning.

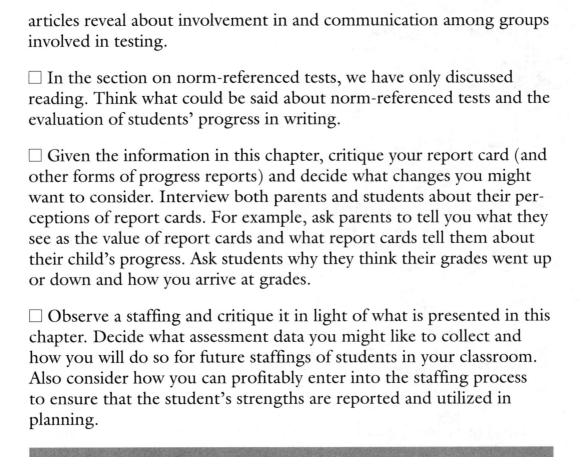

For the foreseeable future, we will continue to be affected by traditional forms and routines of evaluation: standardized norm-referenced tests, grading, report cards, and placement of children in programs like Chapter I and special education. As we have explained in Chapter 1 of this book, we think of these tests as evaluations rather than assessments because they are used to make judgments about students. It behooves us to understand these forms and routines of evaluation well, so that we can challenge them and consider options for using each of them as effectively as possible. It also behooves us to understand these traditional approaches, because they are used to sort and label children in our society. In the United States, those who do not achieve good grades or score well on tests potentially have less choice, power, and influence on the directions of their lives. They have fewer opportunities to participate in higher tracks at school and other special programs that develop talents, or to obtain college scholarships or loans. In addition to the external closing of doors there is the internal closing of doors as learners who receive low evaluations—and their teachers—come to believe less in their abilities. All of us need to consider how to operate within traditional approaches to evaluation in ways that will keep doors open for all children.

norm-referenced tests

Teachers need to be able to cogently discuss several common misperceptions involving standardized, norm-referenced tests, especially with parents and principals. (Hereafter, these tests will be referred to as norm-referenced tests; many tests have standardized procedures but are not norm-referenced.) Only by knowing about these misperceptions and being able to articulate them, will teachers feel more empowered about how norm-referenced test results are used in their schools and districts.

defining literacy

Literacy is often discussed in the media as a single, fixed construct that can easily be measured with norm-referenced tests. According to this method of measurement, there are between 23 and 26 million illiterates in the United States and 23 million more people who function at a marginal level. The examples are typically "worst case" individuals, who can hardly read or write. Using these figures, which are based on a study done by Northcutt (1975), projections are also made about the number of illiterates there will be in the year 2000, and that number is astronomical. Yet, the definition of literacy is problematic:

> The question of who is literate and who isn't has been inadequately answered by politicians, well-intended social activists, the advertising agency for the National Coalition for Literacy, and nearly every local and national news publication in the nation. The result is confusion on the part of many intelligent people about who needs what sorts of help with what sorts of reading and writing. (Mikulecky, 1987, p. 211)

A recent study by the National Association of Educational Progress (Kirsch & Jungeblut, 1986) provides another estimate of literacy abilities. In this study, researchers held ninety-minute interviews with 3600 randomly selected young adults (ages twenty-one to twenty-five) in their homes, and asked them to complete functional literacy tasks. The results showed that all but 6 percent could read at least at the fourth-grade level and thus could perform at least basic literacy tasks. Approximately 80 percent of the total could read at least at the eighth-grade level; however, scores for black (53 percent) and hispanic (71 percent) subgroups were lower. Of the total number of adults tested, 62 percent could read at least at the eleventh-grade level, but again, scores for minority groups—black (31 percent) and hispanic (52 percent)—were lower. It seems that when more functional definitions of literacy are used carefully, there are not as many illiterates in the United States as first claimed (Newman & Beverstock, 1990).

We must remind ourselves that these are figures for twenty-one to twenty-five-year-olds. Illiteracy increases for older Americans because the percentage of Americans with less schooling increases with the age of the population (see Mikulecky, 1987, pp. 223–226). The National Assessment Study reviewed above makes it difficult to conclude that the United States is a nation of illiterates. It does appear, however, that many minority students are not well equipped for the increasingly high literacy challenges associated with being productive and self-sufficient in our society (Mikulecky, 1987).

A related assumption is that all children who do well in school, as measured by norm-referenced tests, will be successful in life. But it is simplistic to believe that societal ills will be cured simply by creating better schools, or that the only reason "things" are so bad is because of poor schools. Family life, employment opportunities, ethnic prejudice, poverty, gender issues, substance abuse, and community violence also play important roles in molding our society. Regrettably, especially for minority children or children for whom English is a second language, a good education is often not enough. Although there is a great need to help all children receive quality schooling, a good education may not result in appropriate employment if racial and ethnic barriers within the job market are not also eliminated.

communicating norm-referenced test results

In Denver, hardly a week passes without a newspaper article decrying the poor state of our schools—either locally or nationally. Although we all need to be concerned about children's learning, rarely do we get a historical perspective about literacy rates, dropouts, number of students finishing high school, and so on. A recent exception was an excellent article by Bracey (1991a).

The truth is that the population we are educating today is very different from the student population at mid-century. In 1950 only half of the eligible eighteen-year-olds graduated from high school. Since 1965, in contrast, graduation rates have remained steady at about 75 percent. When the count includes General Equivalency Diploma (GED) completions and students who graduate after returning to school, almost 90 percent of the twenty-five to twenty-nine-year-olds hold high school diplomas (Bracey, 1991b, p. 107). When students dropped out of school in the past, jobs were available—in factories, farming, railroads, and logging. This isn't true today. Adolescents need to stay in school until age eighteen in part, because the job market cannot absorb them: too many adults, both men and women, need jobs. At the same time, most jobs that pay well enough to support a family require higher levels of literacy than ever before.

One of the authors is trying to help a sixteen-year-old find her first summer job and has found it interesting to look through the want ads for jobs open to students who haven't graduated: retail sales, busboy/girl, fast food worker, receptionist. All of these jobs pay wages, but the wages are not high enough to live on independently or to support a family. Most jobs require high levels of literacy and training.

In addition to these factors, other demographics have changed as well. Public schools in urban settings are becoming increasingly ethnic. There are many single-parent homes, in which the parent cares about a child's education but simply doesn't have the time, or sometimes the background, to provide much assistance with school work. In other families, both parents are working outside the home and time is also at a premium. In some families money shortages make it impossible for children to pay for field trips, materials for school projects, and after school clubs. Drugs and AIDS are yet other problems. It would seem that a return to old solutions has little chance of working because the students and the world have changed tremendously.

For the most part, well-written newspaper or magazine reports on norm-referenced test data are not easy to find. The media fail to discuss test data within a context that encourages knowledgeable interpretation. There are many questions that need to be addressed more thoroughly in looking at scores. How do new scores compare to those of ten, five, or three years ago? What is the makeup of the population taking the test compared to that in previous years? Have norms changed recently and how does that affect interpretation of test scores? What has happened to enrollments over the past few years? How mobile is the school population? What are class sizes in buildings? What resources do schools have? What about parent involvement? What was the absentee rate on the days of the test? Were makeup dates scheduled? Did special education and bilingual students take the tests? Answers to questions like these allow for a more accurate interpretation of test scores, particularly when comparing school or district results.

In January 1989, after the National Assessment of Educational Progress (NAEP) data on reading for 1988 were released, then U.S. Secretary of Education Lauro Cavazos stated publicly that the reading and writing skills of American students remained dreadfully inadequate. Yet Cavazos lacked a historical perspective on literacy and schooling. In contrast two charts (see Table 8.1) appeared in *The Reading Report Card* 1971–1988 (Mullis & Jenkins, 1990), referring to five types of reading:

Rudimentary Reading: the ability to carry out simple, discrete reading tasks.

Basic Reading: the ability to understand specific or sequentially related information.

Intermediate Reading: the ability to search for specific information, interrelate ideas, and make generalizations.

Adept Reading: the ability to find, summarize, and explain relatively complicated information.

Advanced Reading: the ability to synthesize and learn from specialized reading materials.

Change in the Percentage of Students Reaching Levels of Reading Proficiency, 1971 to 1988*

Level		Age 9	Age 13	Age 17
Rudimentary	(150)	+2.5*	0.0	+0.4
Basic	(200)	+4.3*	+2.3*	+3.0
Intermediate	(250)	+1.7	+0.1	+7.7*
Adept	(300)	+0.2	+0.8	+2.6
Advanced	(350)	0.0	+0.1	-1.8*

*Shows statistically significant difference between years, where α = 0.5. The "+" symbol denotes a gain in the percentage of students reaching a certain level of proficiency in 1988, while the "-" symbol denotes a loss.

Percentage of Students at or Above the Five Levels of Reading Proficiency, 1971 to 1988*

Reading Skills and Strategies	Age	1971	1975	1980	1984	1988
Rudimentary	9	90.5*	93.2	94.6	92.5	93.0
(Level 150)	13	99.8	99.7	99.9	99.8	99.8
	17	99.6	99.7	99.8	100.0	100.0
Basic	9	58.2*	62.2	67.6*	61.9	62.5
(Level 200)	13	92.8*	93.3*	94.9	94.1	95.1
	17	95.9	96.4	97.2	98.3	98.9
Intermediate	9	15.3	14.6	17.2	17.0	17.0
(Level 250)	13	57.9	58.6	60.9	59.1	58.0
	17	78.5*	80.4*	81.0*	83.1*	86.2
Adept	9	1.0	0.5	0.6	1.0	1.2
(Level 300)	13	9.8	10.3	11.3	10.9	10.6
	17	39.2	39.1	38.5	40.0	41.8
Advanced	9	0.0	0.0	0.0	0.0	0.0
(Level 350)	13	0.1	0.2	0.2	0.2	0.2
	17	6.6*	6.1*	5.3	5.5	4.8

*Shows statistically significant difference from 1988, where α = .05 per set of four comparisons (each year compared with 1988). No significance test is reported when the percentage of students is >95 or <5. Jackknifed standard errors are provided in the Data Appendix.

Table 8.1   Nation's Report Card Charts

The charts demonstrate that the number of students reading at the rudimentary level has increased slightly over the seventeen-year period in which reading has been measured. There have also been slight increases at the basic reading level at all three ages. In intermediate reading, where there have been slight increases, it is of particular interest that the abilities of seventeen-year-olds has increased over the entire period—from 78.5 in 1971 to 86.2 in 1988. Nine-year-olds do not score particularly well on intermediate, adept, or advanced reading, but this makes sense for their age. The number of students reading at the adept level, the one expected of beginning college level students, has also increased slightly, and it is interesting that these percentages roughly correspond to the number of high school graduates going on to college. Regrettably, few seventeen-year-olds can read at the advanced level, and the percentage has declined over the seventeen-year period from 6.6 in 1971 to 4.8 in 1988. It is important to note that other tables of the NAEP report document the steadily increasing progress poor and minority students have made over the seventeen-year period—not that further improvements are not needed. In light of these statistics, it is difficult for us to understand the dire remarks of Secretary Cavazos about teachers' ability to teach reading. That these scores have risen at all in the face of our changing demographics and difficulties is remarkable. In addition to this data, NAEP also reports that students today read more in school than they did in the past.

Two other points must also be considered. The five levels of reading defined by NAEP are not particularly easy to delineate, and some educators have challenged their validity. In addition, in order to make comparisons of students' progress over long periods of time, as NAEP has done, some items and means for measuring them must remain the same. This is currently a problem, because reading educators have dramatically changed their view of the reading process and how it ought to be assessed. Thus, although students seem to be doing relatively well on the old reading tasks, they do not necessarily reflect current curriculum or new assessment philosophy.

A historical perspective is also useful in teacher's presentations of test data to parents. Dreher & Singer (1985) found that parents preferred to get certain kinds of information about their children's norm-referenced test performances:

- A comparison of results from the previous and current years (for example, of second- and third-grade test results).

- A comparison of results from the previous year's test with a retake of the previous year's test in the current year (for example, of second-grade results with the results from a retake of the second-grade test in third grade).

- Examples of the easiest and most difficult items that were correctly completed.

The first two types of information give parents a sense of their child's progress as measured by a norm-referenced test. Of course, the second type (based on a retake of the previous year's test) requires another test administration, not something many educators would recommend. However, the study does reveal that parents find historical information on individual children useful, just as all of us find it useful in evaluating group data presented in the media.

Teachers are most familiar with norm-referenced, standardized tests. The Iowa Test of Basic Skills, the California Achievement Test, Gates-MacGinitie Reading Test, and Degrees of Reading Power are all examples of norm-referenced, standardized tests. Being "standardized" means that there are consistent "standard" directions for administering the test. Thus, informal reading inventories and miscue analysis are also standardized because there are written procedures for their administration. Unlike the other previously mentioned tests, however, these two types of tests are not norm-referenced.

"Norm-referenced" is the critical term that explains how these tests measure achievement. The idea of norm-referencing is linked to the concept in statistics of the normal curve. On a normal curve, 50 percent of the population falls below the midpoint and 50 percent above. As one gets nearer to the ends or extremes of the curve, the number of cases is fewer. That is, the number of students that score around the fiftieth percentile is greater than the number of students who score either very high or very low on a test.

When a test is normed (or renormed), it is given to a large number of students. Care is taken to ensure that the students represent a balance of racial and ethnic origins, genders, school settings, economic status, and so on. Testing company statisticians determine the average number of correct answers for each grade level; on a well-constructed test, 50 percent of the students at a grade level will score above this number and 50 percent will score below. Questions may be rewritten or changed until this kind of balance is achieved.

Since this is how tests are developed and normed, it is erroneous for educators, parents, legislators, or the public to assume that more students should score above the fiftieth percentile. By definition this should not happen; the test is designed so that half of the population who takes it achieves below the fiftieth percentile. When too many districts report that more than half of their students have scored above the fiftieth percentile, test publishers will renorm the test so that once again only half of the population scores in the top 50 percent.

The renorming of readiness tests is a particularly interesting example of this problem with the normal curve. The letter recognition task in the Metropolitan Readiness Test had to be renormed in the mid-to late 1970s because so many children were correctly identifying most of the letter names. This was probably due to the greater number of preschool programs, including Head Start, and television programs like "Sesame Street." Thus, when higher norms were established, some children began to look as if they were not "ready" when in fact, given a historical perspective, they knew as much or more than past populations entering school.

As another example, the Iowa Test of Basic Skills has been renormed recently. Afterwards, the Denver Public Schools published results that compared the previous year's scores (based on previous lower norms) with the current year's scores (based on new higher norms). Since the new norms are more stringent, it appears that students have made minimal gains. In Denver, this is of concern because the district feels public pressure to have more students achieving scores at or above the fiftieth percentile. More meaningful interpretation of news stories would have been possible if comparisons had been made using both the old and the new norms. Then concern could be more accurately limited to only those subject areas and grade levels where scores dropped in relation to the old norms.

Grade equivalent scores with an exact year and month in school (such as 4.3, meaning the third month of fourth grade) are often calculated from the raw scores of norm-referenced tests. These scores give the impression that students' abilities can be measured to a precise grade level and month within the grade level. This is not the case. When tests are normed, children are tested either in the fall or in the spring and grade equivalents are established. Grade equivalents for other times of the year are mathematically interpolated from the raw scores. No large sample of students ever takes the test each month to establish the precise growth implied by grade equivalent scores. The International Reading Association (Farr & Carey, 1986, p. 154) recommends that only stanine or percentile scores be reported; grade equivalents imply a degree of quantification and measurement accuracy that is not possible.

the ability of norm-referenced tests to measure literacy

As we have frequently mentioned, in measuring reading, norm-referenced tests have many shortcomings. The problem is that most of the general public—and too many educators—are unaware of these difficulties. Indeed, what do teachers and administrators themselves think of the usefulness of standardized tests? In a study completed by the Center for the Study of Evaluation using a large randomly selected national population of teachers and principals, it was found that

> both teachers and principals regard standardized [norm-referenced] tests to be less useful than more locally developed evaluation procedures such as teacher-made tests based upon what the teacher has actually been teaching. Further, both teachers and principals regard the results of these tests as less useful than non-test data (such as student classwork and teacher observation) in making judgments about a student's achievement. (Langer & Pradl, 1984, p. 756)

Similarly, Carey (Aronson & Farr, 1988) found that, in school systems in which students took an average of more than one norm-referenced test per year, many teachers and administrators could provide no clear reasons why the tests were being given other than the need for reporting test scores. In another study of one school system, Carey could not locate any teachers who used test results for curricular or instructional purposes. Only the superintendent favored the testing program so he could report systemwide test scores to the school board and scores on particular groups of students to the state.

In both Michigan and Illinois, new norm-referenced, standardized reading tests have been developed that will eliminate some of the current difficulties (Dutcher, 1990; Jongsma, 1989; Roeber & Dutcher, 1989; Valencia et al., 1989; Weber, 1987; Wixson & Peters, 1987; Wixson, Peters et al., 1987). Let's look at some of those difficulties by highlighting efforts in these states to eliminate many of them.

measuring reading rather than skills

Neither the Michigan nor the Illinois reading tests measure isolated skills. Instead, both concentrate on examining students' abilities to comprehend passages. There are no phonics, word analysis, or isolated vocabulary subtests like those that play a major role in other norm-referenced tests. The thinking is that students' knowledge in these areas is being used in the process of comprehension. Further, since in reading the language cueing systems do not exist in isolation, they should not be tested in isolation.

objectivity

Many people consider norm-referenced tests "objective" and forms of assessment that rely on teacher judgment "subjective." They need to see that, no matter what the form of assessment, someone makes judgments. In the case of norm-referenced comprehension tests, someone made "subjective" judgments about the appropriateness of multiple-choice testing as a way of evaluating comprehension, about what students should read, what questions should be asked, what the answers (and distractors) are, and so on. Although the answers themselves can be objectively scored, the test designers' judgments strongly affect the scores. Parents and educators can understand this (and other issues) by taking a portion of a norm-referenced test and discussing the decisions the test designers made, especially if they discover that they don't agree with all of them.

On the other hand, parents and educators should understand that teachers who use alternative assessments can establish clear criteria and administer these criteria consistently to provide clear and "objective" pictures of what students are able to do. We would argue that such data can be trusted more than data from norm-referenced tests, especially when the teacher collects the data in a variety of situations rather than from a single test situation. Valencia (1990) strongly suggests that we talk with fellow educators and the public about the "authenticity" and "trustworthiness" of alternative assessments. Alternative assessments that take place within real reading and writing events (reading a story, writing a report) have more potential to be authentic than norm-referenced tests. Clearly articulated expectations and standards not only help us make trustworthy judgments about students' reading and writing, they also help us to communicate the information to those who want or need it.

more valid passages

In most norm-referenced tests, the reading passages are short and not necessarily complete. They do not realistically reflect the nature of most reading tasks and therefore do not have high validity: the test does not measure what it sets out to measure. Both the Michigan and Illinois tests are significantly more valid as reading tasks because they use longer passages. These passages are either complete narratives (stories) or expository (informational) pieces. In Michigan, the structures of narrative and expository texts have been examined in detail so that the selected passages exhibit strong structures.

problems of background knowledge

We know today that a reader's background knowledge about a topic affects the quality of her comprehension. (For a discussion of background knowledge in testing comprehension, see Farr & Carey, 1986). On the Michigan test, students' background knowledge is assessed through multiple-choice questions and becomes a loading factor in evaluating students' answers. In Illinois, some ingenious questioning formats have been developed to determine students' level of background knowledge on particular topics, and this also becomes a loading factor in figuring students' comprehension scores.

higher order comprehension

Since the 1920s norm-referenced tests have had a multiple-choice format, which is the most cost-effective for measuring large numbers of students. This format also tends to be more reliable, since questions can be developed from the literal information found in the passage to which there are only right or wrong answers. In the Michigan test, much thought has been given to developing questions that will tap higher order comprehension, yet can still be answered using a multiple-choice format. Higher order questions have also been developed on the Illinois test. In response to at least some of these, students may indicate that more than one answer is plausible.

metacognition

Previously, tests of reading comprehension measured the product of reading to the exclusion of information about the reading processes that students perceive they use. On both the Michigan and Illinois tests, students are asked to identify the reading strategies they would employ to read certain types of material or deal with certain reading problems. One potential problem, however, is that students will learn what they should answer; when one actually listens to them read or tests their comprehension in some other way, it may be apparent that the student doesn't actually apply these reading strategies.

reading attitudes and habits

Until the Michigan and Illinois tests were developed, norm-referenced tests did not address students' motivation for reading. Some students do well on the tests but choose not to read in their daily lives; one can't help but wonder if they should be called good readers. On the other hand, poor readers who develop an interest in reading and read frequently have a chance to become more literate over a lifetime. Both the Michigan and Illinois tests ask students about their reading attitudes and habits, and students may claim that they have good attitudes and habits, although they haven't truly internalized a love for reading. Teachers will want to verify students' self-reports of attitudes and habits by triangulating them with home and classroom observations.

■ ■

test development, staff development, and curriculum

Most norm-referenced tests have been developed by testing companies. It is interesting that this was not the source of origin for either the Michigan or Illinois tests. In Michigan, the new tests were in development for approximately ten years at the impetus of the state legislature, which wanted to measure students' reading progress. There has been close cooperation among members of the State Department of Education, classroom teachers, the Michigan Reading Association, and reading professors at Michigan's colleges and universities. Items were written by teams from these constituencies. In Illinois, such close cooperative development by all groups was not possible because of the brief timetable mandated by the Illinois State Legislature.

Because what is tested is typically what is taught, staff development or in-services about new tests and curriculum is an important part of test development. In Michigan, although little money was made available by the legislature for staff development to accompany the new reading tests, much in-service has occurred about the new state reading test and curriculum, both of which are holistic, process-oriented, and based in schema theory. The test results can now be studied to sharpen staff development efforts and instruction in areas where students have proved weak on the agreed-upon tasks (Jongsma, 1989).

In Illinois, staff development was not put into place to ensure that teachers learned the new views of reading embodied by the test and how to implement them in the curriculum. More than anything, this was due to the short time frame imposed by the legislature to install an accountability measure. In giving the tests, many teachers felt caught off guard, because it was clear to them that the new test was measuring tasks the students had not been prepared to do. In other words, the new test did not reflect the curriculum in place. Use of the test has now begun to influence curricular change. An additional problem is that teachers are also still required to give end-of-unit basal reader tests; although the philosophy behind these tests is in conflict with many of the new views of reading reflected in the state test (Jongsma, 1989).

■ ■

the evolving status of norm-referenced tests

Some literacy experts view the Michigan and Illinois tests as compromises: despite their improvements and their closer congruity with our current understanding of the reading process, the tests do not provide information about what children do as readers in natural settings. For example, Aronson & Farr (1988) argue that adding alternative forms of assessment to norm-referenced tests is not likely to be a solution to the problem of the primacy of norm-referenced tests: "The score from a test administered primarily for accountability tends to take precedence over all the other data collection opportunities that occur every day in the classroom. The most obvious of these is teacher observation of a student's acquisition and application of the behavior that a test can only attempt to depict, engage, and measure" (p. 176).

Still, educators in Michigan and Illinois are to be congratulated for their attempts to measure reading performance in new ways and to tackle the problem of constructing more ecologically valid reading tests (Moore, 1983). Other movements addressing both reading and writing are afoot now, too, in Maine (Guide to the Maine Educational Assessment, 1989), Vermont (DeWitt, 1991; Writing Assessment Leadership Committee, 1989), North Carolina (*FairTest Examiner*, 1988, 1989). Wisconsin (Wisconsin State Reading Association, 1990), and other states, and in several organizations, including the Educational Testing Service (Martinez & Lipson, 1989) and the National Association for the Education of Young Children (1988).

At a minimum, we need to join the efforts of these states and organizations to combat the overemphasis among the general public on norm-referenced testing as the best means for holding schools accountable and improving the nature of schooling. A "Statement of Genuine Accountability" (IRA, 1989) signed by more than forty educational associations was presented to President Bush and all state governors at the educational summit held by Bush in 1989. As the statement boldly declares: "The Governors and the Administration should include, as part of their final plans, the goal of moving from reliance on standardized multiple-choice test scores to use of alternative, authentic and appropriate methods of assessing educational performance and progress" (p. 1).

grading

Grading, like use of norm-referenced tests, is another form of traditional evaluation. Students' grades, usually of interest only to students, parents, and teachers, are often charged with emotion. Done well, the process of grading has substantial power to communicate a teacher's values about literacy. Yet, grading is often considered distasteful by teachers and as a threat by students. In this section, we'll consider philosophical issues, such as the purposes of grading students' reading and writing and guidelines for grading, as well as practical issues, such as what should be graded and how often, and who ought to be involved in grading.

Probably the best way to begin thinking about grading is by to consider what you want to accomplish through grading. Evaluation that results in a grade should help students and parents understand what the student has accomplished in progressing toward more effective literacy. In addition, grading should encourage a continued desire to read and write and to become more effective at it. In other words, grading should be a positive force in students' literacy development rather than a negative one.

Let's consider a story told to us by a parent of a fourth grade girl. The girl and her classmates were concluding a study of insects in science. The girl's teacher asked

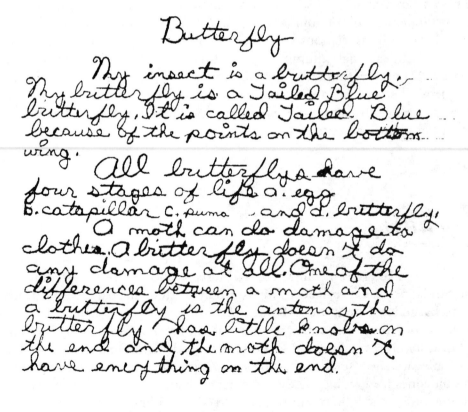

The assignment as given by the teacher:

Exploration

Draw a picture of any insect you choose in its natural habitat and write a paragraph about it. Use an encyclopedia or other book for your information, but make sure your report is written in your own words.

The written portion of the assignment done by the child:

> Butterfly
>
> My insect is a butterfly. My butterfly is a Tailed Blue butterfly. It is called Tailed Blue because of the points on the bottom wing. All butterflys have four stages of life a. egg b. catapillar c. puma and d. butterfly. A moth can do damage to clothes. A butterfly doesn't do any damage at all. One of the differences between a moth and a butterfly is the antenas, the butterfly has little knobs on the end and the moth doesn't have enything on the end.

Figure 8.1   Butterfly Story

the students to choose an insect to write a paragraph about for the following day. She distributed a piece of paper with the assignment written on it and told the children they could use the paper for the report. That evening, the girl reread a trade book about butterflies, composed her report, read it to her parents, revised it, and recopied it on good paper (see Figure 8.1). This took about an hour and a half. The girl then decided to mount her final draft off to one side on a piece of construction paper and to draw, color, and mount a butterfly on the other side of the construction paper so that it appeared to float above the habitat of a garden. This took another an hour and a half. The girl's father said she went to bed beaming because she was so proud of her work.

A few days later the report was returned with a grade of C and no comments. The girl brought the report home and thrust it at her mother, unable to talk about it. Later, when she could talk about it, she said she had no idea why she had received a C. The parents advised the girl to ask the teacher the following day. In response to the girl's inquiry, the teacher said that she hadn't followed directions and kept to a single paragraph.

A number of other issues can be addressed using this grading incident as an example, but what is most glaring is that this was not a positive force in the girl's literacy development. Both the girl and her parents were taken aback by the teacher's decision to value following directions over meaning construction, effort, and care in completing the assignment. Certainly, this incident is not going to encourage the girl to write. On the other hand, the girl did learn something from this incident: to carefully listen and follow the teacher's directions, no matter how arbitrary they seem. Taking risks and going beyond what the teacher has assigned is not valued in this classroom. We hope that this learning is not what the girl's teacher was trying to promote.

In considering grading as a positive force in students' literacy progress, other grading practices, such as the normal curve, must also be reexamined. A normal curve, after all, operates under the assumption that some students cannot learn what we teach. Of course, it's usually the same students who are at the bottom of the bell curve; they learn to expect that they cannot improve their grades because someone has to be at the bottom. Bloom, Madaus, & Hastings (1981) state: "There is nothing sacred about the normal curve. It is the distribution most appropriate to chance and random activity. Education is a purposeful activity, and we seek to have the students learn what we have to teach. If we are effective, the distribution of achievement should be very different from the normal curve. In fact, we may even insist that our efforts are unsuccessful to the extent that the distribution of achievement approximates the normal distribution" (pp. 52–53).

Instead of grading a student in comparison to other students—the premise of the normal curve—we can grade against a set of criteria or against a student's own past performance and what we know we can expect next developmentally. Of course, even these two ways of grading incorporate some attention to what other students of that age are capable of doing. For example, criteria established for report writing in fourth grade are certainly different from criteria for report writing in ninth grade.

Criteria are largely determined by considering what it is that students of particular ages are capable of doing and producing.

Establishing criteria for grading is highly important when it comes to grading the open-ended sorts of assignments that are typical of whole language classrooms. It's easy to rely only on countable or measurable criteria—spelling, punctuation, words read correctly, and so on. It's more difficult to establish criteria for thinking deeply about books, for writing a good report, and for communicating effectively in a discussion. We often know a good report when we see it, but we find it difficult to explain to others the criteria we have used to make this determination. It is also more difficult to establish criteria to grade processes as well as products. If we cannot communicate our criteria, however, we cannot teach students to value or do those things we are looking for when we evaluate their work. Working on defining criteria results not only in more effective evaluation of students' work but also in more effective teaching and learning. If students haven't done what we expected, it's often because we haven't clearly defined what we want them to be able to do and taught them how to do it.

We find two methods that are helpful in clarifying grading criteria. We'll use the grading of literature logs as an example, since grading such assignments is often avoided because responses are so individual and hard to judge. One way to analyze what you value in literature logs is to do the assignment yourself, not just once but for long enough to get a feel for the content of the assignment and the process. Thus, if you require students to write in their literature logs several times a week, you should do the same for a couple of weeks. As you do the assignment, observe yourself closely. Observe the process you are using, your feelings about it, and how that affects your approach to the assignment, and of course, the products you produce. Keep notes about what you observe and use these observations to define criteria for grading literature logs. For example, you are likely to discover that telling the students to "think deeply" about their books requires rereading certain passages and thinking about the book outside of class. You are also likely to notice that you link personal incidents or feelings to incidents in the book and that you link the current book to other literature you've read. Now you know what to teach, and what to assess or evaluate. Next you have to decide which of the criteria it is possible and most valuable to grade.

Another method we like to use to determine grading criteria is to sort students' work into two piles, those we consider excellent and "the others." By analytically comparing the work in the two piles, it is possible to create a list of the criteria you want to use in deciding that one piece is good and another is less so. This allows you to communicate the criteria you generate to students whose work is in "the others" pile, helping them to understand your values and use them to do assignments. This method has two problems. One is that it is more difficult to generate criteria about the process when you are looking only at products. The other is that you are often in the position of coming up with the criteria long after it would have been best to communicate them to students. Defining the criteria after the fact, however, will assist your current students if you are going to give the same or similar assignments in the future. And, of course, it will benefit the next group of students who receive the same assignment because you can make criteria clear *a priori*.

Some teachers grade everything, while other teachers avoid grading certain products. In classes where virtually all work is graded, grading dominates everything, especially the students' approach to risk taking and the teacher's time. When a particular kind of work is not graded, students often assume it has less value in the teacher's eyes than another kind of work that is. We believe that it is most useful to grade a variety of work, especially when the teacher believes that work contributes strongly to students' literacy development. If literature logs are used to help students think more deeply about the books they are reading, it makes sense to let stu-

---

Insect Report Evaluation

1–Woops!   2–Just OK   3–Fine   4–Good   5–Excellent

You included well-chosen details about the insect in your report and about the insect's habitat in your drawing.

_____ × 7 = _____

You wrote your report in your own words. It does not sound like an encyclopedia.

_____ × 5 = _____

You carefully edited your report.

_____ × 4 = _____

Your drawing and report were attractively presented.

_____ × 4 = _____

Comments:

Grade:

Name _____ Date _____

Title/topic of report _____

Figure 8.2   Checkpoint scale

dents know you value such responses through the grading process. On the other hand, we do not find it at all useful to grade everything (or even close to everything) that students read and write. (Thus, if we graded literature logs, we would only grade selected entries.) We don't believe that it is fruitful to *assess* all the reading and writing students do, let alone evaluate or grade it all, if they are reading and writing large amounts of material. If you adopt this stance, however, you may have to help students (and parents) understand that all the work in your classroom contributes to learning, whether it is graded or not. The amount and quality of reading and writing students do has a great impact on the few pieces of reading and writing that are actually graded.

Like writing samples, open-ended assignments of all kinds can be graded holistically or analytically. When grading an assignment holistically, we recommend placing the graded assignments in piles according to the tentative grade you have given the assignments. When you have completed the first round of grading, go back and look to see if you have consistently applied criteria in arriving at the grade for the papers in each pile. See if there are any that should be moved from one pile to another and change the grades of those papers. When you have finished the grading to your satisfaction, record what differentiated one grade from another. If these criteria and values have not already been communicated to the students in advance of the assignment, it is well to do so after you have passed back the assignment. (Keep these criteria for the next time you give the assignment so that you can communicate them in advance or so that students may assist you in grading papers.) In other words, provide feedback to the group about how you viewed the qualities of the assignments, and do it in a way that helps students learn something about their work. Emphasize the positive so that students know what to do in the future, not just what not to do.

Analytic scoring requires that you establish criteria in advance of grading the assignment and that you give multiple scores or grades to the assignment, each of which is weighted according to what you value in the work. Building on the Diedrich Scale developed to score the SAT essay exams, Kirby & Liner (1988, pp. 227–229) have developed writing checkpoint scales that can be made specific to any open-ended assignment whether reading, writing, or both. (See Olson, Kirby, & Hulme, 1982, for a number of checkpoints for different types of writing.) We have simplified their checkpoints (which are for secondary students) for two different assignments. Figure 8.2 is a checkpoint scale that might be used to grade the insect report that was previously discussed. A checkpoint scale like that in Figure 8.3 might be used to grade a student's presentation of a favorite book to classmates as good summer reading.

Because *you* develop the checkpoint, it can relate directly to what you are focusing on in your teaching and what you expect students to be able to reveal on particular assignments. In fact, developing the checkpoint is an excellent exercise in clarifying for yourself what it is that you value in the assignments you give; involving students in developing such checklists over time also serves a teaching function. The specificity of the checkpoint serves to "demystify the final grade and highlight strengths and weaknesses in [students' work]" (Kirby & Liner, 1988, p. 224).

```
┌─────────────────────────────────────────────────────────────┐
│                                                               │
│               Book Presentation Evaluation                    │
│                                                               │
│  1–Woops!      2–Just OK      3–Fine      4–Good    5–Excellent│
│                                                               │
│  You presented the book in an interesting way. You had your   │
│  classmates' attention!                                       │
│                       _____ × 2 = _____                       │
│                                                               │
│  You clearly made your points about why the book was worth    │
│  reading.                                                     │
│                       _____ × 2 = _____                       │
│                                                               │
│  You projected your voice well. We didn't have trouble        │
│  hearing you.                                                 │
│                       _____ × 1 = _____                       │
│                                                               │
│  Comments:                                                    │
│                                                               │
│                                                               │
│                                                               │
│  Grade:                                                       │
│                                                               │
│                                                               │
│                                                               │
│  Name _____     Date _____          │
│                                                               │
│  Title of book _____        │
│                                                               │
└─────────────────────────────────────────────────────────────┘
```

Figure 8.3   Checkpoint scale for a Book Presentation

You can adapt such a checklist in many ways: the content of the statements, the number of the statements, the relative weight of each statement, the descriptors for the ratings, and the total rating. Notice that the Insect Report Evaluation rating totals 100, allowing you to use it as a percentage, while the Book Presentation Evaluation rating totals only 25. The latter might be more useful if you use a point system for your overall grading.

If one of the goals of grading is to encourage more effective reading and writing, then we must consider that goal in deciding who will take part in the grading process. Too often, teachers are the only ones who participate in the process. We are not suggesting that teachers should abdicate their roles as "graders," but we do think that involving students in grading is more likely to lead to greater learning about reading and writing and thus, greater effectiveness. Here are some ways in which students can be involved in grading individual assignments.

- Students can choose the assignments to be graded. For example, they can choose what they consider the best piece of writing they've done in the last two weeks or the best two literature log entries they made on the most recent book they read.

- Students can assist in deciding what elements of reading and writing ought to be graded. Involve them in generating creative ways to grade what you both agree is important (thinking about a book outside of class or communicating effectively in a discussion).

- Students can assist in developing grading criteria. "By using such cooperative criteria, students can see more clearly how to improve and grow as writers [and readers] . . . [It develops] their own critical sense and evaluative judgment (Kirby & Liner, 1981, p. 185)."

- A student can give herself a grade and provide a rationale for that grade. You can structure the rationale by asking the student to base her comments on specific criteria you've established. Although you will need to be the final judge of the appropriateness of the grade, asking students for this information alerts you to differences, when they exist, between the student's values and evaluation, and your own.

- Students may be involved in the evaluation of each other's work. Kirby & Liner (1981, pp. 196–198) suggest various ways to involve students in grading each other's writing. They have found that the process teaches students that grades belong to them and makes them more sensitive to problems in their own work.

Before turning to the issue of progress reports, we want to suggest a number of guidelines to keep in mind as you engage in the process of grading with your students.

- Grade selected student work, work that is selected because it is the student's best work or because it is most representative of the student's reading and writing. Grade a minimum amount of work.

- Grade what you consider important for students to be learning. If learning to make reading an integral part of their lives is important, find a way to grade it.

- Grade both process and product in student work. Students frequently make progress in the processes of reading and writing before the learning shows up in their products.

- Carefully define and communicate to students what you will grade in their work. This is important in teaching, not just in evaluation.

- Involve students in the grading process. If we want to develop students' ability to critique their own work, we must provide opportunities for them to learn how to do so.

- Remember that the fundamental goal of grading reading and writing should be to improve reading and writing. Critique your current grading practices and those you develop in the future with this goal in mind.

progress reports

Progress reports include report cards, conferences with parents, and any other forms of reporting that are done on a periodic but regular basis. Ostensibly, progress reports—particularly report cards—are the reasons teachers record grades; grades are needed to fill in the report card. For this reason, grades on individual assign-

	1st	2nd	3rd	4th
READING				
Level at which child is working				
Phonics and word attack skills				
Word recognition				
Comprehension				
Reference Skills				
Oral reading				
Independent reading				
Completes assignments				
Demonstrates effort				
SPELLING				
Mastery of spelling words				
Application of spelling skills in written work				
Completes assignments				
Demonstrates effort				
LANGUAGE				
Correctly uses language mechanics (punctuation, capitalization, etc.)				
Grammar (word usage/sentence structure)				
Demonstrates creative written expression				
Oral expression				
Completes assignments				
Demonstrates effort				
HANDWRITING				
Conforms to letter form, size, spacing and slant				
Writes legibly and neatly in daily work				
Demonstrates effort				

Figure 8.4   The reading/language arts section of report card

ments frequently reflect the codes on the report card. Thus, if the report card has codes other than the traditional A–F grades, such as H (high quality), S (satisfactory progress), and N (needs improvement), the grades given on individual assignments may reflect that. Where they do not, the teacher must translate the grades from individual assignments to fit the report card.

The philosophy behind progress reports ought to match the philosophy you adopt for your grading practices. If you believe that grading should not only serve the goal of helping students and parents understand what has been accomplished, but also induce a continued desire to read and write and to become more effective at it, you can critique your current report card, parent conferences, and other forms of interim reports with these goals in mind.

A major factor that frequently makes it difficult for whole language teachers to communicate literacy progress is the language used on the report card. The reading and language arts sections of a typical report card (see Figure 8.4) reveal the problem: reading is treated not as a process but as a set of subskills to be mastered. What many whole language teachers would consider writing is given a single line under "Language"—"Demonstrates creative written expression." Spelling and handwriting are not only divided into separate categories, they are given major importance by virtue of the larger bold print. In fact, this makes them far more important than writing.

Many whole language teachers have addressed this dilemma by rewriting their report cards. Although writing a report card is difficult and time-consuming, it is well worth the time and effort if you consider it a process of negotiation and change involving the colleagues with whom you teach. In fact, teachers involved in the process of rewriting report cards have told us that it helps them to consider their values about literacy in ways they have not had to in the past. Especially when it involves more than an individual teacher, the process also encourages a great deal of communication among teachers, administrators and parents about how they value literacy. Figures 8.5 and 8.6 illustrate the reading and writing sections of a primary-level and an intermediate-level report card that better reflect a whole language approach to literacy. The primary card was developed by the first-grade staff at Lukas Elementary in Jefferson County, Colorado. In addition to what is reprinted here, the card also contains a generous space for comments and two inserts that provide parents with information on stages of reading, writing, and spelling development. The intermediate grade card is from Federal Heights Elementary in Adams County 12 School District, Colorado.

Of course, it is possible to get away from report cards that contain grades entirely if teachers or school faculty elect to write narrative reports about children. In these cases, it is necessary to work out together what these reports will address and how it will be said. A useful list of criteria for writing narrative reports may be found in the Province of British Columbia *Primary Program Resource Document* (1990, pp. 77–78). This document, as well as *The Primary Language Record* (Barrs et al., 1989), contains excellent examples of anecdotal reports on children's literacy progress that could be helpful to teachers who add anecdotal notes to grade cards.

Lukas Elementary First Grade Progress Report

Student's Name _____ Teacher's Name _____ Year _____ PAGE 1

KEY: X = Effectively demonstrating / = Demonstrating some of the time ✓ = Not demonstrating NA = Not applicable at this time

READING BEHAVIORS

	1	2	3	4
SHOWS INTEREST IN BOOKS				
Chooses to read for enjoyment				
Participates in shared (unison) reading				
Listens to and enjoys read-aloud books				
Uses reading time appropriately				
Chooses books appropriate to own reading level				
Talks about and is willing to share about books				
INITIATES READING-LIKE BEHAVIORS				
Reads using picture clues, memory, and retelling				
Moves her/his eyes and finger left to right across the print while attempting to read				
Views self as a reader				
Reads reading-like behaviors with familiar predictable text				
Reads with fluency and expression				
DEMONSTRATES PRINT AND WORD AWARENESS				
Accurately reads a word or group of words in a repetitive pattern in a story				
Points to find a specific word				
Recognizes frequently used words in stories				
Notices similarities in some words				
Reads the text in familiar pattern books				
Reads unpredictable text				
Recognizes words from the environment				
USES ALL SYSTEMS OF LANGUAGE TO GET MEANING				
Uses structure of sentence to gain meaning				
Uses overall meaning of the text to figure out a word				
Begins to sound out words				
USES EFFECTIVE COMPREHENSION STRATEGIES TO PREDICT, CONFIRM AND INTEGRATE				
Takes risks by substituting a word that makes sense				
Self-corrects to match what is grammatically acceptable				
Skips a word and reads on				
Refers back to words previously read				
Starts sentence again and rereads for meaning				
Uses picture clues				
Notices miscues if interfering with meaning				
Talks about her/his own reading strategies				

READING BEHAVIORS (continued)

	1	2	3	4
COMPREHENDS WHILE READING				
Relates own prior experiences to the text				
Recalls the main idea of the story				
Retells story in sequence				
Uses story structure to understand the story				
Your child is in the _____ stage of reading				

WRITING BEHAVIORS

	1	2	3	4
SHOWS INTEREST IN WRITING				
Initiates independent writing				
Shows pleasure in writing				
Shares own writing				
Gives and accepts feedback about writing				
USES EFFECTIVE WRITING STRATEGIES				
Conventions of Writing				
Writes from left to right and top to bottom				
Uses spaces between words				
Uses ending punctuation				
Uses capital at beginning of sentence				
Uses capitals for proper names				
Writes legibly				
Spelling				
Uses functional spelling				
Uses some conventional spellings				
Uses letter sound correspondence (beg., mid., end)				
Uses some regular vowel sounds				
Uses words from the environment and favorite books				
Writes for Meaning				
Generates topics and ideas from personal knowledge and experience				
Is able to read back what is written				
Invests time and effort in a piece				
Makes literature connections while writing				
Writes meaningful sentences				
Uses a more complex sentence structure				
Writes story in a sequential order				
Includes beginning, middle, and end in a piece of writing				

WRITING BEHAVIORS (continued)

	1	2	3	4
Attempts to increase written vocabulary				
Uses a variety of writing (stories, letters, lists, etc.)				
Rereads and revises				
Develops story with more detail				
Your child is in the _____ stage of writing				
Your child is in the _____ stage of spelling				

LISTENING

	1	2	3	4
Demonstrates active listening as an audience member				
Responds in an appropriate manner to oral directions				
Remembers specific information from orally presented material				

Figure 8.5 Lukas Elementary first grade progress report

	1st	2nd	3rd	4th
READING				
1. Chooses reading material from a wide variety of genre & subjects				
2. Chooses reading material at various levels of difficulty				
3. Applies prediction strategies				
4. Summarizes information from fiction & non-fiction				
5. Uses a wide variety of strategies to figure out important unknown words				
6. Comprehends at various levels				
7. Reads at different rates (Grades 5-9)				
8. Recognizes when own reading does not make sense				
9. Responds to reading in a variety of ways				
10. Knows vocabulary words and applies that knowledge				
11. Uses steps of study techniques (Grades 4-9)				
WRITING				
12. Chooses to write				
13. Initiates writing				
14. Selects appropriate types of writing				
15. Uses revision strategies				
16. Demonstrates knowledge of mechanics				
17. Makes a final copy				
18. Evaluates own writing				
19. Shares own writing				
20. Provides feedback to writers				
21. Correctly uses appropriate reference material				
22. Spells words appropriate to level				
23. Writes legibly				

Figure 8.6   Reading/writing section of intermediate-level report card

Many teachers find themselves in schools where they are unable to change report cards that are contrary to their beliefs about literacy. In such cases, inserts in the report card may be a partial answer. One type of insert is the "add-on", an insert that adds a subject to those already listed on the report card or adds emphasis to a subject on the report card. The insert in Figure 8.7 allows teachers to communicate children's progress in writing in far greater detail and from a different point of view than their traditional report card (which treated writing like the report card in Figure 8.5).

Another type of insert is one that redefines the traditional terms on the report card from a whole language point of view. In the "Teacher Reflection" in this chapter, Lori Conrad reveals how she defined the terms on her district's traditional report card. Conrad also developed an "add on" to the report card—a checklist of proficient reading and writing behaviors. Together, they allowed her to communicate more clearly what she observed about students within the teaching and assessment system at her school.

STUKEY ELEMENTARY SCHOOL
11080 Grant Drive
Northglenn, CO 80233
(303) 451-6975
Laurence T. Marchant, Principal

School District No. 12, Adams County
James E. Mitchell, Ed.D. • Superintendent of Schools

WRITERS' WORKSHOP PROGRESS REPORT

Name: _____ School Year 19__-__

Dear Parents:

Stukey Elementary has several classrooms using a process approach to teaching writing, know as Writers' Workshop. Your child is involved in this approach. This report will be used in addition to or in place of the language area on the report card. Following is an evaluation of your child's progress in writing. It reflects the areas emphasized in the writing process.

Teacher: _____

Evaluation Key: ⊠ Almost always   ✔ Some of the time   ☐ Working on this skill

WRITERS' WORKSHOP	1st	2nd	3rd	4th
Starts to write independently				
Able to select own topics				
Presents clear, understandable information				
Includes enough information				
Presents well organized information				
Shows openness to suggestions/ willingness to revise				
Edits when necessary (capitalization, spelling, punctuation, and handwriting)				
Takes an active part in writing conferences				
Takes part in share sessions				
Displays a positive, willing attitude toward writing				
Uses time wisely				

Figure 8.7   Stukey Elementary Writers' Workshop Progress Report

It is also possible to design an insert that communicates the curriculum for the grading period. Parents are frequently interested in what their children are doing and learning in school, and a description helps them understand the nature of the assignments used to arrive at report card grades. Figure 8.8 shows an insert developed by Sharon Reiling, a sixth-grade teacher in Douglas County, Colorado. Though Reiling continued to record a grade in the "Reading" and "Language" boxes on the report card itself, she crossed out all terms that were listed under each of these categories

SUPPLEMENTAL REPORT FORM / LANGUAGE ARTS

STUDENT _____ QUARTER _____
TEACHER _____

UNITS OF STUDY	LESSONS	PRODUCTS/OUTCOMES	COMMENTS

Romeo and Juliet
Julius Caesar
 	
British Authors:
  Shakespeare
  Charles Dickens
  Chaucer
  Mollie Hunter
  Margery Williams
  Beatrix Potter
  Susan Cooper
 	
Self-selected novel
	READING:
	Understanding Literary Form: play / fiction / classics
	
	Courteous, engaged listening
	Predicting / confirming
	Strategies for making meaning: Unknown words / reread / read further / ask / read aloud / visualize
	
	Character Development: round / flat
	
	Point of View
	Conflict: internal / external
	
	Leads
	
	WRITING
	Biography
	Essay
	Writing Skills: editing symbols / capitalization / spelling of plural words / possessive nouns / point of view / bibliography / title page / cover / proofreading
	
	Note taking: 3 x 5 cards
	Researching: trade books / encyclopedias / test books
		Plays: *Romeo and Juliet* actor production
		Julius Caesar actor production
		
		Bibliography
		
		British Fair
		
		Learning Log
		Response Log
		D.A.R.E. Essay
		Discussion
		Author's Circle
		
		Independent Project:	

HINTS FOR HELPING AT HOME

Figure 8.8 Supplemental Report Form/Language Arts

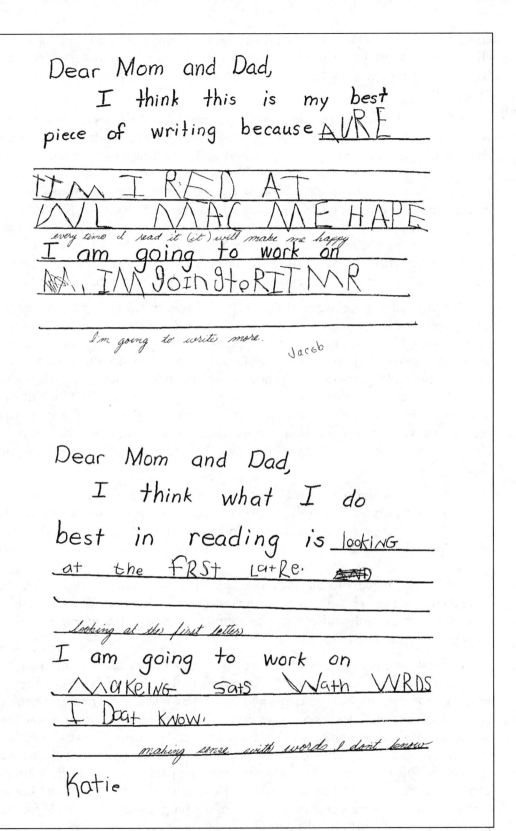

Dear Mom and Dad,
    I think this is my best
piece of writing because AVRE

ITM I RED AT
WL MAC ME HAPE
every time I read it (it) will make me happy
I am going to work on
M. IM 9oIn9toRIT MR

I'm going to write more.

              Jacob

Dear Mom and Dad,
    I think what I do
best in reading is looking
at the FRSt La+Re.

looking at the first letters
I am going to work on
MakeING SatS WAth WRDS
I Doat KNOW.

      making sense with words I don't know

Katie

Figure 8.9   Dear Mom and Dad figures (Jacob and Katie)

and wrote "See attached sheet" in their place. Reiling communicated each student's choices within the curriculum by using a highlighter to denote which particular British authors each student read and by filling in spaces (for example, after "Biography").

A final kind of insert for report cards is students' evaluations of their work. In the week before the end of the grading period, you can involve children in reviewing their reading and writing for the grading period and in setting goals for the next grading period. These self-evaluations can be included in the report card when it is sent home. Even very young children can accomplish this, as the examples from Carrie Ekey's first-grade classroom in Figure 8.9 reveal. (Ekey has rewritten what the child wrote so parents can read it.) The example in Figure 8.10 is from Kathy Hoerlein's third-grade students. The goals students set for themselves are part of the assessment data she uses to make instructional plans during the next grading period. They are also used in arriving at an evaluation at the end of the following grading period.

Parent conferences are another way to communicate literacy progress. The advantages of the conference over the report card are the face-to-face communication about a child's progress and the opportunity for parents to provide information about the child. It's important to build initial rapport with the parents and make them comfortable, particularly if school is a place that has negative connotations for them. One way to do this is to invite the parents to arrive in the block of time just prior to their scheduled conference with you and let them view a videotape of a recent class activity in which they can see their child at work or a videotape of their child's progress as a reader over time (see Jan Bennett's "Teacher Reflection" in Chapter 7).

Because conferences have such potential to help you learn more about your students, it is important not only to provide parents with information about their child's literacy progress but also to seek information from them about the child's literacy. Use open-ended questions similar to those you use to encourage your students to talk, such as "What has _____ shared with you about _____?" Or you can ask parents to fill out a questionnaire in advance of the conference that you can use as a conversation starter (see Lori Conrad's "Teacher Reflection" in this chapter for an example; others may be found in *Literacy Assessment: A Handbook of Instruments* (Rhodes, 1993).

You may find it helpful to have three-way conferences that include you, the parents, and the child. Kathy Hoerlein experimented with three-way conferences and found that her third-grade students and parents gained a great deal from the experience. Hoerlein schedules conferences every twenty minutes during the grading periods in which they take place, so she streamlines the process. The student begins the conference by sharing her work in a way that has been previously structured and rehearsed. This takes about five minutes, with the parents occasionally asking clarification questions. Then she supports and expands on what the child has shared, clearly communicating her views of the child's progress and her goals for the next grading period. For the final portion of the conference, she gives the parents the option of letting the child remain or sending the student out of the room so that the parents can talk more freely about any concerns they have regarding the child's home or school life. Almost all parents request that the child remain while the parent comments on and asks questions about the child's progress. The few who send their children out of the room want to let the teacher know about difficulties at home.

To prepare her students for the three-way conferences, Hoerlein asks them to choose pieces of work or records that will help parents understand their efforts and their progress in reading and writing. Children choose their best two pieces of writ-

---

READING

These are some things I do well in reading.

I am good at reading Beverly cleary books.

This is a problem I have.

my problem is thet I prblums in choling books

This is what I plan to work on next quarter.

To read choling books.

choling – challenging

WRITING

These are some things I do well in writing.

I have lots of ditils in my story. I rember capties and perds

This is a problem I have.

Splling the words I don't know

This is what I plan to work on next quarter.

Wriite it on a pice of paper and see if it looks right

Figure 8.10 READING

ing; in reading, they choose to share such products as a project they have completed after reading a book, some literature log entries, or the record they keep of books they have read. Hoerlein then asks her students to complete self-evaluations of their reading and writing, using the pieces of work or records they have chosen to support what they say. On the basis of this work, Hoerlein conducts lessons in which the children learn to present their work and an evaluation of it orally, including rehearsing their presentation with their classmates and the teacher prior to the conference. A lot of work and time? Yes, but the teacher feels that what the children learn about their own work in the process more than makes up for it.

Following the conference, Hoerlein asks the parents to complete an evaluation before they leave the building, and she asks students to complete one the following day. She has been happy to find that the three-way conferences are appreciated by all parents and students with one exception. Figure 8.11 provides an example of the feedback forms and the responses.

There are numbers of other ways teachers can report progress to parents. An information newsletter can report on general progress made by the class, on reasons why the class is learning about a particular topic, and on specific teaching techniques, especially when they can also be employed at home. Teachers can send home a "Can Do Photo," a picture taken in the classroom that reveals something the child has accomplished. The photo is accompanied by descriptions of the accomplishment, written by the teacher and the student. Periodic work samples are often welcomed by parents, particularly when they are accompanied by a sheet that suggests to the parents what they should notice about the work. Even telephone calls are progress reports when the teacher calls with more than bad news. (For more detail about these and other forms of progress reports, see The British Columbia *Primary Program Resource Document* (1990, pp. 90–95).

staffings

Special education staffings often involve the participation of the assessment and evaluation audiences we referred to earlier: the student, the parents, the classroom and the special education teacher, other evaluators such as the school psychologist, and sometimes administrators. Whether we are talking about the initial staffing or the annual review of a student's progress, decision making in most staffings relies heavily on norm-referenced testing.

Too often in initial staffings, the student's parents and the regular classroom teacher are overwhelmed by the norm-referenced test data, which becomes the central focus of the staffing. This often happens because of the confidence with which the school psychologist or the special education teacher present the data she had collected and because the regular teacher and parents are unfamiliar with many of the tests. Underlying the evaluator's confidence in presenting the norm-referenced data is the belief that the test data are precise, objective, and accurate.

Let us recall, however, that norm-referenced test data have problems, no matter how long the test has been around or how confidently the data are presented. It is also highly likely that the test data are confounded by the fact that the test is frequently given by someone who is a stranger to the student taking the test. This per-

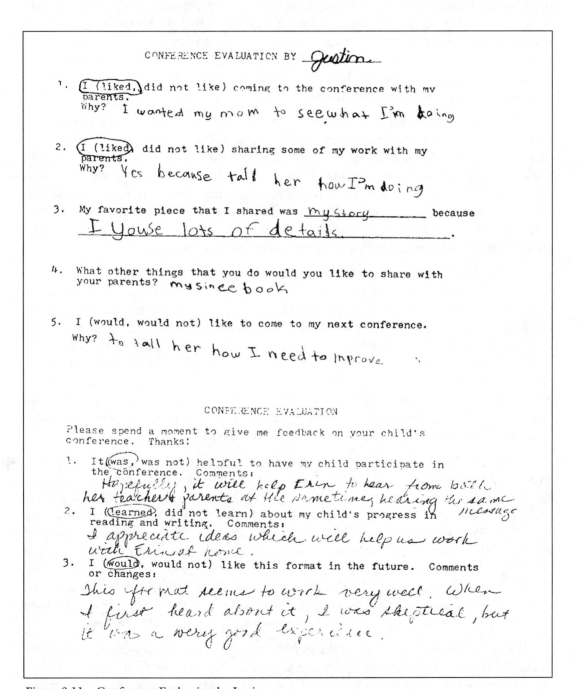

Figure 8.11   Conference Evaluation by Justin

son, often the school psychologist, might conduct the evaluation in a context isolated from instruction and in an environment unfamiliar to the student.

Some students do not perform well on norm-referenced tests; by teachers' accounts, they do better than the tests reveal. Although this is also true for normally achieving children, it is even more probable for children who have behavioral problems or low self-esteem as a result of not doing well in school. Performance is particularly problematic when the test results are relied on heavily—as they frequently are in staffings—to make important decisions about individual students. In light of the problems involved in using norm-referenced tests for students who are experiencing school difficulty (or who are already staffed into special education) a number of actions should be taken. See Mehrens & Lehmann, 1991, pp. 433–455 for a discussion of these issues and possible actions.

If you are a regular classroom teacher, what can you do? First, come armed with your own observational and standardized data and insist on presenting them. Some of the most valuable—and most reliable—data are those you have collected within the context of classroom literacy events. Remember that ultimately it does not matter how a student does on a norm-referenced test; what does matter is what the student does with reading and writing in everyday situations. Find out from the parents if the data being reported are congruent with what they have observed about the child's literacy at home. Make sure their voices are heard as well.

Also collect and present information in the ways we have suggested—observational and standardized data that come from reading and writing whole pieces of text. If the special education teacher presents data, such as the student's scores on reading nonsense words, from the Woodcock Johnson Psychoeducational Battery for example, add information from miscue analysis to the data pool to show how the student reads words in whole text. Encourage the staffing group to decide which is more important—reading real words in text or reading isolated nonsense words. In *Learning Denied*, Taylor (1990) gives a powerful and disturbing account of how an almost total reliance on norm-referenced tests led educators to the wrong conclusions about the capabilities of a young boy named Patrick.

Finally, be an advocate for the student. Keep encouraging everyone to remember that the group is there to make the best possible educational decisions for the student, based on as much data as possible. One possible outcome of the staffing is *not* to label a child, an option often forgotten in the rush to find out what's wrong with the child. Two things are especially important: 1) to be active in seeking out and dealing with the meaning of conflicting data, and 2) to be active in recognizing and utilizing data that show what the student can do, not only what she can't do. In part, this is what went wrong with Patrick, the boy featured in Taylor's (1990) book. The system so intently pursued Patrick's suspected disability, that the participants focused on what the child was unable to do rather than what he was capable of doing.

If it is determined that the child needs special education services and the time comes to create an educational plan, consider the theoretical orientation behind it. Are reading and writing being treated as a system of subskills to be mastered, or as a process of using all of the language systems in concert with each other? If the team agrees to take a whole language theoretical stance, make sure that the Individualized Educational Plan reflects that stance. (See Rhodes [1993] and Dudley-Marling [1988, pp. 68–74] on writing IEPs that better reflect a whole language orientation.) Be careful not to let the behavioristic background of many school psychologists and special education teachers dominate. Remember that many of them have little information about reading and writing development or teaching. Again, Taylor's portrayal of Patrick is instructive here; it was the paradigm used by the educators that led them to conclude that he could only become literate with skills instruction.

In addition to the theoretical orientation of the educational plan, keep the practicality of the educational plans for home and school at the forefront. Too often, regular classroom teachers and parents are told what to do to improve the student's education in the staffing or review. Remember that a staffing (or review) is supposed to be a *team* effort and that the regular education teacher and the parents are often the ones who not only know the student best but are key in carrying out the plan. Some of the educational plans generated by people who are unfamiliar with the classroom or the home in which the student lives ignore the inherent constraints on their fulfillment. Unless the classroom teacher and parents feel that they can carry out an educational plan, it isn't worth the piece of paper it's written on.

Whether or not it is determined that the child needs special education services, if the child needs to receive instruction the teacher or parents do not know how to provide (the teacher is skills-based, for example, and the child needs a holistic approach, as Patrick did in Taylor [1990]), the team needs to create a support system to help the teacher or parents learn new methods. An alternative is to place the student with a teacher who does know how to meet these needs.

Special education staffings were developed to help everyone involved with a student have a voice in how to best assist that student in making progress as a learner. Try to ensure that everyone's voice is heard, that all ways of looking at the child are considered, that the child's strengths are pointed out and that they are the foundation for the educational plan. Remember that the problems may not be "in" the student, or in the student alone, and that it is as important to assess the student's instruction and educational environment as it is to evaluate the student (see Chapter 2). Even when everyone on the staffing team agrees about the data and the resulting educational plan, remember that you have probably only begun to learn about the student; continued assessment in the midst of everyday literacy events is likely to uncover richer data that will help you teach the student more effectively. Remain open to continuing to search for ways to assist the student in becoming as literate as she can be. Always remember that the data about a student are tentative and your conclusions even more so. Assume that the student can learn and search for ways that she learns best.

Teachers continually struggle over grading students and completing report cards. Some teachers can rewrite the report card. Others are in more traditional settings where they must use a report card that does not mirror their beliefs about language teaching or assessment.

Lori Conrad is such a teacher. We met Conrad six years ago as she began her master's program at our university. At the time, she was in her second year as a second-grade teacher at Acres Green Elementary in the Douglas County Schools, a fast-growing and socioeconomically diverse suburb of Denver, Colorado. The district's report card provides a glimpse of the dominant values of the school system. As a whole language teacher whose values were not the same as the traditional values of the district, Conrad did not have an opportunity to rewrite the report card (although she had considerable freedom in developing curriculum for her students). Instead, she worked within the system and generated vehicles to communicate better with parents and allow her to enact her values. One thing we want to point out is how she uses tasks, like designing a report card insert, and the people around her to stretch her thinking and to continue exploring ideas about how to teach and assess literacy.

Conrad has spent the last two school years as a "teacher on special assignment" for the district, working at the district and building levels with teachers who request her assistance in literacy instruction and assessment.

 # Improving the report card ritual

Lori L. Conrad

Every nine weeks, I found myself filling in the myriad little boxes on my students' report cards. It was a regular part of my teaching routine—a part that grew increasingly frustrating each time I attempted it. The discrete marks were suppose to provide parents with clear, well-rounded information about how their child was progressing. I spent hours reviewing the children's writing folders, reading log entries, and thematic unit folders, as well as my own ongoing assessment notes and checklists, trying to portray each child's growth accurately. But, no matter how hard I worked, I always had a gnawing feeling that my desire for a "clear picture" wasn't being achieved.

It was obvious to me that a wide discrepancy existed between what I believed about literacy development, the classroom experiences and environment I provided to enhance and support this development, and the district's reporting format I sent home at the end of each quarter. For example, the report card's single box entitled "Written Language" didn't do justice to the intricacies of the writing process. The section for "Reading" didn't explain the complexities of constructing meaning from print. The fact that reading and writing were graded as isolated learning events was contrary to my understanding of literacy development, and this division certainly did not mirror my students' daily holistic language experiences.

In addition, I never benefited from parents' insight into their children's literacy growth before I passed graded judgments. After all, parents have a different and valuable perspective, one I could certainly use in reflecting on the students' flexibility as readers and writers.

Because of the inadequacies in the way I reported student learning, parent/teacher conferences were spent defining "report card jargon" and clarifying classroom/home behaviors instead of discussing children's strengths and needs. Clearly, I needed to amend my reporting procedures so that they were more closely aligned with my philosophy and the children's daily experiences, while providing more information to parents.

In order to achieve this goal, I began by examining the questions parents asked over and over again about their children's literacy growth:

"Is my child reading where she is supposed to be reading?"

"How do you grade writing? I can't even read much of what my daughter writes!"

"My son doesn't sound out words he doesn't know. How can he be doing well in reading?"

"What does expression have to do with good reading? Do you have the children read aloud a lot?"

"I think my child should spell all the words he uses correctly. Do you teach spelling?"

If I could develop a reporting format that addressed these issues, I knew I'd have a more informative way of documenting and sharing student learning. To accomplish this, I decided to create a three-part information gathering/sharing procedure that included report card definitions, a language process checklist, and a parental questionnaire.

Beginning with what I had

In the best possible situation, I'd be able to make a fresh start in reporting student learning. In reality, I knew I needed to work within the parameters of my district's approved report card (see Figure 8.12). I began by defining each of the report card's graded sections so that both the parents and I would have a common set of understandable labels to use when discussing their child's progress. The definitions explained not only what the section's title meant, but also how I arrive at a grade for that section.

PROGRESS REPORT				
Reporting Period	1	2	3	4
READING				
Reading Grade Level Use of phonetic skills Reads with expression Recognizes words Comprehension				
LANGUAGE				
Written Oral				
SPELLING				
Daily use				

Figure 8.12 Progress Report

Report card definitions

READING

Reading grade level: Using an IRI (Individual Reading Inventory), a specific grade level is determined for each reader. The inventory utilizes words in isolation as well as graded reading passages. This level coincides with an instructional level in our basal reading series (Houghton Mifflin, 1983). Because reading is such a complex activity, labeling a specific level (to the half year) is an approximation at best. This level fluctuates according to a text's structure and a reader's interest and background knowledge.

Use of phonetic skills: Graphophonics (the match between letters and sounds) is one element in written language. Proficient readers rely most heavily on the meaning of language, not on isolated sounds, while reading. When a reader is attempting to understand unknown print, the sounds contained in the word can provide some clues, but those sounds should always be connected to the text's meaning. Over reliance on "sounding out" interrupts a meaningful reading experience. A reader who successfully "uses phonetic skills" understands the sounds letters can make but realizes that English is a phonetically inconsistent language. She uses phonics as it pertains to the intended meaning of a text.

Reads with expression: Proficient readers are able to adapt their rate of reading according to the demands and purposes of a reading experience. They are able to read fluidly, not word by word, expressively reacting to the text's format and punctuation. Even though expression can only be assessed when a child reads aloud, it reflects how fluidly she reads silently.

Recognizes words: As children grow as readers, they develop a "bank" of words that they immediately recognize while they are reading. These words are not learned by rote drill, but instead are learned in the process of language development. This means that readers have learned how language is put together so they can predict upcoming words without having to "decode" each one. Proficient readers take this one step further. When encountering a new word, even one they can pronounce, they use the context surrounding the word to understand its meaning. They don't just read the words, they read the *meaning*.

Comprehension: This is the *most important* part of any reading assessment. It measures understanding a reader gains as a result of an experience with print. Successful readers are able to monitor their own understandings *while* they read and are able to share those insights after they have finished (e.g., major story elements, factual information, writer's style, etc). Proficient readers are able to use a number of strategies to determine unknown words and are able to correct any miscue (wrong word) if it interrupts a text's meaning.

LANGUAGE

Written: Good writing comes as a result of a lot of practice and meaningful feedback from other writers. Growth is measured by the amount of meaningful text a writer is able to produce. This includes an increase in her use of written language conventions (e.g., capitals, punctuation, sentence structure, spelling and text style) as well as an increased flexibility with different topics and forms. This development is demonstrated as she takes first drafts through the revision and editing processes to publication. The goal is to end up with a more complete, more meaningful text as a result.

Oral: This area is measured by a child's ability to express her ideas in complete, meaningful ways. Oral language development is often reflected in written language development.

SPELLING

Becoming a proficient speller is encouraged by frequently creating and interpreting text. Informal spelling instruction occurs continually as children interact with print both as readers and writers. Formalized spelling instruction begins during second-grade because it is at this point that most children are developmentally prepared to look beyond simple letter/sound relationships to the more complex patterns of conventional orthography. A child's spelling proficiency is measured by both weekly test scores *and* improved use of conventional spelling in her writing. In addition to this, each child's developmental level of spelling is determined and reported.

Each definition has a distinctively holistic slant because I defined "reading grade level," "use of phonetic skills," and other terminology according to my own philosophy of literacy development—that children learn to understand, use, and produce print by purposefully engaging in realistic, meaningful reading and writing experiences that are orchestrated and supported by a thoughtful, more proficient written language user. A copy of the "Report Card Definitions" was attached to each report card before it went home.

While developing these definitions, I solicited insight and feedback from my colleagues on their meaningfulness and understandability. The last thing I wanted to do was to create just another piece of educational mumble for parents to glance at and discard. Sharing drafts and receiving reflective feedback supported my own "hashing over" of each report card section. By the time I finalized the definitions, I knew more about the report card, its meaning and limitations, than ever before. This knowledge encouraged my next step in informing parents.

Explaining the reading/writing process

Even though I had very positive feelings about my "Report Card Definitions," I realized that they alone didn't effectively explain or document the process of becoming a proficient reader/writer. Eight discreet grades, no matter how well defined, could not describe the complexities of written language development. I wanted to provide parents with the same pair of glasses, so to speak, that I used on a daily basis in assessing my students' literacy strengths and needs.

I had become very accustomed to jotting anecdotal notes and filling in process checklists while observing my students in various reading/writing situations. Both the format and content of the notes/checklists had evolved as my knowledge of language development increased and as my "kid watching" became more effective. I readily used the information I noted to plan direct instruction and active experiences.

Combining the major elements of the checklists and the anecdotal notations, I developed a "Language Process Checklist," which included behaviors I hoped students would demonstrate given meaningful, realistic reading and writing opportunities (see Figure 8.13). To me, these behaviors more fully described what proficient written language users do while reading and writing than did the report card. The checklist also had the advantage of directly reflecting the kinds of literacy-building activities occurring in my classroom. It was my intent that parents would better understand some of the intricacies of proficient reading and writing while sharing in the kinds of literacy activities their child experienced during our daily language arts block.

To grade these behaviors, I chose descriptors that reflected the "process-ness" of becoming literate. After all, written language proficiency isn't something you do all at once. A reader/writer's ability can fluctuate depending on her background knowledge, comfort level, and interest in a chosen literacy task. It seemed that "consistently demonstrates," "attempts to demonstrate,"

LANGUAGE PROCESS CHECKLIST**

Developed by Lori L. Conrad

C = consistently demonstrates
A = attempts to demonstrate
N = needs to develop

READING	1st Quarter	2nd Quarter	3rd Quarter	4th Quarter
>1. Has a positive concept of self as a reader.				
^#2. Utilizes a variety of reading strategies that cross over the four language cueing systems.				
+3. Exhibits prereading behaviors (i.e., text previewing and questioning).				
+4. Is able to predict a story line as a means of comprehension and evaluation (confirm/disconfirm predictions).				
+5. Self-monitors for meaningful reading.				
+^6. Successfully corrects miscues that interrupt a text's meaning.				
<7. Reads fluidly and with expression.				
>8. Chooses to read for variety of purposes (enjoyment, information, etc.).				
*9. Chooses reading material at an appropriate level depending on purpose/needs.				
>10. Brings books from home, asks to borrow books to read at home.				
+11. Records reading experiences accurately/ reflectively in reading logs.				
+12. Actively participates in reading discussion groups as a means of sharing reading experiences.				
+13. Is able to effectively retell a previously read piece, including major story elements: setting, characters, plot, detailed events, and theme.				
+14. Changes selections at an appropriate rate during quiet reading time.				
>15. Uses all the reading time to engage in purposeful interaction with print.				
>16. Independently rereads books previously read aloud as a shared reading experience.				

Figure 8.13   Language Process Checklist

and "needs to develop" fit my intentions much more effectively than a product-oriented A, B, or C.

As a way of trying the "Language Process Checklist" back to the district's reporting format, I included a key that aligned behaviors with report card sections. This was my way of not only showing how I arrived at specific grades, but also stretching a simplistic label like "reads with experience" into a more meaningful explanation of literacy development.

WRITING	1st Quarter	2nd Quarter	3rd Quarter	4th Quarter
[1. Has a positive concept of self as a writer.				
^[2. Initiates own writing.				
[3. Is successful at choosing interesting topics for writing.				
[4. Composes whole texts that flow well and make sense—is able to get rich ideas down on paper.				
[5. Uses ideas and wording from literature while writing.				
[6. Rereads text frequently to check for sense during and after composing.				
[7. Is willing to revise to create a more meaningful written text.				
[8. Participates in positive rehearsal and conference time with self, peers, and instructor.				
[$9. Shows an improvement in mechanics and grammar when editing.				
[10. Is willing to share writing with the class.				
[11. Offers thoughtful suggestions and comments during sharing time.				
[12. Uses a variety of voices, styles, and contexts.				
[13. Chooses to write for different purposes (enjoyment, information exchange, entertainment, self-exploration, etc.).				
[14. Chooses to write for different audiences.				
[15. Uses all the writing time to engage in purposeful writing.				
[$16. Developmental spelling level.				
[$17. Is aware of and uses conventional spelling of words in the environment.				

**The following symbols match these process behaviors with items noted on the report card:

*	= Reading grade level	>	= Effort
#	= Uses phonetic skills	<	= Reads with expression
^	= Recognizes words	+	= Comprehension
[	= Written language development	$	= Spelling

Figure 8.13 Language Process Checklist
(*continued*)

Again, designing this reporting instrument focused my attention on exactly what I believed successful readers and writers do when they interact with print. It forced me to look at my own ongoing assessment methods and internalize not only what I was documenting, but also why I noted certain abilities and behaviors and not others. I had to know these information-gathering formats well enough to synthesize the "stuff" I wrote down and produce an understandable document that would be meaningful for parents.

Soliciting parent input

As the final way to increase clarity in reporting student development, I asked parents what they saw as their child's literacy strengths, needs, and experiences outside of the classroom (see Figure 8.14). I believed this was an important third step for two reasons. First of all, I wanted to celebrate all the positive literacy experiences parents were providing for their children. All too often, parents dismiss jotting "lunchbox notes" or subscribing to *Ranger*

My Child as a Reader and a Writer

Dear Parents,

    I need your help. To have a fuller understanding of your child as a written language user, I need to know how s/he is using print outside our classroom. Please take a few minutes to share with me your impressions and observations of your child's growth as a reader and writer. These insights will help me provide supportive, individualized literacy opportunities for him/her. Thank you for your help.

Lori Conrad

1. What activities has your child experienced at home that have helped him/her develop as a reader and as a writer?

2. What kinds of reading and writing does your child choose to use in his/her daily life? Circle any appropriate areas.

Reading	*Writing*
books	stories
magazines	letters to friends/relatives
environmental print (signs, labels, etc.)	grocery lists
notes from family members	"Things to Do:" lists
directions to games	notes to family members
recipes	other:
television guides	
newspapers	
other:	

   How does your child share these reading and writing experiences with you?

3. We have been developing a number of strategies to use when the children come to unknown words while reading. Please check the ones you have seen your child use successfully at home.
   a. Make a prediction (a good guess) and check to see if it makes sense.
   b. Skip the word, finish the sentence, and then reread, using the other words in the sentence to figure out the unknown one.
   c. Look at the pictures to see what clues they might provide.
   d. Sound out the word.
   e. Ask someone else to read the word.

4. What would you like to see your child be better able to do as a reader and as a writer?

Figure 8.14   My Child as a Reader and a Writer

Rick as something trivial when compared to school experiences. They may not realize how valuable all meaningful experiences with print are to a child's reading and writing development.

Secondly, the information parents shared with me revealed the kinds of backgrounds my students had with print as well as the parents' own understandings of literacy development. When a parent specified that he wanted his son to "spell all the words he uses correctly," he expressed his valuing of correct spelling as a primary part of any written product. When another parent shared that her daughter read and discussed books nightly with both her and her husband, it was clear that reading was a valuable part of the family's regular routine. All of these insights added to my growing bank of knowledge about each of my students, the bank that I draw on when I make instructional decisions for the class and for individuals.

Because I solicited this information before I completed report cards or conducted parent-teacher conferences, I was able to use parental insights to broaden my understanding of my students' literacy development and build some initial rapport with the other significant teachers in my students' lives.

Benefits of this process

Extending and enriching my methods of documenting and sharing student growth was a time-consuming process, but I gained a great deal as a result of my efforts. Without a doubt, the most valuable reward for me was a clearer, better articulated understanding of written language development. Because I had to decide upon definitions for reading/writing terms as well as delineate and measure proficient language process behaviors, my own understanding of how children grow as readers and writers was deepened and solidified. This increased clarity has made my daily ongoing assessment more focused and, therefore, more effective. I know exactly what I am looking for in my developing readers/writers and am able to plan relevant, purposeful instruction based on well thought-out literacy goals for all my students.

My relationship with parents has also been greatly enriched. Parent-teacher conferences now focus on children and their development instead of on static little boxes. Parents ask more informed questions, ones that move beyond report card jargon. Because there is a two-way exchange of information and insight, we are both invested in developing learning goals.

Finally, the "report card ritual" isn't as painful at it once was. I am still not satisfied with my district's adopted reporting format, but now that I have experienced success with my own revisions and additions, I don't feel that I am betraying what I believe about children and literacy learning.

Conclusion

Perhaps Rex Brown (1989) describes most succinctly what educators face in balancing norm-referenced tests and the development of alternative assessments:

> The task is to keep them from dominating school affairs to such a degree that they distort curriculum and hold back efforts to make schools more thoughtful places. Moveover, professionals in other fields have found ways to aggregate "messy" information systems for policy purposes. This difficult but not impossible enterprise should have high priority in state departments of education and educational labs and centers. (p.33)

Of course, "this difficult but not impossible enterprise" should also receive attention from teachers. It is they and students who will benefit most from reducing the primacy of norm-referenced tests and creating a system in which alternative measures of assessment are possible. Like the teachers in this chapter, we can and should be key figures in creating both local changes and the broader changes in traditional policies and practices that affect our own lives and the everyday lives of students in the classroom.

references

Aronson, E. & R. Farr. (1988). Issues in assessment. *Journal of Reading, 31,* 174–177.

Barrs, M., S. Ellis, H. Hester, & A. Thomas. (1989). *The primary language record.* Portsmouth, NH: Heinemann.

Bloom, B., G. Madaus, & J. Hastings. (1981). *Evaluation to improve learning.* New York: McGraw-Hill.

Bracey, G.W. (1991a). Good news about our schools. *Denver Post,* April 21, p. 1-I and 5-I.

Bracey, G.W. (1991b). Why can't they be like we were? *Phi Delta Kappan,* October, p. 104–117.

Brown, R. (1989). Testing and thoughtfulness. *Educational Leadership, 46* (7), 31–33.

———. (1990). *Schools of thought.* San Francisco: Jossey-Bass.

Delpit, L. (1986). Skills and other dilemmas of a progressive Black educator. *Harvard Educational Review, 56,* 379–385.

———. (1988). The silenced dialogue: Power and pedagogy in educating other people's children. *Harvard Educational Review, 58,* 280–298.

DeWitt, K. (1991). Project suggests alternatives to tests. *The Denver Post,* April 28, 18-A.

Dreher, M. & H. Singer. (1985). Parents' attitudes toward reports of standardized reading test results. *Reading Teacher, 38,* 624–632.

Dutcher, P. (1990). Michigan Educational Assessment Program. Lansing, MI: Michigan Department of Education, Box 30008.

Edelsky, C. & S. Harman. (1988). One more critique of reading tests—with two differences. *English Education,* 20, 157–171.

FairTest Examiner. (1988). *2* (2). (Address: 342 Broadway, Cambridge, MA 02139).

FairTest Examiner. (1989). *3* (4). (Address: 342 Broadway, Cambridge, MA 02139).

Farr, R. & R. Carey. (1986). *Reading: What can be measured?* Newark, DE: International Reading Association.

Goodman, Y., D. Watson, & C. Burke. (1987). *Reading miscue inventory: Alternative procedures.* New York: Richard C. Owen.

Guide to the Maine educational assessment 1989–90. (1989). Portland, ME: Maine Department of Educational and Cultural Services.

IRA (International Reading Association). (1989). Statement on genuine account-ability. Newark, DE: International Reading Association.

Jongsma, K. (1989). Update on state assessment programs. *The Reading Teacher, 43,* 86–87.

Kirby, D. & T. Liner. (1988). *Inside out: Developmental strategies for teaching writing* (2nd Ed.). Portsmouth, NH: Boynton-Cook/Heinemann.

Kirsch, I. & A. Jungeblut. (1986). *Literacy: Profiles of America's young adults.* Princeton, NJ: National Assessment of Educational Progress, Educational Testing Service.

Langer, J. & G. Pradl. (1984). Standardized testing: A call for action. *Language Arts, 61,* 764–767.

Martinez, M. & J. Lipson. (1989). Assessment for learning. *Educational Leadership, 46* (7), 73–75.

Mehrens, W.A. & I.J. Lehmann. (1991). *Measurement and evaluation in education and psychology.* Chicago: Holt, Rinehart & Winston.

Meisels, S. (1989). High-stakes testing. *Educational Leadership, 46* (7), 16–21.

Mikulecky, L. (1987). The status of literacy in our society. In J. Readence & R. Baldwin (Eds.), *Research in literacy: Merging perspectives,* (36th Yearbook of the National Reading Conference), pp. 211–235. Rochester, NY: National Reading Conference.

Moore, D. (1983). A case for naturalistic assessment of reading comprehension. *Language Arts, 60,* 957–968.

Mullis, I. & L. Jenkins. (1990). *The reading report card,* 1971–88. Princeton, NJ: National Assessment of Educational Progress.

National Association for the Education of Young Children. (1988). NAEYC position statement on the standardized testing of young children, three through eight years of age. *Young Children, 43,* 42–47.

Newman, A. & C. Beverstock. (1990). Adult literacy: Contexts and challenges. Newark, DE: International Reading Association.

Northcutt, N. (1975). *Adult functional competency: A summary.* Austin, TX: University of Texas.

Olson, M., D. Kirby, & G.D. Hulme. (1982). *The writing process teacher's guide: Grade 7.* Boston: Allyn & Bacon.

Province of British Columbia. (1990). *Primary program resource document.* British Columbia: Ministry of Education.

Rhodes, L. & C. Dudley-Marling. (1988). *Readers and writers with a difference: A holistic approach to teaching learning disabled and remedial students.* Portsmouth, NH: Heinemann.

Roeber, E. & P. Dutcher. (1989). Michigan's innovative assessment of reading. *Educational Leadership, 46* (7), 64–69.

Taylor, D. (1991). *Learning denied*. Portsmouth, NH: Heinemann.

Valencia, S. (1990). Alternative assessment: Separating the wheat from the chaff. *The Reading Teacher, 44,* 1: 60–61.

Valencia, S., P.D. Pearson, C. Peters, & K. Wixson. (1989). Theory and practice in statewide reading assessment: Closing the gap. *Educational Leadership 46* (7), 57–63.

Weber, E. (1987). Reading standards: The real "bottom line" is not the MEAP. *The Michigan Reading Journal, 20* (3), 2–5.

Wisconsin State Reading Association. (1990). *Toward an ecological assessment of reading progress*. Schofield, WI: Wisconsin State Reading Association.

Wixson, K. & C. Peters. (1987). Comprehension assessment: Implementing an interactive view of reading. *Educational Psychologist, 22,* 333–356.

Wixson, K., C. Peters, E. Weber, & E. Roeber. (1987). New directions in statewide reading assessment. *The Reading Teacher, 40,* 749–754.

Writing Assessment Leadership Committee. (1989). Montpelier, VT: Vermont Department of Education.

Chapter Nine

Literacy Collections

reflections

☐ Begin your own literacy portfolio. What will it include? In what ways does it help you to reflect on, celebrate, and improve your own reading and writing? What insights do you gain from keeping your own literacy portfolio that you might apply to your students' literacy portfolios?

☐ Share your current efforts in developing student reading and writing folders with another teacher. What materials from the reading and writing folders does it make sense to keep in current-year portfolios? What additional data might be helpful?

☐ From items in his current reading or writing folder, ask a student to decide on two items to keep for his current-year portfolio. Ask why he chose these two items. Then share two items you would like to keep in the student's current-year portfolio and share your reasons with the student. What are reasons for the student's choices? What are the student's responses to your choices? What do these activities reveal about the student's literacy development?

☐ Discuss the current-year portfolios of one or more of your students with another teacher who is interested in portfolio assessment. What progress has each student made? In the course of your sharing also point out observations from the portfolios that led you to make instructional decisions to meet students' individual interests and needs. What further changes do you and your colleague think need to be made at this time to meet students' instructional needs?

☐ Share current-year portfolios with parents at parent conferences. Ask parents to compare the knowledge they gain from the portfolios and from standardized tests. Which do they think has more meaning? Why? As an alternative to parent conferences about portfolios, you might write a letter requesting parents to review their child's portfolio with him at home. What growth do they see their child making? What goals do the parents and child think are now appropriate?

☐ It is best to develop criteria for assessing students' portfolios as a collaborative effort. What indicators of growth do you, as a teacher, hope to see in students' work? Discuss the same question with your students. What do they see as indicators of growth? This discussion will probably be most fruitful if, at the same time, students are reflecting on their own portfolios. In your talks with parents, what do they believe are appropriate indicators of their child's progress? Use all of these sources to develop a list of criteria that you will use in assessing students' growth as readers and writers through their portfolios.

☐ Share your efforts in developing current-year portfolios with another teacher. What from students' current-year portfolios does it make sense to keep in their permanent portfolios? In what ways could information be summarized that would be most helpful to next year's teacher(s)?

☐ Use our adaption of the five continuums developed by Valencia et al. (1990), to evaluate your current literacy collections and consider potential improvements. What is the focus of each type of assessment in the collections? To what extent do items in the collections result from authentic literacy experiences? Who makes decisions about what goes into the collections and how work is assessed? Do items in the collections result from both structured and spontaneous literacy activities? Do collections include a variety of student work samples, interviews, and teacher/student observations?

Portfolios are becoming a popular way to solve the problem of creating alternative assessments to norm-referenced tests (Johnson, 1991; Johnston, 1991; Winograd & Paris, 1988; Wolf, 1989). Portfolios allow students to demonstrate what they have learned and what they are learning. Teachers can examine students' portfolios to follow their development and make appropriate adjustments in instruction. Teachers can also use portfolios to encourage other groups, particularly parents, to consider what students are learning as readers and writers beyond their test scores and report card grades.

In this chapter we would like to discuss portfolio assessment along with other types of literacy collections. Right now, "portfolio" is frequently used to refer to any type of literacy collection, but we feel some clarification is needed if teachers are to understand the purposes portfolios serve and how to best construct them. We will explain other types of literacy collections to help teachers understand that portfolios are not the entire picture. Thus, in addition to both current-year and permanent portfolios, this chapter will discuss reading and writing folders, assessment notebooks, literacy biographies, and literacy profiles.

The California Assessment Portfolio Project (Cooper & Davies, 1990) has identified many useful purposes that can apply to all kinds of literacy collections, not just portfolios. We have adapted several from their list of thirty-five that apply to literacy collections of students' reading and writing. Literacy collections can

- Encourage teachers, parents, administrators, and students themselves to focus on reading and writing processes as well as products.

- Document the variety of reading and writing activities that students are engaged in at school, at home, and the community at large.

- Enable teachers, parents, administrators, and students themselves to examine growth in students' reading and writing abilities over time.

- Enable teachers and students to reflect on students' accomplishments and set goals for further improving students' reading and writing, thereby increasing students' feelings of ownership, motivation, and accomplishment.

- Facilitate the examination of students' reading and writing in different disciplines.

- Extend the amount of time devoted to authentic reading and writing in classrooms.

- Serve as an alternative to standardized testing.

- Encourage better communication among faculty and with administrators, parents, and other members of the public.

More specifically, the portfolio idea has been borrowed in recent years by innovative educators, especially as they embrace more constructivist positions (Bruner, 1990; Gardner, 1983) toward learning and knowledge acquisition. In relationship to reading and writing, there are two main types of portfolios: current-year portfolios and permanent portfolios. We will discuss both types. Each kind requires a greater selectivity about the information included and allows more in-depth analysis. If assessment is for program evaluation and policy setting rather than individual instructional decision-making, the portfolios of fewer students per classroom can be analyzed.

A single teacher can use portfolios to guide instructional planning for individual students. These portfolios are often more process-oriented than school or district portfolios. They also involve less quantification but more anecdotal notes than typical school or district ones. Classroom portfolios let teachers chart a child's progress across several drafts or several rereadings of a text. Teachers can encourage individual students to help decide what is selected for their portfolios, which can also include students' own reflections about their growth as literacy learners.

In contrast, the goal of school or district use of portfolios is to learn the effectiveness of the curriculum in general, not to gather information about each student. With district portfolios, random sampling procedures can be used effectively to keep the time and costs of evaluation reasonable (Shepard, 1990). District portfolios are also effective in staff development efforts.

The ways in which portfolios will actually influence classroom instruction for individual children have yet to be closely observed. Nevertheless, Tierney, Carter, & Desai (1991) have reported recent results with over fifty classroom teachers who have implemented portfolio assessment, which suggest several positive outcomes:

- Students from kindergarten to college appear empowered, enthralled, and appreciative of the opportunity to develop, share, and reflect upon their portfolios.

- Students take ownership of the portfolios and have a richer, more positive and expanded sense of their progress and goals as readers and writers across time.

- Assessment becomes collaborative rather than competitive.

- Parents are engaged in seeing first-hand what students are achieving.

- The literacy activities that students pursue alongside of school (e.g., hobbies) or outside of school (e.g., leisure time reading and writing, song writing) have a place to be represented in school.

- Teachers obtained a richer, clearer view of their students across time.

- Teachers negotiated a view of the student that is more fully informed in terms of what each individual child has achieved.

- Teachers have available to them records of what students are actually doing.

- Teachers have a vehicle for pursuing assessment practices that are student-centered and focus on helping the learners assess themselves.

- Administrators have a vehicle for pursuing audits of classrooms and individual performance that represents what their students and classes are doing (p.51)

Regrettably, few principals, district coordinators, or superintendents will nudge teachers to try portfolio assessment or develop other types of literacy collections. They will have to begin with individual efforts that gradually create a grassroots movement. In the rest of the chapter, we will address various kinds of literacy collections, what information needs to be collected in them, how to analyze them, how such analysis can influence instructional decision making, and how results can be shared.

literacy collections: characteristics of different kinds

At first, attempting portfolios or any other kind of literacy collection may seem like a mind-boggling task. But it doesn't have to be! Preparing literacy collections often simply means having students save their work for a period of time and then helping them select pieces that might go into their portfolios. Many teachers want to know how to develop the perfect portfolios before they start so they won't make any mistakes. But there is no foolproof method. Good portfolios are individual to each teacher, classroom, and student. While doing some reading can help to give you ideas about developing portfolios or other literacy collections, good ones are largely developed through trial and error and much risk-taking. Developing good portfolios means plunging in, trying out some things, revising them to work best for you and your students, and gradually getting to a point where you feel that the portfolios demonstrate what students are learning and provide you with the information you need to guide instruction.

We will define six types of literacy collections to help you understand that not everything is a portfolio. We will discuss reading and writing folders, current-year portfolios, permanent portfolios, assessment notebooks, literacy biographies, and literacy profiles. All of these types of literacy collections can be helpful in classrooms.

reading and writing folders

The messiest literacy collections, but potentially the richest sources of information, are students' ongoing reading and writing folders. These folders reveal the "cutting edges" of students' learning processes. A careful review of these folders can help to ensure that subsequent instruction is based on the needs of particular students, not simply what a curriculum guide recommends. We prefer to talk about reading and writing folders and to reserve the use of the term "portfolio" until we are talking about saving students' work over longer periods of time and after a selection process.

Students themselves can do much of the initial data collection and self-assessment of their own reading and writing folders. They can be asked to date all their work, keep all word devoted to a particular piece of reading or writing together, arrange materials in chronological order, and so on. If papers related to students' reading or writing have been sent home or are used in the regular classroom (for example, if students are in Chapter I or special education programs), you ought to periodically make photocopies of final products to keep in students' folders. Thus, students will have copies of all of their work so that at the end of each grading period, they can make lists of all the different kinds of reading and writing they do and select pieces for their current-year portfolios. Having students engage in such activities helps them begin to reflect on their own experiences and set goals for further learning.

By working on their folders students learn how it feels to receive attention for positive actions, which further encourages such efforts. We knew a third-grader who threw all her papers in the trash on the way home from school rather than endure her sense of failure when her parents looked at her work and poor grades. How much this child would have benefitted from keeping a reading and writing folder that helped her celebrate her successes and improve in the areas that caused her difficulty. Used in a caring classroom community, literacy collections can help students build self-esteem as readers and writers and develop a sense that they can begin to work to control and improve the quality of their own lives.

current-year portfolios

Portfolios have long been used by artists working in mediums such as graphic design, modeling, photography, musical composition, voice, sculpture, drawing, and movie production. These portfolios are reviewed by other professionals in the field who know what qualities they value. They do not necessarily use quantifiable evaluative indicators in their evaluation, nor is it assumed that each expert is using exactly the same criteria (Brandt, 1987).

Artists' portfolios contain examples of their finished products. Sometimes actual samples of their work are included; at other times audiotapes, videotapes, or photographs of their work are presented. They attempt to demonstrate the full range of their capabilities and allow observers to make up their own minds about the uniqueness and value of their talents. Portfolios often include rough drafts and the artists' own reflections about their work. This allows them to demonstrate their own creative growth over time. In the arts, this capacity to strive toward higher levels of creativity and excellence is highly valued.

By the end of a grading period, reading and writing folders can become quite full. In his folder, Lupe, a student in a Chapter I pull-out program, had three drafts of his desert poem, a web of what he learned about woolly mammoths from a library book, his questions for his woolly mammoth report, a scratch sheet on which he tried out some spellings, learning log entries on a chapter book his group was reading, his summary of what he learned from a safety assembly, a math paper, notes from two friends, some loose paper, and notes he took from a mini-lesson. Keeping all of these materials in his folder was becoming unmanageable for both Lupe and his teacher. At the end of each grading period, his teacher had what she called a "cleaning" of students' folders. She helped students select materials for their "current-year" portfolios; the remaining papers were taken home.

Students and teachers choose particular pieces from their folders (including all drafts) to include in current-year portfolios. Although portfolios can be maintained for each content area or across all content areas of thematic units, we will consider only reading/writing/literacy portfolios. Current-year portfolios are not usually kept with reading and writing folders. Teachers need to decide if students will have easy access to their portfolios at all times or if their access will be limited to certain times. This decision is likely to be affected by the degree to which the teacher wants students to have input into what is included in their portfolios.

Lupe's teacher first asked students to set aside any work they were sure that they did not want to be included in their Chapter I portfolio. Lupe set aside the math paper that must have gotten into his folder by mistake, the notes from his two friends, and the loose paper, since it was smudged. His teacher then asked students to organize the remaining work in their folders by placing final products or photocopies on top and drafts and rehearsal notes underneath. This work was then placed in students' current-year portfolios. The teacher also worked with students to place any other materials in their portfolio that particularly demonstrated their growth. At this point she encouraged Lupe to keep his spelling tryouts, although they were messy, because they demonstrated that he was beginning to learn to edit. Her anecdotal notes on children's reading and comprehension also went into the portfolios, along with photographs from any performances, such as plays, projects, and parent nights.

If she is having difficulty with a child's behavior or learning, Lupe's teacher finds current-year portfolios helpful in talking with parents or a student's classroom teacher, or at staffings if a child is being considered for special placement. The next step she would like to implement is to develop a method for summarizing each student's growth and then making new instructional plans. Informally, she has noticed that students are very interested in the progress they are making. She would like to confer with each of them about their progress and help them to set new goals.

Linda Rief (1990), an eighth-grade teacher at Oyster River Middle School in Durham, New Hampshire, has implemented just such a plan for involving her students in meaningful current-year portfolio self-assessment. For example, about one student's self-evaluation she states:

I don't have to be the sole evaluator of Nahanni's writing and reading. She's far better at it than I am. And the better she knows her own process as a writer and reader, the better she becomes at both. (p. 27)

Rief requires her students to write a minimum of five pages of rough draft writing per week. Near the end of each six-week period, students are asked to pick the two best pieces from their working folders for grading. She offers students the opportunity to work on reading and writing from their other classes and to include their work in their portfolios if they think the effort is among their best. She bases her grades on the goals set and achieved, as shown by the two pieces selected for the portfolio.

Three times a year students complete self-assessments of their processes and products. At this point Rief asks students to arrange their writing from the most effective to least effective and to evaluate it by considering several questions:

- What makes this your best piece?
- How did you go about writing it?
- What problems did you encounter?
- How did you solve them?
- What makes your most effective piece different from your least effective piece?
- What goals did you set for yourself?
- How well did you accomplish them?
- What are your goals for the next 12 weeks?

At the end of the year, Rief has students complete a reading/writing project that becomes the final piece in their portfolios. We agree with the idea that students include a culminating project, but we would allow students to select which one they wanted to include from those they had completed over the entire year.

permanent portfolios

The next type of literacy collection is permanent portfolios. By the end of the year, the amount of data in current-year portfolios can become unmanageable, especially as students' work accumulates from grade to grade. Permanent portfolios will be turned over to students' teachers for the next year. Because students' new teachers need to look at information on a number of students at the opening of the school year, the number of items in a permanent portfolio must be limited. Teachers may give students free or guided choices about what will go into their permanent portfolios. A teacher may ask students to include their best letter, learning log entry, story, and report, plus two other pieces of their own choosing. Summary sheets that explain the information available in the portfolios are helpful to other teachers who want to review them.

Lupe's teacher found that there was too much information in children's current-year portfolios by the end of the year to keep all of it. But she did want to retain some records because many students were in the Chapter I Program for two years before exiting. Her decision was to keep pre and post miscue inventories, pre- and post writing samples, and the students' educational plans. If she also developed summary sheets for the permanent portfolios, she could keep them as a record of children's performances in Chapter I and pass them to their next classroom teachers. The summary sheets would provide good openers about students who can soon transfer out of Chapter I with extra support from the classroom teacher or begin dialogue about children who will need to continue Chapter I assistance.

Another interesting example of how current-year portfolios can lead to permanent portfolios is *The Primary Language Record* (Barrs, 1990; Barrs et al., 1989). This assessment procedure and the accompanying instruments were developed by British educators over a period of four years. During the early part of the fall term, a teacher interviews each student about his reading and writing. The questions suggested as part of *The Primary Language Record* focus on a student's interests and attitudes toward reading and writing. During the rest of the fall term and into the early spring, the teacher records anecdotal records about a child on another form with a sensible, organized format. Near the end of the spring term, a teacher uses his anecdotal notes, plus other notes and work samples, to compose summative comments about each child as a reader and writer. During the summer term a teacher again holds a conference with the child's parents, makes any further updates that are needed, and sends information on to a child's new teacher for the fall. Although this instrument is called *The Primary Language Record,* we believe the procedures could be used with students of all ages.

Teachers need to consider what the balance between process and product observations, instruments, and work samples, should be in literacy collections that focus on reading and writing. You will also want to decide on the balance between teacher-selected, student-selected, and jointly selected pieces. Ultimately, through literacy collections you can communicate to parents, administrators, and other teachers about your educational philosophy, your knowledge of reading and writing, and your ability to encourage the literacy development of individual children.

Many educators consider collecting evidence of students' reading development more difficult than collecting evidence of students' writing. With reading you must audio- or videotape each student or make notes as each one reads. Students' comprehension, the "product," is also not easily assessed, especially if means other than multiple choice questions are used. To gather writing data a teacher need only have all students write and then collect the products. But the collection of writing samples is equally complex if a teacher also wants to collect data on each student's writing process and consider writing activities that are highly authentic and have less distinct beginning and ending times.

The following charts suggest possible instruments, observations of students' work, and procedures that might be included in reading portfolios. Since processes lead to products, many process measures may also become product measures.

Reading Process Measures

Metacognitive interviews.
Tapes of oral reading.
Self-assessments of processes.
Goal setting.
Strategies-I-Can-Use.
Photographs/videos of
    students reading.
Reading discussions.

Reading Product Measures

Data list of books read:
    Teacher or Student selected at home,
    school, both.
Written retellings.
Reading/learning log entries.
After reading projects:
    sketches, story maps, sociograms, etc.
Photographs of products:
    literacy related art, social studies,
    and science projects.
Videos of student plays.
Self-assessments of products.
Goal setting.
Parent responses to portfolios.

The next chart suggests possible instruments, observations, and procedures to include in writing portfolios. Of course, reading and writing portfolios can be combined.

Writing Process Measures

Hot topics list.
Metacognitive interviews.
Artwork, webs, etc. that assist
    rehearsal for writing.
Drafts: cross-outs, carets,
    other revision strategies
Evidence of spelling strategies.
Authors' Circle/peer response guides.
Audiotapes of Authors' Circle
    or peer conference groups.
Writer's memos.
Self-assessments of strategies.

Writing Product Measures

Writing samples: Teacher,
    Student, both selected.
Lists of pieces written:
    Types of writing.
    Where: home, school.
Self-assessments of products.
Analytic scoring of samples.
Editing strategies.
Goal setting.

Another excellent list of suggestions for inclusions in portfolios can be found in *Portfolio Assessment in the Reading-Writing Classroom* (Tierney, Carter, & Desai, 1991, p. 73). Although these are not reading or writing assessments per se, students might also include in their portfolios:

- Interest inventories.

- Lists of a student's favorite books and authors.

- Quotes and sayings the student likes.

- Other items or pictures the student selects that reveal important information.

The information a teacher wants to collect in portfolios may not be the same for every student. In reading you may want to focus on one student's self-corrections, or on another's growth in asking questions, making predictions, and so on. In writing you may want to focus on rehearsal techniques with some students, but with others tackle usage problems, and with still others content revision strategies. Students will probably work on more than one goal at a time, but not an overwhelming number. Setting and working on a few goals rather than just one is often necessary because not every literacy activity will fit a single goal. By having more than one goal, students can be more assured that a literacy activity will provide opportunities to work on at least one of their goals. As they achieve their goals and negotiate others over the course of a year, the focus of the information in a portfolio may change.

Another reason portfolios may not be exactly the same for every student is related to the stance a teacher takes toward student input into portfolios. When students have great input into the work that their portfolios contain, the results won't be alike. The portfolios will be as individual as the students themselves and their interests and talents in reading and writing.

We would like to suggest the following matrix as a way to decide whether information is valuable enough to include in students' portfolios. When making a decision, we try to keep two questions in mind: 1) What does this information reveal or demonstrate about a student's development? 2) How will this information help to make instructional decisions for this student?

A Matrix for Deciding What to Include in Portfolios

Information Source	What does this demonstrate about a student's development?	How will this information guide instructional decision-making?
1) Story maps	Understanding of story elements	Decide if need to spend more time on certain story elements
2) Student-selected poems	Student is learning to read in a new genre	Encourage student to read even more poems; read more poetry as part of teacher read-alouds; encourage student to write poems and show him various methods

A teacher might consider placing students' story maps in their portfolios. One map reveals little about development; but two or more story maps collected over a period of time will demonstrate development. If maps reveal that students are weak in particular areas, such as sequencing events or theme, a teacher can adjust his instruction accordingly. Or a teacher might notice that a child has decided to include a poem he has just learned to read in his portfolio. On the attached self-assessment, he writes that he "likes to read poems" and only learned about them this year. His teacher now knows that this is a positive developmental step she needs to build upon. She might decide to encourage him to read more poems and to include poetry in the next thematic unit. She also might decide to begin a series of mini-lessons on how to write poetry because she sees that this student and several others are interested.

In the large-scale use of literacy collections across an entire school district, teachers may want to agree upon the inclusion of particular items in portfolios to ensure that certain information will be collected, analyzed, and passed on from grade to grade. However, under these constraints, the value of students' input into selection of portfolio items is often overlooked or dropped. Thus, even when literacy collections are used on a large scale, we would encourage teachers to include in permanent portfolios at least one or two items selected by students. These may not be included in analytic scoring of the portfolios (they could perhaps make interrater reliability more difficult to achieve), but their inclusion adds to student ownership of the portfolio process. At the same time, although teachers may know that the agreed upon inclusions for permanent portfolios are limited, this need not stop them from encouraging students to keep more extensive current-year portfolios that are then simply pared down to meet the requirements for permanent portfolios. Other items in the current-year portfolio can be sent home at the end of the year.

assessment notebooks

Portfolios are most beneficial when students have many opportunities to select items. This will happen most frequently if students have easy access to their portfolios. Information in the portfolios should be relevant and easily understood by students themselves. This all sounds reasonable, but problems can begin to creep in.

Some teachers tell us that they would like to have all the information about each student in one place, that it becomes frustrating for them to consult several different sources in several places in the classroom: their anecdotal notes file, students' work folders, the grade book, reading inventories they gave, and so on. The portfolios might seem like the perfect place to keep everything; but we would suggest that this won't always work.

Teachers do collect information in forms that are not always relevant and meaningful to students. We feel, for example, that miscue analyses or results from the Emergent Reading/Writing Inventory do not belong in portfolios. What meaning do the scoring sheets have to students? Also, teachers do sometimes collect important information about students, but it will only help the child when filtered through an adult. A teacher won't want to keep notes on a student's family problems or calls to the home in a student's portfolio. Such information could be disruptive to the student's self-esteem. Teachers also make notes about instruction, but not all of these notes are meaningful to students either.

A better solution is for teachers to create assessment notebooks. Teachers have found it easy to do so by using a notebook with a divider for each child. Behind the divider are blank sheets to which anecdotal notes can be taped in chronological order. Also included are copies of any important information that won't necessarily be understood by the child. Information about reading that might be kept in an assessment notebook includes:

- Emergent reading inventories.

- Inventories of reading use.

- Notes on miscue patterns.

- Running records.

- Anecdotal notes, especially from reading conferences.

- Developmental checklists.

- Parent questionnaires and interviews.

- Standardized test scores.

Information about writing that a teacher might keep in an assessment notebook includes:

- Emergent writing inventories.

- Profiles of writing in process.

- Analysis of spelling development.

- Inventories of writing use.

- Status of the class.

- Anecdotal notes, especially from writing conferences.

- Developmental checklists.

- Parent questionnaires and interviews.

- Standardized test scores.

We are finding it most useful to keep as much information as possible in student portfolios. If need be, they can always be pared down. Students can benefit from looking over their interest inventories for changes, reading back through their reading and writing interviews for growth, and so on. It is only when information will seem foreign to students that we would put it in a separate assessment notebook. Such an approach encourages us, and the teachers we educate, to work harder to write more and more of their assessment information clearly and in ways understandable to students themselves.

literacy biographies

Literacy biographies (Taylor, 1990) are another type of literacy collection. A literacy biography spans the course of one or more years in a learner's life. In order to create a biography, a teacher collects anecdotal notes as a student is reading and writing and also the student's final products. At periodic intervals during the year, the teacher reflects on the data and writes a narrative description of the progress a student is making. It is these long narratives written by the teacher that most differentiate literacy biographies from regular current-year or permanent portfolios. They represent a teacher's effort to understand a child's literacy learning.

Taylor suggests that teachers begin by trying to write literacy biographies for only five students. She feels that the biographies provide an excellent staff development vehicle that enables teachers to learn about how to observe children's language development. We would tend to agree. Although valuable in helping teachers gain more in-depth knowledge about students' language development, keeping literacy biographies for whole classrooms of students on a regular basis may not be realistic. The idea should be reserved for settings in which rich data will help teachers refine their instruction.

literacy profiles

Literacy profiles capture the nature of students' literacy abilities at a particular time. We think of them as literacy "snapshots" that are verbal rather than visual. While student work and comments are an important part of literacy profiles, the compilation of profiles tends to involve much more selection and analysis by teachers than selection or self-assessment by students. Literacy profiles are useful in reading clinics or in staffings (see Chapter 8) where initial assessments of children's literacy difficulties are made over a short period of time to decide upon a plan of instruction. We much prefer the notion of literacy profiles over "case studies," a holdover from the medical model of remedial instruction.

Triangulation, in which data is collected from more than one source, is a very important concept in creating literacy profiles. To learn about a student's reading interests, a teacher might 1) have the student select something he would like to read from six to ten books on varying topics and at varying difficulty levels, 2) observe the student's choices when given choice time in the classroom: Does the student choose to read? What materials? and 3) ask the parents about their child's interest in reading at home. Information from all these sources helps to establish the student's interest in reading at this point. If the information collected is inconsistent, the teacher needs to keep examining the child's reading interest until he can explain it well.

In our university courses we encourage teachers to collect a wide range of data on students for literacy profiles, which include both reading and writing data. We ask teachers to collect the information in one-hour sessions over an eight-to-ten-week period. Of course, there are other, quicker ways to gather needed information. But teachers need to be careful not to wear students out or the data they gather could be inaccurate. Teachers can collect information on reading from several sources:

Interests:	Informal Interest Inventories
	Interest information from parents, teachers
	Classroom Reading Use
	Informal book selection activities
Strategies:	Reading Interview
	Emergent Reading/Writing Inventory
	Qualitative Reading Inventory
	Reading Miscue Inventory
	Assessments through instruction
	Parent and teacher interviews
	Anecdotal notes from classroom observations
Developmental Level:	Emergent Reading/Writing Inventory
	Qualitative Reading Inventory
	Reading Miscue Inventory
	Assessments through instruction
	Parent and teacher interviews
	Anecdotal notes from classroom observations
	Standardized test scores

Teachers collect information on writing from several sources as well:

Interests:	Informal Interest Inventories
	Interest information from parents, teachers
	Classroom Writing Use
	Lists of hot topics
	Pieces the student has already written
Strategies:	Writing Interview
	Emergent Reading/Writing Inventory
	Authoring Cycle Profile
	Assessments through instruction
	Parent and teacher interviews
	Anecdotal notes from classroom observations
Developmental Level:	Emergent Reading/Writing Inventory
	Authoring Cycle Profile
	Holistic analysis of final products
	Assessments through instruction
	Parent and teacher interviews
	Anecdotal notes from classroom observations
	Standardized test scores

All the information is used to compile a profile of the student as a reader and writer both inside and outside of school. The student's strengths are emphasized and areas needing further development explained. A profile ends with instructional recommendations that will be helpful to parents as they support their child's learning at home and to the classroom teacher or a special tutor. The profile has also proven very helpful when introduced as a part of staffings for students suspected of having particular learning problems.

A recent and interesting application of literacy profiles has been made by the School Programs Division of the Victorian Ministry of Education, Victoria, Australia (1990). Working with teachers, the division has compiled the *Literacy Profiles Handbook,* which suggests many literacy activities in whole language classrooms that can be used for collecting alternative assessment information. (These ideas correspond well to the "assessing through literacy events" section of this book.) In addition, the *Literacy Profiles Handbook* includes descriptors of broad behavioral "bands" for normal literacy development. These "bands" represent a way to create "norms" for alternative assessments. Thus, through careful observation rather than standardized tests, a teacher can determine the band in which a student is currently operating. Over time, students' movement through developmental bands can be documented using means that are much more authentic than standardized tests.

analyzing portfolios

To compile information for portfolios is one task, to interpret it another, especially if teachers' insights are to guide instruction. Currently, student self-assessments, teacher summaries, and analytic or holistic ratings are used to analyze portfolios. How each of these encourages reflection will be discussed in greater detail. What we want to emphasize is that methods for interpreting portfolios are not mutually exclusive. The use of multiple methods of analysis has the advantage of providing more than one perspective. A student's peer, a social studies teacher, the student, the parents, and the teacher who has helped the learner put together the collection may view and comment on the development demonstrated by a portfolio. The comments and conversations provide multiple perspectives on the student's literacy growth so that a much richer, more accurate picture of the student as a learner is possible.

student self-assessments

Engaging students in self-assessment of their own work in reading and writing folders, and subsequently in their emerging portfolios, encourages them to analyze and celebrate their own growth. In the process, students also develop many metacognitive insights into the strategies used by proficient readers and writers. In addition, student self-assessments work to gradually release responsibility for learning to students. Conferences with students over their self-assessments can add insights not revealed by the products alone that are very useful to teachers' instructional planning. In the "Teacher Reflection" at the end of this chapter, Gloria Kauffman and Kathy Short tell how they foster such self-reflection among Kauffman's students.

Student self-assessment can start by asking students to make simple counts of the work in their reading and writing folders: the number of rough draft pages they have written each week, the number of words they have added to a personal spelling list, the variety and number of items in different genres they have read. Students can also be asked to answer other self-evaluative questions. In reading: Why did you choose to read this book? Is it a challenge, just right, or an easy book for you? What did you talk over with your partner as you did buddy reading? What did this book make you think of? In writing: What new ways can you use to help organize your writing? How did you include ideas from the Authors' Circle in your revisions? What new spelling rule have you learned?

Daily self-assessments can gradually lead to assessments of more material over longer blocks of time. In reading: What genres have you been reading during this six weeks? Have you been reading a mix of challenge, just right, and easy books or lots of one kind? What has been the result? What new strategies for dealing with unknown words are you now able to use successfully and on a regular basis? How has your ability to retell information you have learned improved? In writing: What is your best piece from this six weeks? Why do you think it represents your best work? In what ways did you work on your goals this six weeks? In what ways do you think your writing is improving? Such self-assessment at the end of each grading period helps students set new learning goals and become more responsible for their own learning. These can lead up to students' self-assessments for their permanent portfolios.

At the end of the year, Joann Briggs, a fourth-grade teacher in Brighton, Colorado, has students do a self-assessment of the writing progress they have made over the course of the year. She then passes the portfolios on to students' teachers for the next year. Her students' comments show that, with practice, students are indeed capable of assessing their own writing growth.

Two students who have difficulty with reading and writing:

> •   I like to write better now. I think I'm a pretty good writer. Sometimes I have trouble choosing a topic. If I don't finish my story, I go back and read it again.

> •   I think I have improved since third grade. I'm writing longer stories. I'm indenting my stories. I reread my stories more than once and look for my weak points. I think writing is the best subject.

Two good students:

- I think of myself as a good writer. When I'm writing, I try to use my best choice of words so it is not so boring. One strategy that I use a lot when I'm rereading my story is I try pretending I am someone else reading my story. Sometimes I'm not trying my best, but sometimes I am doing my best. My mother and father really like what I write, and I hope I don't lose my writing talent.

- My writing skills have been good. I write a lot of stories. Most of my stories are for kids to read and get ideas. I want kids to be smart and write.

  Sometimes it's hard and sometimes it's easy. All the teachers I had showed me a lesson for writing. If you like writing, read too because it will help you with your ideas and writing skills. As I look back at my stories, I wish I never had some words and added more. But as I grow up, I'll be a good writer I'll look back at my stories.

Briggs also asks students to take their portfolios home for parents to review and students write letters that introduced their portfolios. Briggs includes her own letter to parents requesting that they look through the portfolio, read the letter from their child and their child's end-of-the-year summary, and respond in writing to their child about his or her portfolio and work as a writer. The responses from parents have given Briggs new insights into parents' levels of literacy development and languages used at home. She now plans to have parents respond to the portfolios more than once a year.

In *Evaluating Literacy: A Perspective for Change*, Anthony et al. (1991) suggest an intriguing way to engage students in self-assessment of portfolios, to encourage them to assume more responsibility for their learning, and to communicate results to parents. They have worked with teachers to develop student-led portfolio conferences. As time for parent conferences nears, students pore through their folders to find items they want to show to their parents for their current-year portfolios. The teacher often assists in this process, gaining many insights through the work children choose. Students are encouraged to show their parents not only successful work but also other work that demonstrates the skills they are trying to develop. Students write letters to their parents inviting them to the conferences and outlining the information they want to show them. As time for the session nears, students rehearse their portfolio conferences so they will go smoothly. Depending on classroom size, four to six student-led conferences can occur at a time. Parents who have additional questions about their child's work can ask to have a separate private conference with the teacher. The experience of Anthony et al., is that most parents are very pleased with the student-led conferences and few ask for additional time with the teacher alone.

teacher summaries

Portfolios can also begin with a teacher's summary which is particularly useful in permanent portfolios. Students' teachers for the coming year can quickly read the summaries and then, if they are interested, easily look at students' specific samples. The California Assessment Development Program has developed teacher summary sheets (Cooper & Davies, 1990). Teachers must check off, and then give a holistic rating to, each type of inclusion in portfolios. The bottom of the form has a place for teacher comments. This format allows teachers to scan the summaries to pick up students' general problem areas and then turn to samples in the portfolio for additional information.

Another procedure for gathering and writing yearly summaries can be found in *The Primary Language Record* (Barrs et al., 1989). During the fall term, teachers discuss with parents their son's or daughter's literacy development. The focus is to find out about children's uses of literacy in the home and community and to give parents an opportunity to raise any concerns they have. In the fall, teachers have conferences with students about their literacy in both reading and writing. During the spring term, teachers make observations of students as language users in three areas: oral language, reading, and writing. They record what they have noticed in each child's development and what experiences and teaching have helped or would help development in each area. The questions asked on the form emphasize the close link between assessment and ongoing instruction. Not only does the child's main teacher respond to these questions, but any other teachers involved with the child also add comments. During the summer term, parents are asked to comment in writing on the record, and literacy conferences are again held with children over their progress. The final section asks teachers to do any updating, since the time that the spring section of the record was completed, that may be helpful to next year's teachers.

holistic and analytic scoring of portfolios

In addition to the more qualitative ways of analyzing portfolios, methods are being developed to do more quantitative analysis. Such quantitative analysis seems to be important when portfolios are used to evaluate program effectiveness. Most of the quantitative methods for scoring literacy collections are variations of holistic and analytic methods originally developed for scoring writing samples. Quantification of literacy collections often means that more constraints are placed upon what is included in them.

In the Hawaii Kamehameha Elementary Education Program (KEEP), analytic scoring of current-year portfolios is being tried. Teachers are being asked to include five specific items in portfolios: 1) a questionnaire on attitudes toward reading and

Reading/listening comprehension			
Personal response	1	(2)	3
Response to literature—story frame	(1)	2	3
Voluntary reading			
Contact with books	1	2	(3)
Preferences	1	2	(3)
Genres	1	2	(3)
Appropriate choices	1	2	(3)

Table 9.1   Kehau's profile sheet

writing, 2) a response to literature, 3) a sample of the student's writing, 4) a running record, and 5) a voluntary reading log.

A checklist has been devised for each of the five assessments. Teachers use the checklist results to develop final profile sheets on each student. Ratings on the final profile sheet range from 1 to 3. A 1 means that a student is working below grade level; a 2, scoring at grade level; and a 3, working above grade level. Teachers derived criteria for grade levels (also called benchmarks) from a state curriculum guide, a widely used standardized achievement test, and the scope-and-sequence charts of several recent basal reading programs.

Table 9.1 illustrates the second part of the final profile sheet for Kehau, a second-grader (Au et al., 1990).

The profile sheet lists the criteria (or benchmarks) for reading/listening comprehension and voluntary reading in second grade. These criteria are applied to the five items in each student's portfolio. In communicating a personal response to her reading, Kehau's teacher rates her as functioning at grade level. In her response to literature (defined as being able to write about key story elements, including theme, and to draw relationships between story ideas), Kehau received a 1, meaning that she has yet to meet the standard for second grade. In all areas of voluntary reading, the teacher gave Kehau 3's, meaning that she was above average in her contact with books, preferences, genres, and appropriate choices.

Another example of analytic scoring of portfolios is from the final step in the Vermont Writing Assessment (Mills, 1989; Vermont Department of Education 1988, 1989). Prior to this final step, districts have submitted two prompted writings and a best piece by each student. These are all analytically scored by state level teams of teachers using the same criteria. Then smaller teams of outside teachers visit each school to complete onsite assessments of fourth- and eleventh-grade student portfolios. Portfolios are randomly selected and rated on a 1 to 8 scale for each of fourteen questions. There is also room for evaluators to add additional comments. The questions used to guide the analysis of the portfolios are as follows:

1. Does the writing reflect a sense of authentic voice?

2. Does the writing reflect an awareness of different audiences?

3. Does the writing demonstrate logical sequence of thought?

4. Does the writing show understanding of prose or poetic structure?

5. Does the writing offer evidence of sentence/paragraph revision?

6. Does the writing exhibit editing for spelling and syntax?

7. Has the author used prewriting strategies or techniques?

8. Has the author discussed his/her writing with others?

9. Has the author attempted work in different genres/topics?

10. Has the author produced a final copy and/or manuscript work?

11. Does the folder include work from various courses of study?

12. Does the folder follow a pattern or plan for the reader?

13. Have teachers been involved in the preparation of work?

14. Has the school program material been used as part of the writing?

In order for a school to get ready for the state team visit, all students' portfolios are reviewed by a student peer and a faculty/staff conferee. At the high school level, all teachers are included as potential conferees, not just English teachers. Both the student peer and the teacher conferee assess portfolios using the same questions the formal evaluators use. The only difference is that they use the more informal rating criteria of "somewhat, consistently, and extensively" rather than an eight-point scale. The intent at this level is to encourage dialogue about the portfolios, not to worry too much about reliability on a quantitative measure. Data from the individual writing samples submitted earlier to the state and ratings on the writing portfolios are combined to help individual districts and the state determine what further efforts are needed to improve the quality of students' writing.

A limited number of additional examples of portfolio assessment exist (Cooper & Davies, 1990; Lewis & Lindaman, 1989; Mathews, 1990; Simmons, 1990). Educators need to be particularly careful in reading these examples to decide if the "literacy collections" are truly portfolios. It is also helpful to think about the authenticity of the literacy events from which data have been gathered. The extent to which student selection and self-assessment have been important considerations in determining what is included in portfolios is also worth pondering.

It must be emphasized that all the forms of school, district, and state level alternative assessment we have discussed have only recently been implemented. Procedures may have to be further debugged. Decisions about how much staff development is necessary in implementing new assessment procedures for portfolios and other literacy collections will have to be confirmed. Finally, districts will need to compile results and then decide how findings from portfolios and other literacy collections will influence curricular change.

other issues in implementing literacy collections

Several additional issues need to be addressed before the benefits of various kinds of literacy collections can be realized, but they may be thought of more as shifts in perspective and procedures teachers will need to make than real problems. We will discuss five important areas: the perception that literacy collections are more expensive than norm-referenced tests, finding time to collect and analyze data, developing ways to analyze peer collaborations as part of Reading and Writing Workshops, taking good contextual notes, using literacy collections to fill out report cards, and getting teachers more involved in making their own decisions about literacy collections.

expense

The analysis of literacy collections at the program or district level is expensive but not necessarily any more so than standardized tests. Money is often needed to pay raters for their time, and once data are rated, alternative assessments often require more sophisticated software packages and computer time to aggregate data. In addition, funds are needed to provide staff development in areas that are found to be weak. Each of these potential needs ought to be talked through before a district embarks upon an alternative assessment program. We would argue that the money is well spent if it leads to more focused instruction. Another approach would be for policy makers to consider testing less frequently, thereby saving money that could be used to develop and score more authentic tests at strategic intervals.

Sampling also needs to be considered as a valid research technique that can be applied to the analysis of literacy collections at the program level. For example, if portfolios are to guide decision making about curriculum for each learner, then it is best to analyze individual portfolios. However, if the desired goal is to find out in general how a program is working, then random sampling will work: although all students keep portfolios, only a random sample is fully analyzed. This is very important to consider since it can result in real cost savings. During the 1989–1990 school year, the Seacoast Educational Services of Somerworth, New Hampshire, a consortium of twelve school districts, collected and analyzed the portfolios of fifth, eighth, and eleventh graders by randomly selecting a representative subset (approximately 1,500) of the approximately 4,000 students in the population (Simmons, 1990). These results gave the district information about the writing behaviors of students at a global level. The value of the sampling was that it assessed general problems at various grade levels so that appropriate instruction and staff development adjustments could be made.

Shepard (Johnson, 1991) summarizes these suggestions about cost considerations:

> Cost is a factor. Authentic assessments are very judge/observer intensive compared with standardized assessments which can be run through an optical scanner. Authentic testing is still possible, however, if policy makers would be willing to test less. Rather than testing every student in every grade on every subject, authentic assessments in key areas would be given to a sampling of students and grade areas. The trade-off between quantity and quality is worthwhile, given the corruptibility of standardized tests and their negative effect on teaching stimulating content to students. (p. 2)

time to collect and analyze data

We have made numerous suggestions throughout this book about ways to find time to collect and analyze observations about students' reading and writing. Four suggestions can be applied to literacy collections: 1) enlist students' help to do some of the data collecting and reflecting themselves, 2) plan so that there are times when students are working independently and you can observe and take notes, 3) weed items from your literacy collections if you are not using them to guide instructional decision making, 4) develop a workable plan for reviewing literacy collections on a regular basis for curricular planning. *Portfolio Assessment in the Reading-Writing Classroom* (Tierney, Carter, & Desai, 1991) contains an interview in which the authors discuss creative ways they have seen teachers work to deal with potential time and management issues.

At first, the development and review of literacy collections may seem overwhelming, especially to middle school teachers who see large numbers of students. We would agree that the idea of portfolios seems difficult to implement if you see 120 to 150 students per day and groups change at the semester. Under such conditions, personal knowledge of students as individuals and learners is difficult to come by, let alone keep track of on an ongoing basis. The idea seems much more feasible if middle school teachers work in reasonably small teams, say four teachers, with 100 to 120 students for the year. With all the new uses of reading and writing as tools for learning in areas like science and math, it makes sense for teachers in these subjects to be equally involved in developing literacy collections. In such teams, individual teachers can each take primary responsibility for the literacy collections of 25 to 30 students. Teachers can help students contribute work samples, administer agreed-upon literacy assessments, and take anecdotal notes. A single assessment notebook (containing anecdotal notes, status of the class sheets, and so on) could be kept by the team and would allow them to carry on "written conversations" about students' progress. A reading specialist could then work with all team members when they need higher levels of expertise and additional ideas about ways to help students develop as literacy learners.

growth in ability to work collaboratively

An important goal of literacy collections at the classroom level is to celebrate students' uniqueness, not just to see how they compete with or compare to others. Being overly concerned about whether all work in literacy collections represents individual achievement is an indicator that too much emphasis is probably being placed upon competitiveness and comparisons among students. We would prefer that portfolios include information about learners' ability in areas like using suggestions and giving helpful feedback. Our basic interest is to encourage students to learn to work well together to solve complex problems and not just to compete.

Judy Jindrich, an eighth-grade English teacher in the Littleton, Colorado public schools was not pleased with the quality of her students' peer conferences. She struggled with several solutions and came up with an idea for monitoring peer conference groups. The handouts she developed take students through the thinking and intercommunicational processes she would like to model for them. The class is divided into groups of four to five students. In each group, one student is the author, two or three are listeners, and the last student is the observer who monitors the group's activities. As questions and comments are made to the author, the observer records a slash on the form next to the type of interaction engaged in. Thus, for each author's piece a form is filled out. The form, adapted from *Sharing Writing* (Spear, 1988), contains the following information with one block for each member of the group. Challenging, the most difficult kind of response to make, is further divided into 9 types, each of which can be marked.

Name _____

    A. Sharing writing _____

    B. Paraphrasing/Reflecting _____

    C. Drawing out _____

    D. Connecting _____

    E. Supporting _____

    F. Challenging _____

        Defining terms _____   Clarifying _____

        Reviewing _____   Giving examples _____

        Comparing _____   Testing validity _____

        Citing exceptions _____

        Finding alternatives _____

        Piggybacking ideas _____

When the group finishes responding to a piece, the monitor writes a summary of what she believes went well in terms of the group's responses and what needs more work. After the form is completed, students switch roles before responding to the next author's piece and filling out another sheet. After the session, students are asked as a group to reflect upon what went well in the group and what needs improvement. These sheets can be photocopied, placed in students' writing folders, and used to write summaries and formulate goals as part of student portfolios. Over time, they can demonstrate important development in the ability to collaborate.

the need for contextual notes

One source of concern about whether literacy collections represent individual effort is the frequent lack of contextual notes for work included in such collections. These notes can add greatly to your interpretation of the products in current work folders or portfolios. By recording good anecdotal notes you can capture the strategies a student used during a process and his or her feelings about it. You can record who was involved in interactions and the quality of their exchanges. Students can also be asked to write down details about the context themselves.

In taking good contextual notes you need to consider

- Date of interaction, beginning and ending times.
- What the task is.
- Who is working together.
- What each student's role is in a group.
- What the teacher's role is the exchange was if he had one.
- Why a student took a very long time to finish an activity.

This kind of detail is extremely helpful in team situations in which two or more teachers are developing a collection of anecdotal notes on the children they teach. Teachers who were not present can easily understand the nature of the exchanges that went on.

links between literacy collections and report cards

As we discussed in Chapter 8, it is possible to make close links between assessment data and report cards, but many teachers still feel constrained by old norms about grading. Teachers are looking for new ways to talk about students' progress other than using the standard report terms that are sometimes simply the names of subject areas. Often literacy collections can lead to changes in what report cards measure, the terminology used, and the rating systems adopted.

Literacy collections also suggest new possibilities for helping parents gain insight into their children's educational progress (Flood & Lapp, 1989). Current report card evaluations focus on products of what has been learned and on comparing one child's performance to other students. But when a teacher goes over a portfolio with parents, they can follow the processes the child used to get to the products. Portfolios also tend to offer greater flexibility about what items are used to make decisions, so that a student has a chance to display skills he believes are unique assets.

At its most basic, assessment focuses on analyzing students' strengths and weaknesses to guide future learning. The advantage of literacy collections is that they can encompass a wider variety of standards and focus on processes as well as products. As a result, there is much more to observe and talk about. Let us review two examples: one in which the teacher reviews a student's reading/writing folder with the parents at a parent conference; the other in which the teacher sends children's portfolios home at the end of each quarter.

Dennis was the oldest of four children. His parents, who were administrators in a charitable organization, often had to work in the evenings, and they would take the children with them. As a result, Dennis would come to school quite tired because the family had come home late the night before. He also simply missed school fairly often. His parents were aware and concerned that, as a first grader, he had not done well in learning to read or write. With their busy schedules they found it hard to set aside time to read with Dennis, but they had gotten him some workbooks to practice his writing and spelling.

Dennis's second-grade teacher began the year by having each child start a reading and a writing folder. Since Dennis was a very reluctant writer, his teacher began by engaging Dennis and a few others in written conversations. Answering questions or asking them himself made generating content easy for Dennis; he could now concentrate on how to represent the sounds he heard in the words he wanted to write. He could also sometimes look at what his teacher had written to borrow from her correct spellings. Dennis gradually began to write more on his own and to risk inventing spellings. He was introduced to the idea of writing his own book, and by the end of the grading period had published two: *My Teddy Bear* and *Calling the Police*. He had also worked to read several predictable books, which he listed in his reading folder and made a tape of one to play for his mom and dad at parent conferences.

Using these items in his folder, Dennis's teacher began to talk with his parents about the growth she was seeing in his writing, especially in his attitudes toward writing, getting more on paper, and attempting to spell for himself. In the final published versions of his books, Dennis's text was much more readable, both to himself and others. The folder also contained a picture of Dennis holding his first published book. The teacher talked about how the parents might initiate written conversations with Dennis, exchange notes, and encourage him to write stories. She talked about ways to help him hear sounds in words and how to encourage him to invent spellings without placing undue emphasis on correctness. The teacher explained that these activities would be much more meaningful to Dennis than the workbooks. He simply needed to have writing supplies—paper, pencils, felt-tip pens, scissors and tape—easily available to him. She used the audiotape to talk about the kinds of books that Dennis liked to read, about how important it was for someone to read with Dennis each day, and how a library card could be attained for Dennis and other books selected.

Dennis's literacy collection from the first grading period allowed his teacher and parents to discuss his progress as a reader and writer in more depth than merely reviewing his grades and concluding that he needed to "work harder." The parents learned about the instructional strategies the teacher was trying to emphasize with Dennis and the growth he was making. And she was also able to share some specific ways the parents could better support Dennis's literacy development at home. As the year progressed, Dennis's current-year portfolio let her confirm his continued growth at other parent conferences.

Kathy Hoerlein, a third-grade teacher in Aurora, Colorado, has been experimenting with a somewhat different method of communicating with parents. She sends students' portfolios home with a letter asking parents to respond to her questions. The third quarter portfolios included three entries: children's choice of one story from those they had written; writing they had done in reading; a third piece that was either a literature log entry, learning log entry, or journal entry. Before their portfolios went home, students also filled out self-evaluations. They were asked to respond to four questions about both their reading and their writing. Here are the questions and Michael's answers.

1) These are some things I have improved in for reading/writing.

R: I've mostly improved in book shares.

W: Making a longer story and an interesting story.

2) These are things I do well in reading/writing.

R: Listening and sometimes good and new questions.

W: I used to forget punctuations and sometimes quotations.

3) This is a problem I have in reading/writing.

R: I don't get some papers in, in time.

W: If I go to fast, I forget capitals.

4) This is what I plan to work on in reading/writing next quarter.

R: Not talking or walking around the room.

W: Take my time and don't rush.

Hoerlein also writes her own comments on each child's self-reflection, so that when portfolios go home, the parents see their child's and the teacher's responses. In Michael's case, Hoerlein wrote several responses to Michael's reflections on his reading. About his comment that he listens and sometimes adds good questions, she wrote:

> T: You are participating more in reading group and I know you are a better listener.

In response to Michael's new goal that he's going to work on not talking or walking around the room, she wrote:

> T: This is right and I know you can better use your time. As another goal, how about writing books down on your book chart?

Hoerlein asks parents to comment on their child's reading and writing progress and on the entire portfolios. Here are comments from two parents.

Reading progress:

> P1: Natalie reading very well. (English is this parent's second language.)

> P2: I found Justin reading autobiographic books, which was a nice change from the Hardy Boys. He has improved and seems to know where he is weak.

Writing progress:

> P1: Need to practice spelling and handwriting.

> P2: Progressing but still needs practice. Will start one letter a week writing at home to help him with writing skills.

Portfolio comments in general:

> P1: This is a great idea. I wish every class would do the same things. I'm try my best to help my children on learning. But sometimes it seem to be very difficult. Because English is also my second language. I'm try to let Natalie use dictionary hopefully it will help her.

> P2: Excellent idea, because it involves the student's view of himself, it also teaches him how to set goals, that he can work at accomplishing.

Hoerlein uses student comments about the portfolios to plan the direction of her instruction. Parent comments give her a sense of the literacy within students' homes. During parent-teacher conferences, she discusses the portfolios further, describing how they add in-depth information to report card grades (see Chapter 8). In these conferences, or as part of other parent-teacher forums, she can praise the positive strategies she sees parents using or engage parents in considering better alternatives when their suggestions are counterproductive to children's progress. Now that Hoerlein knows that Parent 1 is a second-language speaker who emphasizes her children's acquisition of skills in English, she can help this parent think through all the other strategies that her daughter could use to figure out new words besides going to the dictionary.

Tierney, Carter, & Desai (1991) review further advice on the use of portfolios for grading, items to include in portfolios, and how to manage them. They also enumerate several ideas used by teachers representing a wide variety of grade levels and curricula in their research on portfolio assessment (see pp. 45-51). In many ways their suggestions are similar to those we have described, but we believe it is helpful to read and critique several different portfolio assessment procedures to find the process that will work best for you.

involving teachers in developing literacy collections

We are often asked to offer workshops on assessment. Teachers and administrators expect that we will bring the alternative assessment ideas and instruments we have developed and help teachers learn to use them in one or two sessions. Is this valuable? To a degree, yes, because it provides teachers with models of classroom assessment instruments and allows us to demonstrate the thinking that went behind their development. But, sometimes we leave these sessions uncertain about whether teachers will assume ownership of their assessments. If assessment is to serve as a guide to instruction, then teachers must be allowed to make it work to fit their own students' instructional needs and contexts. In fact, the ideas and instruments developed in this book and in the handbook may have already done too much thinking for you.

Although it takes time, the benefits of involving teachers more fully in the assessment process, including instrument development, are many (Hiebert & Calfee, 1989). You will understand instruments and procedures better if you have helped to create or to revise them according to your own experiences and knowledge of the reading and writing processes. Working on them will help to clarify your theories of each process and what behaviors you value. Decisions resulting from such creative efforts will often lead to the discovery among teachers, administrators, and parents of significant shared concepts. When you are involved in assessment development and tryouts, you also sharpen your ability to observe and your curiosity about instructional practices that will help students develop in areas you see as important (Stock & Robinson, 1987).

Valencia, McGinley, & Pearson (1990) have developed a scheme that may help you think about the literacy collections you are—or could be—implementing and how these collections could be improved. An examination of your plans will help to ensure that your assessments include a variety of procedures and forms linking assessment to actual instruction. Valencia et al. suggest that alternative assessment strategies be judged on five continuums, which we have adapted as follows:

Focus			
	discrete skills		holistic
Degree of authenticity			
	low		high
Decision making			
	teacher	collaborative	student

Structure			
	structured	semi-structured	spontaneous
Form			
	samples	interviews	observations

There is no right or wrong end to these continuums. The five do, however, act as guides for thinking through the meaning behind each type of assessment you are using and looking for other alternatives you have not yet considered. This is the kind of careful planning that should go into developing literacy collections.

These five continuums can be used to analyze a teacher's assessment program. Let's apply them to the work of a special reading teacher who, with her principal's support, has designed her job so that she teaches students within their regular classrooms. What she teaches is decided collaboratively with the classroom teacher. As you might expect, some classroom teachers are very involved with this special reading teacher in planning and offering instruction and others are not.

This teacher has decided on three key ways to develop literacy collections that guide her instructional decision making. Early in the fall, she oversees administration of a standardized cloze test to all students in the building. From the results of this test, she tentatively selects the students with whom she will work. She keeps these scores from year to year in students' permanent portfolios so that she can monitor students' progress from one year to the next. As part of thematic units taught within the classroom, she usually uses some form of literature log. By reading the logs she can decide if she is pacing lessons well, if she needs to provide more background information on certain topics, or if she needs to teach a particular reading strategy. Children select literature log entries for their current-year portfolios. Her third method of assessment is to hold conferences with students and take anecdotal notes in a conference log. Each class has an assessment notebook with a log page for each student. She fills out the log sheet each time she confers with a student. In some of the classrooms, the regular teachers are also holding conferences and filling in logs for the assessment notebook. After a class period, the special reading teacher tries to conference with the regular classroom teacher about her observations of specific children. At present, she does not record notes about these teacher-to-teacher conferences.

Now let's consider this special reading teacher's procedures for compiling literacy collections using the five parameters we have adapted from Valencia et al. The first continuum, *focus,* attempts to identify areas the language assessments are trying to measure. Is an instrument or procedure focusing on students' knowledge of isolated use of skills and conventions of language? Or are students engaged in tasks that involve using language systems and strategies in a holistic, integrated way?

At present this teacher is focusing her literacy assessment program on portfolios that monitor students' progress as readers. By using the cloze test and listening to children read during conferences, she is focusing her assessment on whether students are using the three language cueing systems in an integrated way. She has chosen not to focus on students' development of isolated reading skills, such as pronouncing all word endings correctly or being able to retell details. This emphasis on students' construction of meaning seems somewhat stronger than the emphasis she places on comprehension after reading. She monitors comprehension only through literature logs, but there are many other activities she could use to collect information about students' comprehension after reading. In addition, the focus of her literacy collections is students' reading but could be enlarged to include students' writing if her goal is to examine students' literacy development as both readers and writers.

The second continuum, *authenticity,* concerns the meaningfulness and relevance of an assessment instrument or procedure to students' lives and the degree to which it is similar to real-life literacy tasks. (See Chapter 2 for an extensive discussion of authenticity.) The assessments this teacher uses have differing degrees of authenticity. The cloze test she administers at the beginning of the school year is a relatively unauthentic assessment. Cloze does not represent a literacy task found in real life; we don't normally run across passages in which every fifth word is a blank. Engagement in the cloze activity does not arise naturally as part of a thematic unit; instead it is assigned by the teacher without linking it to any ongoing study. On a more positive note, however, the cloze test does not take a long time to administer and thus instruction is only interrupted for a short while. Results can be obtained quickly and at least provide gross indicators of children who may be having reading problems.

A more authentic measure this teacher might consider would be to distribute the previous spring a teacher judgment rating scale that contains criteria relating to children's actual classroom reading performance. This would be a more authentic assessment because it asks a teacher to make judgments about students' ability to perform real literacy tasks in the classroom. An example of such a rating scale can be found in *Literacy Assessment: A Handbook of Instruments* (Rhodes, 1993). Information from rating scales can be passed to next year's teacher. If mobility in a school is high, however, this idea, though more authentic, may not be practical, because so many students would be new and have no teacher ratings.

Literature logs are the most authentic measure this teacher uses because they are a part of ongoing instruction in the classroom. Conferring with children and having them read orally is also authentic when done as part of Reading Workshop. However, in the upper elementary grades, listening to students read can become less authentic as students become self-conscious about reading while others may be listening.

The third continuum, *decision making,* concerns who has decision-making power over what assessments are used and what judgments are made. On the left of the continuum are teacher-selected assessments in which all assessment of progress is based on teacher judgment. At the center of this continuum are collaborative assessments, and at the far right student self-assessments. This reading teacher is working gradually to share her decision-making power. Although she does coordinate the cloze test in the fall, in sharing the conference logs with teachers she is attempting to urge classroom teachers themselves to share in decision making in response to their observations of student growth and their sense of what instruction will best fit students' needs.

Currently, this teacher is not sharing decisions about assessment with students themselves. Instituting mini-lessons that ask students to reflect on certain qualities of their literature logs or learning logs would help them to develop metacognitive abilities and learn to reflect on their own learning. She might think about having students set reading goals and make their own self-assessments of their progress during each grading period.

Structure, the fourth continuum, refers to the number of directions or conditions that are required to carry out an assessment. Along this continuum, assessment procedures and activities can be structured, semi-structured, or spontaneous. As tasks become less structured, they provide greater latitude for variety in students' responses and require more personal input from teachers and more interpretation. This teacher's use of the cloze test each fall is very structured. There are exact procedures to be followed in giving the cloze test, and answers to test questions are easily scored right or wrong. Her listening to children read is a semi-structured assessment, especially if children are choosing their own books. The literature logs are again semi-structured. The teacher does not tell the students what to write, but she does tell them that they need to write at least twice a week. If the teacher also kept anecdotal notes about books students are reading on their own and the connections they make between books and life events, she could collect more spontaneous assessment information.

Form, the fifth continuum, refers to the general type of assessment chosen—collecting samples, doing interviewing, or making observations—and its durability. Different types of assessments constrain what information is collected and how permanent a product is obtained. This teacher attempts to use a variety of forms to collect assessment information. The cloze test results in the collection of concrete, durable samples that can be scored and results judged by others. The literature logs again are a concrete, reasonably durable collection of samples. Her use of reading conferences is really a type of interviewing and observing. Anecdotal notes of the conferences are somewhat durable, but they do not capture all of the nuances of the events and, in this sense, provide less permanent records.

We want to reemphasize that there are no right or wrong ends to these continuums. They simply represent different options from which teachers may choose in developing and balancing the effectiveness of the literacy collections they design for their classrooms. As we have illustrated, the continuums become useful guides for thinking through improvements that would make teachers' classroom assessment programs truly exemplary.

In their "teacher reflection," Gloria Kauffman and Kathy Short reflect upon their journey toward developing a portfolio assessment process that would work in Kauffman's classroom. Kauffman was selected as the 1989 Teacher of the Year by CELT (Center for the Expansion of Language and Thinking), a parent group of teachers Applying Whole Language. CELT is composed for the most part of educators in higher education or administrative school district positions. At the time Kauffman wrote this teacher reflection with Short, she was a third-grade teacher in Millersburg, Indiana, a small rural community having a large Mennonite population and a highly regarded private Mennonite college nearby. Currently, Kauffman is living and teaching in Tucson, Arizona.

Short is an assistant professor of language and culture at the University of Arizona. She has worked with Kauffman as a teacher/researcher pair for several years and is a CELT member.

Since getting to know their work with portfolios, we have been following with great interest their development and refinement of portfolios as a vehicle for students' reflections on their own learning. Their work illustrates how portfolios can truly be implemented to inform and improve the quality of instructional decision making in the classroom and students' learning.

Kauffman and Short have chosen to use the word "evaluation" rather than "assessment." They prefer "evaluation" to suggest that teachers need "to value" students' work. We chose "assessment" because "evaluation" for us is so tied to grading and making judgments. Reading Kauffman and Short's piece will give you a chance to decide for yourself which term you prefer.

Self-evaluation portfolios: a device to empower learners

Gloria Kauffman and Kathy Short

As a classroom teacher in a processed centered curriculum, I have constantly reexamined evaluation. For five years I explored evaluation from a teacher's perspective and began to realize that it is not the same as grades and accountability. Evaluation is a gathering of information needed to provide insights into development and instruction so that students can take the next step forward in learning. What I needed was a systematic way of gathering and recording that information. I began using field notes, checklists, anecdotal notes and letters from children. I felt good about the information these devices provided, but I realized that the perspective was my perspective about the students. I needed a stronger system for children looking at themselves as learners.

The children were already writing reflections in their literature logs. They wrote letters to their parents on their progress as learners that went home in their report cards. The class spent lots of time with oral reflections and sharing. But the missing component was a curricular structure to support children in their self-evaluation findings. That curricular structure emerged with the implementation of self-evaluation portfolios.

The portfolios are an opportunity for children to step back and take a look at themselves over time as readers and writers. Portfolios for us are a collection of work that reflects our growth as writers and readers. We carefully select work that reflects our efforts, improvements, processes, strengths and needs as writers and readers.

The students' selections show their growth over time and their range of thinking and exploring. For each item chosen they write a reflection about why they've selected that particular item for their portfolio.

They then step back to write a broad statement about their current understandings of themselves as readers and writers. This whole process is supported by a great deal of brainstorming, sharing, and thinking among class members.

We put together self-evaluation portfolios at the end of each nine weeks. This process of gathering, sharing, and reflecting takes anywhere from a week to ten days. We take time from our regular reading and writing activities to see where we've come from and where we want to go.

When I asked my third-grade class what they saw as the purpose of portfolios, they immediately responded, "To view yourself. To push your thinking. A diary of yourself as a writer and reader. To see yourself as a learner better."

We begin the self-evaluation process by first focusing on ourselves as writers because we have concrete evidence of our growth as writers. Once we have a grip on ourselves as writers it is easier to understand ourselves as readers. This process is difficult because reading and writing are so interconnected for us, but we initially separated the processes in order to focus and see our growth.

Children start their portfolios by gathering all their work as writers. We want to see their range and history as writers. Children spend time alone reviewing their work and getting an idea and a feel for who they are as writers "right now."

As a class, we meet and share what we have discovered about ourselves. I take notes on the board during this brainstorming session. The list on the board helps us state our ideas and offers support when we begin to record our reflections for each item:

I use lots of expressive words, humor, suspense, and
scary stuff.

I use my experiences in my stories.

I've been conferring all the time while I write.

I spell a word five different ways and choose the one that
looks right.

I have paper near me so I can write ideas down to use later.

After our brainstorming and sharing session, the children choose several rough drafts from their author's folders that reflect their growth, improvement, effort, process, strengths, and needs as a writer. They may refer to the class brainstorm on the board for support and as a reminder of their processes as writers.

Once they have chosen several rough drafts, they share these drafts with a partner. They discuss themselves as writers and explain their choices. These discussions sometimes lead children to make changes in their selections. When they feel comfortable with their thinking, they write a reflection for each item that explains why they selected it and what it shows about them as writers. These reflections are written on half sheets of paper and stapled to the piece.

Here is what Adrian wrote.

I chose this story because it is a true story. And true stories
are funnier to write because you know what is going to happen. I
wrote this story because I thought it would be fun to write a true
story and to let people know about this boy.

After the children have chosen and written reflections to several rough draft pieces, they find a new partner and share them with each other. During this sharing they discover many new ideas and raise questions. Often children will revise and edit their reflections.

The children now move on to choosing other pieces of writing for their portfolios. They may put in an article from class newspapers and magazines, personal journal entries, pieces that reflect their work in science, in math, or any expert projects they have researched. Sometimes children will also put in illustrations or other pieces that reflect multiple ways of communicating.

When they have chosen and tagged all the samples the children again share them with a partner. As partners, Jason tells Chris, "You use a poet's voice when you write. Some of your stuff rhymes but not all of it. Since you like poetry, your style is that only longer. Chris, you should have shared more. It would have started more of the class on poetry. I still don't really care for it."

Jason adds, "You really have changed since the beginning of the year. You wrote in a dull and boring way at first. Now you really show your feelings." Chris comments, "I was just adding on to my stories at the end so more people would like my stuff. Now, I like my stories. I think I want to be a poet and not a baker when I grow up." Jason continues, "Now I think you give of yourself. You really try to make your stories good." Chris says, "I use more poetry. I turned all my stories into poems."

Chris tells Jason that he has a "mystery" way of writing. Jason looks at Chris and reflects, "I think what you said about my writing is that everyone thought I was good. I really didn't need to revise. It would have been very easy not to change my stories. I revised to see how it went. Then I found out the more you revise the better your stories become."

When the children have thought out loud with someone else, they synthesize all the information and write a one-page reflection of how they view themselves as writers. Each child ends the reflection with goals they want to concentrate on in the next nine weeks. Many like Adrian below will also add strategies to help attain those goals.

Adrian writes:

When I start to write I get very excited of writing a story that other people can read. I also get excited when I am writing an exciting part in the story. In illustrating I get excited when I get done with a picture that looks good. I get excited that people will give me some very nice comments on the picture.

I have grown a lot in many ways. I have grown a lot in conferring. I use to never conference but now I conference all the time. I like to conference because I know I can get more ideas from other stories for my own stories.

I was conferring with some people and they noticed that I had a style of writing. I saw the style of writing too. I was very proud of myself for having a style. The style is this. I take some of my experiences and things I like to do and make a book out of it.

I have grown a lot in the vocabulary I use. I think that this improves my story. My habits and editing, revising, and having an authors' circle with myself. I'm good in these areas too.

My three goals:

1. Put more feelings in my stories.

2. To use the things I already know.

3. Learn how to use paragraphs.

After the children have looked at themselves as writers they shift their focus to themselves as readers. They begin by choosing and reading one of their favorite books. The children meet with a partner to discuss what they were thinking while reading the book. The class then meets to brainstorm together about ourselves as readers, and I take notes.

I try to get into being a character in the story.

I retell the story to someone to catch what I missed.

I skip a word, read the sentence or paragraph, and come back to unknown words.

I am willing to make a mistake.

I become the author. What word would I use in this spot?

The children read through the list of books they've read and choose five that had an impact on them. They write a tag explaining why they chose these books and discuss the impact the books had on them as readers.

One of the books Megan chose was *The Gold Cadillac* by Mildred Taylor. "I chose this because when I read it, I got a lot of emotion out of it and I think that is a sign in showing that I get excited when I read."

They look through their literature response logs and see what they have written about their literature circle books. The children choose and tag several entries that reflect their efforts, improvements, processes, strengths, and needs as readers. The children then meet with a partner and share their reflections of themselves as readers. This gives them an opportunity to explore their own thinking.

Crystal and Karissa are partners. As Karissa shares, Crystal notices a big change in Karissa as a reader. "You now makes more sense. Your vocabulary is bigger and your sentences are longer." Karissa adds, "I used to just put my thoughts on paper. But over time I can see how I learned to make sense." Crystal shares with Karissa, "I grew as a reader. All my stuff at the beginning of the year was just that I liked books. Now that I am a better reader I relate books to myself. People like my thoughts."

After discussing themselves as readers, students synthesize this information and write a reflection of themselves as a reader.

Karissa writes:

I like to read books. My favorite book is E.L. Koningsburg. I have been growing a lot compared from the beginning of the year. I have also seen a lot of change from the beginning of the year. Some of the changes are just watching myself grow as a learner. I noticed the vocabulary I use is different from the vocabulary I did use. I thought a story always had to start Once upon a time now I found a big difference in myself. I like to be able to read to write and to write to read. I think I can become a better reader if I just hang in there. Sometimes I challenge myself to do what I think I can't do. Like if a book seemed hard to read but I wanted it, I got it and I just read it. When I read to write and I write to read I read stories better. My three goals are to 1. have a better experience with books. 2. To read to write and to write to read. 3. I wish to be a better reader. The literature circle that had the most impact on me was Grandparents because most of the books dealt with the feelings. Most of the books had feelings that said most of the story. Feelings help me understand.

Once the children have finished with their portfolios, they sit alone and read through the whole portfolio. This gives them an opportunity to look at themselves one last time. "Portfolios are a way to see yourself. You can see your goals and plans on paper. You can see what comes next and also see yourself changing," says Megan. Adrian adds, "They can help you see who you are. How did I do this before? Now, how can I repeat my strengths and improve myself?"

The self-evaluation portfolios continue to change over time. We have reached a point where they truly reflect the way the children view themselves as readers and writers. The children have choices about how they will use the portfolios. Some have shared them with their parents at home. Alicia had herself videotaped with some of her peers discussing her portfolio and her parents were invited to share in the video. Some children have shared them with their new teachers.

The portfolios have also changed how I view evaluation and what I look for in students' reading and writing. A lot of people are talking about portfolios as a way to report to parents, administrators, and community. Our focus has been portfolios as self-evaluation and how they empower us as learners.

We really can't write a true conclusion to this chapter on literacy collections. This topic is just now being explored by literacy educators. We hope that this chapter has given you ideas about how you might begin to develop your own literacy collections or refine the ones you are currently using. It is more important to begin than try to have the "perfect plan." In all we have read and in our own work with teachers, it seems that we can begin to plan how to develop collections but that our plans must always be adjusted as we work out issues in context. Even what worked one year may not work the next, not if students are different and we believe that soliciting student input is important. Literacy collections may prove to be a useful vehicle for increasing teachers' and students' sense of empowerment.

references

Anthony, R., T. Johnson, N. Mickelson, & A. Preece. (1991). *Evaluating literacy: A perspective for change.* Portsmouth, NH: Heinemann.

Au, K., S. Scheu, A. Kawahami, & P. Herman. (1990). Assessment and accountability in a whole literacy curriculum. *The Reading Teacher, 43,* 7: 574–578.

Barrs, M. (1990). The primary language record: Reflection of issues in evaluation. *Language Arts, 67,* 244–253.

Barrs, M., S. Ellis, H. Tester, & A. Thomas. (1989). *The Primary Language Record.* Portsmouth, NH: Heinemann.

Bingham, A. (1988). Using writing folders to document student progress. In T. Newkirk & N. Atwell (Eds.), *Understanding writing: Ways of observing, learning, and teaching,* (2nd ed.) (pp. 216–225). Portsmouth, NH: Heinemann.

Brandt, R. (1987). On assessment in the arts: A conversation with Howard Gardner. *Educational Leadership, 45,* 4:30–34.

Bruner, J. (1990). *Acts of meaning.* Cambridge, MA: Harvard University Press.

Cooper, W. & J. Davies. (1990). Portfolio assessment. Spring Conference, National Council of Teachers of English, Colorado Springs, CO.

Flood, J. & D. Lapp. (1989). Reporting reading progress: A comparison portfolio for parents. *The Reading Teacher, 32,* 508–514.

Gardner, H. (1983). *Frames of mind: The theory of multiple intelligences.* New York: Basic Books.

Hiebert, E. & R. Calfee. (1989). Advancing academic literacy through teachers' assessments. *Educational Leadership, 46,* 7:50–54.

Johnson, C. (1991). Lorrie Shepard on assessment. *Perspectives* (Colorado Partnership for Educational Renewal), 2:4:1–2.

Johnston, P. (1991). *Constructive evaluation of literate activity.* White Plains, NY: Longman.

Lewis, M. & A. Lindaman. (1989). How do we evaluate student writing? One district's answer. *Educational Leadership, 46,* 7:70–71.

Mathews, J. (1990). From computer management to portfolio assessment. *The Reading Teacher, 43,* 420–421.

Mills, R. (1989). Portfolios capture rich array of student performance. *The School Administrator,* December, 8–11.

Rief, L. (1990). Finding the value in evaluation: Self-assessment in a middle school classroom. *Educational Leadership, 47,* 6:24–29.

Rynkofs, J.T. (1988). Send your writing folders home. In T. Newkirk & N. Atwell (Eds.), *Understanding writing: Ways of observing, learning, and teaching.* (2nd ed.) (pp. 236–244). Portsmouth, NH: Heinemann.

School Programs Division, Ministry of Education, Victoria, Australia. (1990). *Literacy profiles handbook.* Brewster, NY: TASA.

Shepard, L. (1989). Why we need better assessments. *Educational Leadership, 46,* 7:4–9.

Simmons, J. (1990). Portfolios as large-scale assessment. *Language Arts, 67,* 262–268.

Spear, K. (1988). *Sharing writing: Peer response groups in English classes.* Portsmouth, NH: Boynton/Cook.

Stock, P. & J. Robinson. (1987). Taking on testing: Teachers as tester-researchers. *English Education, 19,* 93–121.

Taylor, D. (1990). Teaching without testing. *English Education, 22,* 1:4–74.

Tierney, R., M. Carter, & L. Desai. (1991). *Portfolio assessment in the reading-writing classroom.* Norwood, MA: Christopher Gordon.

Valencia, S., W. McGinley, & P.D. Pearson. (1990). In G. Duffy (Ed.). *Reading in the middle school* (2nd ed.). Newark, DE: International Reading Association.

Vermont Department of Education. (1988). Working together to show results: An approach to school accountability for Vermont. Montpelier, VT: Vermont Department of Education.

Vermont Department of Education. (1989). Vermont writing assessment: The portfolio. Montpelier, VT: Vermont Department of Education.

Winograd, P. & S. Paris. (1988). Improving reading assessment. The Heath Transcripts. Lexington, MA: D.C. Heath.

Wolf, D. (1989). Portfolio assessment: Sampling student work. *Educational Leadership, 46,* 7:35–39.

Chapter Ten

10

Fostering Change in Literacy Assessment and Instruction

reflections

☐ With other educators, discuss your responses to the questions listed under "Reflecting on Your Own Experiences" (pages 459–460).

☐ Before reading this chapter, use the form "(Your Name) as a Change Agent" (page 474) and the accompanying directions to help you examine what you are currently doing as a change agent.

☐ After reading this chapter, review your responses to "(Your Name) as a Change Agent." What might you consider doing to expand your efforts as a change agent?

☐ After reading the chapter, consider an instance in your professional life when you experienced change. Reflect on that process using Michael Fullan's "Assumptions About Change." What did you learn that might be valuable in future instances when you experience change?

☐ Examine what this chapter has said about fostering change in yourself and others. What strategies did you identify as ones you have and have not utilized? Talk about this with others so you can compare your observations. What did you learn about how you approach the process of change?

☐ Consider what else you need or want to do about literacy assessment. Consider what strategies you might use to foster change in yourself and in others.

To the extent that good ideas or visions of change are not combined with equally good conceptualizations of the process of change, the ideas will be wasted.

Michael Fullan

In this chapter we examine some of the difficulties you might encounter as you attempt to implement what you have learned about literacy assessment under the general topic of change. If you want to change ways of thinking and behaving, these changes will come more easily if you have an understanding of the process of change.

As human beings, we experience constant change. As teachers, our job is to change others. Clearly, teachers already have experience with change but we want to encourage a more conscious approach to the process of change, in particular to the process of changing how literacy assessment is viewed and implemented in schools. Change in the world of education is often uncomfortable, and the more we understand about the process, the more likely it is that we can effect change realistically.

Acquiring new knowledge, understanding, and skills is something teachers do naturally throughout their careers. One of the ways they do this is by thinking about their observations of the students in their classrooms. Assessment is thus a vehicle for learning. It is a systematic reflection on students' processes and products. In fact, most teacher-researcher studies are "assessments" done by teachers to aid in their learning. (For information on teacher research, see Bissex & Bullock [1987]; Cochran-Smith & Lytle [1993]; Daiker & Morenberg [1989]; Goswami & Stillman [1987]; and Myers [1985].)

The more you observe and reflect on children's literacy, the more patterns you see in how it evolves. You most often observe children's reading and writing in the context of the instructional environment you provide; and if you consider the patterns you see there, you can learn about the impact of your instruction on children's reading and writing. As Torbe says, "Pay attention to what really happens [as children read and write] and, perhaps inevitably, one begins to examine one's own practice carefully and critically: it becomes apparent that pupils' problems in learning may be of the teachers' making, not some deficiency in the learners" (1990, p. 150). As you learn more about reading and writing assessment you are more likely to invent changes that "fit" what you know about literacy and how to support it.

If learning leads to change in assessment practices, change in assessment practices also leads to learning. If you decide to use miscue analysis in conducting assessment (see Chapter 4), you will learn to view reading as a process of using a variety of language cues and as a process of making and confirming/disconfirming predictions. If you decide to use a checklist of writing process behaviors, you will learn to look carefully at the process students use in their writing. You may also learn a great deal about a particular aspect of the process, such as students' revision strategies.

Belenky et al. (1986) provide further insight into the relationship between learning (or "knowing") and change in their book *Women's Ways of Knowing*. These researchers found that women college students tend to become immersed in the "knowing" of outside authorities. For them, to learn becomes knowing and implementing the advice of others, a kind of surface knowing that leads to surface change. They interpret the problems they encounter as not-doing-it-quite-right. The fault is in them as learners. What these students do not consider is that expert advice can have problems or that context might require that they make their own adjustments. This is a common mindset in education when "experts" are consulted. Teachers often want experts to tell them what to do to solve students' literacy problems, not realizing that their own experiences and their own familiarity with their students are essential for a sensitive assessment.

At the same time, we do not believe that paying attention solely to one's own interpretations is the total answer. To do so is to base action only on instinct and intuition. Rather, individuals who reach their fullest potential combine what they learn from others with what they learn from their own experiences, an integration of learning that leads to substantial change in practice.

understanding the process of change

"All too often change is guided by reactive initiatives or wishful visions, rather than planning based on sound principles" (Dalziel & Schoonover, 1988, p. 13). Understanding the process of change is important whether you are experiencing personal change, acting as a change agent, or both. Understanding the process of change is vital in situations when the change is complex or involves numerous individuals. We'll review two ways of coming to understand the process of change: 1) by applying principles that guide your teaching to the process of change, and 2) by considering Fullan's (1982) assumptions about change.

applying principles that guide your teaching

The best way to begin thinking about the change process is to consider what you already know about it—how you encourage your students' learning or change— and then to apply the principles you use in teaching children to encouraging change in adults—yourself, colleagues, administrators, parents, or school board members.

Here are some principles we consider. What principles that guide your teaching might affect what you do as a change agent?

- Demonstration
- Ownership
- Opportunity for use
- Risk-taking
- Time
- Choice
- Self-assessment
- Collaboration
- Response and reflection
- Gradual release of responsibility to the learner
- Approximation

Whether all or some of these principles are important depends on the situation. A story will illustrate this point: A classroom teacher was concerned about the literacy assessment and instruction being provided to four learning-disabled students in her class by the special education (LD) teacher. As an initial step in changing the LD teacher's view of reading instruction, one which emphasized decoding, she decided to encourage the teacher to use trade books for reading rather than the phonetically regular basal stories and workbooks the LD teacher had used since the 1960s. In the Reflection Log she kept for her college class, the classroom teacher described what she did:

> I decided that in order to get other material used I had to make other material available. This sounds so simple but I realized it would be the basis on which to make change happen. The learning-disabilities teacher works in a classroom adjacent to our team's trade books. I made a point of always going to choose new books when she was present. By doing this, I found myself constantly suggesting books she might use with the children we both shared, which to my relief she did. She began using books that I had suggested.

It's apparent that the classroom teacher gave this change some *time*: "I made a point of always going" and "I found myself constantly suggesting." She also provided the LD teacher with *choices* (she didn't take a trade book to the other classroom and suggest its use). She provided *opportunity for use* (note the first two sentences from her log). The teacher might eventually follow up by involving the LD teacher in some informal *self-assessment* ("How are the kids doing reading the trade books?"). She might even try to involve the LD teacher in some *reflective conversation* that could further change, perhaps asking what the LD teacher has observed about the differences in students' reading of trade books and the basal materials.

On the other hand, the classroom teacher hasn't applied all the principles of learning. Volunteering to demonstrate for the LD teacher how the students read trade books seemed "pushy" to her; she thought the students would demonstrate the value of the trade books themselves once the special teacher began using them. She uses the principle of demonstration in her teaching all the time, but it didn't seem appropriate or necessary in this situation.

These same principles are important in making personal changes, as the "Teacher Reflection" pieces in this book demonstrate. These stories reveal that teachers gave themselves time to make changes, were involved in risk-taking, and understood that change involved approximations. The teachers also revealed how they self-assessed the change process and the results of change, and often collaborated with others in attempting change. According to most of them, writing about their experiences encouraged even more reflection.

■ ■

assumptions about change

We have also found Michael Fullan's "Assumptions About Change" (1982, pp. 91–92) to be very useful in planning for change and engaging in the change process. As Fullan says, "The assumptions we make about change are powerful and frequently unconscious sources of actions. When we begin to understand what change is as people experience it, we begin also to see clearly that assumptions made by planners of change are extremely important determinants of whether the realities of implementation get confronted or ignored" (Fullan, 1982, p. 91). As we present adaptations of each of Fullan's principles, we'll also provide an example of each principle in action. The examples are taken from a four-year staff development program we implemented in the Chapter I program in the Denver Public Schools that was focused on creating change in teacher's literacy instruction and assessment practices.

1. Do not assume that your version of what the change should be is the one that should or could be implemented. Assume that successful implementation consists of some transformation or continual development of initial ideas.

When we look back on the assessment ideas we originally implemented in our first years of staff development work with the Chapter I teachers in Denver Public Schools, we chuckle a bit. Since the first year, the program's teachers and administrators (sometimes with input from us or from others outside the program) have transformed or further developed the assessment techniques, instruments, and procedures. In fact, it was difficult to do year-to-year data comparisons in the program because the instruments and procedures were continually being refined. Although this created difficulties for those of us who would have liked to utilize data comparisons for research, we learned from Fullan that we should have expected it. That's why we chuckle. We can't believe we were so naive (and egocentric) as to think that the teachers would use our ideas without modifying them. The original ideas were taken over by the users. The assessment instruments, techniques, and procedures evolved in more meaningful and contextualized directions in response to the needs and knowledge of teachers, children, and administrators.

2. Assume that any significant innovation, if it is to result in change, requires individual implementers to work out their own meaning. Significant change involves a certain amount of ambiguity, ambivalence, and uncertainty for the individual about the meaning of the change. Thus, effective implementation is a process of clarification.

Probably the clearest example of "working out their own meaning" occurred after we implemented the use of an interview designed to uncover children's perceptions about reading and writing and their histories as readers and writers. At first, teachers used the interview with all students "as is." Then some of the teachers of emergent readers and writers began talking about how it didn't "fit" their students very well. They soon changed the interview, constructing a different one with a similar intent. In adapting the instrument, they spent hours clarifying what they wanted to ask their students and why. The *Emergent Reader and Writer Interview* in Chapter 7 (and in Rhodes, 1993) truly conveys "their own meaning."

3. Assume that conflict and disagreement are not only inevitable but fundamental to successful change. Since any group of people possess multiple realities, any collective change attempt will necessarily involve conflict.

Like most people, we do not relish conflict. During staff development, however, we could not avoid it. Sometimes it was overt. We remember a teacher shouting at us in the midst of a session in which we were introducing miscue analysis; she was upset by the view of reading that we were presenting because it contradicted instructional practices she had used for years. More often, the conflict was covert. Teachers "forgot" to do something, did it on a surface level only, or avoided it. We realized that we needed to discover the teachers' concerns and then provide them with the time and support necessary to understand these new approaches. We found that naming what we were observing—forgetting and avoiding—often with a sense of humor, allowed us to move into more straightforward discussions about the clashes between their views and ours.

4. Assume that people need pressure to change (even in directions they desire), but it will only be effective under conditions that allow them to react, to form their own position, to interact with other implementers, to obtain technical assistance, etc.

The use of assessment instruments such as miscue analysis was mandated for all teachers in Denver's Chapter I program after staff development on whole language assessment and instruction had been available to teachers for two years. (Although staff development was mandatory, the content of staff development was chosen by individual teachers. Some elected to work on whole language assessment and instruction while others elected topics such as problem solving and parental involvement.)

Mandated use of the instruments constituted pressure to change assessment but also led to a change in instruction. Once they had used the assessment instruments and began to view reading and writing differently, many of the teachers who had not previously sought information about whole language instruction began to seek it. To support this interest in instruction, teachers set up groups to share curriculum and exchange information. They also began to request more staff development focusing directly on reading and writing instruction. Thus, the initial pressure created by the mandated use of assessment instruments inspired greater interest in exploring instructional strategies.

5. Assume that effective change takes time. It is a process of "development in use." Unrealistic or undefined time-lines fail to recognize that implementation occurs developmentally. . . . Careful planning can bring about significant change on a fairly wide scale over a period of two or three years.

The time each teacher needed for change varied considerably from one teacher to another. Some made changes gradually, changing their views or theories in conjunction with changes in the implementation of assessment and instruction. Others made changes rapidly; we had probably given them the support to consistently implement views they already held about reading and writing. Others appeared not to change at all or to change at only surface levels for long periods of time and then, suddenly, made major changes all at once. It was as if this last group had to change their views or theories about assessment and instruction before they could change their behavior with students. We have decided that the two or three years that Fullan refers to is an average and that there are teachers who change their assessment and instruction either much more quickly or much more slowly.

6. Do not assume that the reason for lack of implementation is outright rejection of the values embodied in the change, or hard-core resistance to all change. Assume that there are a number of possible reasons: value rejection, inadequate resources to support implementation, insufficient time elapsed.

One of our discoveries in working with the Chapter I teachers was the tremendous amount of support required in order to put new assessment procedures into place. The teachers learned not only how to collect and analyze miscues and retellings, but also how to give and analyze interviews, collect and analyze writing samples, and, for those who taught emergent readers, how to give and analyze the *Emergent Reading and Writing Evaluation* (see Chapter 7 and Rhodes, 1993). Miscue analysis alone required hours of staff development, including presentations, group work sessions, and coaching, before teachers were able to collect the data with relative ease. Then they spent more hours learning how to interpret the data and to use it to assist children in becoming more effective readers. It was a long time before some teachers could confidently assess students and decide what to do for them instructionally—which was not surprising, given the complexity of reading and writing and its assessment.

Even with adequate resources to support implementation of the various assessments and attendant instruction, change was long in coming. In some cases, change didn't occur at all. Some teachers experienced extreme philosophical and instructional incongruence (Walp & Walmsley, 1989) between the Chapter I program and the schools to which they were assigned. All the teachers were aware of the incongruence between the assessment and instruction supported by Chapter I and the criterion-referenced tests and the basal readers adopted by the district. In addition, some teachers simply had different priorities or wanted to focus on different problems. All of these things (and more) resulted in implementation difficulties.

7. Do not expect all or even most people or groups to change. The complexity of change is such that it is impossible to bring about widespread change in

any large social system. Progress occurs when we take steps that increase the number of people affected.

Having talked with other staff developers and visited staff development programs, such as the Writing Project in New York City led by Lucy Calkins and Shelley Harwayne, we knew it made no sense to spread ourselves thin in order to work with all seventy-five teachers in the program at once. Instead, we initially introduced a smaller group (about twenty-five) to our views of reading and writing instruction and assessment—those teachers caused a ripple effect. By the second year, many teachers who had not been in the first group were asking for the same information and support. Over time and with continuing staff development efforts, all the teachers were affected in some way by the increasing knowledge base of those who were initially introduced to whole language views of reading and writing assessment and instruction. Even so, not all the teachers understood or effectively implemented whole language assessment and instruction. However, years later the same ripple effect continues, this time from the Chapter I teachers to the classroom teachers.

8. Assume that no amount of knowledge will ever make it totally clear what action should be taken. Action decisions are a combination of valid knowledge, political considerations, on-the-spot decisions, and intuition.

One of the most difficult conditions we encountered was the ever-changing nature of the situation in the school system. We were confident about what we knew about literacy assessment and instruction, and we became increasingly confident about engaging teachers within the public school setting in the process of change. We made careful decisions on the basis of this knowledge and on the basis of informal and formal needs assessment data collected from the teachers. Yet we often found our decision making constrained by district politics and by crises engendered by decisions made outside Chapter I. We came to understand that this is to be expected. The bigger the change, the more likely decision making will seem out of your control or quite muddled at times.

9. Assume that change is a frustrating, discouraging business. Instead of being discouraged by all that remains to be done, be encouraged by what has been accomplished by way of improvement resulting from your actions.

Change was frustrating and discouraging, not only because the people with whom we were working did not always want to change, but also because the traditions and precedents of a large school system often made teachers feel as if they could not change. After all, a whole language Chapter I teacher is not always appreciated when her regular classroom colleagues are using skills-based reading curricula. Some teachers would become discouraged after the results of post-test standardized test scores were made available. Although they knew that Chapter I children were reading more effectively and more willingly, the test scores did not always reveal it. In such cases, the other assessment data they had collected helped to remind them of the improvement in their students. They learned to celebrate these improvements while at the same time working to help their students reveal their reading ability on norm-referenced tests.

fostering personal change

In this section, we will explore five basic strategies that allow you to foster and support personal change. These personal change strategies, which create the foundation necessary for you to be an effective change agent for others, are:

1. Reflecting on personal experiences.

2. Creating environments supportive of change.

3. Pursuing answers to questions.

4. Confronting the politics of assessment and change.

5. Developing voice.

■ ■

reflecting on your own experiences

Not enough attention is given to the value of personal experiences, yet reflecting on our personal literacy experiences underscores the complexity of the reading and writing processes and directs our thinking toward what such experiences might mean for our classrooms.

We hope the questions that follow will encourage you to critique the process of assessment in terms of your personal experiences with it. We recommend that you consider your responses as well as our responses that follow each set of questions and then discuss them with your colleagues.

1. Consider your own reading and writing or that of another person you consider to be a highly effective reader and writer. When you describe yourself or that other person as a reader and writer, what words do you use? How does such a description relate to what you are assessing in your students' reading and writing?

When we ask teachers this question, one of the descriptors they often use is "reads a lot." If you agree that this is one important way to define an effective reader, do you assess that aspect of reading in your classroom? What we assess teaches what we value; if we value time spent reading, then we need to consider assessing it.

2. Consider something that you've learned lately. How did you know you learned it? How might "how-you-knew-what-you-knew" inform the procedures by which you assess reading and writing?

Although it's possible that someone praised you for what you learned to do ("That was a beautiful song!"), it's more likely that you evaluated your own learning using standards that mattered to you. If you learned to play a new song on the guitar, you knew the notes flowed well and that you played them correctly because you could sing along. If you were also evaluated by someone else, did that person's words or your own pleasure in your success mean more? What does this mean for the assessment of reading and writing?

3. Reflect on your assessment experiences in school at any level. How did those experiences affect you in positive and negative ways? What can you learn from these assessment experiences about what and how to assess reading and writing?

Most of us have been shaken by an assessment we found unfair, feeling as if there was little or no match between our self-assessment and the assessment provided by the teacher. A student might invest hours of deep thought in trying out a new technique while writing a piece of fiction only to receive a poor grade and no comment. What can you do as a teacher to avoid these sorts of experiences with your students?

Most of us have also had the experience of being pleased by another's assessment of our work. In our experience, the assessments that have meant the most have come from people who have made specific observations (good or not so good) that we ourselves had not considered in our self-assessment of the project. What can you learn from positive assessment experiences you've had?

4. Reflect on the assessments you experience as a teacher. How do those experiences affect you in positive and negative ways? Is your teaching different in any way when you are being evaluated? What can you learn from this about reading and writing assessment?

Most of us don't take risks when the principal or some other supervisor is due to observe our teaching for evaluation. Instead, we do something that we've done before that "works" and fits the value system of the supervisor. Do we want students to treat their writing like this because they know it is to be evaluated? How can we keep the assessment process open so that students will take risks and do work they find valuable?

5. If you are a parent, you've had many experiences from the "other side" with assessment—seeing your children's papers with grades and comments, listening to your children's reactions to assessment, receiving report cards, receiving norm-referenced test results, and so on. What can you learn from these experiences about assessing reading and writing and how to communicate that information to others?

As a parent, no doubt you've asked your child to explain how the teacher arrived at a grade in a particular area and discovered that she couldn't explain the basis of the grade. As a teacher yourself, you know that there are a myriad ways your child's teacher might arrive at a grade. You wonder what tasks, assignments, and tests make up the report card grade, what criteria were used to arrive at the individual grades that make up the report card grade, if some things were weighted more than others, and so on. Even more disturbing than not knowing this yourself is that your child doesn't know either. It's clear that your child is uninformed about what the teacher is doing in evaluating work and that she plays no part in the assessment process.

When you are the teacher, what can you do to help parents and students understand and participate in assessment?

You will think of other personal assessment experiences besides those suggested here. Your reflections can spur changes in your attitude and procedures rather quickly, particularly when you share them with others. Hearing about your colleagues' experiences with assessment can confirm, deepen, and broaden your insights. It is important to honor and use your own reflections on personal experiences as the basis of your work with students.

◼ ◼ *creating environments supportive of change*

In order to make personal change easier, you need to cultivate an environment supportive of change. If your teaching and the teaching of those around you has been founded on ideas like mastery learning and the testing of subskills, it may be difficult to establish a foothold for change even when you are fairly certain about what and how to change. We'll consider several strategies that will enable you to create an environment supportive of your personal learning and change:

- Identifying like-minded colleagues
- Defining the change you want to pursue
- Establishing a comfortable pace for change
- Challenging yourself

◼ identifying like-minded colleagues

As we have suggested, it is helpful to identify colleagues who are open to exploring new assessment ideas or have already begun to reconsider literacy assessment in their classrooms and schools. Working with them will help you clarify your thinking and provide you with the emotional support you need, especially when your assessment processes and products are different from the mainstream.

Working with other teachers often leads to comparisons among teachers. You need to be careful that such comparisons result in reflection rather than judgment. Teachers do not have to conduct assessment and instruction in the same way in order to be effective. Comparing assessment practices is valuable if it leads to reflection and continued growth but it can be counter-productive if it leads to invidious comparison.

When you cannot find other teachers who will join you in creating an environment supportive of change, you can cultivate a supportive environment in your own classroom by confiding in the students (assuming they are old enough to understand). Telling students what you are trying to do and how you hope it will benefit them can pay off in surprising ways. You may find that students suggest better ways to assess their work and progress than you yourself have considered. Inviting students to observe and help you as a learner can pay big dividends by creating a sense of community.

■ defining the change

Another way to create an environment supportive of change is to decide what personal change you want to make and what the starting point for that change will be. It is useful to consider here what starting point is comfortable for you. The goal is to create a situation that is, at least initially, accepting of your efforts at change.

Some teachers find that trying a new assessment in writing is easier than trying one in reading. In many districts, reading assessment has a long tradition that bears little resemblance to what we have suggested in this book. Instead of starting by battling these traditions, some teachers choose to begin with writing because there is less tradition in that area. Other teachers make the opposite decision. They tackle reading assessment head on because it is the area that bothers them most.

Within a particular area you may want to begin with something quite specific. You may find it easy to assess students' use of conventions in writing and difficult to assess the content of students' writing—the development of clarity, voice, and organization. If so, you may decide to focus on that which you are currently having difficulty assessing. Another way to carve out a smaller, more manageable area in which to begin to make changes in assessment is to consider developing alternative assessment techniques for a particular group of students—for example, for your least effective readers and writers.

■ establishing pacing

Another way to cultivate an environment that will contribute to manageable change is to remember that you need to find your own pace. Some teachers will change everything they can about assessment in one clean sweep (and then work out the details). Others will need several years to make the changes they want to make. The changes can be more systematic and controlled, with fewer details left to adjust as the teacher goes along. Some teachers find that making a small change naturally leads to other, sometimes bigger, changes.

The pacing of change is an individual matter and is the result of a number of factors. It may be faster or slower depending on your general approach to change, what forces are driving the change, whether the forces are external or internal or both, what impedes change, what is going on in your life outside teaching, what sort of support you have to make changes, and how you feel about assessment as it currently occurs in your classroom. Try not to judge yourself, positively or negatively, by comparing your pace for making change with the teacher in the classroom next door. The impediments and the challenges are different for every teacher. Be patient with yourself (and others) about the pace at which change occurs. Teachers often have to leave behind comfortable materials and procedures as they move toward new and different ways of assessment. So do students. The older the students are, the more they may balk at being asked to think about assessment in ways that are outside the current school norm.

▪ challenging yourself

An environment that is conducive to supporting change is one in which people feel free to take risks. No doubt you challenge your students to take risks in reading and writing. It's equally important that you challenge yourself. "Force" yourself to try new assessment techniques and procedures, experiment with ways to use the assessment data you collect, and so on. If you fall on your face, you can pick yourself up; it's unlikely that you or anyone else will be hurt by it. You tell your students that they can learn from their mistakes; the same is true for you. If you take frequent risks in literacy assessment, you will make real progress in learning how to utilize assessment to assist you in teaching well.

▪ ▪ *pursuing answers to questions*

I've learned much from my teachers; I've learned more from my colleagues; I've learned most from my students.

Maimonides

Learning is driven by questions. In the case of assessment, your learning is likely to be driven by the questions (sometimes disguised as concerns) that arise as you consider procedures and issues. The more learning you do, the more questions will arise. True learning begets more questions—and more learning.

There are at least three ways to pursue answers to your questions about assessment besides reflecting on your own experiences. One is to consult the experts, the "teachers" Maimonides refers to. Another is to pursue answers to assessment questions with colleagues. Yet another is to observe and consult with your students.

▪ teachers/experts

Educators often seek answers to their questions by turning to experts. Expertise in literacy assessment is available through district workshops, university classes, International Reading Association or National Council of Teachers of English meetings, articles, tapes, and books.

Because experts must generalize to cover a variety of situations and classrooms, they can provide only general answers to your assessment questions, answers that will raise more questions about specific applications in your own situation. Fortunately, there are others—particularly your colleagues and the students you teach—who can help you find specific solutions or answers to your questions; these sources should be given greater credence than they are by many educators.

▪ colleagues

Learning and change occur best in situations of "collaboration and coopera-tion, involving the provisions for people to do things together, talking together, and sharing concerns" (Lieberman & Miller, 1984, p. 16). Teachers who were asked in a study (Fraatz, 1987) what had been helpful in learning to teach effectively often answered as this one did: "Primarily the other teachers. We do a lot—not on a formal basis, but we talk with each other about what we're doing, how we're approaching it . . . This kind of give and take is effective" (p. 202). Though Fraatz does not characterize these informal exchanges as deliberative and sustained reflection, she comments that "they do indicate the promise of dialogue and deliberation" (p. 202).

Teachers have developed vehicles that go beyond informal dialogue and encourage serious reflection about teaching, including assessment. One that is becoming more common is the support group. The support group may be a study group of teachers from a school; a group such as the Philadelphia Teachers' Learning Cooperative (Rich, 1984); one of the many TAWL (Teachers Applying Whole Language) groups (Edelsky, 1988); a CAWL (Coordinators/Consultants Applying Whole Language) group (Rickert, 1990) consisting of Reading, Language Arts, and Chapter I Coordinators and university faculty; or a principals group like the one in Tucson, Arizona (Y. Goodman, 1991). These groups serve to cultivate reflective attitudes (Watson, Burke, & Harste, 1989) or thoughtfulness (Brown, 1988) as group members share ideas and insights.

An assessment study group or support group usually works best with a focus and structure of some kind: a book on assessment, an assessment technique or procedure, student reading and writing data, or some combination thereof. The group can discuss and try out ideas in a book, report back to each other on what they've discovered, discuss new questions that have occurred to them, and consider a variety of solutions. Each person can settle on some assessment technique, try it out, and come back together to share how the technique was employed and what the outcomes were. Or each person in a group can bring something like a child's folder containing a monthly piece of writing and spend time helping each other look for signs of growth and patterns of development.

Educators in a support group can increase the quality of reflection if they raise questions to push each other's thinking. For example: 1) What are we able to observe and comment on easily? Not so easily? What does that mean? 2) Is this assessment instrument appropriate for all children? If not, who is it appropriate for/not appropriate for and why? What does that mean? 3) What is this assessment instrument testing besides what it purports to test? What does that mean? 4) What do our observations about the students' work reveal about our instruction? 5) What else might we want to know about this child? What are some ways to find these things out?

Another way to support learning and change is to spend time observing assessment procedures in each other's classrooms (often using a half day of professional leave). Having another teacher conduct interviews during instruction or take anecdotal records on students, especially students who are not progressing as expected, can give you a perspective it is difficult to obtain when you work by yourself. Or you might ask the other teacher to observe you taking anecdotal records during a language arts instructional period. One key here is that you and the observer spend time in advance of the visit understanding what you want to get out of the visit. Another is to spend sufficient time after the visit pushing each other's thinking.

Pushing each other's thinking is not a concept to be taken lightly—it lies at the heart of true collaboration. It represents a search for language to observe the unnoticed, praise the positive, generate and ponder questions, articulate problems, and devise and try out potential solutions. It involves a contract by both parties to enter into potential change that can be threatening and uncomfortable at first but necessary if learning and growth are to occur. The problem is that human communication doesn't always lead to collaborative transactions.* Just as we "debrief" with students, it is important to conduct conversations with our colleagues that explore how collaboration is going if true collaboration is to take place.

◼ students

As Maimonides stated, "I've learned most from my students." Observation of students' reading and writing can teach you a great deal about assessment.

You may find it particularly useful to talk with students as you first begin to experiment with various assessment techniques and use data to plan instruction. If you tell them what you are trying to do and why, you open yourself to feedback. The feedback is unlikely to be direct (unless you ask direct questions), but students may reveal their reactions to your assessment. A humorous example of this was witnessed in Sue Monaco's first-grade classroom in the Jefferson County Schools in Colorado. When one girl finished ahead of the other girls who were writing at a table, she began to take anecdotal notes on them (see Figure 10.1; the writing resembles Arabic because the child's mother reads and writes Arabic at home). When asked what she was doing, the girl explained that she was writing down what the girls had done well and what they needed to work on. Her explanation provided the teacher with information about the children's perceptions of anecdotal records.

Involving students in assessment will create even more learning opportunities. For example, you could ask students to record and analyze the genres of literature they read over a month and then involve them in planning how to increase the breadth of their reading using this information.

Interviewing students about assessment can also help you learn how your students value the collected information. Ask older students how they feel and what they've learned about themselves as they read the anecdotal notes you've collected over the last month. Ask students to evaluate their involvement in presenting their work at parent-teacher conferences. As we have seen, Kathy Hoerlein's third-grade

---

* For example, female colleagues, culturally expected to "be nice," are often reluctant to offer criticism. Yet "being nice" may not help others reach their fullest potential. In male-female collaboration, a male may be overly sensitive to hurting a woman's feelings. Or he may find it difficult to accept critical comments from a woman colleague. Between two men, the knowledge of one may be interpreted by the other as an attempt to gain power. These are only a few examples of the potential for miscommunication that can involve psychological (Gilligan, 1982; Rubin, 1983; Lerner, 1985; Belenky et al., 1986; Osherson, 1986), linguistic (Tannen, 1990), religious (Ausberger, 1973; Fischer, 1988), and cultural factors (Sanford & Donovan, 1984; Kerr, 1985; Aisenberg & Harrington, 1988).

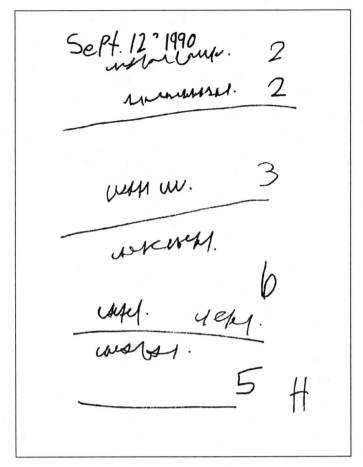

Figure 10.1 Child's anecdotal records

students in the Aurora Public Schools in Colorado responded quite specifically and positively to their involvement in parent-teacher conferences.

Involving students in assessment efforts may seem unusual because the usual student-teacher relationship doesn't support it. It requires a more democratic relationship between teachers and students than exists in some classrooms. Teachers must see themselves as learners in a learning community with their students. This attitude helps create the sort of community and a sense of ownership that serve to increase learning. Students' insights and ideas can often solve problems before they get too big, saving teachers a great deal of time and energy. Then you can look for other ways to involve students in the decisions you make about instruction.

■ ■

confronting the politics of assessment and change

Confront and *politics*—two words that teachers seldom use. Many teachers, in fact, try their best to avoid confrontation and to pretend that they are not touched by political endeavors. As we use the term, being political means grappling seriously to shape the situation in which you live and work so that you can be what you want to be and provide that possibility for others. Because we all live and work in a political realm, we need to consider what our own role is, and in turn how politics affect us, if we are to work around impediments to personal change and be change agents.

Although confrontation has a generally negative connotation, it simply means squarely facing ideas, procedures, and materials that conflict with the ideas, procedures, and materials you want to use. "The easiest, the most tempting, and the least creative response to conflict . . . is to pretend it does not exist" (Schaller, 1972, p. 137). Pretending that the conflict or problem doesn't exist is to give up on the problem and through inaction to let the ideas, procedures, and materials of others reign in your life and the lives of your students.

Another way many of us approach problems is to complain about them. A teacher wrote in her Reflection Log:

> I've become more aware of how much time people spend complaining. As I sat in the [teachers'] lounge last week, I began to make a mental note of how many different conversations were being conducted; and how many of these used an immense amount of energy stating complaints. One group was frustrated with the amount of "extra" things the district keeps requiring us to teach. In another group, a teacher was complaining about a certain child, stating, "I've had it . . . it's hopeless." Yet a third group spent time discussing lack of materials. The amazing thing about this was that when I began to reflect on the situation I realized that these types of conversations are not at all uncommon. I, too, have been guilty of spending an immense amount of energy complaining about various things.

As this teacher explored the idea of confronting problems rather than ignoring or complaining about them, she began to understand how to confront problems. Again, an excerpt from her log:

> I guess if I've learned one thing that has really and truly stuck in my mind this semester, it's that there is always an answer. I realize the solution may be hiding somewhere . . . but it is there. In order to change or make changes in any given situation, one must continually look for answers or solutions. I really found myself awakening to the fact that I often have complained of what I thought was a hopeless situation and I realize now that I probably could have been on the way to the solution if I had used the time to think of constructive alternatives instead of wasting it on complaining. . . . [Now I] think of myself as a person who can influence change in many different situations.

The teacher who was observing the others has found a positive stance that allows her to pursue personal change more easily and to be an effective change agent, to help others arrive at solutions to problems.

A problem-solving approach is a general way to confront the politics of assessment and change. But there are also more specific ways you may find helpful. As you encounter situations in which you experience change, add your own specific ways of confronting the politics of assessment to the three we will discuss next.

getting beyond "but I can't"

Sometimes, when a teacher is asked if she has tried a certain solution ("Develop an assessment that is an alternative to the basal test") to a problem ("I wish I didn't have to give the basal tests"), the answer is, "But I can't do that" ("I have to give the basal tests"). When asked why, the teacher may respond with policy ("The district requires that we give the basal tests") but often can't attach a person's name to the policy. When asked whether the teacher has asked if she can stop giving the basal tests, the answer is invariably "no," but the teacher remains certain that there is an inviolate policy, even if she has never seen it written down.

We all have avoided making changes for similar reasons, but if we are to become change agents, we need to confront this tendency in ourselves to avoid confronting the problem. Try this: go ask someone if you can do whatever you think you can't do. The teacher who wanted to drop the basal tests took this challenge and decided to ask her principal. Grinning from ear to ear, she later related that her principal had given her permission to develop an alternative assessment to the basal test.

In this case, it turned out there was no written policy. There was only tradition, and the teacher's principal was willing to break with tradition. Occasionally, we do get "no" for an answer when we ask to do something in a different way. In such a case, it is well worth asking the same person in a different way or asking someone else. Once it is understood that you really want to do what you are asking about, many administrators are prepared to compromise.

Another reason we may respond to change with "But I can't" is that we are not ready to take what we perceive as a risk or we don't want to fail. Of course, this fearful attitude gets in the way of change. Instead of abandoning change entirely, we can consider smaller changes that feel less risky. Success in implementing a small change could lead to other changes and greater confidence in dealing with the process of change.

overcoming the power of precedent

Precedent may be tradition or it may be written policy. Whatever the case, precedent is powerful and often difficult to change. "The older or larger the organization, the more powerful is precedent" (Schaller, 1972, p. 137).

It is interesting to watch this notion at play in discussions at newly opened schools and at schools that have existed for years. In a newly opened school, where teachers who have dealt with assessment in a multitude of ways come together, generating a healthy discussion about assessment options is relatively easy. There are fewer precedents. It is more difficult to generate such a discussion in a long-established school with a faculty that has used the same assessment procedures for years. In situations where precedent is powerful, "often a part of the change agent's task is to help identify, evaluate and revise . . . customs, traditions, or [the attitude] 'This is the way we have always done it'" (Schaller, 1972, p. 137).

We can begin by generating options other than those currently in place. If we are attempting personal change, forcing ourselves to generate other options often reveals possibilities that we would have not considered otherwise. If we are working with others, they may benefit from a strong demonstration. They are likely to respond with greater understanding if they can experience the details of another possible course of action rather than only hear about it generally.

Convincing the principal to permit alternatives to the basal reader test may mean demonstrating what kind of information you will collect about students' reading on an alternative instrument you've already developed. You (or a pilot group) will need to have tried out whatever assessment procedures or instruments you want others to consider. Certainly, this requires more work in advance, but it is more difficult to say "no" to someone who has obviously invested a lot of thought and effort.

When the assessment procedure you want to implement is rather complex, such as miscue analysis, remember that your goal in the demonstration is to help others understand *the information that can be gained about students* from its use. Explaining the instrument itself may not be helpful. What is usually more effective is to introduce the instrument by sharing the information you've gathered about a particular student. This allows others to achieve a basic understanding of an instrument because they see what it can reveal about students' reading or writing.

uncovering assumptions

Often, when we disagree with people about assessment, the discussion focuses on what is done and what ought to be done. As a result, the discussion may end up where it began; whatever position people had before the discussion began is the one they have when the discussion ends. When we find ourselves in such situations, we try to identify and discuss the assumptions underlying the positions others have taken, which often take the form of reasons for the position the person has taken. If you discuss the underlying assumptions instead of the positions themselves, the discussion may result in someone (or everyone, including you) changing her position or in dialogue that moves change forward.

One way to uncover what a person might believe or think is to put yourself in the other person's shoes. The principal who was consulted about an alternative assessment for the basal reader test might have had one or more of these reasons for denying the teacher's request:

- All teachers need to conduct the same assessments so that the parent community isn't confused by a variety of assessments.

- The principal assumes (or knows) that a policy does exist specifying that teachers must use basal tests.

- The teacher is not perceived to have expertise to develop an alternate assessment.

- The principal does not want to encourage other teachers to ask for permission to use alternative assessments.

- No alternative assessment could be better than the basal tests; the tests were developed by experts.

- Assessment and instruction do not need to be linked.

Another method that can be used to uncover assumptions is to ask why the other person made the decision that was made. It's possible that there may be more than one reason and that the person will name the one that will make you feel the best. Sometimes it works to approach the person with, "I'm wondering if the reason you decided against my developing an alternative assessment to the basal reader tests is that . . . ," filling in what you think is the most likely reason for the decision. Or you might even bring up what you think will be the most likely reason to deny the request when you first approach the person with the idea: "I'd like to develop an alternative assessment to the basal reader tests we are using. I thought a problem you might have with that is . . . and I have some ideas about how to solve that problem."

When you've identified possible assumptions, you have a greater chance to talk about what is important and what is likely to stand in the way of the change you want to make. It may be useful to have more than a single conversation when you sense initial opposition. You might end the first conversation with something like, "I think I understand why you are reluctant to . . . Let me think about whether I can come up with any solutions to [your reason] and I'll stop back to talk about it again." Especially when you need more time to consider possible solutions, setting up another discussion can give you that time. It also leaves the other person with the sense that you recognized the importance of potential problems and that you are open to negotiation.

developing voice

In order to foster change in ourselves, acceptance of change, or change in others, we must each develop the ability to give voice to our own insights. We must find language to communicate our understanding of literacy in ways that are sensitive to others and leave open the possibility of collaboration. This means that you need to speak up about issues of concern to you with *your* words, in a way that others are willing to listen to, and in a way that responds to their concerns.

Women sometimes have problems finding a "voice" to say what they think needs to be said. Culturally, they have learned not to bring up issues that might make waves because these are not considered "ladylike" behaviors (Lerner, 1985). Women need to be encouraged, and to encourage others, to develop assertive voices for educational change. It can be equally difficult for men to be effective change agents but for different reasons. Often men have been raised to make decisions based on rights and justice (Gilligan, 1982). They need to be encouraged, and again to encourage others, to discover the value of other perspectives, and to consider what might work best for all concerned (Keen, 1991). These stylistic differences between men and women create gaps that can inhibit educators in working out positive solutions to educational problems. Deborah Tannen's popular book, *You Just Don't Understand* (1990), can help you to understand and bridge the gaps between the conversational styles of men and women.

When teachers, male or female, first speak about an issue, they often use the words of others, usually the words of experts. Although this is probably to be expected developmentally (Belenky et al., 1986), it is often obvious to listeners that someone else's words are being used. It is more convincing to listen to someone's opinion when it is expressed in her own words. The communication is more sincere, uses less technical vocabulary, and is more coherent.

Several factors may contribute to teachers' ability to find their own voices. One may simply be a greater understanding of the problems they are concerned about and potential solutions. A deeper understanding of a problem allows you to get beyond the surface level of an expert's words in talking about the issue and use your own experience and understanding along with information gained from other knowledgeable sources.

Another contributing factor to the development of voice, one that also affects the degree of understanding, is gaining experience in talking about issues and ideas with someone you perceive to be less threatening. As Lori Wiese, a fourth-grade teacher in the Cherry Creek Schools in Colorado, writes:

> I have been actively instilling change without being aware of it. I am currently a mentor for an exchange teacher from England. This has put me in a role which requires me to constantly be a provider of information, especially about whole language. Working with Sue in this capacity over the last six months has given me confidence. I began to see myself as an "expert" in the area of language arts. I began to understand how to better help others who were not at the same point as myself. In addition to working with Sue, I have also been a support person for a first-year teacher on our team. We discuss our reading programs constantly in an informal manner. This has helped me by forcing me to articulate the whys and hows of a whole language classroom.

Lovitt (1990) also discusses her efforts to articulate new ideas about literacy and instruction as she interacted with her student teacher. What both Wiese and Lovitt found is that it is easier to develop your own voice in the safe role of a mentor and then gradually move to more difficult settings and problems. The "Teacher Reflections" provide other good examples of teachers developing their own voices in the change process. The teachers reveal how they thought about, found language for, and solved assessment problems. The act of writing for the book further clarified their own voices.

Finding a voice contributes a great deal to making personal changes in literacy assessment and instruction. The more we work at articulating what we do or want to do and why, the more we make our learning conscious and explicit. Even in safe environments, we find ourselves stretching our thinking by interacting with others who ask questions or express concerns. Finding a voice also contributes to creating change in others. As we develop our own voices to talk about issues, we need to find one that is appropriate, one that others will listen to. Unless others listen, we cannot foster change no matter how much we care or how much we believe the change will make a difference in students' lives. Clarke (1987) identifies this as one of the constraints on whole language reform: "Some whole language teachers, convinced that they possess a major portion of the Whole Truth, come across as just a bit intolerant, especially in the eyes of veteran teachers who have seen many versions of the Whole Truth come and go. This causes a certain amount of resentment which manifests itself in a lack of total cooperation" (p. 391).

Clarke also proposes an approach that is likely to reduce or eliminate the intolerance and strident voices that some teachers adopt in attempting change. Those attempting change must assume that others are acting in good faith, that they believe they are making the best decisions (or the best decisions possible, given their situations) for their students and for themselves. When we talk with others in good faith, we make an honest effort to see their point of view and exchange views rather than simply promulgate our own.

Using an appropriate voice to talk with others can leave us vulnerable. Listening carefully to other points of view often leads us to change. Even when we initiate change, we must be aware that change can also happen to us. Talking with others and using an appropriate voice creates an atmosphere conducive to collaboration. As Harste says, "When we collaborate, we expect to go out changed in the end, to become a different person" (Watson, Burke, & Harste, 1989).

being a change agent

Teaching means that you are responsible for change in your students. You may be reluctant to consider yourself as a change agent for adults. Or you may never have considered yourself as a literacy change agent. Yet if you do *anything* to influence the thinking or actions of other adults in reading and writing assessment and instruction, you are already a change agent. If you have a position such as building reading specialist, your job description (formal or informal) may necessitate more conscious change efforts.

If you want to encourage others to make changes in assessment, you need to understand that you are assuming that you have a particular perspective you consider meritorious. You also need to understand that those you want to change have their own particular perspectives that are different from (though not morally or intellectually inferior to) your own. Then you can listen to the points of view of others you are trying to encourage to change. Being a listener open to other points of view is more likely to result in change in both you and them.

To be effective change agents, we must devote time and energy to understanding the nature of change and the roles we can play in promoting change. We'll ask you to reflect on what you are currently doing as a change agent and what else you might want or need to do. Figure 10.2, ("Your Name) as a Change Agent," is included to help you to construct a profile of who you are as a change agent. Although we will provide assessment examples to help you generate ideas of your own, record what you do as a change agent in relation to literacy assessment *and* instruction. Stop after each of the following sections and complete the same section of the profile by reflecting on your own experiences. It has been our experience that this is best done in a group setting where participants can share their experiences. Invariably, one person's experience will revive memories in others.

Once you have completed the form, you might want to do two things. First, consider a change agent experience you have recorded in light of the process of change as we have presented it in this chapter. Second, choose one of your ideas about change and consider how to implement it. Now, begin by filling in your own name in the blank in Figure 10.2. It will help you personalize your reflections.

your roles

You are now ready to consider both the formal and informal roles you play as an educator. Formally, you may be a classroom teacher, a special education teacher, a Chapter I teacher, a reading resource specialist, a staff developer, or a principal. Your formal role is what you define your job to be when you meet someone new. But you may also have additional informal roles. Administrators and other teachers may turn to you for particular reasons (for advice or to serve on school committees) because of your expertise in a particular area. Or you may be the faculty liaison for the Parent-Teacher Organization (PTO). Or you may be a good friend of someone on the school board. Informal roles may or may not affect your ability to be a change agent. However, since informal roles often have more potential for fostering change than do formal ones, it is worth considering what your informal roles in the educational environment are.

preparing yourself as a change agent

Before you can foster change in others, you must have prepared yourself as a change agent. Most teachers don't consciously set out to prepare themselves to be change agents, but teachers who are reflective, who keep themselves abreast of current thinking in education, and who have engaged in personal change have already established a foundation. With this in mind, consider our discussion earlier in the chapter. What you do to foster personal change is the same as "How do you prepare yourself as a change agent?"

_____ **AS A CHANGE AGENT**
                    (Your name)

What are your roles?
Your formal role:

Your informal roles:

How do you prepare yourself as a change agent?

How do you foster change among teachers with the same formal role?
Informal ways:

Formal ways:

How do you foster change among teachers with a different formal role?
Informal ways:

Formal ways:

How do you foster change among administrators?
Informal ways:

Formal ways:

How do you foster change among parents?
Informal ways:

Formal ways:

How do you foster change in people other than those listed above?
Informal ways:

Formal ways:

Who are the other people? _____

Figure 10.2   "(Your name) as a change agent" assessment form

Do you reflect on your own experiences by

- Taking courses that are structured to promote such reflection?
- Considering past life experiences with literacy assessment and instruction?
- Talking with others about your life experiences with literacy assessment and instruction?

Do you create environments that are supportive for change by

- Identifying others with whom you can work?
- Flexibly and openly learning from others?
- Defining and experimenting with changes that make sense to you?
- Finding your own pace for change?
- Challenging yourself to try and revise new ideas?
- Creating vehicles, such as portfolios, that will raise the level of dialogue about assessment in particular and education in general?

Do you pursue answers to questions you have about literacy by

- Reading professional journals and books?
- Attending professional conferences?
- Enrolling in university or school district classes?
- Participating in study groups?
- Observing other teachers and being observed by them?
- Observing students' reading and writing closely?
- Involving students in assessment?

Do you confront the politics of assessment and change by

- Going beyond "But I can't . . . "?
- Overcoming the power of precedent?
- Uncovering and dealing with your own and others' assumptions?

Do you use your own voice by

- Finding your own ways to express ideas?
- Listening to and responding to other points of view?
- Assuming that others are acting in good faith?
- Preparing to have your own point of view changed by others?

Consider other things you might do to keep yourself abreast of current knowledge, keep your thinking fresh, and reflect on your literacy assessment and instruction.

teachers with the same formal role

Because teachers who have the same formal role you have (other classroom teachers if you are a classroom teacher, for example, or other Chapter I teachers if you are a Chapter I teacher) are those whose roles you best understand, we'll begin by considering what you might have been doing to foster change in their thinking and practice of literacy assessment and instruction.

Teachers foster change in each other more often in informal than in formal ways. You might display students' drafts along with final products in the hall, which may lead to conversations with other teachers about the importance of using drafts in assessing the students' work. You might take a professional book to the teachers' lounge. A book such as *The Whole Language Evaluation Book* (K. Goodman, Y. Goodman, & Hood, 1989) might inspire some conversation when other teachers ask about it during lunch. Or, if you are brimming with enthusiasm after attending an IRA Preconvention Institute on assessment, you're likely to generate some interest in what you've learned.

In more formal ways, teachers might provide colleagues with in-services on assessment as a precursor to organizing a group to work on rewriting the reading and writing portion of the report card. They might create an informational school bulletin board on spelling development to guide other teachers in observing their students' spelling more effectively. A teacher taking a class on emergent literacy may decide to provide the three best articles she read to those on her primary team and schedule a discussion.

teachers with different formal roles

No doubt you also interact with teachers who have a different formal role than you do. If you are a classroom teacher, you may interact with the special education teacher and the Chapter I teacher over children you have in common. Some of the informal and formal ways you foster change with other teachers are also likely to apply to these teachers. But you might also consider some others.

If you and a Chapter I teacher have conferences in which students' progress is discussed, you can informally foster change by evaluating student work together, calling attention to those aspects of students' reading and writing you consider important, and sharing what students can do and how they have progressed. More formally, reviewing the portfolio of a student from your classroom at a staffing meeting is likely to greatly enhance the richness of the information presented about the student's progress and the situations in which the student's reading and writing appear to be most effective. Such presentations go a long way toward helping others reconsider assessment, particularly the importance of teacher observation in assessment.

■ ■
administrators

You can also act as a change agent formally and informally with administrators. Informally, you might converse with your principal about an article on assessment which you both read in the local newspaper. You might share the progress of a student the administrator has considered a problem. Or you might recommend a journal article on assessment to the language arts coordinator for the next staff development session.

Formally, you might invite your principal to attend the state IRA or NCTE convention with you or suggest a discussion group on assessment after the topic is featured in an administrator's journal, such as *Educational Leadership*. As a group of Chapter I teachers in one district did, you and your colleagues might present a variety of alternative assessment tools to Chapter I principals as a way of helping them to reconsider assessment for planning instruction. As a gift, consider giving your principal or another administrator a copy of *The Administrator's Guide to Whole Language* (Heald-Taylor, 1989) or *Understanding Whole Language* (Weaver, 1990).

■ ■
parents

Informal sharing of students' progress in reading and writing can go a long way toward helping parents reconsider what it is important to assess. A public display of the books that students have read each month during the school year draws many visiting parents into conversations about the importance of reading and of keeping records on what children are reading and how much.

Parents can be formally asked to evaluate their children's work. This can be done on a regular basis, as Bonnie DeFreece suggests in Chapter 6, or intermittently, as Jan Bennett suggests in Chapter 7. Another formal contact with parents that may help them reconsider assessment can occur in the communication of standardized test results. Parents can be provided with other data about their children's progress along with standardized test results, giving the parents a broader view of what the child has learned about reading and writing.

■ ■
others

There may be other individuals or groups for whom you can serve as a change agent about literacy assessment or instruction. You may be the PTO liaison, appear in front of the school board, write letters to the local newspaper, nominate a colleague for an award, have a conversation with someone while waiting for your children to finish soccer practice, work on a district committee or building planning committee, talk with friends over coffee, or volunteer as an adult literacy tutor. In each of these situations, the potential exists for encouraging someone to rethink a position on literacy assessment, for asking broader questions, or at least for realizing that there may be other points of view.

teacher reflection *teacher reflection*

teacher reflection

The final "Teacher Reflection" was written by a teacher who has fostered a great deal of change in her school, much of it related to assessment. We first met Kathy Mestnik when she entered our master's program. She wanted to strengthen her ability to help bilingual children learn to read and write. The school in which Mestnik works in the Denver Public Schools is located in a Hispanic neighborhood and is designated as a bilingual school. Her principal, a Hispanic woman and a former bilingual teacher, is very supportive of alternative assessment and whole language instruction. Mestnik's spirit and involvement in bringing about change illustrate the strengths that change agents need and the situations that teachers face in working with administrators, parents, and fellow teachers to improve educational opportunities for children.

Implementing change: portfolios in progress

Kathy Mestnik

I was anxiously awaiting the coming school year. Our staff had committed to a number of new, exciting projects for the students. A major project we decided to undertake was using portfolios with the intention of abandoning report cards within a few years. Although the change seemed radical to many others outside of our school, the principal supported our change efforts. We felt that parents deserved to see more than test scores and computer print-out sheets of their children's progress. By sharing writing samples, anecdotal records, and checklists we could demonstrate to parents and administrators the progress that students were making. Using portfolios would also allow us to more closely view the processes children were going through in their learning. As a faculty, we decided to begin using portfolios in the fall.

At our first planning meeting on assessment, we made several decisions, among them which items to include in the portfolios. First of all, we felt it was important to include writing samples. We determined that the writing sample could be a journal entry or a story. Because we are a K–2 school [schools in Denver are paired, K–2 in one school and 3–5 in the other, for busing purposes], we decided the sample could be a first draft of the child's writing. We also felt that we needed some established way of evaluating this writing. It was decided that a checklist would be very useful for this. Many teachers had already been utilizing checklists and collecting writing samples. These teachers offered to share the checklists with other faculty members. At midyear, or the following year, we would make a decision as to which checklist the majority of the faculty preferred, and this would become a standard assessment.

Many of us also felt that the samples collected should be more consistent (only stories or only journal entries). Some of the teachers were collecting both journal entries and pieces written during Writing Workshop and evaluating both once a month. However, for many teachers the idea of collecting any samples once a month was an overwhelming task. I felt frustrated, since I knew that collecting and analyzing these samples could aid a teacher in instruction. At the same time I knew we needed to make the transition into more complicated means of assessment slowly. It was decided that we should collect what would be possible for each of us and take it a step further at a later date. Perhaps once the teachers saw cumulative writing samples they would discover their value.

The next item to be included in portfolios was a reading assessment. We looked at what was available and determined that we would use the *Emergent Reading and Writing Evaluation* for emergent readers and the *Classroom Reading Miscue Assessment* for readers. The next problem was familiarity with these instruments. Two of us had already implemented their use in our own classrooms. We volunteered to teach the others how to use them and to continue to give the teachers support as they administered the instruments in their classrooms in the fall. The faculty decided that when school began, faculty meetings would be used to learn how to administer the instruments. We also brainstormed ways to free teachers to work with individual students. Many of the teachers on the support staff, as well as the principal, volunteered to cover classes for the teachers. We also decided to use paraprofessionals to supervise activities with students.

Our next problem was how to determine which books would be appropriate, especially with the *Classroom Reading Miscue Assessment*. We finally decided that the PPA (Program for Pupil Assistance) teacher would spend time searching for appropriate materials to be used with both assessment tools. She put together sets of books to be used with the students. A grade level appropriate set was developed for each teacher. The PPA included typed copies of the text that a teacher could use for marking while giving the assessments. This greatly relieved many of the teachers, who were concerned about when they would find the time to prepare all of the materials necessary for administration of the assessment instruments.

Our biggest dilemma was whether or not to include the scores from the district's criterion-referenced and norm-referenced tests in the portfolios. We did not feel that the test scores accurately represented our students' abilities, yet they were part of the required assessment for our district. After much discussion we came to the conclusion that we would all stand together and put forth our objection to the district-mandated criterion-referenced test administered a minimum of three times per year to all children. We also discussed the Iowa Test of Basic Skills given to all students in the spring of each year. We realized that we were forced to give this test, although we did not like it. We vowed to begin to lobby for the removal of this test district-wide, except for the grade levels mandated by the state.

Spelling was another big issue. We noticed, since many of us stopped giving weekly spelling tests, that parents became concerned that their children would not learn to spell if they did not "study" words each week. We therefore decided that we needed to provide data showing that, indeed, children were learning to spell. We decided to use Richard Gentry's (1985) spelling assessment to determine each student's spelling stage. If we did this two to three times a year, we would be able to provide information to the parents about the stages their child was moving through in spelling. We also thought that counting percentages of invented spelling used in the child's actual writing was a wonderful way to show progress. Parents like to watch the percentage of invented spelling go down as the total number of words the child is writing go up. This was a simple score that could be calculated from the writing sample collected each month.

Finally, we discussed how the portfolio could take the place of report cards. We realized that many other products and assessments would need to be included in the portfolio in order to cover other subject areas such as math, physical education, music, and library skills. It was decided that these teachers would need to design a checklist of the various skills children were expected to learn in these classes. The checklist would be reviewed periodically and shared with parents at conferences. By seeing checklists of all of the things children were learning, parents would leave conferences much more informed than if they had only seen letter grades representing an entire nine-week period of work.

After designing the beginning stage of the portfolio, we realized that it was very important for parents to review the portfolios with teachers. If we did this at conferences, the parents would see them just twice a year. We felt that this simply was not enough. We needed to find some way to meet with the parents quarterly. This however, was going to be very difficult. Conferences are very time-consuming; finding release time for us to meet with the parents two more times each year would be a tough task. We thought about using the support staff teachers to cover while the teachers held conferences. However, the idea still seemed overwhelming to us. It was decided that we would implement the portfolios first and save the conference issue to resolve at a later date.

We agreed that the full design and implementation of the portfolios would take several years. Because of the varying amounts of experience and training among the faculty, the portfolios would be an easy addition for some but a tremendous undertaking for others. We also had additions to our portfolios in mind for the future. We discussed including things such as children reading aloud on videotapes, checklists filled out by parents, and literacy checklists and personal interest inventories to be filled out by the children. It would be a big job to complete, but we felt that, if we took implementation of the portfolios one step at a time and began slowly, we could accomplish our goals.

When the new school year began, we went ahead with training for the *Classroom Reading Miscue Assessment* and the *Emergent Reading and Writing Evaluation*. Once the teachers began to administer the assessments, other issues began to surface. The major one was that some teachers were not using the information to inform their instruction. They saw the assessments as a waste of instructional time. To spend ten minutes with every student in a class of thirty took days! I tried to explain that instead of doing the usual activities to get to know their students, they could use the information gathered through the assessments to begin almost immediately with reading instruction. After all, they would know the reading abilities and needs of every child in their classroom. After much debate I agreed to hold help sessions for specific problems and meanwhile everyone would continue on with the miscue and emergent reader assessments. Soon, almost all of the teachers had given the assessments to their students and some had even begun to comment on how interesting the information they had gathered was. What a breakthrough!

The principal set out to get some support for our project by trying to convince other administrators that portfolios were better than report cards. She took some of our actual portfolios to share with her colleagues and set up a group of principals who were interested in doing some of the same kinds of things we were implementing. She felt that if she could get wider support some changes could be made districtwide.

A final problem concerned what to do with the portfolios at the end of the year. It was suggested that we not put them into the cumulative records, since not all children would have portfolios (due to the high mobility of the student population). Instead, we would pass the portfolios on to the teacher that each child would have the following year. It is my hope that someday we will keep portfolios for all children and we will be able to include them in the children's records, just as we now record grades on the cumulative records.

Toward the end of the first year of implementation, we met and discussed how the portfolios were coming along. Many of the teachers had established portfolios for their entire class and had even included some items above and beyond what was discussed at our meetings. Other teachers felt simply overwhelmed about how to go about evaluating the monthly writing samples that they were collecting; they needed suggestions about how to find the time to both collect and assess. Those of us who felt comfortable and successful with the portfolios tried to explain how we went about it. Other teachers, unfortunately, had not even begun to collect the writing samples. I began to realize how we had missed a step in the process. These teachers seemed to need more background on portfolios. We provided a good deal of training and support, but no background. They didn't share my enthusiasm for the project because they hadn't read extensively on the subject and were not beginning at the same point. They had no point of reference.

If our plan for using portfolio assessment was to succeed, it was obvious we would need to provide further support to those teachers struggling with implementation. However, we lacked the necessary time to do so. We were frustrated about which direction to take. That changed the following October, when we received a grant from the district to continue our efforts. We chose to use the funds to reimburse substitute teachers while faculty were released to work on the portfolio project. We used the release time to redefine our reasons for establishing portfolios (a very valuable activity) as well as to clarify which items/assessments to include. During release time, each grade-level team met and created a progress checklist. These checklists were then compared across grade levels and a master checklist compiled that would follow students from kindergarten through second grade. For the first time since undertaking the project I saw a glimmer of enthusiasm in everyone's eyes! I believe it was the ownership they felt in the checklists. Each one of us shared (and argued) over what should and should not be included. We were beginning at a point at which each teacher had the knowledge and background to contribute.

In addition, we spent a great deal of time discussing a timetable for the portfolio implementation. The faculty agreed that each teacher would conduct sessions to acquaint parents with portfolio assessment and its upcoming use at conferences. Some teachers held meetings after school or in the evenings; others had potluck dinners. Each chose the method with which he or she was most comfortable and thought would work best with parents. We also felt each teacher would need time to experiment with collecting portfolio data, using the checklist, and sharing results with parents in conferences. Following the conferences, teachers gave parents an opportunity to give feedback as to whether they liked the information the portfolios and checklists provided about their children's learning and what further adjustments they would like to see made. The reaction from parents was extremely positive. They commented that they left conferences with a better idea of their child's abilities and needs. These successes were a great motivator for the faculty and, once again, we have a 100 percent commitment.

From our attempt to implement portfolio assessment, we have learned that change is a slow process. It comes easier for some than for others. We have had to be patient and supportive and hope that one day our patience and support will pay off. An important outcome is that we are working together on a concept that most of us believe in. The assessment instruments we are using capture the abilities of the children and give clear pictures of the learning processes taking place. Perhaps in the future the entire district will use portfolios, and less emphasis will be placed on standardized tests. Wouldn't it be nice to see the newspaper filled with samples of students' work instead of columns of test scores?

Final Words About Fostering Change in Assessment

Teachers who engage in working with students in a reflective manner consider teaching to be a never-ending learning process, a process of continual revaluing, renewal, and change. They understand that there is always potential for becoming more effective, no matter how long they have been teaching, and they know that teaching expertise will continue to grow through reflection and change. They have a sense that their understanding of many aspects of teaching, especially something as complex as literacy assessment, is tentative and continually needs to be reexamined. The very act of collecting and analyzing assessment data results in the perception that change may be necessary or good. Reflective teachers are not surprised that they have just as many questions about assessment and instruction today, albeit different ones, as they did when they began their teaching careers. The "Teacher Reflection" pieces throughout this book are examples of reflective teachers in the process of reconsidering, renewing, and making changes in their assessment practices, procedures, and beliefs.

We hope you will consider the literacy assessment that makes the most sense for you in planning for reading and writing instruction for your students. And we trust that, to paraphrase Michael Fullan, you will work out your own meaning from what we have presented and what you have experienced, and transform these ideas to fit you, your students, and your teaching situation.

references

Aisenberg, N., & M. Harrington. (1988). *Women of academe: Outsiders in the sacred grove.* Amherst, MA: University of Massachusetts Press.

Ausberger, D. (1973). *Caring enough to confront.* Scottdale, PA: Herald Press.

Belenky, M., B. Clinchy, N. Goldberger, & J. Tarule. (1986). *Women's ways of knowing: The development of self, voice, and mind.* New York: Basic Books.

Bissex, G., & R. Bullock (Eds.). (1987). *Seeing for ourselves: Case-study research by teachers of writing.* Portsmouth, NH: Heinemann.

Brown, R. (1988). Schooling and thoughtfulness. *Basic Education: Issues, Answers and Facts, 3* (6).

Clarke, M.A. (1987). Don't blame the system: Constraints on "whole language" reform. *Language Arts, 64* (4), 384–396.

Clarke, M.A., & N.L. Commins (in preparation). Whole language: Reform and resistance. Denver, CO: University of Colorado at Denver manuscript.

Cochran-Smith, M. & S.L. Lytle (Eds.) (1993). *Inside outside: Teacher research and knowledge.* New York: Teachers College Press.

Daiker, D.A., & M. Morenberg. (1989). *The writing teacher as researcher: Essays in the theory and practice of class-based research.* Portsmouth, NH: Heinemann.

Dalziel, M., & S. Schoonover. (1988). *Changing ways: A practical tool for implementing change within organizations.* New York: Amacom.

Edelsky, C. (1988). Research currents: Resisting (professional) arrest. *Language Arts, 65* (4), 396–402.

Fischer, K. (1988). *Women at the well: Feminist perspectives on spiritual direction.* New York: Paulist Press.

Fraatz, J.M.B. (1987). *The politics of reading: Power, opportunity, and prospects for change in America's public schools.* New York: Teachers College Press.

Fullan, M. (1982). *The meaning of educational change.* New York: Teachers College Press.

Gentry, R.J. (1985). You can analyze developmental spelling—and here's how to do it! *Early Years: K–8*, May, 44–45.

Gilligan, C. (1982). *In a different voice: Psychological theory and women's development.* Cambridge, MA: Harvard University Press.

Goodman, K.S., Y.M. Goodman, & W.J. Hood. (1989). *The whole language evaluation book.* Portsmouth, NH: Heinemann.

Goodman, Y.M. (1991). Personal communication.

Goswami, D., & P. Stillman (Eds.). (1987). *Reclaiming the classroom: Teacher research as an agency for change.* Portsmouth, NH: Heinemann.

Harman, S., & C. Edelsky. (1989). The risks of whole language literacy: Alienation and connection. *Language Arts, 66* (4), 392–406.

Heald-Taylor, G. (1989). *The administrator's guide to whole language.* Katonah, NY: Richard C. Owen.

Keen, S. (1991). *Fire in the belly: On being a man.* New York: Bantam.

Kerr, B. (1985). *Smart girls, gifted women.* Columbus, OH: Ohio Psychology.

Lerner, H. (1985). *The dance of anger.* New York: Harper & Row.

Lieberman, A., & L. Miller. (1984). School improvement: Themes and variations. Teachers College Record, 86, 4–19.

Lerner, H. (1985). *The dance of anger.* New York: Harper & Row.

Lovitt, Z. (1990). Rethinking my roots as a teacher. *Educational Leadership, 47,* 43–6.

Myers, M. (1985). *The teacher-researcher: How to study writing in the classroom.* Urbana, IL: National Council of Teachers of English.

Osherson, S. (1986). *Finding our fathers.* New York: Fawcett Columbine.

Rich, S.J. (Ed.). (1984). On becoming teacher experts: Buying time. *Language Arts, 61* (7), 731–736.

Rickert, C. (1990). Support groups for reading supervisors. *Journal of Reading, 33* (8), 642–643.

Rubin, L. (1983). *Intimate strangers: Men and women together.* New York: Harper & Row.

Sanford, L., & M. Donovan. (1984). *Women and self-esteem.* New York: Anchor Press/Doubleday.

Schaller, L. (1972). *The change agent.* New York: Abingdon Press.

Shanklin, N.L., & L.K. Rhodes. (1989). Transforming literacy instruction. *Educational Leadership, 46* (6), 59–63.

Tannen, D. (1990). *You just don't understand: Women and men in conversation.* New York: Morrow.

Torbe, M. (1990). Language across the curriculum: Policies and practices. In D. Barnes, J. Britton, & M. Torbe (Eds.), *Language, the learner and the school.* Portsmouth, NH: Heinemann.

Walp, T.P., & S.A. Walmsley. (1989). Instructional and philosophical congruence: Neglected aspects of coordination. *The Reading Teacher, 42* (6), 364–368.

Watson, D., C. Burke, & J. Harste. (1989). *Whole language: Inquiring voices.* New York: Scholastic.

Weaver, C. (1990). *Understanding whole language.* Portsmouth, NH: Heinemann.

Index

LITERACY ASSESSMENT

A Handbook of Instruments

Edited by Lynn K. Rhodes

For every teacher who has sought practical, comprehensive methods for recording and analyzing students' literacy processes, *Literacy Assessment* will be an invaluable resource. The handbook includes in full all the various assessment instruments discussed in *Windows into Literacy*, including:

- interviews and attitude surveys

- miscue analysis

- comprehension checklists

- spelling analysis

- emergent reading and writing evaluations

- and much more.

Most of the instruments have been developed by teachers, or in conjunction with teachers, for use in particular educational situations. Teachers may use the instruments "as is" or adapt them as needed to answer questions about their own students' literacy development.

Contents: 1. Reading: Interviews and Attitude Surveys; Classroom Reading Use; Comprehension Checklists; Miscue Analysis; Self-Assessments of Reading; Ongoing Observations of Reading 2. Writing: Interviews and Attitude Surveys; Classroom Writing Use; The Authoring Cycle Profile; Spelling Analysis; Self-Assessments of Writing; Ongoing Observations of Writing 3. Emergent Reading and Writing: Emergent Reader and Writer Interview; Emergent Reading and Writing Evaluation 4. Literacy at Home: Student Interview; Literacy: Parent Interview; Parent Letter; Data Gathering: Three Perspectives 5. Program Placement: Classroom Teacher Judgment Rating Scale; Kindergarten Teacher Judgment Rating Scale 6. Assessing the Teaching of Literacy: IAP Observation Checklist; Observation Guide; Coaching Form 7. The Assessment and Evaluation of Literacy: Recommended Books; Recommended Instruments.